"In March 1917, Haskell Jones was nineteen years old when he stepped off a train in Akron. He had traveled from Mayfield, Kentucky, traveling north on the news that a good-paying job would be waiting for him when he arrived. After paying $16 for the train ticket, he had six dollars in his pocket. The rubber industry was booming in those weeks before America entered World War I and with employment agents riding the trains, jobs in the tire factories were easy to come by. This proved especially handy for thousands of young migrating Kentuckians who were quick to show insubordination and equally quick to pick a fight . . . an intimate history of the first great migration. Historians have written extensively about African American migration out of the rural south, and Jones seeks to round out the story by including the voices of white Appalachians who also came north for industrial jobs . . . Weaving his grandfather's story with passages providing historical context, Jones has crafted a compelling narrative that left me wanting to know more of the family story."

—Pat Williamsen
Executive Director
Ohio Humanities

". . . Jones puts their words in a rich context due to his extensive research in other sources and the literature. This is good history, but also a compelling story, well told."

—William H. Mulligan, Jr., PhD
Professor of History, Murray State University
President, Jackson Purchase Historical Society

" . . . a fascinating history of the Great Migration . . . this is not just a family tale. The Jones gang provides a peephole to the larger realities of the era, supplemented by Jones' original reporting and extensive research of existing literature . . ."

—Bob Dyer
Akron Beacon Journal

"By the conclusion . . . a person will embrace the Jones as if they were kin . . . and the record of rubber in Akron is all the richer and more complete for it."

—Steve Love
Co-author, *Wheels of Fortune: The Story of Rubber in Akron*

On A Burning Deck.

An Oral History of the Great Migration.

Tom Jones

Previously published and reviewed in two separate volumes as:
On A Burning Deck, The Road to Akron, Vol. 1, 1900-1920 and
On A Burning Deck, Return to Akron, Vol. 2, 1920-1921.

Copyright © 2019 Tom Jones

For permissions contact: Tom@OnABurningDeck.com

ISBN-13: 978-0-578-56270-4

Also by Tom Jones:

On A Burning Deck, The Road to Akron, Vol. 1

On A Burning Deck, Return to Akron, Vol. 2

Waldo Maccabees, In the Footsteps of Christ

Casabianca

The boy stood on the burning deck,
Whence all but him had fled,
The flame that lit the battle's wreck,
Shone round him o'er the dead.

Yet beautiful and bright he stood,
As born to rule the storm;
A creature of he-ro-ic blood,
A proud, though child-like form.

The flames rolled on; he would not go,
Without his father's word;
That father, faint in death below,
His voice no longer heard.

He called aloud, "Say, father, say,
If yet my task is done?"
He knew not that he chief-tain lay
Un-con-scious of his son.

"Speak, father," once again he cried,
"If I may yet be gone,
And"—but the booming shot replied,
And fast the flames rolled on.

Upon his brow he felt their breath,
And in his waving hair;
And looked from that lone post of death,
In still, yet brave, despair;

And shouted but once more aloud,
"My father, must I stay?"
While o'er him fast, through said and shroud,
The wreathing fires made way.

They wrapped the ship in splendor wild,
They caught the flag on high,
And streamed above the gallant child,
Like banners in the sky.

Then came a burst of thunder-sound:
The boy—oh! Where was he?
Ask of the winds, that far around
With fragments strewed the sea,
With mast, and helm, and pennon fair,
That well had borne their part:
But the noblest thing that perished there,
Was that young faithful heart.[1]

Felicia Dorothea Hemans

"The Boy Stood on the Burning Deck
Eating Peanuts by the Peck
Although the Flames, They Licked His Chin
He Kept Cramming Those Peanuts in."

—Children's Parody of the poem *Casabianca*
by Felicia Dorothea Hemans,
as remembered by Haskell Jones.

CONTENTS

ACKNOWLEDGMENTS I

PREFACE III

INTRODUCTION V

PART ONE—GRAVES COUNTY, KENTUCKY 1900

1. "HILLBULLIES" 2
   Relations Between the Races 3
   The Tobacco Wars 6
   A Culture of Violence 8
   Family Ties 9

2. ORIGINS 13
   "Aunt" Kate Kennedy 16
   Robert Cook James 16
   Sarah Ellen Jones 17

3. PUBLIC EDUCATION IN KENTUCKY 30
   School Administration 30
   School Conditions 32

4. EDUCATION 37
   Teachers 42
   Students 47

5. TOBACCO 50

6. WORK 58
   Zack Jones 66
   Elvis "Doot" Gilbert 70

7. HEALTH 71
   Simeon Augustus Carman 75
   "Aunt Fanny" & "Uncle Dud" Magaren 78
   Luther Jones 80

8. THE POLITICIAN 83
   The Political Process 84
   The Daily Messenger and "Democracy" in Mayfield 86
   The "Good Roads" Movement 88

Corruption in the County Sheriff's Office 92

9. RECREATION 103

10. JUSTICE... 109
    May Copeland and Lucian Turk..111
    Bird Choate and Henry Campbell 112
    Tom Tinker 112

11. THE SOCIAL EVIL.. 123

12. MIGRATION 129

PART TWO—AKRON, OHIO, 1917

13. "SINGING SOLDIERS" 138
    The Factory Floor 141
    Housing...142
    The Workforce..145

14. ARRIVAL.. 149

15. THE MILLER RUBBER COMPANY 152

16. FIRESTONE TIRE & RUBBER 158

17. GOODYEAR TIRE & RUBBER 163

18. FIRESTONE TIRE & RUBBER II.. 167

19. ROOMMATES 171
    36 West Miller Avenue 171
    171 West Miller...174
    "Greasing the Growler" 176
    221 Ira Avenue..180
    Summit Beach Park 182

20. WORLD WAR ONE.. 187
    The Teacher 189
    Western Kentucky State Normal School 191

21. THE SPANISH FLU 193

22. CAMP KNOX 196
    The Spanish Flu in Graves County 204
    The Bulldog..205
    Courtship 205

23. RETURN.. 208

106 Brookside 209

140 West Miller Avenue 211

Jones School, Graves County, Kentucky 213

24. PROHIBITION 217

    John Bryer's 218

    Detroit 220

    Mrs. Shelton 222

25. MARRIAGE 224

26. LUCK 229

PART THREE—THE ROAD WEST, 1920

27. "THE LITTLE DEPRESSION" 234

28. THE CLAY PITS 240

29. THE ROAD WEST 244

    Fort Smith 244

    Oklahoma City 246

    Little Rock 249

    Bald Knob 253

30. MEMPHIS 255

PART FOUR—PADUCAH, KENTUCKY, 1921

31. THE "MELTIN' POT" 266

    The Paducah Railway Company 268

    The Routes 271

    Neighbors 273

    Barton Jones 275

    The Cars 277

    The Motormen 284

    Incidents 289

    Rubel McNeill 296

    The High Life 302

PART FIVE—AKRON, OHIO 1922

32. RETURN 312

33. THE MILLER RUBBER COMPANY II 316

    678 Blaine Avenue 324

    Barton Jones 326

34. DUTY AND JONES 329
    High Flight 334

PART SIX—TALLMADGE, OHIO 1926

35. TALLMADGE 336
    Of Autos and Elephants 341

36. THE MILLER RUBBER COMPANY III 343

37. PROHIBITION II. 346

38. GOODYEAR TIRE & RUBBER II 351

39. THE DEPRESSION 356

40. THE HARDEST OF TIMES 360
    Barton Jones 362

41. LABOR 365

42. STRIKE! 368
    Birth 374

43. RELIEF AND PUBLIC WORKS 380

PART SEVEN—TALLMADGE, OHIO 1941

44. THE CIRCLE 396

45. THE TALLMADGE POLICE DEPARTMENT: ONE MAN 402
    Mayor Charles Ritchie 411
    "Queenie" 422

46. "WAR FARERS" 427
    Akron's Wartime Workforce 429
    Housing 431
    Women in the Workforce 432

47. THE HOME FRONT 435
    Rationing 435
    Scrap Drives 441
    F.B.I. Training 446
    Cigarettes 450
    Mayor Vincent Ziegler 453

48. THE TALLMADGE FIRE DEPARTMENT 455

49. THE FURNACE COMPANY 468

50. TALLMADGE CITY COUNCIL 474

51. RETROSPECTIVE 478
    Florence Jones 479

EPILOGUE 486

ABOUT THE AUTHOR 491

BIBLIOGRAPHY 493

NOTES 496

INDEX 565

ACKNOWLEDGMENTS

First and foremost, I want to thank Haskell and Florence Jones's daughter, my Aunt Marjorie, who first suggested "Someone needs to get a tape recorder," as my grandfather launched into yet another one of his stories about the early years of the rubber industry some 40 years ago. Without that spark of insight, this project would have never begun. And the stories the family heard and enjoyed would now just be distant fading memories.

Thanks are also in order Susan E. Burton, Clerk of Council, Tallmadge, Ohio; James "Mike" Clark, Circulation Manager of the Mayfield *Messenger*; Sarah M. Dorpinghaus and Deborah M. "Shell" Dunn of the University of Kentucky Libraries; Miranda Rectenwald of Washington University Libraries, as well as the interlibrary loan staff of the San Antonio Public Library who graciously allowed me to remove microfilmed newspapers from the library so that I could more easily study them at home on my own reader. Also to Mike Tolleson who helped me navigate my way around publishing contracts.

Above all, special thanks to my wife, Steffanie, whose love, support and editorial assistance helped make this work possible. This book is lovingly dedicated to her.

PREFACE

In the early decades of the 20th century, more than twenty-eight million men and women—black and white—began "The Great Migration" north from the Deep South and Appalachia, lured by high wages and the opportunity to make a better life for themselves and their families.[1] As author James N. Gregory noted in *The Southern Diaspora, How the Great Migrations of Black and White Southerners Transformed America*:

> African Americans moved north under intense public scrutiny, accompanied by newspaper coverage that heightened the significance of their move and affected social interactions . . . Meanwhile, their white migrant counterparts remained all but invisible. Although vastly outnumbering black migrants, white southerners were simply another set of moving Americans finding their way anonymously in the thriving northern and western economies of the early part of the century.[2]

Among the white southerners that left their homes and moved north, literally hundreds of thousands migrated to Akron, Ohio, forever changing its culture, history and politics. Who were they? Aside from dry numerical classifications as former residents of West Virginia, Kentucky, Alabama, et al. or simply "hillbillies" (during the second phase of The Great Migration from the mid-1930s through the 1960s), the fact is that historians really haven't had any idea at all. No letters home, diaries, notes or recordings have been discovered.

In Steve Love and David Giffels encyclopedic series for the *Akron Beacon Journal* and their subsequent publication of *Wheels of Fortune, The Story of Rubber in Akron* in 1999, there is not a single quote from one of these rubber workers who made Akron "the Rubber Capital of the World" during the initial boom years of the industry.

In Susan Allyn Johnson's 2006 dissertation, "Industrial Voyagers: A Case Study of Appalachian Migration to Akron, Ohio, 1900-1940," she writes: "Virtually absent from historical narratives are the experiences of the 1.3 million white southerners who left the South before the Great Depression."[3] "Furthermore," she adds, "they were less likely . . . to write letters or keep the sort of personal journals that have served to document the experiences of sojourners of earlier eras."[4]

Finally, in his 2011 work, *The Devil's Milk*, author John Tully notes:

> No rubber worker has left his or her memoirs, and those captains of industry who did write focused on invention and commerce, not the lives of the laborers.[5]

With this seemingly gaping lack of information on these early rubber workers, it is hardly surprising that there is also no body of historical literature documenting the impact of any of these individuals as they moved into positions of responsibility in local government. In fact, for all their contributions to the industrial growth of America in the 20th Century, the individual role of these people has been completely lost and forgotten.

That is, until now.

Based on over 50 hours of unpublished oral histories and hundreds of photographs in the author's possession (unless otherwise noted), this contextual oral history offers the only complete first-hand account of one family of white southerners, that of Haskell and Florence Jones, who helped stoke the fires of northeast Ohio's boom years and left a lasting impact on local governance.

Due to the scope of this project, the retelling of any given incident herein may be a composite of several different conversations over a period of many years that have been edited together. Aside from the elimination of speech disfluencies and filled pauses, as well as the addition of clarifying pronouns and proper nouns, the words are those of the speaker. I have only taken the liberty of combining the details to render as complete a version as possible. After all, they were storytellers. And, as their grandchild, I am of their blood.

Tom Jones
New Braunfels, Texas
2019

INTRODUCTION

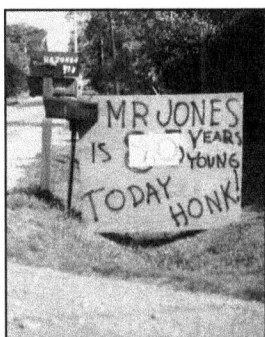

My grandfather, Haskell Jones, stood on his head for his 93rd birthday. Not that this was a rare event, mind you. He had also done it on his 92nd, 91st, 90th and many more birthdays previous to that—when he wasn't tending his orchard, planting his garden or donating the resulting produce to the underprivileged of Akron. What's more, in preparation for these "outstanding" occasions in his back yard in Tallmadge, Ohio, he would also practice in the days leading up to them—just to make sure that he didn't embarrass himself in the presence of the numerous family and friends who would gather to watch him at this annual event.

Just why or when he first decided to stand on his head could be debated as he, himself, never actually said—although I spent literally dozens of hours with him and a tape recorder. As far as I can determine, it wasn't the result of some ancient family tradition that he felt compelled to continue. It wasn't the result of some malady of old age. (I will always contend that after a nap, he was as sharp as any three of my friends put together—for what that's worth.) And, while the majority of his relatives were probably more interested in talking him out of it rather than understanding it, I simply looked forward to it—eventually driving some 2,600 miles each year to bear witness.

Looking back, however, I realize that I didn't have the need to ask the obvious question, so I never did. In the years that I had spent with both him and my grandmother, I had, in effect, relived their lives. I had developed an innate understanding that may have coursed through my veins as much as my mind. But, more than that, I knew about a long-forgotten poem that had remained fixed in my grandfather's mind from his childhood.

Entitled *Casabianca*, this poem about the imminent death of a young cabin boy aboard a burning man-o-war achieved tremendous popularity during the 1800s—despite a theme that today might be best characterized as morbid or macabre. The boy's father was dead. The ship was sinking. The end was near. And the parallels to my grandfather's life, whether he ever realized it or not, are striking. Widely reprinted in *McGuffey's Readers*, the opening words of the poem were required reading by many a schoolboy in the one-room schoolhouses of the day.

> *The Boy stood on the burning deck,*
> *Whence all but him had fled;*
> *The flame that lit the battle's wreck*
> *Shone round him o'er the dead. . .*

Instead of viewing this poem as a tragedy, however, those all too serious words became something quite different in the childhood doggerel of early 1900s rural Kentucky. And it was these words that my grandfather chose to remember.

> *The boy stood on the burning deck,*
> *Eating peanuts by the peck.*
> *The flames rose up and burnt his chin,*
> *But he kept on crammin' those peanuts in.*

In essence, I believe that the revision to those four lines summed up my grandparents' lives. I knew their struggles to stand on two feet in unforgiving places and times. I knew of my grandfather's abusive father who died young, leaving my grandfather as head of the family at age fifteen. I knew the fight to put food on the table amid the loss of a child (along with the near loss of another), a global pandemic, recession, depression, strikes and two world wars. And I knew the peace that somehow later transcended it all with a wry sense of humor. As my grandfather noted, "You think the old man didn't scratch some skinny asses? I have, I'll tell you. Poor ones. Yes, sir."

Neither of them was one to mourn their lives. Instead, they took joy in celebrating them. While the deck burned around them and others were lost, they just "kept on crammin' those peanuts in." Their children, who were carried in their arms, rode on their shoulders and ate from their tables, would become known as "The Greatest Generation." I might beg to differ. They couldn't have become as great if they first hadn't been shown how.

Though one could easily ascribe the stories herein to the genre of "I walked up hill to school—both ways," literally hundreds of contemporary reports, documents, letters, photographs and newspaper articles verified the accounts told here again and again, down to the smallest detail—though my grandfather would have been the first to admit that "dates don't mean nothin' to me."

It was a different world then. But it was the one in which Haskell and Florence grew up. And the one in which they formed their own views of the world. Their lives are not unique. They are not any more special than those of anyone else. They are just documented. As author James Baldwin once noted, "history is not a procession of illustrious people. It's about what happens to a people. Millions of anonymous people is what history is about."[1] This is the history of such a people. Once recognized as "Akron's largest ethnic group,"[2] the natives of Akron, Ohio, would later simply (and disparagingly) call them "hillbillies."

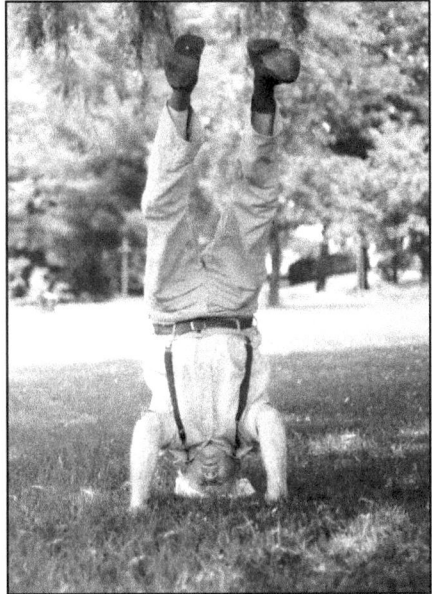

Haskell Jones on his 90th birthday, July 25, 1988.

PART ONE

GRAVES COUNTY, KENTUCKY
1900

CHAPTER ONE

"HILLBULLIES"

It has been alleged, and not without some color of plausibility that Kentuckians are belligerent by nature. We do not deny it. The crest of our state shows two gentlemen in swallow-fork coats, holding each other firmly by the right hand. The intent of the picture is plain. So long as they both hold hands, neither can reach for his hardware.

—Kentucky Humorist Irvin S. Cobb, 1916

Now long forgotten and literally buried under the bluegrass, the history of Kentucky includes numerous acts of violence in the decades following the Civil War. In fact the level of violence was so horrific that even *The New York Times* condemned Kentucky as one of "the most violent states in the union."[1] This was nowhere more evident than in the 6,000 square miles of western Kentucky encompassing Graves County that is collectively known as the Jackson Purchase or simply "the Purchase."

Annexed onto Kentucky in 1818 after President Andrew Jackson took possession of the land from the Chickasaw Indians, The Purchase was isolated from the rest of the state by the Tennessee and Cumberland rivers, which remained unbridged until the twentieth century. Geographically, this meant that many of its earliest settlers were from Tennessee and other southern states, not Kentucky. Economically, it meant that the area relied upon an economy based almost solely on agriculture and slaves (so much so, in fact, that it was referred to as "the South Carolina of Kentucky"). Politically, this meant that it was the most staunchly Democratic and Confederate portion of the entire state, supplying some "ten times as many men to Confederate service as to the Union, in stark contrast to the rest of the commonwealth, which produced perhaps three times as many Federals as Rebels."[2]

Following the loss of the Confederacy, gangs of "regulators" roamed the now defeated, impoverished and aggrieved area serving as "the pulse" of the white community to federal officials. "Usually operating at night and often in disguise," author Marion Lucas notes, "these self-proclaimed disciples of law and order threatened black and Union whites with whippings, burnings, and death."[3] As if this wasn't enough of a deterrent, five of the western Kentucky counties (Calloway, Crittenden, Graves, Hickman and Union) took turns successfully petitioning the commonwealth over the 1880s to legally allow them to reinstate public whippings—even though the practice had been eliminated throughout the State in 1873 and was all but non-existent in the remainder of the United States. In "The Debate Over Whipping Criminals in Kentucky," author Robert M. Ireland relates:

Of the five counties that revived whipping, three (Calloway, Crittenden, and Hickman) could whip any person regardless of gender or age. Graves County could whip any male convicted of petty larceny regardless of age and Union County could whip any male person over the age of fifteen so convicted. Crittenden County could also whip convicted wife-beaters, the only county allowed to do so . . .

Only two counties that revived whipping appeared to have whipped convicted criminals, Calloway and Graves. In Graves, the statute mandated whipping of all males convicted of petty larceny, and the circuit court ordered two of three so convicted to be whipped. (The third, A.B. McAllen, who was sentenced to jail for one month, might have been a woman). Apparently none of the three was an African-American."[4]

Relations Between the Races

By any measure, the white residents of The Purchase were going to do what they wanted, when they wanted and to whom they wanted without much regard to prevailing law. This was particularly true when it came to relations between the races.[5] In *A History of Blacks in Kentucky* authors Marion Brunson Lucas and George C. Wright document that:

Lynchings occurred in all parts of the state in both urban and rural areas. Over 42 percent (149 of 353 lynchings) occurred in western Kentucky . . . More specifically, the Jackson Purchase area, comprised of only seven counties, accounted for forty-nine lynchings. Within that area, Fulton County had at least twenty lynchings and Graves County had thirteen.[6]

In another work, author Wright comments that Mayfield was "a town . . . that richly deserved its reputation as a hostile place for blacks."[7] With incidents of violence steadily growing in numbers since the end of the Civil War, however, the animosity against the black population came to a head in December 1896 with the very real threat of a "race war." This occurred after Henry Finley was called out of his house by a mob and murdered on the 19th, Jim Stone was dragged from the jail and lynched, on the 20th, an unsuccessful attempt was made on the life of Tom Chambers on the 21st, and 18-year old Will Suet was shot and killed on the 24th.[8] As *The New York Times* reported, "the killing of Suet has aroused the negroes to madness, and they swear to wipe out the town."[9] "Telegrams from Water Valley said that the negroes had massed there, 250 in number, and that everyone had some sort of a weapon. News of a similar nature came from Wingo."

The whites in Mayfield, the county seat, panicked as "All women and children were ordered to remain off the streets after 6 o'clock." "Hundreds of farmers came to Mayfield . . . and [were] being armed to assist in saving the town if hostilities commence." To ensure even more reinforcements, "a dispatch was sent from Mayfield to Fulton as soon as the alarming reports began to come in, asking aid of the white citizens. A reply came at once stating that a special train would be chartered and a body of armed men would reach Mayfield as soon as possible." When one group of citizens from Fulton reached town, however, "They reported meeting a mob of 200 negroes, every one armed with a rifle, on the outskirts of the town."

Fortunately, with the passage of night, cooler heads prevailed as "a petition, signed by over 100 negroes, asking for peace" calmed the white citizenry and "many of the armed citizens and volunteers from surrounding towns returned to their homes." By Christmas morning, "nothing remain[ed] to tell the story of the race trouble, but three newly-made graves in a corner of the Potter's field, the charred ruins of four houses and hundreds of bullet holes in buildings and trees."[10] "Regardless," authors Lucas and Wright note, "the show of armed resistance from Afro-Americans clearly demonstrated their discontent with white oppression and a willingness to adopt drastic methods when necessary."[11] At best, it made for an uneasy peace in Graves County.[12] Or, as author George Wright called it, "polite racism"—where one was expected to know their place and act appropriately.[13]

Although Mayfield would witness two more lynchings before the end of the century with the hanging of Richard Allen and Thomas Holmes on February 23, 1898, eventual public pressure and sporadic legislative efforts under the occasional Republican administrations worked together to put a halt to outright lynchings in the Commonwealth.[14] That isn't to say that the public executions ended, however. What had once been extralegal lynchings simply became "legal lynchings" at which trial, verdict and execution took place on the same day—often before a baying mob. The citizens of Mayfield would gain particular experience in this area with the public executions of Robert Blanks on April 18, 1899 and Allen Mathias on July 31, 1906. That of Mathias would gain particular notoriety for the speed of "due process"— or lack thereof.

The truth of the matter was that the scaffold had been assembled in advance of the trial in anticipation of the expected verdict. It was not long in coming. Without any case for the defense being presented, it took only 55 minutes to arraign, try, convict and execute 16-year old Allen Mathias on charges of criminal assault—despite the fact Kentucky law prohibited execution within 20 days of a verdict "unless the safety or welfare of the commonwealth demands it."[15]

As a particularly chilling sign of the times, one of my grandfather's most prized boyhood possessions (until his mother disposed of it) was a piece of the rope used in that last "legal" hanging—by which the defendant had to be dropped five times before he finally expired. "I wasn't more than six, seven years old," Haskell noted decades later. "Maybe eight. My dad took me to town a day or two later— took me down there and showed me where the crowd pulled the fence down that was around this jail yard to see the hanging. The scaffold was still standing there."

With its reputation for swift "justice" solidly assured, law enforcement officials in the substantially larger city of Paducah in neighboring McCracken County would defer to Mayfield as the source of "regulation" ropes ("a hemp rope one inch in diameter and 30 feet in length") to aid in its own criminal proceedings.[16] In fact, Chief McNutt of Mayfield could offer Sheriff Ogilvie of McCracken County his choice of two such ropes that he happened to have on hand. The one Sheriff Ogilvie chose had no doubt to its reliability as *The Daily Messenger* helpfully noted "it had been used previously around two negroes' necks since it has been in Mayfield."[17]

While the execution of Allen Mathias would serve as the last "legal" hanging in Graves County, it would not be the last public one. Less than ten years later, with the lynching of one local felon popularly known as "Tom Tinker," it would become evident that the relations between the races were but one example that "justice" was in short supply.

The Tobacco Wars

Night Riders.

Although the War Between the States was now 35 years past and racial conflict was on a simmer, armed warfare would nevertheless soon again break out again in the western half of the state known as "the Black Patch"—so named because of the dark tobacco that was grown there and, if other stories are to be believed, in soil so poor it was about the only thing that could be grown there.[18] From 1904-1910, members of the "the Planter's Protective Association, who were trying to organize the planters into a collective to stabilize prices, battled The American Tobacco Company, which was manipulating the market through coercion and strong arm tactics to keep prices artificially low. Caught in between were the independent-minded tobacco growers who refused to become members of the collective. To them, The Planter's Protective Association "smacked of loss of control and individual liberty."[19]

As a result, gangs of dozens and even hundreds of horse-mounted members of the collective known as "the Silent Brigade," the Night Riders," or "the Possum Hunters" (because they hunted by night) swept through Central and Western Kentucky in military precision. Dressed in hoods and wielding torches, they issued threats to law enforcement, burned the warehouses of the American Tobacco

Company, and sought to intimidate the independents—by whatever means possible.

Numerous sources claim that the term "hill-billy" (a designation of which my grandfather was always quite proud) originally referred to the independent planters who, stubborn as billy goats, refused to join the Association.[20] Others claim that it was the "hill bullies" that the tobacco trust sent into the hills to forestall their efforts that led to the creation of the term "hillbilly."[21] Wherever the truth may lie, the term "hill bully" could have easily been applied to many of the residents of Western Kentucky.

Although blacks were initially counted among the Planter's Protective Association's membership and rode alongside whites in public parades (being one rare example of racial equanimity in the face of a common threat), the Association's tactics quickly devolved from that of simple intimidation, the scraping of fields and destruction of crops. As tempers flared, it instead became a bloody free-for-all of brutal whippings (of men and women), lawless vigilantism, racial terrorism, and cold-blooded murder.

Located in the very heart of "the Black Patch" and recognized as the largest loose tobacco market in the world, Mayfield remained curiously immune to much of the overt violence.[22] In fact, following a massive fire in the city which destroyed four large rehandling barns filled with over 200,000 pounds of tobacco, editor James R. Lemon of *The Daily Messenger* dismissively commented, "the fact that barns of tobacco had been burned in other counties led many to think at the first moment that it was caused by Night Riders but this rumor was quickly dispelled as any person who is acquainted with the tobacco situation in this county knows that there is no occasion for Night Riders or such reports."[23]

It is debatable whether Lemon's comments implied a tacit acknowledgement that the situation was so well under the control of the Planter's Protective Association that such actions would not be necessary, a winking example of a collective "folk silence" that purposely quashed any mention of the fire's origins or some combination of both. Either way, editor Lemon of the *Messenger* frequently and forcefully made himself very clear on one point: membership in the Association was *highly* recommended.[24]

A Culture of Violence

Regardless of the whys and why not's, the impact of geography, the relations between the races and what are still referred to as the "the Tobacco Wars" a culture of violence was so pervasive in Graves County that the Mayfield *Messenger* estimated that there were some 6,000 pistols in the county by 1909. This, among "a total of 9,000 persons in the county, who are big enough and old enough to own or carry a pistol." The article went on to comment that "if the real truth could be known there are at least 500 pistols in Mayfield on county court day with an ordinary attendance."[25] They often were found in combination with the bootleg whisky (or "bug juice") brought into the nominally dry county from nearby Paducah—which created its own slew of problems.[26]

In an article entitled, "Pistols and Whisky on Easter Day," detailing an Easter Sunday disturbance in which 14 were arrested, the *Messenger* commented "it is getting so that the church people cannot have a public gathering on Sunday without a lot of drunken men and boys visiting these gatherings, getting drunk, cursing, drawing their pistols and raising all kinds of disturbances."[27] Many of the local populace may not have been similarly aggrieved.

"The nearly palpable atmosphere of violence in which the Black Patch people lived and died seemed normal to them," author Suzanne Marshall would conclude in her book, *Violence in the Black Patch of Kentucky and Tennessee.* "Their preachers told them that a harsh God sanctioned violence and its use by fathers against wives and children. People who grow up in violent cultures become socialized and desensitized to the use of physical force. It becomes an acceptable method of instilling discipline, obedience and control."[28]

Acceptable or not, justice would be strained to keep up in the early years of the twentieth century in Western Kentucky—even on the rare occasion a criminal was arrested and put into jail. In the parlance of the times, the county jails in both Graves and nearby McCracken Counties "leaked like a sieve." In fact, escape after escape was documented in the local papers to such an extent one has to wonder why they even bothered with jails and didn't just look for foster homes.[29] The situation was indeed so dire that prisoners were actually celebrated in the paper when they chose to remain behind during a mass "delivery," as a jailbreak was then called.[30]

When Tom Tinker did manage to remain captive in the Graves

County Jail, the law was asked to step aside as the citizenry volunteered their own particular form of "justice." In a sign of the times, the law willingly complied, allowing Tinker to be lynched on the town square. While editor Lemon "remonstrated," as Haskell Jones would have said, he also quoted Scripture as to why such an action had been necessary.[31] Ironically, he then also blamed the elected officials for not doing more to ensure prisoners completed the sentences to which they had originally been sentenced.

Family Ties

Although they were unrelated, Haskell and the woman who would become his wife, Florence, were both Joneses by birth. "There was more Joneses down there than there was peas in a pod, you know. There was just family after family after family of 'em," Haskell would later comment. The roots of both families, however, went deep into the earliest history of Western Kentucky.

The tale was told of a raid by Native-Americans, which resulted in the death of one infant. Another was told of the time a dugout canoe overturned killing that same infant's mother. Later, both sides of the family would come to own slaves. Haskell's paternal family shows ownership of eleven slaves—at least one of which had been given as a wedding gift. Likewise, Florence's grandfather, Joseph "Devil" Jones (also remembered as being an overseer for his in-laws, the Galbreaths) shows that he had ownership of eight.[32]

Joseph "Devil" Jones.

Although at least one family member (Haskell's paternal grandfather William B. Jones) bought his way out of the service during the Civil War, both families would include members who served the Confederacy. At least three of them were killed during the war.[33] One, Florence's grandfather, Simeon Augustus Carmen, became a Union prisoner-of-war at Rock Island, Illinois. And, following the war, yet another relative would take a former slave as his wife.[34] While Florence's immediate family would remain farmers and educators, Haskell's would also choose to serve the community as elected public officials.

(Rear, L-R) Marian Gertrude Carman (Florence's mother), John Carman, Nola Carman, (Front, L-R) Simeon Augustus Carman, Mary (Tooley) Carman, Charles Carman.

One of those elected officials was "Colonel" Robert Cook "Bob" James, Haskell's maternal grandfather, who (when he wasn't working as a carpenter) served as a deputy jailer and acting chief of police in the early 1900s.[35] Recognized as one of the area's pioneers, his actions were frequently a topic of interest for *The Daily Messenger*, which referred to him as "one of the bravest men in the county."[36] Bravery aside, there was certainly ample written evidence he found use for a gun on more than one occasion during the course of his duties.

With the last name of James and living where and when he did, there were also strong rumors within the family (which remain unfounded) that the outlaw Jesse

Robert Cook James and his wife Martha (Keesee) James in front of their home at 204 E. South Street in Mayfield, Kentucky.

Edwin A Jones. Although son Haskell would note that, "Some of my family said they knew [his middle name] was Alexander [as noted on the photo]," he never believed that to be true.

James may have been kin.[37] Even *The Daily* and *The Saturday Messenger* joined in by referring to Colonel Bob as "Jesse" James—frequently.[38] Considering the realities of Western Kentucky, this was not necessarily viewed as a bad thing. At the very least, according to Haskell, his grandfather, along with the entire James side of his family were "gun-happy," with more than one member being involved in fatal gunplay.[39]

Another of those public officials was E.A Jones, Haskell's father, who first served as a trustee of the county schools (where he met the schoolteacher who would become his future wife, Robert Cook James' daughter, Willie) and then as a local magistrate.[40]

A lifelong Democrat in a staunchly Democratic county, he was obviously well read, subscribing to a number of local, regional and national politically oriented newspapers. Unfortunately, he also apparently subscribed to the then-popular belief of "spare the rod and spoil the child" (under which he had most probably been raised). As author Suzanne Marshall would observe of the era, "the earthly father, in the role of Christian patriarch, applied discipline with varying degrees of severity when children (or slaves) disobeyed."[41]

Due to their combined influences, the two-room home in which Haskell and his seven brothers and sisters grew up was undoubtedly an educated, well-informed household (albeit it an occasionally violent one) in which issues such as politics, justice and current events were frequent topics of discussion. Some eight miles from town down an often-impassable road, it was also one of the few homes in Graves

County to have a telephone. That being said, living conditions within the home and on the farm were (to put it kindly) primitive. The family had a roof over their head, but that was about it. Much like their neighbors, there was no electricity. There was no running water. There was not even an outhouse. And an early death from what would be an easily preventable disease today or an accident on the farm was an ever-present threat.

As a result, when Haskell's father, E.A Jones succumbed to tuberculosis at age 51, his wife, Willie Jones, was left a widow with 8 children and precious little else. Within months, even the property on which they lived was put up for sheriff's sale on the courthouse steps for taxes due of $10.15.[42] After its disposal, still clinging onto a barn for which the family had little tillable land, they barely qualified for "dirt poor." And at age 15, the only thing Haskell was left was the expectation that now, as head of the family, he would provide and care for every single one of them. But then, as the eldest son with an often-absentee father, he had been doing just that since he was old enough to wear pants.

Such was life in Graves County, Kentucky, in the early 1900s. And such was the way of thinking that would be carried onto the shop floors of Akron, Ohio, in the early years of the rubber industry by thousands of Kentucky "hillbillies."

CHAPTER TWO

ORIGINS

The young man masters a trade, and soon finds himself able to earn from two-and-a-half to four dollars a day. His sister, pressed by the same necessity, enters one of the few occupations that are open to her sex, and finds that her daily wages are often less than half the sum he receives. He can generally earn three dollars with his hammer, his saw, or his trowel, while she, laboring the same number of hours, with equal patience and steadiness, is thought to be doing well if she receives a dollar and a quarter or a dollar and a half.

The Philosophy of Housekeeping
Joseph B. and Laura E. Lyman

Haskell A Jones.

Haskell: My earliest memory? My dad was unloadin' a load of corn in the crib we had back of the house. And I am too close and the horse kicked at me. It didn't hit me. It hit the end of the singletree and the end of the singletree hit me in the stomach and hurt me. [1] I went bawlin' in the house to my mother where Mom was nursin' my brother Ralph and she said, "Do you want to try this tittie again?" I was a crybaby, you know. I don't know whether I did or not. But I can remember her calmin' me down by tellin' me it was available. I'd been weaned, maybe six or eight months. That's about as far back as I can go. I was about two and a half. Somethin' like that.

One kid I knew (a real smart-aleck)— They were talkin' about how

13

Willie (James) Jones.

far he could remember back. I don't know whether you ought to tape this or not. He said he could remember one time that his mother was in the garden settin' plants. It was cabbage or potato or somethin'. He said, "I was reachin' down and pullin' 'em up." Yeah, he could remember back, too, quite a little ways. The kid was reachin' back pullin' them plants up as his mother went down the row settin' 'em out. He was an ornery bastard. Yes, sir. His youngest brother said, "Well, I can remember when Pappy was born."

My mom, Willie James, went to school in Wingo and then she moved to Mayfield. I can't put my finger on the time they moved to Mayfield. After she finished school (grade school), she went to the academy, which was tantamount to a high school. It was to learn how to teach well.[2]

The first school Mom taught was at a place called Swan, which was in the southeast corner of our county. I can't tell ya' exactly where it was. But it had a post office in those days. It was a grocery store, probably, that had a post office. But it was a school they called "Swan."[3]

She got twelve dollars a month and slept in. Sixty cents a day. That's exactly what she got. Sixty cents. 'Course sixty cents was pretty big in those days. They only had six months of school when I went to school. They might've had five back when she was teachin'. I don't know.[4]

She'd go to your house one week and my house one week and his house one week. She told me she had to sleep with two kids because of the week she had to stay at this house, they only got two beds. The old folks in that bed and her and two little babies got to sleep in this bed, see. It was a little bit rough, but— Ahh, people in those days expected things to be rough. They didn't expect all the fringes and everything.

My dad, Edwin Jones, was the trustee of the schools in Graves County and she came down there to get a school. She taught at Jones School three years and she boarded with his mother three years. The school was named for another family of Jones. A man named Jones gave the acre of ground for the schoolhouse site on the corner of his farm. She married toward the last of November and the school was probably out New Year's. So she probably was still teachin', see. They continued to live there a year or two with my grandmother. All the rest of the kids were married and gone and my dad was the farmer on the place. My oldest sister was born at my grandmother's. But I never had a positive sworn statement as to where I was born.

I got my name from a Methodist preacher who preached at the school where my father went to church. Wright's Chapel. It was an English family—the Haskells were. They moved on west and there's a lot of their names over there. There's a county in Texas named Haskell for him.[5] There was an Indian college named Haskell College.[6]

My dad was Edwin A and I was Haskell A. There was so damn many of the Joneses—more so of 'em than anybody else—they had to nickname 'em. They all had the same name. Tom and Will and such names as that. John and so-forth, you know. And Dad went by "A" [or E.A]. Hell, half– His own closest neighbors didn't know what his name was. He'd been called "A" all his life. He was named for an uncle who was wounded in the Civil War— His name was— Well, "A." Just

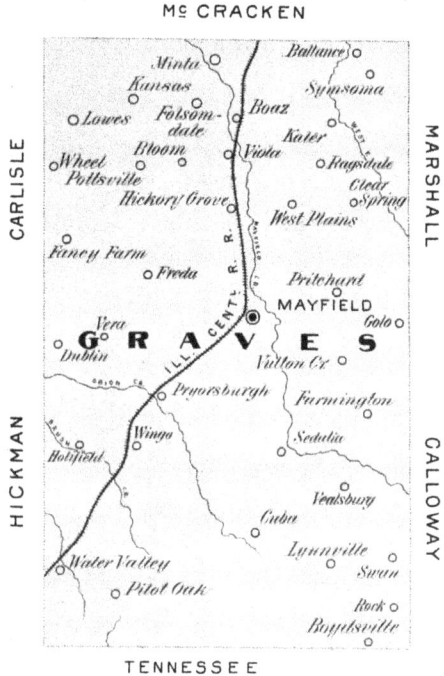

"Graves County, Kentucky, 1897." Located in the extreme southeast corner of Graves County, Swan was one of many small communities in the area that no longer exist. All that remains today of the name is Swan Road, which crosses 97 east of Lynnville (Twelfth Biennial Report of the Bureau of Agriculture, Labor and Statistics of the State of Kentucky, 1897).

an "A." That's all I know. So everywhere I had to go and give my name, I said Haskell A and they said, "What's the 'A'? You gotta' have that." "Gotta' have that." What the hell could I say? So, I adopted the Alan in order to quit answerin' questions.

"Aunt" Kate Kennedy

Haskell: Aunt Kate. Great old lady. That was the midwife that helped with my mother when she had her babies. I wouldn't doubt it if she delivered me and my eight brothers and sisters. I wouldn't doubt she helped deliver every one of 'em. Neighbor woman. She delivered half the kids for five miles each way. When a woman said, "It's about time." They didn't get the doctor. They got Missus Kennedy. Old Aunt Kate. Great old lady.

Aunt Kate kept a little bag behind the door *all the time* full of rags and lotions and whatever she needed—scissors and whatnot, you know. If her husband was home (old Uncle Clay), then she'd get in the buggy and he'd hitch old Mag up to the buggy and they'd take her over to Missus Brown or Joe Blow or whoever needed her. If old "Uncle" Clay wasn't there, it didn't make any difference. She grabbed that bag and took off walkin' and she went there.

She didn't stay twenty minutes 'til the kid was born. She stayed three or four days 'til the woman was able to get up and take care of her own business, you know, and everything. She didn't go home. She never got a nickel for it. If anybody would've offered her money, she would've been insulted to the ninth degree. Never! Not a penny! Nobody would've ever offered her money. That would have been an insult—because she didn't do this for money. She did it for the love of humanity. We don't have that anymore.

Robert Cook James

Haskell: My grandfather James built that little old house we lived in and he was a pretty good carpenter.[7] But he just framed that in and did the inside of the house and built the hall— There was just two rooms. Just a livin' room with two beds in it and a lean-to kitchen. There was an attic. That's all there was there.

My uncle Tom Jones lived in that little old house we lived in. But he screwed himself out of it, see. He had too many kids. He had Grover and Will and Grace and Lawrence. He had those four when he left there. They moved to the Stubblefield place. And then Dad moved in that house and fixed it up a little and finally built another couple of rooms on it. The boys could sleep up in the attic. A little stairway went up there. We slept up there—Ralph and I.

When I was born in it, it just had sheeting on it. It was just poplar boards up and down. Then they nailed a strip about three or four inches wide down over the cracks, you know. They called 'em "box-houses." They called that stuff that they put on the outside (that wide stuff) "boxing." And when they put it the other way, they call that "siding."

I was about ten or eleven years old when I helped my dad put lap siding on the house. We tore these strips off of the cracks. Then, you start at the bottom and went up. The stuff he got was evidently "seconds" or— I don't know what. A lot of it was short. Didn't go clear across. We maybe had a four-foot piece or a two-foot piece. So we had to butt 'em together. You measured this and figured out how much you wanted and cut 'em off that length, you know. Nail 'em up and make it fit. We painted that. Well, I guess it was all right. It stayed on there 'til the old house fell down.

We was a little better off than quite a few. We didn't pay much rent. My dad rented my grandmother's land and paid her seventy-five dollars a year for it. Cut her wood for her and gave her corn for her cows and chickens. Pigs. He looked after her, everything. Kept up the fences.

Sarah Ellen Jones

Haskell: My Grandmother, Sarah Ellen Jones, went to Paducah, which was about twenty-five miles away, to shop during the Civil War. I don't know if her husband was with her or not. I'm assumin' that he was because he wasn't in the army. He hired somebody to go in his place—which was a regular racket.[8]

A lot of 'em did it. Some of those guys would hire three or four times. They'd hire someone to go in their place and they might go into the army and stay there a few weeks and desert. And maybe go on the other side and hire in for somebody over there, you know. Get three or four hundred dollars—whatever they got. Didn't make no difference. It was a lot of money in those days. Then they'd desert there and go somewhere else and go under a different name and enlist somewhere else. That was a common racket.

Anyway, she went to Paducah and bought groceries. She bought a cook stove. And shoes for her husband. The soldiers were in the area. Both sides. And she knew they would take the shoes. Maybe the groceries. So she tied the shoes under her skirt between her knees. And in those days, no man would lift a lady's skirt unless she invited him to—which she wasn't going to do. So, she got home with the shoes.

My grandfather hid his horses in the woods. Every night, he'd take his horses and put 'em in the woods. And every time the word would get around, "They're comin' through," he'd take 'em and put 'em in the woods and hide 'em.[9]

Although the slave days was a little too beyond me, my grandmother had a slave girl.[10] When she married, her mother-in-law gave my grand-mother a girl about twelve or thirteen years old.[11] House-girl. And I guess she kept her 'til slaves was freed. I never did know what her first name was. She never did talk much about it. She did tell me about it though. She never told me any day-by-day things about it.[12]

If she was twelve years old when grandma got married in 1861, she'd've been about sixteen when they were freed in '65. So she didn't have her too many years, you know. I don't think my grandmother

Sarah Ellen (Wright) Jones, and her children. This photo would have been taken some time after 1884 following the death of her husband, William B. Jones in 1871 and son William Robert Jones who died at age 17 of typhoid. She would outlive all except Tom. (Standing, L-R) Lula Catharine (Jones) Bryan, David Luther "Luther" Jones, James Thomas "Tom" Jones, E. (Edwin) A Jones. (Seated, L-R) Sarah Ellen (Wright) Jones, Virginia A. "Jenny" (Jones) Knight.

was a slave owner who was proud of the situation. I don't think she was though she needed one, I'll tell ya.'

You can't imagine how much guts she had. Raised six kids by herself. Husband died when the oldest one was nine. Twenty-eight

years old. If he'd lived to been forty, she'd've had thirty-five kids. But she never complained.

She told me about her boys when they were growin' up, what they wore. They wore a shirt down to their knees. That's all. Nothin' else. Nothin' else. No underwear. No nothin'. Just made out of woven material. She wove it herself on a spinnin' wheel and all that stuff. Made her cloth and made these clothes. Sewed it by hand. Never had a sewin' machine. Did it all by hand. But the kids wore a shirt down to their knees. That's all they had in the summertime. Maybe in winter they might've had pants, you know. Summertime—barefooted, shirt down to their knees and worked in the garden, field, wherever. We don't understand that. That's over our head. We can't believe that.

She was tellin' me one time about one of the kids. They had a dirt fight. They was throwin' dirt at each other or somethin'. One of 'em got dirt in his eye and he was havin' a bad time. So the other one comes over and the guy's cryin'. He pulls his shirt up and he wipes his eyes with his shirttail to get the dirt out of his brother's eye. She told me about it. Laughed about it. Told me it was funny. I guess she saw it happen. He said, "Come here. I'll get the dirt out of your eye."

My dad's brother Tom cut my dad's foot off. Dad was eight and his brother was nine. Their father had died so they each thought they had to be the headman. They go out to the woodpile and Uncle Tom had the axe. You can imagine a nine year old tryin' to chop with an axe. Dad wanted that axe. He said, "Let me chop, too! " Uncle Tom was not giving him the axe so Dad put his foot down on a log where he was choppin'. His brother said, "Take your foot off of there or I'll cut it off!" He said, "Cut 'er off." And he cut 'er off. Everything but the little toe. Cut clear through the boot. Clear through the sole of his shoe. Must've been a good axe.

They put him in a buggy and hauled him about four or five miles for old doctor Merritt to sew his foot back on. Probably put turpentine on it as an antiseptic. Didn't have much else. Sewed it back on and they brought him home. He wore that foot 'til he was fifty-two years old.

They needed a tobacco barn so my grandmother had a barn built. A man by the name of George Leonard built the barn. A mammoth, big tobacco barn. I don't know what she needed with it, but she evidently did. Eighteen-eighty. He spent twelve months buildin' it. She had the trees. He cut the trees down. He hauled 'em to a local mill and had it sawed, brought it back and he built a pen (twenty-four by twenty-four) with a door in each end you could drive a wagon through, see. Got some help to make a barn raisin'—to raise it up and set it there.

Ohhh, I'm guessin' now. Let me— Don't let me guess too much. About eighteen, twenty-feet high. From there, they put the rafters on the thing, you know. He rived the boards. He made the boards to make the roof. He'd take good, straight oak timber and (with a fro) he would rive this board out and make it. And he'd nail the boards on the roof. Then they built a projection on each end and a shed on each side. And it was a great big— It was a good barn. Mammoth, good barn. Good barn. We used it for years. Finally lightning struck it and burnt it down—which was common up there in that country.

It took him twelve months to build it. She paid him one hundred dollars for buildin' that barn. In those days, for one hundred dollars you could buy forty acres of land. Easy. Yeah. A dollar and a quarter an acre, you could buy it. For a hundred dollars, you could buy a hundred and twenty-five— Just— You can't believe— You couldn't believe people lived like that—but they did live like that.

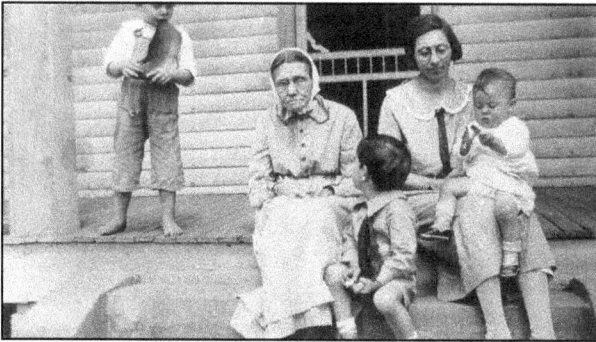

Sarah Ellen Wright with Haskell's sister, Mary Genevieve (Jones) Spalding and her children, John B. Spalding (looking up) and Ralph Charles Spalding (in mother Mary's lap). Child standing is unknown.

Grandma Jones was a great, old lady, I'll tell you. She probably didn't have too much education. Maybe eighth grade. But she had a lot in her head, I'll tell you. She wasn't a dummy. Good, old Methodist woman. Read her Bible every day. A great, old lady. If any kid had got out of line, she knocked him around or set him down—one or the other. She didn't bother with kids' gettin' out of line. They had to follow the straight and narrow. Grandchildren the same way. She used to give us hell if we was wrong.

We had lots of blackberries. Good blackberries. Great big, giant, nice blackberries. My old grandmother, I can see her come in from a blackberry patch red as your shirt. Red all over, you know, and sweatin' clear to her shoestrings, drippin'. Been out there and picked three, four gallons of blackberries and bring 'em in. And then, after she got in, she'd wash 'em and clean 'em up and cook 'em and put 'em in cans. They canned the blackberries or they'd make jam out of 'em, see. One or the other—whichever they had time enough for, you know. But God bless her. She was a great old gal.

She died at eighty-three years old. She never had an outhouse. My dad was only twenty years younger than his mother. Only twenty years younger. He lived with her 'til he married. And they lived in the woods. Hell, they had a hundred and sixty acres of timber when they settled this thing, you know. It was all growed up with great big, oak timber.

I don't know how she made it. I can't understand it. I had a rough time in my life, but nothing like she had. I know I never come close to what she had. Big farm. Nobody to farm it. Oldest kid's nine years old. How in the hell is she gonna' farm? A hundred and sixty acres of land. Not once did I ever hear my grandmother say, "We had it rough." Not once did she ever say that to me. And we were very close. Not once did she say, "We didn't have this. We didn't have that." She never complained.

She smoked a pipe in the evening when the kids was around. I don't know whether she smoked very much when the grandchildren was around, but she thought that was a kind of risqué thing to do. She chewed, too. She chewed tobacco. I don't think she used snuff. She might've had it when she was younger, but she chewed tobacco. She'd take a little bit and put it in her mouth and hold it. Yeah, she did. That was her sole dissipation, see. She had to have somethin' to do. She lived as a widow woman for— Well, from 1871 'til 1926.

* * *

Haskell: When times were good, we burned coal. We'd buy lump—what they call "nut coal." About this big [the size of a tennis ball]. Otherwise, you bought lump coal. Hell, some of 'em must've weighed thirty, forty, fifty pounds apiece, you know. You had to beat it up before you could put it in the stove.

If times were a little hard (we didn't make any money that year), we burned wood. And we went in our own woods and cut the wood, hauled it up and put it in the fireplace. We rode with the tide, you know, like everybody else.

But anyway, we bought that Western Kentucky coal. It wasn't too

(L-R) Mary Genevieve, Mattie Keesee, Haskell A and Ralph Edwin Jones.
Haskell: This picture, the four of us kids when we were little—I can remember
the day that was made. That was nineteen-three. I was five years old.
The first of November.

good. You had a grate in there and you'd throw that coal in there and get a fire started. And that oil and gas in that coal was tremendous. You can't believe it. You'd set here in front of the fire and watch it. There's a lump of coal in there and it starts to burn and gets pretty well goin'. All at once, a bubble would come out of it and it would shoot out a gas flame right out of the coal, you know. And it'd make pictures. We used to watch the pictures.

You could see people, caravans, various ramifications in there. Watchin' this fire, you know, it would develop— "Did you see that? Did you see that picture?" "Look at that camel over there!" "Look at that horse!" "Look at that rhinoceros!" "Look at that carriage!" Look at this— Look at— You could see them in the fire. And that was part of our life to set there and watch the various things develop in the fireplace.

We didn't have a pump. We had a cistern. You catch the water off the roof in a cistern. Have troughs around your gutters and a trough that runs from the house over to the cistern to carry the water into there. Rainwater. You bet your damn life it was filthy [from that smoke]. You'd get down there to about eighteen inches, two feet of

Florence's parents, Marian Gertrude (Carmen) "Mammy" and Joseph Jones with Florence's older sisters Frances Carolyn (left) and Mary Effie Jones (right), c. 1894.

water, and it looks like shoe polish. It was just as black. Dad let me down on the rope and send the bucket down and a broom. And I'd dip out what water was in there and then they'd give me some water to wash it with and scrub it out down there and get it clean. Had to do that every spring. Started doin' it when I was about six years old, probably. It was quite a job.

Florence: The first house that I lived in after I was big enough to remember it— The front part of it was two big rooms. I mean they were big. They was about eighteen or twenty feet square. And between that was a wide hall. And back of the hallway was the kitchen. We cooked and ate in the same room. There wasn't a dining room. There was a stairway in both of the big rooms that went up to the loft. Over one room was just a storage room and up over the other room, we had a bed or two where us kids slept most of the time.

I must've been about twelve or so years old— I can't remember just how old I was, but I was pretty good size kid when they built the house that we lived in the rest of my life down there. And it was pretty nice. It was a nice place to live in a lot of ways. It was right pretty when we got the new house built and the yard all fixed up. We had a lot of flowers in the yard. But back there, you couldn't have a bathroom out in the country like that. You had your little "back-house." So, that's the house we lived in up until us kids began to move away. I was the first one that got away. And the boys, as they got big enough (old enough to go out and work), they went out and worked.

There wasn't much to play with back in those days. Most children like dogs and cats to play with. We always had a dog at home. The first dog I remember, and he lived to be old, was "Nero." I think he was what they called a Newfoundland. He was a real good dog to have around the farm. After Nero died we had a shorthaired dog we called "Rat." He was a rat dog. He caught the rats so we called it Rat.

And we had cats. They stayed around the lot where the corn was. They could keep the rats pretty well cleaned out. Got too many, we got rid of all of 'em but one. Where they store the grain and stuff it was really good to have a cat or two around.

Haskell: We didn't have many dogs. We had one big yellow cur dog. He bit me pretty bad and my dad killed him. We never had another dog. But this dog chewed me up pretty good. I was about five or six years old. I don't know whether it was the dog's fault or mine. I'd had a wheel. It'd been the rim of a little toy wagon. The spokes and everything was out of it and I put it over his head. He turned on me and bit me through the wrist. He kept tryin' to get my throat. Dad was in the house and he run out there with a fire-poker and knocked the dog off me and patched me up. He was a big yellow cur dog. Big crossbreed of some kind. Name was "Rush." But that was the last dog we had around there as long as Dad was there.

My mom went upstairs one time where us boys slept and the cat had had kittens in the middle of the bed. And she blew her top—which she didn't do very many times in her life. Under the bed was some new axe handles. She grabbed one of 'em and killed the whole mess—the old cat and the kittens, too. She threw 'em in a bag and took 'em out of there. My mom was a fighter, but she was pretty well controlled. She could handle herself pretty good. It was out of character for her. Very much out of character for her. But I'll tell you, she didn't back off. If somebody would've tried to mistreat her, I'm sure she would've went to bat. Her family come from that kind of people.

Florence: 'Course we had a lot of chickens. And we killed chickens especially in the summertime. In the spring, the hens always went settin' and you either had to put 'em up where they couldn't run away (and be into things that you planted or what-have-you) or do something about 'em. Long through the winter, they didn't lay very much. But through the spring they laid quite a few eggs. And after so long, they'd set and there'd be a spell that they didn't lay eggs at all— they wanted little chickens. So, we'd put a certain number of eggs under the hens when they started to set—whatever we thought they could cover. After (I think it was twenty-one days. I'm not sure), the little chickens would hatch and we had to feed 'em with fine food so they could grow.

After they got so big, then we ate part of 'em. Parts of 'em would be pullets and parts of 'em roosters. And the pullets we always kept to lay the eggs. We'd sell the eggs that we didn't eat. The roosters— Most of 'em we killed and ate. We'd keep three or four, but most of 'em we'd kill and had fried chicken.

Dad killed enough hogs to make enough meat to last us pretty well through the year. He must've fattened about eight hogs. The first year, they wasn't big enough to make much meat. But the next year, that's when they killed most of 'em and put 'em down in a big box of salt— just cover 'em over good with salt.

After so long, they figured that meat had taken enough salt that it was cured and would be good. So, it would be maybe too salty sometimes, but not very often because they had a certain number of days that they figured on the meat takin' salt. And they took 'em up out of the salt and washed the salt off of the outside.

Then they have a smokehouse. They had rafters across and when they got this meat all washed off and dried, they would put a cord or wire through the shank and hang it up there and build a fire. Seems like they used mostly hickory wood. Some people used corncobs to make the fire under 'em to make the smoke. But, anyway, you made the smoke. Made it with fire under the meat in an old tub or somethin' so it wouldn't set anything afire.

The smoke would go up on that meat and you could tell by lookin' at it 'bout how many days you had to leave it. When it got as brown as they liked, they took it down and usually wrapped it in cloth of some kind so nothin' would get on it—no dirt or flies or anything. It usually hung up 'til we got ready for a different piece of it.

They had two big pieces—all dependin' on how big your hogs was, how big your sides were. But they were a whole side. But when you cut 'em up, you take the backbone out (right down the back) where you cut the ribs off. Then you peel these ribs out of the sides. And that's awful good meat. You use that up when its fresh meat and you just had the hams and the shoulders.

Anyway, they'd have the hams and the shoulders and the sides and— What else did we have? The jowl (that's their jaws). When it was cured, it made awful good meat to cook in your vegetables to flavor them. But anyway, Dad— While we were all at home I don't think that he ever killed less than eight. And they were pretty big hogs.

Haskell: I think my dad did the best job of curin' meat of anybody—except my grandmother. Dad was particular with his meat. I mean everything had to be just perfect. And he watched it. He knew just how long according to the weather to keep it in the salt. If it was warm a little bit, why, it would take salt faster than if it was a little cold. He'd put it down in salt and take it up and cleaned it up and smoked it good. He really put the smoke to it. He didn't mess around. He'd put the smoke to it.

Florence's mother, Marian Gertrude (Carman) Jones with her chickens.

Florence: I don't suppose my dad ever killed the chickens. Mother always killed 'em 'til I got big enough. Then I killed the chickens. My brother Kermit always followed me when he was just a little fellow. I don't know why, but he followed me around most of the time. But that was my job the day we was gonna' have chicken. I had to kill the chickens and pick 'em and cut 'em up—get 'em ready. I don't remember how big he was, but he wasn't very big. Said to me one day, said, "Florence, let me pick some feathers off." I said, "Oh, you can't help pick 'em off." Said, "Well, let me do it." "O.K. Here. You take this one and pick it." So he picked it and didn't do a bad job of it. So, when we had chicken again, he picked it again.

Haskell: We had plenty of food and a house to sleep in. We never went to bed cold or hungry. They used to buy a kitchen stove— The coal stove had about six eyes, didn't it?

Florence: Yeah.

Haskell: Six eyes with a warming closet on top and a hot water reservoir on the side. This reservoir would hold about five gallons?

Florence: More than five.

Haskell: More than five?

Florence: I'd say ten, anyway.

The E.A Jones family, Graves County, Kentucky, in front of the family home. (L-R, front row, seated) Grandmother Sarah Ellen (Wright) Jones, Mattie Keesee Jones, Grace Inez Jones and Lillian Roberta Jones. (L-R, standing) Willie (James) Jones (holding Thomas A.R. Jones), Mary Genevieve Jones, Haskell A Jones, E. (Edwin) A Jones and Ralph Edwin Jones (c. late 1908-1909). Not present is Henry Bascom Jones, born in May of 1911.

Haskell: It was pretty deep and so long. But the heat from the stove kept that water hot all the time, see. The cook had more hot water than she could get out of an ordinary teakettle. Wasn't as hot, but it was pretty hot. It was a good-sized stove. I remember my mother buying one. I'm almost willing to swear that it was forty-eight dollars. And it was a good stove. A good-sized stove. Nickel trim. Nickel legs and the trim around the warming closet was nickel. It had a back on it and this back was just metal, but the back went up and supported this warming closet. And there was a nickel brace that come down and fasten on top of the stove on each side. Just a little ornamental brace and it was chrome. Forty-eight dollars. It'd get pretty warm when you had a fire in there all the time.

The little kitchen we had— Hell, it wasn't near as wide as this room. Had a table sittin' in it. Stove set in the corner. Flour barrel set over in that corner. There was an old pie safe set in this corner. Had a metal panel in the door punched with nail holes or whatever they made 'em with to let a little air in 'em. In the wintertime, they could put stuff in there because it was colder than hell in that kitchen. In the summertime, it wouldn't keep only one day at a time, you know. You cook a pie for noon and you'd be lucky if it wasn't spoiled by suppertime. Hotter than hell.

Mom didn't mess with one pie. She'd make two or three. So, if you got eight kids, what the heck? Ain't much for eight kids and two grown-ups. She baked cookies by the million, you know. Big, sugar cookies. Beautiful and good. Good. Oooh, they were good.

Used to cook forty-eight biscuits for breakfast. She had two pans. Each one of 'em held twenty-four biscuits. She made 'em both full. Well, we had breakfast. With eight kids and two grown-ups, you know, they didn't go too far. But they didn't eat 'em all. Packed the school lunches. We had one biscuit with a sausage patty in it or bacon or a piece of ham or chicken or rabbit or whatever you had.

In the summertime you might have an ear of boiled corn in there. It'd be cold, but we ate it. We didn't have sweet corn. We had field corn. They called it "White Cob Willis" and "Red Cob Willis"—take your choice.[13] They fed yellow corn to the hogs, but humans wouldn't eat it. I used to haul that corn to a local mill and have it ground, bring it home. A half-bushel would last a family of ten a month.

They saved every little jar they got. Every little jar with a screw cap on it was a prize. That was in your lunch box. It had canned peaches or new fruit. Fresh fruit. We had a lot of blackberries. A lot of those people picked blackberries and canned 'em. A cookie usually. We didn't carry anything to drink in our lunches. We had no milk or anything. It would've spoiled in the summertime. In the wintertime, it'd freeze.

One good thing we had was a big orchard. That was a lifesaver when Dad set that out 'cause we ate out of that orchard from when the earliest apples were big enough to fry until the last one was gone in the fall. Every kind. We must've had twenty-five kinds. Liveland Raspberry. Transparent. I couldn't name 'em all. I doubt if they sell some of 'em anymore. They came from Stark's. He got all these trees from Stark's Nursery.

Ahh, we lived pretty crude, but we were happy. We didn't know we were poor. We had a good home. We had good food. Had enough clothes to keep us decent. Mom did the things that happened to make it possible, see. Worked like hell. Umh!

My mom was a hard-worker and a good woman and did her damnedest best. She didn't hate anybody. She treated people nice. She never was spiteful in any manner. She was a good, Christian woman. One of the best. Eight kids to do the hard way. Um! There ain't nobody ever worked any harder than she did—unless my Grandmother Jones. I'll give her credit for bein' top dog.

* * *

Haskell: We had the old "pack peddlers" when I was a small kid—not after I was grown. They'd about quit. But the immigrants (Arabs and Greeks and whatever) come in there and they rode down to various parts of the country. They could buy these things— There were houses in town that would sell this pack peddler stuff. Needles. Threads. Eyeglasses. Shawls for the ladies, you know. Knit shawls. Beautiful. Nice stuff. And a thousand different items. They had a pack this big that they carried on their back.

Later they begin to get a horse and wagon and go around on that,. But early, they didn't have enough money to buy a horse, see. They had to carry it. And they'd stay all night with people on the route and give 'em so many of this and that to get a night's lodging. They called 'em "Old Black John," I don't— Hell, I doubt if any one of 'em was named John. He was probably named Romero or somethin', you know. But I've seen 'em. Needles, thread and sewin' stuff and things of that kind. They had a lot of stuff on their backs.

Those old women didn't go to town. They was more or less land-locked. They stayed there and Old John would come by and they'd buy a bunch of stuff from him. I guess he made a livin'. But, like I say, as I got older they begin to disappear. I don't know when I ever saw the last of 'em. A long, long time ago. But they were operators. They'd set down and haggle with ya'.

If this pair of glasses— They had about fifteen, twenty pair. So your eyes were bad and nobody got an eye examination. Hell, they didn't know you could get one. So you'd put 'em on. You'd try 'em and try 'em and try 'em for fifty, seventy-five cents. Somethin' like that. You needle him down, you might get 'em for forty-five. But they come there to my house. They come to my grandmother's. "Old Black John," that was what they called him. But he carried a pack on his back that was inhuman. You can't believe. My God!

CHAPTER THREE

PUBLIC EDUCATION IN KENTUCKY

For they would be at a disadvantage if they had more of it, and at a disadvantage if they had none, and they are at a disadvantage in the little they have; and it would be hard and perhaps impossible to say in which way their disadvantage would be greatest.

—James Agee
Let Us Now Praise Famous Men (1941)

While art and literature have painted the one room schoolhouse as a beloved icon of American history, the reality in Kentucky was far from the pastoral tones of a Winslow Homer painting or a scene from *Little House on the Prairie*. Educators were undereducated, underpaid and overworked. Schoolhouses were poorly designed, constructed and maintained. And children struggled to learn under conditions that today would merit a visit from protective services prior to their immediate removal. It is a wonder that anyone wanted to teach at all. But, more than that, it is a testament to the teachers and administrators who were deeply committed to the education of their charges that the students were able to learn anything at all.

School Administration

As Florence headed off to school for the first time in 1902, there were 11,364 students in school in Graves County in 104 white districts and 20 "colored" districts.[1] The vast majority of these districts were comprised of one-room schoolhouses in which all students, regardless

30

of age, attended classes together through eight grades.[2] Kindergarten didn't exist.[3] Graded schools (in which the children were separated into different grades) hadn't come into existence.[4] And a High School was yet to be established.[5] There was no county board of education, nor was there anyone overseeing the health of the students who were attending school. [6]

During the preceding 1900-01 terms, teachers had been paid a per capita of $2.50 per student out of the state school fund, with an average monthly salary for white teachers being $38.34 (in the neighborhood of $1,030. in today's dollars).[7] For "colored" teachers, it was $27.35 (or some $738.00) per month.[8] With the start of the 1902 term, instead of being increased, the per capita had instead been cut to $2.32. Despite this reduction, the teachers in Graves County were counted among the top ten highest paid counties in the commonwealth.[9] Even so, their pay was still less than that of an "unlettered laborer" as late as 1919.[10] Unfortunately, that didn't even guarantee they actually received their wages.

The *Daily* and *Weekly Messenger* were filled with notices about teacher's pay being delayed. In 1915, payment in March was only partially made because the dog tax, among other sources of revenue, could not be legally transferred to the state school fund until the end of the fiscal year on June 30th.[11] In another instance, it was because the railroad tax hadn't been as yet collected.[12] In fact, as late as 1919, the Commonwealth of Kentucky would note in a report entitled *Child Welfare in Kentucky*:

> In addition to the inadequacy of her salary, a teacher is further embarrassed by the irregularity of payments. Often she is forced to work three or four months before she receives any money at all, and almost without exception she must wait two months for the first payment. Many teachers report that when a school term is over, they must wait until after their vacation before receiving their full salary for the previous year. This is a considerable hardship. Teachers borrow of their parents or of the bank and can never be certain of the exact date when the money due them will be paid.[13]

Until 1909, when many of their duties were transferred to the county, it was the local trustee (a position which Haskell's father, E.A Jones held) who wielded the ultimate power over the educational system of a district—not that he necessarily came to the position highly skilled or otherwise qualified. As an elected office (with three trustees per district), the requirements for this unpaid position were minimal.[14]

State law only required trustees to be over age twenty-one, of sound moral character and, "when not impracticable," literate.[15]

Qualifications aside, the position was a powerful (and quite lucrative) one. Trustees levied local school taxes to pay for the educational costs of their own district with little to no accounting of the funds.[16] They were responsible for building a schoolhouse, which allowed for its own opportunity for overbidding and kickbacks.[17] They fixed the schedule and term of the school year for each individual district, often opening and closing schools "for the most trivial reasons."[18] They also had the power to hire and fire teachers at will. Trustees were well known to provide a teaching position for a bribe and/or demand ongoing kickbacks from the teacher's salary.[19] Unfortunately, while many of the elections for the position were quite heated and contentious, "many districts chose trustees not for their educational interest or expertise, but rather for their promise to keep taxes low or to favor certain people in the teacher-selection process."[20]

School Conditions

Attendance in the public schools, while compulsory since 1896 for all children ages seven through fourteen (with Kentucky being the only southern state to have such a law at the time), only mandated that the children attend school for at least eight weeks—with "rural schools generally begin[ning] in July and over by the first of the new year."[21] There were, however, no provisions for enforcement of this law. It was just something else that the trustees were expected to take care of.[22] "The trustee naturally dislikes to prosecute his neighbors and friends and so is very slow about enforcing it," author Elizabeth Bliss Newhall reported in *Child Welfare in Kentucky*. "Very often he is not convinced that it is particularly important for a child to attend school regularly and so refuses to co-operate with the teacher in keeping up the attendance."[23]

In 1921, *Public Education in Kentucky* could still report that:

In one instance a trustee closed the school because his son was ill, and he did not want him to lose any time; therefore, other children had to wait until he was well. The teachers themselves, apparently without anyone's knowledge or authorization, also close the schools for days and weeks to do farm work, or visit, or go shopping, or rest. For example, a teacher, on securing her first pay, forthwith closed school for a week and proceeded to Lexington to do her winter shopping. Nothing at all is thought of dismissing school an hour or two earlier than the appointed time. That schools should begin and close regularly at definite hours, and that they should continue uninterruptedly throughout the term, are elementary points in administration that are disregarded at will under the happy-go-lucky, do-as-you-please regime that obtains in Kentucky.[24]

As a result, it's safe to say that school attendance was not among the highest priorities of administrator, educator, parent or child. In fact, within just one ward of Mayfield in 1905, *The Daily Messenger* reported that there were 796 children between the ages of six and twenty years old. Of that only 429 were enrolled. And of that number, the average attendance was just 212, less than 27 percent of the number eligible.[25] Outside the city in the county, where children were required to help with farm work and access to the schools was even more challenging, the percentage was far less.

For those who did find their way to school (be it students or educators) and make an attempt to learn despite the inherent disadvantages, the conditions encountered were, in a word, abysmal. *Public Education In Kentucky* recorded that:

Approximately 50 per cent. of these schoolhouses are painted and in fair repair. The common color is white, which is very attractive against the usual background of green. The other half have in most instances never had even an initial coat of paint, and are in ill repair. The roofs leak, the weather-boarding is off here and there, doors are broken, knobs gone, window panes out, walls stained, floors uneven and cracked, seats broken and out of place, and a pall of dust over all. These neglected schoolhouses teach eloquently the doctrine of shiftlessness, disorder, and indifference. Their silent lessons will undoubtedly be reproduced in the home, on the farm, in the factory and store . . . .[26]

Within the actual classroom, the same report noted that:

Only a few one-room rural schoolhouses have foundations; most of them rest on stone pillars without other underpinning. The biting winter blasts are thus free to sweep under the schoolhouse and up through the thin floor into the classroom to the discomfort of the teacher and children . . . .[27]

. . . . An upright Burnside stove furnishes heat, the fire being started by the first person who reaches school, whether pupil or teacher. As the margin before opening is slight, time is necessarily lost in waiting for the children to warm up. The stove usually stands in the center or front center of the room. In cold weather this method of heating almost demoralizes the school. Although it is not difficult to do, apparently rural teachers have not learned how to build a fire in these stoves so as to produce uniform and continuous heat. Constant use is made of "flash" fires—kindling is piled in, coal thrown on top, and all drafts opened. The fire roars, the stove is soon red hot from top to base, and the children nearby bake. Thereupon the windows are thrown open, the stove door opened, the fire dies down, and the room cools to the point of discomfort. During the course of a single day, this process is repeated again and again. Under these conditions, it is not surprising that almost every affliction known to children visits the rural school, closing them for weeks at a time, nor is it surprising that in inclement weather little school work is done, for the children are continuously on the move from one part of the room to another, either to get warm, or to cool off, amid indescribable confusion and disorder.[28]

Graves County certainly wasn't immune to these abysmal conditions in the public schools. In a scathing 322-page report on *Child Welfare in Kentucky,* it was reported that:

> In Graves County the investigator visited a schoolhouse situated about a mile from the main road on an almost impassable lane. At the time this road was dry; but the only way to reach it was on foot or horseback because of the terrible ruts from the spring rains. The house itself is in a swampy hollow. This is a one-room building without cloak rooms, with cross lighting and heated by an old broken stove (red with rust) in the center of the room. Window panes are broken and stuffed with rags. The stairs leading to the building are broken down.[29]

One school superintendent succinctly summed up the situation when he wrote "hundreds of farmers in Kentucky have more comfortable barns in which to shelter their stock than they have school-houses in which to train the minds and mold the characters of their children."[30]

Even if the school structures themselves may have been short of tolerable, the students would have had a better chance at them being survivable had there been the least effort at sanitation. Unfortunately, that didn't enter into the picture at the time, either. In *Child Welfare in Kentucky,* the National Child Labor Committee needed only four words to sum up the situation. "Kentucky neglects her children," the authors concisely noted.[31] In that report, H. H. Mitchell, M.D., went on to conclude that:

> "Of 41 schools visited in rural districts and cities of the fifth class, only six, or 14.6 per cent. were found with sanitary privies; in seven others the toilets were insanitary and a menace to health, but in a fair state of repair and insuring privacy; in the remainder they were filthy, many with excreta running out upon the ground exposed to flies and small animals. Some had large holes and cracks in the floors, in others the doors were broken off and dilapidated."[32]

As a result, when one child contracted a disease, all within a classroom might equally share in the privilege. *The Daily Messenger* reported in January 1914 on an incident involving Florence's older sister Frances, who had begun teaching in the county schools while still a junior at Mayfield High School:[33]

> Fanny Jones re-entered High School Tuesday morning, after spending the preceding term in teaching. Her school was not quite out, but an epidemic of measles broke out and when Miss Jones arrived at the school Monday she was the only one who did arrive. So she decided it was better to go to school than to teach one with no pupils.[34]

If the students or the teacher wished to wash their hands or otherwise needed water, it may have been drawn from a well (50 percent of the schools had one by 1920). Otherwise, if available, it may have been carried in a bucket from the nearest creek. Either way, all would share water from the same "community dipper." In 1912, the legislature finally outlawed said dipper or drinking cup in public places.[35] However, State Attorney General Garnett protested that the law did not apply to public schools as they "are not publicly frequented places" (neither did it apply to hospitals, he also argued).[36] Editor Lemon of *The Weekly Messenger* wholeheartedly agreed, stating that the law "will work a great hardship on many thousands of people and do very little good."[37] The paper subsequently posted a sarcastic little ditty that mocking the idea that now, "we've got to boil the ice."[38] This, decades after germ theory and antisepsis had become widely accepted within the medical community.

Fortunately, State Superintendent of Public Instruction Barksdale Hamlett prevailed. In an article in *The Daily Messenger* entitled, "Will Banish Cup of Death From Schools," Superintendent Hamlett stated, "I am not questioning the Attorney General's interpretation of the law, but I had something to do with urging the passage of the law, and I knew it was the purpose of its framers that it should apply to public schools. Certainly, if there is one place where it should apply for the protection of public health, it is in the schools."

Consequently, he added, "I do not believe, really, that we need the law to abolish the public drinking cup in the schools. I think we have ample authority in this department to make and enforce such a rule. We have charge of the schools of the state; but if the question is raised, I am determined to test it in the courts, if necessary."[39]

The encouraging news was that the one-room schoolhouses were on their way out. In fact, by 1916, Graves County quite possibly led the state in having the greatest number of high schools in operation, each of which were well on their way to becoming consolidated schools.[40] Even so, a comparative study of the efficiency of the state school systems published in 1921 reported that "Kentucky ranked thirty-fifth in 1890, thirty-sixth in 1900, fortieth in 1910 and forty-fifth in 1918."[41] Eventual progress in the educational system of Kentucky would surely be slow in coming

CHAPTER FOUR

EDUCATION

Haskell: I had kids, little girls five years old that walked two and a half miles to school when I went to school. Two and a half miles! With mud up to your shoe-tops. It was terrible. The situation was bad. But those old Scotchmen and Englishmen, they didn't know there was any different. That's the way they'd done it, see, a hundred years before.

Florence had one little old girl that went to school to her [Florence would teach school from 1917-1920], she walked as far as from here to downtown, I'll tell you. And for the first three-quarters of a mile, she didn't even have anybody to walk with her. A little five-year old girl. A little girl. A little girl. She was small. With a book and a lunch basket. Satchel over her shoulder to carry the book in. Pencils and paper and whatnot. And carried a little lunch box in her hand. If the weather was particular bad, her dad or her mother used to bring her to school—but not very often, you know. Most days she walked. After she walked pretty near a half mile, then there's some more kids would wait on her and walk with her another mile and a half.

Florence: It was a long way to walk to get to school. About a couple miles. And there was no way to get there but to walk unless Dad hitched the horses to the wagon and took us in. We might as well've been walkin' 'cause there was no top on the wagon or anything. When they first began to have any buggies to amount to anything, they didn't have any tops to 'em. Most of us girls was out of grade school by the time they had many buggies. And sometimes the weather would be so bad we couldn't get away to school. But if we could get there at all, we never missed a day. There was that one room school. It filled just about full of kids of all sizes.

We went to school to a schoolhouse that was on the road that went from Mayfield to Dublin. And every once in a while, we'd see a doctor or some kind of a person that would have a car and they'd be going along the road. Teacher could hardly hold the kids down when they'd hear one.

The assembled students of Jones School House about 1908 or 1909. Named for an area farmer who donated the land (and was not a relation to either Haskell or Florence), it was where Haskell and his siblings would all attend school. It was also where Florence would eventually teach school to Haskell's younger siblings. Haskell Jones standing on far left with hand on chin. Sister Mattie Jones standing next to him. Brother Ralph Jones, second row, fifth from left with hat on. Sister Lillian Jones first row, second from left.

Haskell: There was one family of Sellers. There was a bunch of them. There was Will and Roy, Essie, Alta, Albert and I don't know if there was any more. Some of 'em were older than I was. They had to walk a mile and a half with no roads through a lane that mud was knee-deep. Sometimes it would rain. They couldn't get home. The creek was up. If you had a field on one of these old dry creeks, you know, you put a log clear across the creek. You cut a new one and when it rotted, you put a new one in. Clear across from side to side. Well, they put a wire across the top up here so kids could walk this log. It's as high as that door from the dirt. So you had to walk on this log, holdin' on to a

38

wire up here to get across to go walk home. Maybe it's pourin' down rain. What the hell can you do about it? You can't stop the rain. I went when it was pouring down rain many a day.

Very few of those people would come and get their kids when it was pourin' down rain in the evenin'. They wouldn't come and get 'em. Ahh, they come through the rain, so why shouldn't these kids come through the rain? I never had anybody come for me, but we didn't live very far from school. We had probably a quarter of a mile. Not much more than that. So we could run home. Very few kids had a raincoat. Very, very few kids had a raincoat.

Boy, we had mud! Ooh! Ooh! Ooh-ooh! Ooh! The mud. You can't believe. You've never seen mud. You don't know what mud is. You never did see good mud. We had the very best mud there was. I mean, it was really top mud. Umh! No overshoes. You shoes would soak through by the time you got home. Your feet would be wet. Your mom would take your stockin's off. Maybe she'd rinse 'em out, hang 'em before the fire so they'd be dry in the morning. You could put 'em on to go back to school.

We sat in rows. Girls sat on one side of the room and the boys on the other side of the room. Had two rows of seats. One on each side. And as the seat went back toward the back of the school, they got bigger. I think there was three sizes. Three different sizes and four seats each. About twelve seats, I'd guess, on each side. There was two rows and two kids on each seat. They were double desks—had two kids on 'em.

Florence: The county schools were all one-room schools. And you had eight grades in that little room you had to teach.[1] You couldn't do justice to any of 'em because you didn't have enough time. School took up at 8:00 in the morning and out at 4:00 in the evening. There was no lights. Only just plain daylight.

Haskell: When they had entertainment in the schoolhouses at night, the farmers would bring lanterns. Ordinary kerosene lanterns. Barn lanterns, they called 'em.

Florence: Most all had lamps hanging in the barns so they could see about the cattle and whatever else they needed to have.

Haskell: Sometimes they'd have a coal oil lamp up on the teacher's desk. They had benches. Double benches with a desk drawer under here for your books and papers and so forth. Ink well on top for your ink pen. We had old steel pens in those days if you ever had to do any ink, you know. Terrible. Yeah, sometimes girls would set around and somebody would put her hair in the ink. She'd have big, long braid. Pick it up and she wouldn't notice it. Nah, I wouldn't do that.

Had one kid named Gardner Huddleston. He attached himself to me. He was a nuisance, really. He was a good kid. He was a very good kid. Only child in the family. But he couldn't let me alone. He attached himself to me. So he was settin' in the seat ahead of me and I went out and played around somewhere and I come in. I had a couple of those cockle burrs stickin' to my clothes. And I picked 'em off and rolled 'em in his hair. Had a hell of a time gettin' 'em out. But he was a nice kid.

School Books Adopted for the Next Five Years. Their Names and Prices. At Good Prices.

The American School Book Company secured the contract for furnishing for another five years to the children of the public schools of Kentucky their text books . . . . The text books adopted are largely the present State list, some of which the Commission, in submitting to the county boards classed as "antiquated." The books adopted are: Practical Primer, McGuffey's Series of Readers, Modern Speller, Ray's Arithmetic, Harvey's Grammars, Steps in English, Maxwell's Compositions, Natural Geographies, Willis' Physiology, Peterman's Civil Government Eclectic Elementary History, Kincaid's History of Kentucky, and Complete History . . . .

— *The Daily Messenger*
June 28, 1909

Florence: I'll never forget the first day I went to school. We had a man teacher and I was kind of timid and afraid of people anyway. We lived back there where we didn't see people that were strange too much. And I got inside of the door and there stood a great big, tall man in the door. I was kind of 'fraid to go in, but I got along okay.

The big girls and boys sat on the back seats. Then there was some that wasn't quite so big that the next size sat on. Then there was smaller ones that the first and second grades (probably third) sat on.

I used to get to sit with the big girls. Somehow, they took a notion that they liked me and if they was just comin' in or if we'd had recess and we's gettin' seated, there's a couple of 'em would take me and sit me in their seat between 'em. So I thought that was great.

Haskell: We had the little, old local paper—weekly paper. That's what I learned to read out of. My oldest sister had gone to school and she could read. We had the fireplace. So we'd set down there in front of the fire and spread this paper out and she'd teach me how to read these words, you know, in there. And that's where I learned to read—layin' on my belly in front of the fire.

When I started to school at five years old, I could read better than most of the kids that was eight years old 'cause I loved it. At eight years

The school that Florence and her siblings attended, Graves County, Kentucky. Florence Grace Jones (top row, fourth from left), Mary Effie Jones (top row, third from right), Frances Carolyn Jones (top row, first on right), Barton Augustus Jones (first row, second from left), Joseph Huel Jones (first row, third from left).

old, I'm spellin' with the kids twelve, thirteen, fourteen in their class and I'm beatin' their ears off, see, because I could spell. I wasn't a dummy—if I do look like it now. I wasn't then. I learned pretty fast. And I read every book I could get a'holt of. Didn't make any difference what it was.

One night, my mother was makin' a dress for one of the girls (my oldest sister, probably) for some party or school function or whatever. I don't know what. But she's settin' up there with that little, old treadle Singer sewin' machines pedalin' her feet 'til four o'clock, five in the mornin'. And I read a great, big book. Like an ordinary novel today. *Saint Elmo.*[2] I remember that book. He was English—of a good family, but a no-good rat. Cruel and everything else, you know. I read every word of it that night, settin' by her. She had a lamp on the machine and I could set on the other side of the machine and read. Didn't have any electric. We had coal-oil lamps.

But you'd go to school there 'til fifteen or sixteen years old.[3] That was about the end. There was no grade. They didn't grade. They called you a "fourth reader," "fifth reader," "sixth reader," or "third reader"—whatever. That was about the grade they give you, you know—whatever reader you was workin' in at that time. We didn't have a "sixth reader." We had fifth and that was it. After that, everybody was in the same class. Big kids, little kids, anybody that made it through the fifth reader was in the top class. And you could go as long as you want to. Stayed in the same class. Never got any higher than that. And I went to school 'til about 1915.

We spelled and did arithmetic and grammar and whatnot—which I didn't use much. My conversation will explain to you I didn't use much grammar. I had no problem with that. I had no problem because I didn't worry about it. But we weren't exactly ignorant when we come out of those schools. We had a pretty good smatter of history, geography, arithmetic, spelling and reading. How much is there more than that? We knew nothin' about physics or science or anything of that kind. Even the teachers never heard of it.

I was a pretty good student—for a dummy that come up in the kind of school I did. If I'd've had a chance to go to high school or somethin' like that, I would've probably got an education, but I— Nothin' I could do about that. The conditions just didn't do that. But we lived to be ninety years old, just the same, and wasn't considered an idiot by anybody.

I think today they may be better off to go back to old man *McGuffey's Readers* and learn some morals. Every lesson in the *McGuffey's Readers* from the second grade to the fifth reader was a moral story. There wasn't some weirdo story. It was a moral story to teach people to be honest, reliable, and— People that loved their fellow man and did what they supposed to do to be honest. They haven't improved on it, I don't think. Of course, I'm a dummy. It don't make any difference. I'm a dummy. I know they'd say, "That old man is nuts. He's crazy. He don't know what he's talkin' about." So, they can say that. But they can't prove it.

Teachers

It is not often that a maximum is fixed for teachers' salaries, but that has been done in Kentucky for rural elementary schools. Chapter 117, Laws of 1912, provides that not over $70 a month and not less than $35 shall be paid for such service, and that the amount paid shall be based on and regulated by the qualifications of the teacher and the number of children in attendance in proportion to the school population.

—Report of the Commissioner of Education
Made to the Secretary,
United States Bureau of Education, 1912.

Considering the low standard for teachers and the totally inadequate salaries, it is not surprising that one finds the quality of instruction in these schools exceedingly poor. The most noticeable feature is the purely textbook recitation. Questions are asked directly from the book and the only answers accepted are those given in it.

—Child Welfare in Kentucky, An Inquiry by the
National Child Labor Committee, 1919

Haskell: Teachers didn't amount to shit in those days. They didn't amount to anything. All they did was assign lessons. And hear lessons. Hear recitations. They couldn't help you much. If you didn't know what a word was, you'd hold up your hand. And, if she had time, she'd let you come up and say, "What is the word—" "How do I pronounce it?" And whatever it is, you know. But it was about the height of their teaching.

They'd give you a lesson out of the book and say, "We'll have page thirteen, fourteen and sixteen"—or whatever. And you had to study that. Maybe take the book home. And the next day, you'd have arithmetic. You'd have ten or twelve or fifteen problems. You couldn't do that for all these kids. Here you got about six or eight, nine, ten kids in a class. They sat on a bench here. The teacher settin' up here.

She'd say, "Tom Jones, you put that problem on the board." You went up and you said, "There's fourteen apples and ninety-nine seeds in each one of 'em." And how much it is. Whatever the problem was in the book. And you had to put it up there and explain it. But the rest of the kids sat there like a dummy. They didn't know who was gonna' be selected, so they had to study, you know, because they might call on Bill Brown or somebody over there to do this. But if they called on you, that was your job, see. Then, that was arithmetic.

Then, the history. They'd say, "When were the slaves brought to this country? Sam Smith." That was his answer. If he didn't know, he was not considered a good student, you know. This little gal knew over here. She'd tell you 1609. Whatever it was. And then geography. I had that down to a science. I loved geography. When I quit school, I could draw a map of the world on a dozen sheets of paper and put every river nearly in the world on a map.

We had to buy these little dictionaries. They cost us maybe fifty, seventy-five cents apiece. But it's been worth a fortune to me because I can understand— I can't say all the words, but I can pretty well understand what they mean—which helps a whole lot. It helped me in spelling. I'm a pretty good speller. Spelling. History. Geography. That was my reading. That was my four good, favorite subjects. And grammar—which I didn't like.

Florence: That's one thing we had to learn going through school in the country was to read and spell. I remember when one of our adjoining schools thought they was real good spellers and they challenged our school for a spelling match. So, we said, "Okay, where do we spell?" And they wanted us to come down to their school.

They'd just be two spell at a time. And the one that missed had to sit down and the new one spelled against the one that hadn't missed. So, come my turn— I was in the fourth grade and it was up to the ones that was in the sixth, seventh and eighth grade. I can't remember how many I spelled down, but I spelled down the last one. And they was big teenagers! They got so mad! I forgot what it was the last one said. I can't think what it was she said. But she was so mad because I was little and spelled them down.

She got mad at our teacher because she brought us down. Her name was Maude Mason. It was wet and nasty and Maude had left her overshoes in the house and she sent one of the kids back in to see if she could find 'em. So, she went in and to ask. Said, "Do you know where Miss Maude's overshoes are?" And she said, "There's somebody's old things over here!" But they never again challenged our school to spell against 'em.

Haskell: Arithmetic— I was just fair in it. I never particularly liked it. I got my lessons and got the answers most of the time, but I wasn't a mathematician by any means. My mom was a good student of mathematics. Florence was. Florence was very good. But I can't say I was.

When we was kids, if you finished the eighth grade, then you went to the county superintendent and took a test to teach. Some of those kids was teachin' when they were fifteen, sixteen years old. But there was nobody else to teach, so they had to. They was supposed to be eighteen, I think. I think that was the law. But if you wasn't— If you was sixteen, seventeen and you would teach and they needed a teacher, why, they gave you the school. They couldn't prove how old you was anyway because you didn't have any birth certificate or social security card or anything else to prove how old you was.[4] So, I would guess that I never went to a schoolteacher that had more than an eighth grade education.

My teachers? Evalina Key Sellors. She went by Evalina Key. Her husband was George Sellors and only lived a few years and he died. And I don't know— She always went by her original surname. Then I had one named Ann Stephens. Meaner than hell. Annice Wilson. Earl Wright. Aubrey Wilson. Flora Ray. Best teacher I ever went to. I went to her two years. She knew how to teach.

She's the one that taught me the dictionary. She give us a page in the school dictionary. It wasn't a big Webster or anything like that. It was a school dictionary. She give us a page every day. Come up with a definition. You have a class and she'd call on you. "What does 'hippodrome' mean?" What does this mean? What does that mean? It wasn't in the curriculum. It wasn't supposed to be. It wasn't part of the public thing, but she believed that was worthwhile and she did it on her own.

I had Josh Boyd. He didn't die soon enough. He should've died when he was born. He was mean. He was an overbearin' little radical man. Radical. Radical. Radical. He'd beat the hell out of you for anything, you know. He loved to do it. Talkin' out of turn or missin' a word in class or some little thing.

He used to make me sit on the floor and put my feet up on the rostrum, you know. Set there for half an hour. And couldn't put your hands down, either. To punish ya'. Kill ya'. He didn't care. Mean as hell.

He started to whip this great big girl (she was sixteen, seventeen years old) for some minor infraction. It was nothin' to amount to anything, you know. The day that Claude Bright told Josh he wasn't gonna whip that girl, he liked to died with apoplexy. Claude was about twenty years old. He had kind of a mean reputation, but he wasn't a bad guy. He was just ornery. He was dyin' with T.B. then. He got sick. Knew he was gonna' die. So he started back to school.

Josh told Claude he was runnin' that school and he'd do as he wanted to. It was his job and he had to do it. Well, we had a fire poker about this long—as big as my thumb. Claude picked this poker up and went about halfway up to him and said, "Go ahead." Said, "You hit her and it's the last thing you're ever gonna' do 'cause I'm gonna' kill you! Don't you do it!"

Josh said, "I'll expel you from school!" Claude said, "You can do that. But I'll come back here if you ever hit her. I'll come back here and I'll still kill you!" And Josh knew he'd do it, I'll tell you that. Old fella' said, "I'll kill you if it's the last thing I ever do! Don't do it!" Said, "She's a woman. That ain't no little kid. You gonna' get up here and whup her front of the class? In front of the schoolhouse?" Said, "You ain't gonna' do it. That's all."

Jones School House, Graves County, Kentucky. Josh Boyd (far left, in coat and tie), Haskell A Jones (standing to right of Boyd). Brother Ralph Edwin Jones (right of Haskell in cap), sister Mattie Kessee Jones (first row, second from left), sister Lillian Roberta Jones (first row, third from left (c. 1910).

Josh didn't do it, either. But it's a wonder he didn't die, I'll tell you. He swelled up like a poisoned pup. Ooooh-oooh! And all of us kids were holdin' up, you know, laughin' under our skin. We was hopin' he would kill him. I'd holler, "Go, man, go!" if he'd hit him with that poker. He could've killed a horse with that poker 'cause it was quite a club.[5] Old Claude. Son of old Ambrose Bright. Mary Ann Bright. He was the town bad boy. The local bad boy. Old women used to put their kids to sleep, say, "If you don't behave, old Claude Bright will get you!" He was an ornery bastard.

Last time my mom slapped me, she told me Josh Boyd died and I said, "I hope he died a miserable death." And she slapped me—

backhanded me in the face. Not hard. "You ought to be ashamed!" I said, "I ain't ashamed. I'd've loved to kicked him in the ribs while he was dyin'."[6] He wasn't even smart. He was just mean. One of these apoplectic guys. When he'd get mad, he'd get red. His face'd look like a Washington apple, you know. Just get red as fire.

Went to Jim Grace. I think I went to him a little bit. He was a nice man. A little, old guy. He knew how to get along with kids. He never had any problem with any kid. He was really a master mechanic. I got a census record of 1880 and he was teachin' school in 1880. He told us he was teachin' his fortieth school when he was teachin' there at Jones. A woman teacher was about the last teacher I went to. I guess Willie Fuqua.

Florence: He was lucky to go as much as he did—after his dad died and him and Granny [Haskell's mother] and the rest of the kids were big enough to work. Had to take care of what they could on that farm—make enough to live on.

Students

Haskell: We had a lane that went down back of the schoolhouse, over the hill. And after we got to be any size, we wouldn't go in the outside toilet. They had an old outside toilet that was terrible to get in. We'd go down the lanes, you know. Nobody lived down there for a mile.

When two kids couldn't agree, they'd go down the lane and fight. The teacher couldn't see 'em from the schoolhouse. The women teachers, they never went down there. Now Aubrey Wilson was a different. Aubrey was a pretty good teacher. His brother and I, we had a fight. Matt. Matt, his name was. I can see old Matt now. He said "Brother Orbery." that's the way he said it. "Brother Orbery."

Aubrey lived in an adjoining district and Matt wasn't gettin' along at school very well. Matt was my age. We was probably thirteen at that time. So Aubrey told his mother he'd straighten him out or beat his ass good, you know. One or the other. So Matt and I had a fight. And in the fight, some way or the other, I skinned his nose. I don't know whether I clawed him or what happened. But the hide was off his nose. It was bleedin' a little. Dried blood on it.

We come in and Aubrey was a very precise guy. He finally made a preacher. He didn't call him "Matt," like everybody else. He called him

"Matthew." Very proper. "Matthew, what's the matter with your nose?" Matt said, "Why, brother Orbery, I scratched it on a briar."

I was prone to get into a fight every once in a while. I jumped on one guy one time. I thought he was a boy about my age and I found out he was a man. If they hadn't pulled me off of him, he'd beat me to death. Ahh, I was about fifteen or sixteen years old. I felt I could whip anybody. I found out I couldn't.

Jones School House, Graves County, Kentucky. (L-R, back row) Flora Ray, Nora Curd, Etta Moore, Orie Skaggs, Minnie Barnell, Robert Glover, Cecil Barnell, Orville Lassiter. (L-R, front row) Haskell Jones, Courtland Bryan, Etta Morgan, (Unknown) Riley, Genevieve Jones, Lillian Riley (c. 1912).

But I had a lot of buddies. This Ben Middleton, he was a big kid for his years. He was an orphan boy. Lived with people named George Gossett. He was a big, strong kid. A whole lot bigger than the rest of us for his age. We was down the lane there one day and— I don't know what brought it up, but old Ben says, "I can whip every kid down this lane." Well, there was seven or eight of us. But he was about twice as big as any of us. And we didn't think he could, but he did and he knocked us around somewhat. He was too strong for us, you know. So, we kept fightin' old Ben. Every recess and dinner we'd go down the lane. We weren't mad at him. We liked him.

After a while, somebody'd draw a line in the dust and old Ben would dare anybody to get over it. And when they did, he'd clout 'em. He didn't know any more about fightin' than Adam, but he was strong when he hit you. Boy, he knocked you around, you know. Weighed about a hundred and seventy pounds and the rest of us weighed sixty-five or seventy.

I hit him with a stick one day. I had hid me a long stick in the brush and he was fightin' somebody else and I run in and rapped him on the head with this stick. He turned around and kicked me as high as that ceiling. He like to broke my back. Right in the setter. Man, he lifted me off the ground. I liked the guy. We was settin' on the same bench. We had double seats in school, you know.

We wasn't mad at him. But we kept fightin' him and we grew a little faster than he did. There was too many of us. And finally we used to make it pretty tough on him. After he got up about sixteen years old, he left there. Went out west somewhere and stayed awhile and come back. He was as big as a Georgia steer.

Jones School House, Graves County, Kentucky. (L-R) James (Jim) Grace (teacher with his 40th school), Terrell Gilbert, Haskell's older sister Mary Genevieve Jones, Gardner Huddleston, Minnie Barnell, Haskell's brother Ralph Edwin Jones, Vera Carter, Gonza Ballard, Orie Skaggs, Etta Moore, Treva Harned, Lexie Gilbert and Haskell Jones.
Photo taken during his return visit as a non-student (c. 1916).

CHAPTER FIVE

TOBACCO

Nobody on God's earth ever raised tobacco for the sheer fun of it.[1]
— Historian William T. Turner

Like it or hate it, the cultivation of tobacco *was* the defining preoccupation of growers throughout the Black Patch of Western Kentucky in the late 19th and early 20th century. This, because the extremely labor intensive cultivation, harvest and curing of dark fired tobacco often required the complete attention of a farmer from sun up to sun down. It just as often required the participation of every other able-bodied family member as well—regardless of their age or sex. No matter how little "fun" it was. Authors Yolanda G. Reid and Rick S. Gregory note that:

> In comparison to other staple crops, the man hours required to produce an acre of tobacco were roughly eighteen times that needed to produce an acre of small grains, seven times the hours needed for corn, and two and a half times those needed for cotton. Furthermore, the cycle of labor and methods used to raise a tobacco crop had changed remarkably little since John Rolfe raised the weed at Jamestown. Farmers often spoke of tobacco as a thirteen-month crop since by the time a farmer sold his crop the growing cycle for the next year's crop had already begun.[2]

Unfortunately, this lengthened cycle also meant that growers of that era frequently discovered all too late that it had just cost them as much to cultivate the tobacco as they had been paid after hauling it to market. In fact, as a result of the manipulations by the Tobacco Trust, increased competition and changing taste in tobacco products, prices were actually *below* the cost of production in the early 1900s, falling as low as three cents a pound or less in 1904.[3] As a result, most smaller family farms would only grow tobacco in plots from less than an acre in size to only three to five acres, forced to rely on other crops to supplement their "primary" income.[4] As the Mayfield *Saturday Messenger* commented, "The man in the tobacco field fails to be paid for his labor more than any other class of working men at this day."[5]

The growing cycle for tobacco began by preparing a raised plant bed in late winter or early spring and having the children gather and pile brush upon it so that it might be then set afire to kill any weed seeds or insect larvae. Next the soil was plowed, harrowed and hoed until it was finely pulverized. Then the tiny seeds (which would have been saved from the previous year's crop) were mixed with ashes or cornmeal for more even distribution and spread over the ground before being covered with a grid of wire and cheesecloth (which had been sewed together) to protect the emergent plants from insects and frost.

After the spring thaw, the field into which the young plants would be transplanted had to also be prepared. Again, the soil first had to be plowed, harrowed and hoed by hand until it was reduced almost to powder. Following a rain in late May or early June, the seedlings could be transplanted. At this point, the real work began.

Each of the fragile plants was carefully removed from the plant bed and transplanted to the field in washtubs or baskets. There, they were individually set in the ground, watered and had the soil pushed back around them. Far more than a simple prospect one might envision in their own back yard garden, it was backbreaking task as each acre of tobacco numbered some 2,500 to 3,000 plants. Once completed, the farmer and his family would again walk the field after a few days to reset any dead or missing plants.

Once the tobacco plants had been successfully transplanted, the process of continually plowing and hoeing to prevent any weeds that would rob the young plants of nutrients. Referred to as "chopping out," this was performed during the hottest months of the summer, making it particularly arduous and hated.

Around early August, about halfway through the plant's growing cycle, a flower "button" would begin to develop at the top of each plant. These could not remain, however. Each (as well as the bottom leaves of the plant) had to be removed by hand, leaving ten or twelve good leaves. This process, in itself, would only create more work for the grower. Bereft of their top, each of the plants would begin to grow subsidiary plants, referred to as "suckers," at the point where each leaf joined the stalk. As these would rob the remaining leaves of water and nutrients, they had to be continuously removed by hand from the time each plant was topped until it was harvested.

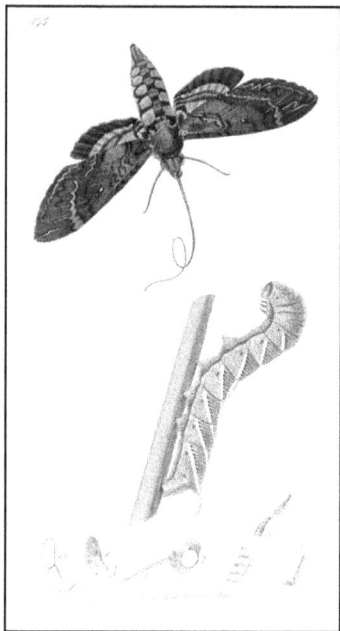

The Tobacco Hornworm Moth. Just two of them could defoliate an entire tobacco plant—and each moth could lay anywhere from 600 to 1,00 eggs.

Lest the farmer then be robbed of his crop and his hard work, he also had to contend with insects, mostly notably the hornworm or tobacco worm—the larval stage of the tobacco hornworm moth. Among the largest of caterpillars in North America, just two could defoliate an entire tobacco plant—and each moth could lay anywhere from 600 to 1,100 eggs.[6] Plants could be dusted with the carcinogenic, arsenic based "Paris Green" to kill the pests ("no danger to the operator may be apprehended provided he does not work facing the wind," *The Weekly Messenger* helpfully notes[7]). But generally it was easier and much cheaper to remove them by hand, as Authors Reid and Gregory detail:

> To destroy the worms, the farmer "wormed" his crop by hand. This process required that he check every leaf on every plant for worms and when he found them, pull the two to four inch pests off and crush them between his thumb and forefinger. This process had to be repeated until cutting time.
>
> Since both suckering and worming had to be done constantly, the grower usually spent the last of July and most of August doing little else. During this period, the average work week for the farmer ran from daylight to dusk, Monday morning until Saturday at noon. If he had an especially bad crop of suckers and/or worms, the grower might work Saturday and Sunday also. To make matters even worse, both suckering and worming had to be done during the hottest days of the summer.[8]

Both of these jobs, it is worth noting, were generally believed to be best done by the children in the family—though one area resident made front page news by training his dog to seek out and eat them.

"The dog goes to the tobacco patch with Mr. Lebre and remains for eight hours and catches more tobacco worms than any person," *The Daily Messenger* reported before helpfully noting, "On account of paris green having been used on the tobacco the dog has become sick several times after going through the performance for several hours, but recovers in a short time and returns to work."[9] As some of these voracious, leaf-green, horned, hairless caterpillars measured up to four and a half inches long, they could easily be as long as a child's hands.[10]

While photographer Lewis Hine is primarily known for his astonishing photographs of child labor in the factories and mills of the Northeast during the early 1900s, he was concerned with child labor throughout the United States. To that end, he ventured into the fields of Western Kentucky in August 1916 and photographed Amos (6) and Horace Neal (4), worming and suckering tobacco, Warren County, Kentucky, 1916 (Library of Congress).

Some six to ten weeks after topping, around late August or early September, the tobacco was finally ready to be cut. Using a specially designed, hatchet-like knife, each tobacco stalk was split from the top to within a few inches of the ground before being cut off at ground level and inverted to wilt. Before the plants could be sunburned,

A tobacco barn near Winchester, Kentucky" (Lewis Hine, Library of Congress).

however, they would have to be put on homemade tobacco sticks and hung on wooden scaffolds in the field to dry. What's more, it was best for the tobacco, if not the farmer, if this was all done during the heat of the day after having allowed the dew to evaporate off the leaves. Far from simple manual labor, each step in this labor intensive, strenuous process had to be carefully planned so as not to damage the quality of the tobacco, reducing the profit to the farmer.

Although the crop was now harvested after months of backbreaking labor, "the most arduous phase of the growing cycle" about to begin. This was housing the crop.

After loading the sticks of tobacco on a flatbed wagon, they were hauled to the barn, which had a network of vertical and horizontal poles five to six poles wide and five to eight poles high. Straddling the poles and working in temperatures of over one hundred degrees, the men of the family carefully placed each stick of tobacco in relationship to the next so that it did not sweat or house-burn.[11] They also had to be alert for any misplaced sticks that might have fallen to the floor of the barn during the curing process. If this occurred, it could start a fire that might burn the barn (and all of the season's crop) to ashes.

With the most labor-intensive phase of the harvest now complete, the one that required the most skill and expertise was just beginning, curing the tobacco. As much an art form as an agricultural endeavor, weather conditions, the type of barn and its location all had to be taken into consideration. If they weren't properly weighed, a crop that looked outstanding after all the work in the field could be completely ruined in the barn. The dark tobacco grown in Graves County could be either air-cured or fire-cured. If it was air-cured, it simply remained hanging in the barn until it was taken down. If it was to be fire cured, however, the process just became much more complex.

The process of fire curing the tobacco began within a few days of housing the crop as fires made of hickory and oak wood and sawdust were ignited on the floor of the tobacco barn. Depending upon the size of the crop and the weather, these fires might be maintained for two to three weeks or longer. To prevent improper firing that could ruin the crop or an accidental fire that might destroy it, farmers might remain in the barn all day and all night.

Once curing was complete (whether it was air curing or fire curing), growers then had to wait two to three months for warm, wet weather for the tobacco to "come into order." This was the point at which the tobacco had absorbed enough moisture from the air to be pliable enough to be safely removed from the sticks, stacked on a wooden floor and covered with a tarpaulin to maintain moisture. If properly done, the quality of the tobacco could actually improve.

Finally, during the winter and spring months, growers would remove the leaves from the stalk or "strip" the tobacco. Perhaps the most enjoyable stage of the entire process, this was when the men of the family could sit, share family stories and have the occasional drink of liquor away from the women. Nonetheless, it still required a high degree of expertise as the dark fired tobacco leaves were carefully sorted into a minimum of three grades—"lug, for the lowest grade which could also be separated into "good" or "trash" based on the amount of dirt or injury to the leaf, "second" for the intermediate grade and "leaf" for the best. They were then tied into "hands" of twelve leaves, pressed together into "books" and either sold loose or "prized" into hogsheads for resale. The dark tobacco of the Black Patch was sold mainly for export as smokeless tobacco for chewing tobacco or snuff and was particularly sought by English, German, Italian, French, Spanish and African dealers.[12]

Despite (or perhaps because of) this incredibly labor-intensive process, authors Reid and Gregory conclude that:

The growing cycle of tobacco gave meaning, direction, and continuity to the lives of the farmers who grew it. The planter thought of himself as a tobacco grower regardless of his other economic pursuits and considered time in terms of where he was in the cycle rather than months or seasons. Thus, late spring was setting time, late summer cutting time, and winter stripping time. The strength of the tobacco culture complex can best be seen in the way it influenced the attitudes and the material culture of the people of the Black Patch. . . .

In the course of raising a crop, the grower would touch each plant dozens of times and each contact forged a bond between man and plant. He loved his mules, with whom he usually spent more time than he did his wife, and found the early morning dew sparkling on the leaves of plants ready to be cut to be a thing of beauty. A well-raised or "fine crop", as it was called, gave him a deep sense of pleasure and accomplishment . . . . Because of this love for the crop and the enormous amount of labor that tobacco culture required, the growers felt an intense sense of grievance when prices were lower than they believed they should be.[13]

As Haskell noted, "We used to make seven, eight hundred pounds an acre. And now they make thirty-five hundred, see. Make thirty-five hundred pounds at $130 a hundred. We could have bought a farm with one crop. I've seen it sell for four cents and two. That is best was four and lugs was two. [14] That didn't pay for the overalls you wore durin' the summer. That was absolute poverty. You could've made more money walkin' up and down the street pickin' up horseshoes."

* * *

Haskell: I was about nine or ten years old I suppose (eleven at the most) and a couple of neighbor boys come down and introduced me to the urge to smoke. Makes me sick to think about it. We went up to my dad's barn and got tobacco and made cigars—rather crude lookin.

It was a March day and we went down in a lane and got behind the bank out of the wind and sat in the sun and puffed away like big shots. I didn't feel too good settin' there, but didn't feel bad as I did when I stood up. When I stood up, why, I'd had it. The fences were chasin' the trees, the hills was after the gullies and my head was goin' around like that.

I had to go to the house and I didn't want to tell 'em I'd smoked. So, I ate some walnuts that were layin' under a tree one day before that and made my stomach awful sour and I think I heaved. So, I went to the house as pale as death and Mom saw me and thought I was gonna' die. Wanted to know what was the matter and I said I ate some walnuts that was layin' under a tree down there and made me sick. I had, but it was a few days before then.

She put me to bed. Dad came in after a while and I suppose he'd come in the room he could smell it because he didn't smoke and he'd been out in the fresh air. Said to my mom, "What's the matter with the boy?" She said, "Well, he said he ate some walnuts that'd been layin' under a tree down there for—got sour." He looked me right in the eye and said, "Yeah, I ate some once myself." He never did mention smokin'. He didn't have to. I didn't want to smoke anymore for a long time. Oooooh! Makes my stomach sick yet! I was afraid I *wouldn't* die!

After I was fifteen, sixteen years old I— All the boys smoked and we used to buy tobacco. You got free papers with a pack of tobacco. And you could buy enough tobacco for two weeks for a nickel. So, it was an "in" thing to do like kids have always done—follow the leader. Sometimes I was out in front. With my Bull Durham and R.J. Reynolds—had a R.J.R on the side of the bag. Big bag full of tobacco for a nickel.

CHAPTER SIX

WORK

[A mule] will draw a wagon or a plow, but he will not run a race. He will not try to jump anything he does not indubitably know beforehand he can jump; he will work for you patiently for ten years for the chance to kick you once.

—William Faulkner
The Reivers (1962)

Haskell: The terrain was fairly steep in that country. When I say, "fairly steep," it couldn't have been too steep with the average elevation was only five hundred feet and it was a thousand miles to the Gulf of Mexico. But the little hills—The water run pretty fast when it run off of those hills because most of the hills was steep. But erosion was awful bad.

It was a type of soil that would wash bad. Didn't have much sand in it and had a hard pan of gravel under all that soil. The water could only soak down so far and, after that, it just didn't go through it. It was just like cement. It'd get soaked, you down, and then come a hard rain and—swooosh it right off like in California. Mud slides.

Some people would let their fields get away from 'em. Man would have a field cultivated down to plough depth, and one of those gulley-washin' hard rains would come. That whole hill would just disappear, swept clear off as deep as it was ploughed. Down to the gravel in some places. Maybe three, four hundred yards wide— Just ruin a field. It took years to build that back up and get that soil any good again.

Since I've left there, they begin to get some equipment they could do somethin' with. They'd bulldoze those hills down smooth and sewed 'em with some kind of grass or vine or vetch or somethin' of that kind that would keep it from washin'. They use it for pastureland or just don't cultivate it at all—just work around it and leave it alone, see. But it was awful bad back in those days. Terrible bad.

We didn't have too much trouble. We were up on kind of a ridge and didn't have a lot of water runnin' on us from anybody else. But we had two drains that went off of there that we had to fight pretty bad. If you go to plow it you'd have gullies three feet deep. That used to be the kid's job—cut brush and throw it in there.

We had a lot of sassafras brush. Fields was polluted with it. They'd pasture that for a few years and the brush would grow. When you got ready to cultivate it— Had to go in there with an axe and cut that brush and haul it away or burn it or take it down and throw it in the ditch. That's where it went. It went in these washes, see.

You know what a cockle burr is? A cockle burr's got spikes all the way around it. And every spike's got a hook on the end of it. It'll hook on anything it touches. It has two seeds in it, side-by-side, like a coffee bean. One of 'em comes up one year and the other one comes up the next year. So, you don't kill 'em one year. They come just as many the next year—so the old-timers told me. I never did plant one to see.[1] They grow rank down in that rich river bottom silt land, I'll tell ya'.

They bound up their horse's tails to protect 'em when they were pickin' corn and had a team on a wagon. I've done it many times—as far as fastenin' a tail up. You doubled it up and then you wrapped it with cloth. That protected the horse. Kept the burrs out of his tail, but it was a mess.

When they'd turn the cattle or young horses in those fields and let 'em eat the fodder up, they couldn't bind up their tails. They might not see 'em for a month after they turned 'em in there. They get sore if they let 'em go out for forage.

Then, doggone horse's tails would get big and solid with cockle burrs. And the only way you could get 'em out was to grease it and use a currycomb. They'd grease those tails and then start at the bottom. You could comb those burrs out and make a pile of "em. But to pick 'em out— It would of took a lifetime, see.

We didn't have many on our farm. Nobody else's water from any other farm come through our land very much except on a little old place up toward the right hand side, back of the pond. And my dad watched like a— Man, every time he's see a cocklebur—no matter what he was doin'. He'd stop and pull it up. Lay it on a stump. Somethin' of that kind. Hang it on a fence. He never let 'em grow.

* * *

Haskell: The first time I remember ridin' a horse was when my dad put me on a horse to go to one of the neighbors. I was quite a small boy. Quite small. And my mother screamed bloody murder because she was afraid I'd get killed. He said, "Ahh, that horse won't hurt him. She's gentle." No problem. I had to go to the neighbors to pass some word along for some reason. I don't remember what the message was, but I can remember ridin' away down there like a king on a horse all by myself with nobody leadin' it or anything. I was probably five or six years old. Somewhere near the same time I got my suspenders.

Mom had made me a pair of pants, I guess. I'd had some before, but I had a button to my blouse. Kids wore a blouse. It bagged at the waist and had a drawstring in it and tie it here, you know. It dropped down over the top of your pants. And under that, you had a little body. That's what they called it. It was made out of brown muslin and buttoned up the front and had a few buttons around it. You buttoned your pants to it. That was little kid's clothes. Then your blouse hung down over it.

Bigger boys wore suspenders to hold their pants up. Put their shirt inside of it. So, when a kid got a hickory shirt made, he could stick it down inside of his pants and have a pair of suspenders, he was quite proud. He'd arrived. He'd gotten to be a big boy now, see.

So, my mom made me some suspenders out of some of the shirting material, folded 'em, and sew 'em and made buttonholes in the bottom and I buttoned 'em to the pants instead of the little body. Tucked my shirt down in the pants and I was quite happy. I can remember I stood on a stump crowin' like a rooster and felt proud as a king.

But I was the oldest. I started takin' care of horses when I was six, seven, eight years old. I fed 'em and cleaned 'em and cleaned the stalls and everything of that kind, you know. Worked 'em, too. We went in the field. We raised tobacco and we raised a strong, dark tobacco. The rest of 'em would use a hoe or whatever. I was the guy that did the horsin'. We had Morgan horses. Copperbottoms. And various runnin' stock. I don't know what. We didn't use a lot of mules. Dad didn't like mules. He hated 'em.

When they set up housekeeping, every country farmer bought a clock. That was one thing they had to have. I don't know why. They wasn't goin' anywhere. Dad looked at the sun and could tell ya' within five minutes what time it was. We'd be out in the field workin' and kids would get a little anxious. Say, "It's about time to go for dinner, ain't it?" "Nah, it's only about 10:30." And he wasn't very far wrong, either, I'll tell ya'. We didn't go 'til 11:30. That was a long hour. We'd go back to work about one, but we'd go to the house 11:30—get a little rest 'cause it was hot down there in the fields, I'll tell you. Man, oh, man, you'd cook down there!

No wonder I'm all banged-up and crippled-up and got bad joints and bad this and bad that. I'll tell ya', I've had some pretty rough treatment in my life. Kicked by mules and bit by mules and— Umh!

We had a mule that was fractious. You couldn't carry anything on him. You could ride him if you just sat up there and behaved yourself and didn't do any monkeyshines, you know. My hat blew off and dumb hired man— He reached out to pick up my hat and started to hand it to me. "Don't give me that hat! Don't give me that hat!" Mule threw me off and I hung myself in the chain. Chain was wrapped right around my ankle. He started to kick me but the chain was hung up on the hame, you know. He was swingin' me away from him and he couldn't get to me. I finally kicked my foot out of there. Then, I spent the next half hour cussin' the hired man out. Uhmm, that mule had me scared. I couldn't get lose.

Boy, I got an awful fall. We had this big elm tree right outside the window. Not thirty inches much from that tree to the window. There's a clothesline was fastened to that window and fastened to that tree. I'm goin' through there with this mule and one of the kids stuck his head out that window just as I come by there. That mule went sideways like this and I go— Clothesline swept me off the—Like to broke me in two. He really dumped me!

One old horse we had was a gate opener. He'd open a gate himself. He could do it faster than you could. You couldn't keep him in a stall, hardly—unless you hid the key where he couldn't get to it. But I was ridin' him. Didn't have a bridle or anything on him. I just rode up and he pushed that bar over and reached to hook the gate with his nose and swung it open. Started through and the gate started to swing shut on him, you know. So he leaned away from it. There was a barbed wire wrapped around the post the gate fastened against. That barb was stickin' right straight out, see. And he'd dragged my foot between him and the post and cut that artery right in two. I don't know what we did with my foot.

Sometime after that, after we'd torn that old gate down, we moved it out of the way and just leaned it against the fence, you know. But it still had three big nails in it that'd been in the piece the gate was swingin' on. I had a wild young horse and I had just got a foot in the stirrup and started up when he took off with me. He dragged my hand right through them nails. Right— Three of 'em against that horn. He cut that— Ooooh, boy! That time, I went to the house and my mom washed it and put some soot on it. I think soot and spider web. Put a bandage on it and that's all. It was torn. Those nails tore it more than cut it. Oooh, it was deep. I got some scars on there now, you can see 'em. They went clear down to the bone almost. I was pretty lucky I didn't get killed.

Florence: When I was in my teens. I had been to take my sister Frances to Sedalia to my uncle's and the only horse I had to drive that day was an old grey mare with a little mule colt. And coming home I got along fine until I got through Mayfield and out about a couple of miles. There was a hill and I started down the hill and was pulling back on "Nell" and the backin' strap broke. The buggy ran down on her, goin' down the hill, and she started runnin'. So there was nothin' I could do but just to pull back on her as hard as I could and try to keep her on the side of the road that she wouldn't run into somebody.

Every little bit I'd look back to see if the little mule was comin' or if we had lost it. But it followed on. And my dad had always told us if ever one of the horse run with ya', whatever you do, don't let 'em turn—keep 'em straight in the road. So I kept her straight in the road. Every little bit I'd look back to see if the colt was coming. Finally I got to the place where I was supposed to turn to go home. But instead of turnin' to go home, I went on down the road. Nell knew she wasn't goin' home so she stopped.

By the time she got stopped there was three or four people behind me that had run behind me just as fast as they could drive or ride a horse—whichever they was doin'.

Haskell: They could hear you swearin'. They thought that was terrible.

Florence: They knew the horse and they thought when they got to the turn they'd find me layin' by the side of the road. But instead, they found I had passed the road and she stopped and I was out talkin' to her. So everyone'd say, "You cain't drive that horse home!" There was one of 'em said they could fix the harness someway so they could drive her home, but says, "You cain't drive her. One of us will have to get in the buggy and drive her home." I said, "No. I can drive her home. She's all right." Says, "She'll kill ya'!" I said, "No she won't. I'm used to her and she's used to me and I'm goin' to drive her home."

Nell and her mule colt.

So I started on home and a couple of 'em followed me home. They was scared, afraid she was going to run. Then they was surprised that I got home without any more. They said to me "Don't you ever drive this horse again!" I said, "Well, I'm gonna' drive her tomorrow. I've got to go to Mayfield tomorrow and I'm gonna' drive her." Said, "You'd better not." Said, "She'll kill ya'!" I said, "Well, I've been drivin' her for years and she hasn't killed me yet."

About that time I looked up and see my dad come runnin', all out of breath. He had been at our neighbor's, across the field, and there was one of the fella's that saw her runnin' and was so scared. He lived there so he went up to this place. And it was there he told him. Says, "You'd better hurry home." Said, "That mare run away with your daughter." And said, "We wanted to take her home and she wouldn't let us." Said, "She is drivin' her home." And Dad ran all the way across the fields to get home and there I was, all in a good shape and Nell was in a good way.

Haskell: I was about nine, ten years old. My dad bought a pair of mules at a sale. They were not young. Small mules. And I was workin' 'em. I turned a harrow over with 'em. It wasn't the mule's fault. It was mine. They had a hinge harrow. And I turned wrong and upset the dadgum harrow, you know. Spikes stickin' up like that. Scared Dad to death. Next Monday, he took the mules into town and sold 'em.

When I was a kid, there wasn't much farm machinery. We had a plow and a cultivator that you hitched the mule to and you went down between the rows and cultivated it, you know. Two mules or two

Driving the double shovel. In addition to his photos of the Oliphant children in the tobacco fields of Kentucky, photographer Lewis Hine captured this photo of Harold Oliphant, 11, driving a double shovel in 1913 (Library of Congress).

horses to plow the ground up with a bigger plow. Then you cultivated it with a smaller one or a "double-shovel," they called it. At ten years old, my dad stuck me out there behind that pair of mules to look at their butts all day.

I'm supposed to do the farmin'. You can't believe the rough time I had as a kid. You can't believe it. Hell, I ain't a man. I'm a kid! A little kid! My dad goes to town. We'd get a hired man to help on the farm—

and I'd try to keep up with the hired man. I'm a little sick kid. I had malaria and wasn't able to work, really. Go out and saw wood all day long with the big hired man, you know—big, strong, bully of a bastard. Big, dumb Jeff Gilbert. He worked for us a couple, three years on the farm. And my dad's gone all day. Go down to the courthouse and shoot the ox with a bunch of so-called politicians.

They had a coal-yard in town along the railroad there and we'd go in there and get a load of coal. You ain't never heard this kind of weight. You'd pay twelve or thirteen or fourteen cents *a bushel* for coal. A bushel weighed seventy-four pounds. The price varied—as oil does or any other commodity does, you know. Twelve, thirteen, fourteen cents. It would depend on the grade. John Shaffer. Good man. Sold fertilizer, coal and a few farming supplies of various kinds.

I went there one time when I was a kid to get a load of fertilizer. We were goin' to plant tobacco and we needed fertilizer. I had a tarp of some sort to put over it. And it was as dark and it r-r-r-r-r-rained! Mister, it rained. I had a raincoat on. It finally got my seat wet underneath. And it rained and rained and rained and rained. It never quit rainin' 'til I got home. It poured down there. It blew in my face. I was so wet that my underwear band was drippin' on my balls. You can't imagine how wet I was. It blew, it rained and it blew. But what am I gonna' do? There is no place to stop. There's no place except some farmer's house or somethin'—who didn't care whether it rained or not. He's inside. Umh! How I can remember that. With a load of fertilizer, tryin' to keep it dry. And that rain blowin' in your face. And I'm a kid! I ain't a man! I'm a kid!

First day I worked for wages I drilled corn for a next-door neighbor all day long and he paid me twenty-five cents. For the day. Not per hour or minutes, but by the day. And I went home for my lunch. That was in about 1908, probably. I was probably ten years old 'bout then. That's the first day I worked for wages. Had a few odd chores now and then for a nickel, but nothin'— No quarters. That's the first day I got a quarter. Then I worked various jobs for fifty cents a day around the neighborhood for farmers. You got your feed, the bed, took your washin' home. You got three whole dollars a week. If you laid off on Saturday, they docked you a quarter. You gotta' work to evenin'. Long days. Hot weather. And hard work.

I was probably ten, eleven years old. Somethin' like that. Ten, probably. I thought I— I was gonna' be real smart. I thought, "I'm gonna' surprise my father with a nice gift." I was sellin' this crap. I don't know what it was. You didn't get any money. But you got a prize, whatever, for sellin' this stuff. It was an awl. Everybody had a harness in those days and they had to repair it occasionally. And this awl had a spool of shoemaker thread or somethin' of that kind, you know. Good, strong thread or somethin' of that kind. And it had this big needle that was in it that you sewed this stuff with. You screwed the cap off of the handle and it had some little drills in there. It had a screwdriver. And it had some small drills.

So I worked my butt off. I went all over the neighborhood peddlin' this crap. And I finally sold forty different orders of it or somethin'. And I get this prize. I was kinda' proud of it. I gave it to him and he laughed at me. "What in the world would I do with that thing?" It hurt me. He didn't understand. He didn't understand. He actually would laugh at me for doin' that. Umh! And I'd walked that whole country over for miles and miles and miles tryin' to sell this crap so I could get this for my father. He let the air out of my bag, I'll tell you that. Umh! And I don't think he ever realized what he was doin'. I don't think he realized— Raised by an old Scotch mother and conditions were bad and so forth and— I don't know what. I just don't understand it.

I was proud of my kids when they come up with any kind of an accomplishment. If it was nothin' but pickin' strawberries for a nickel a quart, I told 'em I was proud of 'em for doin' it and things of that kind. I didn't say, "Well, you're a dummy for pickin' 'em up." I didn't laugh at 'em for some effort they made. I— I wasn't— I wasn't like that. But life keeps goin' on.

Zack Jones

Haskell: We had a tenant farmer when I was about eleven, twelve. Zack Jones. Zacharia, I guess. They called him, "Zack" and that's all I've ever seen in the census records. They lived there around home. Dad was raised with 'em, see. And this guy come out there and conned him. Dad knew he was a no account. He was as big as this table and weighed about three hundred pounds. He was too fat to work and he was awful glad of it.

He had four great big boys. "Hub" and Clyde. Hub was Herbert. They called him "Hub." Charlie and Hollie. Hollie was just my age. Just about. I would say pretty close. But, like little kids, we're a little cocky. Here comes the newcomer and you got to fight. I could whip him anytime. I had a lot of practice. I beat the hell out of him two or three times. But we stayed friends as long as he lived.

They went broke in Arkansas and didn't have a nickel. They went out there and been workin' in wood shops. They had a lot of hickory wood shops. They made wagon wheels, buggy wheels, hammer handles, hoe handles, shovels and all that kind of stuff. But about that time, the automobile was a big thing and that was a boomer, you know. They changed to metal wheels. Wagons went out because the trucks come in. They had steel wheels. Didn't have much business for farm wagons anymore. And buggies went out because they started to use automobiles. So they was out of work and they come back there.

Dad had this new ground of good tobacco land. Too much for us. Zack come back there beggin' Dad to let him have that farm that year. Dad had to stand good for a team of mules for him, furnish 'em food and everything else. He should've known better. He should've told him that he was gonna' sell it or somethin'. Anything to keep from givin' it to him. But he felt sorry for him so he give it to him.

So they didn't work, take care of their crop. They didn't make any money and the end of the year when it was time to settle up, they didn't have enough to pay their grocery bill and pay for their team. Dad had to pay that. So Dad took the team.

Nice team of mules. "Tobe" and "Dick." They were full brothers. Iron gray. That Tobe was the best mule that ever went in the field. There ain't nobody ever had a better mule than he was. Tougher than wool. You couldn't kill him. He stayed longer than you did. He was a little tricky. He'd kick you. He'd bite you. He'd jump all over you. You had to be kind and quiet with him. If you was, he was all right. He was a tough son-of-a-gun. You couldn't kill him workin' him.

He used to like to jump fences. He'd jump over there and graze awhile and jump back over and graze awhile. The minute he'd get hung, he'd just stand there and bawl. Go, "Waaaaaaah, ha-lah, ha-lah, ha-lah!" You'd go over there and take his foot out of the fence and he was just as gentle as a dog. He'd never bother ya'. Never nothin'. He knew he was hung and he didn't fight it. He didn't get excited and hurt himself. He knew he was hung up. He needed help. When the family decided to leave the farm, they had a sale and they sold that mule. My brother Ralph cried like a baby. He loved that mule like one of his brothers. But that mule was really tough.

The other one was spoiled. That one was Dick. Dick was the

ornery one. He was a bad one. As crazy as a bedbug. He'd been abused when we got him. If you turned around and looked at him, he'd run backwards clear down to the road. He'd never stop runnin' backwards 'til he hit a buildin' or a tree or somethin'. Nuts! Somebody beat him over the head and he was nuts! Good mule. Gentle. He wasn't that particular mean, but he was nuts! And he was balky. He'd work pretty good by himself. Put him on a cultivator or a plow or somethin' by himself and he did pretty good, but you put him with the other one and he wanted to balk.

After my dad died, we'd cleaned up a big piece of timber and had a lot of tops. We'd cut these tops off up to where you could use the lumber for somethin' and then we'd leave that top 'til we get ready to work them. So we hooked 'em up. You'd throw a chain around the top of this piece of timber and hook this in it and drag it where you wanted to. So, I had 'em all hooked up and ready to go and I call on the team to go and the one mule goes and that other one, he backs up. He don't want to go.

So, I got them big, heavy lines on him and I give him a rap across the rump with the butt lines and he jumped right over the other mule in the harness just like a monkey. Well, he fell over on the other side all messed up in the harness. I finally get him up and straightened out and get him up on the feet. And he ain't fightin'. He's just standin' there. But he'd pulled the bridle through his mouth way up on the side. The bit piece and mouthpiece is up here by his ears, the strap's in his mouth, and I want to slide it back without takin' off the bridle, you know.

I slide it in and I slide my finger in his mouth and he bites me. Well, he hangs me and I can't get loose. He didn't bite down on me anymore, but he bit me 'til I can't get out. And he feels his mouth all over my fist, you know. He's got great big thick lips and everything and I can't see how much he's got. But it feels like the whole thing is in there.

So I try to get him loose. I put my hand on his nose and try to shut his air off so he'll gasp a breath and I can get my hand out and it didn't work. And I choke him. Don't work. And I had a big knife in my pocket. I went in and got my knife and was openin' it up and Ralph said, "What are ya' gonna' do?" I said, "I'm gonna' kill that son-of-a-bitch." I said, "He's gonna' bite my hand off!" He said, "If you stick that knife in him, he <u>will</u> bite it off. That's for damn sure!" Said, "Wait a minute."

We had a rod that went through the tailgate of the wagon—the two sides, you know. They called it a "tailgate rod." It was just about a half-inch iron. Threaded on one end and a loop on the other. He went down and got it and slid it in his mouth. A horse has got a gap in his mouth where the bit goes. No teeth. They're never in there.

In the meantime, I'm standin' there with my hand in his mouth. He slipped that rod in there and pried him off my— I'm about five minutes with him standin' there with my fist in his mouth, you know. It felt like three weeks. I'd think every minute he was gonna' bite it off. I didn't know how much he had. I couldn't tell. The mouth was covered up. The big lips covered up my hand. Ooooooooooooooooooooh! Man, was I glad to get out of there.

I'd've killed him though. I'd've cut his throat if Ralph hadn't've been there because I didn't know what else to do. But I'm scared. I'm scared! I'll tell you.

They had a sale and we sold him to a fellow by the name of Doyle who had a road-gang. Worked 'em in a road-grader. Three, four head on the road grader. But he had problems with him, too. He was always havin' trouble with him. So the war come along in 1917, they begin to buy mules to send to the army. And they sent Dick to the army. I can imagine the soldiers had a little trouble with him.

They say a mule'll kick you any time he's got the right-of-way. I had one kick me one day. I had one foot on the ground and one up in the air. And he kicked me on the one I had up in the air. Had a load of brush and weeds and crap I took up along a fencerow. I was loadin' it on the wagon. And I guess I must've raked him with one of these switches or somethin' in that bunch. He kicked me and I must've— I must've made two turns when he kicked me— Just standin' on one foot, you know. Kinda' made me laugh, but it hurt like mad. That was my fault, I guess. He was pretty tough.

"100 Mules Wanted," *The Daily Messenger* (University of Kentucky Libraries. Special Collections Research Center).

Elvis "Doot" Gilbert

Haskell: As my old friend Elvis Gilbert says, "Four o'clock. Ten minutes 'til." "Three o'clock. Quarter after." "Five thirty. Half past." "Five o'clock. Half past." They called him "Doot." He worked for us a couple, three years on the farm. He bought himself a nice watch— one of them huntin' case watches. He had a watch-pocket on the front of these bib-overalls. Me and Ralph, we winked at each other. About twenty times a day, we'd ask him, "What time is it, Doot?" He was as dumb as an ox. He'd look at his watch and he'd say, "Eleven o'clock. Nine minutes after." "Ten o'clock. Quarter 'til." He'd give you the hour. Then he gave you the minutes—whatever they were (one way or the other, you know). "Eight o'clock. Half past." I can hear him say it yet. He was a dummy, I'll tell ya'. He went to school one day and got stabbed in the back by Troy Dill, I think it was. There was three or four of 'em—Sterlin, Troy, Fred and Boge. Anyway, Doot never did go back.

The Brown guys—Silas and Earnest. Brothers. They were livin' with their grandfather not too far from us—old man W.P. Jones. William Pinkney Jones. Not related, but a neighbor. They were pretty good-sized boys. Sixteen, seventeen years old. Doot was about fifteen years old but bigger than they were. His mother had died when he was young and his grandmother, old man Hardy Glisson's wife, raised him over there on Meridian Road. Well, Doot used to get milk at old man Jones'. He'd go over there in the afternoon and get a gallon of milk. They'd give it to him because they had milk and Doot didn't have any. That was the system.

These kids [Silas and Earnest] know he's comin' so they get an old, double-barreled, muzzle-loader shotgun and decided to fix him up. They overloaded this shotgun with powder. Put a double charge in it. When he shows up, they're out there lookin' like they're lookin' for a blackbird or somethin' in a tree, you know. "Ahh, what do you want?" "Lemme shoot the gun." "Ahh, you're too young. You ain't old enough to shoot it." They tease him along. "You're only fifteen (or somethin')." But he keeps beggin' and they finally agree. This gun kicked him across the road, stomped him three or four times. Like to broke him in two.

70

CHAPTER SEVEN

HEALTH

The United States Census reports show that Kentucky has repeatedly had the second highest tuberculosis death rate of the whole United States registration area. Its typhoid fever death rate last year was nearly twice that of the average of the United States registration area in 1916, although it has been reduced more than 50 per cent in the past nine years . . . .

. . . . Although considered a southern state, Kentucky probably has not as much malarial territory as many of the others. Nevertheless, it ranks among the five states with rates well above that of the remainder of the registration area.

—Child Welfare in Kentucky: An Inquiry by the
National Child Labor Committee for the
Kentucky Child Labor Association and
the State Board of Health (1919)

In an era when the merits of simple sanitation were still being publicly debated, communicable disease was endemic, "patent medicines" were generally not much more than alcohol and antibiotics were nonexistent. A broken blister or a scrape from a farm implement could kill—and often did. As a result, malaria, tetanus, whooping cough, pneumonia, flux (dysentery), typhoid, diphtheria, small pox and consumption (tuberculosis) were of nearly epidemic proportions.[1]

The easily preventable communicable diseases, however, were only part of the problem. The perhaps more exotic (by today's standards) kick from mules, runaway horse and buggies (or horses just scared by parked cars), train accidents, explosions, cave-ins in the clay pits, fire and "deadly black damp" encountered while cleaning the bottom of cisterns were all equally threatening—as were the more curious fatalities from toy cap pistols, the slamming of a door and the occasional explosion of a gasoline iron used to iron clothes.[2]

If you were lucky, you passed through the fire. If you weren't, the public was duly informed in the pages of *The Messenger* that "the silent messenger of death" had just paid yet another visit, guiding another soul "across the dark river" with its "icy hands."

Haskell: Oooooh, I had it. I had it one time. "Pink eye," they called it. I was home from school. Eight, nine, ten years old. Your eyes get as big as one of them Washington apples and about that red. Wake up in the morning and they'd be sealed shut, just like concrete, you know. You have to pick the scabs out of it to get it open. Sore! Terrible! It's contagious. It went through school, see.
We had a telephone. People would call and the neighbors— Some of the neighbor's family had died. I don't know if it was Miss Annie Lassiter's mother or father or somebody. I think it was her mother. And they wanted to know if some of us would go down and tell 'em, see. They didn't have a phone. So, there's nobody there to go but me. Mom's got a baby. Snow on the ground and a bright sun shinin' on it. It'd kill you if your eyes was sore, you know.

So, she took a stocking and pulled it down over my head and I could see through it. It was stretched. It wasn't a new stocking, anyway—worn out one. Old silk stocking. Well, that killed that glare so I could see how to get along. And I went down there and knocked on the door and they thought I was a "booger man" or something. I come down dressed like that. But it hurt my eyes, even that. Your eyes would be so red. Oooooo boy! They'd water all day and matter all night. Umh! It lasted about a week. It was a contagious thing. A lot of kids got it. One and another. I don't know. Kind of a strep infection, I guess.

Me and my brothers slept up in the attic. There was no screens up there at all. They had some screens downstairs, but we didn't have any. Mosquitoes were terrible. They had two kinds of fevers that come from mosquitoes—Intermittent or Remittent Fever.[3] I had it about three years.

They gave me everything. Horseshit to Shinola. All home remedies and everything else, you know. Doctor pills and this, that and the other. Saw Doctor [George] Fuller. He was a good doctor. He made a "chill tonic," they called it. A little bottle about that high and you took ten drops of it. The name of it was "Hell to Take." If you don't think it was, you're crazy. When you took ten drops of that, you didn't speak for the next twenty minutes.

Well, they get me a bottle of it and after a dose or two, I throw it away. I'd make like I was takin' it, spill it and make an awful face, you know. Not even taste it. First time I got a chance, I'd get the bottle and throw it away. They'd get me another one. They had four-hundred-thousand remedies for that. None of 'em worked very good. He finally gave me a pill that was about that long and damn near that big. As big as a lead pencil. With blue stone of some kind in it. I forget what they called it. But it broke it up.

I go to school in cool weather. I'd have a coat on settin' in school. Little jacket, you know. And I'd go to sleep. The teacher would let me sleep on the desk 'cause she knew I was sick. And I'd wake up and that jacket's wet. My clothes were wet. My pants were wet. I'd just sweat like hell.

Now this malaria that I had, every third day you had a chill. My dad made me work. He didn't think there was much wrong with me. I don't think he'd ever had it. He didn't know what it was like, I'd go out in the morning about ten o'clock. That chill would come on me and I'd just (SHIVERS) like that—freezin' to death. I'd go to the house, go to bed, and the next morning get up and go back to work again. He didn't have much mercy on me. He didn't realize how sick I was and how weak I was. I was weaker than hell.

Dad bought that land across the road with sixty acres on it. Right due south of the house. We had thirteen acres of virgin timber on there and we cut that down and had it sawed and built a big barn and some other buildings.

Mined the rocks out of a rock outcrop about a mile away from there or more. There wasn't any rock in that county, only an occasional outcrop. This one was in a field over about a mile from us. My dad and I went over there. We drilled holes in there with a big iron rod. Drill the hole deep enough to get some black powder in it and take a fuse and put in there and shoot it. It'd crack the rock apart. Then beat the corners off with a sledge and get 'em somewhat in shape and load 'em on a wagon. It was heavy, too, I'll tell ya'. We used to pay fifty cents apiece for gettin' those rocks out. That was a day's work in those days. And I'll tell ya', that was quite a bit to have to pay for a rock you had to get out yourself. Then we had to roll 'em up a skid plank to get 'em in the wagon.

We'd get up four or five and haul 'em home to build the barn and dump 'em and go back and get four or five more. It was hard work, I'll tell you. I was about twelve, thirteen years old. He died in fourteen. This was about 1911, 1912, 1910. I might've been about twelve years old. I can't remember when it was.

Hard work for a poor, little, old sick boy—and I was sick. I had that damn malaria. Beat my brains out. Umm, if I had a chill, I went home and laid in the bed all afternoon. The next day I went to work again.

Ever since, maybe five years apart, something upsets me and makes something happen. I don't know what. It comes back on me yet. One of the effects of it is night sweats and stink. You can't believe. But I wake up in the night soakin' wet. My bedroom's smelled like a goat pen. Umh! Terrible! Even I couldn't stand it. Umm, I had a rough time. I ain't cryin' about it. I had a rough time. I lived and I'm still livin'. I managed to make it. But I don't know how. I don't know how.

Florence: My Uncle Charles was moving out West and we all went up to spend a night and a day in that neighborhood. Grandpa and Aunt Nola lived in one house and Uncles Charles' folks on their place. But they'd sold it and was gonna' move away. So, us kids were all in the living room and the others were playin' something. I don't remember what. Anyway, they was playin' and I was watchin' 'em. I squatted down in front of the fire in front of them, between them and the fireplace. And a coal had popped out on the hearth and my dress got on that coal and after so long, it started to blaze. So Edwin and Mary and Fanny see it and said, "Florence! Your dress is on fire!" And Edwin jumped up and run to the door and opened it and said, "Run outside!" Aunt Nola and Grandpa was in the kitchen and they hear this. And they rushed in there and Grandpa heard that and said, "Don't you do it!" And he run between Edwin and the door so I couldn't get out if I tried to and grabbed me and put me on his bed and wrapped me up in the blanket to smother the blaze out.

So, when he unwrapped me, and took me off of the bed, Edwin goes back and he started to, you know, pullin' the blanket and things back and Grandpa says, "Get away from that bed!" He says, "I gotta' see if she set Grandpa's blanket afire." Grandpa says, "What if she did?" Said, "You want her to burn up?" Or something like that. Said,

"That's the way to do if you see somebody on fire. You can wrap 'em up and smother that." But said, "Don't ever open the door for somebody to run outside if they get afire!"

Simeon Augustus Carman

Haskell: Old Grandpa Carman [Florence's grandfather] was a schoolteacher. He taught school for a long time. Of course he was in the army and was a prisoner, but that was only a short time in his life. He lived to be ninety-three or four years old. But he taught school.

(L-R) Simeon Augustus Carman, Edwin Ferguson,
Mary Enola "Nola" (Carman) Ferguson.

That was a family of schoolteachers. Edwin [Florence's cousin] taught school. She taught school. Her sisters both taught school. My mother was a schoolteacher. My wife was a schoolteacher. My daughter Marjorie's a schoolteacher.

Florence: My grandfather and Aunt Nola lived south of Mayfield on the Cuba-Sedalia Road. And he has walked a many a time from where they lived to where we lived. Maybe at times he would start out and walk a little way and then Aunt Nola would come along and pick him up and he'd ride the rest of the way. But he could walk like everything. He had a walkin' stick and he could out walk most kids.

Grandpa used to come to our house and stay for two or three weeks at a time. Him and Aunt Nola and Edwin lived together but he

75

liked to come out to our house because there was a house full of grandchildren instead of just one. He liked to see us play and talk to us. He'd tell us stories about things that happened to him when he was in the army. He was in the Civil War and he's tell us about places that he went, things he saw. We was just always thrilled to death when Grandpa come 'cause he could always entertain us. Some men when they're old—women, too—didn't have any patience with children. But he did. He liked children and was very patient.

Haskell: [Having served in The Civil War on the Confederate side,] Florence's grandfather was a major hater of the Yankees. Spent about a year and a half, two years as a prisoner-of-war over in Rock Island, Illinois, in a Federal prison.[4] And I know that he had pretty rough treatment. He told me some stories about the life in the prisons. The outside walls was made out of tree trunks set in the ground, in a row, you know. Made spikes sharpened on top. Set down and tamped in the ground all the way around.

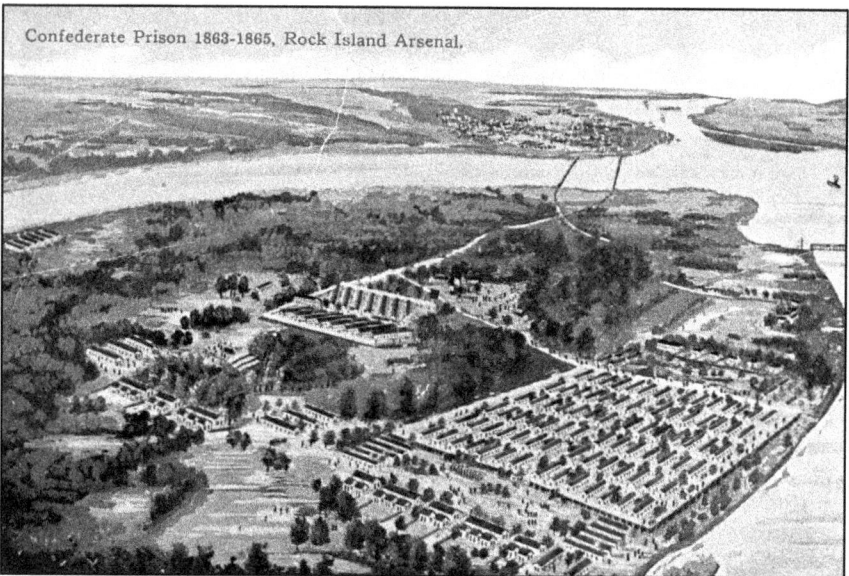

The Confederate Prison at Rock Island, Illinois.

Florence: Their food, of course, was pretty short and not too good, but they lived through it.

Haskell: The feed was lousy. The Yanks didn't have any feed to give 'em much. He said for months and months their food was one pint of shelled corn per day. You can eat it like it is. You can beat it up. You can roast it on a shovel and eat it like that. You can beat it up and make a soup out of it. You can eat it anyway you want to, but that's all you get.

He said, "You'd think civilized people won't eat a dog, but don't tell me. I know." Said these posts didn't always fit tight together. They had openings in 'em. Small openings in 'em where you could get your arm through. Said, "We'd lay by one of those openings for hours, waitin' for a little dog to come down. And, 'Hey! [WHISTLES] C'mon. C'mon. C'mon. C'mon. C'mon here.' If we got a hold of him, he was a goner. We'd pull it through that hole a piece at a time or all together. It didn't make any difference. And we ate him." He said, "Don't think they ain't good. When you're that hungry, they taste pretty good."

Florence: They had given him up before he came home from the war. They looked out one day and here he comes, walkin' home.

Haskell: His wife might've known how he got home from Rock Island, Illinois to Tennessee—which is a long ways. But Florence never knew whether he walked, whether they give him transportation, whether he rode a freight or how he got home. They never knew. They thought he was dead. They'd hadn't heard from him in a long time. So one day he comes walkin' in, down there in Middle Tennessee.

Florence: He wouldn't've worn a suit the color of the clothes that the Yankees wore for nothin'! You couldn't put 'em on him.

Haskell: The kids used to tell him that they was gonna' have him buried in a Yankee uniform when he died. He'd get mad and just rave! Just go crazy, you know. It'd aggravate him. But anybody with a blue suit on, that looked blue, was an enemy to him 'til he died—many, many years afterward.

He had a mini-ball in his "hiney." A mini-ball was a round bullet they used in those smoothbore rifles. They was about like a shotgun. I think he was runnin' away. I don't know how he could've got shot in the butt comin' towards you, you know.

Florence: Never would have it taken out.

Haskell: He wouldn't have had anything to talk about if he'd had that. No, I guess it didn't bother him too much only when he sat on something hard.

Florence: He died after we married. Must've been twenty-one because he was at our house stayin' awhile after we married. Haskell went out in the field to help him hoe tobacco and he give up [working] with him— And Grandpa would've been in his nineties. He never stopped as long as he could go at all. He wouldn't give up. You just can't believe anybody that old could do it. In spite of him crippled, he didn't let it bother him. He went out and enjoyed his workin' outside.

Haskell: But he never got tired of hatin' the Yankees. He was a Rebel soldier 'til the day he died at age ninety-three years old. If they'd've put him in a blue coffin, he'd've jumped out of it. Yes, some people get such a funny hate, you know.

"Aunt Fanny" & "Uncle Dud" Magaren

Florence: Grandma Jones, I guess, died a year or so before I was born and Grandma Carman died when I was three, I think it was. But we didn't live too far away from Aunt Fanny. Oh, about a mile and a half, probably. And we thought as much of her as if she'd been our grandmother because we didn't have one. I've said a lot of times, "If I ever envied anybody of anything, it was their grandmothers." I just felt bad because practically all the children I knew had a grandma and I didn't and I thought that was awful.

I had erysipelas and was real sick when I was three years old. Kind of a blood disorder. Had sores. Run a high temperature.[5] And Aunt Fanny just dropped everything at home and came and stayed with us 'til I got well enough that I didn't need as much attention. But I wanted my mother to do everything for me. I didn't want

Frances Catherine "Aunt Fanny" (Jones) Magaren.

anybody else to. And Aunt Fanny would want to so Mammy [Florence's mother] wouldn't have to do it and I didn't like it. I think she said I scratched her. But anyway, she told me that when I got well, she was gonna' whip me.

Many's the times she'd say to me (every year or so), "Well, I haven't whipped you yet." Said, "When you was so sick, I told you when you got well I was gonna' whip ya'." And said, "Well, I haven't whipped ya' yet." And she never did whip me.

But she was so good to us. She was good to everybody. She was just kind of like a nurse for all the sick around her. No matter who it was. If they really needed somebody, she'd go help. We thought Aunt Fanny was the greatest.

Aunt Fanny never had any children and if there was anybody in the families, the relatives, or even anybody in the neighborhood— If their children got sick, Aunt Fanny would go and help take care of 'em 'cause her husband, Uncle Dud didn't need her and he was cranky anyway. She'd make us cookies or candy or do somethin' for us. She was more like a grandmother than an aunt. But Uncle Dud we never liked.

The cooks during a wheat threshing at the farm of Frank Rogers, south of Mayfield. (L-R) Lela (or Telia) Warthan, Mary Will Tucker, Mrs. Mattie Shreve, Mrs. Ila Clark, (baby) J.W. Clark, Aunt Fannie McGaren, (baby) Amy Rogers, Ret Rogers, Florence Grace Jones, Mary Effie Jones, Gladys Tucker Clapp.

My dad was a farmer and he raised tobacco. And there was always somebody that could help. Farmers helped each other. At dinnertime (wherever they were cuttin' tobacco) they'd fix dinner for 'em. And we had to fix dinner that day. There was just enough people, counting the help and the family, that two pies made enough for the bunch. That was twelve pieces. You know, you cut pies in six pieces. We had made two jam pies and they're real good.

Well, we cut the pies and when they ate the other food and got ready for dessert, we gave 'em all a piece of pie that helped. So Uncle Dud— He ate one piece and reached over and took the second piece and ate it. That left five pieces for six people. And we were all very put out.

It was a hot day and he wasn't too ambitious anyway. The men went back to the field to work and when he got out in the field, he said, "Confound, something's making me sick!" One of the boys said, "How much of that *chocolate* pie did you eat, Uncle Dud? He always said he couldn't eat chocolate pie (just made him sick) and he said, "Confound! Was that chocolate pie?" They said, "Sure!" So, he was very sick then and sat down in the shade and wouldn't work anymore that day.

Hugh Dudley "Uncle Dud" Magaren.

Luther Jones

Haskell: My uncle Luther was a dairyman. He owned a dairy. He milked cows, cooled the milk, and peddled it out of a horse and wagon.

When they first milked in the evening, the milk was warm. It was right out of the cow. He cooled this milk with a water cooler. He had a well near one of these dairy barns. And they put the milk in some kind of an apparatus that had an agitator in it and stirred it. Then he pumped this water up on top and it run down the outside. This thing was made out of bright, nickeled tin. That cold water from the well run down the outside and took the heat out of the milk.

I wasn't too familiar with the operation. He didn't peddle milk but once a day in the morning, but he must have had some way to keep that milk. He might've had ice, but there was no electric refrigeration of any kind in those days. So, I don't know how they cooled it and kept it.

But he had a route. He peddled it up and down the street from house to house. You didn't deliver. Women used to come out in the street and get the milk. Had a big horse and wagon covered like a mail wagon or whatever. They had a platform in the front end big enough to set two twenty-gallon cans on there with a spigot on the bottom. One had milk in it and one had buttermilk. That's usually what they loaded.

You just drove up and down the street with a bell on the horse and he jingled up and down. They could hear him comin'—like an ice cream wagon, you know. All the kids in town knew the horse. They'd pet him as they went by 'cause he was gentle and nice. Pretty, beautiful horse. He must've had that horse on that wagon for fifteen, twenty years. That old horse knew every stop. Never had to talk to him all day long. Just go 'round that route, you know, and stop in front of this house.

A child driving a milk wagon in Bowling Green, Kentucky

As it come jinglin' down the street, the people would come out to the wagon and get their quart or half-gallon or gallon of milk— whatever they wanted. Wasn't very sanitary. If the people come out of the houses with a bucket or pan or crock or whatever they wanted their milk in all he did was stick it up there and open the spigot.

My uncle Luther probably had a phone. Took orders and so forth. I don't remember seeing it but I kind of believe I remember it. He didn't live near us. We lived on the north side about eight miles from town. And he lived on the south side right out at the edge. Farm was out there. We went there occasionally, but he come [by our house] quite often because my grandmother lived there by us. He used to hunt there every year. He was doin' quite well, but he died quite young of typhoid fever.

Typhoid was prevalent down there. It was common as freckles on your back, you know. Everybody had it. Dirt, filth, no sanitation. Everybody had typhoid fever. If you didn't have it, you was lucky. They couldn't figure what was wrong with you if you didn't have typhoid fever, see. Spread from one person to another from human shit. The flies bring it in here and there. Contagious, you know. He was about forty, maybe.

His wife, Josephine was a suicide. She was a big, healthy woman and she got pregnant by another guy after he died. So she's ashamed. She's already got a boy ten, twelve years old. Whatever. I don't remember how old. He's about my age. And her family's gonna' be disgraced. She's gonna' be disgraced. People didn't do that in those days. You didn't see much of it. Some hillbilly that couldn't read and write or somethin' of that kind back in the brush, why, they— They got pregnant, you know. But not decent people. They didn't— They didn't— They legally got married and then they lived like that. And they didn't cheat and stuff like that.[6]

She was a good woman as far as I know. But she had hot pants. And after he died, why, she got to foolin' around. So she walked out in the pond and drowned herself—which is a pretty hard way to go. There wasn't much publicity about the thing. It was pretty well quieted down, you know, because she was of a prominent family and they didn't make any big to-do about the thing, see. It's over and let's forget it. Let's don't talk about it, see. That's the way things were done.

CHAPTER EIGHT

THE POLITICIAN

Esq. Jones Will Be A Candidate For Judge

Editor Mayfield Messenger

Permit me through the columns of your paper to say to the voters of the 5th district that I shall not be a candidate for re-election to the office of justice of the peace . . . .

Several good men who would like to represent the 5th District in the Fiscal Court have asked me concerning my candidacy for re-election and to them this statement is due.

Also I expect in a few days to formerly announce myself a candidate for County Judge of Graves County, and if elected I shall make the same efforts to safe guard the interest of the county that I have as a member of the Fiscal Court.

—E.A. Jones
The Daily Messenger
December 9, 1912

Haskell: Dad read a lot. He subscribed to a lot of magazines, newspapers and stuff like that. I guess I got my thirst for reading from him, maybe. Mom didn't have time to do much readin'. She had too much other stuff to do—raise eight kids. But Dad read. Political papers. *The Commoner. The Commoner* was William J. Bryan.[1] He was editor of a paper in Kansas, I guess. But he ran for President two or three times. Ahh, he used to get a paper out of Pennsylvania. *The Yellow Jacket?* It was a Democratic paper.[2] But he got the *Saint Louis Post Dispatch* and the Louisville paper.

Before we had rural routes, you had to go to a store somewhere and get your mail, you know. We had to go clear to Pottsville—about three or four miles. I would go to the mailbox and get an armful. Most of 'em was weekly papers in those days. They didn't have many daily papers. They had weekly papers. We had the little, old local paper—weekly paper. That's what I learned to read out of. But he had a thirst for knowledge. Would always read.

He was the school trustee when he was a younger man when my mother got the school down there. Heck, he was thirty years old when he got married. He wasn't a kid. But he was a good citizen. And people admired him and they considered him a little better than the average citizen. He could read and write and open the doors and tell time and stuff like that, you know. He was a little better than some of 'em. He was a school trustee for years and then he was a magistrate.

Dad had political aspirations in his head. He never told me that, but I knew that he did have. He was a Democrat. Voted Republican twice. He never did forgive himself for it. He thought he was an elite citizen. Top dog. But, as a magistrate, he was considered a very capable man and did a good job. People came to him for any kind of problem, you know, and he could help 'em with their problem. That's about the only political job he ever had. I think eight years he had that job. Two four-year terms.

The Political Process

Haskell: Our county had Democratic office-holders all the time. They never had anything else.[3] When I was a kid, I know it was true. They had two Republican office-holders since the Civil War in the whole county, see. Well, the nomination for Democratic was tantamount to an election. All you had to do was get nominated and you was it. Well, it was always a big slate runnin' for sheriff or county judge or whatever, you know. But if you could get to be nominated, you was it.

Well, twice they nominated a man for sheriff who Dad could not vote for. Democrats. Lousers. They had a game. You and I are runnin' for sheriff. You're a city man. You know everybody in town. And maybe you've been in business and everything. Know all the farmers and so forth. But I'm a farmer. Pretty good farmer and well thought of and well known, you know, and I run. Let's say for sheriff.

So you'd get about four or five guys scattered around the county of some note— You'd pay their way. Give 'em a little money and a few jugs of booze to run for sheriff out in the county. So they'd take votes away from me because they were gettin' the county votes, see. And I would take a few guys in town and (if I could afford it) I would get a few guys around town runnin', you know, to help take the vote away from you. So that was the kind of deal. Well, it wasn't always the most honest, clean guy that got nominated because it was a deal. It was a racket, see.[4]

There was a fellow named Brand who ran around town—gambler, whoremonger, wagon and buggy salesman for his brother and a big loudmouth, happy-go-lucky, hand-shakin', everywhere. Always was like that. He was raised right out there at Lowes. He got nominated for sheriff but he didn't get elected. He got beat. The Republican got that job. Dad voted against him.

The guy that beat him was John T. Roach, a nice man, but he was a dummy in this respect. He went out around the county here and there and he said, "Tom, I know you know a lot of people around here. If you'll help me get elected, I'll give you a job as a deputy sheriff"—which was a little better job than farmin' or anything of that kind.

So he goes out and talked to Sam Galloway (young fellow, had a crop started and was goin' along) and he says, "Sam, I'll give you chief deputy if you'll sell your crop to somebody and get in there and help me get nominated. Why, if I get elected, I'll give you the job." So Sam did. And [John T. Roach] got elected. But he had promised too many people that. He didn't realize what his budget was—what he could afford, you know. He was so anxious to get elected that he lost his grip. Didn't know what to tell people.

So he got elected and they get in office and Sam's his chief deputy and they run about three months and he's out of money, see. Got no money to pay him. He's only got so much budget—whatever the commissioners give him. So he calls Sam in and Says, "Sam, I've got bad news." Said, "I'm gonna have to let you go because I just don't have enough money to keep you goin'." Well, Sam was hurt because, hell, he worked his ass off. He got the man elected. Helped do it and was expectin' to have four years of salaried work, you know.

So they argued about it and Sam went home and come back after a while and set down there. And they were talkin' about it some more. And the sheriff's safe is standin' open with his gun layin' right in there. And Sam just picked it up and killed him right there—dead as a mackerel, see. Well, he got seven years in the pen. It was about the time I left there. I never did know how much time he served. But he burnt him down right there because the guy had ruined his life. He messed him up. But it was a matter of not understandin' or not bein' aware that you can't have everything. John T. Roach. I think (if I remember right) he was a schoolteacher.[5]

The Daily Messenger and "Democracy" in Mayfield

If Mayfield was solidly Democratic in the early years of the 1900s, *The Daily Messenger* under editor James Robert Lemon (who was also a member of the Democratic Campaign Committee of Graves County) was gleefully so. And once editor Lemon purchased the *Index Democrat* in 1901 and the *Mirror* ("the 'only' democratic paper published in Mayfield") ceased publication in 1905, *The Daily Messenger* and the Democratic Party became virtually indistinguishable.[6] The masthead was reworked to notify readers (in case any were daft) that the paper was "Democratic" and "Democracy" in Mayfield was assured.[7]

Between the two, Republicans generally never had a chance at the polls. Nor would the largely Republican black populace ever be allowed a voice, with one front page editorial questioning, "Shall Negroes or White People Name Governor of Kentucky?"[8] For editor Lemon, it would have been a "political crime to depart from his party's ticket" and act otherwise.[9]

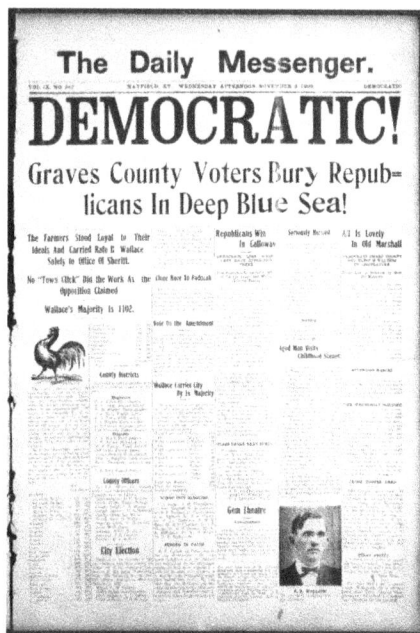

"Democratic!" *The Daily Messenger*, Wednesday, November 3, 1909 (University of Kentucky Libraries. Special Collections Research Center).

"Runaway horse" on the streets? Editor Lemon might refer to it as a "Republican horse."[10] On the front page. In a news article. Candidate selection process for the parties going on? Republicans weren't just "digging their own grave." They were "preparing to take voyage up memorable Salt River Stream."[11] In fact, the odds were so stacked against Republicans that in the general election of 1909 in which E.A Jones was first elected magistrate, they only fielded one candidate on the ballot in the entire county—that of J.W. Green for the position of county sheriff.[12] Historically, it was the only race in which they ever did field a candidate on a regular basis.[13] And certainly quite coincidentally, it was also "said to be the best paying office in the county."[14]

When Mr. Green subsequently lost in an extremely close election by only sixteen votes, editor Lemon still used half of the front page to roast both him and the Republican party.[15] And when he chose to run again in 1913 (and lose by a more substantial margin of 2,369 votes), editor Lemon mercilessly noted "the sweeping majority of W.B. Sullivan over his Republican opponent, J.W. Green, for sheriff, was such a shocking defeat for the Republicans that there will probably never be another man who will offer himself against such great odds. The overwhelming victory for the Democrats should be conclusive for all time to come."[16] However, it was not to be. The Republican challenger for sheriff in 1917, F. Marion McCain, won a decisive victory over Democrat A.L. "Art" Brand. "Strange things are happening," the paper noted, but took consolation "in the fact that the other democrats in the county had no opposition."[17]

Haskell: In my home, the Townships was organized in Magisterial Districts. A magistrate was the fiscal agent for the district. They had a county clerk and registrar and treasurer and all those things, you know. But your magistrates were the guiding hand that set up the salary for the county attorney, the clerk, rules and regulations and so forth. I think it had eight magistrates and they tried people.

They had court and they let contracts for all the county business. They bought all the supplies for the county. They took care of the bridge and roadwork. Had to look after improving a road or building a bridge or whatever in their district, see. What I mean, "look after 'em"— If somebody screamed loud enough that they needed to have to have a bridge repaired out here, he went down and looked at it and let some contract. They even held trials if somebody in the neighborhood had a family fight or stole chickens or bootlegged or somethin'. They had the hearing and fined 'em and they had to go to court or jail or wherever, you know. The county judge was the presiding officer of that.

This magistrate job paid him if he fined somebody ten dollars or fifty dollars for bootleggin' or whatever it was. He got a percentage or court costs. It was established by the state how much he got, you know.

It wasn't much. It didn't amount to a hell of a lot. If he married somebody, they'd give him a couple dollars. Somethin' like that. He married quite a few people. Things of that kind.[18]

I used to run around with Dad. We'd go out and— Well, he had a bridge here so he had to meet two or three fellows out there and they give him a price on repairin' or rebuildin' or maybe buildin' this bridge or whatever. And then he'd take it into the county court and he'd give 'em the recommendation of what he thought was right. (And, of course, they always went along. There wasn't much fight among themselves. They were all Democrats, anyway.) They'd give the contract to whoever had the best price or the best figure or the best plans or whatever suited him.

But you— You can't believe the conditions. You can't believe. He was so interested in good roads. He's been born and raised in mud all his life. He never got out of it. In fact, he never got out of it 'til the day he died. But he was far-sighted enough to see automobiles had come in and the traffic was heavier and people were thicker and everything. And the roads was atrocious, I'll tell you. They were terrible! Terrible. Terrible.

The county had a road grader that they loaned out to the various districts. You'd get it in your district and the people in the neighborhood, they worked on the road. They'd put their teams of mules on one of them big graders—'bout six head. All they did was ditch 'em. They'd cut the ditches—cleaned them out and pulled it up in the middle of the road.

That ground washed awful bad down there. They used to put an angle ridge in the middle of the road to run the water off into the ditch as it went down the hill and keep it from washin' down the ruts so bad. And they cut the brush back a little bit—keep it from rakin' the top of your car or buggy or whatever. Some of it'd almost meet in the middle in a year's time.[19]

The "Good Roads" Movement.

When E.A Jones expressed an interest in "good roads," it wasn't just his own personal concern. It was a major political movement of the late 1800s and early 1900s. Begun by early bicycle enthusiasts (or "wheelmen") in the northeast, it quickly grew into a national organization with public demonstrations, conventions and lobbyists. To help further spread the idea that good roads were important to everyone, not just bicyclists, The League of American Wheelmen began publishing *Good Roads* magazine, as well as *The Gospel of Good Roads, A Letter to the American Farmer*.[20]

With its publication, the Wheelmen contrasted the good roads of Europe to those of the United States and through illustrative examples and statistics made it clear that good roads didn't cost farmers money. It was bad roads, instead, that were costing them a tremendous amount of money by limiting the distance they could carry their goods and limiting the actual amount of produce they could carry, as well as increasing the wear and tear on both wagons and livestock while also decreasing the value of their land. Convinced of the value of the arguments, the farmers began to come on board, as did the local politicians and a new player to the scene—the automotive industry.

In Mayfield, under the leadership of editor J.R. Lemon, *The Daily Messenger* took up the cause as early as 1902, but political will and progress lagged for another decade.[21] With 1912, however, following the coldest weather ever recorded in the area and the heaviest rains in forty-two years, the situation was reaching absurdly dire proportions.[22] The very least of it was that mail delivery on some roads ceased altogether and farmers couldn't haul their tobacco to market.[23] It was threatening their livestock and their way of life. Over the next several months, coverage on the conditions of the roads would be almost a daily occurrence.

In March, one horse fell in a mud hole near Pryorsburg and died shortly after being pulled free.[24] In a separate instance, it required several men to extricate another horse. "The horse lay there for about six hours inundated save its nose, which was held out by means of a rope which had been tied to the horse by Mr. [Hal] Tubb and persons who happened to be passing."[25]

In April, it was reported on the Fancy Farm Road "that five or more horses got stuck in [a] deep hole and would probably have died had not they received assistance in getting out."[26] The magistrates of the fiscal court took emergency action in letting bids to repair roads and replace an iron bridge over the Wingo Road that had been washed away.[27]

In May, those who went out to repair the Cuba Road got distracted by the abundance of fish swimming in the road and went fishing instead, catching a sizable number of "nice perch and catfish."[28]

In July, editor Lemon found himself editorializing about "The

Value of Deep Mud Holes." "While the fire department was fighting the fire that consumed the warehouse of Adair & McClain," he noted, "the fire horses got away with the fire wagon and went south at a 2:40 speed on the Mayfield and Sedalia road and was not found or caught until they went down in one of our famous mud holes near Harry Wimberly's on the Farmington road, three miles south of the city."[29]

By August, crops were in sorry shape due to the continued rain and "the largest appropriation ever made in Graves County by the fiscal court for road and bridge purposes was made."[30] It would not be enough. The mud holes had become "money pits."

After another winter passed, Editor Lemon was forced to point out what so many of the farmers already knew. In an article entitled, "Roads So Rough Eggs Cannot Be Brought Here," he noted:

> A general complaint is beginning to go out against the condition of the roads in this county.
>
> Farmers residing only a few miles north of town find the roads too rough and bumpy to bring their eggs and other produce to town, and instead take them to Paducah, which city may be reached over smooth, graveled highways. One man stated that eggs could not be hauled over some of the roads leading to this city without a large percent of them being broken in transit.
>
> The bad roads of this county, it is said, is the main reason why so many of our farmers are making Paducah their trading point instead of Mayfield, and the local merchants are contemplating the presentation of a petition to the county authorities.[31]

Just days later, Editor Lemon tweaked the locals a bit by noting that the city which was already stealing their business, Paducah, had begun experimenting with putting crude oil on their city streets to settle dust and keep the roads in better condition.[32] The competitive spirit was sparked. And by the end of the summer, the movement had come to a head. On September 2, 1913, in a truly remarkable announcement, the Mayfield and Graves County Commercial Club invited every citizen of Graves County to come together over a two-day period with one goal—reworking all the roads of the county.[33] The results were nothing less than astounding.

Within days, *The Daily Messenger* reported, "out-of-town papers all over the state are talking about the Graves County two days' road working," with even the *Paducah News-Democrat* reporting "the big County of Graves has caught the good roads fever all over."[34] Automobile transportation was soon arranged for dozens of speakers,

"Thousands of Men Are at Work on the County Roads," *The Daily Messenger*, Wednesday, October 15, 1913 (University of Kentucky Libraries. Special Collections Research Center).

including E.A Jones, to be sent throughout the county to inform the farmers that they "were paying $80,000 a year for new buggies and wagons on account of the very bad roads over which no vehicle could travel any great distance without being more or less damaged."[35] Massive public meetings were held in the city at the courthouse at which every store in the city and county were strongly encouraged to close for the day (with any holdouts branded "a traitor") and schools were encouraged to be dismissed.[36]

Should anyone doubt the momentum behind the project, Road Engineer J.E. Carman noted, "already more than three hundred wagons have been pledged to haul gravel on the Fancy Farm and Lowes Road." The newspaper even printed a letter from one of its "colored" readers who noted that while they had not been invited to attend or asked to participate, "I am sure that many of our colored citizens will use their influence to help in the work."[37] When the project kicked off on October 15th, it was estimated that there were over 6,000 men and boys at work.[38]

When the two days of work were completed on October 16th, Editor Lemon could proudly record:

Many miles of roads have been graveled, thousands of bad places have been repaired, and scores of bridge abutments leveled. All this will mean much to

91

Graves county. It will mean a saving of about a hundred thousand dollars in the county's money which would have been paid for our future road work.[39]

Following his suggestion to set aside the same two days every year for the purpose of reworking the road, Lemon recorded the name of every single person who had been recorded working on either or both of the days. There were thousands of names listed, both white and "colored," working together for the common good.

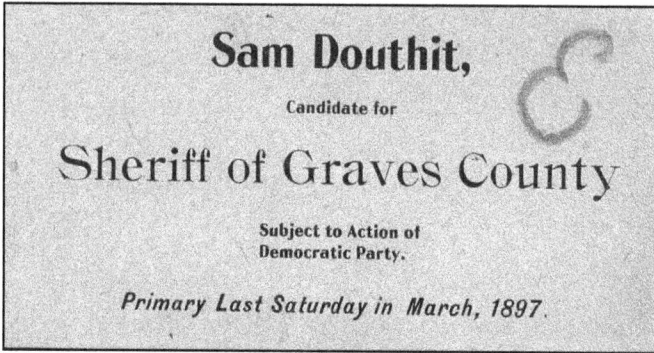

Sam Douthit,

Candidate for

Sheriff of Graves County

Subject to Action of
Democratic Party.

Primary Last Saturday in March, 1897.

Corruption in the County Sheriff's Office

Haskell: Durin' my dad's administration, this man Douthitt, had been sheriff. Well, my dad, the prosecutin' attorney and I guess the county attorney and the county judge and some of the other members of the court started an investigation of the sheriff's office. They found out the sheriff had been stealin' 'em blind for several years. Several years. Quite several years.

There was also a fellow by the name of Brand, Will Brand.[40] They ripped him up real good. My dad put the skids under him and broke him.[41] It took about everything he had to repay all he stole.[42] And there was one other one. So help me, I can't think of what his name was. I think he was in office at the time and they ripped him up a little bit.

But they moved. Douthitt had some farms way out around Sedalia. He sold out and went to Jackson, Mississippi, after that thing got cleared away and he got paid-off. This Will Brand came to Akron later, oh, about 1924 or 1925. Somewhere around then. And he got some kind of a little insurance debit. He was hangin' around the poolroom where the Mayfield boys hung around tryin' to sell insurance to these guys, you know. He didn't know me. I knew him by sight, but that's all. I didn't know him.

So one day he come, sat down beside me and said, "You from Mayfield?" I says, "Yeah." He says, "I don't believe I know you. What's your name?" "Jones," I said, "Jones." Well, Graves County is full of Joneses. They had more Joneses than they did sparrows, you know. And he says, "Which Jones?" I said, "My father was A Jones." He turned about three colors and got up and walked away. He never did speak to me again. But my dad was one of the instigators of the investigation.

* * *

With the one party system so firmly entrenched in the region, corruption became inevitable. And, once entrenched, it was all the more difficult to eliminate, making the position potentially quite profitable. This was particularly evident in the operations of the sheriff's office, which was wholly responsible for the collection of property taxes. As even editor J.R. Lemon of Mayfield's *Daily* and *Weekly Messenger* opined "the sheriffs of this county go out of office in good financial condition."[43] And it wasn't simply because the office was among the highest paid in the county.

In fact, a sizable number past and present sheriffs of both Graves and adjacent McCracken counties would eventually each be placed under indictment and tried for embezzlement—not that this was the easiest thing in the world to accomplish given prevailing public opinion.[44] One investigation foundered in 1905 simply because the foreman of the grand jury refused to take any steps toward an investigation or issue subpoenas.[45] Unfortunately, there would soon be a new, even greater opportunity for the sheriff to increase his personal income.

When authority over local school districts consolidated in 1909 from the offices of the trustees to the county, the sheriff became the responsible for collecting those taxes, as well. The system, in fact, was so woefully ripe for corruption that *Public Education In Kentucky* later noted, "a local school tax may or may not be levied, and, when levied, the sheriff may hold it in his own hands for as much as two years . . . . Cases are known where the collector has not made a settlement within five years. Evidence of petty graft, inefficiency, and the free play of personal and partisan interests abounds."[46] The authors may well have been talking about the sheriff's office in Graves County.

Almost as soon as the change was initiated, however, State Auditor Frank P. James, recognized that there was substantial tax revenue being collected that was not being turned into the state treasury. As a result, he initiated a massive, sweeping investigation of every Kentucky sheriff in every county for the past 15 years.[47] Although the proverbial wheels of justice would indeed turn slow, the investigation eventually worked its way through every county, finally reaching Graves County two years later in the summer of 1911. It soon ensnared former sheriffs Samuel R. Douthitt, J. Newt Harris, and W.L. Brand, as well as the current sheriff, Rafe B. Wallace.[48] The first suits were filed in February 1912.[49] What was discovered would make the accounting systems used by the trustees and the county superintendent appear a model of propriety.

Two months later, in an open letter "To the Citizens of Graves County" printed in *The Weekly Messenger,* County Attorney M.B. Holifield outlined the results of their investigation:

The people of Graves county are familiar with the fact that in 1911 there was an investigation of the books, records and settlements of some of the ex-sheriffs of Graves county. When the auditors came to make this investigation I was out of the city, and on returning was surprised to find that they could only locate one cash book and forty-five (45), or less, receipt stub books for all the ex-sheriffs of Graves county. By investigating I learned that there was no specific provision of law requiring the sheriff to retain in his office the stubs to his tax receipts, and that it was a doubtful question as to whether said stub books were public property or the private property of the sheriff. I further learned that the sworn statement of the sheriff as to the amount of taxes collected by him, and which statement he was required to file in the County Court on the first day of May, June, July, August, September, October, November and December of each year, as set forth by Section 4147 Kentucky Statutes, had not, in a single instance, been filed, since the days of Sheriff Frank Houseman; that the only way by which we could gain the information desired by the Fiscal Court as to the exact amount, or more correctly, approximately the amount of taxes collected by our ex-sheriffs was to employ auditors for an indefinite time at an enormous expense to Graves county.[50] By further investigation, I learned that every year a large number of tax payers had been and were being omitted from the assessment books by the Assessor and the County Board of Tax Supervisors; that most of this omitted tax was collected, but only a small amount of same was ever paid to the County and State.[51]

Despite the obvious shortcomings in the system, investigators found a shortfall of $348.91 in former Sheriff Douthitt's receipts, which he promptly paid in full. When former Sheriff Harris was found to be in arrears for some $10,365.71, he quickly settled for $7,000.00.

The case against former Sheriff W.L. Brand, however, was not to be so simple. With claims against him totaling $19,165.32, *The Weekly Messenger* noted that it was "reported that he will not make any proposition, but on the contrary will fight the collection of the claim to the bitter end."[52] Although that particular investigation may have concluded, that didn't mean that either the Commonwealth or the County was finished. And the *Messenger's* words regarding Sheriff Brand would turn out to be spot on in their description.

As the year progressed, it was the Commonwealth's turn to levy embezzlement charges against former Sheriff J. Newt Harris, as well as the current Sheriff, Rafe B. Wallace. In November, Harris was acquitted "on pre-emptory instructions from Judge Bugg."[53] And Wallace, who was charged "in 14 counts of receipting or collecting for taxes not listed" was assessed a fine of $400 "in the nature of a compromise."[54] The case against Brand, however, still stood.

With Sheriff Brand still resisting any attempts to cut a deal (and every member of the regular panel of circuit court announcing they had already formed an opinion on the charges), a special venire of fifty men was summoned from nearby Fulton County the following March to hear charges that he had embezzled $2,384 in school funds.[55] After a jury of twelve was empanelled and the case went to trial, *The Daily Messenger* pointedly noted on March 13, 1913, "there is much interest centered in this case, especially in Graves County. It will require several days probably to complete the trial."[56] Inexplicably, however, the trial ended just two days later. And *The Daily Messenger* simply reported the verdict without further comment, "We, the jury, find the defendant not guilty."[57] Although the case then completely disappeared from the pages of the paper, it hadn't disappeared from the minds of those involved in its prosecution.

County Judge J.W. Monroe (with whom E.A. Jones and their spouses had once traveled to St. Louis to see the World's Fair) decided, "to fire the opening gun at Folsomdale" on March 29th as he announced his own candidacy for the sheriff's office. After relating his work in the investigation of the sheriff's books, he declared, "they have whitewashed crime in courts in Mayfield." The *Messenger* then went on to relate, "attention was called many times to the deplorable condition of justice, declaring that he did not like the farce that had been pulled off in the way of trials."[58] The charge, which should have been sensational given the public's interest in the recent case, was buried at the very end of a very long article.

When Judge Monroe and Sheriff Wallace met in public debate on the campaign trail, charges began to fly. After apparently having previously made the accusations at numerous venues, the paper finally noted Monroe's charges on April 19th. "Judge Monroe, it is said, intimated or accused Mr. Wallace with having made an effort to use his influence to prevent an investigation of his and of former sheriffs [sic] books, and to this Mr. Wallace defended his record in vigorous style, denying declarations made by Judge Monroe with reference to his actions since he has been in office."[59]

While the campaign for sheriff was being played out (with both Monroe and Wallace eventually losing after a bruising primary), one final investigation of the sheriff's department was underway. Virtually ignored by the *Messenger* was one being undertaken by E.A Jones of the magistrate's fiscal court. Although he had already been forced to abandon his own candidacy for Judge Monroe's seat due to failing health, "Squire" Jones had one last campaign in him.

"On motion of Justice Jones," the *Messenger* reported on September 5th, "it was ordered that R.G. Robbins be allowed $1,250 on his account for taking depositions in the cases of Graves County against W.L. Brand."[60] Curiously, in the staunchly Democratic *Messenger*, this information was disclosed in an article headlined, "No Road Machinery Will Be Bought." Although E.A Jones launched the final prosecutorial efforts, he wouldn't live to see closure of the case against W.L. Brand, dying on January 27th of "pulmonary tuberculosis."[61] Exactly one month later, on February 27th, newly elected County Judge Voris Gregory announced a settlement of $14,000 in cash on the original suit of some $19,000.[62] On March 5th, the investigation finally came to an end. It had cost over $6,000 and the records involved contained over 6,500 pages.[63]

"At least three sheriffs were found to be behind in their accounts," *The Daily Messenger* duly recorded. "All paid up and settled except W.L. Brand who, according to the investigation, was found to be behind with the state about $5,000 and with the county $14,472.84. The county brought five suits against him, one for $4,545.61, another for $2,882.97, another for $2,448.89, another $1,871.42 and another in the interest of the Board of Education for $2,723.95, making the above total." "Thus ends an investigation and an expensive litigation that has engaged the minds of the people of this county for several years,"

Editor Lemon concluded, "and it is hoped that another such will never be necessary."[64]

On December 9th, 1914, a small notice was posted in *The Daily Messenger* regarding the "commissioner's sale" of W.L. Brand's property to pay his outstanding debts.[65] On the same page in the very next column was the notice of another "commissioner's sale." That one concerned the sale of the estate of E.A Jones to pay his.[66] W.L. Brand had been broken.[67] Through his pursuit of politics over the work on his farm (which he left to his wife and children), E.A Jones would die broke. The property sold for ten dollars—the exact same cost of the plot on land on which he had been buried some eight months prior.[68]

Haskell: I knew a lot of those politicians through my dad. I used to go into town and go to the courthouse with him and mill around and meet this guy and that guy. And Dad would tell me who they were and I knew 'em. I knew *a lot* of those people. I had friends in Mayfield. I knew hundreds of people. I knew what most of 'em did. From the taxi driver to the mayor of the town. I knew the whole program. I doubt if there's anybody in that county that knew any more people than I did. Just by accident. Not necessarily planned or anything like that or because I was particular smart or anything.

I never forgot. That's one good thing. I had a good memory. I can remember who we saw, where we saw 'em. Almost to the crossroad where it was, you know. And I was lucky. I had a memory that's a little better than the average, I guess. A lot of water's gone over the dam since then, I'll tell ya'. Oooh! Seventy-five, eight years ago. I was fifteen years old when my dad died.

Justice E.A. Jones was in the city Thursday and is yet quite feeble. He has not recovered from his affliction of bronchitis, and unless he improves very rapidly he will hardly be able to make the campaign for the office of County Judge, which he would like to do.[69]

— *The Daily Messenger*
Friday, May 2, 1913

Haskell: He had been a magistrate and he had been elected a couple of terms or three and decided he'd like to be the county judge. So, he announced his candidacy and started in on the campaigning and became ill. He realized that he wasn't going to be able to handle the job, so he withdrew as a candidate. A year later he died.[70] The man who was running against him was elected. He was a man named Voris

Gregory who went to the U.S. Legislature and was a congressman for years. Finally died. Probably had thirty years as a congressman. But Dad was better known. He probably would have been elected.

Florence: I never saw his dad but one time. I was in Mayfield. He was runnin' for office. He was runnin' for county judge and the Mayfield paper was havin' a contest. They paid the one that got the most subscriptions to the paper so much money.[71] Fanny decided she wanted to try gettin' subscriptions for the *Messenger* and she went to

Florence Grace Jones and Frances "Fanny" Jones (L-R, front), Mary Effie Jones (rear) (Collection of Marjorie Jones Knapp).

Mayfield one Saturday afternoon ('cause that's when all the farmers went to town).

So, there was this man and he said he had already subscribed for the paper. Says, "I'd like for you to do something for me, though." She said, "What's that?" (He gave her a card) and said, "Well, I'm runnin' for county judge and I would like for you to speak to your father about me." It was A Jones.

So, I found out just exactly for sure, when I went to teach school down there, that that was the man (these kid's dad) that I had seen that day. It wasn't more than a year 'til he died from the time he was runnin' for office. I know he had to withdraw because he was sick and wasn't able to do it if he'd been elected.

So then, when I went down to Jones School to teach, I had his children—Mattie and Lillian and Grace and Tom and Henry goin' to school to me. From his pictures, I think Ralph is very much like his dad. And Haskell's like his mother.

Haskell: He'd been sick for a couple of years. Died with cancer, probably. They didn't know what was the matter with him. He'd been sick for a long time. He knew he was gonna' die. Yeah. He went down to skin and bones. He was a pretty big man. He wasn't fat, but he was a big man.

There used to be a fallacy that if you went out West, it was good for your health, you know. We had so much

"Prominent Citizen of County Died Tues. Night." When E.A Jones died at age 51, the occasion merited a large photo on the front page "above the fold" of *The Daily Messenger*, an extreme rarity at a time when the paper generally didn't even run photos at all. Because of his near constant involvement in area politics and recent success in uncovering corruption at the local sheriff's office, he was a local politician who left an overwhelmingly positive image behind in the public's mind upon his passing. On the other hand, his wife, Willie Jones, was left a widow with 8 children and little else (University of Kentucky Libraries. Special Collections Research Center).

T.B. down there. The doctors didn't know how to do anything about it, only bury you. Go to Texas or Arizona. My dad was gettin' ready to go and he finally got so bad he couldn't go.

They wrote "complications" on his death certificate. But to me, I guess, he had cancer of the lung 'cause I've seen a man die with cancer of the lung just like he died. But it could've been T.B. They doctored him for hardening of the liver and for pellagra. I don't know. It was either T.B. or cancer and I don't know which. They wrote "complications."[72]

* * *

Haskell: My dad didn't drink very often. Very, very seldom. But when he did, he'd get too much. He didn't know when to quit— every time. He'd come home about half-high, you know. My mom used to comb his hair pretty good. She'd really give him hell. But he didn't keep booze at home very often. He'd go into Paducah once or twice a year and come back with a bottle—<u>one</u> bottle, you know. Hell, it wouldn't last very long.

He wasn't rough with my mom. But he was rough with me. I think he resented the fact I looked like the Jameses. Maybe I'm wrong. I'm the oldest boy. He thinks I'm gonna' have a great, big boy that looks like him with black hair and nice features and so forth. And when I arrive, I got a big nose and look like my mother's people, the Jameses. I don't look like him. He favored Ralph over me all the time. And I remembered that. Maybe he couldn't help it. I don't know. Maybe I'm wrong. But I think I'm right. 'Cause he beat the hell out of me for anything. For anything or nothin' at all, I'll tell ya'. For sneezin' out of turn. Oooh! But good. He was a pretty good man. He could do a pretty good job of it. I went around with straps on my back half the time. Umh! He beat the hell out of me.

He was pretty cruel. He was always knockin' the hell out of us kids—especially me. Been raised like that and I was, too. So it kind of comes first nature. He apologized the day he was dyin' on the bed. He called me in. He said, "Son, I know I have been rough on you. I hope you can forgive me." I told him I did. But I lied somewhat. I ain't too sure I ever did. I tried. I honestly tried. A many and a many and a many, many time I've thought about that. And I thought, "You lied to him. You told him you'd forgive him. But did you?" So, I don't know yet. I still think I tried. I truly tried. I still try.

I think maybe he didn't know— Being brought up by the old Scottish method, they used to have a saying, "spare the rod and spoil the child." And that was their belief. Beat the hell out of him and make him be good. Way back four hundred years ago, five hundred, six hundred years ago, that was a Scottish belief that you beat the hell out of 'em, they'd be good. And it didn't necessarily work. Umh! I wonder.

This is ridiculous. I think about it now and I resent it. I resent it. But it— Well, I saw it happen. And I know it happened. Some of the neighbors had outhouses, but my dad didn't.[73] He couldn't have time. He had to go do this or do that, run up and down, go to town every day and mess around.

My grandmother didn't even have an outhouse. Never made an outhouse. Never made one for his own wife. And I'm fifteen years old and the second in. My sister was seventeen and never had an outhouse. You can't believe this. But it's a fact. And it was no problem. You had all the room in the world. You could build a barn, a corncrib or whatever he needed, you know. He had lumber, cut it down. But he couldn't build an outhouse.

Well, for a thousand years, they hadn't had any outhouses. So why should we start buildin' 'em now? It was an old Scottish habit. When you get ready, go out there behind the barn, in back of a tree or someplace, you know. Nah, the women used to go in the chicken-house down there. Go in the chicken-house and the chicken would eat this stuff up, see. You got rid of it that way.

Corncobs. That was the main— And it did a good job. You used two corncobs. You took three corncobs. You used two red ones. When you got them clean, why, you read a white one to see whether the red ones did the job or not. See whether you was clean or not, see. Couldn't tell on the red ones. You could tell on the white one. That was the old story. Nah, this— People don't know. Nah, they lived like the Indians.

I got some old boards and I had a saw that wasn't worth a damn. I couldn't cut with it. I tried, but it wouldn't cut. I had boards that stuck out over the eave of that outhouse four feet because I couldn't cut 'em off. But I tried. I worked like hell to try. I hated to see my mother and sisters have to go in a place like that. And I built 'em an outhouse. Fifteen years old. My dad died when I was fifteen. But nobody ever said, "Thank you." Nobody ever cared. They found it. They used it. And they were glad. But that's it. Nah, you can't believe people lived like that. They did!

I don't know. I can't understand. Dad was a fairly decent citizen. Educated—up to a point. And considered a civic-minded person around there. But as far as his family's concerned, the hell with it. They lived or they died. I don't understand it.

But I lived. And I'm still here. Ninety years old plus and happy and I don't hate anybody. I don't hate my father. I don't hate anybody. I can understand that things didn't go exactly like I wanted 'em to. But I couldn't do anything about it then. I can't do anything about it now. But I tried. But I sure worked hard as a kid, I'll tell ya'. I worked like a bastard! Umh! Done my best.

CHAPTER NINE

RECREATION

Haskell: I took a fishin' trip one time down to a town called Berkley in Carlisle County (in the Mississippi River bottom). This was summertime. July, probably. June, July, August. We went to a lake to fish down in a place they called Fish Lake. It was a pretty good-sized lake as lakes went down there. They really were sloughs. They had an outlet that went out to the river. And, in the spring of the year when the water would get up, the water would come in that outlet and fill the lake up. Then they'd get full of fish. As the water went out, it went out slow and the fish stayed in there. Then, all summer, that thing was loaded with fish, you know. It was pretty good place to fish. We used to take a net and go down there and fish.

They had a lot of big timber at that time. Big, tall gums and sycamores and what-have-ya'. And man, the lightnin' was poppin' all over there. Every once in a while you'd see a crack up the creek here a little ways and the doggone tree would just burn! Just the fire would hit it all over! A streak of lighting hit that water and it would've killed every one of us, but we was dumb enough we run out in the water. We didn't know any better, you know.

We wanted to get fish for supper and we caught a big feedbag full of shovel-bill cats. A shovel-bill cat is built kind of like a catfish. He don't have bones in him. They were considered "junk fish." When they took a bunch of kids down there, they fried 'em up for the kids and give 'em to them 'cause they didn't have any bones in 'em. They weren't the worst things to eat. They was better'n a carp. We ate carp down there. Out of that fresh water, carp was good. It was greasy, but— Full of bones. Ooooh, man! A carp's got more bones than you can imagine! A million of 'em in one carp wouldn't be too many. Man, it was terrible!

They used to catch them with their hands. They'd go in the water and feel around the logs. They'd call that "noodlin'." The heat of the day was a good time. A fish'll get in the shade in the shallow water. This water wasn't too deep in there. Some of it was ten or twelve feet, but most of it was five or six or less.

You get in there and find a log and get on the shady side of the log. And just start easin' along and finally you touch one. Well, if you jump like this— He'd go like lightnin'. But you just kept your hand on him— Then you felt him. And you felt which end was which of him, you know. So, you finally discovered where his head was. Then you took your thumb and finger and you rubbed him—like rubbin' a puppy or a dog.

As he breathed, you stuck your finger and thumb in his gills. Then you felt his tail. And you got him back just above his tail. Then you bent him. If you kept him bent, he couldn't flop. He was a pretty good-sized fish. Ain't a little fish. Ten, twelve, fifteen pounds. If you let that tail loose, he'd pull loose from ya.' But if you keep a kink in his backbone, then you could bring him right up out of the water and throw him in a boat, see. You had him all right, like that. But if you ever let him flop once, he was a goner. You couldn't hold him.

But we made a drag with a seine. We'd take a seine that was a hundred feet long and put it in the boat and leave one end here—to shore. Not shore, but as far out as you could walk. These fella's would wade out there and they'd hold that. These seines had a staff on each end of 'em. Inch and a half. Somethin' like that of pole. Then, they had a rope tied to the top and the bottom And the seine had floats on it and lead on the bottom.

A guy would take a boat— Two guys. One would row and one would pay the seine out. They'd go out and make a circle. And there was some guys that would go behind the seine and pick it up in case you hung up. Then they'd make a circle around to where they could take the ropes on the other end back to the crew that was on the shore, you know—or in the shallows. Then the whole crew on both ends would start pullin' toward the shore with this seine.

We couldn't land these seines up on the shore. The shore is full of cypress knees. Look like a post, stickin' up here. They was all thick down there. So, you couldn't get in there with a seine. There was no shore. So what you had to do was to pull the two ends together and then start workin' it and workin' it and workin' it 'til you got the seine down into a six or eight foot circle. Then you got in there and caught the fish with your hands and threw 'em in the boat, see. That wasn't bad if you knew what you was doin'. But we got some pretty rough lookin' fish in there. We got a garfish that was five foot long in there with a mouth that long and eeeee— If you stuck your hand in his mouth, you would never get it back. He'd bite you. But we knew a little bit about how to handle 'em. And you'd keep 'til you got everything out of there. Sometimes you'd get a big turtle. Sometimes you'd get a snake. But, in the meantime, you got fish.

One boy was named Johnson. They called him "Drap." He wanted to get in the seine to help catch. And the old man was kinda' in charge of the party. He was the oldest man of the bunch. Old man Kelley Holland. This boy was bout fifteen, sixteen years old. He said, "You'd better not get in there. First thing you get ahold of, you'll jump over that seine"—let all the fish out, see. Smash the seine down, they go out. "Oh, no Mister Holland! I won't come out! I won't come out!" The old man was pretty rough. He argued with Drap. Finally, he said, "O.K. But don't you come out of that seine! I don't care what you find in that seine. Don't make no difference. We've worked to get this thing up here to get the fish and you ain't gonna' jump on top of it and claw it all over and let everything out!" "I won't. I won't." "All right."

He had a devil in that seine with him—a fellow by the name of Ben Morris.[1] And Ben knew this boy was scared to death. He found a block of wood in there that had been sawed off about this long and it was waterlogged. The seine picked it up and brought it in, you know. Pretty soon Ben gets this block around where he knew he can touch Drap with it and he says, "Watch out Johnson!' Said, "There's a turtle in this seine with a hand as big as mine!" And Drap said, "Ooooh! Ooooh!" The old man only said, "Don't come out! Don't come out! I'll drown you! Don't you come out of there!"

So Morris got around behind him and he shoved that block between his knees and out of— out of there he come! Old man Holland got on Drap and I thought he was gonna' drown him! I'll tell ya', I got nervous. I figured he wasn't ever gonna' let him come up again. And he— I betcha' Drap never come out of another seine, 'cause that old man really gave him a treatment. But Drap come out of there screamin'. That— That Morris was a character. Umh!.

These things, you know, they ring bells. Clide King. This Clide King was a big, husky, young guy. Older than me. Let's see. He was born in ninety-three. I was born in ninety-eight. He was five years older than I was. They had a circus or fair— I don't know which. Anyway, they had a wrestler and a boxer.[2] And any guy could stay with 'em for five minutes got five dollars or ten dollars—whatever the prize was.

Well, this King, he wasn't a professional wrassler, but he was an awful strong farmer boy, you know, and wrassled a little around the neighborhood. So they get the match. This Jap he was wrasslin' wasn't as big as he was. But he was a professional wrassler. I think they said the Jap weighed about a hundred and thirty, thirty-five pounds. Well, Clide King weighed about 165. But the Jap would wrassle anybody that didn't weigh over 150, you know.

So the Jap says, "How much you weigh?" Clide says, "About 150 pounds." This Jap feels his legs, you know, and he says, "Man—" Says, "You a big 150 pounds." But he needed a customer to get the show goin' so they could sell tickets to get in there. He knew how to wrassle. He would've finally downed Clide 'cause he was eely. In about four minutes he was gonna' let it go and then he was gonna' lay him down. They appointed me timekeeper. So I see he's gonna' get my buddy and I called time on 'em for five minutes. Nobody else was keepin' time. So we got the five bucks.

We had one boy in town— His name was Robert Norman. Bobby Norman. A nice-lookin' kid. Only child of the family. Queer as a three-

MATTY MATSUDA.

Lightweight champion wrestler of the world, with the Metropolitan Shows here next week. Matty will meet all comers up to 150 pounds. His weight is 130. If you are a lover of the boxing and wrestling sports you will be sure to see some of the best at the fair next week.

"Matty Matsuda." *The Daily Messenger* (The University of Kentucky Libraries Special Collections Research Center).

dollar bill. I heard it through the grapevine—not directly. After he was seventeen, eighteen, nineteen years old, his folks discovered that he was. I knew him somewhat.

I hunted with him one night and it was a shame. The guys from town brought him out. And they shouldn't've done it. They should've known better. But they knew him and he was a neighbor boy or friend or somethin'. He was about sixteen, seventeen years old. So they conned me into goin' huntin' with him at night with some dogs. And we go out treein' opossums and whatnot, you know. It's a wet fall night. The dew is drippin' out of your ears, it's so wet out there. It didn't rain. It was <u>dew</u>. And the conditions are bad. We got briar-thickets that's a mile wide, you know. It's terrible in the woods. I can't remember the guys that brought him out there. But Bobby was one of 'em. Had a high-pitched voice—squeely voice. Eeeee-eeee, ahh-ee, you know. Well, he come out there with a Palm Beach suit on to run through these briars. He don't know what the hell he's gettin' into. He should've been in town in bed.

Well, I'm in there with a pair of knee-boots on and a raincoat. I know what the conditions are. So the dogs will tree from here to the street down there or twice that far. We can hear 'em way over there—oooh, ooooh,

"Have a Standard — Young Men." The advertising for the W.E. Norman company of Mayfield would infer that its clothing was the perfect attire in which to pick up a shotgun and go hunting. However, the owner's son would gain an unfortunate understanding regarding truth in advertising. *The Daily Messenger*, Friday, November 19, 1909 (The University of Kentucky Libraries Special Collections Research Center).

ooooh, ooooh, ooooh, ooooh. They've got it up a tree. We can tell that. You can tell by the different bark when they was treed and when they was runnin' still. It was a game, you know. I wish Joe Price was here to tell you this. Old Joe knew exactly. He could say it just like a hound. Ahh-oooh, ahh-ooh, ahh-oooh, ahh-ooh, ahh-oooh, ahh-ooh, ahh-oooh—he's still runnin'. But finally he gets this thing up a tree and he goes ahh-ooop, ahh-ooop, ahh-ooop, ahh-ooop.

So this kid would— He couldn't make it. I've got a flashlight. Some of 'em got lanterns. Well, he attached himself to me and we start to— on this barkin'. It might be from here to the far side of the street. There's nothin' but a briar thicket. Terrible! Well, these guys would go around it. This one would go around that way. And, so, I went through because I had this tough raincoat on and my boots and so forth. He'd stick his head under my raincoat tail and we'd go through one of these briar-thickets. He could get by by doin' that, you know—without gettin' scratched all to pieces.

I can hear him yet. I can hear him to this minute. [In falsetto] "My Lord! Let's go back to town!" Poor kid. I didn't know this guy. I heard of him, but I really didn't know him 'til that night. I wouldn't know him yet. He's dead and gone, but I— But I— But I felt sorry for him. I didn't know he was queer. I thought he was a sissy. But I learned later that he was. His folks finally told him, "We don't want you around." They finally give him some money and told him to go to San Francisco or somewhere where you'll find congeniality and get the hell out and don't ever come back.

That must be an awful thing to do. You're shocked. I can imagine that. I can imagine bein' shocked, you know. But he's your own blood and you produced him and— Why don't you say, "God bless you. I'll do the best I can for you. I can't help what you are. I can't help what I was, either. So behave yourself. Don't expose yourself any more than you have to. Live your life the best you can. But I still love you." Why can't they do that? I grant you I wouldn't like it, but I would never say, "I disown you." I would never say that. No.

CHAPTER TEN

JUSTICE

There are now in Mayfield fifty-one dives, a number that is not only a disgrace to the municipal administration, but a menace to the morals of the community at large as well. No effort is made to break them up.

The Paducah Evening Sun
Friday, August 27, 1897

Hades Discovered
The Mayfield Monitor Gets Hot in the Collar.
It is said the bawdy house in the east end of town has opened. There is either no law to reach such institutions or it is ignored, as they are permitted to run without let or hindrance. Mayfield seems to be on the down grade as to morality and Christianity. She now has about everything in the line of sin that can be reckoned, and very little effort appears to be made to check any of it. A few years ago the St. Louis Republic said that ever since the days of Adam efforts had been made to locate hell, and that it had at last been found in Mayfield, Ky. With forty or fifty blind tigers, a bawdy house or two, and any number of gambling places, together with the numerous other evils that are permitted, it is not very strange that the St. Louis paper should make such a statement as the above. Once Mayfield was the leading town in the state in point of morality and Christianity, but that can no longer be said by any one who has any regard for the truth.—Mayfield Monitor.

The Paducah Evening Sun
Saturday, January 29, 1898

Haskell: I can remember when I was younger, they used what they called a "road gang." They sent the petty offenders. Bootleggers, chicken thieves and a few things of that type. Fightin'. Swearin' on Sunday—they used to put 'em in jail for that. And they used to put 'em on the city streets to work—and on the county roads. They did ditchin', built bridges and stuff of that sort on county roads. Cut the brush back.

Graves County Court House, Mayfield, Kentucky

The Graves County Court House, Mayfield, KY.

Brush would grow to the middle of the road back in those days. And they trimmed it up. But they kept the city streets cleaned and worked up in shape. They always had a dozen or more of 'em. They called 'em a "chain gang." But it wasn't a chain gang. They didn't wear chains unless they'd run away. If they'd run away, then they'd put a ball and chain on their foot.

I know one fella' that lived in our neighborhood—Johnny Curd—wasn't too bright. And they had Johnny for somethin'. Stealin' chickens, bootleggin', or somethin'. I was on the way home from town or on the way to town. They were workin' on a bridge about halfway from my home to town and they was havin' a lot of fun there. I think my dad was along. So, we stopped, anyway, and wanted to know what was goin' on. Said Johnny tried to get away. He jumped in the creek with a ball and chain on his leg. He wasn't just exactly all put together. There wasn't much water in there.

Back when I was living at home, when I was a kid, we had murders all the time. For anything. Everything. No reason at all. Kids. School kids would cut each other all to hell with a knife, you know. It was a thing to do. It was a kind of a hillbilly thing. They didn't know any better. For no reason at all. Nothin'. Crazy stuff.

They had two or three murder trials. We had what they called "Circuit Court." We had Commonwealth Attorney and a judge who traveled from one county to the other. They would come, like, to Graves County and they'd hold court for three weeks or more. Then they'd go to Calloway County or somewhere and they'd have court there. They had a regular attorney, a commonwealth attorney and a commonwealth judge. "Circuit judge," they called him. And every time they'd come to our place for three weeks (which was about three times a year because they had four counties) they had three or four murder trials. But the most senseless crimes.

May Copeland and Lucian Turk

May Copeland Said She Killed Hugh Atchison
. . . . At this juncture a pistol was presented to Miss Copeland and she recognized it, saying that she had seen it before. "It belongs to Lucian Turk and it is the pistol that I shot with that night. (She demonstrated to the court that she knew how to shoot it.) . . . .

— *The Daily Messenger*
December 1, 1913

Haskell: We had one crime—There was a woman from our county who was visitin' her sister down in Ballard County. This Turk, Lucian Turk lived in the area and he started goin' with her and givin' her a little meat in the other end. Her name was May Copeland. Pretty woman. So they'd been pullin' up in the driveway by this guy's house (her brother-in-law) and shackin' up in that car. So he ordered 'em to get the hell out of there. Quit that. Told her if they didn't cut it out, he was gonna' make her leave, you know. She was stayin' there with her sister.

So those two bastards [Lucian Turk and May Copeland] pulled in there and went up to the window where he usually set and read the paper and shot him right through the window and killed him deader than a mackerel. This Turk come from a very wealthy family. Very, very wealthy family. Very, very wealthy. They owned a big wholesale grocery company in Paducah. And they owned a lot of land. A lot of lumber business. They was well to do.

So anyway, they killed this poor guy— Well, we probably had the best defensive lawyer in the state of Kentucky at that time. A fellow named Pete Seay who came from down there right close to where we did. Between us and Lowes. Down in that section. His name was Bernard, I think, but he was known as "Pete" by everybody that knew him. But he was a— He was a defense lawyer deluxe. He didn't let 'em go to the pen.

I went to this trial. I listened to some of the evidence. This guy was shot with an automatic. A .45 automatic. They had trained this May Copeland how to take that gun apart and put it together with her eyes shut, you know. She's an expert. So she claims her brother-in-law had raped her and threatened to do it again so she killed him. Pete Seay got 'em off. They never served a day in the pen. Not one. But he defended a lot of murderers around there. They ought to put him in jail for some of the jobs he did.

Bird Choate and Henry Campbell

Haskell: A guy by the name of Bird Choate. Him and a fellow by the name of Henry Campbell had been buddies. Campbell was a kind of n'er-do-well and Choate was a veterinary and had some property and was fair-to-do guy. But him and Campbell were friends and they went on a fishin' trip. Took their families. Went down to Reelfoot Lake in Tennessee or somewhere. I don't know where they went. I don't remember that. So after they came back, Choate's wife told her husband that this Campbell had raped her while they were down there.

So he drove down the road one morning by Campbell's house and threw a gun on him and put him in the buggy. Handcuffed him. Took him down the road. And Choate said, "Now, I'm gonna' take 'em out [Campbell's testicles] or I'm gonna' kill you. You got a choice." And the guy knew he'd do it. He wasn't a man that kidded around. He was a responsible citizen. So Choate said, "Take 'em out" and Campbell did. And this Choate cut 'em off and throwed 'em over in the field. Well, they gave him seven years in the pen.[1] He served maybe two and Pete Seay got him out on a petition.[2] Campbell was the first guy that signed the petition to get him out of the pen.[3] He wasn't too smart, you know.

Tom Tinker

Mayfield News
Yesterday's Messenger
Robert James is acting chief of police in place of Chief McNutt, who was called to Chicago last night on business.

— *The Paducah Sun*
Thursday, February 14th, 1901

Tinker Caught
One of the Folsomdale Burglars Safe Behind Bars
Tom Tinker Confessed and a Part of the Goods Recovered —
Another at Large.

Constable Peary of Boaz station Saturday night arrested Tom Tinker, white, for breaking into the Garton and Sellers stores at Folsomdale Friday night.

Tinker has acknowledged to having been one of the housebreakers, and says that Will Roberts, white, still at large, is his accomplice. Tinker has served two terms in the penitentiary, one from Hickman and the other from Graves county, for stealing bicycles. He seems to have a mania for stealing wheels, and when arrested had a new one which he claims he bought. He lives near Hickory, and has been out of the penitentiary several months. An Investigation of the robbery led to the opening of several packages of goods left at the Boaz station by Tinker, and the contents proved to be some of the goods stolen.

Tinker was taken to Mayfield and lodged in the jail there. Marshal McNutt was called in to interview him and found him to be Tinker, although he had given a fictitious name when arrested. Marshal McNutt was in the city yesterday and last night looking for Roberts, but was unsuccessful in catching him. Tinker had been in Paducah all day Saturday.

— *The Paducah Sun*
Monday, June 2, 1902

Three Escaped
Prisoners Made a Break for Liberty at Mayfield

Mayfield, Ky., July 11—Three white prisoners escaped from the county jail here. They were Tom Tinker, Lee Goins and Norman Walpole. The hall door leading to the back yard was left open while the deputy jailer was carrying quilts from the cells. The prisoners from the back yard climbed a sixteen-foot fence and made good their escape. Tinker has been in the penitentiary. He was awaiting trial on the charge of breaking into a store at Pryorsburg recently.

— *The Paducah Sun*
Friday, July 11, 1902.

The Jail is Unsafe
Guard May Be Necessary to Keep Mayfield Prisoners in
Dave Johnson of McCracken, Declined to Escape with the Others Saturday
Tom Tinker Playing Bad

It is claimed that the Mayfield jail is unsafe now that the only way to prevent the prisoners from escaping is to keep a guard around it night and day. The delivery mentioned exclusively in The Sun Saturday, in which five of the prisoners escaped, took place after the jailer had set up nearly all night to keep guard, previous developments in the discovery of saws, rope and other things having aroused his suspicions.

The men had threatened to get out before July 24, when the July term of circuit court begins, and it seems did so. Two of them, Ed Carter and Bull Holyer, were charged with maliciously cutting a young man a short time ago, and the others, Tally, Sawyer and Dick were charged with liquor selling.

One man who could have gone was Dave Johnson, of this county, who was arrested by Sheriff Potter a few weeks ago on an old charge of horse stealing, after he had been away for two years. He seems to be pretty well satisfied and remained in jail.

Tom Tinker one of the men who escaped several days ago by running past the jailer when the door was opened, is said to be hovering about the neighborhood

113

trying to play desperado, a la Tracy, the Oregon fugitive. A reward has been offered for his capture.

— The Paducah Sun
Monday, July 21, 1902

Night Guard at the Jail

Robert James has been appointed deputy jailer at Mayfield, to guard the jail at night. Since the escape of prisoners last week a constant guard has to be kept there.

—The *Paducah Sun*
Thursday, July 31, 1902

Tom Tinker Caught

Tom Tinker, who broke jail at Mayfield some time ago after being arrested for house-breaking, has been recaptured. He had been at large in that section for some time.

—The *Paducah Sun*
Friday, August 29, 1902.

Another Attempt

Deputy Jailer Bob James this morning in searching the jail found a 10 inch meat saw in the cell of Tom Tinker. It was only last Saturday that tools of every description were found in different parts of the jail and places where saws and knives have been used in cutting the bars. A careful eye is being kept on the inmates. They have been exceedingly quiet for some time, but Mr. James says it is not quiet ones who are necessarily innocent.

— The Daily Messenger
Tuesday, September 23, 1902.

Tom Tinker Still Tinkering

Deputy Jailer Bob James made another search at the jail yesterday and found a 10 inch flat file in the cell occupied by Tom Tinker.

— The Daily Messenger, Wednesday
October 29th, 1902

Life Term
Tom Tinker Gets Heavy Sentence This Time

Tom Tinker, white, who has twice before been in the penitentiary, was yesterday sentenced at Mayfield to the penitentiary, this time for a life term. He was indicted and convicted of housebreaking at Folsomdale and was yesterday morning tried in the Graves county circuit court.

— The Paducah Sun
Friday, November 21, 1902.

We Are Seven
Mayfield's Latest Contribution to Eddyville Society

The seven prisoners convicted at the term of circuit court just closed at Mayfield were sentenced yesterday and are as follows:

Tom Tinker who was captured after running amuck in the wilds of Graves for

114

several weeks, was sent up for life, as he had previously served two terms. He burglarized a store and broke jail a time or two, going armed constantly and dodging about the county instead of escaping to other parts . . . .

— The Paducah Sun
Thursday, December 11, 1902.

Haskell: My Grandfather [Robert James] was putting a roof on a house—an addition he was building for it. And he saw this Tinker coming down the road. I didn't know who he was. But Grandpa, he remembered him. I asked him why he got the gun. He said, "That was Tom Tinker."[4] I said, "Why?" And he said, "Well, I shot him once. I thought I might have to do it again if he recognized me."

He had been in jail and my Grandfather was a jailer. And he went to open his cell for something and the guy made a dive at Grandpa and Grandpa shot him. This guy was one of these birds with a low brow. His head just went back like that. He didn't have much forehead, just enough. Looked like a roof. And that cheap little gun my Grandfather had— He shot him here [pointing to the his hairline] and the bullet just went around his skull. Left his hair parted forever and his hair died on that strip. It was plowed loose from his skull, you know. He had a part 'bout half an inch wide right around his head.

Tom Tinker, sent from Mayfield to the Eddyville state prison about ten years ago, has been paroled. Tinker is almost blind and was sent there for a life term on a third conviction of larceny.

— The Daily Messenger
Friday, July 4, 1913

Haskell: He was in for life. I don't know what he had been sentenced for. But I do know he had been sentenced a third time for the same offense. If it ain't nothin' but stealin' chickens—you go up for life. They call you a habitual criminal. They had no way of doin' anything with you only lock you up to keep you from stealin' chickens—whatever it might be. Burglary or robbery or various things of that kind was a felony.

Some years afterwards, why, he'd been in jail but he'd been paroled because his eyes were supposed to be goin' out. He was released because they said he was going blind. He'd told somebody that he'd rubbed soap in his eyes and feigned that he had a problem with his eyes and they paroled him.

Tom Tinker, who was recently pardoned from the Eddyville State Prison, is back in Mayfield furnishing music with his violin.

— *The Daily Messenger*
Friday, August 8, 1913

Haskell: He wasn't a kid. I would say he was in his fifties. His hair was thin. I went to a dance and him and his buddy made music for the

"Tom Tinker Lynched Here Last Night." Perhaps one of the most notorious "double hangings" in U.S. history, the lynching of Tom Tinker has been all but forgotten—perhaps purposefully so. Microfilm copies of the newspaper have disappeared from the Mayfield Library, the offices of the Mayfield *Daily Messenger* and the Kentucky Historical Society, as have any images of the hanging itself. This photomosaic image of the February 10, 1915 issue was pieced together from several separate photocopies of the front page in the files of *The Daily Messenger*.

dance. His buddy's name was Ed Rogers.[5] They met each other in the pen. I guess he was doin' time for stealin' a horse and a wagon from my grandfather when he met old Tinker. He had started over toward Murray and they caught him over there somewhere. The horse wasn't worth seventy-five cents. It was mostly the price of the hide. Big, old, flea-bitten horse. She was a mess.

After the dance, they broke into this store and two deputy sheriffs went to arrest Tinker. One went in one barn door and one went in the other and they— Tom was up on a wagon loadin' tobacco in the wagon and one of these sheriff's tell him to come down. He went down on the other

116

side and grabbed his gun and run out the back door. This young fellow tried to catch him as he come out and Tinker killed him.

So, the other guy run him down and run him in a house and upstairs. And when he got up there, Tinker was on his knees by the trunk huntin' more shells for his gun.

The guy took him out and he took him to jail. On the second night, why, they took him out of jail—the mob did. He said, "Let me get my shoes on." They said, "Where you're going, you don't need any shoes!" They took him up the street, about a block away in the courthouse yard and hung him to a maple tree. Deputy that was killed was one of the sheriff's deputies, you know, and the sheriff was all for it. Couldn't say that. He couldn't publicly say, "Go ahead and hang him." He could remonstrate with his fingers crossed.[6]

I knew about that. I was gonna' go and see it. I heard the rumor— The neighbors were talking about it. It was general knowledge that they were gonna' hang him that night. I don't know whether he knew about it or not. Anyway, my brother Ralph told my mom that I was gonna' go and see it. And she threatened me with extinction if I went. So I didn't go.

Unseen for over 100 years, this photo of Tom Tinker was acquired from a descendent of Dick Tart, the constable murdered by Tom Tinker.

Sheriff went out there in the morning— He hung there 'til morning. He went over in the morning and cut him down. He was laying there on the ground waiting for the coroner to come and declare he was dead and some photographer come and wanted to make pictures. So, some of the boys around there accommodate him. They hung him back up so the photographer could take pictures.

Florence: Well, my sisters, Mary and Fanny, were going to high school at that time. And they were staying at Aunt Anna's. And they walked along the west side of the square going to school and they saw him hanging there.

Haskell: Saw him hanging there?

Florence: Yep.

Haskell: I imagine if you offered a reward for one of them pictures, you could find some of them. They was made around Mayfield. There was quite a bunch of 'em made. But I don't know whatever become of 'em. I've seen one of 'em. But I don't remember where I saw it. They sold 'em. Probably fifty cents apiece. Something like that.[7]

Killing

Along with many others, another bloody chapter was enacted at the "Red Shack" just east of the city this afternoon just before 2 o'clock in the shooting of B.S. Thurmond of Water Valley and Bill Houseman of this city shot by John James. Thurmond lies dead while Houseman is seriously shot through and through.

Eyewitnesses say that James was in possession of the "Shack" and had been for some time. They say that Houseman came down there and said he was going to take possession when he was ordered out by James. Houseman then made a threat towards James and James pulled a pistol on him and told him to stay off. Houseman continued to advance and succeeded in grabbing the pistol, knocking it up when it went off, the ball striking Thurmond . . . in the head killing him instantly.

James succeeded in shooting again and hit Houseman in the upper part of the hip passing through and through. Houseman succeeded in getting away to his home in the eastern part of the city where he now lies. James was placed in jail.

Mr. Thurmond was about 65 years of age and was a clever old gentleman, liked by all who knew him. He had one fault, like many others, the love for strong drink. He leaves a wife, one son, Allen, who live at Water Valley.

The inquest will be held this afternoon. Houseman is a noted character and was fined $300 only this morning for selling liquor and turned out of jail, where he has been for some time, upon his promise to leave the county.

— *The Daily Messenger*
Tuesday, March 3, 1903

Haskell: My grandfather's family was— They was gun-happy. They'd shoot you. My Uncle John James was a bartender in— They called 'em "blind pigs" in those days.[8] It was nothing but a bootleg joint.[9] And this man, Bill Houseman, come on the warpath for some reason. I don't know what started the argument. They were gonna' shoot at each other, anyway, and Uncle John shot at him, missed him, and killed another man. He was exonerated because this Houseman was a known killer.

A lot of the territory all the way around—Southern Illinois, Tennessee, Kentucky, Indiana was dry. Graves County, where I was raised, was dry. Always been dry since the Civil War almost. But they could go over to Paducah and get legal whiskey anytime. So, there was some bootleggin' goin' on around in our neighborhood. But it was mostly manufactured still-house whiskey. It wasn't moonshine, see— wasn't made out in the bushes.

There was a lot of bootleggers. They'd go to dances and sell it out the dance or some meeting of some kind or some political meeting or somethin' of that kind. But they always kept it at home. They sold it out of their homes. They didn't have stores. Livery stables— Guys would be around a livery stable workin' the livery stable. A lot of 'em would keep a few bottles around there in the hay somewhere, you know. Farmer'd come in and wanted a bottle, why, they'd sell it. Stuff like that. I never bought a bottle of booze in our county. Didn't care much about it.

Editorial
Beer and Whisky for "Personal Use"

Saturday afternoon the Louisville accommodation mail train, which arrives here at 4:45 p.m., brought and delivered to the express agent at this place about twenty-five kegs and several cases of beer and about thirty-six packages of whisky, consigned to various parties, all for "personal use" . . . .

This was only on one train, but other trains are said always to bring more or less each time, especially those which arrive from Paducah. In conversation with parties who observe the "drinking" habit in Mayfield and Graves county, a Messenger reporter was told that the trains, in one way or another, either by express or privately, would bring to this county in a year at least $100,000 or more worth of whisky and beer . . . .

Although this county has the local option law in every precinct in it, where these beverages cannot be bought or sold according to the law, yet it is claimed by many that at least a quarter of a million of dollars is paid out annually for intoxicating drinks by our people.

About half of this is shipped here under the "personal use" law—a law which permits thousands to violate both the spirit and letter of the law and go unpunished.

About one-half comes into this county in wagons, hacks, buggies and automobiles, with no restrictions whatever . . . .

— *The Daily Messenger*
Monday, June 26, 1916

Haskell: They had one train that come through Mayfield on the Illinois Central. They called it "Whiskey Dick" because of all the bootleggers in Graves County.[10] We could have whiskey in Graves County. You was entitled to as much as you wanted. Couldn't sell it. So that made it an open thing. And some of these bootleggers would go over to Paducah and come back on the Whiskey Dick with a burlap bag over their shoulder with 15-20 bottles or more in the bag. Take it home. Everybody knew they were bootleggin', but if they didn't catch 'em, they didn't care much, you know. Some kind of a deal like that.

They used to have a system— They had automobiles when I was a kid. Livery stables (who had been in the horse livery business, you know, before) bought a bunch of new Fords. I don't know what they did before that. That was before my time.

You go to the livery stable (four or five guys who wanted to go to Paducah) and it cost each one of you a dollar apiece to go down there and back in a Ford in those days—which a dollar was about that big [spreading his hands apart], you know.

It was twenty-five miles from our house. The guy that owned the car (the livery man), he paid the guy that drove the car a minimum. Maybe a dollar. But you was supposed to buy him some drinks and maybe give him a tip. Somethin' of that kind. Saloons were open then, back in those early days when I was around there. I never made the trip but a time or two, but I did. I have been down there.

They'd take you down to the saloon. People that didn't want to go to the cathouses, you didn't have to go. They'd pick you up though wherever they knew where you was gonna' be and take you home, see. But you could go to the saloons and have a few drinks and buy a bottle, take it back with you. Whatever you wanted. It was kind of an evening out, you know. It didn't cost much. Booze was cheap. Girls were cheap. A couple bucks.

They had the condition pretty well under control back in those days. They had "cathouses" in Paducah. (There was always a few girls around Mayfield, but there was no— There was no "line." There was not enough people there like Paducah had. They had a real red light district all the time.)[11] Operated very methodically and orderly. The customers would come in— They had one of them pianos. You put a dime in it in and you could dance about three minutes to four. They sold booze in there. They sold beer or a shot of whiskey, you know. And they had a place for operations upstairs, in the back room or somewhere. Usually

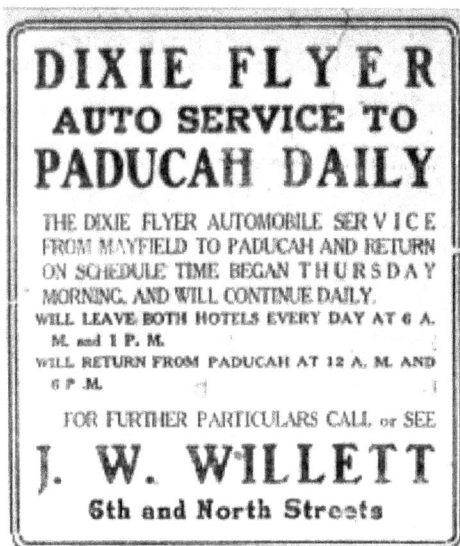

DIXIE FLYER
AUTO SERVICE TO
PADUCAH DAILY

THE DIXIE FLYER AUTOMOBILE SERVICE FROM MAYFIELD TO PADUCAH AND RETURN ON SCHEDULE TIME BEGAN THURSDAY MORNING, AND WILL CONTINUE DAILY.

WILL LEAVE BOTH HOTELS EVERY DAY AT 6 A. M. and 1 P. M.

WILL RETURN FROM PADUCAH AT 12 A. M. AND 6 P .M.

FOR FURTHER PARTICULARS CALL or SEE

J. W. WILLETT
6th and North Streets

"Dixie Flyer." *The Daily Messenger* (The University of Kentucky Libraries Special Collections Research Center).

upstairs. And they were clean. They were inspected by the health department periodically for venereal diseases and things of that kind.

The madam who was in charge was usually a big, strong woman. Not a little, skinny one. And she usually knew how to handle herself. She'd ballbat you or whatever when you got out of line. You had to behave yourself just like you would if you was in church. You didn't get out of line. Didn't get drunk and raise hell. But they had six, eight, ten gals (somethin' like that) work around there, you know. They still had their hair long. Didn't smoke cigarettes. Behaved themselves.

One of 'em was pretty close to the river. Old Jenny Lytton.[12] She had the scum-bums. They had three sisters in Paducah—Emma, Ruth and Bess Martin.[13] Each had their own house. Big women. Maybe it was Ruth— She was goin' to Dyersburg, Tennessee, to work a fair. There was a place out south of Mayfield there they called the "Red Cut," where the railroad cut through a hill and the soil was kind of red. There was a railroad crossin' went across there in that cut, you know. It was a dangerous place. They didn't grade it down so you could see.

She had a Model T. Her and her P.I. (that's a pimp) drove in front of a train and it cut her leg off. And it was a common practice— They didn't want a pocket book to be bothered with. They carried their money in their stocking, you know. They all wore stockings up to here [indicating mid-thigh] with a belt of some kind to hold it up. If they got money, they put it in the stocking. They might have three or four hundred dollars in there. Whatever.

Well, they're not close to a hospital. There was no ambulance. There was nobody— Nothin' they could do with her only let her bleed to death. There was no doctor nearby or anything. It was [SLAPS HANDS TOGETHER] like that, you know.

But they said she crawled about twelve, fifteen feet over to the leg, took that money out of that sock and put it in the other one before she died. Of course, I didn't see it. One of the Martins. I think it was Ruth. One of the Martin girls. I never knew her. Never saw her, but I heard of her a lot.[14]

They had an old man in Paducah— Old man Iseman. Had a lot of rental houses. Had strings of 'em. Rented to colored people generally. Mostly. But not all. Not all. Some of 'em was white. He collected the rent himself. And when you rented a house from him, you signed a contract to pay the rent every week. You didn't pay by the month. You paid by the week. They couldn't get a month's rent ahead. Rent was probably six dollars a month. A dollar and a quarter a week or somethin' like that, you know. I don't know. Never rented one. I don't know.

He drove a mule to a buggy. He drove up and down the street and he'd stop here to go in and gets his dollar and a half—or whatever they got comin'. Whatever it was. If you didn't have it, he had a contract with you to throw your furniture out in the street. You'd better have it. Wore an old beard. I've seen him a time or two. I didn't know him.

He'd go to the saloon and get himself a beer once in a while. He'd take a bottle of beer out and give it to the mule. This mule was trained like your dog. He'd go out and give this mule the beer and he'd take it in his teeth, turn it up like that. It was quite a show. Everybody wanted to see old man Iseman get his mule a beer. But he did it regular, I guess. I never saw it happen. I heard of it.

His brother got killed in a hold-up.[15] He only had one arm. Guy come in a saloon, hollered "Everybody, hands up!" And this guy stuck this one arm up. He couldn't get this one up. He didn't have any. Stuck the one arm up and the guy shot him. Killed him. Pitiful thing. Pitiful thing. He was a double loser. He lost his arm. He lost his life.

CHAPTER ELEVEN

THE SOCIAL EVIL

"Paducah has one public prostitute to every thirty-five of her adult woman population."
"There is no other city the size of Paducah, so far as we have been able to learn, which has anything like the number of prostitutes as are here."

"Existing Conditions"
Report and Recommendations of
the Paducah Vice Commission.
Paducah, Kentucky, 1916[1]

With the progressive movement of the early 20th Century, public efforts at reform in Graves County took many guises, whether it was in the battle to eliminate a common drinking cup to prevent disease among schoolchildren, the eradication of child labor or battling corruption in office. One of the biggest challenges for the era, however, was the elimination of "the social evil," which could encompass all manner of vice. Being technically a "dry" county, Graves County generally only had violations of the "local option," the occasional "blind tiger," public pool halls, skating rinks or Sunday sales of soda with which to contend.[2] Neighboring McCracken County, and its county seat, Paducah, however, was another story. By the time Haskell first visited the city as young man, even the city fathers considered it to be "wide open."[3] Although efforts were underway in 1916 to change that situation, they would ultimately prove to be just as unsuccessful as they had in the past.

Following the Civil War, when Paducah was still a village, the "red light" district was allowed to exist along the riverfront on South Second Street. Eventually being seen as a "public nuisance," however, the denizens of the "disorderly houses" weren't ordered to leave. They were just ordered to move, eventually settling on the outskirts of town on West Court Street (with the "negro" practitioners a block further back on Washington Street).[4] As the city continued to grow and expand in all directions, West Court Street (now renamed Kentucky Avenue) was to be found in "very nearly the center of town." What's more, the "latticed porches, in themselves an open sign of the character of the house," made the area "possibly the most conspicuous spot in the city of Paducah."[5]

After a fatal shooting in 1906, the first serious efforts at reform were initiated. With Rev. D.C. Wright taking up the crusade and Circuit Judge William Reed providing the legal backing, the residents were once again ordered to move.[6] While Kentucky Avenue was eventually cleaned up, the efforts didn't do much for the rest of Paducah. The "bawdy houses" of "Paducah's leper colony" simply spread throughout the town in almost every direction, making them even harder to control—not that there was much interest in the proposition among the citizenry—unless it was in queries to the local cab drivers and accommodating police officers as to exactly *where* the houses had relocated.[7] Despite their best tub-thumping editorials, even the editors of *The Paducah Evening Sun* had to eventually concede:

> That the "red light" district exists in any city is not so much the fault of the police as it is of the citizenship generally . . . . The Paducah police will start a crusade against the "red light" whenever a positive, vigorous public sentiment demands it, that public sentiment in Paducah has not been stirred as yet into an active force . . . . There are still disorderly houses in Paducah and the fault lies in her citizens who have and do permit such a condition to exist, except when it encroaches on their individual rights."[8]

Failing that approach, the city subsequently tried medical inspections of the ladies, which, at best, only offered a false sense of security at the ten houses that made a pretense of going through the motions.[9] When those efforts faltered, city fathers next enacted, "An Ordinance Relating to Penal Offenses Committed within the City of Paducah, Kentucky, and Prescribing the Penalties Thereunder" in 1909.[10] Among other things (such as prohibiting the flying of kites and ringing of bells on the city streets) the new ordinance attempted to proscribe "any indecent, immodest, lewd or filthy act," "to utter or speak any bawdy lewd or filthy word or discourse within the hearing of any other person," "any indecent, immodest or lascivious books, pamphlets, papers, pictures or statuary," "any picture of any female person with exposed busts," and "any two or more common prostitutes to walk or be in company together on any street, side walk, alley or other public thoroughfare in the City of Paducah."

By 1916, however, it was obvious that the ordinance's enactment was just as successful as previous efforts had been. Even though some two hundred major American cities would initiate their own vice campaigns between 1912 and 1920, shuttering their own red light districts, the fight against prostitution in Paducah would not be so easily won.[11] Effectively thumbing their noses at both the ordinances and reform efforts, Paducah's houses of ill repute simply collected the exiles from the other cities and put them to work.[12]

In March 1916,"after lengthy discussion by the Public Welfare Commission, it was unanimously voted that the Mayor appoint a Vice Commission." Reverend Clinton S. Quin, the new rector of Grace Episcopal Church, was to serve as its chairman.[13] Other volunteers would prove slightly harder to impress into service, however, as the nascent committee found that it was not without "some little difficulty in securing citizens to serve on this Commission."[14] Once it was established, the Commission hired two investigators who held "numerous private hearings" and "used every known, legitimate means of securing information which would show to us the true conditions in our city." It would soon become obvious that there was plenty of opportunity for reform.

Within the city confines, the commission discovered four or five public dance halls (viewed as the "ante room to hell itself" in other cities), 12 poolrooms, 67 saloons and 60 brothels (which also sold alcohol) located throughout Paducah or within the district known as the "Gash" (not to mention 174 "professional sporting women").[15] What's more, fifteen of the "sporting houses" catered specifically to boys under 21 years of age.[16] Therein, the lads from Mayfield might even occasionally recognize girls from back home among the residents of the "red light resort's."[17]

Upon further investigation, the Commission members were appalled to discover that schoolgirls, just barely in their teens, were being openly recruited off the street on their way to and from school.[18] Police officers were openly consorting with the prostitutes.[19]

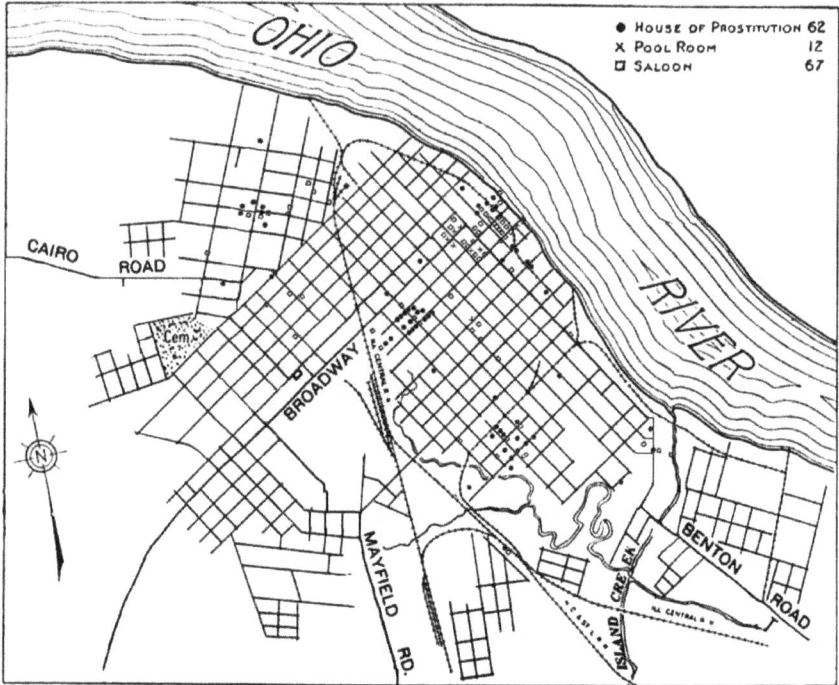

Houses of prostitution, poolrooms and saloons in Paducah, Kentucky, 1916.
Report and Recommendations of the Paducah Vice Commission (The University
of Kentucky Libraries).

Syphilis and gonorrhea were of epidemic proportions in the filthy houses.[20] And after the Madam took her cut from the proceeds of the player piano (to which every visitor was pressured to contribute) and beer sales (including Sunday, the only days the saloons could not legally make it available), it was determined that the women were paid an average of $4.85 per week—for working "morning, noon and night every day of the year."[21] In his private diary, Quin would liken Paducah akin to "ancient Damascus, and Sodom and Gomorrah."[22]

As a result of their investigation, the Commission came up with 32 recommendations including enforcing existing laws and establishing new ones through medical care, vocational training and rehabilitation. However, even Chairman Quin appeared to have understood the nature of the battle ahead. In the Commission's report, he noted, "We are fully aware that other men and women, equally intelligent and honest, and equally devoted to the welfare of our city, will hold opinions different from those which your Commission, in view of the evidence obtained, have felt compelled to form." "We believe," he continued, "that, for too long, the general condition of vice in our city has been winked at, not alone by the police administration, but by the public, the citizenship as well."

Considering their work complete, the Commission disbanded, hoping the light they had shown on the topic would begin the process of immediate and lasting change. Little progress was made, however, until Police Chief Henley Franklin was unceremoniously demoted back to patrolman status and replaced by James W. Eaker.[23] Finally, on July 27th, after personally visiting every known house of prostitution, Chief Eaker made his agenda known. He ordered an immediate stop to the playing of pianos and the sale of beer and announced the brothels would be forcibly closed on September 18th.[24] Unfortunately, he had neglected to consider the legalities of such a pronouncement. When five women (including Queenie McClure and Emma Martin) appeared before Judge Caswell B. Crossland for violating Eaker's initial edict just two weeks later, Judge Crossland dropped all charges against the women declaring "there is no law against piano playing, and that he did not propose to fine women for such offenses."[25]

With the day for shuttering the brothels fast approaching, little progress was to be seen. To help support Chief Eaker in his efforts, a Morals Commission, which included Reverend Quin and Sanders E. Clay, Commissioner of Public Safety, was appointed on September 5th. Just three days later Reverend A.A. Myrick of Calvert City was shocked to be offered female companionship when he took possession of his room at the Southern Hotel.[26] When the deadline for closing the brothels came and went without any arrests, charges of stalling began to fly, spilling over into that fall's election. Affidavits were even filed (one, oddly enough, signed by brothel owner Emma Martin) that Commissioner Clay and Mayor Lackey were allowing houses to operate if they kept the player pianos quiet and the porch lights turned off—despite earlier assurances to Reverend Quin of their full support.

Although both Lackey and Clay were swept from office following the election, it was to little avail. In mid-December, Judge Crossland dismissed all warrants against the proprietors of 22 brothels "and virtually killed the whole crusade against reopening of the vice district. In doing so, he declined to call the police to the stand to testify saying, "Crowds of men might visit any private house." The next day, in a speech criticizing "so-called Christians," Judge Crossland "told the crowd he would not put the women in jail and felt sure they had no money." The newspaper flatly concluded that, "The police are nonplussed as to what to do to close the district."

With the locals fully embracing this unexpected holiday gift, future business at the brothels was so assured that one madam contracted to add ten more rooms to her resort within days of the announcement.[27] Even Commissioner Quin finally gave up. It would not be without one final parting shot, however:

> In a letter rebuking Mayor Frank N. Burns, Commissioner Eugene Graves and Don P. Marton for their alleged failure to co-operate, Rev. Clint S. Quin, rector of Grace Episcopal church, resigned from the morals commission. He said that the mayor promised before election he would do all he could to remove public prostitution from the city, but that he had refused to turn his hand in fulfillment of his promises. Concluding, Rev. Quin said: "Assuring you that I have enjoyed every minute of my time spent in this distasteful task, thanking you for past audiences, and regretting very much to sever my connection with a work which must either triumph or the city go to hell, I remain, most respectfully, "CLINTON S. QUIN."[28]

He preached his final sermon at Paducah's Grace Episcopal church the following Sunday before moving on to a more receptive congregation and far greater accomplishments in Houston, Texas.[29]

CHAPTER TWELVE

MIGRATION

Detroit and Akron Mecca For Work Seekers

Detroit, Mich., and Akron, O., seem to be two of the busiest places in the United States at this time.

It is said that over a hundred thousand persons have gone to these two places to get work and that all who were capable and willing to work got a job.

Over 100 persons from Paducah and probably a hundred from Graves county, to say nothing of those from the surrounding counties in Western Kentucky, have gone to these places to work and most of them are there yet.

Another colony of ten or fifteen left Mayfield today for Akron, Ohio, seeking employment, which no doubt they will get, as some of our best young men are drifting away to these industrial cities.

Such a demand for labor has never been known before at any two cities as there has been within the past two years at Detroit and Akron.

The industries and manufacturing establishments of these two cities are paying out millions of dollars every month or so for labor.

— The Daily Messenger
Saturday, August 26, 1916

Coming Back Home

We notice in many of the state papers that large numbers of the boys that went to Detroit and Akron to work are returning home. Some got homesick. Some got sick. The work is too hard for some, and others are satisfied with the trip, while board and other expenses are beyond all reason. The roads have been kept hot both ways for months.

— The Daily Messenger
September 11, 1916

Returns From Akron

Wayne Slaughter has just returned from Akron, Ohio, where he has been at work for a year or more . . . . He says he had rather be at home on less wages than at Akron with greater wages.

— The Daily Messenger
October 24, 1916

Haskell: I'd done a little, a few odd jobs. Dug clay. Worked with a hay baler. A few odd jobs like that. But mostly just farmed.

Florence: Farmer's sons always worked on the farm.

Haskell: The rehandling of tobacco for shipment and sale was seasonal. It's only lasted three, four months a year and then there wasn't anything to do if you worked in the tobacco, in the factories, you know, in the rehandling.

Florence: Raise a field of tobacco and not get very much money for it. And it was a lot of hard work.

Haskell: After the farmer sold his tobacco, it was carried to these rehandling barns. This tobacco was conditioned to the right moisture content by steam chest. They put it in there and steamed it and got it in the right "order," we called it. Then they put it in these big barrels (we called 'em "hogsheads") which would hold close to a ton of tobacco.

They had a man that stayed down in that barrel and a boy that worked on a bench up alongside. He threw it into this barrel one "hand" at a time (you threw it head first). If he was a good boy, he could almost throw it right where the man wanted it, see.

They went 'round and 'round. They had to put several layers in. They started on the outside of the barrel and put the heads of the hands of the tobacco against the outside. Then they dropped back a little way and put the head on the tails 'til they got the barrel so full.

Then they had a big, heavy screw jack. They'd put a head in the top of this barrel and they pressed that tobacco down in there.

"Delivering Tobacco in Mayfield, Ky." With over 30,000,000 pounds of tobacco received in 1916, alone, Mayfield was the largest loose leaf dark tobacco market in the world.[1] The work of processing it, however, was only seasonal at best.

Then they'd put in another amount 'til they got it up to the top and then they'd press it again. Then they'd fill it up and press it again. That tobacco was pressed in there real tight, in that whole barrel. And a lot of it— Most of it went overseas. It was exported.

There wasn't any public work. There was very little, very, very little public work. A few stores in town and the storekeeper's friends and kids worked in them. But, women— There just was nothin' to do.

There was no work for young women. A few of them worked in millinery stores. They'd have a lady's millinery store where they sold hats. Every woman wore hats in those days. Dresses, corsets, whatever, you know. Underwear and so forth. They didn't sell that in the department store. They sold it in the millinery store. And any stockings and so forth. Women could get a job in that kind of a store. But, heck, they only got two stores in each town! And they got three hundred women! They can't get a job there.

There was two woolen mills there. But they were not considered the very best. If you didn't have to work in there, you didn't. We had the Merit Pant.[1] We had the old Woolen Mills, which was a <u>big</u> outfit. A great, big outfit. They spun the thread, wove the cloth, cut it out, fitted it, sewed it together, finished it and sent it out to the stores, see. It was a big outfit. The Mayfield Woolen Mills. Some of our people owned some of it. The Wrights. Yeah, old Uncle Ben and his family.[2]

At Mayfield, in Graves County, a public health nurse was found struggling with the problem of poverty-stricken, advanced tuberculosis cases living in one-room houses, with large families of children. Some of these patients were even doing home-work on pants for the woolen mill.

—*Child Welfare in Kentucky: An Inquiry by the National Child Labor Committee*, 1919

Haskell: Women could work in the mill, but they were looked on as harlots if they worked in a mill. No matter how bad— If they were starvin' to death, if they worked in a mill, they weren't no good.

It was just one of those old fallacies. A lot of women worked in there. They *had* to. Some women would go to the mill and bring clothes home and they did sewin'—put in pockets or whatever they had. Now, they weren't too bad. They were "pieceworkers." But the ones that stayed in the mill and cut and sewed and did whatever in there, boy, they were— They were really ostracized. It was terrible.

Women could teach school if it was open. They could do that. But there was so many of 'em, there wasn't half enough room for all the girls, you know. There was just one here and there that had the ability or had the appearance of a capable person that'd get a school. This girl

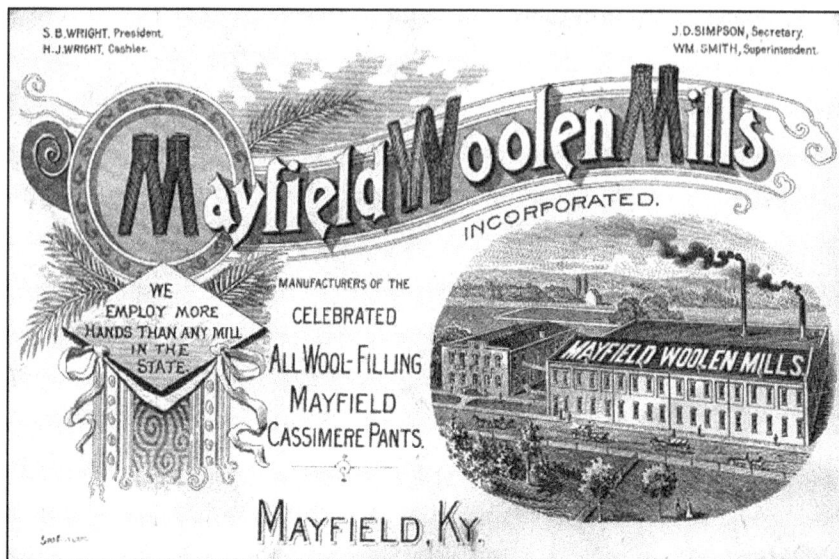

The Mayfield Woolen Mills, Mayfield, Kentucky. Although the Mayfield Woolen Mills was the largest employer in the area, and the largest plant of its kind in the United States, it was not the most desirable location in which to work. Locally, women working there were "looked on as harlots."

might be too fat for the trustee or too skinny or whatever. Any reason he didn't like her, he wouldn't give her the school, you know. But this one that was a pretty, shapely-lookin' gal got the job.

A lot of girls went out with a definite plan. I'll move out of my neighborhood and go teach school and I'll meet some young man and I'll get married. That was the ultimate motive was to get out away from the Joe Blows we know here in the neighborhood. "We don't particularly like them. Maybe I can go down here and I'll meet some capable, young man and we'll get married."

It was a common thing. It happened to thousands of 'em because that was the way— That was not necessarily the little, old twelve dollars a month they made. But they had somethin' else in mind, you know. And, well, times were rough in those days, I'll tell ya'. Women had a hell of a rough time.

Florence: Teaching was about all there was for women to do down there in the, out in the country that far. When you got out of high school, the only thing you had to do was take a state exam at the county

The Graduating Class of Mayfield High School, 1917. Florence, the class salutatorian, is in the top row, second from left.

superintendent's office.[3] If you passed, and somebody would hire you, you had a school. If you didn't pass, well, that was it. You still didn't have anywhere.

Haskell: You went to town and they give you an examination. They said, "When you're facing north, which way is east?" And, "Can you read and write and are you big enough to whip all the kids that come to school? If you are, why, we'll give you a school." And that's

Florence's students while teaching.

about all the qualifications they needed. I went to school-teachers that didn't know the way home in the evening.

Florence: Well, I know some of the teachers I went to didn't know there was a high school.

Haskell: No, no. Never had seen one. They only had one high school in town and they hadn't had that but seven years [when Florence started teaching in 1918]. They had had a little bit of an "academy," they called it. But it was a "subscription school." Some teacher or some girl around the neighborhood would go around and get up subscriptions among a bunch of parents and they'd have a spring school 'long in May, you know for the younger kids. You subscribe to a course and I subscribe to a course and they get enough, why, they have a school, see. You paid the tuition. I don't remember what it was. It couldn't have been very much in those days. They used to do that with the country schools. The girls that didn't work in the fields and stuff like that would go to a spring school. Boys mostly had to work. They didn't go.

Florence: But it just so happened that the school next to our school didn't have a teacher hired for that year. We was very well acquainted with the principal. So I went to see him and told him if he didn't have a teacher, I'd like very much to be their teacher. Said he'd love to have me. So, I taught my first school, in 1917, in the district that joined our home district.[4]

Haskell: They called it "Dublin"—a school there near her home. About two miles and a half. She had to walk across the fields to get to it. But that was a common practice. Nobody bothered about that, you know.

There wasn't much— There was lots of people, but not much work. As the new machines began, more modern farming methods, you didn't need all this help, see. You didn't need four people on a little farm. One was enough. We had a small farm but not enough land for Ralph and I both. I had to get out of there. He was younger, so I left to come to Akron.

There was many, many people from our area was coming to Ohio for work because there was lots of work here and the word drifted back, you know. I had a friend who came here first. Him and his girlfriend had a spat and he came up here and wrote to me and told me about the conditions so I decided that was for me. I came. By the time I'd got here, he'd gone home. He went back and married the girl and lived with her some fifty years, I guess, pretty close, before she died. But I stayed. Then, later on, they all followed me see. When I got married, her brothers followed us.

I've never been sorry the day I left there. Never.

PART TWO

AKRON, OHIO
1917

CHAPTER THIRTEEN

"SINGING SOLDIERS"

Too, it is the man who can sing at his work, light hearted and carefree, who works best.
Their labor then is not drudgery. When man sings at his work, it is a labor of love.

—"Which Shall it be Home or Hovel?"
The Goodyear Heights Realty Company

As one of our country's original boomtowns, Akron first found success during the early 1830s to the 1860s with the development of the Ohio and Erie canals—making Akron an international inland port.[1] As trains replaced the canals, the city reinvented itself and boomed again. Thanks to a local abundance of high quality coal and easy access to the Great Lakes, it soon gained national renown as a manufacturing and trade center for such products as iron, mechanical mowers and reapers, flour, stoneware, gunpowder and matches—with the small local companies that would become Diamond Match and Quaker Oats still household names today. Soon, however, Akron would realize the biggest boom in its history. This time, through an extremely unlikely commodity for the Midwest—rubber.

While B.F. Goodrich would be Akron's largest rubber company in 1917, with fifty-nine buildings taking up some sixty-three acres and employing 20,000 workers, other major players had come along, as well.[2] These included the Miller Rubber Manufacturing Company (founded in 1892, reincorporated in 1898 and later purchased by the B.F. Goodrich Company), the Diamond Rubber Company (founded in 1894 as The Sherbondy Rubber Co., renamed in 1896 and purchased by Goodrich in 1912), Goodyear Tire & Rubber Company (1898) and the Firestone Tire & Rubber Company (founded in 1900, though originally purchasing its tires and supplies from B.F. Goodrich).[3]

"Akron Works." Taken in 1907, the title on the photograph actually refers to International Harvester's Akron Works plant, which manufactured harvesters, motor truck parts, tractors and harvesters. Although the factory would have burned and been rebuilt by the time of Haskell's arrival, this iconic image of Akron taken by photography pioneer George R. Lawrence gives a gritty indication of the sprawling boomtown.[1] The James Hotel, in which Haskell Jones spent his first night in Akron, would have been located in the lower right corner.
This photograph, as well of those of dozens of other American cities, was taken by Lawrence in the early 20th century from the "Lawrence Captive Airship." Using 17 Conyne kites strung together by piano wire, he lifted a massive 49 lb. camera into the air to a height of 400 to 2,000 feet before clicking the shutter through an electrical cable (Library of Congress).[1]

To provide those factories with labor, Akron's population more than tripled between 1910 and 1920 to over 208,435—making it the fastest growing city in the entire nation.[4] Of those, over 75,000 were employed in the rubber industry, working twenty-four hours a day, six days a week, pumping out thousands of tires in addition to hundreds of thousands of other rubber items.[5] This was a number greater than the city's entire population had been just ten years before and more than had been employed in every plant in every industry in Akron's history to date.[6]

So dominant was this industry that a contemporary author wrote,

"No steel city, no cotton center, no packing city, no grain or ore or tobacco or sugar city has the proportion of predominance in a particular industry possessed by the chief rubber city of the world."[7] "There are twenty-four rubber companies in Akron," he calculated, "and if you want to start an argument there, ask which of several is growing fastest, which makes the best tire."[8] All arguments aside, the means by which they produced their products was not a pretty one.

"World's Rubber Center, Akron, Ohio." An early postcard view of Akron. As if the images didn't already depict enough of the gritty reality of Akron, they have been obviously retouched to add more smoke to the pictures—even where there aren't any smokestacks. Whether it was added to the picture as a hallmark of pride or a badge of shame could be debated.

"If there is an uglier city," *The American Mercury* magazine noted, "it must exist only in the imaginations of industrial visionaries. Akron is not a city which supports industries; it is an industry which supports a city . . . . Akron makes tires, and tires made Akron . . . . The town swelled and smelled."[9] In fact, the air was so rank that a walk to the garbage disposal works along the open sewer of the Little Cuyahoga River was considered a "breath of fresh air" compared to the sulphurous molten rubber that was carried in the wind as far as thirty miles away.[10] And in an era when cities were built on the reputation of their industrial might, it could boast that what passed for sky above the crowded city streets rivaled even Pittsburgh's claim of "darkness at noon."[11] In winter, the snow was black.[12]

In a scene that today would be viewed as something out of a post-apocalyptic world, the portions of discarded automobile tires which could not be reclaimed were "trucked to the outskirts of the city where they are burned in great piles, to the accompaniment of huge volumes of black smoke, the fierce indignation of all the downwind housewives and the dismay of town councilmen who are trapped between fear of the big industries and of their irate constituents."[13] Area boosters at the Chamber simply smiled and referred to Akron as the "City of Opportunity" or the "Wonder City of America."[14]

The Factory Floor

Inside the colossal factories, sprawled over hundreds of acres, the conditions were even more appalling than many of the "constituents" or the boosters could have ever endured. Authors Howard and Ralph Wolf would later note in their groundbreaking work *Rubber: A Story of Glory and Greed* (1936):

> It was still the era of dust and flying soapstone loading the lungs; of workers nodding drunkenly in the benzene vapors above cement tanks; of unventilated calender rooms [the machinery used to evenly coat cotton tire fabric with rubber] below the street level where men withered in the heat and the skin peeled from their bodies; of hell-hot pits where the toilers yet slipped about in the wet underfoot. Mills had no hoods to carry poisonous fumes away and the result was lassitude and loss of appetite on the job, a splitting headache to carry home every day. 'Blue men' baffled physicians who had not yet penetrated the jealously-guarded compounding secrets of the gum mills to discover that aniline was in use. Lead poisoning doubled up compounding and mill room workers with agonizing colic and fuddled them mentally.[15]

That was to say nothing of the massive equipment running at high speed in a web of whirling belts, pulleys and steam. Lacking such basic safety items as "fast acting brakes and clutches, guards and other safety devices," authors Wolf and Wolf continued, "It was no uncommon thing for a careless mountain boy to have a hand trapped by the treacherous rubber and be pulled, screaming, into the rolls up to his elbow or his shoulder, and, in a few cases, beyond."[16]

As if the lack of the basic rudiments of safety weren't bad enough, there was no union to protect them.[17] And violence among the workers raised amid different cultures, languages and beliefs was just as much a threat to the workers' lives as the equipment and working conditions.

141

This would only become all the more apparent as the companies began recruiting "hillbillies" from the South—an area with an ancestral "culture of honor" where cold-blooded murder was considered the appropriate response to a spoken insult (and not necessarily even considered a crime among one's brethren).[18] In fact, at B.F. Goodrich alone, the company counted nine homicides on the workplace floor during the period of 1918 to 1920—two more than the number they reported killed in industrial accidents during the exact same time period.[19]

In defense of those brought to justice, B.F. Goodrich executive C.P. Ufford noted that, on the whole, the individuals brought to Akron "at the solicitation of the factories" were a good group. He blamed the deplorable living conditions. "[M]any of them are living in kennels that some people would not permit their pet poodle to live in. They are without their families, a great many of them." It was the housing situation—and nothing else—that had forced many into crime."[20] H.C. Spicer, Akron's domestic relations court judge echoed this opinion when he concluded that men "are prone to go wrong when they come to Akron to work and fail to find homes here to which to bring their families. They are very apt to become entangled in affairs with young girls or else take to gambling or drinking . . . . Anything that will encourage more home building in Akron will encourage morality and the permanency of marriage."[21]

Housing

In 1916, the *Akron Beacon Journal* had editorialized that newcomers were "left alone till they either blundered into some solution for themselves, went to the street and the saloon for human companionship and comfort, or gave up the struggle and went back to their home town."[22] By 1920, the *Beacon* was lamenting, "Our housing conditions are damnable . . . . They are a menace to growth, prosperity, sanity."[23]

"Growing by leaps and bounds, building could not keep pace with the demand. Prices rose and quality diminished . . . . Attics, sheds, every semblance of shelter was turned into use. To the newcomer of moderate means, it was not a case of what they wanted, but what they could get."[24] "One family," it was noted at the time, "has preempted, for eight dollars a month, half of a henhouse, and the rightful occupants now roost in the other half, back of a board partition."[25]

Tent cities sprung up on empty lots with the resulting tens of millions of empty tin cans so abundant and colorful that they were simply referred to as "Akron wildflowers."[26]

In a city where, as one national magazine of the time headlined, there was "Standing Room Only," many were forced to sleep three to a bed—if you could find a bed.[27] And that was just one shift for that bed. In fact, "Laborers worked the factories in three shifts and slept in rooming houses the same way, often on soiled sheets . . . . The man who oversleeps is dragged from under the covers by the roomer who has the next ticket," writer Edward Mott Woolley noted.[28] Another commented that "a certain landlady was known to brag that . . . the sheets in her house were never cold."[29] As a result, it wasn't just the workers who were making money. The landlords profited handsomely, as well. As authors Wolf and Wolf were to later note, "One of the record cleanups of those years was made by a lad yanking down $6 ½ a day in each of two gum shops while at home the wife was doing $125 a week with boarders."[30] Not all were successful in finding sleeping quarters, however, as "hundreds of men have come to Akron intending to settle, but have left after a week or two spent in hopeless search for living quarters."[31]

Unlike the auto industry of Detroit, which largely let workers fend for themselves, both Firestone and Goodyear initiated their own immense residential development projects to meet their endless employment needs (and to ensure a workforce which didn't flee back to their home states or factories in other cities).[32] The result of their efforts would be respectively christened Firestone Park and Goodyear Heights, and encompassed literally hundreds of acres and thousands of homes, making Akron the country's first "company city."[33] Goodyear Heights alone encompassed some 450 acres divided into 1,937 lots, including a forty-six-acre park, athletic fields and playgrounds. It was so large, in fact, the city limits were extended to include it all.[34] "It is not charity," a publication of the Goodyear Heights Realty Company assured their proud workers. It instead was "above all, good business."[35] In doing so, the company promised a new, happier class of workers, "Singing soldiers!"[36]

"Too, it is the man who can sing at his work, light hearted and carefree, who works best. Their labor then is not drudgery. When man sings at his work, it is a labor of love," the publication continued.[37] A

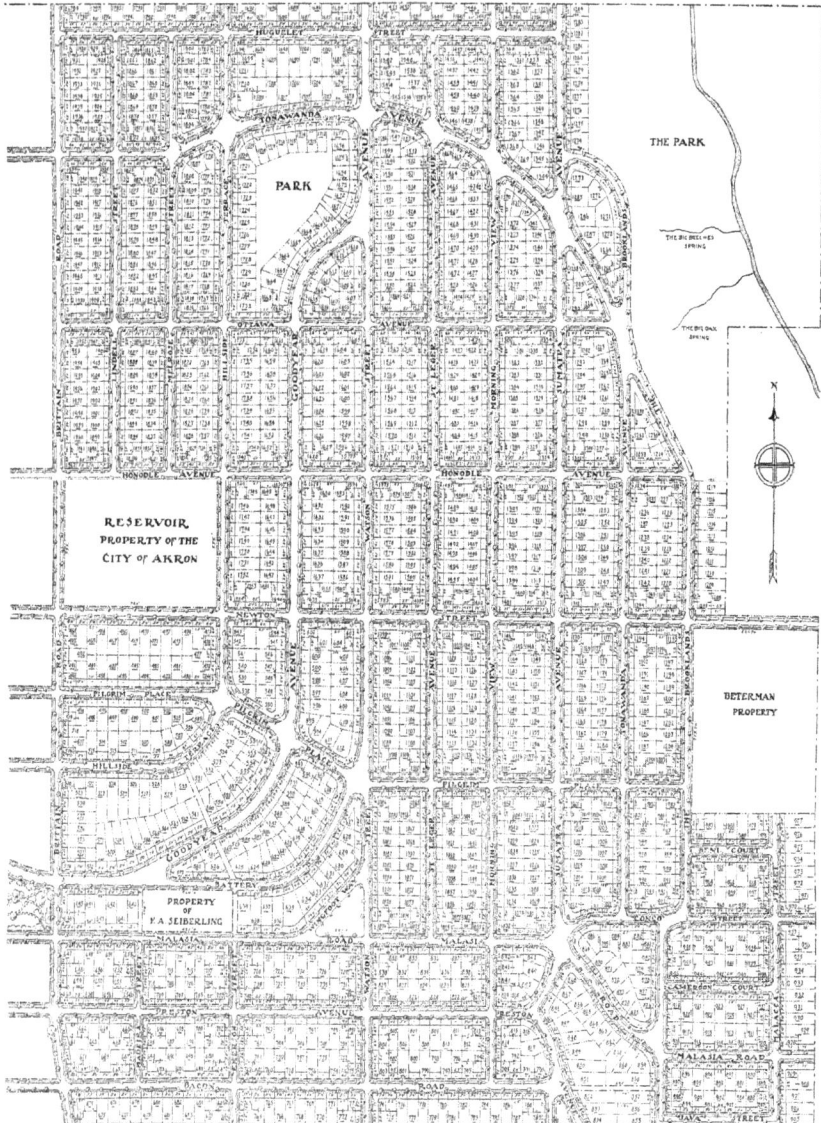

GOODYEAR HEIGHTS No 2
AKRON·OHIO
PLAN FOR DEVELOPMENT

WARREN H.MANNING LANDSCAPE DESIGNER,
BOSTON & NORTH BILLERICA,MASS· OCTOBER 1916

"Goodyear Heights No. 2" The initial phase of Goodyear Heights opened in May of 1914 and offered 400 lots. This second phase, begun in 1916, was substantially larger leading to the completion of more than 1,200 homes.

contemporary and arguably less poetic version of the same general idea stated that "the life of the hand built tire depends very materially on how the builder's wife felt at breakfast."[38] Either way, that potential of happiness was only extended to white workers.

Blacks were banned from skilled labor positions at the plants and banned from the housing developments.[39] Although the neighborhoods of well-built homes with oaken woodwork and hardwood floors would indeed prove to be a success for those allowed to participate, the gritty and dangerous daily reality of life in Akron and the gum shops in the early days of the rubber industry would prove to be a far different proposition to tens of thousands of "Singing soldiers"—no matter what their sales brochures, advertisements in backwoods newspapers or the recruitment agents working the aisles on the trains headed into Akron might say.[40]

The Workforce

Day by day, the factories' monstrous appetite for "singing soldiers" was only growing. Due to conditions on both the factory floor and in acquiring suitable housing, recruiting (and maintaining) a workforce was no easy task for the personnel managers. "Indeed, one company reported hiring 642 new employees during one week of 1916, only to have another 652 quit."[41] In 1918, the Miller Rubber Company "hired 10,742 new workers—out of which 9,433 quit within a year."[42] A third company, which employed 18,000 men, was forced to employ 88,000 men over the course of a year. What's more, two-thirds of all employees who quit never bothered to notify their supervisor or foreman that they were leaving.[43] At a projected minimum cost of $64 per employee, the rubber companies were losing $4,000,000 per year simply because of labor turnover.[44] Goodyear alone had to hire 60,000 people in 1920 just to keep 33,000 on the payroll, costing the company nearly two million dollars.[45] This, despite the fact that the tire builders were among the highest paid laborers in the country.

For each of the workers who chose to remain in Akron on the shop floor (and, as Haskell did, send money home to support his family), the money was more than good, as authors Wolf and Wolf recorded:

> By 1916 the probationary wage while learning a rubber "trade" was up to 32 ½ cents an hour, ordinary iron-muscle labor to forty cents. Farm and mountain boys only a month or two away from field or hollow knocked off $5, $6 and $7

a day as expert tread room workers, rim painters, tire strippers who hauled the new casing from their iron cores with bull strength plus quickly learned knack. At the height of things pay of $60 to $70 a week was common in the tire departments. Daily wages with no overtime went as high as $15 and $16 a shift, weekly wages as high as $100 and more. The records show payments as $28.07 to one man for a one-day double shift, $102.35 to a curing room hand who worked three double tricks that week. Hot for big money and eager for overtime were the workers and there were numerous cases of coin-crazed toilers traveling under two names and simultaneously holding man-killing jobs on different shifts in different factories.[46]

As a result, one contemporary writer noted, "Akron is inclined to be 'wide open.' Almost everybody has plenty of money and many are quite disposed to spend it."[47] The combination of an abundance of work, high wages, and some 138.9 men for every 100 women resulted in an astonishing "silk shirt period" in the soot blackened city—when even the grimiest worker would clean themselves up on the weekend and don the coveted apparel as a sign of newfound riches to impress the ladies.[48] This, when silk shirts went for more than a day's wage at fifteen dollars apiece.[49] In fact, they became so desired among rubber workers that the Miller Rubber Company chose to award silk shirts to employees who attained the highest records for efficiency.[50] One young rubber worker, Clark Gable, made the most of the situation by moonlighting in a men's clothing store, where he sold Haskell Jones his first suit of clothes. "He worked at the Goodrich and worked for a firm called Gates and Kittle on the side—a men's clothing store, Haskell later remembered. "Saturdays and evenings and time off shift-time, see. A very good-lookin' young man, when I knew him. He didn't go to California direct, I don't think, but he finally wound up out there and got in the movies and made a big name for himself."

As if the factories and its workers weren't already busy enough, they shifted into an even higher gear when the United States entered World War One in April 1917, turning out countless numbers of truck tires, gas masks, balloons and blimps. At Goodyear alone, "production of solid tires for trucks zoomed from 250 a day in 1916 to nearly 4,000 a day by war's end."[51] With the war also curtailing immigration and thousands of employees either volunteering for service or being drafted, the challenge of maintaining an adequate workforce only increased.[52] This was compounded by the fact that many factories also chose to embrace a policy of "100% Americanism." In fact, Goodyear went so far as to establish a policy of hiring only Americans whenever possible and requiring anyone who was not to take steps to become one.[53] That didn't mean that all Americans need apply, however. While women and even a substantial number of deaf-mutes workers found employment (with Akron earning yet another nickname, "Crossroads of the Deaf"), outright racism still barred entry of black workers to any skilled, higher-paying jobs. [54] This was not, as author Steve Love notes, unique to Akron. It was simply and unfortunately, "the tenor of the times."[55] As a result, the rubber shops cultivated a ready workforce in Southern white males—in the parlance of the times, "hillbillies," or, as they would become known in more polite circles, "Akron's largest ethnic group."[56]

The Goodyear Tire and Rubber Company's Office as a tchotchke.

Readily available from neighboring southern states, southern white males were preferred over even locals by the rubber companies as "they were hard workers and often individualistic in outlook, reflecting their origins as fiercely independent small-owners of farmlands."[57] Best of all, it also made them less susceptible to unionization and meant they could be easily "returned" home when production slackened. It was that very mobility, however, that meant that they were resented by the locals who saw them as having no city pride and being interested only in taking their wages and returning home, leaving their passage a blight upon the landscape. As a later study of a similar population would show, they were actually looked upon as less desirable by the local white population than either blacks or foreign immigrants—with only "criminals and gangsters" being less desirable.[58] In fact, distaste for the "hillbilly" "outsiders" was so high that it led to recurring variations on the joke: "Did you realize there are only 48 states now?" "No, how did that happen?" "All of Kentucky moved to Ohio and Ohio went to hell."[59]

Despite the prejudices of the locals, many of these same "hillbillies" chose to remain, working to change the way of life in Akron to the betterment of all. So many became a part of the community, in fact, that nearly half the residents of Akron in the 1970s were counted as either from Appalachia or had parents who originated there.[60] One of those Kentucky "hillbillies" would be Haskell Jones, who arrived in Akron on Saturday, March 17th, St. Patrick's Day, 1917, just three weeks before America's entrance into World War One.

CHAPTER FOURTEEN

ARRIVAL

Haskell: They had employment agents ridin' trains. They'd get on like at Columbus. Catch a trainload of us hillbillies with one of them dollar and a half suitcases and a straw-hat on in the wintertime. "Where ya' goin' son?" Nice-lookin', young man, you know, or middle-aged. "I'm goin' to 'Aykron'." "Have ya' got a job there?" "No, sir. I haven't got a job." "Well, I'll tell ya' what. I know of a Mister Hannah over at Firestone (he was an employment man).[1] Here's my card. You take this over to Mister Hannah and tell him I sent you." 'Course, had his name on it, you know. That's the way he got paid. Said, "You tell him I sent you. I like the looks of you. I think you'd make a good man." You thought the guy was a prince. They did it for all the companies. They rode various trains. They figured out where the labor was comin' from, you know. Pennsylvania. West Virginia. Alabama. Georgia. Kentucky. Tennessee. That was the big influx into Akron.

Haskell Jones, c. 1917.

I think I had six dollars. Not much. The railroad fare used to be sixteen dollars and forty-four cents from Mayfield to Akron. Took about twenty-four hours to get there. Let's see. A little more than that. We used to leave Mayfield after 6:00 in the evening. Six-fifty-four, I think. And we got into Akron about 10:00 at night the next day. We'd go to Louisville, layover awhile, and come on to Cincinnati and layover

149

awhile. Trains didn't go too fast in those days.

First night I was in Akron, I slept with two other guys. Strangers. I didn't know either one of 'em. There wasn't any rooms. There was just not any you could get ahold of unless you was acquainted and knew how to look and where to look. On the train I got acquainted with two guys. We get off the train and we had already heard the news, "You can't get a room in Akron." We've been ridin' for twenty-four hours. It was 10:00 at night. So I suggested we get a cab and get the cabdriver to get us a room because a cabdriver usually knew where these things were. That's part of their business. He said, "I believe I can find you a bed." He apologized. "It ain't somethin' fancy, but it's clean and you can get to sleep." So we went and the guy said he only had one bed. I said, "That's good enough." The room wasn't as big as a shoebox. Two of us had to stand out in the hall while the other guy undressed and got into bed it was so small. The James Hotel on James Street. If you don't know where it is, don't feel bad about it 'cause it ain't there anymore. Little, lousy hotel. They called it a "hotel." It was nothin'. Flophouse. The three of us slept in that bed. Three total strangers. We didn't know one another from Adam.

But we stayed there that night and the one guy, Hawkins, knew where he was goin'. He had an address. He was a little older than me and the other guy. So, he took off the next morning. He got a cab and went where he was supposed to go. He knew where he was goin'. He had people or somethin'. But this Georgia "cracker," he had a friend that lived on High Street. So, he had the number. So, we go up and down High Street and there ain't no such number on South High or North High. There's no such number. And he keeps sayin', "I know—" And "I've got written down—" And he looked at it. I didn't look at it. Sixty-four hundred or fifteen-thirty-one or sixty-two High Street. And I noticed something after we'd walked for hours. This is Sunday. I got suspicious he wasn't sayin' "High Street." So I said, "Let me see that address." He give it to me and it's H-O-W-E. That's a Georgia "Howe" Street. So, we asked around and we finally found out where it was. It was out back of the Goodrich off— It used to be the Bowery street car line. So, we got off the streetcar and went out there and he found his people.

That left me by myself. I come back downtown and I wandered around. And I didn't have much money. So, I got down there by the Goodrich and there was a hotel across the street from the Goodrich on Main Street called the Richmond Hotel.[2] And ten, eleven o'clock at night I went there and tried to get a place to sleep. The guy said, "Nah, son. They're ain't a place to sleep in the United States. There ain't no place in Akron you can get a room tonight." So, I asked him if I could set in the lobby (had a few chairs in the little lobby) and sleep in the lobby. Said, "Yeah, you can set there. It's perfectly all right." Said, "Every once in a while, somebody has to do it 'cause we just don't have rooms in this town for the people that's here." So, there was a little restaurant two or three doors away and I went down there once in a while to get a cup of coffee or somethin' to eat. I made the night in that hotel and the next day I found somebody I knew up on Miller Avenue. Hollie Jones. He was down there at one-seventy-one. That's where he was stayin'. So I found him and he took me down to the Miller where I got a job. He was workin' at the Miller. Then I was all set.

CHAPTER FIFTEEN

THE MILLER RUBBER COMPANY

The danger of contracting *communicable diseases* was considered bad in 2 places, fairly so in 7 others and practically nil in the 3 remaining. The hazards here were the use of common drinking cups, improper washing places and toilets, spitting on the dusty floors, the absence of cuspidors, the lack of physical examinations and of first-aid provisions.

—"Rubber—Calendering"
A Survey of Industrial Health Hazards
and Occupational Diseases in Ohio, 1915

Haskell: All you had to do was hit town in those days and they grabbed you. Rubber factories was going full blast and they was hiring every one of us hillbillies that come into town. Thousands. When I first came here, they couldn't get enough people. That was durin'—just before World War One, you know. World War One was fomentin' over in there. We hadn't gotten in it, but we were gonna' get in it next week.

Jobs were no object then. You had to fight people to keep 'em from hirin' you. That was a ruination of a lot of us guys. We didn't realize the importance of keepin' a job because you could get another one in a minute, you know. It was no problem.

I came here on a Saturday.[1] Monday, I went to the old Miller Rubber and got a job. We didn't make much money. Wages were pretty low. I think I was makin' fifty-six cents an hour. It was better than fifty cents a day, I'll tell you that. That's what I got around home. Went to work at 2:30 in the afternoon in the calender room. Dirtier than hell.

Awful dirty. Awful dirty. Lampblack and soapstone.[23] Sometimes the air would be so dirty you couldn't see the lights over ya'. Where I worked it was particular noisy. I worked about two weeks and had the measles and almost died.

When I went back to work, why, I'd worked about another two or three weeks and a man got killed. It was only about twenty feet from me. He got pulled into the machine. Got his arm pulled in there and pulled his arm off. Some guy run a steel bar in between the rolls and cracked the machinery to get him out of there.[4] But the poor guy died. That's the first job I had. Don't want to see it again.

"Miller Tires. Geared-to-the-Road. Produce Mileage" (c. 1917).

It was on a Saturday evening. On Monday they assigned that job to me. You know what that song says about "You can take this job and shove it." That's what I told them 'cause I wasn't gonna' do that job. I said I wasn't gonna' work there. So, the foreman said, "You're gonna' tell us what you're gonna' do around here, are ya' son?" I said, "Nah, I'm gonna' tell ya' what I'm not gonna' do. And I'm not gonna' work on there." And he says, "All right. Clean out your locker. You'll get paid at 3:00." So, they literally fired me.

So I went over to Firestone and got another job and got examined and was back in an hour and a half later to get my pay. Firestone and Miller was only a block apart. That's how it worked in those days. You just walk out of one job and said I want another one and the man gave it to ya'. Not maybe at the same place. I probably could've got one down at the employment office if I'd asked for one right there.

"A Modern Tire Factory." This photo, as well as others in the series which follow, are from *Rubber. Its History And Development*, published by the Firestone Tire & Rubber Company in 1922. While they cannot capture the actual conditions on the factory floor, they give an idea of the labor that went into building early tires (All public domain/ author's collection).

"Calendering Tire Fabric." After tightly woven, cotton cord fabric was manufactured in New England, it was then transported into the calender room of the factory. Here, the fabric was saturated in rubber and coated in pure gum as it repeatedly passed through a series of rollers. The resulting plies of gum-coated fabric were then rolled up into stock which varied in width from 60 to 84 inches and 150 to 300 yards in length.

"Vulcanizing The Tire Beads." The tire beads, which hold the sides of a straight side tire to the rim, were created by first braiding fine piano wire into narrow flat lengths, resembling a wire tape. These lengths were then impregnated with compounded gum, covered them in fabric and then vulcanized to a semi hard state, cut to length, formed into rings and dried. Finally, they were placed into molds and vulcanized again.

"Building The Tire." Once the fabric and beads are prepared, the process of actually building the tire begins. Here, seen in the far left, the fabric is tightly stretched over a core that is made to the exact size of the inside of the tire. In the center, small wheels on each side of the tire, called stitchers, work the fabric to ensure no bubbles or creases are formed. This process is repeated as each new layer of fabric is applied. After the second layer of fabric is applied, the bead is pressed into each side of the core, as shown to the right. Remaining layers of fabric are then applied and folded around the bead, securing them into position.

"The Side Wall." After the core of the tire is built up, the sidewalls, made entirely of gum compound are applied. The tire worker uses a metal squeegee or hand roller to avoid bubbles or wrinkles.

"Applying The Tread." With the carcass complete, the tire is passed onto the finisher who mounts it on a stand. After first applying a cushion and breaker strips, he carefully applies the tread, spinning the wheel with his knee, again avoided creases or air bubbles. Even at this stage, however, the tread is still smooth rubber. The actual tread design is created during the vulcanization process that follows, as the pressure of the mold forces the rubber into the design engraved in the inside of the mold.

"Vulcanizing The Tread." After the smooth tread has been applied, the tire is ready for its final step of vulcanization, which hardens the rubber from a soft, plastic condition to hard rubber, cured to the form of the mold.

Depending upon the type of tire, a pressurized air bag may be placed inside of the tire, forcing it against the inside of the mold and stretching the fabric evenly to the finished size. The uncured or "green" tires are placed inside iron molds that are then placed on top of each other in vertical, cylindrical steam heaters approximately 15 feet deep and 54 inches in diameter. After 20 to 30 of these molds are placed inside, the lid of the heater is placed into position under hydraulic pressure. Live steam of 286° Fahrenheit is then turned on until the tires are cured. Following this final step in their actual manufacture, the tires are inspected, wrapped and shipped.

CHAPTER SIXTEEN

FIRESTONE TIRE & RUBBER

Dust in the atmosphere was observed in all places. In 10 it was present to only a fair degree, while in 11 places it was bad. The dust consisted of the dry ingredients (Al, Fe, Ca, Zn, Pb, Sb, Soapstone, etc.), which go into rubber—lead ranging, according to one analysis of the finished product, as high as 25%.

—"Rubber—Mixing Mills"
A Survey of Industrial Health Hazards
and Occupational Diseases in Ohio, 1915

Haskell: I went to Firestone next. That was in the latter part of '17. They put me on supervision because I'm able to converse with everybody in there by signs. Firestone was worse than anywhere else. Boy, it was so dusty in there you couldn't see twenty feet sometimes. A dust storm. It was awful bad in the stock and mill room.

It wasn't much of a job as far as the skill of doin' the job was concerned. They milled this stock in the mill room and brought it down on trucks in sheets about twenty-four by thirty and they stored it either in the bulk on the floor or in a bin. We handled stock by number. Man, they had hundreds of kinds of stock. Heavy. Light. Tacky.

We stored it and kept it a day or two in steel bins about thirty inches deep. Maybe thirty inches wide. Three in a row on steel bins. Side-by-side. All bolted together. They had an aging date. The bin was supposed to keep this particular stock twenty-four hours. One forty-eight hours. One seventy-two hours or whatever it might be, you know. They had to age that and then they went from there to either a calender room where it went into tire stock or a tube machine that extruded treads or sidewalls or some other solid tires.[1]

Sometimes the stock wasn't soaped good enough with the soapstone. So it would stick together like glue. We had to cut it apart. We had handsaws with the teeth ground off of 'em. You'd take a bottle of water, pour the water in. That kept your saw from stickin' in that rubber, you know. And you could cut it pretty fast with 'em. They kept 'em sharp with an emery wheel all the time. Just a big knife blade only it had a handle like a saw.

We had a hook. Something like what a farmer uses when they're pullin' hay up in a loft with a pulley. It's a double hook made out of metal about as big as my finger and sharp on the point with a big eye in it. You'd take a chain block, hook it on something, hack it in there and chain that out of there, you know.

They used to make a lot of solid truck tires. They were not pneumatic at all. They were one solid hunk of rubber and they rode rather rough. But it lasted well. It wasn't as noisy as a steel tire would've been on a truck, you know, and had more traction. So the stock went out to the calender rooms or whatever and we had to see that the stock was the right stock when the truck came down from the calender room to be loaded. It had a requisition with it that they wanted 403 or 221 or whatever the stock might be. And that happened to be two of the stock numbers, too. Four-oh-three was a solid tire tread stock. Two-twenty-one was a fabric impregnator.

They run it in the calender room and pressed it into this stock while it was hot. This stock was not cord stock like they got today in a tire. It was one solid fabric like a rug or burlap bag. It was one weave, you know, weaved both ways. It didn't last too well. Had no expansion.

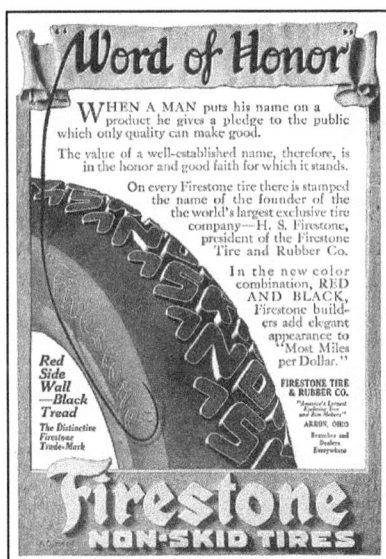

"Word of Honor." The Firestone Red Side Wall Cord Tires were seen everywhere along the roadways of the country shortly after they were introduced—both on and off the wheels of the cars (c. 1917).

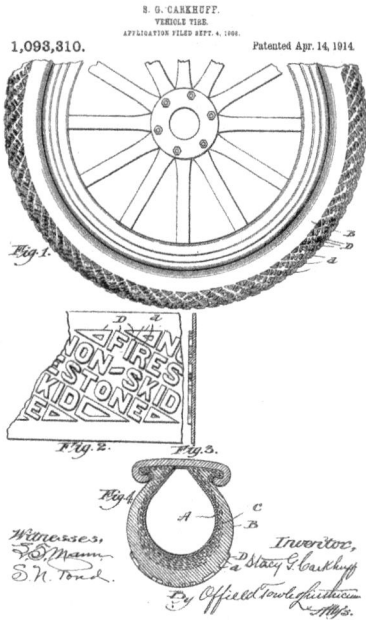

S. G. CARKHUFF.
VEHICLE TIRE.
APPLICATION FILED SEPT. 4, 1908.

1,093,310.

Patented Apr. 14, 1914.

Patent 1,093,310, Apr. 14, 1914,
Application Filed Sept. 4, 1908, Vehicle
Tire. Stacy Carkhuff, of Akron, Ohio.
While functional as an early tread design
among the dozens of different ones
offered, the Firestone "Non-Skid" was
also a brilliant advertising ploy.
Capitalizing on the commonly used term
"non-skid" by incorporating it into the
company's tread design and patenting it,
the product's name would clearly
imprinted along every dirt road on which
the car travelled—while also precluding
other tire manufacturers from using the
term without also identifying a prime
competitor.

They couldn't give. And, you hit a sharp spot in the street— Boom! You had to go buy another tire.

Tires weren't worth much, I'll tell ya'. Firestone built a tire with a red sidewall. Two twenty one. Two-twenty-one was the stock number. It was red, real red. But it wouldn't stay on the tires. The whole countryside where there was any automobiles was a scrap of this red sidewall. They'd just come off. They wouldn't stick to the tire.

The tire was cured with no tread or sidewall on it in those days and it was perfectly smooth. Then, they brought it out and buffed it. And they cured a tread on a drum instead of puttin' it on green. The drum had the indentation on it that made the name of the tread, whatever it might be. Firestone Non-Skid or they built one they called a— Can't think of the name of it now. Firestone built one with an arrow on it. Can't think of what the name of it was. But it was white tread. Miller built one. "Rellim"—that was Miller backwards.

Then they'd buff this tread— They'd put it on a mandrel, see. Two wheels here and a power— One of 'em was powered and it was upside down. You had a wire brush that you pulled down with a lever. It brushed that tread as it went round and round—roughed it up. Then they took it over into the finishin' room and they cemented the tread. They buffed this tire with a file down to a sidewall line. They had a little line cured in the mold. And, you buffed it right down to that line.

Then, the sidewall went from there up to the tread. That sidewall wasn't very thick. But the tread was thicker. "Finishers," they called 'em. "Tire finishers." After it was cured, they cemented that and put it together. They took mud made out of soapstone and they filled these indentations in this tread. They were already cured, see, but they filled 'em. Then, you put it on a machine that wrapped it with a rag about two inches wide. It was heavy fabric. And they put it on a truck and rolled it in a horizontal heater and cured it again. That cured that gum where it was cemented. Cured the cement. It was supposed to hold it together, but it didn't hold those red sidewalls.

I sent out the last load, I know. When the truck come in, the foreman said, "Don't send anymore. This is the last load. That's the last load." They're gonna' quit usin' this stuff, see. We still had some of it and they scrapped it. I don't know what they did with it. It wasn't very much, but some. So, I sent the last load out of that red sidewall.

You could see it layin' up and down the streets where it'd fly off the tire. Just a strip about two inches wide. I've seen great big hoops of it. Junk. It was junk. The tires were junk. But, they did the best they could with 'em. They didn't know much about compoundin'. They didn't have the technical skill. So, they did the best they could. It was way ahead of a solid tire. Never could've did the automobile business with a solid tire. It just wouldn't've been possible to ride in one at high speed, you know, with that solid tire.

* * *

Haskell: I was a little on the muscle. I was— I *thought* I was a pretty fair fighter. Big, foreign man. I don't know whether I started the fight or what happened. But we got into a jangle of some kind. And he grabbed me by the throat and pushed me back against a post. That post had bolts in there to bolt timbers against. And he was making a pincushion out of me against those bolts. I hit him and it didn't do much good. He was a much bigger man that I was. And I pounded him in the mouth for a while and *that* didn't do any good. So I stuck my thumb in his eyes and I lifted his eyeball out of his socket. Didn't take it out, but it just hung loose on the outside. He turned me loose then. They had to take him to the hospital and put his eye back in. He went over there holding his eye in his hand.

My foreman, who was a prince of a man was an old ex-pug. Name was G.W. Schneider. A big Dutchman from Cincinnati. When they took this guy out of there, he said, "Jonesie, about the next hunky comes around here with a fat lip— You hit him, I'm gonna' beat the hell out of you."

He had gotten fat. He was a bigger man than I was by about twice, but he had developed a pretty good tummy and didn't look in too good a shape. And I said, "I don't know of a better time to start than right now." And that was the wrong thing to say. He immediately backhanded me in the mouth and stuck that big stomach out for me to hit. And I hit at it and all I hit was his elbow. He gave me a good lesson in what not to do. He didn't mean— He didn't hurt me, but he slapped me around to teach me a lesson and let me know there was a lot of people I couldn't lick. A lot of 'em.

Yeah, he was a prince of a guy. He liked me and I liked him. I saw him a few times after I'd left over there. He was a real, real good man. He got in somebody's hair at the Firestone and they laid him off— fired him as a foreman. They got the department in such a mess that they didn't know heads or tails, so they enticed him to come back. He went back and straightened them up and they laid him off again. He went from there to the old Akron Lamp. And I used to run into him once in a while. We thought a lot of each other. He was a good man.

He used to laugh at me. We used trucks, big heavy trucks—put a ton of rubber on one. I was idle for the minute and one was setting in the aisle. It wasn't really my job, but I was idle for the minute and I said, "Do you want me to carry this over on the other side?" He said, "Yeah, if you can." I said, "Don't you think I can?" I was a smart, young kid, you know—nineteen years old—and I thought I could.

So, I immediately took hold of the truck, pushed it over on the other side, come back smilin' and he said, "You didn't carry it!" Said, "You pushed it!" Says, "When you carry anything, you put it in your arms and carry it on your shoulder!" And I— That— He— He'd laugh at me every once in a while about carrying stuff around there. But I— I didn't know the difference.

Had foremen in there named [Oliver] Hites and Schneider. Hites wasn't a bad guy. And the day shift foreman, the department foreman, the headman was McCarter. John McCarter. Big Scotchman. Didn't care for him much. E.N. Sherman. After he got out of Firestone, he worked for Carlton Clothes for years and years 'til he died. He was a store manager for Carlton Clothes. Had that Falls store at one time.

CHAPTER SEVENTEEN

GOODYEAR TIRE & RUBBER

Buffing at a machine which has no air exhaust to carry off the dust is both dirty and dangerous. The usual method of buffing tires is to place the tire on a revolving wheel and hold a file against it as it turns, but in one New Jersey factory the workman slipped a tire around his body and over one shoulder and held it against a revolving file. He and four others were working in front of a window and around them were fully three bushels of rubber dust, which represented the accumulation of four days.
— Industrial Poisons Used in the Rubber Industry, 1915

Opportunities for inhaling rubber *dust* were bad in 4 places and fair in the 2 remaining. But 1 place supplied respirators and these were unwillingly used. Many of the workers were as black as coal heavers, due to the dust.
—"Rubber—Buffing"
A Survey of Industrial Health Hazards
and Occupational Diseases in Ohio, 1915

Haskell: I was there in '17—not very long. I've forgotten. I quit. They had a lot of supervision in those shops that didn't have much training. Some of 'em didn't have much judgment. I don't know how they were selected for supervisors—unless they were "brown-noses." But I worked for supervisors that you wondered how they could find their way home.

When I worked at Goodyear the first time, I buffed tires— That was this job buffin' these old two-cure tires. They had a supervisor whose name was— Ahhh, it skips me. But he'd steal from ya'. We used to buff these tires and stack 'em behind your machine back there in the alley-like area. And you had a card that hung on your machine with

163

various sizes. Great long card, like that, had six hundred, five hundred, four hundred, three hundred, whatever their size was, you know. And they paid different prices. Then he counted 'em (the tires you'd buffed) and then threw 'em on a truck. That was his job. Somebody else hauled 'em away. If you didn't watch him and you had ten tires of four hundred size, we'll say (whatever the size was), he'd give you nine or he'd give you eight. You got to watch him like a hawk and check your card every time he punched it. He had a punch like a milkman or a paperboy—punched the numbers out on your card. So, he stole from me a couple of times and I caught him and I cussed him out about it. He didn't like me too well because I did.

So they had a rule— No eatin' durin' workin' hours—which was all right. So, I go to the lunchroom at noon or quittin' or lunchtime (whatever it was) and I eat my lunch. And they had some peanuts in a little package—a nickel bag of peanuts. So I buy a bag of peanuts and I come back. And we're standin' out in the hall out here waitin' for— They rang a bell for time to go to work. So, I'm eatin' on these peanuts and finally the bell rings and I threw the rest of 'em in my mouth, start walkin' in the department to my machine and he jumped all over me for eatin' durin' workin' hours, see.

So finally one day we had a— We didn't have much safety in the shops in those days. Instead of individual motors on the machines, you had a drive shaft runnin' all the way through the shop with a great big motor on it. And that run that shaft there. They had

"Goodyear" (c. 1918).

a bunch of pulleys on that shaft where every machine had a belt run down to your machine. So we had strict orders that— (Every once in a while, you'd put too much pressure on one of these tires and you'd flip that belt off of that pulley. It'd jump off.) Don't get on that machine to put that belt back on 'til that shaft quits runnin'! It was a safety feature. It was all right. Nothin' wrong with it. But I shut down the whole line if I did that, you know. That had twenty men on that one shaft. And every time one guy flipped it and had to stop the line, everybody cussed him out, see, 'cause he's takin' money out of their pocket. I'd do it myself.

I had flipped the belt off. Well, the control was over here about six feet from me on a post. Big switch. I went over and pulled the switch and this thing— Of course it's got a lot of momentum and got all these pulleys. It's still slowin' down, but it still was haaaaalf-way turnin', like this, you know. So I stepped up on my machine— You had a position there you could get on and get up there to grab that belt and put it back on so everybody could go back to work. And he come up and cussed me out for gettin' on that machine.

So I used this big rasp to buff these tires with— I took that rasp and hit him on top of the head with it and knocked him out. And he laid there for a minute and got up with a lump on his head like an egg and headed for the office. Had a good man— I can't think of his name. Mac-something. Scotchman. Was a foreman. So he come up to my machine. He says, "Well, Jones, what in the world happened here?" I said, "Well, this guy cussed me out and I hit him with a rasp." He said, "You might have killed him! I said, "Well, I didn't much care if I did!" He said, "I ought to fire you!" "That'd be all right with me. There ain't nothin' I could do about that. But people don't talk to me like that. Where I come from, people don't talk to you like that. If they do, they expect to get hurt." "Well," he said, "You're a rash young man. You gonna' get yourself in a lot of trouble." I said, "Well, I could be." So he said, "Don't you do anything like that again or I'll have to let you go." I said, "all right."

So they had a left-handed machine in this shop. They had this row of machines that went clear across this wall. All of the rest of 'em were right-hand machines. Up at the end, they can't put a man between the machine and the wall, so it's a left-hand machine. You have to work on the left-hand side of it, see. So this supervisor come down and he said, "How about you workin' on that left-handed machine?" I said, "Well, I'll go up there and I'll work on it if you leave me on it." Because I worked pretty good left-handed, see. That didn't bother me. I said, "Don't take me off of it. Leave me on that machine. I gotta' break in on the thing 'cause it's gonna' be awkward for a day or two." "I won't take you off of it. Oh, no. You break in on that machine, you can stay on that machine."

I'm on there about two weeks, come in one night, start to go to work, and he said, "I'm gonna' have to move you off the machine." I

ON A BURNING DECK

says, "What's the matter?" "Well, this guy—" Name was Bennett. Bennett moved back from the other shift. He had more service than I had. So he'd been workin' on this left-handed machine on the other shift and he changed shifts. So he got more service. So he bumps me off the machine, see. Well, I said, "You know what you can do with this machine." And I explained it to him in a few adjectives, you know, stuff like that. And I said, "Give me a pass out of here!" "You can't get out of here." "What do you mean I 'can't get out of here'?" I ain't gonna' give you a pass." I said, "You want to get hit on the head with another rasp, don't you." And he said, "You got to check your tools in at the tool shop." I said, "Well, there's my tools layin' right there. You can have 'em. And I'm goin' out of here." Said, "You can't get out without a pass." I said, "The hell I can't!" "Well," he said, "you got to check your shoes and check your tools in." I said, "You check 'em in. And if you don't check 'em in, I'll come and get you later!" I said, "If they take 'em out of my pay, I'll take 'em out of your hide!" I said, "You bastard, you told me I could stay on that machine and so what happened?" I said, "There they are. They're your tools. They ain't mine!" So I walked out. Went out to the police department and guy said, "Where ya' goin'?" I said, "I'm goin' home." He said, "How come?" I said, "I quit!" He didn't say anymore. I went on home. I didn't stay at Goodyear very long. Then I went back to Firestone.

CHAPTER EIGHTEEN

FIRESTONE TIRE & RUBBER II

Skull is Crushed by Negro
Trivial Argument at Miller Plant Likely to Be Fatal

Boldizres Riffner, 32, 979 Ido av., an elevator operator at the Miller Tire and Rubber Co., is dying in the City hospital as a result of being hit over the head shortly after 1 o'clock with a heavy wrench by a negro held by the police who gave his name as Moses Wotts, 21, 66 e. Thornton st.

Witnesses told the police that the two men had had an argument about going to the third floor of the factory, and after having been on that floor Wotts returned to the elevator and the argument was again taken up.

Wotts, it is charged, then picked up a heavy wrench lying on the elevator floor and struck Riffner one blow over the head, which crushed his skull.

After having struck Riffner witnesses said, the negro made no effort to escape but waited calmly for the police to come to arrest him.

— Akron Beacon Journal
June 26, 1919

Haskell: I went to Firestone next. That was in the latter part of '17. I was workin' in the Firestone as a supervisor in charge of a bunch of men—loadin' and unloadin' stock because I could understand English and knew what was goin' on and some of these guys are raw immigrants, you know.

We had a passageway under a mill base that was cut in there through a big concrete wall. And it was like a tunnel, almost. It was probably fifteen feet through there and just wide enough to get a truck through. We used a truck to load stock with. And this man named Bartholomew,[1] a small man, was coming through with a load of stock. And he met a big— I think he was from Montenegro. Mammoth big

167

man. Not fat, but <u>big</u>. And it was customary when you met a man— Both of you wanted to go under there— Why, the man with the load went on through and the guy with the empty truck always backed out and got out of the way. But the big (We called 'em "hunkies")— He just pushed his way right through and pushed Bartholomew back against the wall and he had to back out of the way and let this guy through.

When he comes back, he had to stoop a little to get under this base. It was just barely good enough for a six-foot man and he was about six foot six. He come in there pushing that truck with that big load and Bartholomew was waiting for him with a piece of gas pipe. And when he stuck his head through there, [Bartholomew] could readily come down on his head. Had he hit him dead center he might have killed him. But he hit him over the ear on the side and he scalped him. A piece of skin as big as your hand was hanging down over his ear and he took that whole side up. They had to take him to the hospital and do a repair job on his head. So, they gave Bartholomew three days off. That was World War One. They didn't fire anybody in those days. They just give you a day or two off and hoped you'd hurry back.[2]

By chance I was ordered to run the elevator on Christmas Eve, 1917. It was a freight elevator—not a passenger elevator. I don't know why the supervisor picked me, but he did. The common practice was we got paid at 10:00 or 10:30 and went out at 11:30 to get lunch. So, another practice was to go to the saloon instead of the restaurant. Get a big cheese sandwich and a glass of beer. And, now and then, they'd buy a bottle. You'd buy one or I'd buy one and sometimes we all bought one. Then we'd have too many bottles. This night I bought one and I couldn't get anyone to help me drink it. So I drank the most of it myself. A quart of "Old Overholt"—a rye whiskey. I wasn't used to drinkin'. I didn't drink much. I very seldom drank a whiskey. I drank a beer occasionally, but I wasn't a drinker. But, I was a kid. I was nineteen. The upshot was I got completely blottoed.

So, the supervisor finally found it out and he come and took me off of the elevator and put somebody else to run it. Told me to go somewhere and lay down. And I crawled into a greasy hole that was filled with grease and lampblack. When I come out of there the next morning, frozen and dirty as a man could be. No other clothes to put on. And I had to walk about ten blocks, maybe, on early (Six o'clock we got off, in the morning) Christmas morning down that cold street with that grease and lampblack all over me. I was the filthiest man to ever walk down the street of Akron. And it was quite an experience, I'll tell ya'. Taught me that wasn't a good place to sleep.

I worked at Firestone, I think, seven different times. I walked out. I got fired. I quit. Worked out a notice. Half a dozen different ways I left out of there. We had an argument with a supervisor. Foremen went on strike— Went sick or vacation. Shift foremen. They put some hunky in there as an employment supervisor. I was a supervisor myself. Put him as foreman. So they changed our pay. I was workin' day work as a supervisor. As a supervisor, I was makin' a hundred and ten dollars a month—as a supervisor. This is World War One days, you see, and they didn't pay much money. So they put the guys that was workin' for me on piecework and they're makin' ten, twelve dollars a day. So I said, "Well, I ain't gonna' work out here. I gotta' run a gang. I had a hundred men! Some of the time. "I ain't gonna' work here for a hundred and ten dollars a month workin' over guys makin' ten, twelve dollars a day! I want to go back on workin', see." So this smart-ass bastard wouldn't let me do that, see. "Can't do it!" I said, "Well, I can quit!" So me and another supervisor walked out.

Well, he went out to the Labor Department and made up the report. He maybe didn't go out there, but he sent in a report that said we went on strike. We didn't strike. We didn't stay there. We didn't do nothin' only walk out. That's all we did, see. So I went back out the next day to— Not Hannah, but a man by the name of Spitznas who was another employment man.[3] Second in line. Prince of a guy. Nice little dark-haired little— He was a Serb or something of that kind. Nice little man. So I went out and I told Spitznas what the story was. I said, "This guy told me he'd see I never got another job at Firestone as long as he was in there." But Spitznas said, "Well, I hired him and he don't have any say-so as to who we hire in Akron." Said, "Well, I'll send you up in the tread department." So I went up in the tread buffin' treads and I get fired out there.

This was the thing. We cured the treads on a drum. Two cures. They built the tire and they just smoothed gum strip over the breaker. That's all was on there. Cured in a smooth mold on an iron core. Then they buffed that. They took it off the core and they buffed the tire. And the guys that built these treads on these drums, they put it on there and stitched it on, see. They'd push about three truckloads in one of these heaters. Cure 'em right on the drum. And they stripped 'em off the drum and you'd put it on a buffin' machine and you buffed that tread real good. Then they took it into the tread room and they cemented that. After so many minutes or hours or whatever (I don't remember how long), you put this tire on a spindle (It was a "spider", they called it) and they buffed that. You had a line on the side in the mold (cured in the mold) and you buffed down to that line. That was your sidewall. Then they put this tread on there and they stitched it down all the way around. Then they rewrapped it and they run it in these heaters and they cured it again, see. So they had a helluva lot of work. They cost more money than they do now.

They had two kinds of tread at Firestone. At that time, they had a second rate and the second class was a— I can't think of the name of it. But it had an arrowhead design on the tread. It was a white tread. Not a black tread. It was white. So a guy by the name of Watson was workin' with me— Can remember him as long as I live—'cause he got me fired. He brings this tread over to me and he says, "Hey, look! This guy's gonna' get fired." He'd put a white tread on a black drum or black tread on a white drum—whichever it was. I don't remember. But it was junk because that kind of tire— It's junk, see. He said, "Why don't we buff the number off of it?" It had little old aluminum tags on, you know, they put on. Various numbers. Each guy had his own number. When they wrapped this stock on this drum, he'd put his tag in there and it was cured right in the stock. Tell who built it, see. So I said O.K. And I just pick it up and held it against the buffin' wheel and buffed that number off and throw it in the stack [to stop someone from bein' fired].

So after a while, a guy by the name of Buckmaster come and said, "Who did this?"[4] "I don't know." Nobody knows. So they put the heat on. They take Watson up in the office. He goes up there and tells old man Frase who was our foreman (was my next door neighbor) that I did it. Old man Frase called me in the office and, "Jonesie, what do you know about this tread?" I said, "You probably already know the story." He said, "I do." He said, "Well, you know I'm on the spot." And said, "I think a whole lot more of you than I did of him." Said, "He's a rat and I don't like rats. But I'm on the spot. There ain't nothin' I can do but let you go." And says, "I'll recommend another job." So I said, "O.K." I went out the next day and Spitznas gave me another job, but he had to fire me because it was the right thing to do. He hired me back the next day.

CHAPTER NINETEEN

ROOMMATES

. . . . it is necessary to mention industrial stimulantism which is usually alcoholism, coffeeism, or drugism. Stimulantism is promoted by subjection to one or more of the above health-hazards; or, because of the absence of good drinking water; or, because of a tradition among workers in certain lines that alcoholic liquors tend to stimulate them and to protect them from the effects of poisons, dusts, gases, or hard work to which they may be submitted; or to the fact that the employers promote alcoholism among their workmen by permitting the drinking of intoxicating liquors while at work; and, finally, to the fact that there is an absence of a welfare attitude, or an industrial efficiency department in connect with an establishment. Coffeeism, in females, may represent alcoholism in males.[1]

—"The General Principles of Industrial Hygiene"
A Survey of Industrial Health Hazards
And Occupational Diseases in Ohio, 1915

36 West Miller Avenue

Haskell: First place I roomed was thirty-six West Miller Avenue—which is right off of Main Street. South Main. A lot of guys from my home roomed there. I roomed with two other guys. We had a room with a cot and a bed. Paid a dollar and seventy-five cents a week a room. But had an attic and they had about ten or twelve, fifteen guys up in the attic. All the drunks were up in the attic. Our little room had three. That end of the house had two. This one over here had four—a big room. Two beds. Two beds. That one over there had two, I think. They was small rooms. Downstairs, they turned the dining room into a bedroom and they had two in it, see. Old lady Jackson.[2] Good woman. Great big, fat, happy West Virginia hillbilly. Mrs. Jackson.

I originally roomed with a fellow named Dick Landrom. Then a cousin of Florence's who was named Laban Jones—him and I roomed together a short time (not too long) and he left. A guy by the name of Handsel Ballew (from down in Florence's neighborhood, out in the country—a hillbilly from out in her country), he came in and I roomed with him. He was a nice guy. Handsel was clean as a pin. But he'd get drunk and he'd steal. Come home one night with two pair of shoes. He bought one and stole one exactly the same like it and in the

36 West Miller Avenue, Akron (July 1988).

same size. And I have yet never been able to figure out how he could get that salesman to show him two pair of shoes, exactly alike, same size. He was disturbed about it. He used to steal every glass he drank out of all evening. He'd come home with his overcoat pockets full of glasses, you know. Up to a beer glass like this, you know. He didn't like that. He hated it, but he'd do it when he was drinkin'. But he didn't stay too long. Then Tom Payne come in. Then I got the measles. Maybe it was before Ballew. I think it was.

They used to quarantine for measles. If you got measles in this house, they put a big red sign on the door. "Do not enter." Contagious disease," see. I had the measles and Tom comes home and they got a quarantine on the door. He was a dumb bastard and the other guys knew he was gullible. Tom said, "What goes on? I see that quarantine on the door." And they said, "Well, Jonesie got small pox." And he was scared to death. They give him a long line. He couldn't go anywhere. He had to stay there 'til I got well. Yah, yah, yah, they told him. Maybe they're gonna' take him to the pest house and all this, you know. These guys were pretty good with this b.s.

So about 2:00 in the morning, he goes downstairs and pounds on old lady Jackson's door and said, "Mrs. Jackson?" "Yeah. Yeah. What do you need?" "Has Haskell got the small pox?" She said, "No, you damn fool! Go back to bed! He's got measles. What in the hell's the matter with you wakin' me at two, three o'clock in the mornin'?" She cussed him out. She could do it. Poor Tom. Tom was there and Lee was there. Tom Payne. Lee Payne. Joe Lee.

The old houses are still there. Go down Miller Avenue from Main, west, toward Summit Beach Park area, down there, and there's about five or six of these little houses on the left hand side. They're just alike. They were built way back before I came to Akron. They weren't new then. But they were rental homes—most of 'em. I know some of them down fifty-six where we used to eat.

Mrs. Pennington.[3] She served meals. The houses weren't very big. I doubt if she kept any roomers. But she served dinner. On Sunday, she served dinner and supper. I can't remember. But we used to go down there and get a home-cooked meal once in a while and get away from the restaurants. She served at certain times of the day. Four 'til six or somethin' of that kind. Whatever. I don't know. You couldn't get a boarding house hardly.

She had two good-lookin' daughters. Young, sixteen, seventeen year old girls. Like that. I think her number was fifty-six Miller Avenue. I could guess where Clarence McClure got burned was forty-four. Could've been forty-four. I don't know. Clarence got burnt in a gas fire in an outside toilet on the back porch. It just had a toilet in it. That's all. Nothin' else. No sink. No nothin', you know.

56 West Miller Avenue, Akron, Ohio. The one-time residence of Mrs. Pennington, who was known among the rubber workers for her home-cooked meals—as well as her two attractive daughters (July, 1991).

He walked in this place and the light was out but the gas was on. It had blown out. One of these old mantles. He struck a match and stuck it in there and it blew him out in the yard and burnt him—clear around from his collar to his hat. Had a straw hat on. From his cuffs to the end of his fingers. The skin was just hangin' off of 'em when he come up the road. Terrible shape! It was probably '18. Early '18. Sometime. Seventeen or '18. I don't know. It was in a home, but they rented rooms. The toilets were on the back porch.

I go down there once in a while and look at these old buildings where I lived back in 1917. That's over seventy years ago, you know. That's a long time ago. Some of those old buildin's are down there. The one I lived at 140 West Miller burned down evidently. It's gone. There's still an empty lot. Nothin' there. I don't know how many years ago it burned down because I wasn't in that part of town when it happened.

171 West Miller

Haskell: I lived at one seventy-one West Miller. That's the second place I lived. Probably four or five months. Then I moved down about two blocks. George Ball and his wife had that place. And he had a niece or sister that lived there. And there were two or three of us boys from Mayfield there. Wilson Wright. I don't know whether Bob Wright (his brother) lived with him or not.

We moved to this place the corner of Celia Avenue and West Miller. They finally changed it to Victory Street. But it was Celia back in those days. One-seventy-seven? I think. It couldn't be seventy-eight 'cause seven-eight was on the other side of the street. I lived at 140 later. Anyway, the corner of Celia and West Miller. You had to climb a mountain to get in it. The street's down there. You come up about six or seven steps to get in the yard. You come up here, there's about six, seven steps. And you go in here and you go six or seven steps up to the second floor where your room— You felt like you was climbin' up a mountain, you know.

I don't know who I roomed with there. Maybe Hollie Jones. I don't know. But I know Wilson Wright roomed there in another room. Wilson was a big guy—big, strong guy. And he was a distant relative. He had a brother Bob and a brother Clarence. I roomed with Clarence a lot of times, but I don't think I roomed with him there.

I remember one time I went in the saloon and Wilson was drunk. And he was a big man. He weighed two hundred and ten, twenty, thirty pounds. And this bartender's sellin' him everything in the store. He had a basket set out there and Wilson'd say, "Gimme that and gimme that and gimme that." He's drunker than a hoot owl, see. I was the caretaker for those guys—and thank God I was. None of 'em remember it, I don't think. But anyway, I did.

I jumped on the bartender. "What do you want to sell him that for? He's drunk now! He don't need that stuff! What the hell? He lives down here in a room. He ain't got no business with a basketful of booze." "Well, he wanted it." So he sold it to him. You know how some greedy people— They'll sell you poison if you want it, you know. They know you're gonna' kill yourself. "Get that stuff back and give him his money back." And he went along with it. I could talk like that. So I said, "C'mon, Wilson, I'll take you home."

Wilson lived at the corner of Victory Street and West Miller Avenue. Eleven-seventy-eight West Miller. And it was <u>hot</u>. It was summertime. It was hot. So I drag him and I carry him and I pull him and I steer him. And I worked like hell to get him up to that thing. I mean, I almost had to drag him, you know. He's bigger than I am. I weighed 140 pounds.

You talk about takin' people places— I took him. I carried him— Practically carried him down West Market Street and that's two long blocks down to Edison. Then the next one was Carrie Avenue (now it's Victory Street). And he lived up on a bank as high as this ceiling. The house was there and you went up in this porch and on the second floor. And I've got to lug him all the way up there, see, one or two o'clock in the afternoon. Hotter than Hades.

So, I finally got him up in his room. I'd undress him and put him in bed, take his keys out of his pocket. And he had a great, big trunk. I see a trunk key in there. I take his shoes and I put 'em in the trunk and I lock 'em—take the keys with me. This is about two-thirty, three in the afternoon. About six, seven o'clock, I went back around there. And he is on a warpath. He was snortin'. Needed a drink pretty bad. Couldn't get out to get it—barefooted. Somebody stole his shoes. He'd never looked in the trunk. He wanted to get out of there and go somewhere. Ahh, I made him sweat a little and I said, "Well, I'll get your shoes." And I opened the trunk and give him his key and took his shoes out of there. I said, "Here's your shoes in there. I didn't want you wanderin' back down the street again 'til you've sobered up." But that was a job to carry that big guy down there.

Clarence Wright. "Hoolie," we called him. He was the best roommate I ever had. We roomed together a dozen times. He'd leave town and go somewhere and come back. And we moved together. If I was livin' with somebody else, I moved in with him. We moved. We liked each other. And he was a good roommate. Clean as a pin. Never used your material. If that guy got up in the morning and you had a full pack of cigarettes on that dresser and he didn't have any, he'd never open that pack. If it was open, he might take one. But he didn't wear your ties. He didn't wear your socks. He didn't steal your stationery. He didn't steal your stamps. He didn't steal your handkerchiefs. And that's much better than a lot of 'em did. A lot of guys you'd room with, man, they was into your stuff all the time.

Almost anything they could get their hands on, they'd take it and use it, see. They wasn't stealin' it. They just used it. You'd meet him down on the street and he had your favorite necktie on. "What are ya' doin' with my tie on!?" "Oh, I just thought I needed a change." Thought it was a big joke. And good station— I bought *good* stationery. Lot of them guys used a

Clarence "Hoolie" Wright. Photo taken at 224 Ira Avenue.

tablet, see, and they'd see my box of stationery. Used to pay a buck and a half for pink stationery—nice lookin' stationery. They'd take mine and use it. Steal your stamps. But old Hoolie never did.

He used to get drunk and he'd come home sometimes and— The milkman used to come around midnight and put the milk out on the porch, you know. Everybody got a quart or a half-gallon or whatever they needed. And Hoolie'd get drunk— He'd come home and have about three or four bottles of milk. He'd pick 'em off people's porches and bring 'em home. I'd say, "What the hell you gonna' do with 'em?" He said, "I don't know. I don't know why I got 'em."

"Greasing the Growler"

Haskell: Men were pretty over-bearing in those days. They'd send their wife or they'd send one of their kids down to the local saloon to get a bucket of beer. We used to have a bucket that held about a gallon and cost maybe a dime or fifteen cents to get a gallon of beer. So, to cheat a little, they'd take a little butter and wipe around on the inside of the bucket—down a little ways from the top. When the beer hit that,

that grease would kill the foam. The bucket they called "the growler." I never did know why, but that was a common name for it. I never did it. We never lived near a saloon. Didn't drink beer around it. But it was a well-known fact. Everybody did it around the saloon area. If you didn't do that, the guy'd draw it full and you'd have three inches of foam on top, you know. When you got home, you hadn't much more than a half-bucket of beer. If you greased it, it would be all beer. There wouldn't be any foam on it.[4]

They wouldn't sell a kid a bottle of beer or booze or anything, but he could come in there with a bucket and get a bucket of beer for his dad. Probably some of the bigger kids took it down in the back of the barn and drank it or somethin'. They did it all over. All over the country. It was a common practice. It was very common.

Beer was cheap. It wasn't much more expensive than water. You could get a glass for a nickel that would hold a quart if they filled it up and it didn't have too much suds on it. If you didn't like it, you'd tell 'em to "put a head on it." In a lot of saloons, if you'd come in there and have a couple beers, then the bartender would buy one. It was cheap enough, you know. It was an advertisement or matter of good will that he'd buy one, too, see.

You stood up and drank. No women. Never saw a woman in one of those bars except the boss's wife. And she didn't mingle. She come in that front door and went right behind that bar and there was a chair there for her anytime she come in. She'd come in, talk to him, set around there. Maybe pass the time of day with some of the people she knew (if she happened to see 'em), get up and go out and never mingled around.

The restaurant on the back end was for the ladies of the evening and the old women of the neighborhood in the afternoon. They'd come in there and maybe have a sandwich and a glass of beer or two— whatever they wanted. Ethnic groups generally. More so than Americans.

In those days, there was a saloon every other door almost from the Goodrich to the Firestone. Every corner had a saloon. I bet there was twenty-five saloons between the Goodrich and Firestone. At least twenty-five.[5] And some of 'em was "hunkie" saloons. They'd have these foreign-speakin'— They had their own gang. You could get a drink in there if you went in, but you couldn't understand what anybody said. They were all aliens, you know.

177

Old Hoolie was bad. He'd get so drunk that he was as limber as a rubber band. Worked at the Goodrich and I worked at Firestone. I got off at Firestone at 10:30. They had a 10:30 shift in those days. Six-thirty, 10:30, 2:30. They didn't get off down there 'til 11:00 at the Goodrich. Well, he had a couple of drinkin' buddies that got off the same time he did.

I used to hurry out of Firestone and run to the poolroom. The poolroom was there a couple of doors north of Firestone Bank. Eleven hundred and five.[6] I hustled down there and we played pool 'til midnight. Then we'd get our supper, see, next door at the Manhattan Restaurant. Hoolie'd start out for the Goodrich and he didn't get up there 'til— The saloons closed at 12:00 and he had an hour from the Goodrich up to the poolroom. By the time he got there, he was higher than a Georgia pine. I mean a tall pine. I never went out with him hardly in the evening. We roomed together I don't know how long. I never went out with him. Him and Dewey Smith was drinkin' buddies. They had been raised together there in Mayfield. They'd drink together a lot. They didn't work together. Couple a' more Mayfield boys. But I never— I never went out with him. I didn't drink much and I didn't enjoy hangin' around those saloons. I'd take a beer when I wanted it or a shot if I needed it, but I didn't drink much.

But by the time he got there, he'd be so loaded sometimes— He'd be so drunk he couldn't hardly eat his supper. We lived on Miller Avenue at that time and I'd hustle him down the street and get him to bed, you know.

We had a big fight in one saloon Halloween night. Umh, I can't remember the name of that old saloon. I know where it was. Right by Firestone Bank. Across Miller Avenue from Firestone Bank in the middle of the block where High Street goes up over the ramp goin' to Firestone. You turn right there and went on across Main Street. There was about six or eight of us guys—all diked out in costumes and out havin' a big time, you know. They had straw hats and beards and— All crazy-lookin' guys, you know.

One guy with us was a professional boxer. Big, heavyweight guy named Wolfe. Ray Wolfe. A fellow named Mason. He was a Tennessee boy. Good friend of mine. Richard Mason. Everybody called him "Slim." Good-lookin' guy. He had lost his teeth. He had about four teeth. Two down. Two up. Somethin' on that order. But it was all gold. The whole thing was solid gold bridge, you know. He looked like a railroad when he was comin' down the street. He really was shinin'.

We run into a bunch of Alabama guys. We used to call 'em "Alabama sycamores." Nearly every one of 'em was six feet or more tall. Slim was drunk and he'd fight. And I was gonna' stick a knife in a guy or somethin'. I can't remember what the deal was. He had one of my buddies down on one of these benches against the wall. He was poundin' him and I went in to help him. I can't think of who it was. But this Wolfe, Ray, he run right by me and hit that guy on the chin. I bet he didn't come-to for an hour. He really cold-packed him. The guy had a sucker-punch. He didn't know it was comin'.

Somebody hollered, "The cops is comin'!" Slim started to run out through the kitchen to get out in the alley. And this dago that was in there was cookin' somethin' on the stove in a skillet. He run in front of the door and put his arm— He wasn't gonna' let Slim get out, you know. Slim picked up that skillet and dumped that hot grease right in this guy's face. You could hear him yell from here to Pittsburgh. He really took him out of that door, I'll tell you that. Ahh, we get into these messes, you know. We got out. We got away. We all took off out the back door. If we had costumes on, we yanked 'em off.

There was three or four of those Mason boys. Was Slim and Jack and Lee and another one. This Slim was a character. Slim was a good lookin' man. He was a lady-killer. Always had two or three women on a string. Had one big, hard-lookin' hillbilly woman that he shacked up with occasionally. She was a waitress in the Manhattan Restaurant. Pretty, good, husky, West Virginia girl. What the heck was her name? I don't know, but somebody cut her with a knife. She had a great, big scar across her neck. He never lived with her. She was his regular girlfriend. Shacked up with her, but he didn't live with her. Always lived in a decent roomin' house somewhere.

But Slim had a habit— He'd get drunk. He'd get crazy drunk. Violently drunk. Crazy as a bedbug. He'd go down there and he cut her clothes into strings—everything she had. Take 'em out of the closet, take a knife and cut 'em all to pieces. Throw 'em out and leave her stark naked. Anything she had on— "Take it off!" you know. And she'd be in the room there with nothin' else to put on (Not even a handkerchief, you know) except these rags. After a while, he'd sober up and he'd go buy her somethin' to put on so she could go shoppin' and buy some more. He'd give her some money. But he was nuts!

One Saturday afternoon, him and I was in a saloon together and

ON A BURNING DECK

we started drinkin' and we both got drunk. I got drunk. I was just a kid. The poolroom where we loafed around there (a bunch of us)— That Greek was in there was a good friend. And he was a nice man for a poolroom operator. He was one of the best. He looked after us kids. He was a good man. Jimmy. I can't think of his last name. He had a Greek name. He told it to me and I've seen it. But I never kept it up long enough to remember it.[7]

I went over there and I went back in the poolroom. It had them great, big seats that set around the tables around there. And I was settin' on one of them and I heaved on the floor. He cleaned me up, got me straightened out.

I went out in the back and they had a little, old— This buildin', it once had a delivery porch on the back of it to deliver merchandise— whatever it had before it was a poolroom, you know. This had a railin' around it made out of two by fours—pine.

I hear this noise and I went out there and Slim's down on his back on this floor and his brother Lee's tryin' to control him. He's gone berserk. Of course, I ain't feelin' too good. I'm sick. But I see what's goin' on. Slim worked his way over there and a piece of one of these two by fours— He bit a chunk out of it that big, out of that— Grabbed it and pulled it over and bit it—just like a mad dog, you know. With that thousand dollars worth of teeth he had in his mouth, I thought, "Here they go!" But they didn't break. I guess the dentist must've done a heckuva good job. But he was a good guy except when he got too much to drink. He was a drunk. Just drunk. Just went crazy. I just got sick. I wasn't use to drinkin'. Just once in a while I'd do that.[8]

We were buddies. We used to walk at night. We'd walk all over town. Work 'til 11:00 at night or 10:30. Didn't want to go home and go to bed. Nice summer nights. Both hillbillies. He come from down in Montgomery County, Tennessee. So, we'd just take off and walk. We'd walk all over town (clear downtown a lot of times) from South Akron. Richard "Slim" Mason.

221 Ira Avenue

Haskell: I stayed there until the fall of '17. I moved over on Ira Avenue with Jim and Gladys Wooldridge. Two-twenty-one. It was a flat. Four suite job, you know. Called 'em "flats." There was two up and two down. Brick place. Still there. Me and Clarence Wright roomed together there. "Hoolie." Ahh, I had two or three roommates

180

there. I had Jack Allen. He roomed with me. He was a nice, little dude of a guy and a nice roommate—clean and everything. I roomed with Hoolie and I roomed with a fellow named Blancett. Emmet Blancett. He broke out with smallpox in the bed with me.

I say, "He broke out." He didn't break out. He got sick. You get sick with smallpox. You get in a high fever and you get in trouble for three or four days. Then you break out. Then you can give it to people. But 'til you got pus out of these sores, you don't give it to anybody. I knew where his brother lived. I'd been out there with Emmet one time. So I went out there and I tell him— He wasn't home. I told the lady, I said, "Emmet is sick. He don't want me to have a doctor for him, but he is sick. He's very sick. He needs a doctor. And I don't want to order a doctor for him because he's tellin' me he don't want it, see. And we get along all right—him and I." So the lady said, "O.K., we'll get a doctor for him. We'll send a doctor out there." So the doctor came.

He walked up and stuck his nose in that room and said, "Holy Smoke, he's got smallpox." He could smell him. Said, "Get him out of here!" They took him over to City Hospital. They used to have a big, old house over there next to City Hospital. They called it "The Pest House." They took him over there and kept him 'til he was able to come back. I never got smallpox. I was pretty lucky.

I give him a little shaftin'. He had a beautiful, new suit. Tailor-made. Him and I were almost identical same size. A black and white check. They call 'em "pepper and salt" or somethin'. I think a black and white check. Somethin' like that. But he'd had it in a suitcase and he had a bottle of ink in there and it froze and broke and it got on this suit of clothes. Beautiful. Beautiful. Tailor-made suit. Good material. Lovely suit. So I saw it and one day I make him a deal. I said, "I'll trade ya'—" Well, before I made him a deal, I cheated him a little. I talked to a tailor down there that had a dry-cleanin plant. I said, "This guy's got this suit and it had ink frozen on it. Can you take that ink out of there?" He said, "Hell, yeah, we can take it out of there—as clean as a pin. No problem."

So this guy thinks the suit's ruined. It had it on the coat. It had it on the pants, you know. It had a vest and it was on that. So I banter for a trade. I traded him, I think, a pair of workpants, a couple of old blue shirts. I don't know. It wasn't very much I traded him, but he thought he was, "I'm rid of somethin' that ain't worth a shit," you know. So I get the suit and take it to the tailor and he runs it through

181

the mill and it comes back clean as a pin. Ahhhh, he said, "Well, I didn't know they'd take that out of there." I said, "Well, I didn't either"—'til I checked.

So I wore it the rest of that year and I went home that fall and I left the suit down there for Ralph. And he wore it a little while and then— I don't know what happened, but Mom cut it up. She made a suit for Tom or Henry or both of 'em out of it. I don't remember just how it worked. But she made some clothes out of it for them. It was a beautiful suit.

I went to a place with another friend of mine and I was lookin' for a room. And we worked in the shop where we got dirty and we took a shower in the shop every day. Well, this old woman was a chinchy son-of-a-bitch and didn't want to furnish hot water. So she asked us how often we took a bath. Thinkin' that she would want us to be clean, you know, I said, "Oh, a couple, three times a week." We didn't take a bath at home at all. We took a bath in the shop. She said, "Don't you think once is enough? It takes an awful lot of hot water." So, I turned around to my friend and said, "Let's go." We didn't want her room if we had to be policed that well. It was in '17 or '18. 'Bout '18, '19 maybe. I don't remember. It was one of those years before I was married.

Summit Beach Park

Although public amusement parks had quickly become the country's favorite recreational diversion by the early 1900s (with Ohio offering dozens of fine examples), Akron and Summit County itself had relatively little to offer to the thousands of workers pouring into the city. In fact, offerings were so slim that the Goodyear Tire & Rubber Company was forced to hold its employee picnics at Cedar Point, over 60 miles away.[9] This all changed when Summit Beach Park opened its gates on Summit Lake in Akron on July 4, 1917.

Known as the "Million Dollar Playground, "Akron's Coney Island" or its "Fairyland of Pleasure," Summit Beach Park was immediately hailed as one of the finest parks in the Midwest. For the recreation-starved workers, its midway was awe-inspiring. Within fifty Spanish colonial themed stucco buildings, there were more than one hundred attractions. This, in addition to a $25,000 hand carved carousel with forty-six horses, tigers, lions and deer, a submarine exhibition, a Ferris wheel, whip ride, penny arcade, shooting gallery, a boat and canoe livery, free circus acts, the largest roller skating rink in

With Akron overwhelmingly populated by single men during the teens and twenties, the photographic backdrops at Summit Beach Park that were undoubtedly designed for more romantic uses often found other willing subjects. (L-R) Bob Johnston and Haskell Jones.

the Midwest, a motordome and the "Dixie Flyer" roller coaster, said to be over a mile long.

While more than 50,000 patrons entered its gates in just its first two days of operations, eating over five thousand pounds of hamburger from just one concessionaire, the park struggled during its first year due to its relative late opening and America's entry into the war. Contractually bound by the owners of the land to increase its investment in the park by $25,000 per year, however, major expansions were still planned for the 1918 season. The adjoining Lakeside Park and Lakeside Casino were acquired and an additional carousel was acquired. The biggest and best new attraction for 1918, however, was the "Over the Top" rollercoaster. Making its debut in May of 1918, it was advertised as the fastest and steepest rollercoaster in the entire country. Within just two months, it would make news for an entirely different and deadly reason.

Haskell: I almost got killed down at Summit Beach Park.[10] We lived right up the street from it and one Sunday night Slim said, "Let's go down and ride the roller coaster." I said, "Okay." So we walked down there. We'd just went through the gate when we met a guy we knew. Well, we was standin' talkin'. We don't have time to go over and get our tickets and get on this thing, see. We talked maybe for six or eight minutes and all at once we hear this big commotion, then this bang.

When the chain picks the car up, you know, on the roller coaster it goes in a socket on the bottom of the car. When it jerked, it jerked the front wheels off the track. And they went on up and nobody knows. It's very gradual, you know. Got up just about to the top and thing it went off. Pulled off the side and it went through the railing and dumped over. I don't know. It killed two or three people or four or five. I don't remember how many, but it hurt a bunch. But we— We was sure tagged to be on that car! Umh![11]

Coaster Car Derailed by Block of Wood Placed on Incline Track.
Roller Coaster Accident at Summit Beach Sends Three to Death,
With Others Doomed.
Four Cars Being Drawn Up First Incline of "Over the Top" Leaves Tracks
and Plunge 50 Feet Down Carrying 15 Passengers With Them.
Thorough Probe is Promised.
Police and Firemen Aid in Rescue Work and
Send Injured to Both Hospitals,
Where Three More Victims are Reported in Critical Condition.

Investigation of the cause of the accident on the Summit Beach roller coaster, "Over the Top," which caused the death of three persons Sunday evening and may result in three more fatalities, is likely to center around the responsibility for the placing of a block of wood on the left tack of the incline about 10 feet from its beginning. This piece of wood, about 4x6x8 inches in size was run over by the front truck of the train, derailing the wheels, which then ran on the ties and running board of the incline up to the point where the train finally crashed over the side to the ground 40 feet below carrying its human freight to death and injury below. This piece of wood was found this morning, and bore marks of the wheel flanges. . . .

The cool weather, with the smallest Sunday night attendance since the park opened, probably prevented additional casualties as the cars have a capacity of eight people each, or 32 for the train of four cars. The train was just half full when the accident occurred, which was the heaviest load carried all evening . . . .

—The *Akron Beacon Journal*
July 8, 1918

Haskell: They had an opera house down there at Summit Beach Park they called it The Casino.[12] It was a road-show theater. And it got good road shows. I used to go down there in the afternoon a lot of times. You could get in there for about fifteen cents in those days and go to the show.

I went down there one time and there was three German brothers named Howard. Willie and— I can't remember the others.[13] I think it was him. One of 'em. I went in there in the middle of a storm outside and lightnin' shut the lights off. Man, it was dark in there. And he was on the stage entertainin' when this thing happened. So, he kept right on talkin', crackin' jokes about this, that and the other. And I bet it was thirty, forty minutes before the lights come back on. When the lights come on, he was settin' on top of the piano down in the orchestra pit still crackin' jokes. He was a good entertainer.

I saw some pretty good singers down there. They had a lot of trick fun houses and a skatin' rink and all the carnival stuff. That midway was a solid carnival. Big! Then you had a big swimming pool and a roller rink like a farm. Big thing.[14] I saw a skater skate against a motorcycle down there.

We had the best roller skater in the world in Akron for years, but he'd gotten a little old. He skated before the crown heads all over Europe and Japan and everywhere in the country. Australia and

(L-R) Haskell's brother, Thomas A. R. Jones, (Unknown), Florence's brother, Barton A. Jones.

everywhere. He was uncanny. Little bit of a guy. Name was Lowther.[15]

He was floor manager down there at Summit Beach on this roller skating rink. He was an old man when I first knew him. Not terrible old. He wasn't gettin' the big play, anymore, you know. That guy could've skated on a spool of thread from here to Chicago. He was— He was just as much at home on a pair of skates as anybody could ever be anywhere. Backwards. Forwards. Sideways. Or anyway you wanted

(L-R) Haskell Jones and Holly Jones (no relation) at Summit Beach Park.

to go. He— He just simply glided around. Just looked like without effort. He really was so natural.

He had a race down there. I was down there that night to see that. Had a guy on a motorcycle try to beat him on roller skates around that thing. It was three, four, ten laps or what. I don't know. But he beat the motorcycle. Maybe it was part of the game. Might've been pre-staged. I don't know. But that floor was pretty slick for that motorcycle. He didn't get much traction on it. He couldn't go wide open and make the turns.

After he quit skatin', this Lowther was deputy sheriff here for years. He used to ride a three-wheeler and serve papers. Witnesses and juries. All that stuff. Nice little guy.

CHAPTER TWENTY

WORLD WAR ONE

Haskell: Old man Moore's daughter was Addie. She married John Shaver who was a coal dealer in Mayfield. He had two boys and a girl. Their son Lelland was a hustler. Sold tickets at circuses and carnivals and stuff like that. He was a short-change artist. He used to pay six, eight thousand dollars a year to get a job sellin' tickets at a main gate of a Ringlin' Brothers circus. He'd paid that to get the job, but you short-change people, you know.

They had a big rush and a lot of farmers come in there. He said, "How many you got?" Said, "Got four kids and the wife." Well, the price was two dollars for each one and seventy-five cents for the kid. And he looked at him and he said, "Twelve and a half." The guy pays and away he went, you know. The next day he began— "Hell, I got clipped a little bit, didn't I? For two and a half or somethin'." But this guy made the fast deal, you know. Him and H.P. Ferris, Jr., they were operators. They sold tickets. They couldn't get the big gate. They took the best sideshow they could get. They did that. Whatever, you know.

Come to Akron durin' World War One— Didn't get a job. Didn't want a job. Go down to the poolrooms, this, that and the other, pick up newspapers. We got a new newspaper about every three two or three hours. The paper only cost three cents. New casualty list for the whole area, right where you were—right in Akron, Canton, Cleveland and around. So, you go down the street and the newsboy said, "New casualty list! New casualty list!" So you give him the nickel and forget about the change and you take the list and you look and there ain't anybody you know on it. So you lay it down somewhere. You get rid of it in a poolroom or wherever.

So, Lelland would pick 'em all up and straighten 'em up, and put 'em in his arm and run down the street and, "The new casualty list." It might be two hours old or three hours old or a day old. It didn't make a damn bit of difference to him if he could sell it, you know. He'd sell it for a dime. He never had change. If you had a nickel, he'd take it. But he'd rather have a dime. He made a livin' at it dur— He didn't stay too long, but he worked it durin' the war there, you know. He come up and worked it. He had a— What was his brother's name? Lelland— Can't think of the brother's name. I don't know. But they were nice people. We used to buy coal from 'em. They had a coal-yard in town

They had quite a problem durin' World War One—like some other German settlements. The rabble-rousers. I have to call 'em that. Here's a man. He's a German. We're fightin' the Germans. But he's a citizen. He's been over here for thirty, forty years. Why in the hell should I pick on him? My people come over here, too. There's people that want to push somebody. Some of these lard-heads, they forget their parents or grandparents were immigrants, too, you know. And regardless of where you came from, why, it didn't necessarily put you down on a low shelf. Most of us in this country (you and I) and most of the other people that's been here, their family's been here for two hundred years. They're all mongrels anyway. Nearly all of 'em got French and German and English and Dutch and whatever mixed up in 'em. That's what makes America.

I hunted out here in Portage County somewhere with a group. Couple, three fellows. And we hunted on a farm over there that a German had owned it. Did own it. He still owned it. He was an immigrant. Unmarried. And the neighbors burnt his house down. Burnt it down. He moved into a chicken-house about as big as that garage. He had never built it back. When I hunted with him was when I was workin' at Goodyear in the thirties. Fifteen, ten, fifteen years after the war was over, you know. He never had built anything back. He just— Piss on 'em and moved into that shanty and fixed it up and was livin' in it. But he let us hunt there.

The Teacher

Among the younger teachers, especially among those who are graduates of the high school, there is often an earnest effort to meet these problems intelligently. Unfortunately, such teachers are still too rare. This, however, is not the fault of the teachers. They are poorly trained and hopelessly underpaid, they have an unadaptable course of study and no proper equipment, their program is heavy and there is no opportunity for departmental work, and finally there is a lack of any kind of supervision.

—Elizabeth Bliss Newhall, "Schools," *Child Welfare in Kentucky:*
An Inquiry by the National Child Labor Committee
for the Kentucky Child Labor Association
and the State Board of Health (1919)

Florence: The first year I taught, I stayed at home. That was the winter that there was so much snow. It snowed around the first of December and the kids couldn't get back to school 'til January. You couldn't get anywhere. If you did, you rode a horse or maybe the farmers could hitch a couple of horses to a wagon if they'd put runners on and made into a sled and get out.

But, they'd just delivered a good load of coal before the snow came up. Well, when I got back to school, there's wasn't any coal. Maybe a scuttle full or something like that. So, there was no way of knowing, just from seeing it, who got the coal. But there was a family that lived pretty close. They were so poor. They hardly had anything to wear or eat, either. There was another family that lived across the road the other way. They always had plenty and I knew that they'd have coal or they's just run out.

Florence's wristwatch while teaching school.

So, when I got back to school and saw the coal was gone, I said to one of these little boys, "Did you see anybody get in the coal house?" He looked kind of funny. He didn't want to say. Said, "Yes, ma'am." I said, "Who was it?" And he told me.

I couldn't feel too bad about them getting the coal, only we had to have some coal. They had to have some way of getting warm or they'd froze to death. They couldn't buy it. Couldn't get out if they could have.

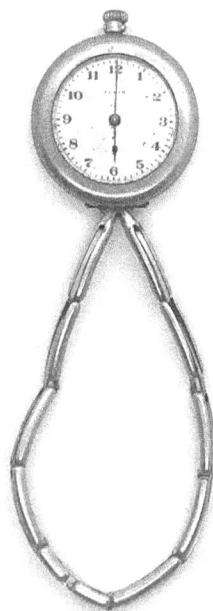

189

So, the little boys came back to school. I said to the biggest one, "When's your gonna' bring back the coal he borrowed?" He says, "I don't know. I'll ask him." So, in a day or two, he brought the coal back.

I told the county superintendent about it the first time I went up to Mayfield and he got the biggest laugh out of it. About that time, one of the other teachers came in. Said, "You know, we had a time about our coal." Said, "Somebody took the coal while we was closed down." He laughed and he said, "Why don't you do like Miss Jones

Florence Grace Jones.

did?" She said, "What'd she do?" Said, "Well, she found out, in a nice way, who got it." And said, "She told one of the kids to ask their father when he was gonna' bring back the coal he borrowed and he brought it back." They all got a big laugh about it.

But they— These folks— It was pitiful. There were so poor. They hardly had anything to eat or wear or warm the house. They lived in just a little house. But, takes coal and stuff to make heat no matter how little it is.

One of the little girls burned to death that winter. She got her dress afire by the stove. They had a little heater and (from what I got) they had the door to the heater open and she got her dress afire from that stove and she run outside. And, of course, when she run outside her clothes just burned that much more. Somebody coming along the road saw her and stopped and ran to her. But it was too late. She died from her burns.[1]

I had a pretty nice bunch of kids, as a whole, down there. Had a few that was pretty dumb and couldn't do much to help 'em, but most of 'em was pretty good kids.

190

Western Kentucky State Normal School

Florence: In January of 1918, I went to Bowling Green to college.[2]
Went that session from then on. I guess I stayed for two what they

Robert P. Green, teacher at Western Kentucky State Normal School, Bowling Green, Kentucky.

called quarters then. And we got a few days in between.   Had light-housekeeping rooms—a kitchen and a bedroom. At that time, it wasn't a full-time college. It was a teacher's college and you could go part of the time and teach your year. Then go back and teach and go back to school when your school was out. It was pretty nice. You had to work hard though, I tell you that. Kind of hilly around. If you went for a walk, you knew it.

Some of the teachers were good and some of 'em— I was telling Dad [Haskell] the other day about one I went to. They never taught agriculture in schools until about the time I was in school at Bowling Green. I think that was the first year they'd ever had to teach it. And the girls had to take it just the same as the boys did. We had a teacher by the name of Robert Green. During class, when we'd be discussing the different things in the lesson, some of us would say, "Well, Mister Green, what about (so and so)?" And he'd say, "Well, I don't know. We'll come to that later on." And we never came to it!

Haskell: Not yet!

Florence: That got to be kind of a password, a phrase—"I don't know. We'll come to that later on." But it had never been taught in the schools. They had the books just issued to 'em that year. I wasn't surprised that he didn't know it. Some

The Women's Basketball team at Western Kentucky State Normal School, Bowling Green, Kentucky. Frances Jones is third from right.

The Cuba High School Basketball Team, Graves County, Kentucky, where Florence's sister Frances Jones taught and coached basketball.

of it, I think I knew more about than he did 'cause I'd lived on the farm all that time. No sir, "We'll come to that later on."

When my sister Fanny was going to school at Bowling Green, the girls had a basketball team and the boys had a basketball team. So, that's the way she got her exercise. It was on the basketball team.

Haskell: So, when she went down there to teach at Cuba, why, she coached the basketball team.

Florence: Yeah.

Haskell: 'Cause she knew something about basketball and those hillbillies never had seen the game, see. She introduced it down there. She'd played basketball and knew the rules, so she coached the team.

Florence: She taught another place or two before she taught at Cuba. But Cuba being, you might say, just a spot in the road, their high school was very few students in it. She taught in the high school and even taught a basketball group. They didn't have any boys that knew anything about it and they wanted a teacher so she told 'em that she'd try it. "O.K." They got along pretty good with her. I don't think Fanny taught any after she married. She had too much to do around that farm.

CHAPTER TWENTY-ONE

THE SPANISH FLU

If would be difficult, if not impossible, to overstate the impact of the "Spanish Flu" in 1918-1919. It is just as difficult to explain why so few are aware of its impact as what some have referred to as "the most devastating epidemic in recorded world history"—surpassing even the "Black Plague" of the Middle Ages.[1] In The United States, within the span of just six months, this virulent combination of influenza and the pneumonia that was often associated with it killed more Americans than all of the wars of the 20th Century combined.[2] Within just twenty-five weeks, it took more lives than AIDS has in over twenty-five years.[3] Within the time it took to circle the globe once, it killed at least 50 million and possibly as many as 100 million.[4] Adjusted for today's population, that toll would be between 175 and 350 million.[5] What's more, each of these numbers may be grossly underestimated due to poor reporting and inaccurate diagnoses. And all along its deadly path, it affected the lives of countless millions of others. Worst of all, no one had the slightest idea how to even treat it, let alone stop it.

The first wave of flu began in the spring of 1918 at Camp Funston, an Army camp in Kansas. Due to wartime censorship, willing cooperation of the newspapers and the fact that the strain did not appear particularly virulent at the time, the Public Health Service was not even notified. Nor was the camp quarantined. By the time the disease swept around the world to reenter Boston in early September, 1918, it had been renamed the "Spanish Flu."[6] It had also become deadly—though that, too, was little noticed at the time. Surgeon

193

General Rupert Blue of the Unites States Public Health Service issued only routine precautions.

"On 11 Sept 1918 Washington officials disclosed that the Spanish Influenza had arrived in the city. On the next day 13 million men . . . lined up all over the United States and crammed into city halls, post offices, and schools to register for the draft," one account noted.[7] One of three registration dates, it was the day all men ages 18-45 were required to register.[8] "It was a gala flag-waving affair everywhere," another account noted, where men lined up by the hundreds to sneeze and cough on one another.[9] One of those men who stood in line was Haskell Jones.[10]

Having boarded a train out of Akron to return to Mayfield for his older sister Mary Genevieve's wedding, he also decided to register for the draft at home, thinking that he might be drafted into the service alongside his friends. Then, having little to do afterwards and needing money while he waited for his draft notice to arrive, he decided to go to Camp Knox in search of employment. Under construction as the new "hands-on" field artillery training location for Camp Taylor and located just outside Louisville, it would eventually grow to become present-day Fort Knox.[11] He had no way of knowing that the places he went, the things he saw and the people he met on his way there would soon be forever altered.

A little more than one month later, on September 27th, the Spanish Flu first appeared in Louisville, Kentucky, carried there by troops in transit on the train to Camp Taylor. "The situation . . . was clearly dire, as the Public Health Service calculated that the city had about 1,000 cases during late September . . . By the second and third week of the epidemic, Louisville was experiencing about 180 deaths a week from influenza . . . Camp Taylor was harder hit than the city itself . . . During the week of October 19th, there were 3,772 cases at Camp Taylor alone, which would indicate an extremely high rate of infection."[12] Doctors were called in from throughout the state to rush to the camp "to assist in treating the thousands of cases of Spanish influenza among the soldiers . . . The situation is said to be serious at this camp as many are dying for want of attention on account of the scarcity of doctors."[13]

Dr. Carl Skinner was one of the doctors who helped to care for those stricken at Camp Taylor and his daughter later recalled the conditions in Louisville at the time, "I remember that late at night, we would be wakened by a rumbling noise on the cobblestone pavement outside our home on First Street. They waited until late at night to take the bodies from Camp Taylor down to the 10th Street (Union) Station. And down there, all around the station, the coffins were stacked up. It was terrible . . . It was very grim."[14] "The dead were hauled away from the camp in trucks and on horse-drawn vans," another witness recalled. "Pine caskets were arranged in pyramids—10 on the bottom, nine on the next layer, until they reached the top, where one lonely casket was positioned." There would be many such processions. By the end of November, with well over 12,000 sick, some 800 would be dead.[15]

CHAPTER TWENTY-TWO

CAMP KNOX

Haskell: Kinda' talked about enlisting. I was workin' in Akron. And then I decided to go home and register down there. I didn't know the ropes or anything else, you know. I thought, "Well, if I go down there and register, a lot of guys from my area will go with me," you know, "and we'll all be in the same group" —which is a big fallacy. It ain't true. First thing they do is send you to California and me to New Jersey and another guy to Arkansas and one— They split you up. Deliberately. They don't want too many guys from the same neighborhood. They don't want a big killin' from one neighborhood. They could have a catastrophe and half a dozen men killed. They don't want 'em all to be from there. So they break it up. Well, I didn't know that.[1]

You started out of Akron on the Pennsylvania. You went to Cincinnati on the Pennsylvania, from there to Louisville on the B&O and from Louisville to Mayfield on the Illinois Central. You had to change. The B&O ran here, but the connection was better on the Pennsylvania goin' down. Sometimes you'd come back from Cincinnati on the B&O. I can't remember why, but we did. But I made a boo-boo. I worked an extra shift and caught the train out of Akron at ten-ten at night. And I'd worked about twenty-four hours before that. Between bein' drunk and bein' asleep on the train, I finally got home.

I slept with a stranger in Louisville. We met on the train. We got in there about seven in the morning and missed the fast train goin' south. We were gonna' be there for hours. It was four o'clock or five 'til we get another train goin' out of there. So we went up to the old Seventh Street Hotel and got a room and slept together 'til one or two o'clock in the afternoon. A guy by the name of Gorman. I remember his last name, but I don't remember his first name. He was a young lad about my age. Young guy from Shreveport, Louisiana. So we got up about one o'clock and thought we'd get somethin' to eat.

Well, we couldn't get anything to eat downtown. They had two big camps out there— Camp Knox was under construction but Taylor was a big camp. And it was on Sunday and everybody was in town. They'd made a bunch of— What's these college boys that take R.O.T.C.? They'd made a bunch of them second lieutenants and they were in town with their girlfriends and the mothers and fathers and so forth. And downtown was just jammed with soldiers.

So we started goin' out and look for somethin' to eat. We get to a restaurant, start in— "Whooa, wait a minute. We don't have any food" or "We don't have any seats" or "We don't have any room" or we're out of this or that. So we run around town there awhile and stopped at half a dozen places. I said, "Let's get on the streetcar and go out to the edge of town somewhere and get away from downtown." So, we didn't know where we were goin'. Didn't care, you know. Just got on the streetcar and went out to the end of the line and went to a little restaurant.

I said to the waitress, "You got any food?' Said, "Not much." Said, "What do you got?" "Well," said, "I've got two pork chops." I said, "Well, give each one of us a pork chop. What else you got? Got any potatoes?" "Nah." "You got any eggs?" Said, "Yeah, I got some eggs." "Well, give us a couple eggs apiece with the pork chop. Give me a glass of iced-tea." It was hot summertime, you know. Said, "Don't have any." I said, "Give me a glass of milk then." "I don't have any." "You got any coffee?" Said, "I can make some." So we got somethin' to eat and went back downtown.

The jail in Louisville is a ground floor jail. Ain't upstairs like it is in most places, you know. The porch all the way around it and the rooms are a little higher than this floor here, but not much. And they had all the whores in Louisville and that area locked up in Louisville. They were havin' trouble.[2] We went by and they was, "Ayyyyyyy! Come here, Charley!" you know. They couldn't pay their fine and get out of jail. The only way to get out of jail was for you to pay their fine and take 'em—sign up you'll take 'em out of the state, you know. So they was beggin'. Said, "Come here, honey! Come here!" Said, "Get me out of here, you won't never have to work again as long as you live," you know. They was gonna' take care of you from here on in. And we bull-shitted with 'em there a little bit.

But I got home and I am exhausted. I have worked about twenty-four hours before I started and then I was up all day and got loaded in the evening. Get on the train and I'm up and down and here and there and everything. When I got home I was so tired— Nobody can believe how tired I was! I was really worn out. Ride six hundred miles on the train at slow— They didn't move too fast. Twenty-four hours to get there.

Haskell Jones—on the fence at his girlfriend's house.

My mom wanted to get me out of bed. I was supposed to go with my sister to this church down at Fancy Farm for her wedding. They come in and try to wake me up and I said, "Ahh, the hell— I ain't goin' to a wedding or anywhere else. Let me alone." I'm gonna' sleep, see. My sister told me she had a girl for me to go with. Well, I didn't care about girls. I was beat to the bone. So after the wedding, they came back to his father's. And they had a kind of a dinner party. So they finally get me awake and I shave and clean up and Mattie— Mattie? Yeah. I took my sister Mattie and we went over there and we went to this. And here's a beautiful babe, you know. Lovely. I liked her. And I think, "What a dummy you was! You should've been here yesterday!" She's a real chick, you know. That was my old friend Mary Vincent Spalding. So we got acquainted and we liked each other very much. She would've been a sweetheart for me. Me and her would've got along fine if it wasn't for a religious situation. They were Catholics and I wasn't.

Her father was raisin' hell with her 'cause she was goin' with a Protestant. That was another religious fanatic, you know. He was rather a really radical Catholic. I worked for him a little bit cuttin' corn and stuff that fall before I come back. And anytime I wanted to rest, all I had to do was start a Catholic argument and he'd shut the job down and go into a dither.

I don't think he complained any about my sister marryin' [her brother] Bernard. Should've been glad to get rid of him. He was as dumb as an ox. But the old, old Catholics don't mind that, see. They say if you're a Catholic boy and you marry a Protestant girl, you're gonna' be the boss and they gonna' go through Catholic school. Everybody's gonna' be Catholic. But if your daughter marries a Protestant, he's gonna' be the boss and then they're gonna' pull away and go to the Protestant church, see. They thought that was breakin' down the order.

Well, her father was raisin' hell. He was on her back all the time. All week. All night. Every time I'd go over there, she was afraid to get out of the house. Once in a while, I'd go to pick her up in the evening and we'd start out the front door. The barn and the stable was across the road. We'd get out toward the front porch and she'd say, "Wait a minute." I didn't realize what was goin' on for a little while. She'd wait until he'd go back in the barn. She was afraid he'd say somethin'. Afraid he'd jump on me about it. I talked to her mother about it after I found out what was goin' on and she said, "Don't pay any attention to him." Said, "Do as you please. You don't have to run from him." She's Catholic, too, but she said, "Don't worry about it." She liked me. Me and her got along pretty good.

Haskell and Mattie Jones and Vera Buchanan called on Mary Vincent Spaulding Saturday night.
    Mrs. Lena Scott and children and Miss Florence Jones attended the sandwich supper at Boswell school house Saturday night.

—"Hickory Route One"
The Weekly Messenger
October 10, 1918

Haskell: Mary was in a Catholic high school in Owensboro, Kentucky, before I met her. She'd been up there four years. Hadn't hardly been home. Didn't know as much about the world as that dog. Didn't know anything. Pretty gal. Pretty as she could be. I'd talked to her. I'd been talkin' to her for a long time. I knew her, the whole family.

We'd go to a picture show or somethin' of that kind. Go into Mayfield to a picture show. Cost a whole quarter to get into a show. It was a big one if you got thirty-five cents. We didn't have much money. It cost a whole dime to get one of them big bags of popcorn.

They tell this story about this Wilson boy who was a known chiseler. Tighter than hell. He comes up with his girlfriend up the street

199

and here's a popcorn wagon there. He parks back here. He sat there awhile. And she said, "That popcorn sure smells good, don't it?" He said, "Yes, it do. I'll pull up a little closer so you can smell it better." I don't know whether it happened, but they told it on him anyway. Yes, sir, "I'll get a little closer."

Celebrating its grand opening on July 18, 1913, The Princess offered "the instrument equivalent to a 14-piece orchestra." It was only one of the theaters in Mayfield. The Dixie Air Dome open-air theater had opened in June, The Unique Theater opened in September and the Dixie Theater opened in August of 1914 (Postcard courtesy of Ronald Morgan Kentucky Postcard Collection, Kentucky Historical Society).

But Mary and I, we loved each other. There ain't no doubt about it. We did. We thought a lot of each other. And had conditions been proper, why, we might've made it. But the girl was havin' a hell of a time. He was really givin' her a bad time. So, one day, I took her to the show. And we was comin' home. I said, "Mary, we better hang up our tools." We had no intention of gettin' married because we was both kids and I didn't have a dime and she didn't either. I said, "You're gonna' live miserable with him. I'm gonna' go back to Akron again." And, so, she didn't want to. She wanted to hang on. But I said, "No." I said, "I ain't just gonna' put you through that torment." And, so, we cut it out.[3]

* * *

Haskell: I registered in, I think, the first week in August—somethin' like the 12th of August.[4] So I loafed around there a little while and I didn't get called. And another neighbor boy lived there. I said, "Let's go to Camp Knox and get a job." Well, they were buildin' the camp then. They was just startin' it. There was some buildin', but not much. So we went up there. We each took a few carpentry tools. I took that tape measure and a six-foot rule and old framin' saw. It was my dad's tape. Lead pencil.

Civic Center and Barracks, Camp Knox, Kentucky, November 13, 1918
(National Archives).

We didn't know any more about carpentry than Abraham did or any man did. Nothin'. Nothin'. Couldn't saw a board straight in a vise, you know. But it was a time and materials job by some big contractor who was buildin' that camp. And he got so much percent over what it cost.

So, we went to the window to get a job and the man said, "What do you do?" "We're carpenters." Carpenters got six dollars and sixty cents a day. A laborer only got four dollars and forty-four cents a day. Yeah. We're carpenters. And we didn't know from shit. And they didn't want to know. They sent us out on a labor job—but we was gettin' carpenter's wages, see.

So we was out unloadin' cars and doin' various other labor jobs around the camp. Mostly, we were workin' in the freight yard unloadin' stuff. Boilers and equipment of various kinds. We unloaded poles (sixty foot long) off a flatcar and loaded boiler parts out of cars and unloaded stuff into the bakery.

Offloading, Camp Knox, Kentucky, September 4, 1918. Taken during its construction from September through November of 1918, this photograph (and the one on the following page) captured Camp Knox as Haskell Jones saw it. The boiler parts seen on the flatcar could have easily been the same ones he helped unload (National Archives).

We were buildin' these barracks, but they didn't have any soldiers except about ten thousand misfit colored guys—bow-legged and ruptured and one-eyed and legs so crooked they couldn't get a uniform on 'em. They put 'em in what they called a "limited service."[5] That meant you didn't fight, but you worked. So, they had 'em up there buildin' highways and doin' camp garbage work and latrine work and anything that they could work. Instead of bein' out workin' for five, six dollars a day like everybody else, they was workin' for thirty dollars a month—while gettin' their feed and clothes and hospitalization and stuff of that kind. They were in the Army. They got Army service, but they didn't fight. They didn't wear a uniform. They wore a dungaree.

All they had was a provost guard in there. Not very many. Just enough to keep order, you know. They were gettin' fifteen dollars a month in those days for army duty. Not long after that, they raised 'em to thirty. A dollar when they started. Fifteen dollars a month. Fifty cents a day for army duty. Raid the crap games and things of that kind. Bootleggers. I had a friend (only I didn't know he was up there 'til I got up there)— He was one of the guards in the M.P. situation. John Austin. He's dead and gone forty years. Good friend. I liked him.

John told me what they used to do— The guys used to shoot craps in these barracks. They'd take four or five blankets, hang 'em around here and make a "tent" in the middle of the barracks. Get a lantern down in there and shoot craps at night. The cops used to raid these and steal all the money. They'd grab the money if there was any available.

John said, "We raided this place and we was takin' 'em down to the lock-up and the one guy said to me, he said, 'Hey, would you do me a favor?'" And John says, "What do you want?" Said, "I haven't got any money. I lost all my money in that game. But I've got some pictures and this, that and the other in my pocketbook. I'm afraid if I go in the lock-up, somebody'll steal it and I'll lose the stuff." Said, "If you'd keep it for me, I'd appreciate it." "Yeah, I'll keep it." So the guy gives him his pocket book and he stuck it in his pocket.

When he went in at night to go to bed, he said, "Ahh, I'll look and see what the hell is in there." He opened it up and there's two twenty-dollar bills in it. So the guy don't know he's got any. He thinks he's lost his money. Told him he had. So he took one of 'em. He said the next day or two they let this guy out and he come lookin' for his pocketbook. Come over and John said, "I thought you told me there was no money in that pocket-book?" He said, "There wasn't, was there?" I thought I lost it all in the crap game." "Well," he said, "there's a twenty-dollar bill in there." And the guy said, "Gee, I didn't know that." Said, "Hell, I'll give you half of it." He said, "I took half of it." I said to John, "Well, you louser—" "Ahhh," he said, "what the hell. He's workin'. He's gettin' wages."

Well, I was there until I got my notice to appear for a physical examination. They sent it out to my home and my mother sent it to me. It took about a week for me to get it up there in camp. But the day I got it, the war was over. In a couple of days (they paid us off on a Saturday) we went home. Everybody had the flu. I had it. Was in bed about a week with the flu. It wasn't just me. Died by the thousands. It killed people overnight almost. Grown people. When I was able to go to town to get my examination, the doctor said, "Get the hell out of here! The war is over!"[6] So, I never was examined. That's how near I come to bein' in that one.[7]

The Spanish Flu in Graves County

"When the full import of the Influenza-Pneumonia plague 1918-1919 is understood, we stand aghast. At no time in the history of death registration was there ever accumulated such a widespread death rate in the same length of time."
— *Preliminary Vital Statistics Report for 1918 and Tables for 7 Years, 1911-1917 Inclusive.* Bulletin of the State Board of the Health of Kentucky. April 1919.

With the Commonwealth of Kentucky releasing its first flu advisory on September 29th, subsequent issues of *The Messenger* lay out the toll as the community and surrounding areas are overwhelmed with death and disease.[8] Even as doctors were summoned to Camps Taylor and Knox, schools were shuttered, jury duty was cancelled and the death toll mounted.[9] *The Messenger* struggled to even put out a paper, reporting on October 17th:

> It takes about fifteen persons to run this paper and there are only two left, the editor and a young man, Hobart Coleman, in the back. Of course it is impossible to get out a paper with only two persons. Both of our linotypes are idle; our job department is also idle. Our make-up man is sick, our pressman is sick and our mailing galley man is sick. The reporter and three of the carrier boys, which of course makes it impossible to think about getting out a paper . . . We ask our friends to bear with us in our troubles, because they know we would not miss an issue of the paper if it were possible to get it out.[10]

By December, as cases began to decline in Mayfield yet still raged throughout the county, all public meetings in the rural districts were forbidden by law. "[T]his includes schools, churches, public indoor funerals, sales, courts in the city where they require the attendance of individuals from the country districts."[11] Though hundreds of cases of flu and pneumonia would still be reported over the following months and the Commonwealth would tally well over 18,000 deaths from influenza and pneumonia, it would be January of the following year before life began to return to normal.[12] By then, the county schools will have been closed for nine weeks, an untold number in the area will have been ill or died and the Herculean effort to put out the paper on editor Lemon's part will be his last.[13] He, too, dies that month "after a two weeks illness of complications and paralysis."[14] "Democracy" in Mayfield would never be the same.

The Bulldog

Haskell: My brother Ralph kept a little bull dog for a cousin of ours durin' the World War One. I'd go around the neighborhood at night and come back home. I only stayed there a couple of weeks. We had a gate in the yard and he wouldn't let me come in that yard. He didn't know me so I'd have to wake somebody up to get out to come and let me in. So, I said I was gonna' kill him. I took a shotgun and I put it down in the corner of the garden down there. When I come back, I load the gun and come walkin' up. And never heard the dog. Never see him. He— He sensed it some way or another. He could feel or smell me, I guess.

So Ralph had sold a wild cow. She wouldn't breed. She's run in the pasture 3 or 4 years and never been handled and she's wild as a deer. He'd sold her for beef and we had a rope on her. We was drivin' her to the place where we'd sold her and she was fightin' and buckin'. Havin' a lot of trouble with her. Finally, we came to a bridge in the road and I was in front with the rope tuggin' on her and Ralph was behind. Finally, she took a notion to go and she run by me and jerk me down with that rope. When I fell, she turned on me—just headed for me with one of those horns pointed right at my bellybutton. And I was layin' in that bridge and couldn't get up that quick.

This little bulldog was along. And without anybody sayin' a word, he run in and grabbed the cow by the nose and turned under her and just pulled her down. She kinda' struck me as she fell, but it didn't hurt me. She would've pinned me to that bridge with her horn if he hadn't a' done that. After that, me and the dog got along pretty good. But I'll tell ya', he saved my life. Good thing I didn't shoot him, I'll tell ya' that. He'd a' fixed me up.

Courtship

Haskell: Well, I was there for a little while longer and I met Florence then. I went to a schoolhouse one night after I told Mary I'm gonna' quit because I don't want to be in a jangle. Went to this schoolhouse and they had a party. A schoolhouse party. She met me. I didn't meet her. She was lookin' for a boyfriend—

Florence: You! I sure wasn't lookin' for one down there!

Haskell: —and her sister was teachin' a school down there close to home. So I went to a party and she was there and they had some kind of a drawing that you draw names for the girl for your partner. Partner for the night.

Florence: They called that a "box supper" and every girl that went was supposed to take a box with lunch in it.

Haskell: She was lucky enough to draw my name. So we had supper together, didn't we?

Florence: Yeah.

Haskell: It was a supper, wasn't it?

Florence: No. It was a *box* supper.

Haskell: Box supper! The girl brought a lunch—a shoebox or whatever they put it in, you know. Chicken and cake and pie and whatever. And you bid on that. The auctioneer up there put it up for sale and you bid fifty, a dollar, whatever you had.

Florence Grace Jones

And when I get the basket, it's got her name on it, see. Then you went back and got acquainted. Got introduced. Then we had a candy drawing.

Florence: I believe we did have.

Haskell: Yeah. Yeah. The boys throw'd candy. Well, each threw candy. You went up and picked blindly out of a bag or something. Couldn't see what color you was gettin'. But if you got the same color as the girl you got to kiss her up in front of the whole place. But she was watchin' what I was doin' and didn't get the same kind. I was a little high on hard cider that night and she thought I was a little simple. She said that she thought I was crazy. I thought she was crippled. I guess the house must've been settin' up on edge.

Florence: No, I'll tell ya'. I had on a new pair of black shoes with white soles on 'em. That was "all the go" back then for the girls. Black shoes with white soles on 'em. He thought I was crippled.

Haskell: Probably too small for her.

Florence:　I guess he thought that was a bandage on my foot.

Haskell:　So, we didn't see each other then for—

Florence:　A couple a years, I guess.

Haskell:　I expect it was two years. Yeah, longer. She started teachin' school down there in the district where I was raised.

Florence:　And this district where we met was between the one where I taught the first year and the last three years I taught school.

Haskell:　So, we got acquainted. Saw I was a real good catch, see. I had a pretty steady girlfriend, but she talked me into turnin' that girlfriend down. This other girl didn't like that from nothin'. She met Florence on the street one day and she jumped all over her. Said, "I'm gonna' get even with you!" And Florence always said she did. "She let me marry you!" But anyway, I didn't see her for a while. I left there. I come back to Akron. But you was jealous!

Florence:　Jealous! I'll tell you— Oh, oh, oh.

Haskell:　Yes, sir! You're jealous!

Florence:　I've never seen one minute when I was jealous of that gal.

Haskell:　Don't tell me you wasn't jealous of her.

Florence:　No, I wasn't and don't think I was!

Haskell:　'Cause every time I looked at her, why, you started to color up!

Florence:　You got things kind of mixed up. If I'd go anyplace with him, or be anywhere, she just come up and stick right by us—be in between us if she could.

Haskell:　Wonder why she noticed it?

Florence:　And I didn't pay any attention to her.

Haskell:　Wonder why—

Florence:　I didn't, but— I didn't like her and I wouldn't have if she hadn't been trying to take him.

Haskell:　Green-eyed monster!

CHAPTER TWENTY-THREE

RETURN

In 1917, when Haskell Jones had first arrived in Akron, the hordes of hopeful newcomers were greeted by a large billboard erected by the Chamber of Commerce welcoming them to "the City of Opportunity."[1] This, adjacent to "the little Union Station hiding back of monstrous heaps of trunks and boxes."[2] Upon his return, many of the same workers were leaving. "Pine boxes, homeward bound, cluttered the baggage coaches."[3] The Chamber's optimistic billboard was of cold comfort. Akron, and the surrounding area, had been devastated.

In Akron, "The overcrowded conditions in the city's rooming houses were exactly what was needed to make the flu a great death-dealing machine."[4] In fact, the toll became so severe that the newspapers actually ceased reporting the epidemic's toll following November 7th after the 209th victim—"evidently figuring that by ignoring the disease, it could be conquered."[5] By the spring of 1919, however, there were at least 919 confirmed deaths that couldn't be ignored. As the population was highly transient and the holiday season would have seen many returning to their home states, it would be safe to assume (as the Metropolitan Life Insurance Company calculated) that the true death rate was substantially higher.[6] An additional 5,000 others were reckoned having become ill in Akron and recovered.[7]

106 Brookside

Haskell: I moved with the Wooldridges to Brookside. A hundred and six Brookside. I can remember the number of the house there. And that's been many, many, many, many, many years ago. A nice, clean room and everything. A beautiful place. Then I roomed with Hollie Jones. He gets married and he comes into town and leaves his wife in Kentucky and comes up there.

106 E. Brookside, where Haskell Jones roomed with Hollie Jones. One of the first homes built by the Firestone Tire & Rubber Company in Firestone Park (Dec. 2011).

They had one particular point where everybody met. Five hundred guys come through there every day from my county. They come by and got cigarettes or whatever lookin' for somebody they knew. "Well," he said, "who's roomin' with ya'?" I said, "Nobody." He said, "How 'bout I could room with ya'?" I said, "O.K."

I'd just got rid of a mess of crabs. I had a helluva' time with crabs. I went home with 'em. I didn't know I had 'em. I gave 'em to my brother Ralph. I was sleepin' with him and we got rid of 'em. I went up to Camp Knox and worked and slept in those crummy beds up there and got 'em again and I brought 'em back and give 'em to him. He said, "Why don't you go somewhere and stay? Don't come back and bring me crabs back here." We got rid of 'em.

I'd been back there a month. Somethin' like that. I ain't been around a woman or anything. So I take him home with me and we go to bed. And along two or three o'clock in the mornin', I feel one of them turtles walkin' across my belly. And I knew what it was. I'd had 'em. It wasn't any accident or somethin' else or a cockroach or nothin'. I knew what it was. So I get up and turn the light on and skin my underwear down and I check— He's as big as a grain of wheat. He's an old-timer. He wasn't new.

I pulled him out of bed. I said, "Get out of that bed, you bastard!"

You've got crabs on you!" And he said, "What's crabs?" I said, "You got 'em. I know you got 'em." And he'd just been married for maybe less than a month. About a month. Married a big, dark-haired, husky woman. I said, "Get out of that bed!" He had on long underwear—sleepin' in a union suit. I said, "Get that Goddamn clothes off of you!" And he said, "What do you mean?" I said, "I mean what I say." He pulled them off and actually he looked like a handful of wheat hit him. He had a pint of crabs on him! That guy was covered! He had sores all over him where he'd scratch and where it had bit him, you know. I said, "Out of that bed and get dressed!"

This is about two or three o'clock in the mornin'. I said, "Get the hell out of here and go to the drug store. And you be standin' against that drug store in the morning when they open up! And you get some blue ointment." That's what they used back in then for a quick kill, see. It was a blue salve with a blue vitriol in it or somethin'. I don't know what. But I wouldn't let him come in the house. I made him get the hell out of there at two or three o'clock in the mornin'. I run him out. So I watched and we got cleaned up—him and I both.

That night after that we got cleaned up, he said, "Do you suppose my wife had those?" I said, "What do you mean, 'Do I suppose'? I know she had 'em." I said, "Where'd you get 'em?" He said, "Off of old (some French gal around town who was a pig and he'd had relations with her before he married, see—not long before he married)." I can't think of her name. Janie LeMay. Janie LeMay, I think. It was a French name. I never knew her.

Well, this people where I lived had an attic. So maybe two weeks later his wife came up and they fitted up the attic for them for a light housekeepin' room where they could cook and a bed and so forth, you know. So what does he tell me after a day or two after his wife comes? "You know, my wife didn't have one of them." "Maybe she's smarter than you. She might've got rid of 'em." So they didn't stay long. She didn't like Akron and so— I think this might've had somethin' to do with it. She was ashamed or what. But they went back to Kentucky.

Jim (the guy that owned the house) said, to me one Saturday morning, "Let's go up and clean this place up and get it ready. I want to rent it again." I said, "O.K." So we go up and lookin' through the drawer and there's a box of blue ointment in the drawer, see. Well, he didn't need it when she came there because I sandpapered that guy. I'd check him every night to see if there was anything on him. But she had it—no doubt. She was lousier than hell and she didn't know what the hell was wrong with her. She never heard of a crab, see. But you have all kinds of experience as you go through life.

I remember one guy whose feet was so cold— That man had the coldest feet I ever saw in my life. I roomed with him once. Harvey Chester. When he put his feet on ya', you could feel the water runnin' down in his toes.

Me and another guy roomed together. I was sick and he was lazy. He didn't work very much. He didn't have any money. So we had a system. In the morning when we got up— This game run almost twenty-four hours a day. Take a couple dollars and go down to the crap game and win fifteen, twenty dollars and come back. We had enough money to pay our rent and eat for a couple days, you know. And maybe next morning, he'd go. And he'd win ten, fifteen, twenty dollars. But if we went together, we broke every time. We wouldn't go together. So we kept that up for about a month. Then he went back in the navy. I got rid of him. I got to feelin' better and I got to workin'.

I just simply was run down. I don't know. My doctor said I had T.B when I was younger and I might have had it then. I don't know. But I wasn't able to work. That's the truth. Didn't feel like workin'. That was after the war was over. Early '19. Well, I got straightened out. I felt all right from then on. I never felt particular bad. I did a lot of hard work though, I'll tell you. My God! But it didn't kill me.

140 West Miller Avenue

Haskell: I stayed with the Wooldridges awhile and then I got me a roommate named Ralph Haines. He was double ornery. We were livin' on 68 East Archwood Avenue. He had a girlfriend. A great, big, husky, hundred and eighty-five pound Effie Malone (God Bless her. I loved her) from Shreveport, Louisiana with an Irish and Southern brogue. Had the most catchy voice you ever heard. She could walk in a room and sneeze and everybody in that room would stand up and applaud, you know. She had the most catchy, beautiful voice. She used to sing around the cabaret. She'd hustle her butt. She was ornery as hell. Great, big woman. Fight like a tiger. So we roomed together for quite a while. Ralph and I.

Part of the time Eff would work. Part of the time she wouldn't work. She hustled Jews—old Jews. Come out of the room one mornin' and she's broke. She don't have any money. We called Ralph "Gob."

He's been in the Navy. He was a Navy man. She said, "Gob, I need a little money. I got to go downtown and see if I can pick up some change." And he said, "The hell with you. I won't give you anything." And they'd fight. They were always fightin'. I got 'em out of jail twenty times. She'd fight a circle saw—fresh filed. Anytime. At the drop of a hat. She was ready to go. She was ornery.

He was a flirt. Women liked him. He was a beautiful guy. Great, big blonde with a nice head of curly hair. Looked like it had been done in a shop, but it wasn't. It was natural, you know. Big, broad-shouldered, nice-lookin' guy. Every woman that saw him liked him. So he'd be sittin' at a table in a saloon—him and her and I or somethin'. And he'd start flirtin' with some woman over there. Well, very soon Effie would catch on. She found out who he was flirtin' with. And that was bad. She'd go over there and grab this woman by her hair—by the hair and just sweep the floor with her like this—back and forth. "Don't mess with my man!"

About every other week, he don't show up. He didn't sleep with her. He laid up with her, but he didn't sleep with her. He come home and slept with me. But if he didn't show up by 12:00, 12:30 Saturday night, I know he's in jail. So I get on the streetcar and I go down to the police station and I go in and here's Effie sittin' behind the police desk—the sergeant's desk back there, you know. She was half-drunk. They didn't lock her up. They'd lock *him* up. I come in the door. "Hi, Jonesie, you bastard! I knew you'd come and get us out of here! I knew that!" So I'd tell the sergeant, I said, "Get her buddy out of here. I'll put up the bond for 'em." I only had to put twenty bucks apiece for each one of 'em for appearance Monday morning. I said, "I'll get 'em out of here." I get 'em straightened out and I take 'em back where we lived on Archwood. But she thought a lot of me and I did of her. I liked old Effie.

They had a fight. Up on Main Street around Miller Avenue. Him and I lived in a nice room. Nice people. Old people. We had a room up there. So we go up there and we both shack up with her. And you could hear her makin' noise from here to the street down there. 'Bout four o'clock in the mornin', I said to him, I said, "We better get the hell out of here. I ain't gonna' let that old woman wake up in the mornin' and throw me out here. I'm gonna' get out of here right now." So we packed our suitcases and left. Two or three o'clock in the morning. Didn't owe any rent. Went down on Miller Avenue. A hundred and forty West Miller. We stayed there for some time.

Well, I guess I had two or three roommates there. Ralph left. "Hoolie" Wright moved in, my old friend. "Hound Leg" Owsley. He moved in. We finally got thrown out of there for havin' a crap game on the bed one Sunday mornin'.

I woke up one morning and they was shootin' craps on the foot of my bed. Three or four guys whom my roommate had gone out and got—a few of his buddies. And they come up there in the room and was havin' a crap game on the foot of the bed.

The old man come who owned the house and knocked on the door and I opened it.[8] He wanted to know what we was doin'. "What's goin' on up here in this bedroom?" And I said, "Well, we're playin' cards." We weren't playin' cards. We were shootin' crap on the bed. And he said, "Well,

Haskell A Jones and Florence Grace Jones, during their courtship.

I don't like this mob up here. You guys had better pack your suitcases and get out of here." So, we left. Where did we go? I can't remember where we moved to.

The next spring I guess I went home. And Florence was teachin' school at our old school down there in my neighborhood, see. So, one day I went to school before lunchtime— just "by accident," you know. I went in and talked to her. We got acquainted pretty good and I get a date and we begin to chase around together.

Jones School, Graves County, Kentucky

School at Jones' is progressing nicely under the management of Miss Florence Jones.

—"Hickory Route One"
The Weekly Messenger
April 15, 1918

Florence: The district that joined our home district was a good district to teach in, but I just wanted to teach where I didn't know so

Florence's Students at The Jones Schoolhouse in Graves County, Kentucky. (L-R, standing) Haskell's sister, Graces Inez Jones and Allene Kennedy. (L-R, sitting) Ola Jones, Opal Kennedy. Note the bell on tower to summon the students.

many of the kids. I thought it'd be easier. So I went to the superintendent's office and was talkin' to him about it and so he said that he didn't have a teacher at Jones. They wasn't rehiring the teacher they had had that year and— There was another place or two, but they were farther away from home. And at Jones School, I could drive down and come back on a weekend. Some of 'em [family members] would take me.

Haskell: It was named for another family of Jones. A man named Jones gave the acre of ground for the schoolhouse site on the corner of his farm.

Florence: My side of the Jones lived just about straight west of Mayfield and his [Haskell's] lived, I guess you'd say, northwest. So, I went down there and got that school.

You just had to look for somewhere to stay. You could ask whoever you had to make the deal with to teach if they knew where you could get a place to stay or stop at a house and inquire.

So then, when I went down to Jones School to teach, I had Haskell's sisters and brothers Mattie and Lillian and Grace and Tom and Henry goin' to school to me.

Haskell: And me.

Florence: Tried to teach you something. But I hadn't been able to do it.

Haskell: Us kids used to go to school and we always had apples in the

(L-R) Haskell's brother, Henry B. Jones and neighbor Neil Jones at the well of the Jones Schoolhouse.

fall—from early to late. My brother Tom, he went to school to her. These kids would stand there and slobber, watchin' us eat 'em. They bothered him. They'd want a bite. One day, Tom come to school with a big bag full of apples. Florence said she had to laugh. It was before school takes in, but while the kids were around there ready, you know. Tom just took this bag and stretched 'em out like he was throwin' 'em to hogs. These kids really went mad for them apples. Their people had lived there for generations and they don't have an apple tree.

We had apple trees my grandfather planted. He died in seventy-one and he already had an apple orchard, see. Today, you can go through that country and you look behind the house and you don't see an apple tree. You don't see anything. They raise wheat and oats and soybeans and whatnot, but they don't raise any apples.

Florence: The first year I taught, I stayed at home. And the next year, I stayed at Lena Scott's. Just her and her three daughters. Her husband was dead. But it was kind of a long walk. The road from there to school was pretty bad if it had rained or snowed or anything.

The next year, I wanted to stay closer to school at the Lassiters. I went to see if I could get a room with her because they lived right close to the schoolhouse and I knew a lot of teachers had stayed with 'em.[9] But she said, "I'm sorry, but I just can't keep you now because (this sister) is real sick and she's gonna' die at any time." But said, "When everything's over, you come back and you can stay with us then."

So, I stayed with Lillian and Clarence Jones and they was just as poor as anybody you ever heard of in life. But it was a place to stay. It was clean and what little they had to eat was all right. I stayed with them

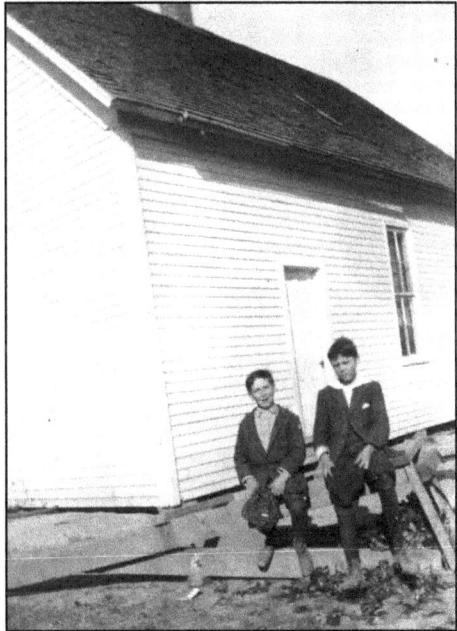

(L-R) Haskell's brother, Thomas A.R. Jones, and classmate Kevil Lassiter on the now fallen bell tower at Jones School.

until Miss Annie's sister died and was buried and she sent the word. I went back and stayed with them 'til school was out. And then the next year I stayed with 'em.

After this sister died, her husband came to school to see me. He asked me if I would let his son James go to school. He said, "He's not old enough. He's five." But says, "I don't have anybody to help take care of him."

Haskell: The father was Oscar Jones and his mother was Cordie Gossett.

Florence: He was doin' the cookin' and farmin' and everything by hisself. Some days the weather was bad and he didn't want him to have to follow him all the time. As a general thing, they didn't let kids go when they was five, but I told him to let him come and I'd manage. I didn't think he'd be any trouble and, like I said, he was a good child. So, he started to school just after his mother died when he was five years old. There was Ola and James and Neil—the three children. They was good kids. All three—the girl and the two boys both were real good children.

CHAPTER TWENTY-FOUR

PROHIBITION

Men who work the greatest number of hours per day seek in the use of their spare time, first, rest and then recreation that comes cheaply and easily—and the saloon usually furnishes the latter in the most effective fashion possible.

—Charles Stelzle
Why Prohibition! (1918)

Haskell: I believe Prohibition started on the 19th of July 1919, I guess. Eighteen or '19? I don't know. But it had been voted in, you know, and everyone knew about it.[1] So, for a few days before the end, the good saloonkeepers sold out and quit. You'd go in a saloon and they'd have market baskets—half pecks and bushel baskets. They'd set 'em on the bar and they'd fill 'em up. They didn't have fifths like they got now. They had quarts or pints. Two or three bottles of whiskey, some gin, gin rickey, rum and so forth. They'd stack this up and sell it to the highest bidder. They want to get rid of this stuff. They're goin' out of business. They got to clean up. And they cleaned it up. Some of us guys would go buy a bag of that and take it down and put it in the room. Gonna' last ya' for six months. It lasted about three days 'cause you'd have a lot of company.

Then, after they cleaned out the saloon and everything, they got rid of the beer dispensers and so forth— Then the old breweries started to make beer they called "near-beer." It was made under the same process only it had no alcohol. I don't know how they got it out. In fact, some of it I don't think <u>did</u> get it out. But anyway, they got away with it by labeling it "near-beer." Same size bottle. Same bottles, in fact. But they'd open up and have a cooler in there. They didn't have refrigeration. They had ice. Had a great big thing with fifty bottles of beer in it. Ice on it. Crushed ice. And they'd open a little— They called it a "cabaret." They had a dance floor and maybe they'd have a two-piece band or one of them ten-cent pianos in there. You could put a dime in and could dance around in there. And you could get a sandwich.

They had bootleg joints all over town. Everywhere. Guys I knew drank it. Once in a while, I'd take a little, but I didn't like it. Terrible stuff! I didn't like whiskey anyway. I didn't drink whiskey in those days. I didn't want any whiskey. I drank a little wine. I didn't ever care much for beer. Before Prohibition, I used to drink beer. I didn't drink whiskey in the saloon. I'd drink beer. I <u>have</u> got loaded a few times on booze, but it wasn't a habit or anything. But after Prohibition— The good saloon-keepers— The good, honest saloon-keepers (And there were a lot of them. Good businessmen), they quit.

John Bryer's

Haskell: Had one guy— I don't know what his name was, but his last name was Schaefer. At the time, there was also a champion pool player named Jake Schaefer.[2] They wasn't related and they didn't even know each other, you know. But they always called this guy "Jake" because of this similarity of names. Cross-eyed. Here's the pool table and he's shootin' over there and he's lookin' this way. He looks like an amateur, but he wasn't. He was a slicker. Dumb in a lot of ways. He was a hillbilly, too. But he'd go out and make himself a hundred bucks a day shootin' pool—hustlin' nine-ball or whatever it was with the hillbillies around there.

He'd go over to old John Bryer's, who had a gamblin' joint upstairs, and set down in a poker game and lose every nickel of it, see.[3] Didn't know any more about poker than a dog. Half the time (after a crap game broke up) he'd sleep on a pool table. He didn't even have a room. He made a hundred bucks that day playin' pool, but he hasn't got a place to sleep.

One night he goes broke in the poker game and he starts over to the pool table (They had a crap layout on the pool table, you know) and finds a quarter on the floor. So he shoots a quarter and he hits. He let it ride and hit. Let it ride and hit. Let it ride and hit. And it goes pretty fast, you know. Finally, he's got a hundred and twenty-eight dollars.

They had a ten-dollar limit. You ain't supposed to shoot over ten bucks, you know—unless you bring money. If you bring money and come in there and show your money, they'll let you shoot more. But if you come in there with your money in your pocket and shoot a quarter, they ain't gonna' let you shoot over ten bucks. So the guy that's dealin' dice there, he called the proprietor.

Said, "John, cross-eyed Jake just found a quarter on the floor and he's got it run up to a hundred and twenty-eight dollars." Well, they know he can't keep runnin' forever. He's gonna' lose it if we'd just let him. So old John Bryer said, "Oh, the hell with you. I'll shoot a quarter." And he throwed a quarter down and throws craps—for a lousy quarter. Dice jumped that high. He said, "Well, you lucky so-and-so." Well, old Jake went over to a poker game and lost it anyway. It didn't make any difference. But John probably didn't get it all. Some of the poker players got some of it.

There was a guy from over around Wingo—not in my county. Young guy. Evidently a mama's boy or somethin'. I don't know. Great, big bully of a kind of guy. He went up there and got in a crap game and lost his money. He left and come back, cryin' about losin' his money in there. And old John Bryer was a pretty good hunky. He said, "How much you lose, son?" Oh, seventy-five dollars or whatever it was. "O.K., here's your money. Now you get out of that door and don't you ever stick your head back in this door again. <u>Don't</u> come back in here! I'm givin' you your money back. You can't afford to gamble because you've proved you can't afford to gamble. You come up here cryin' for your money back. I don't question how much you had. There it is. Get out of here! Don't come back!"

So, he stayed away for a few weeks. And this is a stairway— You had to come up a stairway and come in— They had a peephole in the door so they'd know it wasn't the police or somethin' comin' up. It was a little off-color although the police knew it was goin' on. So one night this guy thought he'd sneak back up. Maybe old John ain't there or somethin', you know. John's workin' the crap game. He always kept a half a pool stick leanin' against his leg there so he could handle it if anybody grabbed the money or somethin'. This guy come there and knocks on the door and the guy at the door don't know the story and he opens the door and let him in. Old John took that stick and he threw it end first right at him and he stuck it in the wall through the lath next to his head. This kid went fallin' back down the steps. He never come back in there again. Old John would've killed him because he told him, he said, "There's your money. Get out of here. Don't come back. <u>Don't</u> come back."

Old John did pretty good. Had a lot of money. He wasn't a kid. Man, he must've been fifty years old. I don't know what nationality. He was a European of some kind. Hunky. Pollock. Romanian. Lithuanian. Dinf-fing. I don't know. But when Dempsey and Willard fought, he bet a mammoth amount on Willard. He lasted about two rounds with Dempsey and Dempsey knocked him out. He never could get— He never could get things goin'. It seemed to break his luck. Every time he made a bet he lost it.

He had a yen for some friend's wife. Him and this woman was evidently playin' footsie. Well, I guess she decided to break it up or somethin'. I don't know what happened. But he killed himself. Old John.[4]

Detroit

Haskell: Me and "Hound-Leg" Owsley went to Detroit once from Akron and rode freight backwards and forwards—both ways. He had the crookedest leg you ever saw. His [real] name was Dennis. Dennis Owsley. He called himself "Ol' Hound" just like everybody else, you know. He'd be talkin' about somethin'— He'd talked about "Ol' Hound" was doin' so-and-so. He was about as mis-made as they make 'em. I don't know how. We both had a job and we thought maybe we'd see somethin' big up there, you know.

[We] started to Detroit and we had to change trains over there at Carey, Ohio. We grabbed a train and I see way back down the line a cop get on the train—a dick. We're tryin' to hide and he finally comes up and we jump off—me and old Hound Leg. So we start up the railroad track runnin'. This guy's grabbin' at my shirt tail. He's that far behind me. And I'm runnin' like a bastard. So finally the cop fell down.

When he fell down, I went over the fence over in the field. There was a right-of-way fence along the thing. He didn't try to get over there. But I took off out through the bushes and old Hound Leg is right ahead of me and I'm beatin' his butt off tellin' him to run like hell, you know. So we got away from him.

That night we slept under a big poplar tree out in the field. It wasn't bad. That was summertime. It wasn't too bad. It was August, but at that time, it wasn't too cold. There was lime kilns— They burned lime up in that country. They dig this lime rock and they rack it up from here to that street down there. They put a lot of wood under it. Then they pile this limestone around that wood. Then they set it afire and they burn that. And that burns this rock. Then they put it in water and it breaks it up into dehydrated lime. They had lime kilns all along over there—a whole bunch of 'em. They were down in a field somewhere down there.

We went to Detroit and we come back and we rode with the same brakeman we rode up with out of Toledo. He said, "I thought you guys was goin' to Detroit." I said, "Well, we did. But we didn't like the town so we're goin' back there." And we're on top and it's cold. It's August, but it's cold. And he said, "Well, I'll tell ya', it's too cold to ride on top." Said, "When we get out of the railroad yard, stay on top 'til we get out of the puzzles (he called 'em). Then go back about three cars." Said, "I haven't got any empty cars on the train except a coal car with a flat wheel on it." Said, "But, get back there and you can get out of the wind." So we rode that flat wheel on in to Akron. I can hear it yet when I go to sleep. Thunk-thunk-thunk-thunk-thunk-thunk-thunk-thunk-thunk-thunk-brrrrrrr, like that. We finally get to Akron.

This guy that I'm with is a big b.s.er. He'd never rid a train a whole lot. A little. Now, I hadn't either—as far as that's concerned. Not a lot. And I told him, I said, "When we get back there to South Main Street, I'm gonna' get off this train." Ahh, he's a smart-ass, you know. He said, "You'll get off and fall down. I'll get off and stand up." I said, "Well, that'll be fine." I said, "I'm gonna' get off. I don't care how fast it's goin'."

Well, it was goin' too fast. When we hit that crossin', I dropped off and I bounced and I landed on my knees in the cinders. But I got off anyway.

He don't get off. He's hangin' on the car behind me on the side. So I [go to a] restaurant where we ate all the time. I could go in there and get a meal anytime. I didn't have to have the money. I was a regular customer. So I went in there and ordered myself a steak and some potatoes and whatnot. I was hungry. I hadn't had anything to eat to amount to anything. In about forty minutes or an hour, he come back.

He'd gone clear downtown to Exchange Street 'til the train slowed down. Then he got off and walked back—from there to South Akron. We lived there by the Firestone Bank, at the corner there. We lived right next to it. I said, "I thought you was gonna' get off and stand up, sucker." He said, "I saw what it did to you and I didn't want any part of it." I sure bounced, I'll tell you. That thing was goin' faster than I thought it was. That was before I married. That was August nineteen-nineteen, probably—before I went home.

Mrs. Shelton

Haskell: Times got tough and I didn't have much work. So, I roomed with some people. Gladys and Jim Wooldridge. His mother was Mrs. Shelton. A very nice "lady" type woman. Real nice old lady. She was not a kid. Not young. This was embarassin'. I had a hole in the seat of my pants. As big as a cue ball. They're worn out. Mrs. Shelton said, "Haskell, I believe you've snagged your pants. If you'll pull 'em off, I'll fix 'em. I'll fix that place." They weren't snagged. There was nothin' to snag! They were worn out!

It was cold wintertime and I went to the poolroom one day. And "Jimmy the Greek"— Jimmy run the poolroom. And a prince if one ever came out of Greece. He was a dandy. He monitored and advised every young guy that came in the poolroom to behave themselves and look like a gentleman—which he was, you know. He didn't like rough tough. He didn't let the kids drink too much. He didn't want gamblin'. He was strictly a "do-gooder"—in his words. A nice guy. And I liked him very much. Went in there one cold day and Jimmy says, "You got an overcoat?" I said, "Nah." He said, "I got one hangin' in the back of the poolroom that's been here for four or five months. Somebody left it. Why don't you go get it and try it on and see?" And I went and got it. It's beautiful. Big, loose overcoat with raglan sleeves—what they call 'em. Big, loose sleeves. Beautiful coat. Dark. Dark with some kind of figure in it. Some stripe or somethin'. I don't remember. He said, "Take it. It's been hangin' here for months. Whoever— Might be in the army or be in Chicago or be here." Said, "They didn't come back after it."

So, I took it and I was a little leery. 'Fraid some guy'd walk up and say "Whadaya' doin' with my coat on?" So, we had a tailor. He had a cleanin' and pressin' shop and made clothes. His name was Harry Haberman. I had bought some clothes from him. Had a business near Miller and Main by Firestone Bank.[5] Catty-cornered across the street. So, I took it down to Harry. And I said, "Harry, I've got this overcoat. A guy give it to me, but I'm a little leery about it because I don't know where it come from. He said it'd been in a poolroom for months and he give it to me. What it cost me to get it dyed?" I think it was three dollars, in those days, he said. Labor was cheap. It didn't cost much. I said, "O.K." So, he dyed it solid black. A real good dark color. It was a lovely color. I wore that coat three or four winters. It was lovely. But it covered up the hole in the seat of my pants. I could get by Mrs. Shelton without her seein' my ass, you know.

CHAPTER TWENTY-FIVE

MARRIAGE

Haskell A Jones. His appearance had changed considerably from the time he stepped off the train in Akron in 1917 to the time he mailed this photo to Florence during their courtship in 1919.

Haskell: I was writin' to Florence in 1919 all the time. I was livin' at 140 West Miller when we was makin' our romance heat up pretty good. And we was writin' pretty hot letters. Sometimes the mail would smoke when they brought it in the buildin'. I was a pretty good bullshitter. I could lay it on pretty thick. She was kinda' gullible. She believed it, see. It wasn't necessarily so.

I went home in the fall then and— Well, the first of December. We were gonna' get married and I went home 'bout— I guess I got home about the 15th and I'd made up my mind I wasn't gonna' get married. I don't know how to get out of this— this contract we agreed on, you know. I think, "Well— If I can— I don't know if I should do this. I'm broke and what the hell? I ain't got nothin'"

Ah, I went down to see her on the night before we married. But she insisted we go ahead with it. So I went ahead with it. The best I could. Did all right. And she was glad and I was glad. I was walking back from where she was staying over to my home, which was a short distance. I only had one single dime and I threw it away. Borrowed enough money to get married on and come back to Akron. Been broke ever since! I borrowed seventy-five dollars from my sister and her husband. We got married and I got enough to get back to Akron on.

I got home about the 15th of January, I think. Her school was out the 16th and we got married the next day—after school was out.[1] The roads was atrocious, I'll tell you. They were terrible! Terrible. Terrible. The day I married, my brother Ralph took me to town to meet Florence and I'll tell ya', I almost had to swim a horse through mud-holes. My God, they was that deep with mud! January and the farmers been haulin' tobacco to market and the roads would freeze every night and thaw every day. Oh, boy! Oh, boy! Nobody can believe how bad the roads were. Nigel and Ed Tucker went with us. Nigel was a Sullivan, but she was Ed Tucker's wife. Nigel was used by both men and women. They married when she was about sixteen. Went to school to Florence. Pretty little girl.

But it was so bad I wouldn't go by the house and pick Florence up. She met me in town because the roads were just so bad. It was out of my way to go to her house by several miles. She said, "I'll meet ya' in town." In fact, she didn't want her folks to know she was gettin' married. She was stealin' the march on her folks. They had no idea she was gettin' married. I'd never been in her house. They didn't know me from Adam. I wrote to her all the time. But most of the time, she was away teachin' school. Her sister knew about it. I guess Fanny went with us to get married. She met us in town. But she was teachin' school down on the Tennessee line. She catched the train, comes back into Mayfield.

We got married in a farmhouse out in the country. Country preacher. We went to town to get married and they were havin' a big funeral and all the preachers had gone to the funeral. They was buryin' the mayor of the town.[2] He'd been mayor for some time. Quite prominent man in a little town. All the preachers went to the funeral so we couldn't find a preacher. We got a cab and the cab driver was supposed to take us to find a preacher and he went a half a dozen place and he couldn't find none of 'em.

Finally this cab driver said, "I know a preacher out here in the country that will do the job." And I said, "Well, that's all right as long as we can get the job done." So, we drove out there two or three miles. This farmer was down in the barn workin' the tobacco and this cab driver sent the kids down there and brought him up. We told him what we wanted and he said, "Well, I'd better clean up and change clothes." And I said, "No, don't worry about that. You can do it just as well with overalls on as you can with any other thing and we're behind time now." He said O.K. So, he married us with a pair of overalls on. Cost about four dollars. Two dollars for a license. Two dollars for a preacher.

His name was [Thomas] McNutt. We got a marriage certificate here somewhere that's got his name on it. Didn't work very good. We've only been married fifty-nine years [At the time of the recording]. His son's name was Haskell. Haskell McNutt.[3] That's how I remembered. I remembered he had a son by that name. My mom knew. My dad was dead, but my mom and all the kids knew.

Florence: Well, I didn't tell mine because I knew Dad wouldn't like it because I was older than him.

Haskell: She was marryin' a kid.[4] If you'd told him you was adoptin' a kid to raise, he might've put up with it. No, she was old enough to get married. She was twenty-two years old—old enough to make up her own mind. But she didn't tell 'em. She thought they'd beat her if they found out she was marryin' a guy younger than she was.

Florence: But I didn't tell 'em. I knew if I got married and went home everything would be O.K. in a few days. Or weeks. And it was.

Haskell: Yeah, he always treated me right. I never could complain.

Florence: He always thought lots of Haskell.

Haskell: Her mother and I got along real good. We were buddies.

Florence: My brother Kermit said Mammy said that George [sister Frances' husband] was Daddy's son-in-law and Haskell was hers. But Dad liked him after he got to know him. But he never said anything in the world against him only that he was "just a kid"—as old as I was. Dad was ten years older than my mother and George was about that much older than my sister Fanny. So, I thought, "Well, I know after a few days everything will be fine and I'll just not tell 'em." So, everything went O.K. They was kinda' shocked

Haskell: I let her go in and tell 'em. I didn't go in the house. Her brother Joe come out and was gonna' take the horse out and put it away in the barn so I helped him unhitch the horse and put it away. I had actually slept with Joe

(L-R) Florence's brother, Kermit E. Jones, neighbor Thelma Duncan and brother Barton A. Jones.

the night before. He came down after her on Thursday evening and stayed all night with me. After her school was out Friday afternoon why, he took her home. That was the end of school, see, and he took her clothes and everything she had where she was boardin' and took her home.

But I had told him on Thursday that I was goin' back to Akron pretty soon and said, "Why don't you go back with me?" He said he had some tobacco to strip and I said, "Well, I might come out and help ya'." So, when he saw me, he thought I'd come to help him strip tobacco, see. So, we put the horse away and, in the meantime, her and Fanny went in the house and spread the news.

Well, when Joe and I went in they were all hugged around a big coal fire, you know. Florence just introduced me as "Haskell" all the way around. She didn't say, "This is my husband." She was afraid to say that—hadn't got used to that yet. And, so, nobody said anything. Well, Joe's in the dark. He don't know from beans about it yet. We set around there for an hour and he don't know we're married. He don't know nothin' about it. Mrs. Jones got dinner ready and she come out and said it was ready. And said, "This isn't much of a wedding supper, but it's better than you deserve for not lettin' us know." Joe's ears went up and his eyes got big and he got up and eased in the kitchen and he said to his mom, "Are they married?" He didn't believe it.

Florence: They had never seen him, but they liked him from the beginning. The only thing Dad didn't like was that he was a "kid." But Haskell would go out with him and help him hitch up the horses—do

227

any little thing he was doin' out— He thought he was pretty nice. Then he had to come to Akron to get a job and go back to work because if you'd leave and wasn't back by a certain time, you was out of a job and you had to get another one. So, he went to— What, about a week after we married—

Haskell: Yeah, week or ten days. Somethin' like that.

Florence: —you went back to Akron? Might've been two weeks but it was about a week. And then it begin to kinda' be talked

Haskell and Florence Grace Jones, sometime after their wedding on January 17, 1920.

around behind my back they thought he had left me.

Haskell: Well—

Florence: Two or three different people asked my sister Mary, "Has he left her already?" Said, "What's the matter?"

Haskell: I hadn't abandoned her. I just left her.

Florence: Mary said, "Nothin' in the world the matter." Said, "He's just got to be back for work by a certain time so she's gonna stay home with us a little while and then she's gonna'—" So, that was the end of that. A friend of Haskell's was comin' home. His wife was sick. I guess she'd had a baby and they lost the baby. So, Haskell wrote and told me that Harvey Chester was comin' back home at a certain time— for me to be ready and come back to Akron with him when he came. So, I came to Akron—

Haskell: —with another man.

Florence: —with another man.

Haskell: Yeah. Made a good story.

CHAPTER TWENTY-SIX

LUCK

Florence: At the end of two years at Jones School, we got married in January. I was going to make that my last year in school because Haskell didn't want me to work anymore—that he wanted to make a living for us. He went back north to get a job.

Haskell: My brother Ralph came with me and he got a job at Firestone where I was workin' when I left to get married.

Florence: Well, that was fine, but then him and Ralph got laid off the summer after we married. We didn't have a dime and no way of making any.

Haskell: There wasn't any jobs! You couldn't buy a job if you had money cause nobody wanted anything done. It was right after World War One and they had an overproduction and everybody was loaded with merchandise.

Florence: We went back to Kentucky. We went home.

Haskell: Yeah. We all went back together. They were layin' off whole shifts, you know. I guess I asked for it. I didn't have much service 'cause I quit when I went down to get married and come back and hired in again. Ralph got laid off and I went to the foreman and I said, "My brother got laid off and I know I don't have much service. How much more time I got here?" He said, "Not a helluva' lot, I'll tell ya' that." I told him, "Why don't you lay me off, then, and I'll go on home with him—if I'm gonna' get it anytime soon, you know."

Florence: When we got home, we went to somethin' in a church, I believe it was, on a Sunday afternoon and wondered what in the world we were gonna' do with neither of us doin' anything. And here, who should walk up was the trustee of the school that I had taught two years. He says, "Oh, Miss Florence, I'm so glad you're back." Says, "You come back to teach our school again, didn't you?" And I said, "No. I guess not. Haskell says he don't want me to work anymore since we're married." And I said, "Well, it's time for school to start. Don't you have a teacher?" "No," said, "I have three applicants and I wouldn't let either one of 'em teach in our school if we don't get a teacher." Says, "What about you comin' back? Said, "The children all get along good with you and I know they'll all like to see you back." I said, "Well, we'll have to talk to Haskell." And about that time he walked up.

So, I talked to him and he said, "Well, you know I don't want you to teach again!" I said, "I know you don't. But look at this." I said, "You don't have a job. Ralph don't have a job. Nobody else to work. Granny [Haskell's mother] don't have anything." And I said, "I am not going to stay here and eat off of her!"

She was just as poor as they ever come and depended on what Haskell and Ralph made with the farm there until Haskell got old enough that he left home. And he wasn't makin' enough to help too awful much. But she got by from rentin' what little ground she had.

I said, "You and Ralph don't know when you're gonna' get anything to do and I know I can make enough to keep us. I think it'd be a foolish thing for me to turn this down." He said, "Well, I don't want you to teach again, but if nothin' else 'll do ya', go ahead this year." I said, "Well, O.K., I'm goin' to teach." So, that was it. I taught school the first year we was married. And if I hadn't, we wouldn't have had a dime to go on for a few months.

Haskell: She said, "Can I teach?" I said, "If we want to eat you'd better."

Florence: I stayed with Granny there and with the rest of her kids and taught school and that fed us 'til we could manage to get something.[1]

Haskell: We would've went to the poorhouse. The war had been over some time, but they had over-produced, in this country, about everything. They had a surplus of everything and they just quit producing anything 'til it was used up. The country really — Labor had a rough time in '19— The fall of 1920 and '21 was rough.

Florence: We didn't make very much teaching school at that time.

I believe the last year I taught I made seventy dollars.

Haskell: Eighty-six!

Florence: Eighty-six?

Haskell: Eighty-six dollars. I remember it quite well. It didn't make much money, but it fed us. Fed the whole family. It fed Ralph and the girls and everybody else. It fed all of 'em because she was the only one that had any money comin' in, see. It was bad. But eighty-six dollars would buy a lot of stuff in those days.

I'd buy a twenty-four pound sack of flour for thirty-five cents. You could buy three cans of salmon for a quarter. Pink, three cans for a quarter. Red, two for a quarter. Food was so cheap. You can't believe. But we didn't have much money to buy it with. That was the hell of it. It didn't make any difference how cheap it was unless you had a little money. Nah, it was pitiful. It was terrible.

Florence: I guess it was about the luckiest thing that ever happened to us was them not havin' a teacher at the school and runnin' into that head of the school and that gave him a chance to get out and look for somethin'.

Haskell: I wanted to come back to Akron. I always wanted to come back. When we left here, we was making pretty good money. And down there, you wasn't making anything. So I was anxious to come back.

PART THREE

THE ROAD WEST
1920

CHAPTER TWENTY-SEVEN

"THE LITTLE DEPRESSION"

Every time the clock ticks off a minute enough tires to equip seven and one-half automobiles are made in Akron. It took less than five months to swing tire production from a stage that was dwindling to a rate even lower than that of 1913 to the "Tire every two seconds" gait now in effect, says the B.F. Goodrich Rubber Company.

One may perhaps more easily visualize the magnitude of Akron's tire production by a comparison with Detroit. Akron makes tires enough in one minute to equip all the cars turned out in Detroit in seven and one-half minutes. This is based on recent reports from Detroit, which say that the city is now back at the old automobile-a-minute stride.

And now Akron is getting ready for even bigger expansion. She is preparing to meet the full demand of the tire buying American public with a production schedule that will eclipse all pre-war records. The transition from a war basis, when dirigible balloons, gas mask, army rubber boots and raincoats were turned out in tremendous volume, was made in Akron without a dent in the remarkable industrial organization of the city.

Unlike many other cities, Akron has a distinct labor shortage. This sign near the entrance of the Goodrich employment department characterizes the situation: "We have a job for all returned soldiers and sailors." Intense activity in building homes to care for the workmen needed to fulfill the labor needs of the city is substantial evidence of the prosperity ahead for "the world's rubber center."

"Akron Hangs Up Tire Making Record"
Hardware Review, February 1920

Croakers warned—an omen!
"The boom is outboomed—it can't go higher"
"So we thought five, ten, fifteen years ago," said the old residents. "But now we're easy. This is a permanent boom. It will never stop."

"The City That Blew Itself Up"
The American Mercury. February 11th 1926

Anticipating a great peacetime rush for goods which were no longer restricted and undeterred by the loss of wartime government contracts, the rubber industry fully extended itself following the war—and so did the city. Or, as *The American Mercury* would later ruefully comment, "Akron got drunk."

"Seldom has any city in the world's history experienced such a condition of expansion as that which held Akron in its throes in 1919 and 1920," *A Centennial History of Akron* would note.[1] Construction had hit a new high in 1919 with 6,891 building permits being issued valued at more than $600 million—nearly half of which was required for new housing as people poured into the city at the rate of 1,190 per month.[2]

Envisioning a boom that would last forever, The Chamber of Commerce developed an extensive plan of growth for the city with new schools, parks, and thoroughfares.[3] The *Akron Beacon Journal* was filled with full and even double-page ads offering readers the chance to buy into new housing developments—each more exceptional and offering better services than the one before. Neighborhoods which still define portions of the city today such as Silver Lake Estates and the Wooster Avenue Allotment were just being developed, as were dozens of burgeoning dreams of development—including Victory Park, Forest Hill, Martin Heights No. 2, MaGennis Heights and the Maplehurst Allotment.

If one was not of a mind to speculate in real estate (or had already purchased their piece of the dream), they could also speculate in the rubber industry itself. Equally large and spectacular in their promise were ads offering stock in the yet-to-be-built (yet already successful, if you were to believe the ads) rubber companies such as The Cleveland Rubber Corporation Company (offering "The Wonder Stock")[4] and Akron Maderite Tire and Rubber.[5] Their promises certainly sounded good—especially when all you had to do was read the paper, drive around the city or talk with your neighbor to know how well rubber was doing. In fact, by the spring of 1920, the employment rolls of the existing rubber factories had reached an all-time high of 70,000.[6] The boom looked and sounded like it would never end.

"From every part of the country an avalanche of orders descended upon the rubber plants, by letter, telegram and phone. The demand for tires was beyond all reason. Motorists begged for them; dealers grieved when their orders went unfilled for a day or so. No one complained about prices—the only thing demanded was quantity."[7] Goodyear, the largest rubber company in the world at the time, proudly boasted that they had "sold more stock to employees than any other corporation in the United States, with the exception of the United States Steel Corporation."[8]

As orders from the Far East took some two to four months to arrive, a constant six-month supply had to be ordered in advance—even though customers could cancel orders with just a phone call.[9] At Goodyear, the largest rubber company in the world at the time, "Fabric requirements were three million pounds per month at $1.50 per pound, and a workable inventory was a three-month supply."[10] To meet this demand, Goodyear began commercially producing its own cotton for sixty cents a pound at a 37,500-acre plantation in Arizona and locked in long term orders for rubber at fifty-five cents a pound.[11] Lauded for his foresight (even as he emptied the company treasury in exchange for production inventory, expansion and dividends), company founder and president Frank Seiberling made a cool $20 million profit before rubber and cotton reached their peak prices.[12] Trying to remain competitive, Firestone was attempting to do the same. Then, with millions of dollars in commitments outstanding, and no established relationships with larger New York finance houses at either Goodyear or Firestone, the bottom fell out.

Nearly a decade before the Great Depression hit, Akron (and the United States as a whole) first had to weather what would subsequently be called the "little depression."[13] While many have heard about the "Roaring Twenties," no one remembers the devastating economic downturn from which the country had to roar back to make those years possible. Whether the cause was a surge in the civilian workforce as troops returned home, overproduction, tighter monetary policies or the lasting effects of the Spanish Flu, the result was the largest drop in industrial production during any recession since 1873, the greatest drop in wholesale prices since the American Revolution and the most extreme one year period of deflation in 140 years of United States economic history.[14] Industrial production fell by 30 percent and automobile production declined by 60 percent.[15] The effect on the tire industry was devastating.

Almost overnight, consumers stopped buying, the orders ceased. And the layoffs in the rubber industry began. Eighty-three percent of the city's manufacturing workforce had been employed in the rubber industry in 1919 reaching a record high of 73,490 rubber workers in

From the purely image oriented ads Goodyear had run before the recession (Pg. 164), the once great company was forced to defend its value and quality in ever more descriptive ads. Finally, in its struggle to survive, Goodyear was forced to advertise that it was slashing its prices with the most basic price/item ads (all c. 1922).

April 1920 (out of a total adult population in the city of 152,050.[16] By March of the following year, nearly 54,000 workers had been discharged from Akron's factories.[17] This represented an astonishing 46 percent of all adult, head-of-household names listed in the City Directory for the combined area of Akron, Kenmore, Barberton and Cuyahoga Falls in 1920.[18] By the time the next City Directory was printed, over 31,000 of them would no longer be counted among Akron's population.[19] Those that remained turned to the only full-time occupation that remained: "On the sidewalks of the City of Opportunity stood beggars in $18 silk shirts putting the bee on passers-by for a thin dime. The boom was over."[20] The elaborate City Plan envisioned by the city fathers was shelved.

At Goodyear, in particular, the impact was devastating. Seiberling could only watch with horror as the price of rubber crashed from fifty-five cents a pound to ten cents. And cotton fell from $2.50 a pound to as low as 12 cents a pound.[21] "Rubber brokers, fabric mills, equipment manufacturers, and other Goodyear suppliers wanted their money. Banks recalled their loans."[22] With little in the treasury, the great Goodyear faced bankruptcy. The New York financiers (who had once been shunned as "pirates") took control. And Seiberling was forced out.[23]

At Firestone, company president Harvey Firestone eliminated 73.9 percent of his workforce, ordered remaining salaries and wages cut by 10 percent and reduced company expenses by 78.7 percent.[24] Accompanied by a massive advertising campaign that stunned the competition, he also slashed tire prices by 25 percent to quickly generate sufficient revenue for the company to survive. In doing so, Firestone was a good month ahead of its competition—while simultaneously giving the company an opportunity to completely clean out its existing inventory of tires with the outdated

> **20%**
> **Price Reduction**
> **on Goodrich Tires**
>
> Endorsed by Users and Dealers
>
> The decisive reduction of 20% on the prices of Goodrich Silvertown Cords, Goodrich Fabrics and Goodrich Inner Tubes, which took effect Monday, May 2nd, received the endorsement of both tire users and dealers throughout the country.
>
> It was accepted at its full face value as a helpful economic move in tune with the times.
>
> It conforms to present conditions and carries out in a straightforward way constructive merchandising methods.
>
> Goodrich Tires have earned their reputation and standing with motorists by sheer quality of construction and complete dependability of service. Quality in a tire rests not only upon the materials of which it is made, but also upon the experience and skill of its makers.
>
> Every advance in construction and improvement in making, with many exclusive betterments, is in the Goodrich tires you buy today.
>
> Your Goodrich dealer is ready to supply your needs.
>
> **The B. F. Goodrich Rubber Company**
> Akron, Ohio

"Non-Skid" tread design. At the expense of thousands of employees put out onto the street, sales boomed, reaching an all-time high of $115,000,000—even while the devastating write-downs on the value of inventory eliminated all possibility of profit.[25] The other major tire manufacturers soon followed suit, slashing prices anywhere from 10 to 30 percent. Consumers could now purchase tires nearly 15 percent cheaper than they were before The United States entered World War I.[26] Harvey Firestone would later look back and note, "Although I date the foundation of the company historically from 1900, I regard the first twenty years only as a period of preparation for the real test of 1920. A business is not a business until it has been hardened by fire and water."[27]

Across the country, some 100,000 businesses went bankrupt as profits plummeted by some 75 percent. More than 450,000 farmers lost their land as the price of agricultural products fell by as much as 40 percent, never to fully recover again.[28] Almost overnight this recession had turned into one of the most devastating in U.S. history.[29] Some 15 percent of the total workforce in nonagricultural industries were later estimated to have been thrown out of work without the benefit of such modern-day niceties as unemployment insurance—although this number is only an estimate as no entity was keeping track of the actual numbers.[30] In September of 1921, Secretary of Labor James J. Davis would make an attempt to humanize the disaster by noting, "that according to the best estimate that could be made there are 5,735,000 fewer men, woman and children on the payrolls than there were in March 1920."[31]

Today, it would be called a severe recession. While that terminology didn't exist in 1920, it was then merely reckoned to be a financial disaster.[32] This, in a time when the husband was usually the sole wage earner—and families depended upon him for their survival. Among those forced to find any means to survive were Haskell and Florence Jones, who fled Akron to his home in Graves County, Kentucky, when his well-paying job in the rubber industry disappeared. As she could teach school in a one-room schoolhouse to pay the bills, she could help his mother and six siblings survive. He nearly didn't.

CHAPTER TWENTY-EIGHT

THE CLAY PITS

"There are several pits of potters' brick and tile clay in the county, which are being worked with profit. Vast quantities of this clay has [sic] been shipped to the East for the manufacture of ironstone china, fancy tiling, etc. A plant at Mayfield is manufacturing a very superior and handsome brick from clay found two and a half miles east of that city."

"Graves County"
The Commercial History of the
Southern States Covering the Post-Bellum Period

Florence: I guess it was about the luckiest thing that ever happened to us was them not havin' a teacher at the school and runnin' into that head of the school. That gave him a chance to get out and look for somethin'. After a while, Haskell and Ralph got a job working in the clay pit. That didn't last very long.

Haskell: I dug clay for three dollars a day in a pit about twenty-five feet deep. Maybe about forty feet long and thirty feet wide. Then they'd move over and dig another one. The clay pit was potter's clay that they dug out of the ground. The vein of clay was quite thick—anywhere from twenty to forty feet.[1] We skinned the top off of this clay, gravel and red clay with a team—slip scraper. Then they went in there and dug that clay by hand with a mattock and a short-handed shovel and shelved the bank—made ledges along the bank. As they went down they'd leave a shelf. You'd stand on this one and throw it on that and he'd throw it back on the other one and they finally got it up on top. If you don't think that was hard work, you're wrong. They didn't have any machinery. They just done it all by hand, see. The hard way.

Then they loaded it on wagons and trucks and hauled it to the railroad, about three miles away, and dumped it over there. They had a platform alongside the loading dock and you went in there with a dump wagon.

The whole truck bed would collapse. You could break it down, spill this stuff out on this platform. You had two-by-fours all across the bottom. They weren't fastened. They were free. They were just loose in there. They had a cleat on each side where they fastened on the wagon, so they wouldn't slide each way.

Had sideboards—maybe twelve inches wide. And one on the front end. One on the back end. You'd pull the sideboards off and a lot of it would spill out. Then you'd start at one side and turn these two-by-fours over and just set it up on edge. In the meantime, it's falling down on this platform beside the boxcar. Then you pulled away and they shoveled it into the car.

Some other crew loaded it into cars and then they hauled it to a factory where they used that potter's clay for various insulators, pottery, crocks, jugs, and even some good porcelain made out of some of it. So, it was man-killing work. Paid thirty cents an hour for ten hours a day. But, there wasn't any other work. So, that was better than nothing.

They did shoot some of that, once in a while, with dynamite. They'd hit a hard streak in the clay and they couldn't dig it with a mattock. So, they'd put a charge of dynamite in there and break it loose where they could have an edge to work on.

I used to do that kind of work. You'd take an iron bar and you'd keep at that 'til you got through and get down in there. You had to be a little cute, too. If you got it too deep, when it exploded, it'd just make a pocket down in there like a hornet's nest. If you got it too close to the top, it'd blow a few pieces out of the top and it wouldn't break it up. So you had to kinda' be able to figure out the consistency of what it was—whether it was really hard or half-hard or whatever.

I was skinning top with a team of mules and a friend of mine, "Stud" Wilkerson, was loading the truck right beside where I was working. This layer of clay had gravel on top of it. About ten, twelve feet of gravel on top. We had to move that off before you could get into the clay.

Out on the edge was a box half full of dynamite. Had a package of caps and a roll of fuse laying on top of the dynamite and a box of parlor matches. Fifty pounds, I suppose was in a box. I don't know how much. It's a *very safe*, *very safe* way to work. And they shot this dynamite— Somebody shot it. It wasn't me. And it blew a lump of clay, a small lump, out and up in the air and it come down on that box of matches and set 'em off.

Well, I looked and old Stud was loadin' his truck. I said, "Get the hell out of here, Stud! The dynamite's on fire!" And I hollered down in the pit. I said, "You guys, don't come out! Stay in that hole! The dynamite's on fire!" I busted these mules on the butt with a "buttline", we called it, took off down the— I was two hundred yards from there when the dynamite finally went off. Knocked one of the mules down. The boom and the shock, you know. Didn't do much damage. It was on top of the ground and it blew some gravel in the hole. It made one helluva' noise, though. Whoo!

Florence: You dig in that clay— Sometimes it'll fall on you if you're not pretty careful. Haskell's brother Ralph bruised one of his hands. Had the awfullest time. Had blood poisonin' and had to have his hand operated on.

Haskell: Had blood poisoning. Boy, his hand was as big as a country ham. Uhm! Black as heck. I fed him aspirin like givin' him peanuts. I asked the doctor, I said, "How many aspirin can I give him? He's sufferin' death with that hand." They'd lanced it, see, and had a great pussin'. "Oh," he said, "he's young and got a good heart. You can give him quite a few." Man, I gave him about two every hour. Poured the doggone aspirin to him and kept him knocked out 'til the pain kind of subsided.

They never had any antibiotics. They didn't shoot anybody with a needle or didn't even give ya' anything. Sulfur molasses or quinine was about all they could give you. Aspirin. But they put a poultice of some kind on it. Nah, there was people down there that lost arms or legs for no reason at all because they had no idea what to do with 'em— with a thing of that kind, see. Terrible. Terrible.

Florence: Ya' don't know what might happen. Haskell almost got hurt. The bank caved in and almost caught him. Well, after that happened, he quit. I didn't blame him 'cause there was always someone gettin' hurt in there.

Haskell: A big chunk of dirt fell off of the top from about thirty feet up and come down right beside of me. A chunk about— Weighed about one hundred pounds. The edge broke off. It was in the fall and it was soft. I figured that was enough.

Florence: Somebody had told him there's a lot of work out West and if he'd go out to a certain place he could get a job. So, he told me if I'd let him have enough money to get tickets, he wanted to go out there. And I said, "Well, if you feel sure you can get a job I'll let you have enough."

Haskell: She gave me money. Forty, fifty, seventy-five dollars. I don't know how much.

Florence: I let him have the money to go on and we didn't hear from him. We didn't hear from him.

Haskell: There wasn't any work! When you got out there you found out you couldn't buy a job if you had money cause nobody wanted anything done. It was right after World War One and they had an overproduction and everybody was loaded with merchandise. Farm products went down to nothin'.[2]

Florence: Granny [Haskell's mother] and me, both, worried to death. And Ralph hadn't got able to go back to work. He was really sick. That blood poisoning had got in that hand and had to have it split and everything. So, we was both beginnin' to really worry.

CHAPTER TWENTY-NINE

THE ROAD WEST

Fort Smith

Haskell: I went to Memphis on the Illinois Central and then I got on the Rock Island and then I went through Arkansas into Oklahoma and various stops and everything. I don't remember all of 'em. We rode Rock Island on the freight comin' back.

Couldn't get a job. You couldn't get a job if you had the money to pay for it. Nothin'. Ooooh! The only jobs I could get that was offered was the one job carrying timbers out on a bridge about a half a mile high across a river and another one pickin' cotton.

Construction of Albert Pike Bridge, Fort Smith, Arkansas (Fort Smith Museum of History).

I went from Mayfield to Fort Smith first of November. They was buildin' a bridge across the river there. That bridge was about two hundred feet above the river and what they wanted was men to carry timbers out on that bridge. They did it by hand. They get a big board and you'd get on one end and I'd get on the other and you'd walk out on this thing, see. Three dollars a day for ten hours. That didn't look very good to me.[1]

244

The farmer told me he'd give me the cotton if I'd pick it and pay him three dollars a week for board. Before pickin' cotton, they'd turn the cattle on it and let the cattle eat it. It just wasn't worth anything. Farm products went down to nothin'.[2] That was in Oklahoma somewhere. Down in Oklahoma City, I think.

I ate dinner in Fort Smith, Arkansas with some people name Miller in 1920. On Thanksgiving Day. I was in the depot studying the timetable and figurin' out where I was goin' and a man passed by and I noticed his hand. He had a finger— One or more off. Well, I looked up at him and I knew him His name was Rollie Frey and I'd known him here [in Akron] and I knew of him before I came here.

Him and his twin brother had been put in a lodge home of some type that his father had belonged to. Rollie and Roy. That was their names. When his father died, they had some kind of a plan that the lodge would take the boys and raise 'em and teach 'em a trade. They had learned the cabinetmaker's trade.[3] In the meantime, he stuck his finger in a saw and cut some part of his hand off. I think it was just one finger. I don't remember.

So, I stopped him and we talked and he said, "Where ya' goin'?" And I said, "You know as well as I do. I don't have much idea." "Well," he said, "you wait a couple days and I'll go with you." Said, "I'm buildin' a table for my aunt and when I get that finished, why, I'll go with you wherever you want to go." So, I said O.K. I hustled pool (I was a fairly good pool player) durin' the meantime and he told his aunt that I was there and was a friend of his. So, anyway, when Thanksgiving come (a day or two), why, she invited me to come and have dinner. So I had dinner with 'em.

I saw the table which was really somethin'. His uncle worked in a furniture factory and he brought home scrap off various types of wood. Exotics and every other kind. Everything that they had. Snow white and blood red and black and everything of that kind. And he'd brought these little scraps home for years. So, his uncle had woodworkin' machinery and Rollie took these scraps and fitted all these things into a checkerboard design. It was an octagon library table some three feet across. Beautiful thing. Beautiful. He had it all done except some varnishin' and rubbin' out the lacquer or whatever he put on it. So, he got it done and we took off.

Oklahoma City

Haskell: Well, we got off the train in Oklahoma City. It was an old wooden depot in those days just like a freight shed. In fact, the freight shed was on one end and the depot was on the other end. I looked down along the platform and I see a guy standin' all hunched up with his hands in his pockets and his back towards us. And I recognize him.

I said to Frey, "You see that guy standin' down there?" They didn't know each other very well, if ever. He said, "Yeah." I said, "That's Reed Douthitt." He said, "Might be, but you couldn't tell it from here if it was." "Well," I said, "I betcha' that's him. Let's walk down." We walked down and here's old Reed standin' down there. I knew of the family and I'd seen him before he came to Akron. His father was sheriff down there and my father was on the County Board of Magistrates.[4]

The Rock Island Station, Oklahoma City, Oklahoma.

Turns out somebody'd stole all his clothes. Work was bad and he'd gotten a job on an oil-drillin' outfit somewhere from some employment agency or somethin'. He went back to his room and asked to get his clothes and somebody'd stole everything he had. So he was stuck. He didn't have much money and no clothes and he was in bad shape. So he didn't go to the job.

We milled around together for a few days and Frey got a job. He had an uncle there who was workin' for some oil company and he got a job paintin' oil tanks, railroad cars and the rest. Me and Douthitt hung around Oklahoma City. We couldn't find anything to do. You couldn't work if you worked for free. They didn't want you. Didn't want anything done.

So we go to the railroad depot and a cop come through and threw me out. Said, "You got a ticket?" "No, sir." "Well, get the hell out of here. You can't sleep in here." So some old bum saw the guy throw us out. Said, "You guys got any money?" "Well, we got a little, but not much." Said, "You can buy a ticket over here to Saint John's (or whatever the name of the town was) for thirty-five cents. You buy yourself a ticket. Stick it in your pocket and anytime he comes through here and says, 'You got a ticket?' 'Yes, sir!' 'O.K.' That's all there is to it. You can stay there for three weeks on it. You don't have to catch the train. You can stay here as long as you got that ticket in your pocket."

He spotted that we was "greenies." We didn't know this deal. But he's an old-timer. So we could sleep in the chair back in the waiting room in the depot. It wasn't too bad in there. It wasn't too bad. Had a little heat. We'd go in there and sleep 'til morning and go out and get something to eat and go look for a job. We was lookin' for work all the time. We wasn't just bummin'.

They was havin' a big manhunt in Oklahoma—a "womanhunt." I can't think of his name to save my life. She had the same name although she was a distant relative. She wasn't very close. They'd been shackin' up together. She worked for him as a secretary. He was married to some other woman and she'd been playin' footsie with this guy for several years. I guess he was supportin' her and so forth as well as her wages. But he got a big idea of being a candidate for some government office. Vice-President or somethin' of that kind. I've forgotten what it was. So, he had told her she'd have to cut out and stay away from him. Well, she didn't like that. After he fired her and told her to scram, why, she went in his office and shot him. Killed him. She disappeared and they was lookin' for her when we got to Oklahoma City. This happened in El Reno, which is near Oklahoma City. Not too far away. I don't know just exactly. She— She gunned him down.[5]

Went to one place. Big Smith. I can remember that guy. A.I. Smith.[6] They were a big wholesale hardware out of Oklahoma City. So we went in there one day and they showed us in to the— I'd guess you call him the manager or the president of the company. He said, "Sit down. Sit down, boys." He was as broke as we were. There was no work.

We told him what we was lookin' for and he— He'd never been anywhere. He was born and raised there and he'd never been anywhere. He didn't know anything about the rest of the United States personally. So he begin to ask us about where we'd been, what we'd done, here, there and whatever. And we'd covered the waterfront. And he was interested in it. He talked to us and he was nice. Finally he opens a big box and gives us a cigar—which I didn't care anything for because I didn't smoke cigars. But I smoked it tryin' to get a job.

He takes us around the various departments. Shippin', this, that and the other. Mammoth big buildin'. Said, " Could you give a guy or two a little job down here around the—" "No, my God, Mister Brown (or Smith or whatever his name was). We're layin' men off now. We don't <u>have</u> any work." "O.K." We go to the next place. Same story, you know. We went to half a dozen different departments around there. "Well," he said, "boys, I'm sorry. I'm sure you're sorry. But if you'll keep in touch, I'm sure this thing will break up some day. I'd like for you guys to work for me. I like your looks. I like your attitude. And if you're still available when things begin to pick up, contact me and I'll see what I can to do give you a job." I said, "I don't know where I'll be." And Reed said, "I don't know where I'll be either.

They weren't hirin' anybody for anything. We bummed around there and this one night we were gonna' sleep in a freight car. We didn't realize what was in there. It was bales of cotton. And that cotton's all over everything on a bale of cotton. They wrap it with a burlap and it's got as much on the outside as it has on the inside almost. It sticks to everything. Lint. We got woolen clothes on. Next morning we looked like two sheep. Good sheep. Lot of wool. Man, all morning we're

"Cotton Compress, Oklahoma City, Okla." The open freight cars filled with bales of cotton offered a comfortable place to spend the night for free—if you didn't mind a little extra work in the morning.

pickin' ourselves like we was lousy, you know, tryin' to get the dadgum fuzz off of us.

I slept under trees. I slept out in the field. I slept in various places when I bummed on the road. Well, you had to do the best you could.

Little Rock

Haskell: We bummed around out in that country and finally wound up in Little Rock, Arkansas. We had a little cheap hotel room somewhere. I was readin' the paper lookin' for a want ad for somebody wantin' somethin' done. Douthitt went out and prowled around and come back and said, "I talked to the Navy recruiter down there and I'm gonna' join the Navy." His folks lived at Jackson, Mississippi. They had moved from my area.

I said, "What the heck you goin' in the Navy for?" He said, "I ain't gonna' get in the Navy." Said, "I come out of the Army with a sixty percent disability of heart trouble in World War One. I know I can't pass the examination." Said, "I can go to Great Lakes, Illinois or New Orleans." Choice. You got a choice for final examination. " I know I won't pass. So I can ride a cushion from here down to New Orleans. Then they'll give me a ticket home from there. "

He said, "How much money you got?" I said, "I ain't got very much." But he'd been workin' out there in Oklahoma some and he give me three or four dollars. I don't know what it was. Said, "This will feed you, maybe, 'til you get home." We walked out to the bridge and went across the river out there. I'm goin' out to catch a freight. We don't have no more money to buy tickets with. We had shipped our clothes to Memphis from Oklahoma City by Express.

He said, "When you get to Memphis, you go to the Express office and transfer my clothes to my dad in Jackson, Mississippi." He gave me the address and so forth. So I did. The next time I heard from him he was in Pearl Harbor in the Navy. He'd passed the examination. He stayed in the Navy two years for a train ride. He could've walked home in two or three days.

So I get out there and I look the situation over. Here's the railroad runnin' down here and over on that side is a hobo camp. They had a fire back there and fifteen, twenty guys there, anyhow. This train is gonna' come this way. So a young lad comes up and he don't know what's goin' on, either. He wants to put in with me. "Can you help me?" and so forth. He wanted to go to Poplar Bluff, I think. I said,

"Well, you stick around with me. But, I'll tell ya', we ain't gonna' catch a train here because there's about six railroad dicks out there walkin' up and down on that side over there." They were worried about those guys in the hobo camps—not so much for us. That was Rock Island. That road was rough. The cops was mean. They had a railroad detective that rode the cars and he'd kick you off or shoot you or do anything. He was a mean bastard. Called him "Rock Island Slim."

There was some cotton gins along this side of the railroad. Three or four of 'em. So we come up behind the cotton gin. I said, "Now, when the train comes, those guys are gonna' try to get on that train, but these cops are gonna' stop 'em. So we'll be over here in the boondocks and we can get on." I told 'em, "Hang on the side. Don't go on top 'til you get away from here. Because they can't see you if you're on the backside hangin' on the ladder. Just hang on there 'til you get a mile or so down the tracks and get out of sight. Then we can get on top. We get in and stay hid as quick as we can. Get in a coal-car or somethin' and stay hid." Finally, a freight comes draggin' out of there. We nailed the side of it and go up in the coal-cars and go down and get hid. We looked back and the cops are gettin' on the train. It's a long train and way back down there, they're gettin' on the train. I said, "Stay hid! Stay hid! Stay down!" And we stayed down.

We got in a car, me and this kid. We had to crawl in the end up in here and get down in there It was open. We climbed in that and I got afraid. It was loaded with carpet. It probably was five-foot thick carpet—just laid in there one on top of the other. Nine by twelve or whatever they were. We laid in there and toward morning I begin to get the jitters. I said, "They catch us in here, we're gonna' be in trouble." I tried to stay out of local jails. I didn't want to get in them.

I don't know how far we went. Two towns ring a bell. One of 'em was Bald Knob, Arkansas. And the other one was— I don't know. We come to a place where he wants to get off and go over to Poplar Bluff, Missouri. I lost him. So, he was a nice kid. And younger than I was. Hadn't been around the world like I had.

I come into this one town. I don't know what it was. The train stops. It was Sunday night. It was gettin' late. I met a guy on the street and I asked him where to get cigarettes. Said, "You out of cigarettes?" I said, "Yeah." You couldn't buy 'em in Arkansas. You could buy papers or tobacco, but you couldn't buy cigarettes. Legally. Everybody sold 'em, but you couldn't buy 'em legally. Said, "I work at the insane

asylum, but odd times I work in this pool room here and barber shop."
So he went down, opened the job and gave me two or three packs of
cigarettes. Wanted to know where I was goin', how much money I had.
We had a long conversation.

Finally he said, "I know the train crew." Said, "They'll be in here

The Van Noy Railway News and Hotel Company, Newport, Arkansas—just north
of Bald Knob on the Missouri-Pacific Railroad.

in a half an hour or so. They always hang up here and come in this
restaurant and get something to eat." He said, "Come on down and I'll
buy you some food." We went down and he bought me somethin' to
eat. They had a restaurant in a railroad depot in those days. [Van Noy
Railway News and Hotel Company]. He wanted to know which way I
was going. I told him. He said, "Train crew will come in here in a little
bit." Said, "They're goin' to Memphis or that direction." Said, "I'll put
you in the engine." He evidently knew these guys, see. I don't know
how, but he did. Maybe it was a regular thing. So, he said, "I'll talk to
the train crew."

So, when they came, they made a food stop there. Freight train.
Come in and get a coffee and sandwich or whatever. He went over and
talked to them and said, "This guy's goin' east." Said, "Put him in the
engine when you get ready to go." They said, "We need somebody to
pull down coal."

When they got ready to leave, I was right there and they said to ride up in the engine. "Young man, you're gonna' have to pull down coal 'cause we're just about out." I said, "O.K." That was a job. They was gettin' low on coal. The tender is kind of long, you know, and they're generally firin' out of the front end of it all the time with fresh coal. They had to go, maybe, seventy-five, a hundred miles and they'd used all the loose coal in this place. I had a pick and was pickin' that coal that was as hard as concrete almost. Some of it had been in there for twenty years, I think, all run together. I picked it down and shoveled it up to where the fireman could throw it in the boiler.

He let me try it. I didn't do very good. It was a pretty tricky job for a grunt. You have a foot pedal and you put your foot on that pedal. The boiler's door is controlled by air or steam, whatever. I don't know.

One of the trains operating in Arkansas on the Rock Island Line at the time Haskell made his return trip. Chicago, Rock Island and Pacific 1889 Camelback, former Choctaw, Oklahoma and Gulf, 101 Vauclain Compound. Built by Baldwin in 1901, photo taken June 1910 (Collection of Harold K. Vollrath).

Pressure. You put your foot on here and those doors would fly open. You throw the coal in and they'd slam shut just instantly. You didn't watch, they'd catch your shovel—like they did mine a few times. Ahh, I got to where I could throw 'em in there a little bit. We finally got to a place where they could get some fuel and I had that coal tender swept out pretty clean, I'll tell you. There wasn't much left in there.

What the heck? I didn't mind that. But they were good to me. If you kept yourself clean when you're "on the bum," you know, why, look halfway decent— Well, you don't have much trouble. But if you're dirty and crummy, why, then you're— You're in trouble. Nobody wants you. Not even the bums.

Bald Knob

Haskell: The next stop I get off the train, a place called Bald Knob, Arkansas. Why, we coasted in there with no coal in that thing. I cleaned it out. Just clean as a pin. They went coastin' down in there to where they get some coal. But that's where I picked these two kids up, I think. Yeah. They're goin' somewhere else. They ain't goin' my way. I pick up two young lads. Sixteen, seventeen, eighteen years old. Didn't know the way— Didn't know east from west. They knew nothin'. Hungry and starvin'. Don't know any more about bummin' than Adam knew—not as much.

"Where ya' goin'?" "Portsmouth, Ohio"—which is way up on the northeast part of Ohio. They had gone to Saint Louis in a brand new Ford lookin' for work, got broke, didn't have any money. Didn't hock the Ford. They put it in storage so they could come back and get it. They were tryin' to beat their way home. And they knew no more about beatin' your way home than your mother knows. No more. No more.

So I took 'em under my arm and I said, "When'd ya' eat?" It had been three days. They hadn't had a bite. Nothin'. I said, "Well, I'll get you somethin' to eat." And this railroad yard, they had one of these little railroad restaurants where they have 'em for the train crews and so forth. "C'mon." So I go in and we sat down. I said, "What do you got to eat?" Well, this, that and the other. "Got any beans?" "Yeah, got a great, big—" She had a pot that big, that deep full of beans. Soup beans. I said, "Well, give these guys all the beans they can eat." I said, "I'm gonna' pay for it, but I can't buy steaks. And I'll take a dish, too." They had a little other stuff with it. I don't know what.

Well, the one guy— I can remember him like yesterday. He drank six cups of black coffee before he started to eat. Why it didn't kill him, I don't know. He hadn't eat for three days. It should've killed him. It didn't seem to hurt him. So they get filled up. We went out and finally we caught a train. We went on in to West Memphis. And we got off and walked across the bridge—across the Mississippi there out of Arkansas.

The brakeman tells me, "Don't try to go across the river. Get off on the Arkansas side, see, and walk across the bridge." He knew we were ridin'. He didn't care. He was a good guy. They wouldn't let you ride across the river on a freight train. They'd shoot you on a railroad goin' across the river. I don't know what the hell was the difference, but you couldn't ride across the river. There was a footbridge or traffic bridge across for railroad and automobile traffic, too. So we walked across the bridge.

"The Great Bridge and Train at Memphis, Tenn." If you were on good terms with the engineer, you could ride in the engine and shovel coal. But you always had to walk across the bridge on the Mississippi.

CHAPTER THIRTY

MEMPHIS

Haskell: When I got to Memphis, I went to the Express office and went down there and re-routed Douthitt's clothes and shipped mine on to Mayfield. Two pair of socks and a change of underwear and one shirt probably. I don't remember. It didn't cost much. It was all I had, so might as well send it. Wasn't very much, I'll tell ya', in those days. Boy, times was tough.

We don't know where to go. I know I want to go north on the Illinois Central, but I have no idea about Memphis. I've never been in Memphis only goin' through there the other way on a train and ridin' a cushion. So I got to find out where we go to catch a train. I don't know. We were down to the nub. So we go up on Main Street and we got a sandwich or somethin'. Cup of chili or a bowl of soup or somethin'.

Old colored boy— They always knew the way to get around. I said, "Hey, Pop!" We want to catch the Illinois Central out of here goin' north. Where do we catch it?" "Well," he said, "you got streetcar fare?" I said, "Yeah, we got streetcar fare." He said, "Catch the streetcar that goes to Hollywood."[1] And Hollywood's way out here in the boondocks. River bottom. It's a little establishment at the end of the car line, see. Said, "You get off the streetcar there and you walk straight ahead. Right down that road about three-quarters of a mile and you come to a railroad crossing in the valley down there where two tracks cross—one east-west, one north-bound." But I didn't get the information about which was north and south. So we got on the

255

streetcar and went down there.

It's in November. It's black as hell. There ain't a star. There ain't a moon. There's no buildin's. There ain't nothin' or any people livin' out there. Woods. Jungle. Swamp. River-bottom. There's nothin' only railroad crossings out there. A row of leaves alongside. And these two kids are tired. They are worn out by the nubs. They pile up in these leaves and go to sleep instantly.

I'm standin' around there and finally a train comes. They always have to stop and flag these crossings, you know. They don't just barrel across. Stop back there seventy-five, a hundred feet and the flagman, I guess they call him, he comes down and looks both ways to see if they can go ahead with no interference. I went up to him and I said, "Sir, I want to catch the Illinois Central freight goin' north. Which one of these tracks is north?"

He just stuck up his hands and said, "Get away from me, buddy. I'm afraid of you." "O.K." And I turn around and I'm surrounded by about six guns. These railroad dicks was down there and I didn't see 'em. I don't know where they came from. But they had guns all over me and then I was the guy who put the hands up.

Kills Jailer; Escapes With Pals
Posse Closely Pressing Bandits
George Reeves Dies After He Wounds Slayer

George Reeves, county jailer is dead and three gunmen and safe blowers—known as the "dandy bandit" trio—are at large pursued by every available officer in the city following a sensation but hurriedly planned jail delivery at the county jail Tuesday shortly after 11 o'clock . . .

The News Scimitar
Tuesday, November 30, 1920.

Haskell: They're lookin' for a bunch of outlaws that had escaped from jail. Somebody had smuggled 'em a gun so they had a jailbreak. They'd had a shootin' match out there. They killed the jailer and his daughter and the deputy sheriff. These guys were loose in the railroad yards and we come wanderin' in there cold turkey. We don't know from nothin' and we get a hot reception. We're lucky they didn't shoot us down right there and then ask questions 'cause they were scared to death—the officers were. And they had a right to be.

So they were pretty decent except one old buzzard about seventy-five years old. He was an ugly son-of-a-bitch. He was scared to death and he began to abuse me. I hadn't done anything to him. I showed

Receipt and Waybill Tag From American Railway Express. While these didn't belong to Haskell, they would have been the same ones in use at the time.

'em who I was. I'd shipped my clothes out of Oklahoma City I'd shipped my clothes by Express. I had a receipt for it. And there wasn't any question about who I was. I wasn't one of the guys they was lookin' for.

He kept wavin' that gun under my nose and cussin' me out. I'm a stupid guy. I finally boiled over and told him if he'd throw that gun away I'd run him out of that river bottom. Then I thought he *was* gonna' shoot me! One of the other guys said, "C'mon. C'mon." Said, "What's the matter with you? You got the jitters. Put that gun in your pocket. He ain't doin' anything." And he said, "Who's these guys?" They had never woke up. They was exhausted. "Oh," I said, "a couple of kids I picked up over in Arkansas. They're on their way to Portsmouth, Ohio. They was destitute and I'd fed 'em a little and brought 'em this far and gotten 'em on the road." Well, he went over and kicked one of 'em and said, "What are ya' doin' here?" He scared 'em to death. They jumped up and started to run and I

"Posse Closely Pressing Bandits."
The Memphis *News Scimitar,* Tuesday, November 30, 1920.

thought sure he was gonna' kill 'em.

I slapped the gun right down. I thought sure he was gonna' shoot that kid in the back. I said, "Don't shoot that kid! Hell, he's only a kid." I hollered at the kid. "C'mon back here!" So he come back and the old guy searched them. They had their receipt for their car.

Burnished Gun Barrels Greet Scribes on Trail of Escaping Murderers.

. . . A reporter from The News Scimitar and four other men, were in a Cadillac automobile conveying the officers over the Horn Lake road. The newspaper men seemed to travel only a few miles behind the news and in various towns which they passed through, they were taken for the bandits. The word had been flashed ahead that a Cadillac car containing the bandits was speeding through the swamps in the direction of Tunica.

Hit Sixty Miles.

At 3 o'clock the press car, driven by Johnny Gammon, owner of the 529 Taxicab Company, from which the bandits got their getaway car, came to the Delta highway and for the first time in two hours they were able to make any speed. Gammon opened the car and within a mile of Tunica it was tearing along at 60 miles an hour.

As the flying car crossed the corporation line at Tunica, the occupants saw a Ford touring car parked along the roadside, and from the rear end of the Ford protruded the glistening barrels of a half dozen rifles and shotguns. Gammon barely had time to bring his car to a stop before Sheriff Cox, of Tunica, and five deputies leaped to both sides of the highway and had covered the machine with their guns.

The Cadillac was brought to a standstill while the hands of every man in the car, excepting the driver, were extended skyward.

The sheriff and his posse closed in on the big machine, but after careful scrutiny of the occupants, decided that they were not the ones he was looking for. . . .

The newspaper men then proceeded into Tunica to wire back to Memphis for news of the bandits . . . .

The big Cadillac, however, was still identified as the bandit car and at almost every little village on the highway it was halted by armed posse.

The News Scimitar reporter was carrying a camera, and this, in the majority of instances, identified the occupants as everything but bandits.

While well on the home stretch and about a mile north of Lakeview, the front right tire of the Gammon [car] received a puncture. Three of the occupants walked back into Lakeview to telephone into Memphis for a service car. As they walked into the general store at Lakeview they were met by the proprietor and a six-shooter.

The proprietor said later that he was ready to start the fireworks immediately had the newspaper men and Gammon acted suspiciously.

The News Scimitar
Wednesday, December 1, 1920.

Haskell: So after they finally checked the kids, I thought they was gonna' lock us up. I didn't want to go to jail. I wanted to go home but I knew he was kind of touchy. So finally, I said, "Well, I don't care if we go to jail." I said, "Maybe we'll get something to eat. We haven't had anything for some time." Said, "You won't get a helluva' lot in there." I said, "Well, we ain't gettin' any out here." He said, "You want to walk out of here?" I said, "Nah, I'm ready to go to jail." I wanted to walk, but I don't want him to know it, see.

He said to these two kids, he said, "You want to walk?" Said, "Yessir." "Well," he said, "that railroad heads north Get goin' and don't look back." I stood there. I think they're goin' to put me in jail, but I ain't too sure as I cared. So finally he looked at me and said, "(So-and-so) you— You go, too. And I *hope* you look back." He wanted to shoot me, you know.

So I took off and we wore our shoes out walkin'. We walked twelve miles up that railroad and it's dark as ink. It's November and there ain't no lights from one end of that road to the other. Twelve miles we walked to the next little town. You can't imagine how dark it gets in that wintertime in that river-bottom. Timber all around. Um-uh! I wore my shoes out walkin' up that railroad. If you ever had rough walkin', buddy, that's it. The ties are set together at the wrong space to step two and too short for one. It's the most miserable place in the world to walk. If you could see and get out on the side, it wasn't as bad. But you couldn't see.

When we got up this twelve miles these kids was hungry. There was no place there. It was a little old town. Lucy or Millington, one or the other. They were close together. And I said, "Well, you kids are hungry." I said, "There's a work train right over there." Big string of work train cars where they kept these guys on the track. They fed 'em, slept 'em, did everything else. They had boxcars all lined up and ready so they could live in 'em and they had a cook's car.

I saw the big colored guy standin' in the door over there with an apron on. I said, "Now, I'll tell you kids— You don't know how to hustle." I hadn't too far to go yet. I can make it. I said "You go over there and tell that cook you're hungry and you want something to eat." They're scared to death. They're afraid to go over and ask him. I said, "Go on!" I said, "You ain't gonna' get back to Portsmouth, Ohio, without hustlin'. You got to hustle a little. I got to tell you how." "Well, he don't know us." I said, "He don't care. He's had a lot of bums. He's fed a lot of 'em." I said, "You go over there and tell him you want something to eat and that you're hungry and he'll give you something to eat."

So they went over there and in a little while they come back and they had almost half a pork shoulder. Great big hunk of roast pork, see, and half a loaf of bread. And they sat down and they was gonna' eat it all. I said, "Wait a minute. He put the bread in the bag. Make yourselves some sandwiches and put 'em in the bread and put it in the bag and don't try to eat it all at one time. You got a long ways to go yet."

I said, "I ain't goin'. I can't take care of ya' any further than where my home is"—which is only two hundred and fifty miles or somethin' like that. I said, "You may be on the road for two more weeks and you'd better make yourself some sandwiches."

You had to be respectful. You didn't go up and be brusque like you was demandin' somethin'. You act like a gentleman. You didn't have to cower and feel like you was smashed down. But you— You approach the people in a reasonable manner with a politeness and they was mostly cooperative. They'd give you somethin' to eat if they had anything. You couldn't go up and be demanding. But these old cooks on the railroad shanties, they're used to it. Every day some bum comes by for somethin' to eat. And it wasn't their food in the first place. Had plenty of it. They didn't hesitate.

I don't remember which one was first, but I think we caught the train out of Millington straight to my home. So, when I got off the train at home, I had three cents left. I said, "Here, I got three pennies. I'll give you one, you one, and I'll keep one." Said, "Just for luck maybe. I hope you'll get home." Never saw or heard of 'em again of course. I never knew whatever happened to 'em. Whether they got there or not. I hope they did. But I got those kids through there. And I hope to God they got home all right. I've thought about 'em a million times and wondered how they made it. 'Cause I couldn't do anything for 'em. I didn't have any money and I wasn't even full of information. I was a "greenie," too, see. But I sent 'em on their way and I hope they made it.

Jailer's Slayer Killed In Gun Battle
Slain Murderer and His
Captured Bandit Pals
Pals Captured Without Fight By Winona Men
Gun in hand, Clyde A. Hamilton, gunman and bandit, murderer of Jailer George

Reeves, was killed Wednesday at Winona, Miss., in a pistol battle with officers. Alden Shaw and E.B. Kelly, companions in the "dandy bandit" trio, who escaped Shelby county jail Tuesday, after the fatal shooting of Reeves, are in custody in Winona, and will be taken from there Wednesday afternoon. Their destination is unknown.

Hamilton fell wounded four times. Sheriff R.F. Smith, of Montgomery county, and City Marshal Joe Glenn, of Winona, each fired two shots, inflicting wounds any of which would have proved fatal. Lying prostrate with two bullet wounds, Hamilton raised his gun arm and fired a single shot at the two officers. Glenn's pistol then spoke twice and Hamilton fell back. He died within a minute.

"Jailer's Slayer Killed in Gun Battle."
The Memphis *News Scimitar*, Wednesday,
December 1, 1920.

No difficulty was experienced in capturing Shaw and Kelly, both of whom were in a coal car during the firing. They were not armed.

One of the two men taken confessed, according to Sheriff Smith, that they escaped with Hamilton from the jail here. This statement, the sheriff added, said that the dead gunman fired the shot which ended Reeves' life . . .

Mary Dodd, 17-year-old telephone operator of Winona, first saw the bandits and tipped officers of their presence. The trio had gone to the home of her father, H.R. Dodd, and asked for a drink of water. Miss Dodd had been reading descriptions of the escaped trio in newspapers when a knock came at her door.

She answered. She recognized Hamilton. But she coolly furnished the men with water. Then she telephoned Sheriff Smith and Marshal Glenn, when the three departed.

Hasten to Yards.

Hurrying to the railway yards, Smith and Glenn came on Hamilton as he was boarding a coal car. His companions were already aboard. The officers asked the men what they were doing and who they were, adding a question about the killing of Reeves. Hamilton exclaimed that they knew nothing about the occurrence here.

"We will search you, anyway," declared Smith as he grabbed Hamilton.

The bandit jerked free and reached for his front trousers pocket, pulling a pistol, barrel up. The sheriff and Glenn drew and as Hamilton squared away with his pistol. Smith fired twice. Hamilton fell.

It was then that Hamilton duplicated his feat of Tuesday when, lying prone, he fired a single shot which brought Reeves' death. Hamilton fired once. Sheriff Smith said he could not say whether this shot was directed at Glenn or himself. Both officers were together and within four feet of the dying yeggman. The bullet did not touch either.

The News Scimitar
Wednesday, December 1, 1920

Haskell:　　When I come back into Mayfield on the freight I went down to a fellow I knew. Marcus Greene. He was a telegraphic operator and hotel night clerk. I went down and borrowed a couple of bucks from him and went to a restaurant and got a meal. I hadn't had anything to eat.

So I walked home that night from town eight miles in the drizzlin' rain. It was muddy. Ay-yah-yah, yah-yah. I'd walk a mile and pull up under a bush or tree alongside the road and rest a little while and then I take off again. I got home about midnight, I think. One or two o'clock. It was in the middle of the night. My feet were that big and almost that wide with that mud all over 'em.

Florence:　　I heard somebody knock on my door 'bout midnight or past—after we had worried so. And I thought, "Well, I know that's got to be him comin' home because nobody else would be knockin' on this door." So I went to the door and sure enough, it was him. Feet loaded down with mud! You never saw shoes with such a hunk of mud on 'em! I'm tellin' you, his shoes, each one of 'em would, probably weighed at least ten pounds. And it was rainin'.

So, he pulled off his shoes. And I said, "Why in the world didn't you get a cab to come home!?" He said, "Well, I didn't have any money to come on." Said, "I've spent enough of your money so I was gonna' get home the best way I could." So, he found his way home by "hookin'" himself onto a train. When he got off the train at Mayfield, he started walking home and he walked all the way. If he'd just got a man to bring him home— But he wouldn't do it 'cause he'd already spent so much money— He'd worked his way home that far— Boy, he was tired and give-out.

Haskell:　　Florence and I had the back room where we lived there at Mom's house. She said my brother Henry— I was Henry's father, almost. He'd never had one, see. Dad died when he was a little tyke

262

and he always followed me. I took care of him. And he loved me. He wanted to wake me up. He wanted to wake me up so bad. Florence said, "No, you're not gonna' wake him up. He needs sleep." I slept 'til about five o'clock in the afternoon.

PART FOUR

PADUCAH, KENTUCKY
1921

CHAPTER THIRTY-ONE

THE "MELTIN' POT"

The location of Paducah makes this city one of the most important inland ports in the United States. Geographically, few cities of Paducah's size in the country can boast a more ideal situation. At the mouth of the Tennessee river and only 12 miles below the mouth of the Cumberland, Paducah is the terminus for two great rivers which flow through some of the richest agricultural and mineral land in America. The city's location on the Ohio, and her proximity to the Mississippi, make her a central point along a thousand miles of waterway which links the coal and oil fields of Virginia and Pennsylvania with the southern corn and cotton belt . . . .

Paducah is a central point on lines which link several of the largest cities in the middle section of the country. By rail, Paducah is only a few hours from St. Louis, Louisville, Memphis, Nashville and Chicago. A night's ride and the traveler out of Paducah can reach either the lakes or the Gulf. The city's wholesale territory reaches out for 150 miles in all directions. Paducah is the retail hub of a territory including more than a hundred thousand people, her stores drawing trade from both sides of the Ohio for a distance of fifty miles east and west.

"Did You Know These Things About Paducah—Your City?
Get Acquainted With the Place You Call Home and Appreciate It."
The Paducah Evening Sun
Tuesday, October 25, 1921

Despite a nationwide recession, the only employment challenge in Paducah was actually finding people who were willing to work. As the *Evening Sun* noted in its August 22nd edition, "One Paduchan made an effort last week to get a hundred workmen for a special job, and went up the Tennessee river to obtain them. Not a single man was interested in his offer. In fact, a little less than two months later, *The Paducah Evening Sun* could only find a total of 110 people among their readership who *were* out of work—or "about two-hundredths of the total population."[1] It wasn't that they were all gainfully employed in Paducah's wholesale or retail trade. It's just that they had a different concept of commerce. They were all involved in making moonshine."[2] What's more, as a result of this bustling, albeit largely underground economy, Paducah was in a near constant state of transition as visitors passed through its busy terminals even as its products passed over their lips.

During the year and a half that Haskell and his brother Ralph would work there, the newest dance craze, "the shimmy," would be seen on the paddle-wheel steamboats plying the city's waterfront—even as it was banned in the (perhaps) more refined city of Louisville. The first women to ever sit on a jury would have the opportunity to witness the first "colored" attorney to ever act as defense counsel in the city—who, incidentally, won the case.[3] And the city's "Negroes" would be allowed to celebrate Emancipation Day by holding their first fair—to which the city would donate $100 and proclaim the day an official "Negro holiday." "In the opinion of officials, as well as leading Negro citizens," *The Paducah Evening Sun* proudly noted, "the first Negro fair will constitute a progressive step for the race in this section of the country."[4]

Haskell Jones viewed the city as a "meltin' pot." If so, it was an unbelievably stratified one in which everyone "knew their place." The newspaper article about the first woman juror and the first black attorney to appear at a public trial was not celebrated but buried on page 5. The first Emancipation Day Fair blessed by the city fathers was offset by the city's first annual Paducah-McCracken County Exposition a little less than 3 months later ("A Brilliant Spectacle . . . Thrown Open For Public's Inspection")—to which the city's "colored folk" were only belatedly invited "at their request." And only after it had been open 3 days.[5] And only on their own special day at the end of the event so they would not mix with the white citizens. "The Negro citizens of Paducah will have a day and a night at the building for themselves," the *Sun* helpfully noted, "and their day will be Monday." To further ensure the separation of the races, *The Paducah Evening Sun* even went so far as to publish advertising for the event headlined, "Notice to White People" followed by an accompanying notice "To Our Colored Patrons."[6]

In one regard, however, Haskell was absolutely spot on. The world in which he worked was perhaps the one place in the city in which everyone freely mixed every day—whites, blacks, criminals, conmen, revenuers and bootleggers (or "leggers," by which they were commonly referred).[7] That was on the streetcar line of the Paducah Railway Company, on which he, his brother Ralph, and friend Rudolph "Stud" Wilkerson found employ.

In much the same manner that the *Sun* warned fairgoers against the mixing of the races, however, management first attempted to warn them away from employment because of the color of those with whom they'd have to associate. Persisting in their pursuit of employment, they were indeed hired—but only after an equal number of those same "colored" workers were fired to open the new positions.

The Paducah Railway Company[8]

Florence: After Ralph recovered from the accident at the clay pit and got so he could do anything, him and Haskell went to Paducah and their uncle gave 'em a job on the streetcar tracks. I stayed with Annie Lassiter until school was out because Granny [Haskell's mother] and Haskell and Ralph and the whole bunch moved to Paducah.

Haskell: Went out West and took that "sashay" and didn't find anything. Come back home and this uncle of mine (married my aunt) was the superintendent of track construction and maintenance. I never thought of it. Until I got desperate, then I thought of him, see. Always tryin' to hope my way into somethin', you know.

I said to Ralph "I'm goin' to Paducah and see if I can get a job from [Lovett Bryant] Uncle Love"[9] and he said, "Get me one, too." Well, he had a friend who had a T-model truck who had been working in this clay where we'd been workin'. Fella' named Rudoph Wilkerson. And he said, "I'll go with ya' if ya' can get me one." So Wilkerson and I drove down there in his truck between Christmas and New Years and I went to see my uncle. I said, "I need some jobs." And he said, "Whadaya' mean?" I said, "I don't want just a job for me. I want one for my brother Ralph and this other guy. I want three jobs." And he said, "You don't want to work out here on this track with these n-ggers!"

Florence: That's what they said then.

Haskell: I said, "We ain't got no privilege. I got to work wherever there's any work. It doesn't make any difference." I said, "I— I've got to have a job. It's the end of the year. The wife's school is out (would've been in a few days) and we've got to have some work." Things were tough, man. You couldn't buy a job.

This was his answer (now this is history), he said, "When do you want to go to work?" I said, "Yesterday." He said, "Well, how about Monday?" I said, "That's fine." We'll be here." And he said, "Well, I'll lay some of these n-ggers off and give you a job." Now you think that don't happen. That happened down there whenever a colored boy was in the way. He got laid off and a white guy got the job.

"Broadway—Looking South on Ninth." Road crew building trolley tracks, Paducah, Kentucky, 1906.

We lived in a room and started workin' for the streetcar company. We had a few dollars left. Florence had a payday or somethin'. And we managed to eat and all that. Then here come the rest of 'em. Ralph come down and got the job and there ain't anybody there at home to make any money anymore. So he agrees that Mom and the girls ought to come to Paducah and he rented a house and they brought 'em up there and they lived there 'til '24.

This Wilkerson was a truck driver, so they put him on the truck and put me on as a helper. Ralph worked on the track for a very short time. They wanted all three of us to go on cars as car men. Well, I didn't want to go on the car. I thought I was comin' back to Akron. I couldn't believe that things would stay bad very long. We'd been away from here [Akron] since July and this is the first of the year. Akron's always been good and is bound to pick up again, see. So I said, "No. I'm not gonna' be here too long. I figure I'll get out of here in two or three months."

When I first went there, I took this job on the track. This was the first month or two I was there. It was January or February of '21. And we had a big snow and ice storm. We had an old snowplow built on a trolley car and we plowed this snow off the tracks and then we shoveled it out of the switches and put salt on 'em. We went to the river and picked up barrels of coarse ground salt, had a chute over each wheel and we had these grocery scoops like they use to scoop up stuff in a grocery store. And we scooped the salt out of that barrel and (just by hand) we shook it as the thing moved. We shook it on the tracks, see, to melt the snow and ice off the tracks so the cars could go.

I can't remember who was on that car except a guy by the name of Bill Young who was hard run and hard up and never had had a good meal in his life. My uncle give me the job to feed 'em. So, we had to go down to the river, which was about six blocks from the restaurant, to pick up salt. He told me anytime they wanted to eat it didn't make any difference. They were gonna' have to work all night, so feed 'em. This Rothrocks restaurant—[10] I'd get off there and they'd go down to the river, load the salt. They'd put about eight barrels on at a time. Then we'd come back to the restaurant and just stop the car in the middle of the street because there wasn't any traffic anyway. There wasn't hardly any cars. And eat and go on.

When I'd drop off, I'd say, "What do you guys want?" Well, after the first big meal in the morning of ham and eggs, they didn't want a lot. Maybe a cup of coffee and maybe a sandwich sometimes. A piece of pie. Bill Young said, "I want the biggest steak they got." And I bet you he ate ten steaks in that thirty-two hours 'cause he never had a steak in a restaurant before, I don't think. He really went for 'em.

We stayed on the job for thirty-two hours without goin' home. Well, if we went home, we didn't stay. We might've went home for a change of clothes or socks or somethin', but we didn't stay at home. We went on back. We did go into the car barn at two or three o'clock in the morning and set in the chair and maybe lay on the pool table or somethin' and sleep a few minutes, but not very long like gettin' a change or something. It was pretty rough, but I wasn't runnin' a car at that time.

They had a lot of freezin' rain on top of that. It had sleeted and froze. It'd freeze on the front windows of the streetcars. Well, you had no way of keepin' it off. Had no heater. There was no heat on the cars at all. They'd have a man downtown with buckets of warm saltwater. So, when you'd get down there, he'd wash your windows with this saltwater—wash all the ice off. But, by the time you got to the other end of the line, you'd have to get out and scrape it off so you could see. We used to blow and make a hole we could see through—blow our breath on the window. When it'd fog up, we had a little spot so you could see through to see the passenger on the side wantin' to catch a ride. I have run a car when we had sleet.

They'd have to put a (they called it an 'ice wheel") on the trolley instead of the regular grooved wheel. They'd put an ice-machine thing on there that broke the ice up on the trolley line so you could keep contact, see, 'cause ice would insulate from the trolley to some extent. You'd get stuck. You couldn't move. You'd have to get out and beat on the trolley pole to start that ice. Once you got started, you could keep goin', but you get dead stop a lot of times you couldn't move.

Finally, everything ya' hear from here is bad. So I took a job on the car and later Wilkerson took a job on the car.

The Routes

Haskell: We didn't have that many passengers. You'd get a big rush once in a while or a pretty good group going down early in the morning. I didn't catch the early runs much. I'd have to go in the morning—take the people to work. But I missed the heavy traffic. Kind of lucky. I caught the car at 11:00 in the morning on my regular run that I had for about a year and worked 'til five. At 5:00 I went home for lunch. I didn't live too far away—most of the time.

My run was eleven hours and fifty minutes with an hour off for lunch—which made twelve hours and fifty minutes. I had to be at the barn an hour before 11:00—which made thirteen hours and fifty minutes. When I lived three miles from the car barn, I had to leave about twenty minutes after nine to get down there by ten.[11] Then I had to walk home twenty-eight blocks. Maybe further than that. So, I put in a pretty long day—seven days a week. Not once in a while, just seven days a week is all. If I got in a fifteen-day pay, I drew fifty-five dollars. For fifteen days at twelve hours a day. You think the old man didn't scratch some skinny asses, I have, I'll tell you. Poor ones. Yes, sir.

It was quite a deal. You went there and you had to buy a uniform, hat, changer and work eight days. We had eight different lines. Broadway and Guthrie Avenue went out Broadway. That's two. Avondale's three. Union Station's four. Sixth Street's five. Third Street is six. Rowlandtown is seven. Cemetery's eight. We had eight lines. That's what we had to work. Eight days.

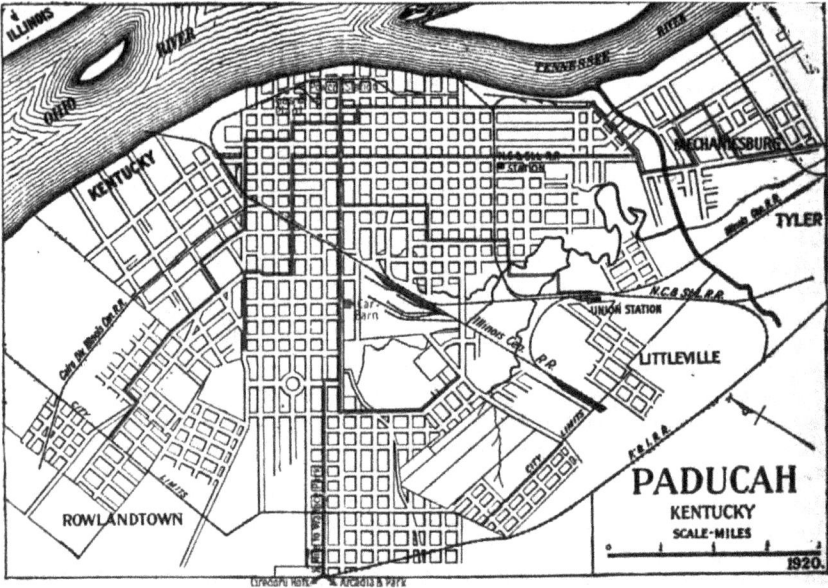

"Paducah, Kentucky, 1920." Haskell's route went from the Car Barn (left center) towards the Ohio River and then northeast toward Mechanicsburg and Tyler before it turned around at the end of the line and returned ("Paducah Electric Company. Paducah, Kentucky." Stone & Webster, Boston: 1920).

You had to work one day on each line for free (didn't get a dime for it) to break in on each line so you'd know the stops and everything. They took every drop of blood they could get out of ya'. Then they started you off at thirty-four cents an hour. You worked thirty-four cents an hour for six months. Then you worked for another year for thirty-five. Then you got thirty-six and that's as high as you could get. That was it. There's an old man— He drove mules down there. He had over forty years service and he was gettin' thirty-six cents an hour. Billy Bethel.[12]

Florence: But we lived on it. Rent wasn't that high.

Haskell: So there was sixteen men goin' out in the mornin' and if I was off, somebody took my turn. If nobody's off sick, they'd make somebody take off. They'd sign your run to somebody else the day before and you'd have to give the extra man a chance to make a livin' so they could stay there. If you could get in a sixteen-day pay, why, that was a real wizard. You could get about fifty-five dollars for a sixteen-day pay.

A transfer ticket from to Rowlandtown Line to other points on the track system.

That extra board was a bastard. You had to go there in the morning to be there at 5:00 when you was on the extra board. They signed you out and you was signed up to make the 5:00 report. If you didn't get a job, you had to come back again and make the 10:00 report. Then you might get out and you wouldn't get back into the barn 'til close to midnight. Or might not get out then. Yeah. A lot of times you wouldn't get out so you didn't get a day. Didn't get nothin for showin' up or anything like that.

Neighbors

Florence: We lived in three different places there. The first place we lived was ready to fall down when we lived in it. Then we lived in a place on Sixth Street. Was a pretty good house. Two-story house. We had the second floor. Had a big bedroom and a kitchen. Then, at the back, there's a porch on the ground floor—

Haskell: There's a porch on the front—

Florence: — couple of rooms off of it.

Haskell:—all the way across. Then we rented a little house.

Florence: It was pretty nice.

Haskell: Ahh, what was that? Three rooms. A kitchen and a bedroom and the livin' room. We never did furnish the one room. We just furnished the bedroom and the kitchen.

Florence: Better've not done it 'cause we didn't stay there too long 'til we left Paducah.

Haskell: It was a pretty good little house. I think we paid— We paid twelve dollars a month for that house. Three rooms.[13]

Florence: There's a family lived next door to us (they was nice) and they had a woman come in and wash and do a few things for her. And she'd bring her little grandchild with her once in a while. This was in the Spring and I was mowin' the front yard. She says, What ya' cuttin' that muuustard for?" I was mowin' off the grass and weeds and the weed was "muuustard." "What ya' cuttin' that muuustard for?"

She lived in a little house in the block behind and she worked at the hospital. I guess she did the cleaning (part of it) around the rooms. Haskell just happened to come in while she was in the room [one] day and he just asked her about the children. And said, "We watch 'em climbin' around on that fence and wonder if there's anybody a lookin' after 'em because it looks like it's so dangerous [It's a] sharp fence." She said, "Well," I have to work and they just have to stay by themself. They don't have anybody to stay with 'em." He said, "Well, where's their father?" She said, "I don't know." Said, "I told him to go to hell and I guess he went for I haven't seen him since!"

Haskell: Dan Sladon and old Pres' Lindsay lived next door. Pres' Lindsay. He was an old bachelor. His house was about five feet off the ground. Plenty of room underneath for the dogs—if he had any. I don't know if he had any. Old Dan's wife was hollerin' at the kids. Mom [Florence] used to mock her. She did laundry. She'd be out washin' and she'd tell the kids, "C'mon you young 'uns. Get out from under my feet! Go away from here! Go somewhere! Go— Get out of here! Go!" They'd take off up the sidewalk and get about fifty feet from the house and she'd start screamin' at 'em, "C'mon back here! You know I can't do without you chillun'! Don't you go wanderin' off!"

Florence: There was the grocery man that we bought groceries from in Paducah. I bought flour by the twenty-five pounds because I made biscuits all the time and used quite a bit of flour in bakin'. So I got sick after I had bought this and I'd had an operation. Anyway, I couldn't go back to that store to buy groceries anymore for quite a long while. I just wasn't able to do it. It was months.

Finally, I decided I felt good enough I could go back to this grocery to do some tradin'. And I got to my flour on the list and I said, " I want a twenty-five-pound bag of flour." I believe it was Omega. And he said, "Well, I'm sorry, but, you bought a bag of (so-and-so) the last time you bought any." And it had been weeks and weeks!

But he remembered your name if you ever came in there to buy anything. The first thing he wanted to know is what your name is. And when you go back there or wherever you happen to see him over that, he speaks to you and calls you by your name. I never saw anything like it because there's lots of people go through a store that way. But from the very first time you go in there and buy somethin' from him— He knew you. Yeah, "You bought (so-and-so) the last time you bought flour."

Haskell: Florence had worked like a beaver. She had some female trouble because of hard work, probably. And she walked about two miles to teach school under very bad conditions. Mud. Snow. Whatever. She had the flu durin' that time—which was a bad thing in those days. That Spanish Flu. She had that while she was teachin' school over there. So that affected her, too. She begin to improve and come on after we married.

Barton Jones

Haskell: We went from Paducah down to Mayfield to Florence's father's. And they were having a schoolhouse play, I suppose it was. One of the country schools. Florence and I went down there with Florence's brother Barton and her sister Mary and I don't know who. Florence's younger sister Ethel. Anyway, we went to the schoolhouse. And, during the intermission, I went out on the porch to smoke a cigarette. While there, I hear an argument start down at the other end of the porch. Somebody was gonna' beat somebody up. So, I eased down there and I see who's gonna' get beat up was Barton—who was a kid about fifteen years old and weighed about seventy pounds. And there was three young men and their father.

So, I stuck my big nose in and said, "If there's anybody gonna' get beat up, let it be me." Immediately one of these guys pulled a big jackknife and I was backed up against the wall surrounded by the four of them. But I bluffed my way out of it by making 'em think I had a gun—which I didn't have, which I was glad I didn't have later. But I really prayed for it at that time. I had had my gun and picked it up and was gonna' take it with me. So, had I had that gun, I probably would have blown that bunch off of that porch and been in jail the rest of my life. But I didn't have it.

They accused Barton of throwing a cat in the window. They had the windows open in this schoolhouse. It was in the Fall of the year and the weather was fairly decent. And it was a big crowd, in the schoolhouse, so it was hot in there. There was no air-conditioning or fans or anything. To this day I don't know whether he did it or not. He swore to me he did not. And that's it.

Barton: I think I'd've been in trouble if I'd had to— If I'd been alone.

Haskell: He'd like to get me killed that night, I'll tell you.

Barton: I believe if I'd've been alone, I'd've had trouble. But when they found out I wasn't alone— He says, "Well, we don't want any trouble. Let's just quit." I think your Grandpa got little scare on to 'em.

Haskell: And Wilson Wright was the guy that saved our ass, I'll tell ya' that 'cause they had me backed up against the wall where I wasn't gonna' get loose.

Barton: If I'd been there alone, I— I— I'd— They— They'd— I don't know what they'd've done to me.

Haskell: I don't either. They was kind of a lousy bunch, wasn't they? Wilson Wright was my friend, a relative, but a friend. Not a close relative. But he happened to be in the neighborhood. Big, rough and tough. So when they had me backed up against the wall and the one guy's got a knife and he's talkin' about how he's gonna' make his initials on my hide and old, big Wilson happened to recognize me. And he stuck his head into the group and he said, "What's the matter, Jonesie?" I said, "Look like these guys is gonna" cut me up." And he said, "Don't guess so-and-so they will. Not long as I'm here."

Barton: They made about three.

Haskell: That give us a little edge.

Barton: About three— About three to five. Something like that.

Haskell: Something like that. But they didn't know who I was and they didn't know how mean I was, see. They— They— They didn't— They said if I— If they'd have a little idea of who I was, they'd known how to handle me. But they didn't know 'cause I was a stranger, see. They didn't know how tough I was.

Barton: The old man was in it with 'em.

Haskell: Yeah.

Barton: And he says, "Well— Forget about it. Let's just let it drop.

Haskell: I still believe Barton threw that cat in there.

Barton: I did. I pitched it in the window, but it didn't hit nobody.

Haskell: I thought he did it but he'd never admit to me before that he did that. But I was pretty sure that he did. But that didn't make any difference to me. I wasn't gonna' let 'em chop him up—if I could help it.

Barton: I pitched the cat in the window, but it just fell in the aisle. It didn't— It didn't hurt nobody, touched nobody. And I was alone. They didn't know it was me anymore than anybody else, but I was the only one around there. Happened to be in the wrong place.

Haskell: Well, they— They get ganged up on ya', why, they could be tough, see. And that was— That was their way of playin' ball. They'd gang up on ya'.

The Cars

Electric Journal Praises Paducah Railway Co. for Safety Campaign

The "safety first" campaign conducted by the Paducah Railway company has won wide attention. Railway publications published in a number of cities have commented on the effective sign displays placed at Fourteenth and Broadway by Manager Alfred S. Nichols and Superintendent of Transportation J.W. McNeely.

In its July issue of the Aera, a magazine devoted to electric railway interests, says:

"This is the record of the Paducah Railway company, operating practically all its mileage within the busy Kentucky city. It indicates that the railway is remarkably free from accidents.

"It 'got that way' by dint of persistent education of the public and employes as to carefulness on the highways and in operation of vehicles. Manager Nichols makes might good use of signboards and his originality is well displayed by his using a battered old auto to help drive home the safety-first lesson.

"Mr. Nichols has made successful use of sign boards in driving home the safety-first lesson.

"There is an open space on the Paducah Railway company's car barn property on Broadway, in Paducah, and here Mr. Nichols has erected his signs. They are on the main artery of travel in this lively Kentucky city and are seen by thousands of persons every day.

"Mr. Nichols changes the signs frequently and keeps them lighted. A rather novel demonstration is made in connection with one of these signs. An automobile much the worse for having been in a collision is placed beside the sign as visual evidence of the danger that always menaces the careless or chance taking person.

"These signs are but features of a safety first campaign which had been conducted by the Paducah Railway company for a number of years, and they have helped materially to reduce the number of accidents resulting from collision with street cars.

"Mr. Nichols says that during the five months ending May 31, 1922, his company, operating over nineteen miles of single track equipment, practically all of this in the city of Paducah, had paid out just $7.50 in claims for accidents. This is a most unusual showing and testified to the efficiency with which safety first measures are carried out in Paducah."

The Paducah Evening Sun
July 7, 1922[14]

Haskell: The big car we had down there come out of Saint Louis. They was down there for the World's Fair in 1904, see. That's where the streetcars we run in Paducah came from.

After Saint Louis World's Fair was over, they had more streetcars than they needed. Then they doled them out to the various other companies that needed cars. So, they were pretty good cars. They were pretty big cars. All yellow. They had lights in 'em. They had about six lights on each side.

There were different types of cars. Thirty, forty and a hundred series. They were built a little different. The forty series had a sliding door. It slid back into the framework. The old hundred series is bigger. I can't remember how many different numbers they had on 'em. But I remember ninety-two 'cause I operated it quite a bit.

The big cars, we had a double truck job. They made some small cars. They called 'em single truck.[15] But man, they'd buck up and down when you hit a rough place in the street. We had a lot of gravel streets and the joints would sink in the track.

They'd have the name on the side and they had this destination signal up in there. It might be Tyler or Cemetery, Rollin' Town or Guthrie Avenue or Broadway. Avondale Heights. Union Station. You just rolled 'em around. You could see through it from the back.

I think there was a grab handle on the side of the door, too, for people that was heavier or handicapped or somethin'—package in one hand. They could grab both sides.

Had all the advertising up on the side. A guy by the name of [Barron] Collier got a patent on that card that goes in the streetcar, buses and whatnot yet. He made so much money he bought a county in Florida. Collier County down by Naples. The whole county—he bought it.[16]

"Order Number 969." In 1912, Stone & Webster ordered five new streetcars from The St. Louis Car Company for one of its subsidiaries, The Paducah Traction & Light Company (renamed The Paducah Railway Company in 1919).

Consisting of five new 21-foot single truck cars numbered #20 through #24, they would be among the last new streetcars to ever run in Paducah. This photo and the ones that follow, document the interior and exterior car #21, which was built in April of the following year.

Although its construction was based on designs by both Joseph M. Bosenbury and Charles O. Birney, it was popularly referred to as the "Birney Safety Car." This was because Birney worked for Stone & Webster (which owned many of the railway lines on which they were used) and because this 29-passenger trolley could be safely operated by one motorman—as opposed to older, larger cars which would require both a motorman and conductor.

The first mass-produced streetcar in North America, it was popular in smaller cities because of the reduced capacity and in larger cities on less traveled routes (Washington University in St. Louis, St. Louis, Missouri, St. Louis Car Company Collection photos).

Weighing about 13,000 pounds (about a third the weight of conventional cars) the Birney Safety Car was economical to operate, managing a top speed of about 20 mph.

The car's light weight on a single center-mounted truck, however, could prove troublesome in snow. It also often resulted in a rough ride for passengers—particularly when budgetary considerations meant that track maintenance was deferred.

The entry and exit of passengers through one door also often led to the bunching of passengers, which could result in uneven weight distribution at one end of the car. No small matter, this could derail the rear wheels, throwing the car off the tracks.

While car #21 may not be the exact car that Haskell drove in Paducah from 1921-22, it certainly is of the same design and construction.

Motorman Haskell Jones at the controls of his streetcar. A little worse for the wear than the car manufactured and delivered by the St. Louis Car Company some eight years earlier, it is easy to imagine it being the exact same car. "Tyler" in the upper window refers to the streetcar route (Author's collection).

Haskell: Everybody rode streetcars in town or walked. There wasn't no other way to go. They'd take a pretty good crowd of people. They weren't segregated. We didn't have that many passengers.

We had a lot of fog down there. We had a big front window and you could drop it down into the body of the car in front of you. We left that down and just ride and try to see. If it wasn't too cold, why, you could stand it. You could always have heavy clothes on anyway if it was that kind of weather. Used to wear a big heavy pair of shoes with a silk sock, then a wool sock on my feet to keep my feet warm. The front end

Haskell's watch while he was a motorman in Paducah. Although the chain was added later, the larger coin is actually an Indian Head Nickel, which he collected in change at the time. An example of "hobo" or "convict" art, it is highly collectible today. The smaller coin is a fare token used on the streetcar line.

of that car was cold. I had heavy underwear. The door openin' and closin', see, all the time.

They had an Avondale Heights line. They didn't come downtown. They stopped way out on Broadway. It went to an allotment and a big golf course out in the section out there. They'd put this line out there and had a franchise to run it. Some days you wouldn't have a customer at all. You'd just run back and forth 'bout once an hour, I think, and set the rest of the time. Some of the help that worked out there— colored people that worked out at the golf course, kitchen help and yard crew and stuff like that. They'd ride the car.

The streetcar company had a park [Wallace Park].[17] Only way you could get in it was ride the streetcar. It was a pretty nice park. Wasn't much in it. Good lot of benches to sit around out there. Lot of nice trees and everything. And a few little carnival midway cat-racks and pop-stands and a hamburger and a few things of that kind. But the main attraction was a big dance hall. The streetcar company paid for the band. I think only two nights a week. Friday and Saturday, I believe.

But we used to go out there as car men. Get off work at 9:00, sometimes, catch the car and go out to the park and watch 'em dance. I didn't dance. It was nice. But this band was marvelous. It was well known. There was no "mikes" in those days, anything of that kind. No amplification. The band played and they had a singer. And they sang with a megaphone. He'd sing the blues through that megaphone. Man, he'd stand your hair on end! He was a good singer!

The motormen of the Paducah Railway Company gathered on Easter morning, March 27th, 1921, near the car barn at North 14th and Broadway for their annual photo. Seated (L-R) "Uncle" Billy Bethel, who had more than 40 years of service at the time, William Huff, Haskell Jones, Lexie Phillips, Edward R. Ferrell, J.W. Fletcher, Felix Walters, Frank James, Julian Cole and Harry Harper. Standing (L-R) Dell Wallace, inspector, Thomas E. "Tom" Arant, John "Happy" Williams, Ralph Jones, Lonnie Ragland, Emmet Johnson, William Parks, Sylvester Denny "Vester" Ward, Mr. Radcliff, Lee Travis, Saul W. Andrews, William Bryan and Duke Williams, Inspector. **Haskell:** This was made early in the morning before we went to work on Easter Sunday. First car left the barn, I think, five twenty, went downtown and left the downtown terminal at five-thirty.

The Motormen

Haskell: I was on the streetcar in 1921, '22 with Walters. Frank James. Julian Cole. Cole worked Union Station. Harry Harper. Dell Wallace. "Happy" Williams. Happy John Williams. He was runnin' on Rowlandtown. Ralph. Ragland. Emmet Johnson. William Parks. Old man Huff had Guthrie Avenue. Rudolph Wilkerson. Old "Stud" worked Third Street. "Duke" Aikins. He was a slicker. He was a character. Every time we got paid, he tore his pay slip in two. Tore it up. Put part of the money in one pocket and part in the other. He said, "My wife will never know how much I make." He wasn't makin' very much, but he didn't want her to know how much he made. Old man Parks. Him and Mom lived in the same house—a duplex. Parks lived on one side and Mom lived on the other. Lexie Phillips. He had the same number on his badge as the Fire Department in the town. In those days they just had two numbers. Dial ninety-five for fire, you know. And old Lexie used to take off his cap and hold that sign and say, "In case of fire, call ninety-five."

I worked Sixth Street—me and old man Bryan. Bill Bryan— Meanest son-of-a-bitch that ever run a streetcar. Everybody in town hated him. He'd been petitioned off three or four, five or six different lines. He was so hateful to the customers they'd get up a petition and ask the company to move him off of the line. He carried pennies in his pocket. He carried five dollars worth of pennies all the time. Fare was a dime.[18] If anybody got on and give him a five-dollar bill, he'd give 'em four dollars and ninety cents in pennies, see. It's a wonder somebody didn't kill him 'cause he was a bastard. Nice lookin' old man. Neat. Clean. He wasn't dumb, but he had a mean streak in him.

Little Girl, 5, Is Crushed to Death Under Street Car
Lillian Beasley, Returning From Grocery,
Stumbles and Falls on Track, Lives Few Minutes.

Lillian Beasley, 5 years old, daughter of Mr. and Mrs. Lube L. Beasley, 1909 Guthrie Avenue, was crushed to death under a street car at Seventeenth, Tennessee street and Mayfield road this afternoon at 1:40 o'clock. She died almost instantly.

According to witnesses, the little girl was returning from the grocery and started to cross the car track in front of a Guthrie trolley car which had stopped at the end of the line. The car started just as she reached the track and according to persons in the vicinity, the child stumbled and fell. Motorman Walters heard a woman scream, and applying his brakes stopped the car. He had moved only a few feet from the point where the car had been standing. The little girl was crushed across the stomach and her head was bruised. Men who were in the car rushed out and took her from under the car, but she died before they could carry her to her home a short distance away.

Traction company officials said the wheels did not touch the child's body, attributing the fatal injuries to pressure of the brake "shoe." Motorman Walters had his car under perfect control and had hardly started.

The child's mother was prostrated. Motorman Walters was unable to continue work and asked to be allowed to go to his home.

The Paducah Evening Sun
Monday, May 16, 1921

Haskell: Walters run over a kid and killed it. Like to kill him. He had a run that the back end was short. He had a lot of time at the end of the line. And he'd just go out there and lay until the right time to leave, see. He loved the kids. And all the kids in the neighborhood— They was always comin' around the car and he'd talk to 'em—set in the door of the car and yack with 'em. So, this day, why, he'd been talkin' to 'em and he said, "All right, now. Let's all go back on the sidewalk and get out of the way. I've got to go." They all left and he started up and this little girl run right down right in front of the car. He didn't see her. Run over her and cut her in two. Like to kill that old man. He didn't work for a long time. It really shook him up.[19]

This Kolb Park (alongside of that on 6th Street), we had a passin' switch where we crossed (two cars passed each other) and we went around the turn. There at the corner of Bridge and Broad Street, I was goin' home one day and Matlock relieved me to go home for supper. I had to go back with the same guy that relieved me and get off. (Florence would have supper or dinner ready for me and I'd run in there and eat and I'd have to catch it to get back down there.) So, we're goin' back— It's in the spring and the farmers were pickin' strawberries. They had a shippin' yard down in the railroad where they shipped these strawberries to New York or Boston or wherever— Timbuktu, you know. And they had kind of like a co-op. They raised the berries and this one man sold the berries for 'em and saw to the shippin' and that they brought decent berries and things like that.[20]

They had twenty-four quarts in a crate. Made out of light wood like an orange crate or somethin' you see. And they'd stack 'em on those old cars just as long as they could tie one on. They'd have 'em tied on the runnin' board. They have 'em tied on the hood. They'd have strawberries tied everywhere. They had to ship at five o'clock in the evening or somethin' like that. Six o'clock, whatever.

So, Matlock, he relieved me and we're goin' back and he's talkin' and we have a corner up there. You had a set of trucks in the front end of the car and a set of trucks on the back end and this middle would swing way over. And there was a telephone post right there in the corner. He made the turn as this guy drove in this corner. There wasn't room enough for this car between the pole and that streetcar and he made a big strawberry omelet. He really smashed 'em up. You never saw so many smashed strawberries in your life! Man, it knocked all the crates off. Matlock squealed like a pig. He hollered. He thought he'd killed these people.

Didn't hurt the old folks. It was an old couple and a boy. The boy was drivin'. He was about fifteen, sixteen years old and he was drivin'. This old couple was in there with him—mom and dad. Matlock saw what was gonna' happen. But you couldn't stop one of those cars on a dime. They had old hand brakes on 'em. You didn't have air. He screamed like a panther. I can hear him yet. He— He thought sure he'd killed 'em. And all it did was smash up the car and mash up their strawberries. They got paid for 'em. The company paid for 'em.

We played pool in the car barn. We had a trainmen's room they called it, or the poolroom or waiting room for the men. We played pool for a Coke® or something of that kind. They didn't gamble. But I was the champion pool player of the barn.

So, two young men (who worked in the main office downtown) came to the barn every afternoon to pick up the cash. The trainmen brought the cash in and put it in a safe. And the boys came and got the cash and took it downtown. They played pool occasionally and I played with 'em once in a while.

So, somebody said, "How 'bout you boys come out some Saturday night and we'll have a tournament?" There was a man named Bill Young who played fairly good pool and worked on the track. So, we set up the date. And Bill Young and I was to play these two men. One of 'em's name was Duke Williams and the other I can't remember. When they came out, they had gone to the hotel bar poolroom and picked out nice long ones and was all set to trim the "yokels" at the barn. Our sticks had been broken off and repaired 'til we didn't have very good sticks out there.

Well, when Bill Young sees these boys come out with a collar and a tie on (all dolled up) and these long sticks, he got chicken and wouldn't play. And what are we gonna' do? So, old man McNeely, which was our boss ("Mister Mac," we called him)— I said, "How about you?" He said, "Me? You'd play with me?" I said, "Sure." He didn't play too bad a pool. He was a man up in years, but he played fair pool. And he said, "O.K." So, we trimmed the boys downtown quite thoroughly. They never came back to play pool with us again.

Duke Williams would bet you on anything in the world. If there was a sparrow sittin' on a wire, he'd say, "I'll bet you ten dollars that sparrow will fly that way or he'll fly that way. You take your choice." It didn't make a difference. He— He just loved to bet. He couldn't help it, see. He liked to play cards for a nickel a game. He just got a big kick out of playin' for a nickel. Played for a Coke, anything, but he wanted to gamble on everything there was. He's the guy that beat me on the horses.

Negroes to Hold Fair, Races on August 10 to 12.
City Sanctions Effort, 10th to be Official Negro Holiday.
Negroes of Paducah Will Present a Fair and Racing Meet for the First Time in City's History, on August 10, 11 and 12.
The Paducah Evening Sun
August 3, 1921

Haskell: The colored people had the fair and they had old cheap horse races. These horses look like they come out of a plow team somewhere, you know. I'm off in the afternoon and Duke says, "Let's go out and get a load of n_ggers." They rented the fairground. Had a pretty good-sized fairground there and a good half-mile horse track. Come in with all the skin games—the cat-racks and the chuck-a-luck and the three-card monte and all the gamblin'. Everything, they had it. Nobody bothered 'em. They let 'em alone. They had a good day all by themselves.

So, he went out with me. I went to the barn. I got one of these antique cars. It's the only time I ever run one. All open on the sides and they had a register up here with a rope and you pulled it when you'd collect the fares. You had to go around the end on a catwalk on each side and go between the seats to collect the fares. You had a motorman on one end and I'm conductor. Ding, ding the bell whenever you collected the fare.[21]

We got out to the track and there was a sidetrack out there where ya' could park the car and the other cars go on by and pay no attention to it, see. He said, "Well, we might as well go over and watch the races.

The motormen of the Paducah Railway Co. on Easter morning, April 16, 1922, gathered in front of the car barn at North 14th and Broadway.[1] (Front Row, L-R) William H. "Uncle Billy" Bethel, Frank James, Andrew "Duke" Aikins, Julian Cole, Lonnie B. Ragland, John B. "Happy" Williams, William Parks, Walter Doyle, John Bernard Spalding, Etheledied "Lenny" Futrell, Haskell A Jones, Ralph Edwin Jones, Rudolph John "Stud" Wilkerson (Back Row, L-R) Dell Wallace, Felix Walters, (unknown), Lexie W. Cross, E.C. Matlock, Sylvester Denny "Vester" Ward, Lee Travis, Thomas E. "Tom" Arant, Saul W. Andrews, Riggs Ashbrook, Clarence C. Rose, William Huff, Emmet Johnson.

Haskell: This picture was made in front of the office. There's a car sittin' back in there. We went in through here and in the back was a repair shop, paint shops and storage where they stored 'em at night, stuff of that kind.

Had a great big yard out there—went clear to the next street.

Down behind the office was a trainmen's room. We had a pretty good sized room. We had a pool table and card tables in there. While you was waitin' for your time out or waitin' for a run if you was extra man, why, you played pool or whatever and play after night after we'd quit.

There was a stockroom [on the left] where they had all the parts for the cars and stuff of that kind. Every Saturday night, they had a big poker game in that room.

It's a little early." So, we went over and they had four harness races. We get against the fence and he says, "Well, make a little bet for two bits?" "Um, O.K." He said, "O.K., I'll give ya' first choice. You take first choice. I'll take second. You take third. I'll take fourth." "O.K., for a quarter."

So, both of his horses beat both of mine. And he was a ribber. He'd needle ya'. He'd give ya'— tell ya' how dumb ya' was for not knowin' how to play (bet horses) in a good manner. Next race he said, "Well, I'll give ya' a little better break." Said, "I'll let ya' pick two. I like to give a sucker a break." He like to really needle ya'. I said, "O.K." So both of his beat both of mine and he rode me some more.

The last race was two halfway decent lookin' horses (nothin' that looked like any prizes, but they looked able-bodied), a little bit of a horse (it was awful small) and an old grey horse. He was old. His ears down almost crossed, you know. He was old flea-bitten, old grey and he had a problem they called "string-halted." The leaders in his legs get bad and when he starts out, he steps way up high—can't get his feet down. He's goin' like crazy.

So, he said, "O.K., H.J., I'll give ya'— Like to give a sucker a break. I'll give ya' three this time." I said, "O.K. I'll take the two good horses—the two good lookin' horses and the pony. I'll give you that old grey horse. He'll never make it around there." It was a mile race on a half-mile track. Two loops.

So, they made two or three false starts. With harness races, if they're not even enough when they cross the startin' line, they call 'em back. Make 'em go back and do it again. So they did that couple, three times—got this old horse's legs warmed up.

When he finished, he was ahead of those two good-lookin horses and that pony hadn't come in yet. He's still on the track somewhere. Well, this guy, he really needled me good about that. He was always kiddin' me about bettin' the horses.

Incidents

Haskell: I was working the old cemetery line, which dead-ended at the cemetery.[22] There was no loops at the end of these lines to turn the car around. When you got to the end, you locked your door, picked up the fare box and your controller handle, went to the other end of the car and took your trolley. You could pull it down, walk around and put it on the other end of the car on the trolley wire. Then you went the other direction, see.

So, I was in a hurry because I was late. We had hand brakes on these cars. Operated a shaft that went down to the brakes. At the floor, you had a dog. So, when you'd get ready to set your brakes, you'd kick your toe against that little trigger and set that in that dog. And then your brakes was tight. They wouldn't release 'til you kicked the other end of that little dog, down there. You put a little pressure on it, kicked it, it's come out. Then the wheel would go around. It had a spring, that dog did.

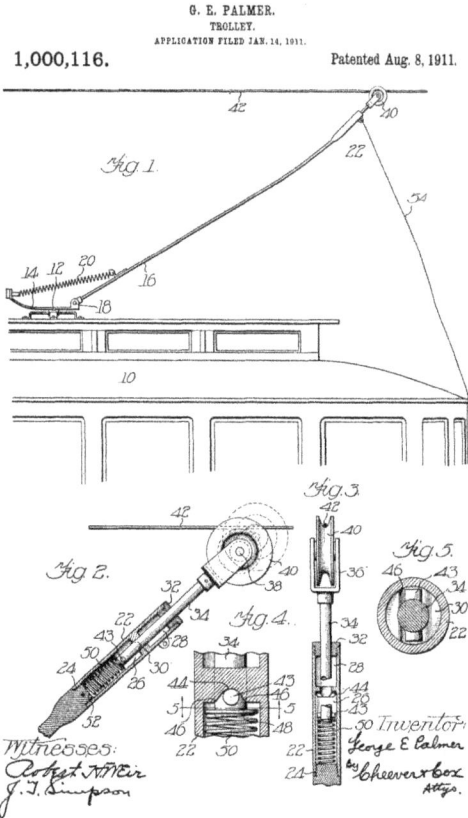

G. E. PALMER.
TROLLEY.
APPLICATION FILED JAN. 14, 1911.

1,000,116.

Patented Aug. 8, 1911.

U.S. Patent No. 1,000,116 by George E. Palmer for a streetcar trolley (USPTO).

So, I was sailing down to the end of the track and I wind the brakes up and kick the dog in and step off the car. By the time the car stopped, I would be at the other end where I could grab this trolley rope and run around and set the trolley back on— ready to go the other direction. When I got within about twenty-five or thirty feet of end of this line, I had this thing set. I knew about how long it'd take to stop. I stepped off and the brake chain that went from this rod to the brake shoes broke. So the car continued on out on the gravel street. Well, of course, it bogged down pretty fast in that gravel street. Didn't go very far. I had it slowed down pretty good anyway. It was clear off the rails.

Well, the streetcar runs on a circuit between the trolley car and the rail. The rail's the ground. The trolley's the positive. They have to be connected through your motors. And the trolley and the rails is connected to both. We had a switch bar. We threw switches with this bar. And it had a wide end on the end of it and it was thin. It was only about four feet long. If you had to switch the car off of that track, why, you went out and switched that bar with that switch so you could go that direction. So I was just close enough that I could put one end of it on the rail and one end against the wheel of the car. You put the bar on the wheel first and then touch the rail and that made the circuit, see. When you took it up, you took it off the rail first. Then, that eased you back on, see. You had to run to catch the car, though. 'Cause you were down at the back end. You didn't want to get in front and get run over by the durn thing. Then, I inched it back onto the rail again, see. So I set my controls and got it back on there. No problem.

If you hear anybody say, "I put 'er around on nine," you know what he means? That was the fastest. That was against the post. One. Two. Three. Four. And then there was a gap. Six. Seven. Eight. Nine. Well, when you started, you had this thing setting on one. That just barely moved your car. Just a little bit. Well, that's where you'd set it, see. But this nine had a brass block on the end of it. And when you was against the post, you was on nine, see. You supposed to feed it. You give it time between each one. You didn't wait all day, but, you didn't just zzzzzzzt — like that. But a lot of times we did.

I remember one time I hit a car. They was havin' a trial at the courthouse. Dark rainy day in the wintertime. Not snow or anything, but a dark day. This guy killed his father and threw him in the Ohio River. The old man had a lot of money. He was a prominent farmer [Joe Daniels]. The kid [Van Daniels] couldn't get it fast enough, so he figured he'd knock the old man off. He'd get it, see. Eighteen, seventeen, twenty years old. So they was having a trial that day and the cars was parked all around that courthouse. The courthouse was a square city block. Nothing else in that square but the courthouse.[23]

So, I'm, going downtown and I'm late. I don't have any more stops to make because I'm within two or three blocks and you hardly ever picked up a passenger going to town. They walked if they was that far. Fare was a dime and dimes was hard to come by. You'd drop somebody off once in a while, but you hardly ever picked up on the last two or three blocks. So, I'm "ballin' the jack" down through there, they've rendered a verdict and all the farmers was goin' home. That guy backed that straight out in front of me— That T Model.

This guy's got side curtains and those side curtains was just solid. Had a little strip of mica so anybody in there could look out and see if whether it was daylight. That's about all you could see. I couldn't see him in the car because of these curtains. I didn't know he was in the car. The minute he started that thing, he just zooooooooom—And here he come back. He ought to know there ain't nothin' I can do. I was from fifteen feet away. No way to stop. I hit him pretty hard. Knocked him back up in the courthouse yard.

So, I set this brake, kick the dog in, throw the thing in reverse. It scared me because I knocked him clear back in the courthouse yard. I knocked that car from here out to the other side of our garage, up in the yard, across the sidewalk. Wonder that it didn't kill somebody 'cause there was people all around that. So, I 'm jumped out of the car to run and see about him. It didn't hurt this old fat guy because he was pretty well padded in there and he's— It hit him in the back and pulled him against the back, see. The backs were high enough it didn't hurt him. Old Model T Ford.

We had a pad and I went back to get the pad and I could smell the car. I've got the brake set up, and I've got it setting in reverse and setting on nine. If that brake would've come loose, it would've been clear to the other end of the line. But it scared me because I didn't know who was in the car, how many, or anything. Men. Women. Children. Or what.

He never reported it as far as I know. If he ever made a claim for damages I never heard of it. Nobody ever questioned me about it after I made out the written report and I got it in the shop. I got his name and address and so forth. I had to write a letter on what happened. I worked there, um, let's see, on the car about sixteen, seventeen months, I guess, and as far as I know, I never caused an accident that cost the streetcar any money. I was pretty careful.

Editorial. Service.

Thousands of our patrons are working people and depend on our cars to carry them to and from work, to church or the lodge or theatre.

Do you ever give a thought to the men and machines that make the service possible? Some of our boys must get up before dawn to provide service for the man who goes to work early. The young chap who takes his sweetheart home from the dance or theatre late in the evening wants transportation home. A few men must work until after twelve o'clock at night to provide this service. Then there are the engineers and firemen at the power plant where the turbines revolve ceaselessly and the boilers are always under load. There is many a grump and crank among the host of riders. And every car must during every minute of the day guard the safety of his passengers and public, and try and maintain a pleasant attitude towards all patrons.

Our men are above the average. You will find them courteous and considerate. Compare them with employees of other systems. There is a reason— they know the Company's problems and we try to understand theirs.

The men understand that they are public servants, that service of high quality, courteously rendered [sic], makes the work more pleasant, encourages riding and helps Paducah grow. Say "Good morning" or "Good afternoon" to the motorman when you board the car—he will appreciate your courtesy. If you like the service he is rendering tell him so. He is trying to be courteous to you and encourage you to ride on his car. A kindly word from you, Mr. Street Car Rider, will be as welcome as your fare.

The Paducah Electrac News
A Journal of Information Concerning
Paducah's Electric Utilities
Wednesday, June 28, 1922

Haskell: My old ninety-five. I used it a lot and hundred-and-one and hundred-and-four. We went South Sixth Street from downtown Broadway. We went up to Broad—about a mile and a half. Made about a block turn and then went about three blocks on Bridge and cross the river. Then you went north on Clements—two long blocks. Then turn right on Yeiser. Then you went two blocks on Yeiser. Then you turn right again and went back on Hays. You went up to Hays and you go the other way to Bridge Street. That's the one you come off of originally. You're goin' out to the end of the line, see.

That old ninety-five— You couldn't throw it off the track. I've tried it. We had one place. You went up to Hays to the end of Hays and there was an "S" turn. Just quick, like ka-boom! Zing! You get there and you make this (about the length of the streetcar) and you go the other way. Just a short turn. Very short turn. "S" turn there. No graduated curve. We had no brakes to amount to anything on these streetcars. It was hand brakes. You had to wind it up with a great big wheel here with a handle on it. No air or nothin' of that kind. Man, you went right up and went right around that curve, I'm tellin' you!

I'd get mad once in a while. The kids used to grease that track and you'd zoooooom! They'd take a can of gear grease and go out there and grease that track and your brakes couldn't do anything only slide on the rails. You'd fly when you hit that thing. Lot of times that trolley'd fly off and break the rope and you'd have to crawl up and retie the rope. They knew you'd do that, see. They'd been doin' it for years.[24] Then they got to throwin' rocks at my car.

There was a mean guy that lived in the neighborhood. He was known in that neighborhood as "Don't mess with Goebel Brian." I got along with him all right. He got on the car one day and I said, "Listen, I wish you'd do me a favor." He said, "What's that?" I said, "Those kids up around that 'S' curve have been throwin' rocks at the car. They broke out two or three windows. They're gonna' knock somebody's eye out with that glass. It might be mine and it might be a passenger's." Says, "I'll take care of it." It never happened again. He put out the word, "Lay off the streetcar." And they didn't mess with him. They knew he'd kill 'em if he had to.

He rode the car and got into a fight one night and I broke it up. I wasn't mean or ugly or anything with him. I just broke it up. One Saturday night I'm takin' a load out. There was an old gentleman (old man [Rinaldo] Barnett), he come runnin' out on the front end of the car and said, "Hey, stop the car!" I said, "What's the matter?" He said, "A guy's killin' another one in there." I said, "What do you mean?" "Go in there! Go in there!" He's in a frantic. "Go on!" So I stop the car and go back and Goebel Brian's got some boy by the throat and he's chokin' him. And his tongue's stickin' out about that far. And I pulled him off. I said, "C'mon. What's the matter? Somebody's gonna' get hurt here." I don't get mean or ugly. I don't want to fight with this guy. "C'mon, Goebel." I said, "Get up. What's goin' on?" "Ahhh, these two country boys want to pick a fight with me." I said, "Well, that was wrong for them, but they didn't know it." So I get him off of there and he only had to go from about here to the corner to get off—his regular home stop, see. off.

They had got to pickin' at him. He was a city kid. They was a couple of big, husky farmers. They'd been downtown Saturday night and we're goin' home and this guy's sittin' back— He never was rough or loud or nothing. He was quiet as ice. They want to have fun with somebody. That's all the fight started on. That's the way ninety percent of 'em started over nothin' anyway. I can remember that kid's tongue was stickin' out about this far. He had his thumbs on his windpipe and he had him down on one of them long seats and he was chokin' the hell out of him. He would've killed him if I hadn't've pulled him off of him. But he didn't care. He didn't mess with 'em.

So I go on out and these two country boys come out on the end and come in. They come over and tell me what they's gonna' do to him the next time they see him. I said, "I'll give ya' a little tip. The next time you see him, run like hell. Because that guy will kill you." I said, "He ain't gonna' mess with you. He knows how to fight. And you just know how to start a fight." I said, "He knows how to fight and he will kill you. Don't bother with that guy. Let him alone. Stay away from him. Don't mess with him." "I said, "He'll cut you in two! He'll kill you! Just stay away from him. Don't go botherin' with Goebel and you'll be all right. You don't have to be a coward to stay away from him because that guy is tough! He's a killer!"

I heard the story— He didn't tell me, but another guy told me about it. Said when Goebel was about thirteen, fourteen years old, he was ridin' a bike down the sidewalk and he hit a guy—a great, big bruiser named Joe Green. Railroad man. He bumped into him. And Joe slapped the hell out of him. Slapped him off the bike and hurt him. Nothin' he could do about it. Joe weighed about 250. Said when Goebel was about fifteen, he come along that street one day and Joe's standin' out there talkin' to somebody. Goebel hit him with a knife up here about the top of his head and cut him clear down. "That, you son-of-a-bitch," he said, "is for slappin' me when I was a kid."

Well, Neil Jones (who owned Tallmadge Lumber), he was a good friend of mine—almost a brother, but he wasn't related.[25] Neil worked for old man King who owned the King Mill Lumber Company.[26] They had a herdin' yard where they floated logs down the river. Then they'd pull 'em up a conveyor and into the mill and sawed 'em—made the lumber. He was a tyrant. Ugly, mean, overbearin' old bastard, see. He hired this Goebel Brian to drive a truck and he drove a little while. So King buys a new truck and he sends him out on the truck. He parks the truck while he's makin' a delivery somewhere and somebody run into it—mashed the fender and messed it up. Nothin' he could do about it. He's in the buildin' gettin' the deliveries.

But he comes back in the yard with the truck all messed up. Brand new. And old man King really started to comb his hair. "Dumb so-and-so and so-and-so and so-and-so. You don't know how to drive. Take a truck and mess it up the first time you drive it. Yah-dee, yah-dee, yah-dee, yah-dee." Said this Brian beat the hell out of him. Neil told me that old man shit himself 'til he had to go home and take a bath. Said he just beat the hell out of him. Told him to "Take that truck and shove it!" and walked away. And everybody in the mill was tickled to death. They was ready to give him a pension, you know. Neil told me he really beat the hell out of him. Neil worked for this guy at that time. He didn't know I knew Goebel Brian, but I did. He was all right with me. I treated him all right and he treated me all right. What the heck? I never had trouble with him.

Rubel McNeill

**McNeill is Cheerful Though in Jail,
Mail Order Youth Talks Calmly to Reporters.
By Sidney Snook.**
Perhaps, after all, that optimistic proverb which tells us that "stone walls do not a prison make nor iron bars a cage," really holds true in the case of Rubel McNeill—scarcely more than a school boy in years but with a list of federal charges against him that might well make the most callous of criminals pale—who laughs and talks just as freely from behind the iron bars of the McCracken county jail as he would under circumstances somewhat more cheerful than those which the thought of a jail usually calls to mind.

The Paducah Evening Sun
Saturday, October 15, 1921

Haskell: Old man Barnett— I'll never forget him. He had two big jug-legged daughters. Pretty as they could be! Looked just like turnips! They went up just like this, you know—pretty girls.[27] They had an uncle who was the United States Marshall down there. Fellow by the name of Ollie Barnett.[28] He used to tell me about that Rubel McNeill. It took him two years to catch him.

I can't tell you how many charges he had usin' the mails for defraud.[29] He'd order anything he could order on free trial and sell it to somebody for whatever he could get for it. He run ads for tobacco and baby chicks and he ain't got one chew of tobacco and no chickens. And he'd run 'em in all the papers all over the country.

Lot of people used mail order and stuff in those days. All the farmers had chickens Get a good price on a high-grade leghorn or whatever it was. Twenty-five pounds of tobacco for five bucks. Barnett told me that the mailman wouldn't deliver Rubel's mail to anybody but him. Said that mailman would carry that mail for so many days before he returns it to the sender. But he's got to carry it for so many days. Said, "We ride with that mailman. We follow the mailman." But said, "Let us miss and that kid would stop the mailman somewhere around the neighborhood there, in the woods some place, and come out and get his mail." And says, "I've seen a time when he had as many letters with five dollar bills in it as you could put on your arm and hold like this. Believe it or not. This guy is a— He's a master. He writes the nicest ads you ever saw—beautiful. He will write to a newspaper and get their rates for advertising and send just the right amount of money and everything. Write his own ads."[30]

* * *

Haskell: I had a lot of experiences on that job. I had a bunch of guys got on the back end of the car one time. I see this guy climb in the window in the back end. It was summertime and we got the back window down—great, big window. And they jump on the coupling back in the back and climb in the window— Save a dime. I had a mirror up front. I could see him climbin' in. So I stopped and I threw them off the car. "C'mon, get the hell off here." It was Saturday afternoon along toward evening.

That night (the last trip), they waylaid me out there at the end of the line when I went to change the trolley. They'd've killed me that night. They should've killed me, but they didn't know how. They wanted to talk about it. An old man named Rudy Streit— I'll never forget that man. He saved my life that night. He's doin' some repair work in the grocery store 'cause he rented it. He didn't own it. He didn't operate it. A fellow by the name of [John] Nolan operated it. And he hears these guys out there givin' me a bad time. He had a grocery store right at the end of the car line and he was in there doin' some carpentry work—puttin' in some shelves or somethin'.

There was about four of 'em— Four brothers. And some of 'em were men. Not kids. I got nothin' but my bare hands. One guy got half a brick. One got a whole brick in his hand. They was gonna' really clobber me, but they want to talk about it. That's where they made their mistake. They was swearin' and raisin' hell about what they was gonna' do to me and old Rudy heard it and he come runnin' out there with a hand-ax and said, "What's the matter, Jones?" I said, "These guys are figurin' on killin' me, I guess." And they knew him and knew he had the ax. So they took off.

I knew they're gonna' come back. So I've got a gun at home. I bought it from some guy who was a watchman over at the Miller Rubber when I was workin' here before I went back down home. Every day in the morning when I went to work, I'd take that gun and put it under the car seat. In the evening, when dark come, I put that gun in my pocket. I know they're gonna' wait for me. So on a Saturday night (Maybe the next. I don't remember), I see 'em settin' on this store porch. I recognized 'em. And I've got to change this trolley so I can go back to town. I go back and change the trolley, go up to the front and get ready to go and they pull the trolley down so I can't move. I see this guy out there holdin' that trolley pole. I get this gun and I go bam! Right beside of him. The bullet bent in that sheet metal. If you ever seen gravel fly, that son-of-a-bitch took off up that road in high gear. Man, he hoed that road up, I'll tell you! He really "skinned ass"! Never did see him around that corner again. He thought that old hillbilly had killed him!

I never had any more trouble with 'em. I never had any more trouble. They knew I would shoot 'em if they messed around with me and they didn't bother me. But they would've beat the heck out of me, see. Four of 'em.

I'd've been messed up, I'll tell ya'. You run right up along the river and a bunch of river rats lived up in there. They weren't the high-class people in town. A lot of 'em were hillbillies come in out of the countryside and come in to Paducah to work. They never had much education or anything else. They were pretty rough characters, I'll tell you. Ummh! I had some experiences that I can't even relate. No, sir.

> When Mary starts to board a car,
> Just see how brazen bad men are!
> Why don't they turn their heads, I beg?
> Why should they look at Mary's hat?
>
> Those high steps are a disgrace;
> They are entirely out of place;
> The distance truly should be half;
> Then Mary wouldn't show her animosity.

"Some Rhymes"
The Daily Messenger
March 19, 1914

Haskell: That was the day of the hobble skirts. You've seen women naked. They run around now with no clothes at all on. But in those days, they didn't do that. They come up with a skirt that was tight in the knees. And these damn steps on those old streetcars were about two feet high. They weren't low.

To get on a streetcar, the only way to get on was to pull it up and step up. And they exposed the meat in New York. One little old Dutch girl— Her name was Koch. I don't know whether she was married. I think she was single. She was short to start with. But she got on that car, you really got a— You really got an eyeful, I'll tell you. They had regular stockings, but they only come up to their knees. They had a garter around their knees. Then they wore a loose, like a balloon pants for men, only they were cut up short in the crotch. There wasn't much in there. When they stepped up there, hell, they was exposed like a camera film.

One old colored girl, she used to pick up laundry. She would go out to your house and get the laundry, take it home, wash it and bring it back, you know. A common way of bringin' it was tied up in a sheet. And I'd help her. Hell, the first step was this high. She'd come up to a car with a bundle of that laundry and I'd pick it up and stick it over in the back-end side out of the way. And she'd come on in and go back and set down. Quite several times I'd helped her. I kid her along a little. She was probably fifty-five years old, maybe. Had a great big wen right on her forehead. Right dead center up here at the hairline. Look like your thumb stickin' out of her head. I've seen a lot of 'em. Various kinds. People get 'em on their hands and here and there. I don't know what causes 'em.

Anyway, she gets on the car out by the end of the line with this big bundle of clothes. And I help her on with it and she gets up there. I says, "You oughta' get a man to take care of you. You're gettin' too old to run around here draggin' these big bundles of clothes around. But," I says, "you're probably too old. A man wouldn't want you. You're probably too old to satisfy a man, anyway." And I kept givin' her a lot of bullshit. I kind of got under her skin a little. There was woods alongside one side of the road— The streetcar tracks down toward there. Used to have a lumberyard there years before. She said, "I'll tell you somethin', white boy. You go down there in this woods with me. When you come back, you'll know you've been somewhere." She was all right. I treated 'em all right. I had no problems.

Ahh, I did have a problem with a couple of 'em. One woman was gonna' cut me with a razor 'cause I didn't stop where she wanted me to. She was a colored woman. She wanted to get off in the middle of the block. So, just as she passed the stop, she rang the bell. If she'd've been an old, crippled-up woman, I might've stopped in the middle of the block. But I knew where she lived and I went on down to the stop. She said, "Why didn't you let me off when I rang the bell?" I said, "That ain't a stop. This is. You have to come down here and stop." So, she started to give me some badmouth and I said, "C'mon, get off the car." So, she reached down in the front of her dress, here, and come out with a straight razor.

U.S. Patent 691,809 of January 28, 1902 by William B. Potter for an electric streetcar controller. The heavy handle and rod would be lifted out of the socket and carried to the other end of the car when the motorman changed directions—or when he simply needed to protect himself (USPTO).

We had a controller handle that we used to shut the doors with that you took off and carried to the other end of the car when we changed ends of the car. Always kept that shaft greased. It was kind of a half-moon thing. So, I grabbed that up and I said, "Don't open it! I'll kill you!"

I said, "You get off of this car." That rod weighed about two pounds. I would've really clobbered her. Broke her arm, anyway. If nothin' else.[31]

There was a guy, colored fella', got on with a phony silver dollar he'd hammered out of a piece of lead. Hammered and cut it to the right thickness about. Hit it on one side with a silver dollar and made an imprint on it. I was busy, so he slipped it to me. And when I got to the end of the line, I checked my money and I see what I've got and I know who gave it to me. That trip or one trip immediately after that, there was a city detective got on the car. I told him, give him the money and told him where this colored boy lived. He was a crippled fellow. He was easy to identify. So, when I got back there, he had him out by the side of the track waiting on me. Says, "Is this the guy?" And I said, "Yeah, that's him." So the detective says, "Well, you'd better give this man a good dollar or I'm gonna' throw you in jail." So he gave me a good dollar and old Franklin told him he could go.[32] He said, "Don't I get that other dollar back?" He said, "You are trying to get into jail, ain't you?" Said, "You don't get it back!"[33]

I think I told you this story about the big, slim guy that rode the streetcar with me. This guy worked for a milling company who sold feed, flour, meal. And he delivered. He was the truck driver. I think he had a wagon. I don't think he had a truck. I think he had a team to the grocery stores, here and there. He delivered this stuff. About six-foot-four or five. Big, thin, tall guy. Black guy.

But every Saturday, about noon or a little later, he'd catch my streetcar. And under his arm he had a bag wrapped in newspaper—twenty-four to forty-eight pound bag of flour. He was headed for Allen Street. There's about ten houses in there with all colored women. Not many men. Colored women. This is in the depression of 1920 when there ain't no way to get food only earn it—one way or another. It don't make any difference. The streetcar track stops right here at Allen Street.

So Slim would get on the streetcar about twelve or twelve-thirty (Whatever time I got down to Main Street) with this bag under his arm wrapped in newspaper. He'd stole it durin' the week sometime. I say, "Where you goin', Slim?" I'm goin' over to Allen Street and get me some of that smoked ham." He'd laugh about it. I didn't get in any hurry to leave when he'd get off the car with a bag under his arm. About eight or ten of these houses along the side of the street. None on the other side. They had a ballpark down in there.

Slim'd get off of that— I can see him yet. He'd get off of that, start walkin' up that bank and every one of these houses some head would pop out. "Hello there, Slim!" "I know you, Slim!" "How are y'all, Slim?" Everybody wants to see Slim for the weekend. He is the selector. He's got from seven or eight houses anybody he wants up there to spend the weekend with. Monday morning, Slim would come out all but draggin'. He felt worn out. He probably made three or four houses in the meantime. "How you make out, Slim?" Said, "Well, I didn't do too bad. But I'll tell you what, I shore is tired." Yeah, he was a character. I liked him. He was a great guy. He was a lot of fun. "I'm goin' up and get me some of that smoked ham." And he did, too. No doubt about it. No doubt about it. He got it.

I can't believe in all the years I was gone from there— There wasn't any business on that street from one end to the other. Three miles. That streetcar line was three miles long. I'll give it (and I'm stretchin' it a little bit) six or eight mom and pop grocery stores. One slaughterhouse. Jones slaughterhouse [T.A. Jones & Sons].[34] They butchered and sold meat downtown. They made wieners and stuff of that kind, see. One day a week (I don't remember if it was Saturday or when it was) a colored kid would go downtown with one of them great big wicker baskets full of wieners. Just right out of the boilin' water.

301

Hot. He'd get on the streetcar with 'em to take 'em downtown to scatter 'em around down in the restaurants and hamburger joints. I used to get a half a dozen of 'em and eat 'em. Beautiful. Fresh, good meat. Jones slaughterhouse. "Cold storage," they called it.

One colored guy— Was gonna' kick him in the face. We stopped at a downtown stop with a big Catholic church. And they had a pretty big eave. If the weather was bad, the women would hug the church to stay out of the weather 'til the streetcar come. Then they'd all gang up. It was a busy time of day and they'd been shoppin' or somethin'. I don't remember. But anyway, he was standin' back there in the church and these women all started to get on the car. And he was just elbowin' right through the crowd. He was gonna' come on— I saw it.

Well, these platforms was high out there. I drew my foot back. I was gonna' kick him right under the chin. He saw what I was gonna' do and he backed up. He waited 'til all the women got on and come over and said, "I guess I made a mistake." I said, "I guess you did." That's all that was ever said. I would've kicked his head against the church. And not particularly because he was black. I'd've done the same thing to a white man. I got along with blacks all right. Treated 'em like a human bein' and they treated me all right.

The High Life

The excursion boats are largely frequented by prostitutes and their male comrades, so that decent people avoid them. Surreptitious drinking goes on in them, as well as vulgar dancing and more or less open solicitation. No bedrooms are on board, but one boat has a small room which may be locked, and acquaintances made on these trips often lead to serious consequences later on. In addition, open gambling goes on constantly on slot machines, and secret gambling by card games and dice is allowed at times. For certain excursions beer is sold on several of the boats.

Report and Recommendations of
the Paducah Vice Commission
Paducah, Kentucky, 1916

Haskell: Went on what they called an "excursion." It was an outing in a river steamer. It'd leave about seven o'clock at night or eight and stay 'til midnight. Pretty good size boat. Carry four or five hundred people. They had a bar and everything. They had boot-leggers. And the "chippies" in town (They were the prostitutes), they always went on this excursion boat. That night they were out in force.

My sister Grace went along with Florence and I. And that's when this "shimmy" was big—great big dance. They shook all over like a Quaker. Mom [Florence] and Grace got quite a kick out of seein' a bunch of hustlers out there shakin' it up. I can remember when Mom looked at the women and said, "I didn't know there was that kind of people in the world!"

Florence: Grace didn't know we was goin' anywhere and when she got up there and found out where we were, said she's goin' home. No, she wasn't goin' home. She was goin' with us. So, she didn't think she wanted to, but she liked it.

Haskell: Paducah was a meltin' pot. They all come in there to get booze and there were girls always where there was booze. You bought a pint of good whiskey for a dollar, a pint of cheap whiskey for a quarter. And it wasn't very good. Oooooh! Like chill tonic. Man, it was awful. "Barrel whiskey," they called it. You could buy a quart of booze for two dollars. Good bourbon for two dollars. "Bar whiskey"— Bar whiskey at the bar cost a nickel for a shot. If you wanted bonded whiskey, it was a dime. And they'd throw a little mix of some kind in. Ginger ale or somethin'. Whatever. No ice. Throw that down. Then you wash it down with a little glass of somethin'.

When Ralph was runnin' the streetcar there, he said he picked up a travellin' man one Saturday afternoon. He said, "I'm back in old Paducah again." Said, "I used to like to come to this town." Said, "Not long ago, I was here and I went down and registered at the—" I think they called that the Southern Hotel.[35] "Thought I'd go out and pick me up a girl for the weekend."

Said, "I went down in front of the ten cent store and some big hillbilly gal was standin' down there in front of the ten cent store and I engaged her in conversation and asked her if she'd like to spend a 'happy weekend.'" "Ahh-ll right."

Said, "I took her up to the hotel and we get in the bed and she had a package in her hand. I got on top of her and put the works to her and she ate a pound of peanuts while I was workin' on her." Said, "I never did want to come back to this town again." She was pretty interested. Layin' there and eatin' peanuts.

My brother Ralph run a line that went out to Union Station. There was a woods not far from the Union Station out there. They had a lane out there. Anyway, he said this young guy and his girlfriend got on the car late in the evening another time and this guy was tickled. He was laughin' and laughin' and laughin'. He could hardly pay his fare. And Ralph said, "What the hell's goin' on?" Said, "Well, I had this girlfriend— We was out in the woods there and I took the car seat out (In those days, you could just lift the car seats out. It was no problem.). We had some pastime and I come back and the car's gone." Somebody stole his car while he was out in the brush.

He said, "I went up to the house there nearby and carried this seat up. I didn't want to lose it. I thought maybe I could find my car again. I knocked and the guy come to the door and said, 'Mister, could I leave my car seat here?'" he said, "That guy just laughed like hell." He left his car seat there and he was still laughin' about it. They'd walked over to the Union Station and was catchin' the streetcar back to town.

Generation's Time Needed, Make Nation Wholly Dry
[Prohibition Commissioner] Kramer Says Cannot Be Practical Statute While
Taste Is Known, says Country Is Really In Favor of Prohibition Enforcement
The Paducah Evening Sun
January 7, 1921

Seize Moonshine on River Front
720 Gallons Mash Stored in Tiny Houseboat, Owner Arrested
The Paducah Evening Sun
March 20, 1921

Seize Five Stills in Business District
Police Raid 5 Still Plant, Believe Huge Shipping Plot Nipped
Most Complete Plant Unearthed in District, Two Arrested, Both Deny Guilt
of Operations
The Paducah Evening Sun
July 21, 1921

Liquor Traffic is Growing, Police to Redouble Efforts
Claim "Hootch" Comes in From River Stills in Quantity
The Paducah Evening Sun
August 22, 1921

Oh Lucky Fish; 176 Gallons of Shine in Ohio
Police Dump Contents of Jugs Seized by Raiders
The Paducah Evening Sun,
September 30, 1921

Police Court
It is the first day in some time that a drunk failed to appear on the docket.
The Paducah Evening Sun,
November 17, 1921

Haskell: When we went back to Paducah in 1920, they had quite a lot of people that bootlegged. Quite a lot. That was a big deal. I never knew all of 'em, but I knew a few of 'em. They had these places where you knocked on the door. They always had a bottle. They'd dump it in the toilet if the police come in. A peephole through the door. If the police knocked on the door with a uniform on— If they didn't know him, why, they'd take their booze and dump it in the toilet and flush it and let him in. They didn't keep very much. They kept it out somewhere hid. They'd go get it if you needed it or when it run out. They'd keep it at the neighbors or somewhere else. There was all kinds of rackets in that thing.

They had a man named Rickman who had a bunch of stills and he'd hire young guys to operate 'em. He was a moonshiner. Not a bootlegger. He was a moonshiner. He sold it wholesale. He'd furnish the still, the location, the material to make it out of. Mason jars to put it in and give them a dollar a gallon for runnin' the still, see. They were makin' a lot of money. You got fined, he'd pay your fine. But if you had to go to jail, there wasn't much he could do about it—only you had to go to jail. It usually was fines. The city wanted the money. They didn't want you in jail. You cost money in jail.

Just before I went on the car, they hired a young kid. He was just a homeless kind of a tramp. Young lad, seventeen, eighteen years old and he was workin' on the track. Well, when I was runnin' the car, he used to ride the car with me occasionally. I knew him, talked to him. I hadn't missed him because I didn't know him that well.

One day he got on the car out at the end of the line. He started to pay his fare and he pulls out a roll or money a show dog couldn't jump over—really nice big roll. I said, "Man, where'd you get all the money!?" Because I used to give him money to eat on! And I didn't have much money. But I'd give him fifteen cents to go to the store and get a loaf of bread and some bologna, see, when we was workin'.

He said, "I'm workin' for Rickman." And I said, "What are you doin', runnin' a still?" He said, "Yeah," said, "I'm doin' all right." He said, "I'm goin' down to the riverfront to the Mill and Mine Supply. I got to pick up some copper tubin'." They were makin' up some new stills, see. And he said, " When I come back I want to carry it on the streetcar out to the—" I said, "O.K., you can carry it." We carried packages like that. After about the second trip, why, he met me out there with this big burlap bag with a great big roll of tubing in it. Probably had a hundred pounds in it. He put it on the car and we talked 'til he got off the car. Never did see him again.

Officers Seize 2,000 Gallons of Moonshine Mash
Police and Sheriff Join in Visit to Farm on Said Road

City and county authorities cooperated in a liquor raid late Tuesday at the farm of James Rickman, on the Said road, 12 miles from Paducah. Nearly 2,000 gallons of mash, evidently the product of a giant still or series of stills, rewarded the officers for their search. The mash was stored in 18 tanks each holding 50 gallons and nine large containers or troughs. No distilling equipment was found.

The police and county authorities received a tip several days ago that a still was being operated on the Said road at or near Rickman's farm. Yesterday the officers questioned Newman Sledd, 19 years old, who was suspected of aiding in the marketing of illicit liquor made at the Rickman place. The questioning of Sledd hastened the raid but did not prevent a hasty removal of the manufacturing apparatus.

Sheriff Roy Stewart and former Sheriff George Alliston accompanied Detectives Jack Nelson, John Dunaway and Kelly Franklin to the Rickman farm. They found no one on the place.

Rickman operated a store at Benton a number of years ago and Marshall county authorities suspected that his place was a rendezvous for moonshiners, the police say. One night Rickman's store in Benton was wrecked by a dynamite explosion and Rickman and some of the members of his family were slightly injured. Later Rickman filed a suit in United States court against several Benton citizens.

The seizure yesterday afternoon was the largest single discovery of liquor in the making yet achieved by the authorities in McCracken county.

The Paducah Evening Sun
Wednesday, January 4, 1922

Haskell: They finally got to raidin' Rickman and they give him a bad time. They'd fine him pretty heavy every time they'd catch one of these stills. They finally broke him up. He had to quit. He was makin' this whiskey and shippin' it on the river by powerboat at night. He'd load a big load of it and take it down to Cairo, over across to Metropolis, or up the river to Paris or someplace like that, see. Was a pretty big operator.

Federal Officers Arrest Dickerson
Allege Violation of Dry Laws In Possession Of Whisky

Clarence L. Dickerson, proprietor of a soft drink stand, 109 North Fourth street, was arrested by federal prohibition agents yesterday afternoon on charges of having whisky in possession and with delivery of whisky. Federal agents raided his place on Fourth street.

Dickerson was arraigned before United States Commissioner Walter A. Blackburn, and waived his examining trial. He is held under $200 bond for his appearance before the federal grand jury at the April term of Court.

The arrest of Dickerson followed that of Neal Ogles, taxicab driver, who delivered a pint of grain alcohol into the hands of federal agents Thursday night. Dickerson is alleged to have delivered the whisky to Ogles.

Officers raided the soft drink establishment of Dickerson yesterday afternoon but found nothing in the way of illicit liquors. Officers searching the place were J.W. Clark, prohibition enforcement agent, T.L. Whitaker, Louisville, prohibition agent, and R.W. Kimbell, deputy United States Marshal.

The Paducah Evening Sun
Saturday, January 15, 1921

Haskell: But Clarence Dickerson ("Poker Dick")— He killed a guy. I knew the guy he killed. This guy was a bully. They were kinda' friends, I guess. He come in there drunk and on the muscle—like some drunks. I don't know what the argument was about. It didn't make any difference. I didn't care. I didn't really know either one of 'em closely. He picked that big beer mug up and he was gonna' throw it at Dick. Dick says, "Don't you throw that. I'll kill you." So the guy threw it and Dick ducked under the bar and grabbed the gun and killed him dead as a mackerel.

But he was a poker player. They wouldn't let him deal. Nobody would play with him and let him deal. He was too slick. They knew he knew how to handle cards. They'd play with him in a game, but not if he dealt.

I saw him one night tear the top off a convertible. He had a Buick convertible. Red one. Nice, beauty. In those days, cars were not like that too much. Our Broadway was from the river to Twenty-first Street. Twenty blocks. Straight as an arrow. Flat. And kids used to race on there at one o'clock in the morning. There was nothin' else on the street but them.

They had a lot of awnings over sidewalks down there. It was hot, you know. They'd have a post set right at the edge of the walk, up here, and then a flat roof over the top of it. Slope it a little. So people could walk under it. A big store would have maybe three of 'em. A little store, two. I don't know whether they belong to the city or belong to the store. I would guess it's the city. But he was crossin' Sixth Street (It come out of the River) and he was flyin'.

A guy come out of Sixth Street— I think he had a pick-up truck or stake-body truck or somethin'. But he come out of that street and Dick's comin' this way. He cut around him to go in front of this drug store over there. He set that car up on the edge and he caught that convertible top. Just ripped it off. It was still hangin'. And he never slowed down. He just kept goin'. That top was floppin' around behind that car as he went on down the street. But I'd seen him a lot of times. I knew him when I saw him. Clarence Dickerson. Known all over as "Poker Dick."[36]

I see a guy named Dell Dowdy one night. He was from Mayfield. He ran a poker game in a bootleg joint. Upstairs over some kind of business. I don't know where. Over on Trimble Street. I knew where it was, but I never was in there.

I happened to be workin' off a different line from my regular line that time. I don't know. I guess I was still on extra board. I don't remember. We come up this block and made a turn to go toward the river. Well, this type of car we had, they called the single-truck outfit. It was small. When you made the turn, it'd swing way over that front.

I come up here and I almost caught him between a parked car as he went through there. He had four or five of those jellybeans from a cathouse somewhere in the back end of that old touring car with the top down. They didn't have a stitch of clothes on. About eleven o'clock at night. The town was pretty well put away. They rolled up the sidewalks about nine-thirty.

One night I was runnin' Broadway.[37] A colored that I knew was a houseboy out there on one of those big homes on Broadway. He said, "I'm gonna' get a bottle when I get down to the river. Would you want a drink?" And I said, "Ahh, I'll take a little drink." So, while I'm changin' the trolley, he runs in one of these dives there and come back with I guess a half a pint, though it should've been a pint. I don't remember. Hands it to me and I took a slug of it and went on about my business.

In about 30 minutes, I'm almost paralyzed. I could see my hand work. I could kick that gong. And I couldn't feel my foot hit the floor. It had some ether or somethin' I don't know what. But I managed to shake it off after a little— Wonder I didn't run over somebody and kill 'em. Umh! I never wanted any more of his booze.

City "Bone Dry" as Police Grip Liquor Traffic
The Paducah Evening Sun
January 4, 1922

Still Boiling on Stove When Officers Came
Attempt to Pour Out Bubbling Contents Thwarted
The Paducah Evening Sun
Tuesday, January 17, 1922
Officers Find "Mule" Hidden Beneath Floor[38]

2 Soft Drink Stands Raided for Alleged Violations

The Paducah Evening Sun
Tuesday, January 17, 1922

Dry Men Seize Booze At "Stag"
Keep Watch From Office Across Street

Swooping down upon soft drink place at 115 North Fourth street, after a three-hour vigil from the darkened windows of an office building across the street, prohibition enforcement officers seized five half-pints of moonshine whisky last night at midnight.

Warrants against Clarence Dickerson, proprietor of The Stag; George Bondurant, bartender, and John Shaw, a Negro porter, were written following the raid. Dickerson was arrested on a charge of selling liquor, and Bondurant and Shaw on charges of aiding and abetting in the sale of whisky. The defendants were released on bonds of $300 each. The cases will be set for trial in McCracken county court.

County, city and federal officers watched The Stag from 8 o'clock until 11:45 o'clock last night, from a darkened office on the west side of the City National bank building.

Members of the raiding party were L.F. Morris, federal prohibition agent for the western district of Kentucky; Sheriff Roy Stewart, Chief of Police Charles Whittemore, Deputy Sheriffs Charles Clark and Bob Bannerson, and Night Police Captain Lige Cross.

The Paducah Evening Sun
Saturday, June 10, 1922

Haskell: The police didn't pay any attention to it. Then, they elected a do-gooder for a mayor. He tried to put the heat on the bootleggers and had 'em all troubled.[39] That was just about the time I left when he got elected. I knew people and I heard about it. I think he got old man Rickman. He kept knockin' him off 'til they finally broke him down.

Old man [Benjamin] Moredock (who was this friend of mine in Paducah's dad, lived in Paducah at that time) told me about this incident. He was a hardware salesman.[40] He went all over the area there peddlin' hardware for some big wholesale outfit in Saint Louis for years. Sold merchandise to this man who was the banker for the moonshiners. He furnished the metal for the stills, the pipe, the copper. They needed money for the mash, he'd furnish the mash. But was considered a very conservative businessman. He had a big store, general store (not just a hardware store). And got no picture in the thing. He was workin' in the back door.

This do-gooder (He was a preacher), he gets another man and they go up there and are gonna' clean out this bootlegging that was between the Cumberland and Mississippi River. It's a strip up there for quite a little ways. Some places, it isn't too wide. Other places, it might be 15-20 miles wide. So, he went to this store, flashed his badge, said, I'm from the Internal Revenue. I'm up here to clean these shiners out." The old man said, "I think it's a good idea. They've been here for a long time. I don't know any, but I have nothing to do. If I could help you, I would, but I can't. But I've heard there's a lot of it goin' around down here." "O.K."

So they take off. In the meantime, the word went out immediately. "G-man's in the area," you know. So they're drivin' along a ridge along the bank of the river and about three or four of them hillbillies are up in the brush with a Winchester rifle. When they come drivin' up there, they start shootin'. They shot the motor right out of that old Ford. They broke it to pieces.

These two guys barreled out of that and down over the riverbank and run down the river and found a boat. Took off down the river in high speed. Never came back. Old man Moredock said that car sat in that road for a week or ten days before they ever sent anybody out there to get it. It just set there. Everybody was afraid to go after it. Finally, the Feds sent somebody up there to tow it back to Paducah. But he said they really tore it apart.

Boy, I had a lot of friends. I did 'em little favors like that and they liked me. It didn't cost anybody anything. Long time ago. Long time ago. Holy smoke. Almost eighty years. Almost seventy years. Almost seventy years. Nineteen-twenty-one, '22. I stayed there until July '22 when we quit and come back here.

Florence: I'll tell ya', we had some pretty rough times then for two or three years. Finally, work started up again. We came back to Akron and "Hack" [Haskell] went back to work.

PART FIVE

AKRON, OHIO
1922

CHAPTER THIRTY-TWO

RETURN

One outstanding result of the recent depression was an outgrowth of real efficiency in the factory, office and sales forces of the rubber companies in the Akron manufacturing district.

Through a reduction in personnel in all departments and an increased output from the employes remaining, the Akron companies are averaging three tires a day for each person on the payrolls. In the boom times, a rough estimate was one man for each tire made.

Nine of the larger Akron factories report 27,000 rubber workers are turning out 80,000 tires daily in comparison with 100,000 tires produced by 75,000 workers during the peak of employment.

Employment figures from Akron business bureaus show that the low ebb in the rubber industry was reached in December of last year when the nine factories employed only 18,500.

The peak of employment was reached when these same companies employed between 95,000 and 100,000 workers, including office forces.

"Factory Efficiency Improves"
The Rubber Age, Vol. 9
April 1921

From Akron, Ohio, came the report that business is steadily increasing, both in activity and volume. The rubber industry in that city is said to employ at the present time 45,000 hands, compared with 35,000 during last year. One of the prominent rubber companies there is turning out 25,300 tires per day with 11,425 employees at work; whereas, at the same period in 1921, the labor of 7,500 persons was necessary to produce a daily output of 7,000 tires.

"Employment"
Industrial Management
June 1922

Haskell: I wanted to come back. I've always wanted to come back. I made pretty good money in Akron before when I was here. When we left here, we was making pretty good money. Down there, you wasn't making anything. Well, I didn't realize they wasn't making anything in Akron anymore, either. But I thought they was. So I was anxious to come back. It was picked up. It was picked up some.

After we come back here in '22, we got a house. We lived on this corner. Twenty-seventh and Childs. We had a room about twice as big as a table. I am tellin' you, it was little. Florence had a great, big trunk she brought to Akron with her. We didn't have room for it in that place. I guess we took it upstairs. I don't think we had room for it on that floor 'cause that room was small. I'll tell you, it was a small bedroom. You had to put a bed in it and a chair. And that's about all the room you got in there. No more. She would pay 12 dollars a week for those rooms.

We cooked upstairs in the attic. They had a great, long attic up in the top. Not too wide, but it was roomy. Well, we cooked up there and we could stay up there only when it wasn't real hot. My brother Ralph come up and she made him a bed in one end of the attic and he slept there. But he ate with us. The Davises ate in the basement in hot weather. They had a stove down there

They told Florence if we wanted to eat in the basement we could take our food down and warm up what we wanted to eat. Somethin' like that. In the evenin', after they got through, we'd go down there to eat our dinner. They had a table and everything down in the basement. So we ate down there quite a bit.

Bill Davis. Him and his wife lived there. Worked for a big department store. He was a shippin' clerk. Shipped stuff. Seein' it shipped out. They hauled a lot of stuff to houses in those days. He drank a little and his wife give him hell. They'd both been married before. What the hell was her name? He called her "Biddy," but I don't know what her name was now. I can't think of it. They had a parrot.

They would get in an argument and the parrot would scream. The old man would tell Missus Davis to shut up and the parrot picked it up, you know. They'd get in an argument and the parrot would holler, "Shut up!" They'd get tickled and laugh and quit their arguin'. They had an adopted daughter. Marie was the girl's name. Marie. Little, fat blonde. This parrot would yell, "Marie!" You could hear it a block.

We had a milkman when we lived in Firestone Park. He had a big route. He used to collect in the evenin'. Nine-thirty, he'd be collectin' for milk. You paid so much a week or month or whatever. I don't remember what the deal was. But it was a lot. That guy would have a pile of bills that big in his pocket. I said, "My God, aren't you afraid somebody'll hold you up along the route?" "Ahhh," he said, "Never occurred to me." But he'd had two, three thousand dollars in his pocket at nine, ten o'clock at night prowlin' around out there. Today, he couldn't do that. Hell, they'd fry him in oil and take it away from him. But in those days, things weren't so bad.

When we lived on Archwood, we found out the man and the woman took a bath in the same water because they didn't want to heat that much water.[1] They just heated the water long enough to take a bath and then turned out the gas. So, we never had hot water unless we heated it on the gas stove and poured it in the bathtub with a teakettle or bucket. She thought we oughta' take a bath in the same water 'cause it took gas to heat the water.

She didn't furnish much heat at all. Her and her husband both worked and she kept a big police dog in the basement. We was actually afraid to go in the basement to the furnace. Florence was. He wasn't very friendly. Some days the house would get pretty cold.

193 East Archwood, Akron, Ohio. When Haskell, Florence, Ralph and Jack Jones lived here in 1924, the landlords, Mr. & Mrs. J.T. Wynn, were adverse to furnishing heat. Or water. Or the use of the toilet. Or even the carpet. This home was on the northern edge of the original section of Firestone Park built by the Firestone Tire & Rubber Company (July, 1991).

She didn't want us to have company. Said she don't want us to wear out the carpet. Said she'd had that carpet for sixteen years and she didn't want to wear it out.

The old man used to come home from work and go in the bathroom and set on the john and read the paper for an hour. There was only one bathroom in the house. Sometimes you had to get in there. My brother Ralph and "Jack" Jones lived there with us and ate with us.[2] And one of 'em had to go shit and the old man's sittin' in the bathroom readin' the paper. He had to go down to the gas station. They didn't have any water in the kitchen. We had to get kitchen water out of the bathroom. So, we didn't stay there long. Very short. We lived there about ten days. We all moved.

Florence: You can run into all kinds of people when you move around from place to place that way.

Haskell: Forty-six Ido Avenue. Florence and I lived here for a short time. Very short. That's where our first baby was born, in that house. We lost the first baby there.

CHAPTER THIRTY-THREE

THE MILLER RUBBER COMPANY II

Inasmuch as the curing used to be done in cylinders sunk in pits in the ground (usually in the basement), the 'semi-cure' process room retains its name, "the pit" . . . . The work is *laborious* and on this account big powerful workmen were usually seen. In three places the piecework was promoting exhaustion, while in 1 large plant, the men, though working in 8-hour shifts, were hurrying along, many of them, half stripped, and dashing from steam heated to draughty areas in what appeared to be a killing pace.

"Rubber—Steam Vulcanizing"
A Survey of Industrial Health Hazards
And Occupational Diseases in Ohio, 1915

The second upheaval has been in the labor situation. With the supply of experienced tire builders completely exhausted, tire companies have begun to bid against each other for men. The Firestone Tire & Rubber Co., started the movement with a ten-per-cent increase in all factory wages, effective May 29. The B.F. Goodrich, Co., in order to salve a feeling of dissatisfaction among its men reduced its shifts by two hours and gave the men a readjustment in wages which averages about 77 cents an hour for them. The company offered 71 and the men demanded 80. The Miller Rubber Co. has followed with a commensurate upward revision of wages and it is considered certain that other companies will have to do the same, for every company needs men and cannot afford to lose any it now has on its payroll.[1]

"Labor Supply Scarce"
The Magazine of Wall Street
May 13, 1922

Haskell: They wouldn't hire me back at the Firestone, 'cause they said I had quit without notice. It was a raw deal, but I was better off, I guess. Ralph got laid off and they were layin' off whole shifts. I didn't have much service 'cause I quit when I went down to get married and come back and hired in again. I went to the foreman and I said, "My brother got laid off. They're layin' 'em off and I know I don't have much service. How much more time I got here?" He said, "Not a helluva' lot, I'll tell ya' that." I told him, "Why don't you lay me off, then, and I'll go on home with him—if I'm gonna' get it anytime soon." When I come back, he had me wrote up as havin' quit without notice. They wouldn't hire me. So I went over to the Miller.

Wages were awful low. They cut wages to the bone. First day I went to work, I went to work in the pit at Miller. I'd worked about an hour and some big hillbilly come up to me and said, "We're gonna' shut this place down at 10:00." And said, "How do you feel about it?" Well, I don't know. I didn't know what the story is. He says, "Well, we want to. We ain't makin' enough money." I didn't ask how much we was makin' 'cause all I wanted was a job, see. When I left here, I was makin' about twelve dollars a day—which was a buck and a half an hour, see.

So, I said, " I didn't even ask what, how much the job paid. I was experienced and worked at Firestone at the same kind of work." He said, "Well, you know how much we're makin'?" I said, "No." He said, "We're makin' twenty-seven dollars a week. Forty-eight hours." So, "I can't blame you for shuttin' 'er down." They shut it down and went to the office and told 'em they had to have enough to make 'em forty dollars a week.

They promised, promised to give us forty dollars a week. It went on for about ten days and no change. They had a system. When the rate changes is when they post it on the wall. They had a production sheet. They drew a line through it and everything below that was the new rate. Everything above was the old rate. Right at that same time, they put the sheet up first and then put the line. So, they shut it down again.

Went to the office and the superintendent, the department foreman, turned around to his office boy and says, "Didn't you post those new rates?" And the boy very meekly said, "No, sir." "Well, you

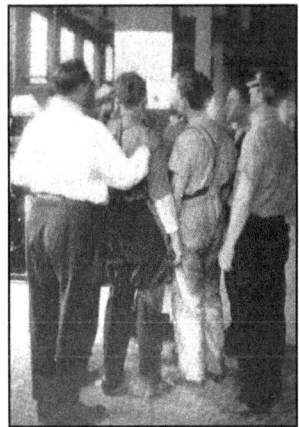

Posting the departmental efficiency ratings at The Miller Rubber Co.

317

get down there and post 'em!" He had held out just as long as he could to get the last tire made at the old rate. They wonder why they've got unions.

* * *

Haskell: I put the rings on the green tires that shaped the bead in the pit. That's the curing room where they cured tires. They had two rings that fit around the bead (one on each side). The bead had to be forced into this ring. We put a bag in 'em and clamped these beads together with a little "U" clamp. Some of 'em were bolted together. You had an air hose there and you blew the bag up on the inside to see that your bead was in place all the way around.

Then they took them and put 'em in the mold. That mold had the tread design on it. They locked the top of the mold shut. Then, they put twenty, twenty-one, two, three tires (dependin' on the size) in these big, deep pit heaters. Some of 'em, you could only get about eight in— the big truck tires.

They built a tree of fittings in the middle of those molds. They'd set these fittings on top of the other and they kept buildin' that up. Each one of 'em had a leader that went over and fastened to a tire.

They had a sheet of steel ('bout half inch thick) that went on top of the top mold. This top leader went over to an air connector and this piece of steel had a cut in it about eight inches wide. You put your leader through it so it wouldn't get smashed. Then they'd lock the top on.

Finally, you'd raise up your ram and put about two hundred pounds of air pressure in there to force that tire out against the mold. Then they turned live steam on it and cooked it for anywhere from forty-five minutes to an hour to three hours, dependin' on the size of the tire.

These big heaters, they were about six foot across and went down in through the floor. The head of it only stood up about twenty-four inches to thirty inches above the floor. You worked with the ram and all the hooks and steam fittings and everything that were coming out from the bottom down below. I think we had nineteen or twenty on our side of the room. And I think there was one more on the other side of the room. We had twenty and they had twenty-one. Then in the middle of the room, they had (I'm guessin' again) six, seven big heaters that they cooked truck tires in. We had forty-by-eights and forty-two-nines and forty-four-tens. That's the way they measured the tire. They didn't have all these micrometric systems in those days. They all used inches.

I run a gang downstairs. Oh, couple, three years. I was runnin' a gang in the old Miller pit on the seventh of July and it was a hundred and twenty degrees in that room for about a week, ten days. Ooooh, it was hotter than hell. It wasn't warm. No air. No ventilators. The guys would knock the windows out as soon as it got hot in the spring. Somebody was always throwin' a bolt or a clamp or somethin' through the windows. They finally had them all knocked out.

They sent me a young man his first day. Come from down close to Cincinnati. Big, farm boy. Nice, young man. They sent him down there to work for me. It was hot weather. And it was hot in that basement. I said, "Who sent you down here? [Frank] "Red" Balderson?" "Yeah." I said, "Well, you go back up there and tell him to send somebody else down here. This is too hot for you here."

He looked around and "Does this guy do it?" "Yeah, but he's been here for years. He's acclimated, you know." And he felt bad. He said, "I'm used to hard work. I'm a farm boy. I've worked on a farm." I said, "Yeah. And you was always out in the fresh air. You could get a little breeze occasionally. But you've never worked in a place as hot as this is." I said, "This is hot."

I said, "See that little old four-foot fan on the end down there?" It wasn't high speed. I said, "That is the ventilation they got here." They had like a French door down in the corner where they moved machinery in. Big, twelve-foot door. We could open the top of it. And stand on the lattice down here where the stuff was nailed—wooden door. You could stick your head out once in a while and get a little air.

He was insulted. He thought if anybody else could do the job, he could do it, see. I convinced him that I was gonna' make him go back so he went back up there. And he was up there a couple weeks and they sent him back again one day. He went to work and I had a bunch of hogs that was workin' for me. They worked piecework and they all got the same pay. They got paid for production. And they drove a hard row. So he worked about a half a day or three or four hours. Whatever.

He come around to me and he said, "I want to apologize to you." I said, "What do you mean? What's wrong?" I had forgotten about this other incident. He said, "I was pretty mad at you when you sent me back upstairs the other day. I felt like you didn't think I could do the job." Said, "I wouldn't've been able to make it." Said, "I know now. I wouldn't've been able to make it."

I saw another guy. Come out of the army in World War One. Come up to our gang where they stripped these tires. They were cord tires. But they stripped 'em by hand. They had a big post like that tree. They'd take the tires out of one of those heaters and the guys would roll 'em up and stand 'em up against the post until they come back out about this far. And they pulled 'em out of those heaters pretty hot.

So you'd get in the front of one to work. You worked right at the end of this row and that was like a storm comin' out of there. That heat comin' out of that thing— Gettin' out right up in your face.

This guy was a nice, big, young man. A hundred and eighty-five, ninety pounds. And they brought him around to work. They stripped 'em right beside of where we was workin'. I was puttin' the rings on 'em. And the foreman said, "Now, I'll tell you, young man. This is pretty hot job. And you're makin' minimum wage now. Don't try to kill yourself." Said, "Take it easy 'til you kind of get acclimated." "Oh, I'm used to work."

Had a little Irishman named MacMillan, I think. Mac-something. This guy looked at him and said, "Does he do it?" He was short, but he was a man. He didn't look too big, but he was much a man. The foreman said, "Yeah, Mac's been here for several years. He gets along." "If he can do it, I can do it." Well, he said, "Don't try to keep up with 'Mac' because it's hot."

So he give him his tools and started him in, showed him how to do it. Second shift. We went to work 2:30 in the afternoon. He worked about an hour. I saw him straighten up and take a big breath and he went, "Who-o-o-o-nk!" And he just started to double like this. Looked like a string you'd turned loose. Fell right on his butt down on the ground and they picked him up and put him on a stretcher and took him out of there. I never did see him again.

We had one guy come in there and he was wanderin' around. Didn't seem to be doin' anything. And we run and we hollered. We had to carry these tires from where we ringed 'em up on a table. Well, if it was a good-sized tire, you both carried it. And if it was a smaller tire, the helper had to carry it. He'd throw his glove on top of his shoulder and keep that hot ring from burnin' him and run down there and put this tire on a rack. They had racks for different sizes where you stuck 'em on. Well, you'd yell at anybody that was in front of you because you was runnin' at top speed with this thing. "Yo!"

This guy stood around there a few days. We thought he was a time-study man. And one day, some guy run in behind him and yelled at him. He crawled right up on one of those hot heaters on his hands and knees. Burnt his hands. Well, it looked kind of funny.

They took him in the office and after a while, the supervisor or foreman come along and we asked, "Who was that guy?" He said, "He was a shell-shocked veteran. He come in here and we hired him with the provision he could work in the noise and the steam hissin' and the air blowin' and the people hollerin' and yellin' and the noise of the machines." And said, "Now, that proves he can't do it, see." Said, "He might get killed or hurt himself some way or another because he's under stress." Never saw him again.

One big, rough guy come in there and got a job. We didn't have lockers. We had a coat hanger with your number on it—your clock card number. And we had an old Hungarian guy (an old retiree) that worked in the coatroom. You'd go to the window there and say, "I want number six-thirty-one." And he kept 'em in order and could go and pick up your clothes and hand 'em to you.

We had some sinks alongside of the office where we could wash our hands. Some of the guys didn't even change clothes. They went home to take a bath. They'd wash their hands there to get the soap and dust off. And then we had a shower—big, long shower and a room outside where we could change our clothes. We'd bring our clothes, throw 'em on the bench, go in there and take a shower, come back out and put our clothes on. Or wait 'til you got your shower and then go to the window and get your clothes. I don't remember which system. Both, maybe.

But this guy checked his clothes and he come in there and worked an hour or so and he saw he didn't like that job. No way. He didn't want any part of it. Well, this screwball, the day shift active foreman, he's a skinny-faced, blonde, ugly bastard. He had brought the guy down and told him where to work. So this guy said to one of the other guys, "I'm goin' out of here. Where's that guy? Tell me how to get my clothes out of here. I'm gonna' get the hell out. I don't like this job."

The guy said, "Well, you see old Frank up in the coat-room." He said, "That ain't the guy I want to see. I want to see that guy that looks like a young whippoorwill." And that was as about a good description as you could've made of him.

I almost got in trouble— A guy by the name of Rinehart was our supervisor in the Miller pit and he was Catholic.[2] The nicest guy I ever worked for. And some of the hillbillies, they want to run him out of the job. Run him off the job 'cause he was a Catholic. They're talkin' the thing and I hear about it and I said, "I don't know what's the matter with you crazy bastards." I said, "You'll never work for a nicer guy that Rinehart. He never did anything wrong to any of you. If you're gonna' try to throw him out of here, you're gonna' throw me out with him." I don't know whether they were Ku Klux or not. I don't know who they were.

* * *

Haskell: We cured the overflow of tires when they had too many upstairs they couldn't keep up. We cured the small tires. And we cured the air bags that went inside of the tires, cured 'em on. They held the air that forced 'em against the mold to give the design in there and keep them the right shape and everything. High pressure in 'em. Made out of heavy fabric. Not rubber, but rubberized. Yeah. Rubberized fabric. Heavy. Thick. Used 'em over and over.

I see old Jess Devine, that big Indian, kick one of those bags in two one day. It was a small tire. Went on a Model T. Got stuck in a tire and he had a helluva' time getting it out. They used soap. It was hypo-something else. I can't remember, but they called it hypo.

A lot of times, it didn't do the job. And those bags would stick inside those tires terrible. You had a barb was about so wide with a shoe that was about that long and scooped. It was thinner on the point. But not thin enough to cut the tire or the bag. You slipped that down behind the bag and broke it up. And then you took the tire and put your foot in it and kicked it out of there, see. Sometimes, it didn't want to come.

It was hot and you were workin' piecework. You're in a hurry. You're mad. Big Indian kicked that out. He could swear— You could hear him for three miles. You son-of-a-so-and-so. You'll never stick in another one. And he kicked it right in two. Nobody else could do it in the shop, I don't think. He was a horse. Kicked the bag in two.

I remember a guy, he worked for me. This guy's name was MacMullin. A good man. Good, hard worker. Good man. Well-trained. Knew his business. But a drunk. He'd work here three of four months. Then he'd go on a drunk. And he wouldn't come back. You'd wonder where "Mac" went and you wouldn't know. And after a while, you'd find out. Sometimes he'd come back.

So Mac was workin' for me and he disappeared. Nobody knew where in the hell he was. So, one night, one of the guys come in and said, "I saw Mac today. Hired in at Firestone today." Ahh, they'd hire him anywhere he went 'cause he was a good man. He was a good mechanic. He did the job. He was a hard worker and knew his work. The employment men knew him and knew he would do it. They'd hire him. Here. There. He'd been half a dozen places.

So, the next night, Mac come in to work for me again. He hired in back at my job. And he come down to work for me and I said, "I thought somebody told me you hired in at Firestone yesterday." He laughed like a madman. He said, "I didn't last long." I said, "What's the matter?" "Well, I went in on second shift yesterday afternoon (three to eleven). I get in there and they— (The man who laid the tires in the mold was the head man in the gang. The "layer," they called him.)" Said, "He didn't come in to work. So the super's come around and he said, 'Mac, how 'bout you layin' tires today. You know how to lay tires.'" And he said, "Sure, I know how." So, "O.K., you lay the tires."

At that time, we had a lot of mixed heats. Very, very similar. Early days of the cord tire. Five-twenty-five. Five-seventy-seven. Five-ninety. I don't remember all of the sizes myself. But they were very close. So Mac laid the wrong tire in the mold. And, when it come out, it was ruined. Probably cost the company seven or eight dollars. So he knew it'd come out before the end of his shift. But he went home. The next day he come in and— "Slim" Stout. What was his name? I can't remember. He was about six-foot-seven. Stout said, "Jim Speers wants to see you in the office, Mac." Speers was the general superintendent of the department.

Said, "I went down to the office." And Speers knew Mac. Mac had been in there half a dozen times. "Well," Speers said, "Mac, you didn't stay with us long. Might as well clean out your locker." Never mentioned the tire. That's it. That's the way you got fired. "You didn't stay with us long." He probably did seventy-five or a hundred tires but he spoiled one.

So Mac, in the meantime, he gets fired, he goes over to the Miller and hires back in and comes over to work for me that night. He didn't lose any time, but he lost a job over there. But that's the way they fired ya'—for sneezin' out of turn or combin' your hair wrong. It didn't make any difference. It was awful. Fired you for nothin' or no reason at all. The foreman didn't like you, he fired you. He didn't give a damn whether there was any reason or not. He didn't have to have a reason. He didn't like you. Umh!

So, we needed the union. But then when the unions got in the driver's seat and got the whip, they couldn't level off. They had to keep grindin' and grindin' and grindin' to get one more grain of sand in their pockets. And they still do it. They still can't realize they're— We got half a dozen unions in our area up there in Akron and that section. They've shut this plant down because they couldn't compete because the union wages was too high. I don't know how many. Half a dozen or more in the area. Canton. Akron. Around Youngstown. Steel mills. This, that and the other. Whatever. These guys are sittin' on the sidewalk, ain't got a job and say, "The hell with 'em. We got to get a raise." They ain't got a job.

678 Blaine Avenue

Florence: We came up and then after a while Haskell's brother Ralph came. He couldn't stand it on the car down there anymore. Us up here and Haskell back in the shop making good money and him making such little down there. So, he wrote and asked Haskell if he thought he could get a job then. And he wrote back and told him he was pretty sure he could. So he came back.

Then Haskell's sister Mattie got sick. This doctor told her she had tuberculosis. And there was a doctor that lived in Kenmore. People we knew knew of a person he had doctored for tuberculosis and cured it. So, Ralph and Haskell talked about it and they said to Mattie, "Come up here and take treatment from this doctor." So, after just a few months, he told her she was well and she could go to work. So, she got a job at the Firestone and went to work.

She wrote home to Haskell's sister, Grace, told her about how much more she was making than they made in the cigar factory (Her and Grace had worked in the cigar factory). So Grace came up. There we had 'em—Ralph, Mattie and Grace —all in a way dependin' on us.
Haskell: Our daughter Jean was just a baby. She was born at fifty-one Brookside in March of twenty-four.

51 East Brookside. The home where Haskell and Florence's daughter, Barbara Jean Jones, was born on March 14, 1924. One of the first homes built by the Firestone Tire & Rubber Company in the original section of Firestone Park (July, 1991).

Florence: Then, in just a few weeks, Granny [Haskell's mother] wrote this letter and said she didn't care what they said—she's gonna' get rid of what little stuff she had and she's gonna' bring the kids and come up. She had Tom and Henry still at home. Henry wasn't much bigger than your fist. But Tom was maybe fifteen—somethin' like that. Said she wasn't stayin' down there with just them two kids. So, here they come up — in July of nineteen twenty-four.

Haskell: Mom and her mob— The whole bunch come into Akron. They fouled out in Paducah. Ralph had come here and Mattie had come here and Grace had come here. My sister Lillian had married and went somewhere else. Tom and Henry were small. They've got to have somewhere to survive. So, "Come on. I'll help." Florence and I.

Henry was about ten and he was a prowler. He had to go see everybody on the train. He was runnin' up and down the aisles from one car to the other. So Mom missed him and she couldn't find him. And she told Tom, the older brother, said, "Go look off the back of the train and see if he fell off!" The train goin' sixty miles an hour! Maybe he was hangin' on or runnin' along behind!

Florence: When we knew they's comin', we had to have a house big enough that we could live in. We had enough room to squeeze in this one with the people that we was rentin' the rooms from, but they got up here and we found a house that was big enough for us to rent.

Haskell: We moved way over on North Hill and rented a great, big home over there. Beautiful home. Six-seventy-eight Blaine Avenue.[3]

Florence: Well, we lived over on North Hill almost, together, for about two years. And we all lived in the same house together.

Haskell: The lot was three hundred feet deep or more. Great, big lot. Houses were close together, but the lots were long. We rented that house for sixty-four dollars a month. And that was a lot of money. But there was a lot of us in it. We rented this big, old house and all moved in there.

So, we lived together from about first of July '24. But our son Donald was born there. We stayed there 'til November '26 and there was too many of us. Florence's brothers Barton and Kermit come in and Jack Jones came in. We had the house full. Jammed to the eyeballs. Mom and Florence was workin' their butts off feedin' that bunch. The old

Florence and Haskell Jones with baby Barbara Jean Jones (c. 1924).

man that owned that house— I can't think of his name was. He wondered what in the hell was goin' on— There was so many people in that house.

Barton Jones

Barton: We raised a little corn and stuff one year [in Graves County]. I hadn't even counted on comin' 'til Louia Jones— He had been up here, worked awhile and he went back there and got married.[4] Said, "How 'bout goin' to Akron with us?" I didn't give it a thought in the world. He said, "Well, you can get a job." He told me what he was makin' up here and I says, "Well, if I can get the money, I'll go."

Haskell: Sound better than what you was makin' there, huh?

Barton: So I mentioned it to Dad and he said, "Well, if you want to go," says, "I'll get the money for your train fare." So I came back with them on their honeymoon. Me and his wife's brother and his wife's cousin came back with 'em.

Barton: I was— I was the last one of 'em to get a job.

Haskell: The only one who stayed, huh?

Barton: Only one that stayed and the last one to get a job. And I was gettin' awfully discouraged. Boy, the snow was that deep. Ice was everywhere. They didn't even use salt then. When it come down, it stayed 'til it— Spring

Haskell: — melted.

Barton: I'd get on the streetcar out on North Main Street and down to the Firestone and the Goodrich and the Miller and the Goodyear, a couple of little old rubber companies down on Howard Street. What was they?

Haskell: Swinehart was one.

Barton: Swinehart.

Haskell: Williams. They had a Williams or somethin'. I forget what the other one was.

Barton: All day long, I'd be goin' from here to there lookin' for a job. Two weeks from the day I started lookin', I went through Firestone and walked in. "Nothin' for you." Never even asked me a question. They didn't— After the first day, Hannah never asked anybody anything 'cause he knew what they'd said before. "Nothin' for you." So I starts on through. "Now, wait a minute," he said. "How long you been a' comin' through here?" I says, "Two weeks." "Would you work that long if I give you a job?" I said, "If I hadn't wanted a job, I wouldn't a' been a' comin' through here." "I'm gonna' give you a job."

So, I went to work midnight 'til six in the morning. I worked on 'til

(L-R) Haskell Jones with Florence's brothers, Joe and Barton Jones.

327

Louia quit Firestone and gone on over to Goodrich and he was makin' more money and things was goin' good. Said, "They're makin' more money at Goodyear than they are at Firestone." I decided I'd quit and go to the Goodyear, too. I quit and went over to the Goodyear. They'd done quit hirin' by the time I worked my notice out. I worked my notice out at Firestone—two weeks notice. Goodyear had quit hirin' anymore.

So, I went everywhere else and finally went to Falls Rubber and told 'em I was a tire-builder. They hired me. I worked two days out there. I decided I wasn't a tire builder.

I went back down to the Firestone, walked in, Hannah said, "We're not interested in a boy that'd quit and walk out on us—a time like we was havin' two weeks ago!" I said, "I didn't quit and walk out. I worked a notice." "I know," but said, "We needed you then. We don't need ya' now." So, I kinda' felt discouraged. Next day, I went down— Instead of goin' in through the line, I went in the back and went into his office. "O.K., Jones. I'll put ya' back where you was."

Haskell: This guy had a photographic mind. He was the employment manager at Firestone. When you went in there and he asked you half a dozen questions, he knew everything about you— Where you come from and how old you was and how much you weighed. I'll tell ya'!

Barton: You could go back two weeks from then when he had never seen ya' since and he could tell you everything you told him.

Haskell: A month. A year. Yeah, he— He didn't forget.

Barton: Years after I worked around there, after Howard [Barton's son] grew up and married— Talk 'bout a memory! Howard was married and was lookin' to an apartment in the Falls. Wanted to rent. And it belonged to Hannah's wife. And Hannah was talkin' to him and says, "Well, where's your dad work?" Howard says, "Firestone." he says, "What's his name?" Howard says, "B. Jones." "Oh, yeah! Barton! I hired him in two or three times."

Haskell: He really— That guy had a memory, I'll tell you! Never forgot you.

Barton: He had the best one that I— of anybody I ever knew of anywhere. He hired me in three times.

CHAPTER THIRTY-FOUR

DUTY AND JONES

Haskell: I worked there at the Miller three or four years and I quit. I wanted to get out of there and learn a trade. Well, that wasn't the smartest move I'd ever made.

Everything anybody does, they have to start at it sometime. In about '25 sometime (I don't remember what time of the year) I bought a half interest in a little electric company. An electrician, Homer Duty, had a little business. We'd had light-housekeepin' rooms in the house with him at 124 Brookside.

Sam Thomas and him had been partners. Sam had bought in it. Sam got a job on the police department. So, I bought his interest in the business. It was Duty and Jones. We had business cards. Ahh, his name was probably listed in the telephone book. I don't know. I can't remember if we had a telephone under our name or not. We used his basement for a storehouse.

I worked with the guy for a while, but I couldn't get along with him. I didn't approve of his business methods. Steal! Steal anything he could get his hands on. A pack-rat thief. He'd steal tools from other men on the job. Steal material off of the job. I don't think he

(L-R) Haskell A Jones, brother Ralph Edwin Jones, family friend Vodrie "Jack" Jones and Homer Duty.

would've stole money. I think if he'd've found your pocketbook, he would've hunted you up and give it back to ya'. But he was a nickel thief. He'd worked at Firestone as an electrician. He got fired there for stealin'.

That guy'd steal anything in the world. He had bundles of shingles out at his house and five or six different brands. Some of 'em was red and some was black and some was green. Some was grey. Just take a bundle wherever he could get it. Some of 'em was a hexagon shape and some was this shape or that shape.

Finally built a garage out there out of rubber boxes. You used to get rubber out of South America in a box about, oh, twenty-two inches wide maybe and that high. About four feet long. It's a native rubber they got out of the jungle in South America. They shipped it to Firestone and you could buy these boxes for a song because they didn't want 'em. Whatever they could get for 'em, they'd sell 'em. Lumber was cheap. Good lumber was cheap. So, he'd buy 'em and he built a garage. I helped him.

He worked for the Ohio Edison before I worked with him and he knew the guys on the Ohio Edison.[1] At that time, they didn't run cable like they run here. They run a cross arm. Cross arm about ten feet long and four by four. Good material. Good stuff. And these guys on the line crew would throw 'em out if they'd get a little split place or somethin'. They'd let him know where they were and he'd pick 'em up. So, he made studding out of them. We took those boxes for the siding

330

and then he covered it with these shingles. All kinds. Looked like a crazy quilt.

He'd broke his neck before I knew him. When he worked for the power company, he did what you call "burnt a pole." You start down and your spurs cut out and you come down, see. Well, he come down part way and his spurs hung—pitched him off on his head, see. Broke his neck. So, he had a permanent injury. If you hit him, he'd lay on the floor and just flop around on the floor like a chicken with his head cut off. He'd finally snap out of it.

But I've seen him knocked out half a dozen times. One of the first times I was ever in Tallmadge— They had a town football team back in those days and they played across the street from the high school. That was all open field down there then. I think the school board owned it. They owned clear on over to the Falls Road—a great spot over there. They bought where the fire station is now. All that. So they played football over there. But we come down the road and they got a football game goin' on over there. So, "Let's stop and see it." There wasn't kids playin'. It was men. A bunch from Akron, down in the valley there.

You couldn't keep people off the field. Crowdin' in, crowdin' in, crowdin' in. I pulled him back a dozen times. He was gonna' get hit. "C'mon back here. Get back here." Finally, a guy makes an end run around somebody there and he's out there in the field about two feet. And this guy knocked him as far as from here to the corner of that room. He just went through the air like a kite. And he's layin' down on there, just a kickin' and a thompin'. He's just like a chicken with a head cut off—just floppin' all over the ground and everything. Took him about a minute and a half, two minutes, to come to after he got a good shock. I didn't know it before, but I saw it then. I saw it several times afterwards.

We had a contract on a place called Lawrence Court of about six houses. This old man, he had gone bankrupt and he did business under his daughter's name—Alice Lawrence. And we're wirin' these houses. Never been wired before. Big houses. Big, old roomin' houses. Most of 'em was rented. He rented all of 'em and some people re-rented 'em. At this one house, some widow woman was the proprietor of the house. It had roomers and so forth.

I was just startin' to work. I didn't know how to watch for anything. We had to take the floor up upstairs and go through to get down to a light in the bedrooms and here and there. And I stepped through the ceiling. He give me hell. He really chewed me out. There wasn't much I could say about it. It was plain carelessness. It was lucky. I catched myself. All I did was break the plaster loose from the old wood lath. And, about an hour later, he steps through the dining room ceiling.

This woman, she was followin' me around. She kinda' shined to me. I was a young guy and she was about thirty-five years old—a widow woman. She was followin' me around. Talk, talk, talk. So we go downstairs and we look at this ceilin'. It's cracked like the one I did. It just knocked loose from this lath good. It was a spot as big as a table. Bigger. He's standin' under there and he didn't know she was around there. He had a sayin' that he said quite often. He looked up at that, said, "Wouldn't that scrawl your grandma's balls." And just then, that piece turned loose and come down on his head.

He's layin' on the floor, just a floppin' around and she said, "Oh, my God, he's dyin'! He's dyin'!" I said, "I hope he is." She said, "What do you mean?!" I said, "You didn't hear how he talked to me when I went through there. And there wasn't anything I could do about it. I was just awkward enough to step in there." I said, "If he dies now, I'll kick his dead body." I was mad. I couldn't say much because I was guilty for steppin' through there. She said, "My God, you're the meanest person I ever knew!" And she wouldn't come close to me from then on. She stayed the hell away from that guy.

A little hunky gal (she was married to an old man) was followin' me around. She was a little hungry for affection. She was a young woman. She was probably thirty at the most and he was about sixty. They're livin' in this house although it's never been wired. They built it and was shackin' up in there and livin' in it. It wasn't finished inside. There was just outside walls. And we were wirin' it. Had a floored attic up in it.

We're down in the basement. I was goin' up to the attic to finish puttin' on switches and plugs and so forth up there. I'm ready to go and I pick up what I need and I said to Duty, "Don't you come up there." We ain't doin' anything. We were shootin' the shit. I'm busy. I'm workin'. She's followin' me around. And I hear that son-of-a-bitch sneakin' up the steps. He thought he could catch me in bed with her or somethin'.

We were workin' in a house over on Locust Street. Over back of Children's Hospital. Dirty old attic. Oooooh! It was an old house and we were up in there doin' wirin'. Dust was flyin'. It was hot! And he jagged his head on a nail in the sheeting board on the roof or a roofin' nail. He threw his hammer just as far as he could throw it. Swore and threw his hammer against the end of the building. That wall was open and his hammer— Hah! His hammer went down the wall and he lost his hammer!

He was a rat. But he had a bad nerve or somethin' in his neck or head. Somethin'. That's one reason I quit. I knew I was gonna' kill him someday if I didn't quit. I told him that. I told him a couple times, "If I wasn't afraid I'd kill you, I'd beat the hell out of you!" So I finally got enough of him and I told him one day, "I'm fed up with this bullshit. We'll inventory our stock. Whatever I owe, I'll pay. Whatever I got comin', I want. But I don't want anymore to do with you. I want out." So we measured up the stock and I owed a little to the wholesale house. And I didn't have a dime. I didn't have a job. I was puttin' everything I had in that thing.

Well, I went down to the hardware supply and I told the man, I said, "We're split up and I owe you so much." I said, "We've inventoried our stock and everything else and agreed to disagree and I'll pay you this. But I can't pay you now." Talked to the credit manager. A nice guy, I thought. Great big, son-of-a-bitch. He was about six-foot-five or six. Big, tall guy. I can't remember his name. But the day I told him, he said, "I'm glad you come in." Said, "We understand each other. And you will never get a bill. You pay it as you can." And we agreed on that, shook hands and I left.

Ahh, it was a month or six weeks later and here come a little collector out there one day. Little, short bastard with a derby hat on. I can remember it. I happened to be home and he come out and he flashed this bill on me and I said, "What do you want?" Said, "We got to get a payment on this." I said, "What are you doin' out here?" "Well, I'm the collector for [unintelligible] Hardware and Supply." I said, "Who the hell sent you out here?" "The credit department." I said, "The credit department?" I said, "The credit manager didn't send you out here 'cause he told me that I could pay on this whenever I could. I've made two payments on it. I know it isn't up to date or anything like that. But," I said, "you son-of-a-bitch, you get out of my yard and don't you ever come back here! Get now! Right now!" And he took off, too, I'll tell ya'. 'Cause I was fed up. I was mad. I'd done my best tryin' to get even. I made that guy go. He never showed up again, I'll tell you that. But I finally got it paid off. I don't owe 'em a nickel for these many, many years. I don't owe anybody. I don't want to owe anybody.

High Flight

Haskell: I was out to Akron Municipal Airport before they had an airport out there. It really never amounted to much as an airport until they put that Goodyear hangar in there. Before that, it was a cornfield. Oooooooh, ooooh, it was in the thirties. Way back. Way back in the thirties, yeah. I would say thirty-five, maybe. Thirty-four. Maybe earlier than that. I don't remember. Way back.

Ralph and George Thomas and Sam Thomas and I went out there and Sam and I was gonna' take a ride. "Shorty" Fulton, who originated that airport out there, had a plane out there that he was takin' up passengers but I don't think he was flyin' that day. I'm pretty sure it was a monoplane. I'm pretty sure it was. I can't tell ya'. So, Ralph and George was afraid. They wouldn't want to [fly].

Sam was a city policeman—Akron policeman. He wasn't in uniform, but they always had their badge, anyway. So, we got in this plane and I said to the pilot, "Give us everything you can." And he said, "I can't do much. The police'll get me." Sam just pulled his badge out and said, "I'm the police. Go ahead." He didn't realize what he was gettin' us into, see.[2]

[It was a good thing] we'd strapped in this thing 'cause this guy did some fancy didoes with us. He did some roll over some loops, some hairpin turns, and this, that and the other. Ralph and George was down on the ground and when we got back they were both white.

They said, "Man! That guy's crazy! What was he doin' up there!?" Said, "Who— He was doin' this and he was doin' that—!" I said, "I told him to." He said, "Well, then, you're crazy!" That was the first time I'd been up. I had confidence in the pilot or I wouldn't't've went in the first place.

PART SIX

TALLMADGE, OHIO
1926

CHAPTER THIRTY-FIVE

TALLMADGE

Founded in 1807 as a faith-based agricultural utopia (some 18 years before it's more famous neighbor) on the very edge of Indian territory, the Township of Tallmadge literally fueled the success of its neighbor, Akron. The village of Middlebury, which would eventually become Akron, was created with the purchase of a 54-acre tract out of the original 16,000-acre Tallmadge Township.[1] From there, it saw its initial success as a regional shipping center with the opening of the Ohio and Erie Canal in 1828. However, it was the discovery and subsequent mining of high-grade coal in what is the present-day city of Tallmadge (recognized as "the first account of surface mining of coal in Ohio") that made Akron's growth as a regional and then national manufacturing center both possible and profitable. [2]

"Had the coal fields proven to be as 'inexhaustible' as originally boasted, it is not outrageous to consider that Tallmadge might have become the first major city in the county instead of its neighbor," author Judy Anne Davis noted in "A History of Tallmadge Coal: A tales of Woodchucks, Welshmen and a Canal." However, that was not to be. After some 1,000,000,000 tons of coal were taken from "Coal Hill" above what it now called Thomas Road (and was then the track bed of first railway line in Summit County), the mines played out.[3] The coal that remained was only of sufficient quantity for local consumption.

Once Akron and the neighboring communities had mined Tallmadge of much of its coal below ground, they next began the process of annexing the land above, reducing the township in size by over 40 percent over a period of just 18 years—even as Akron increased over 200 percent in size between 1910 and 1920, from 11.48 square miles to 23.8 square miles.[4] In 1930, there was actually a movement on the part of Tallmadge residents to have the entire village annexed to Akron.[5] With little other industry to speak of other than commercial kilns of U.S. Stoneware (which mined the local clay deposits, ranked among the finest in the nation), Tallmadge was instead slowly relegated to the status of a rural bedroom community for its now richer neighbor.[6] As a result, it saw its own population also grow from 1910 to 1930, exploding from 1,159 in 1910 to 5,207 in 1920 and 6,437 in

Haskell and Florence's home was located at 74 S. Thomas Rd., the very base of "Coal Hill." Occasionally, pits would open on the hillside to the long-abandoned mine shafts below. The coal-miner's carbide lamp pictured here was found on their property on which the last active mines were operated. When the last miner turned off the last light in the tunnels and shut down the coal industry of Tallmadge, this may have been the lamp that was used.

1930. As would also be expected, however, that growth would take a dramatic turn when Akron's boom turned to bust during the Depression.

Florence: After a while, I begin to wonder if Haskell and me were ever gonna' get to live by ourselves.

Haskell: Her brother Barton had come in and this one and that one and everything. And the girls were grown. I said, "We ought to break this thing up and split up. We don't have to live together the rest of our life." Ralph was workin' and Mattie was workin' and Grace was workin' and they were able to take care of their own expenses. Mom and Florence was workin' their butt off feedin' that bunch.

Florence: Our son Donald was born on the last day of '25.

337

Haskell: In the fall of '26, why, there was too many of us. Finally, we decided that we ought to split this thing up and get the hell out of there. We moved to Tallmadge and they moved to South Akron in November '26.

Florence: Donald wasn't a year old.

Haskell: Well, I went to work for a fellow by the name of Patterson and wired two or three houses. He was a little contractor. Then I went to work for old lady Krauss—Jake and Polly.[7] Over on Bowery Street. I worked piecework over there. That's when I found this place in Tallmadge. The women that owned this house wanted a price on gettin' it wired. Polly gave her a price and I went out and did the job. I found out the house was gonna' be for rent.

Florence: He came home and he said, "I want you to go with me out to a place where I've been workin' today." I said, "Why?" He said, "Well, it's gonna' be vacant before long and the house is gonna' be for rent." Says, "Out in the country out in Tallmadge." No water in the house. No electricity. Said, "It's just the country is all it is, but," said, "I think it'd be a good place to raise the children." And I said, "Well, I'll go with ya'. We'll look at it."

I went out and we looked at it and we both decided we'd been raised up in the country without electricity and a bath in the house. We could do it again if we's wanted to. We could have a place to ourself and get away from a few things. Seems like it was twelve dollars a month and we'd been payin' sixty or somethin like that.

When the people got moved out of the house so we could move in, we got things cleaned up and moved out to Tallmadge. Scrubbed and washed and did everything we could so it was clean and we could move in. The rest of 'em moved over to Firestone Park. And, so, when we moved out in this house, we didn't know how long we might stay or anything. We didn't know anything about Tallmadge. We liked it though.

Haskell: People that was in it was buildin' the next house up the street there. So, I rented it in the summer and we moved out here the last of October 1926.

I did some fancy [electrical] fishin' in that house. That was a fishin' masterpiece! They framed the chimney all the way down. And I crawled up in that— Man, how I got up in there, I don't know. Had to put loom. Didn't have any Romex® in those days. You had to loom the wires all the way over to wherever you could make a connection. The walls were open. It was pretty handy that way.

That kitchen back there— That's where I like to roasted. That old Mrs. Keller[8] was cookin' for harvest hands with a big coal stove. I didn't know and I cut a hole in the back end of that house there by the chimney between two studs. Big enough to crawl in. Crawled up in there so I could fish in there with a snake. So, I was fishin' back in there, and workin' in there, tryin' to get a little light on that back porch. All at once I realize I'm gettin' too hot. I crawled over to that little hole I had dug in there— It was ninety degrees outside. But when that fresh air hit me in the face it was like a bucket of ice water. Man, I would just gasp. I said you'd better get out of there, Charley. And I crawled out and waited for it to cool off. It's a wonder I didn't pass out up there. Um-uh-uh.

Florence: Don and Jean were just little kids, but they got big enough that they could run around outside and play. The people across the road from us (the Sacketts) they were friendly and nice people and they loved those kids. When they was goin' anywhere, if they thought the children would enjoy goin', they'd holler over and want to know if they could take 'em along. The kids just loved that. There was a lot of open space in back of our place and to one side and they kept horses over there in one of the fields. And, so, we lived in that house until Jean had finished grade school and was startin' high school.

Haskell: We lived out there in the country almost twelve years—from '26 to '38. We didn't get to the store every

Florence and son Donald Jones in the yard of their home at 678 Blaine Avenue in Akron, Ohio. **Haskell:** Donald and the car. Somebody stole it out of the yard [after we moved to Tallmadge]. That was all the money we had to buy that thing for him for a little Christmas. Somebody took it out of the yard. I think the Millers. Had a bunch of thieves named Miller that stole everything they could find around Tallmadge.

day. She bought groceries from Jewel Tea Company. This guy would come by every day at two. They didn't have a full grocery line. They had light groceries. Coffee, tea and ahh— Not pork and beans and stuff of that kind. They had coffee and sugar and this, that and whatever. A lot of things. Sold a lot of things. But every time you bought anything, they'd give you a ticket for seventy-five cents or a dollar on a premium. And they had a premium book. They'd give you the book and you could look in there and count up and see what you could afford and tell 'em to bring it.

I remember she got a linoleum rug. Put it in the dining room. That thing lasted for a hundred and fifty thousand years. We used it in the dining room all the time and everybody had to go across it from the livin' room to the kitchen—go right through the dining room over that piece of linoleum. It was about a nine-by-twelve rug. It was a small dining room.

When we moved, we moved it up by the schoolhouse and it was on that floor as long as we were there. I think we threw it away when we left there. I don't think we moved it down where we were down on Thomas Road. But it was a good piece of merchandise. Tough as whalebone. A wooden clock. Somethin' else she got. Some other kind of prize. I don't remember what that was.

Used to buy bread from the bread man. The bread man come right to the door, see. City Bakery man used to come there. And later on, there was a bakery in Canton. They used to come after City quit.

The Jones family home, 74. S Thomas Rd. in Tallmadge, Ohio.

There was two Canton bakeries that peddled up in here. One was Nichols and one was somethin' else. I can't think of it.

Of Autos and Elephants

Haskell: I had an Oldsmobile way back. The first car I owned. A '20 model, I guess. It wasn't new. It was a good car. A guy killed somebody with it. He run over somebody and killed 'em. They sent him to the pen and I bought his car.

He went out to East Market Street to some cat-house out there about four o'clock in the morning, him and some more boys, and comin' home he was gonna' turn in South Main Street there at Market and Main. His brakes were disconnected so he couldn't make the turn. He went on down to Howard Street and made a flyin' turn on two wheels. Some poor old hunky was goin' across the street and he run over and killed him.

Well, he went on home and the police come out there and when they got him out of bed and examined his car they found out, hell, the brakes ain't even hooked up. I think they had a clevis pin in where they were hooked up. And I think one of the pins had come out of inside it.

My next car was a "T" model Ford. Twenty-five, I think. It was another one of those things. I was lookin' for a car and some finance company had a lot out there on South Main around Crozier Street. I went up and looked at this car. It was a fairly new car. The guy that bought it (some young guy), had put gadgets on it instead of makin' payments. So, they'd taken it away from him.

It was cold. Colder than hell. I went in and asked him I said, "What do you want for that Ford coupe, out there?" Said, "Two-hundred and seventy-five dollars." I said, "Will it start?" He said, "Yes, sir!" I said, "What'll you take for it if it won't start?" Said, "Two-hundred and twenty-five." I said, "Let's start it." Went out there and it wouldn't start. We pushed it about twenty feet down the little grade and it started. The battery was all right. It was dirty. The terminals were dirty. I had it for several years until finally the steering post broke off of it. It absolutely rusted out. You couldn't steer it. So I junked it.

Bought a Chevrolet then. Twenty-nine, I think. It was fairly new. I bought it from some hillbilly. He was a Tennessean. He wanted to go back home. He owed a little money on it and I went and met him downtown at the finance company and give him the pay for it and get the papers straightened up.

We come back up there by Leon's (comin' down that grade)— There was a great, big, old red barn there back in those days.[9] They remodeled it and made a shop out of it. Some travellin' circus had been broke down and run out of money and they was keepin' the animals over there. They had some dogs and a camel and two or three elephants and other stuff. I don't know just what. They were feedin' 'em down in that swamp down in front of where we lived down there on Thomas Road. Take 'em down there in the mornin' or afternoon or whenever and let 'em graze awhile down there in that briar-thicket.

We broke over that hill up there and there was two or three of those elephants goin' across the road down there. And this hillbilly— "By God! Look at the elephants down in there!" I said, "Oh," I said, "there's a lot of 'em around here." I never did tell him any different. That poor guy's tellin' people in Tennessee to this day that them woods is full of elephants.

CHAPTER THIRTY-SIX

THE MILLER RUBBER COMPANY III

Haskell: I worked for Jake and Polly for more than a year probably. I worked a long time for them. But I got mad at Jake and quit. When that blew up, I went back to the Miller and wanted my old job back. It was a pretty good job. It wasn't too bad. I knew everybody there. Well, I'm afraid— They stripped you, weighed you, and put you on the scale naked, see, and everything else. But the guy that was a doctor down at the Miller was a drunk. So I told him I never worked there before. I used an assumed name. Alan Jones, see, and hired in again.

Had a good buddy that was the foreman. He's the guy that put me back on supervision. Name was [Elisha H.] "Dice" Dickson.[1] One-armed man. He had his arm cut off in a press there. They made a foreman out of him. But him and I got along swimmingly. We got along all right with no problem. Never had a criticism or anything from him in all of my years. I did my best. I worked my butt off. And he appreciated that, see.

The general foreman, Carl West, had a brother-in-law that was a day shift foreman. His name was— What in the hell was it? But he was an idiot. I think they were all from West Virginia. Anyway, we broke down one night. The power went off in the whole room 'bout four o'clock in the mornin'. Well, somebody called the general foreman and he come in the shop about four o'clock in the mornin' and went up to his office and doin' nothing. What could he do? But he was there. And you couldn't see in there. So we couldn't even take a bath. We couldn't get our clothes. We couldn't do anything. It was black as pitch in there. All you can do is stay where you are.

And this— What the hell was that stupe's name? But he was Carl West's brother-in-law. About six-thirty, they begin to break a little light so you could see a little bit. Here come this screwball sailin' up to the office, stuck his head in the door and said, "Carl! Oh, Carl!" Says, "The lights are out!" They'd been down half the night and Carl had been in there for two hours or longer. He had to <u>tell</u> him that the lights were out—like he'd made a big discovery.

Hah, we got in a jangle out there one time. Big, old Southern guy. I can't think of what his name was. I never knew him too well or worked with him. Well, we're in the shower bath and you got hot water all comin' on you, tryin' to get clean. And this Rebel from down in Alabama, somewhere, he's throwin' cold water. He's got cold water runnin'. He'd take a handful and put it on your back.

Purley Gill said, "Don't throw that cold water on me. I don't like that." So he turned his back and this guy throws some more on him. Gill turned around and hit the guy. Well, they started to fight right in the shower. Gill hit him and missed and hit the faucets on the wall. Broke his fist. Terrible.

So we come back out and get out of the bathroom and Gill said, "What am I gonna' do? What am I gonna' do?" I said, "Why don't you go to a doctor outside and have him look at it—rather than go to the company hospital and tell 'em you hurt it fightin'." So he did.

Then he come back to the Miller and went to the doctor. He told 'em that he fell down and broke it goin' home. And the guy asked him, "Who saw it?" Well, without thinkin', he said me and a fellow by the name of Yates.

So, the next mornin', he come to my house and he said, "I fouled up." I said, "What do you mean?" He said, "I went in there and they asked me how this happened and I told 'em I fell down. And they wanted to know who saw me and I told 'em you and Yates.' He said, "They're gonna' call you in. What am I gonna' do?"

I said, "Go down and tell the man the truth. Go down there and tell 'em you had a fight. You broke your fist. Tell 'em why and everything. And I'll back <u>that</u> up." So he went. Yates and I met about nine o'clock somewhere and we went in there and reported to the labor man. And he said, "I don't need you guys. Gill was in here and told us what happened. Forget about it. Go on."

So, he was off from work for about a month. He had a bad broken hand. Well, we had the one job— As the conveyor come around (the end, down there) they had a connector on each one of these end tubes that this thing was cured on. And they set 'em up and made a tree out of 'em when they put 'em back in. But they had to come off as the tire come around. The tire was cured.

It was not a bad job. And they had an old guy by the name of Dick Woods (son-of-a-bitch), he had that job. And we were all makin' the same money. We're in a pool. But old Dick, he'd had a little break. He had a brother-in-law that was a supervisor. And he was an older man, farmer, lived out there at Johnson's Corners toward Clinton, down there.

They took him off of that job and give Gill the job 'cause he could do it with one hand—a crippled hand. His own brother-in-law did it. So this rat, he goes to the office and tells 'em the whole story and everything. Made a big deal out of it. They never did anything about it. But he got his tail in a crack because the rest of the guys wouldn't have anything to do with him from there on 'cause he ratted. But Gill had a pretty bad fist. It busted in here on the knuckles.

Oh, that's the way it goes. I'll never forget that day. But I'm the fall guy. I was always up at somebody in some way, somehow, doin' somethin'. If they was hurt, I'd help 'em. If they was broke, I'd help 'em. If they were in trouble, I'd help 'em.

CHAPTER THIRTY-SEVEN

PROHIBITION II

Haskell: I was workin' back at the Miller in '24 up to '27. Had two boys from down south of Mayfield there named [Grover and James] Andrus. Two brothers.[1] They had a poolroom where the railroad crossed Main Street. There was an old hotel building there. It wasn't too old. I remember when they built it. The Frederick Hotel.[2] But they had a poolroom— a pretty big poolroom in there. Maybe eight, ten tables. They run a poker game downstairs and a dice game downstairs and a tin dice game on the counter up by the cigar case.

I put lights on that pool table down there so the guy upstairs that's on the cigar case— If the cops come in, he's got a foot pedal underneath the case here. He'd put his foot on it and blink the lights on the pool table so they get cleaned up down there (downstairs) before the cops could get down there, see. The stairway's way in the back. I put it in there myself. I did little moonlightin' jobs like that. Pretty good pay for it. Never did much gamblin' in those places, though. They were too "up" for me. I couldn't afford to lose and I didn't do much— Very, very little. They'd had a bottle under the counter, pour it out and give it to you.

Some people couldn't take one drink. They couldn't stop. They wanted to drink all there was in town. One guy drank pretty hard. Him and his wife was goin' through a town and there's a big distillery (all lit up at night) makin' booze. She said, "Now, see, John. You can't drink it all. They're workin' nights." And he said, "I'm workin' on it. At least I've got 'em workin' nights."

I may have gone ten years and never have a drink of whiskey after I was married. Never drink it. Didn't want it. Never made home-brew. Everybody made home-brew in their homes. After Prohibition, they advertised all the ingredients and everything. You could go down to half the stores— They sold the bottles. They sold the mash. They sold everything that went in it. And it was legal for 'em to sell it. Used to set it up in a fifteen, twenty-gallon crock.

I never made it. I don't even know what they made it out of. I have known— But anyway, you put all the yeast and everything in there in the water and you let it sour. And it stayed in there so many days. Then you strained it off and then you bottled it. And they had bottles with these caps like a bottle of Coca-Cola® or somethin'. And they had 'em a press. You'd set the bottle under there, put the cap in there and put it on. Press this down and it'd force that cap on there and hold it. Sometimes. Sometimes, you'd have too much yeast in it. It'd blow up.

I remember my brother Ralph and George Thomas used to make homebrew all the time.[3] Florence and I went over there one Sunday night— They was livin' at my mom's. I look at the ceilin' in the kitchen— There was spots all over the ceilin'. I said, "What the Sam Hill's goin' on?" They had opened this beer and it'd explode like champagne. It went clear to the ceilin'. They was both high as a Georgia pine. My mother oughta' poisoned 'em. She was a teetotaler, I'll tell ya'.

One time I was over at George and Mattie's (and that was in the home-brew days) and these two Akron policemen— Father was a bootlegger. MacAleese. MacAleese was their name.[4] They used to raid places and take the beer in for evidence, but they'd drop some off to the old man and he'd sell it.

So, it was about noontime. This was on a Sunday. And I said, "George, let's go over and get a bottle of beer." So we walked over there and there's this policeman settin' there readin' the Sunday paper in uniform. Badge on him. Mother was fixin' his lunch. We had a beer and went on about our business— "We don't care." Jim. Jim MacAleese. I can't think of the other one's name. They was on the force for years and years and years. Retired off the force.

Able Street was a big market with bootleg— Down off of South Street. And Washington Street was another street. Crozier was another bootleg area. Anyway, Barton had a new '26 Ford. They improved the Model "T" and made a Model "B" out of it (I think they called it). But better than the old Model "T". This paint on these old "T" Models was good. It was tough paint! You couldn't get it off with a blowtorch hardly.

Barton and Bill would go out somewhere and get drunk.[5] Shack up with anything in town. It didn't make any difference. Black, white, green or yellow. Old, young or vice-versa. It didn't make any difference. Never got problems. Never got any problems. They'd drink that bootleg whiskey. And that stuff would kill an elephant.

Barton A. Jones.

They went out one night and got drunk. One of 'em heaved— I guess Bill. Barton was drivin'. Heaved over the side, down the side of the door on the outside. It took that paint off clean to the metal. Just as clean as— Right down to the runnin' board. Even off of the runnin' board where it hit on that. And that runnin' board was tougher than pine-knot! I don't know why it didn't kill him. It was lye! They used to make this whiskey with a little synthetic stuff and some lye. It was terrible stuff! Killed people! It killed people!

New Law To Limit Selling Of "Jake"
Federal Regulation Become Effective Tomorrow, To Issue Prescription

Popularity of "Jake" has reached its crest and of absolute necessity, though maybe not choice, the wave will begin to recede after today. A federal regulation will go into effect tomorrow which will make this come true and no longer may the ginger drinks be bought at will.

According to a federal law enacted three months ago, to become effective February 16, the extract of Jamaica ginger may not be sold in any instances except upon physician's prescription. Not more than two ounce quantities may be sold, and none can be purchased except upon doctors' orders.

Perhaps physician won't issue their prescriptions for Jamaica ginger to be used for medicinal purposes upon the many cold drink stands. This looks like a decline in the "jake" business for the soft drink establishments, according to federal officers. "Somehow, I guess the doctors won't send their patients around to the cold drink counter to get their prescriptions filled," Enforcement Officer Clark stated this morning.

A big decline in the number of sales is expected as a result of the new federal regulation. The extract as an "imitation" drink has been a popular substitute during the dry days of prohibition.

The Paducah Evening Sun
Wednesday, February 16, 1921

Haskell: They had one concoction that they bought— You could buy it at the drugstore. It was Jamaica Ginger. It was a rum with ginger in it. It was used for medicine, but it was about ninety-five or ninety-nine percent alcohol. That's what it was. They called it "Jake." It was great stuff. They used a lot of it. I think I tasted it. They had some juniper juice in it. They made a gin out of it with this rum and ginger.

But people— Everybody drank a little. Not everybody, but a lot of people. A lot of people. Prohibition was a curse to this country. Women never went into a saloon before that. Very few of 'em ever drank. Very few women. The old women from Europe drank beer mostly. They didn't drink booze. Even the hookers didn't drink much. They didn't drink much. If you'd buy a drink, they'd take a drink. And charge you for it. But they'd pour themselves a little, short drink. They didn't want to get drunk. They didn't do that.

We had a lot of bootleggers in Tallmadge. Man, we had bootleggers all over the place. The house where Gus Stillenbauer lived. They was bootleggin' in there. Bootleggin' at the Greeks. They had lived in there and had a bootleg joint in it. I don't know whether they made it there or not, but they sold it anyway. They got in a fight in there one night and killed another Greek. I think he stuck a knife in him. I remember when it happened. I was livin' here then. Happened in around 1928, '29, '30—somewhere after we moved out here. They was bootleggin in the old brick schoolhouse out on Northeast Avenue.[6] They was bootleggin' two places out north of that on Munroe. They was bootleggin' on Eastwood in two or three different places. Gene Fritsch was bootleggin' in the corner across from the swimmin' pool down there on Falls Road—little house set right across the street.[7]

* * *

Haskell: Anyhow, I stayed at Miller Rubber 'til '27, I guess. December '27. I had got transferred— Things got slow and I had no service because I'd been gone and didn't have much seniority. So I got transferred into a department that made bathin' shoes and bathin' caps—cuttin' material. They cured that stuff, molded it.[8] In '27 I got

349

laid off in that job. It slowed down. I went to Goodyear and went to buildin' tires. Built tires for ten years. All through the Depression.

CHAPTER THIRTY-EIGHT

GOODYEAR TIRE & RUBBER II

"In this large body of workmen it was of course possible to find some anemic or sickly *looking* workers in practically all the places. The chief *complaints* were headache, dizziness and stupefaction, due to breathing benzene fumes. Many claim that this bothered them only at first. We have commented upon this toleration to poisons in a previous part as decidedly unphysiological. Many cases of anemia were seen which were undoubtedly due to the chronic effects of benzene. The workers; disregard of the fumes and the tendency of many of them to scoff at their effects is unfortunate and can only be met by enlightment, particularly upon degenerative diseases."

"Rubber—Tire Building"
A Survey of Industrial Health Hazards
And Occupational Diseases in Ohio, 1915

Haskell: I think we built eighteen tires in eight hours. Today [the early 1980's], they build ten times that many. A hundred and eighty. One man. When I was buildin' 'em, it took about four or five men to build one and cure it and get it back out. So there was a lot of labor in a tire in those days. Today, there ain't much. They pop 'em out like popcorn.

Had one foreman out at the Goodyear. He was a Scotchman. Joe McGrath. I worked for him several years. They'd imported him from Scotland over here as a foreman. Scottish and English foreman, generally, was heartless. They took care of themselves and to hell with the help. They'd drive 'em to death. Joe wasn't like that. A lot of guys didn't like Joe. But I liked him very much. We used to talk. Never found him to be unfair in any way.

They had a guy named Kirk. He was an asshole. I messed up a tire. Our stock was on the rack behind us. This stock's all tacky, sticky. Had to handle it with gloves almost. You had to be very careful. We had a drum about so wide— You operated the drum with your foot then. Had a foot pedal down here. You cemented this drum first with a brush and cement. Let it run for a minute or two to dry it so it wasn't too sloppy and wet. It dried pretty quick because the drum rotated pretty fast. You stopped the drum. Then you pulled the stock down and placed it properly on your drum, eased it along, and got it nice and tight on the drum. When it come back to the end, then you tore it off so just enough margin to splice. Then you pulled it up and spliced it. Then the next ply come off a different row and it was pointed the other way. This stuff's cut on a bias, see. First one went this way and that one went that way—across the drum.

Well, we had been told forty times, "Don't pull your stock down 'til the drum stops." There was a reason for that, but we all did it because we worked piecework. So I pulled this roll down and I dropped it on that drum and naturally, it stuck, see. And it rolled about eight or ten plies around that thing and then the stitchers come up in it and stitched it together good and tight. I've got to reach over that stock to get my controller to stop this drum and that stock was goin' up and down. And I'm not gonna' stick my arm in there. So I finally got it leveled off and I got a hold of it and stopped it. I had a mess. I had about twenty plies on there all stitched together. And Kirk come over and said, "Get a benzene can!" So, we had to get a squirt can, squirt all the way around right in there and pull that stock apart. It would've been a day's job. For free. He walked away.

I'm standin' there lookin' at it. Joe comes by. He looks at this mess there. "What are ya' buildin', Jones, 'specials'?" I said, "Yeah. I got a twenty-ply job here. A good one." Said, "Give me your shears." They had a big pair of shears on the machine all the time. I give him the shears, he cut it in two and threw it on his shoulder and walked away with it. Kirk come back and looked and said, "What'd you do with that?" "I didn't do anything with it." "Well, where is it?" I said, "Joe McGrath took it away from here." "Ohhh." He never said any more. But he was a prick. He didn't have to do that. He could've done the same thing Joe did. He could've said, "Well, cut it off and go back to work."

Barton: Well, that guy didn't do like Harry Bittner done me when me and my buddy cut this stock off and threw it over on top of Burger Iron. It wound around the roll and we couldn't get it off and the only way we could get it off was to cut it off. And you didn't dare have scrap then. So we took our knives and cut it off from the roll and didn't want anybody to see it. So, we went back to a window that was open and Burger Iron was just across an alley. They had a row of garages with plastic roofs on 'em. He goes back there and I give 'er a sling out the window and it lands right on top of that roof.

That was on Saturday and we was the last shift workin' on Saturday. So they looked out there they find that stock layin' out on that roof. And me and my buddy was the only one that worked on that machine that could've done it. They had us clear. So Harry Bittner never mentioned it to me. He never said a word to me about it at all. He did talk to my buddy—ask him about it. And the supervisor said that he said when I come back in, he was gonna' fire us both. He never mentioned it to me and he still hasn't.

But later on we got into an argument with our supervisor. We was buildin' bands and we'd worked in one wing awhile and then they sent us over in another wing and worked awhile. We're still buildin' bands. But one of 'em was in one wing and the other one was in the other. Well, the first wing we worked in before we'd leave there, we kind of upped our production, oh, twenty-five or thirty bands in that one. And we moved over in the other one and we got enough over there to make us all we could turn in—honestly.

We made our card out (our time card), put our production on it, turned it in and the supervisor, he disputed how many bands we'd built over in this one wing. And he had us in the office to see Harry Bittner. And we both told him that we absolutely run every band that we turned in over there. He never questioned what we'd run in the other place where we'd stolen about twenty-five or thirty. Never questioned that. But he's questionin' where we turned in exactly what we'd run. And old Harry says, "O.K." Says, "I'll see it goes through." And he turned around and he says— He says, "Bob," (Never said it to me. Said it to my buddy) Said, "Bob, you'd better be careful." Says, "I've got that stock you and Jones cut up."

When I quit there in nineteen-twenty-seven to go back home, he went and opened a cabinet in the corner of his office and pulled the door open and here come that roll of stock comin' out of there wrapped up in— He still had it.

Haskell: Every vacation had to be taken by the 1ˢᵗ of September. They give you all May, June, July and August to take your vacation. So you can call and ask whenever you want it and get your vacation. I had a week comin'. So they come around and said, "When do you want your vacation?" I said, "I don't know yet. I'll let you know." So, they never come around anymore. They didn't question me and I kept my mouth shut. Everybody else is takin' vacation, takin' vacation, takin' vacation.

The weekend before huntin' season starts, I go in the office and I said, "Joe, I'd like to get my vacation next week." He said, "What do you mean!?" I said, "I'd like to have my vacation next week comin' up for huntin'." "Well, you've had your vacation!" I said, "Oh, no. I haven't had my vacation." "Well, I know you have! Everybody in the shop's had their vacation. Had to have 'em by the first of September." I said, "'Jonesie' didn't have his." He said, "I don't believe it!" he reached in his desk and got the book. He said, "I'll say one thing. You're the only guy in Goodyear that hasn't had his vacation time. Good luck to you! I hope you have a good time huntin'!" I said, "I just didn't talk, Joe." He said, "That's fine."

So, durin' that week they have a one day work for United Fund. They called it Community Chest, then, I believe. Well, everybody was supposed to work a shift for that fund, see. So I go in there and Joe comes around. "What are you doin' in here, Jones? I thought you was huntin'?" "Well," I said, "isn't this the night they work for Community Chest?" He said, "You mean you come in to work for Community Chest?" I said, "Sure." "Well," he said, "You was the only guy that had a vacation to get to go huntin' and you're the only guy in Goodyear that would've come in here on his vacation and work for nothin'!" Said, "I'll give you credit." So, I worked that night for Community Chest.

Joe McGrath had had ten thousand men that worked for him over the years he worked at Goodyear. I'll bet you the day he walked out of there he could tell you every one of 'ems clock card number.

We had four shifts. The foreman worked eight hours and the help worked six hours. So, they alternated. I think they worked three months from seven to three. The next three months, they worked from three to eleven. The next three months, they worked from eleven to seven—but the men didn't change. Periodically one of 'em might, but not very many. So during that time, he had one hundred and sixty-five men or more. Probably 200 men all totaled with the day help. And he was their foreman. Then the next shift he had that many more. Then the next shift. That's four times two hundred. Eight hundred people.

So, you skinned a finger or something, you had to go to the hospital. Said, "Joe, I need a hospital pass." Picked up a hospital pass and wrote, "Jones. Six-thirty-one." And he had your clock card number on it and the whole story. He didn't ask you, "What's your number, Jones?" Never. That guy never asked anybody. He knew what everybody's number was. He knew everything about you.

I never knew a man with a memory like that. I didn't work for him too long. I worked at Plant One five years. Then I went to Plant Two. And he was down at Plant Two five years and he was periodically my foreman. He wasn't all the time. But we liked each other.

CHAPTER THIRTY-NINE

THE DEPRESSION

In 1929, the economic outlook in Akron was bright. The city could boast "two-thirds of all the tire and tube manufacturing in the United States; the highest wages in the industry; 90 per cent of the town's population American-born; 50 per cent of its homes owner-occupied."[1] With the sale of tires a record high in 1925, "the value of rubber sold in the country surpassed a billion dollars, with more than 70 percent of it used to manufacture tires, about fifty million of them a year" by the end of the decade.[2] As a result, Akron's largest tire companies broke all sales records in 1929. "Goodyear's $256 million was followed by Goodrich's $164.4 million and Firestone's $144.5 million."[3]

With the start of The Depression in late October of 1929, however, all of these gains would soon be shattered as the sales of new automobiles collapsed. The price of crude rubber plummeted from a high of $1.20 a pound in 1925 to a low of 3 cents per pound in 1932. And orders placed months before could arrive at the factory valued far less than their agreed to purchase price. The result was nothing less than horrific for the rubber company stockholders. Goodyear common stock plummeted from 106 on October 15th, 1929 to 10 on March 1, 1933. Firestone's dropped from 271 to 10. And that of B.F. Goodrich fell from 69 to 3 ½. And the number of tire manufacturers fell from 166 at the start of the 1920s to just 35 by the early 30s.[4] Miller Rubber was among the losses, having been merged into Goodrich in 1929.[5]

Initially, to avoid wholesale layoffs and spread work to as many people as possible, Goodyear adopted a six-hour shift in 1930. And, within three years, the remaining major rubber companies followed its lead.[6] And hours weren't the only thing that would be cut. The workers that kept their jobs also saw their wages drop from a weekly wage of $37.18 in 1928 to $21.17 by 1933.[7] As the rubber companies struggled (with Firestone actually turning a profit every year of The Depression), they had to do what they could to survive.[8] And that could only come at the expense of the workers. From a record high employment in 1920 of over 70,000, the total number of full-time clock card workers was reckoned to be 25,500 by September of 1932.[9] And, unbelievably, "Akron's industrial unemployment rate hit a staggering 60 percent."[10] The national economy, with unemployment of only 23.6 percent (which didn't include some 11 million farm families), looked almost robust by comparison."[11]

The homes that were once so proudly owner-occupied now were going into foreclosure faster than the sheriff's department could serve notices. During 1933 and 1934 alone, the eviction notices were served on at least 3,000 families and, in hundreds of instances, their possessions were also piled on the curb.[12] In fact, so many people were forced to leave the area in search of work that Akron was no longer referred to as "The Rubber Capital of the World." Instead, it was being referred to as the "Ghost City of America."[13]

While it would be simple to ascribe these losses solely to the impact of The Depression, the truth was much more complex. The first of these factors in declining employment numbers began ironically enough, in Graves County, Kentucky, as well as countless other rural communities some 20 years earlier. That was the "Good Roads" movement, of which Haskell's father had been such an avid proponent. As a result of its success, the mileage of paved roads across the country had increased dramatically over the intervening years, dramatically reducing wear and tear on the tires.[14]

The second factor that was also of great benefit to the consumer, if not the rubber worker, was that the tires that were being manufactured were of a far superior quality. In *Rubber. A Story of Glory and Greed* (1936) authors Howard and Ralph Wolf record:

> Between 1910 and 1916 . . . the casing makers had been selling the average motorist seven or eight high-pressure cord or fabric tires a year. With the cord being brought to a reasonable degree of perfection by 1916 and with the

compounds steadily being improved, the tire engineers and chemists employed by the manufacturers succeeded in chopping this figure to three by 1919-20 . . . . Today [1936], with the steady development of the balloon into the still lower pressure tire now vended as the "air wheel," "low pressure" or whatnot the figure is between one and 1.18 and the continuing growth of retreading should carry it still lower. . .

Nor has the motorist profited only by a tire life increasing from an average three thousand miles in 1914, to an average eight thousand plus miles in the early 1920's, to today's average of twenty thousand plus opportunity to add ten thousand to fifteen thousand more by doing business with the retreaders.[15]

The third factor was that new labor-saving equipment was making the tire production process much simpler. As authors Wolf and Wolf noted:

Altogether, the Bureau of Labor Statistics of the United States Department of labor finds a total of 28,189,000 man-hours eliminated by the tire industry between 1922 and 1931 exclusive of the reduction caused by the production drop after 1929. From 1921 through 1931 there was a net actual increase of 21,393,000 tires produced which should have necessitated an increase of 35,536 employes [sic] by 1921 standard or output per man. Actually there was a reduction of 7,155 employes [sic] or a total of 42,691 technologically displaced. Between 1928 and 1931 six leading factories dropped as surplus labor 14,735,000 man-hours or forty-one percent of their 1928 total. And as indicative of a trend still continuing it is of major interest to note that of the men who lost their jobs because of this labor surplus only twenty-nine percent were unemployed because of the drop in production. The remaining seventy-one percent were technologically unemployed.[16]

The fourth and most critical factor Wolf and Wolf cited, however, was, "a new menace to the physical and mental health of the workers that would make carelessly handled poisons, soapstone snow and open cans and cups of benzene seem minor indeed. This was the man with the stop watch."[17] It was the "time-study man" that Haskell had referenced while working at Miller that was responsible for:

. . . . the even more continuous driving and rawhiding of the worker at new speed records eliminating all "waste time and motion"—the thing that so far outweighs the machine elimination of bull-strength work that casing making (and most of the other rubber trades) has become among the industrial world's most dreadful jobs. . .[18]

In fact, the time-motion studies (such as those of Charles E. Bedaux at B.F. Goodrich) were more responsible for the increased output per man-hour than any other single factor.[19] As a Congressional hearing in 1938 was informed:

> A worker made 25 percent more rubber tires per day in 1935 than in 1929 although he worked fewer hours in 1935. If you translate it to an hourly basis, one man working 1 hour produced 72 percent more than in 1929.[20]

Finally, and ironically for the tens of thousands of workers who had moved north in search of work in the factories, management was looking into yet another way to cut costs. In search of still cheaper labor, they had begun to move their plants south.[21]

CHAPTER FORTY

THE HARDEST OF TIMES

Haskell: I'd've been just as well off if I had've been laid off because a lot of that time durin' the thirties, I worked one day one week and two days the next week. And we made about five dollars and a half a day for six hours. So we averaged about eight dollars, eight and a half a week with a family. Had to keep an automobile up so you could drive to work and pay rent and try to feed 'em and clothe 'em. If I'd 'a been on relief, I'd 'a been better off. But nobody wanted to be on relief. Nobody wanted to be on relief and today that— It isn't any stigma to be on relief. But in those days it was avoided by all honest, hard-workin' people. They didn't want to be on relief in any manner.

I used to pick up a little electric work. A day now and then. A little bit. Do a little wirin' here, wire there. Used to get ninety cents an hour for that work back in those days. I picked up a dollar here and there but not very much. Not very much. I helped put on a roof or something of that kind. Do the labor work. I wasn't a carpenter. I couldn't do carpenter work. So it was a pretty rough row to hoe.

I had to whip Jim Hazen once.[1] He owed me money. Electrical work. And other. I did the whole thing. I built an apartment over a garage. Put the floor down. Put the studs up. Put the drywall on. Put the plumbing in. Put the wiring in. Built the cupboards and the cabinets. And dug the hole in the ground and made the septic tank. Built a septic tank out of brick. Did the whole thing. I went down for Christmas to get some money. He told me to come and get it when I needed it. He owed me about a hundred dollars for fifty cents an hour.

He was a good mechanic who worked for this Akron City Water Department, but he was a drunk. He had a habit, when he got drunk, of hittin' people. He'd hit you for no reason at all. Tenants were movin' into that building that night. I went down there with old man crippled Sparhawk. He drove me down there. I went up and we had a drink with him. I said, "Jim, I've got to have a little money. It's Christmastime and the kids don't have anything and I don't have any money." He said, "How much do you want?" I said, "I need twenty dollars." Said, "I won't give you twenty dollars. I'll give you ten." I said, "I don't want ten. I want twenty—because I've got three kids down there and I've got to have a little Christmas for 'em." So, he mouthed about it, but he finally give me the twenty dollars.

I started home and he followed me out in the yard to his car. His car was settin' out there. And he sucker-punched me. Ooooooh, like to knock my head off. Hit me right here over the eye. And I ain't too sure yet whether he knocked me down or not. I don't know. But I know I got up and beat the hell out of him. His wife was with him and she knew his habits. He's hit her many times and she knew— I turned him around, took him over to his car and I said, "You son-of-a-bitch, you get in that car. I should kill you!" So he swung at me again. But I was lookin' for it then. He hit the window of this car. I grabbed him around the neck and I really wore him out. When I finally got through with that and I turned him around. I started kickin' him in the butt with my knee. And I kicked him as far as from here to that door. He was as limp as a dishrag. He was drunk as a hoot owl. She said, "Jonesie, you've killed him!" And I said, "I know it. And I *should* kill him." She said, "I know that, too. But don't do it!" So I took him and threw him in his car.

I didn't see him for three or four weeks, a month. I don't know how long. He lived in town, but he owned that property. So, one day I was settin' there in the gas station and he drives up and got some gas and come in to pay for the gas. And he starts mouthin' off to me — about half drunk again. And I liked the guy. I said to Jim, "What do you want to do that—" I said, "I had to whip you once. I don't want to do it again. You never saw the day you could whip me, so don't try." But I said, "You keep on and I'm gonna' give it to you again!" He said, "I'll just pay you what I owe you." I said, "That's gonna' make me awful mad." He owed me about sixty, seventy dollars—whatever it was. So he went out and got the money from his wife [Kathleen] and paid me.

His wife finally died. She told me once, says, "I'll outlive him. I'll get what money he's got." And said, "I'll take these beatin's and—" But she didn't. She died.

Barton Jones

As the Depression deepens, letters were written home by Florence's brother, Barton, to their sister, Mary, clearly show the personal impact of the growing crisis. From discussions of feeling "luck" to have a job as an inspector, the outlook slowly darkens until worries about making payments "on the place" become mention of "rooms" and "rent" even as he is relegated to the job of pushing a stock truck. Finally, five years later, work is good again.

Akron Ohio
Feb. 23, 1930
Dear Sister:
. . . Work isn't getting any better here yet. They laid off four of my men last Monday but Hannah gave three of them another job and told the other one he would have a job for him in a few days. I don't know if he has another job to get or not. I think they are expecting work to pick up before long. We still have too many men but Glick (the foreman) said he wanted to hold all of them if he could cause he thought he might need them before long. We've been sending men to every dept. in the shop nearly this last week. We haven't had anything for them to do so if any other dept. could use a man we would send them one. Glick said if we could keep placing men in other departments that we could hold the others. I don't think my job is good for very much longer now. I'm expecting to have to go back on piece work most any time now. I'm the youngest inspector on now so I'll be the next to go off if they take any more off. They took two off this last week. Well I think there is one younger than me yet but I'm not sure. If they only took two off there is still one younger than I am but he was still on second shift and I don't know whether he was taken off or not . . .

Love to all
Barton

Akron O.
June 2, 1930
Dear Mary:
How are you all at home by now? . . .
Work is no good now and I don't believe it will be this summer. I haven't worked since last Wednesday night but go to work again tonight. This is usually the busiest time of the year too. I hate for holidays to come any more we always have so much time off. Maybe I'll get to work pretty steady this month though being as there are no holidays but is a lot of talk that we are going on four days per week. I sure do hope not for I could use six days a week from now until Nov. 1st awfully well. If we go on four days I just don't see how we'll ever make the next payment on the place . . .
Well, I don't know anything to write so I guess I have to quit.

Love to all
Barton

Akron, Ohio
Feb.24—1931
Dear Sis:
How are everybody at home by now? We are all getting along pretty well I guess . . .
 Florence, Hack [Haskell] and the kids were here Sat. night and we played bridge until 1:00
. . .
 Work is still awfully slow but I done a little better last week than I usually do. I made $29.^{00},
worked a little over every day . . .
 I don't guess milk or eggs are worth anything there now are they? We get fresh eggs here now
for 19¢ a dozen and milk 10¢ a quart. That's the cheapest milk has been here since 1917 so the
papers say. We usually pay 12¢ but it went to 13¢ last fall. Butter is from .28¢—.35¢ a pound so
the farmer can't get very much. We can get Florida oranges [illegible] for 12¢ a dozen. I don't see
how they can pick them and ship them for that. The grower sure don't get much for them. Has
anybody started doing any farming except burning plant beds? I'm thinking now that we won't even
get to come home this summer. If work don't get a lot better we'll never be able to make the next
payment on the place. We sure can't save much money the way I've been working. I feel luck though
to even have a job that I can make a living at. There is so many people that can't get anything at
all to do . . .
 I don't know anything to write so I guess I might as well quit trying.

Love
Barton

Akron Ohio
May 6, 1931
Dear Mary:
. . . Our rooms look real nice now but we are paying too much rent for the way times are now. I'm
sure we could get rooms as nice as our for $5.00 or $5.50 a week if I'd get out and look but I hate
to move we have had such places before. We pay $6.50 a week here for two rooms and I believe I
could get three rooms for that if I'd look around. We may have to get three rooms this summer. I
start working 8 hrs a day today and have to work third shift from11:00 P.M. to 7:00 A.M. and
will have to do all my sleeping in the daytime . . . it's going to be a pretty hard job if work don't get
any better than it is now. Of course it don't cost as much to live now as it did a year or two ago but
if you don't make any money you can't save it. I've been making from $25.00 to $30.00 a week
all this year and had one pay as high as $35.00 but it looks like we are out of so many things we
can't save anything much. We have to go where we can save a little more now if nothing happens but
I will be off two weeks in July and that will ruin one month. The whole factory will shut down for
two weeks, and it will cost just as much to live as if I was working. Well I've written all I know
and that isn't much but will have to do for this time.

Love to all
Barton

Akron
May. 25. 1931
Dear Mary:
How is everybody at home by now? We are all getting along pretty good I guess. I am working eight
hours a day now and worked six days a week the last two week but they gave me a good "Hunky"
job now. "pusha da truck" and I'm only making .62¢ an hour now. That lacks .08 cents a day

363

being as much as I was making in six hours. We have moved now and get our rooms $1.50 a week cheaper than we were getting then.

. . . I'm making $4.96 a day now and paying $5.00 per week room rent. When I was home I was making $7.99 a day. I've been cut .32 cents per hour within the last year. . . 22¢ of it coming at one time. If I can get six days a week though it won't be so bad . . .

. . .They really have me working now. By the time I push that truck for eight hours I feel like I've done a day's work. I'm trucking stock up to the tire room. The stock is rolled up in big rolls weighing anywhere from six hundred to a thousand or eleven hundred pounds each and I have to keep going all the time except the twenty minutes we have for lunch. The first few nights almost ruined my feet and legs but it isn't quite so hard now that I've kinda gotten used to it. Well I guess I'll have to quit being as I don't know anything to write. Write me and tell me all the news down there.

Love to all
Barton

Akron Ohio
Dec. 20, 1935
Dear Ma:
. . . I am working pretty good now. Worked 33 hours last week but don't think I'll get but 30 this week but don't think I'll be off but one day for Christmas . . .
Love — Barton

CHAPTER FORTY-ONE

LABOR

In response to the deepening depression and the unrest among both the employed and the unemployed nationwide, Washington attempted to help with the passage of the National Industrial Recovery Act (NIRA) in June of 1933. Although it would only be in effect for two years before The Supreme Court declared it unconstitutional (only to be replaced by the National Labor Relation or Wagner Act), it would subsequently be referred to as the "Magna Carta" of the labor movement as Title I, Section 7(a) stated:

> ...employees shall have the right to organize and bargain collectively through representatives of their own choosing, and shall be free from the interference restraint, or coercion of employers of labor, or their agents, in the designation of such representatives or in self-organization or in other concerted activities for the purpose of collective bargaining or other mutual aid or protection . . .[1]

One month earlier, the local Central Labor Union in Akron had as few as 400 members. By November, a little more than six months later, that same union would count more than 30,000 members. Much of the growth would be in the rubber shops. Even though Goodyear would initially see low union representation among its workers, some of the smaller shops would see as high as 90 percent of their workers signing up. By the end of the year, it would be estimated that some 60 percent of the rubber workers in Akron were union members.[2] By the end of the decade, the union would count over 100,000 members.[3]

Over the next two years, union membership dropped substantially as differing unions argued over whom they would represent, jockeyed for membership, staged small strikes, and accomplished little. Then, in September of 1935, rubber workers broke away to form the United Rubber Workers of America (URW). Shortly afterwards, Goodyear decided to return to the 8-hour day, laying off over 1,000 workers in the process. It also announced both hourly and piecework wage cuts that the company promised would be offset by the longer shifts. Their promise wasn't worth much. "By one estimate, a tire builder making $122 a month on the six-hour shift would make just $125 a month on an eight-hour day."[4] Afraid of even more layoffs because of the longer shifts, the stage was set for the fledgling union's first major strike.

On February 17th, 1936, in the midst of a blizzard, the union shut the plant down. And it was the Southern whites, which were initially hired in the belief they were not prone to unionize, that led the strike. Now, with massive unemployment outside the walls of the rubber factories and stronger ties to the community, their view of union membership was quite different, despite being the highest paid workers in the country.[5] Local journalist Ruth McKenny noted, "These mountaineers, union organizers will tell you, are hard to convince, but once convinced, they take their union very seriously."[6] Or, as Wolf and Wolf clarified, "The iron had entered into the gummer soul."[7]

The technique the strikers chose to use was both highly effective and highly illegal—a sit-down strike, which prevented other workers from taking their places to carry on production and reduced the chance of violence in the streets. In fact, this technique which would later become the signature technique of the labor struggles in both the auto and steel industries during the late 1930s was actually first used in the United States in the rubber factories of Ohio and perfected on the shop floors and streets of Akron.[8]

Despite bitter cold as low as nine below zero, picket lines strung out for eleven miles over nearly five weeks—proving to be a formidable presence for any strikebreaking action by local law enforcement.[9] Surrounding the entire Goodyear complex, it was the longest line of pickets in U.S. history.[10] Work was suspended in all of Goodyear's Akron plants and 13,800 workers were idled. At the start of the strike, there were less than 500 members in the Goodyear local of the URW. Within a week's time, some 5,000 had joined.[11]

Strike! Goodyear workers went on strike on February 17th, 1936. Despite temperatures as low as nine below zero, their picket line eventually surrounded the entire Goodyear complex—some nine miles in length—for nearly five weeks. It was the longest picket line in U.S. history. And it set the pattern for strikes in other major industries for years to come (Special Collections, Michael Schwartz Library, Cleveland State University).

As common as strikes would be later to other industries such as automobile manufacturing, iron and steel and coal, the strike at Goodyear took on national importance as the test case for a growing national labor movement. As author Maurice O'Reilly noted in *The Goodyear Story*:

> Veteran union leaders from other industries invaded Akron to lend strength to the obvious all-out strategy: crack Goodyear, the largest rubber company, and destroy its history of amiable labor relations. With this accomplished, the other rubber companies could more easily be brought into line and organized.[12]

Coming from "other industries," the ultimate goal of the other union leaders (including John L. Lewis, president of the United Mine Workers) was obvious.[13] Soon, the techniques first used in Akron would be carried across the country. And, according to the historical plaque in Akron commemorating the 1936 "sit down" strike, it was "instrumental in the founding of the industrial union movement in the United States."[14]

CHAPTER FORTY-TWO

STRIKE!

Haskell: There was no union in Goodyear. I'd been there ten years and I didn't know one man that belonged to the union. Not one. Not one man did I know. There never was talk. Nobody talked. Nobody would. I'd never been approached. I'd never heard anything about it. Everybody was anxious to try to make a livin'.

Long November '35 or something like that they first organized and got an office.[1] There was a skeleton union across the street. They had an office and there was a few people around that belonged to it I know. Well, we went on strike the first of February '36. But the company made a boo-boo. I mean a wholesale boo-boo. A big boo-boo.

In '36, they wanted to go back on eight hours. It was costly for the company to maintain four shifts. They had more employees. They had more insurance and more worker's compensation and everything else. They wanted to get rid of that shift. They'd done that early with good intent to spread the work so more people could work durin' The Depression when there wasn't much work. So they got cute. They'd come through every night and say, "You want to work a couple hours over?"

Everybody wanted to work eight hours 'cause everything they had was worn out. They'd had almost ten years of Depression. Furniture was worn out. Clothes was worn out. Everything they had was worn out, but them and their wife—and most of them were. So they needed every nickel they could get. Most guys would say yes. I worked two nights and I said, "This is a bunch of shit. What they're gonna' do is to see if we'll work eight hours. And then they'll dump this night shift." We worked on second shift. I was workin' from six to twelve. Six hours, we was workin'. And I wouldn't work anymore. I didn't work but two shifts.

Well, they did that a few nights. Maybe three weeks. Had no problem. So they come around at midnight one night when the night shift come in. They were dirty bastards. They could've done it in the morning after they'd worked the shift. They didn't have to go in there at midnight. They laid-off 174 men—with men workin' overtime on the machine next to 'em. Well, the men blew up. They sat down. They wouldn't work.

PLANT 2 TIRE WORKERS IDLE
Two Goodyear Shifts Affected As 150 'Sitdown' In Layoff Protest
AGREEMENT IS REACHED
Employees Return to Jobs This Afternoon After
Hearing Is Promised
BY JAMES S. JACKSON

Tire builders reporting for work in Goodyear's plant two at noon today were delaying for a time the actual start of production while considering whether to lend support to the fourth shift's protest. No layoff notices have been given on the afternoon shift, the company said.

Tire production was to be resumed at plant two of the Goodyear Tire & Rubber Co. this afternoon after a "sitdown" of 150 tire builders had caused a halt in operation from 3 a.m. until noon.

The protest was against the layoff of 60 builders on the fourth shift.

The stoppage of the production line quickly affect 250 other persons in the tire division on the fourth shift. When the 500 first shift workers reported at 6 a.m. they were turned back by the company at the gates.

Fourth Akron 'Sitdown'

This was the fourth "sitdown" in major Akron factories and the second at Goodyear since this new form of labor protest was tried successfully at the Firestone Tire & Rubber Co. less than three weeks ago.

The 150 protesting tire builders all left the plant during the morning upon the promise that a committee from their number would be permitted to present their grievances to Fred Climer, factory personnel manager, at 3 p.m.

The "sitdown" began at 3 a.m. after layoff notices had been given to 60 men, the company said. . .[2]

Akron Beacon Journal
Friday Evening, February 14, 1936

Haskell: So, in the morning, the first shift come in—the old men. They had a lot of old sixty, sixty-five year old men in there then. They couldn't figure they could ever work eight hours again. Piecework. You worked like hell. So they was in sympathy with the guys because they didn't want to go on eight hours. We wouldn't give a damn. We wouldn't've cared if whether we worked eight hours or fourteen. If they'd've done it right, you know. There was no overtime pay. It was straight time. So the first shift sat down. They wouldn't work. Night shift went home finally. We was the second shift. We went to work at 6:00 in the evening—worked 'til midnight. Third shift started at midnight and worked 'til 6:00 in the morning. Well, when we come in, we hear what the story is and wasn't gonna' be scabs. It wasn't union. Wasn't nobody talkin' union. Nobody said a word about union. So we wouldn't go to work.

Biography in Brief. Fred Climer.
By Kenneth Nichols

So it seems even more amazing, in view of this array of evidence, that Fred has the reputation of never getting sore. He's always as calm as the president is when he makes a radio address and as cool as last week's weather . . . . The big thing about Fred is his air of understanding a man's problems. Maybe "air" isn't a good word. Fred does understand 'em. A man or woman can pour out his or her troubles to Fed and walk away with the feeling that—even if nothing is done about them— he or she has had a fair hearing, anyway . . . .[3]

Akron Beacon Journal
Sunday, June 21, 1942

"Fred Climer was a decent man but he was working for an indecent company."

E.K. Bowers
The Once and Future Union
The Rise and Fall of the United Rubber Workers, 1935-1995
Bruce M. Meyer

Haskell: By that time, Goodyear was gettin' desperate. They had a man who was head of the Labor Department named Fred Climer. So he was— He was— He didn't know what to do. He was scared. He had never had a situation of this kind develop. Never had had it so he was gonna' try to bluff. Then he got hostile. He got up on a truck and he said, "I'm gonna' tell you guys somethin'. If you don't go back to work, I'm gonna' fire every damn one of you!" That was his words. So we didn't go to work. So they fired us. Give us a pass out. We didn't go home. We stayed there.

The rest of the management (the foremen, the superintendent, supervisors and what-not), they kept millin' around through the crowd. We was all friendly. Nobody was mad or anything. "Why don't you guys go back to work?" "We can't go back to work. We've been fired." "Well, they don't— Don't pay any attention to that. Go on back to work." Nobody would go.

Joe McGrath come over and talked to me. Said, "I can't understand." Said, "These guys have all been here for some time. Got some service. Can't understand what's goin' on." I said, "One thing that's goin' on, Joe, was that the place is too damn big." I said, "You and I can't settle anything. If I've got a problem, I go to my supervisor. And he don't want to look bad so he paints me as bad. So he goes to you and he tells you that Jones is an asshole and he's doin' this and doin' that and bellyachin' about this or that and everything and you believe him. So you go to your superintendent and you tell him the same thing." Said, "By the time it gets to the labor department, I look like a radical outlaw of some kind." I said, "I've got no representation. And you can't hire me. You can't fire me." I said, "Joe, you ain't nothin' but a messenger boy!"

Well, he looked at me for a minute. He said, "I never thought about it that way." "But," I said, "Isn't that a fact?" He said, "Yes, it really is." Said, "They expect me to run the department on a budget. They give me 'x' number of dollars to run that department and build so many tires and that's what I'm supposed to do. I got to do it within those figures. But," he says, "I can't hire a man or fire a man." He says, "You're right. I ain't nothin' but a messenger boy." That was a good man. That was a good foreman, I'll tell ya'. A lot of guys hated him because he was a little rough. If you persisted in being rebellious, why, he'd get rid of you. But he'd be fair as long as you was. He was tough, but he was fair.

When it come time at the end of the shift and the other shift came in, we built two tires apiece. That made agreement— We build two tires apiece and go home. I've still got the check somewhere that I got for those two tires that day. That was the beginning of the payday and those two tires. Seventy-four cents, I think it is. It's layin' around here now. In the trunk or somewhere. Goodyear sent me about ten letters askin' me to cash that check. It fouled up the bookwork. And that check was never— I never did cash it. The hell with it.

Ousters Seen After Sitdown.
Jobs of 140 Goodyear Tire Builders are Hanging in the Balance
Workers Quit, is Claim
'Don't Dare Fire Them,' House Declares, As Company Acts
BY JAMES S. JACKSON
Jobs of 140 Tire Builders hung in the balance today as the culmination of a series of "sitdowns" at plant two of the Goodyear Tire & Rubber Co.

The company held the position that the men had quit Friday night after they had defied a warning that unless they resumed operations within a half hour their Goodyear connections were terminated.

The fact that just before midnight, two hours after the warning was given, most of the men finally operated their machines for a brief period was recognized as "a possible technicality" that might alter the picture.

Meanwhile, however, the 140, many of whom have 10-year service records, are considered as former employes [sic] and their cards probably will not be placed in the rack when work resumes Tuesday after the week-end shutdown, the company spokesman declared. . .

. . .No layoff notices had been given to the third sift men who are now considered as having quit, the company said. These men explained their protest as being in sympathy with the fourth shift. . .[4]

Akron Beacon Journal,
Saturday Evening
February 15, 1936

Haskell: The next day, we begin to go to the union office. There wasn't anybody else to go to. They was the only people we had any strength with. We signed up with the union after we got fired. Not before. I didn't even know they had a union. Nobody ever talked about it.

We had a couple of guys in there— A guy named "Whitey" Bethel was the supervisor.[5] Old man Litchfield was a great guy to take graduates out of M.I.T.[6] He was a graduate of M.I.T., see, and he thought anybody graduated M.I.T. was a world-beater. Some of 'em was a world-beater nut. This Bethel was a supervisor and he was a double-dyed asshole of the first water.

So during this strike, five or six of us guys were settin' around the gas station up here at Tallmadge, talkin' about the strike and so forth. A stranger come in, went over and set down on and oil can or box or somethin'. Just set there. Never said a word. And we kept on. Finally the personnel question come to the front. Talked about the supervision and the foremen and this, that and the other.

The guy that was our department superintendent was named Bill Denny and he was a triple-dyed asshole. He was a prick that long. So we just expressed our opinion of 'em. And I said, "Well, I get along. I always got along. I never had any particular trouble with the help. But," I said, "There's one bastard in there that I don't like and I think he's a no-good bastard. Whitey Bethel." "Whitey," we called him. He was blond. I can't remember his first name.

This big bastard that was settin' there in the corner got up and stuck out his hand. And he said, "That's my sentiments exactly." Said,

"I'm his brother. He always was a bastard."[7] I thought, "If he'd a been real fond of his brother, he might've combed my hair." But he put out his hand. He said, "He always was an asshole. He was when he was a kid. And he isn't any better now." Well, what this guy was doin' was workin' for the *Beacon Journal*. And he was goin' around, settin' around, where crowds was talkin' and just gettin' the sentiments for the stories in the *Beacon*. He later bought this old H & H Restaurant down there (him and another fellow). Ran that for a couple of years.

Blockade Goodyear; 8,000 Idle.
Hundreds Fight Police Move to Take Workers into Plant 2
Layoff Fear, Demand for Notices Blamed
'Don't Know What Strike is For,' Says Company; Won't Confer until Men
Return; Schroy Insists on Order
BY JAMES S. JACKSON

The roar of labor strife sounded through East Akron today, as a strike at the Goodyear Tire & Rubber Co. threw 8,000 employes [sic] out of work . . .

The 1,200 workers who met last night also were angered over the apparent refusal of company officials to promise 3-day notices if and when the 180 tire builders are laid off and refusal to permit the employes to share the work, instead of ordering some laid off. . .

Company executives said they would not confer with any representatives of the employes not working, but that if work was resumed a conference would be agreed to.

Company official declare they do not know why the strike was called, as most of the workers' demands were met . . .[8]

Akron Beacon Journal
Tuesday Evening,
February 18, 1936

Haskell: It was cold, cold, cold. So, they had a few riots. Goodyear would put the heat on the sheriff. The chief of police of Akron was a pretty levelheaded man and he had some sympathy for the men and he did not get aggravated with his policeman out there like the company wanted him to. They finally got hold of the sheriff who was an eager beaver and he collected a mob down at Case and Market and marched up there to break up all the picket lines. He was just ready to start marchin' with armed men when the chief of police came down and said, No, this is my territory. Don't you start any riot over here in my town. And he stopped him right there. It would've been a mess. It would've been a bloody mess.

I can understand their theory. They're in business to make money. We had four shifts. Four six-hour shifts. Well, you had to carry insurance and everything, pension, everything that went with the overhead on this extra shift—which you didn't need. In other words, you're in there workin' eight hours and your insurance don't cost the company any more than a guy workin' six hours, see. Then they had medical bills and various things to take care of. You could understand their point, but they did it in a very— In my opinion it was callous and stupid. They could've handled it with a little more finesse. If they would've cut out the overtime, went along for about a couple of months and started layin' these guys off a few at a time, instead of wholesale— If they'd laid off 50, wait a couple weeks, lay off 50 more 'til— Then clean out the place, there would've never been nothin'. Then, after a few weeks say, "Well, we're goin' back on eight hours, boys." And everybody would've been happy and would've been tickled to death. But they didn't— They forgot about the guys that got laid off. It was bad handled, I thought.

Birth

While Goodyear may have been on strike and Haskell was out of work, both he and Florence had more pressing concerns. Florence was pregnant again and ready to deliver their third child, Marjorie. The delivery at home would not go well. And it would soon prove that past history was not on their side.

Haskell: Florence had an operation when we was first married. Hadn't been married too long. She got a tubular pregnancy. So they had to operate on her after we lived in Paducah. Well, that found that her womb had sagged. So they fastened it up. Evidently the job was not perfect. They— They raised the amount of the womb too high. So when she tried to have a baby, it wanted to come out up here instead of comin' out down there where it belonged. The route was misguided, see.

Marjorie: The uterus would not drop properly into a birth position. With the smaller babies, you were O.K. But with the larger—

Haskell: Jean, we didn't have much trouble with her. She arrived pretty good. Donald was a rather long baby, but he wasn't fat. We had him at home and had some problem with him. They had to drag him out of there with the tongs. His head was about that long when they got him out of there. But he come out all right. Got straightened right

up in a few days. But Marge was a big baby. She weighed almost ten pounds.

Jean: When the time came that mother knew it was close, we were in the midst of one of the biggest snowstorms that ever hit the area. So they were afraid that we might not be able to get out when she needed to go.

Marjorie: Yep. Roads were all blocked and all. They planned to have me at Aunt Margaret's in Akron [Barton's wife]. Mom said every day dad would go out in the car and see how far he could get. Then the first time he was able to get through he said, "We're not going to take any chances. We're going tomorrow."

Jean: So we packed up and Dad took Mom to Barton and Margaret's. Donald and I were left with Uncle Ralph and Aunt Ruth.

Haskell: We were goin' to Barton's and Margaret was gonna' take care of her.

Marjorie: Mom and Dad were working with her for quite a little while. She was exhausted and wasn't getting anywhere.

Haskell: They started about six o'clock in the evening. And they screwed around with her all night long. So about nine, ten o'clock, we called the doctor and he came over there. And he messed around there 'til one, two o'clock in the morning. Didn't know what in the hell to do. The only good thing he said was, "We better take her to the hospital and get a specialist"—which we did. But they had one hell of a time before they got her out of there.

Marjorie: The nurse told Mom afterwards, "You don't need to thank that doctor for you having a live baby." She said, "She wasn't breathing. She was just laid over to the side. He was working with you and there was an intern in there that asked, "Would it be ok if I worked with the baby and see what I could do?" He did this thing of dipping me in and out of cold water, which now I've read about it as suddenly a new thing. But he tried that and got me going, got me breathing.

Haskell: Never knew anything about him anymore. Never saw him. Don't know what his name was. He just heard the conversation and he asked if he could come in and watch. I said, "If you can learn anything, you go ahead." I said, "You can't hurt anything." Well, I was lucky that I did that, see. If I'd've said, "Get the hell out of there," why, I wouldn't've had a baby. She never would've lived. This nurse told me that. These other guys were ready to lay it aside. "It's dead. Let's don't bother with it. Let's take care of the woman," see—which they did.

Jean: But she came through it and Marge came through it. Every-thing was O.K. after that.

Haskell: See, we lost our first baby. They— The doctor let her lay there 'til she killed him. He was a boy and big like Margie. Finally she— He just— He never touched her. He just let her— He said, "Let nature take its course." And it did. And she come out— The

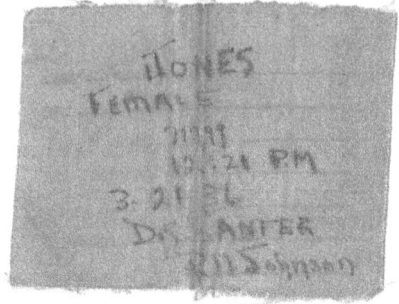

A Scrap of fabric saved from the birth of Marjorie Jones. The attendants didn't put her name on it. They didn't expect her to survive (Collection of Marjorie Jones Knapp).

baby was a breech and it had the cord around its neck and he was too stupid to send her to the hospital.

I'm a kid. Hell, I don't know what to do. He'd been recommended to me by a guy I knew. I never had a doctor there. I didn't know anything about doctors. So it was an unfortunate thing.

But you think back. That kid've lived, he'd've been the first guy drafted in World War Two. He'd've been the proper age just then. Maybe the Japs would've fried him, killed him or tortured him or done anything else, so you don't know whether he got a break or not. You wonder. You wonder about these things—what fate will do to you. You don't know. So you couldn't feel— Didn't— At that time, when it happened, we didn't think anything about another war. But it would happen.

Goodyear Production is Resumed.
Thousands Go Back to Jobs.
5-Week Strike 'Forgotten' as Great Industry Reopens Plants.
Restore Old Schedule.
Company Expects to Have All Schedules Restored by Tuesday Midnight.
By James S. Jackson

Akron's biggest factory, the Goodyear Tire & Rubber Co., was swinging back into production today. The strike that had lasted nearly five weeks was at an end . . .

During the weeks that a chain of pickets had encircled Goodyear's three big East Akron plants, more than 14,000 of the total 16,000 employees had been idle.

They lost a payroll of approximately $2,500,000, the company estimated. No figures would be hazarded as to the company's loss. . .

Akron Beacon Journal
Monday Evening
March 23, 1936

Haskell: So after— I think we went out on the 8th of February and on the 21st of March (almost on the hour that Marge was born), we got an agreement, a settlement and we went back to work. I was at the hospital when she was bein' born when they voted down at the Armory and got a settlement from the Goodyear to go back to work. That was the beginning of the labor movement in Akron. The big labor movement. We've had unions. Electricians had unions and various trades had unions and things of that kind. But the gum shops hadn't had an organized union by the company. So that was it. Then work was pretty good.

* * *

With the end of the Goodyear 34-day strike on March 21st, the United Rubber Workers union did more than just ensure a six-hour day and a thirty-six hour work week that would last until Goodyear's closed its Akron plants in the 1970s.[9] Now with tens of thousands of members, it also became a major force in union activism, setting a pattern of sit down strikes in other industries around the country.[10] As author Ruth McKenny noted in her novelized version of the strike, *Industrial Valley*:

> Seaman and subway workers, girls in textile mills and boys in the great radio factories, clerks behind busy department-store counters, garment workers, fruit pickers, electrical workers, men and women in mills and mines, factories and field, enrolled in the organized labor movement. Akron, a brave but lonely outpost in 1936, had become by the summer of 1937 only one of many C.I.O. [Congress of Industrial Organizations] cities. The United Rubber Workers of America, 70,000 strong, stood side by side with the 200,000 organized auto workers, the 250,000 steel workers, the millions in newly organized unions.[11]

The rubber companies got the message loud and clear—even as Goodyear held off on signing a union contract until late September 1941.[12] Author Susan Allyn Johnson notes:

> In 1936 and 1937 alone, nine new rubber factories were established outside of Akron, reducing the city's dominance as the center of rubber manufacturing. Whereas in 1929, the city had manufactured two-thirds of all tires in the United States, by 1938, sixty-five percent of all tires were made outside of Akron.[13]

Haskell: But they were dirty, son-of-bitches labor people. Dirty as hell. Dirty as hell. One year before that, they were layin' off a few guys and I wanted to go to Kentucky. I had two or three years' service. And Florence wanted to go home. I wanted to go home with her. So I went to the office to ask for time off. Well, they're layin' guys off and these guys ought to be glad to work in our place 'til we get back. The foreman said, "Ahh, we can't let you. We got the schedule down to where we got just the right production and we ain't gonna' let anybody off."

There was a man in there with more service than I had cryin' for his job. He was gettin' layed-off. And seniority meant nothing. One of 'em said, "We can't keep you in here" and "You can't make out. You weren't gettin' your schedule out." He said, "You know I've been off sick. I've had two or three operations in the last year and I'm gettin' back on my feet, but I can't— I can't cut it like these other guys. But I've got—" And he told how many years' service. Much more than I had. "There ain't nothin' we can do about it." And he was cryin'. Tears come in his eyes. He turned around and walked out. And I was the next one up. I could hear the argument.

One of these— There was two Charleys in there. Charley Brewer and Charley Sowers.[14] Charley Sowers was the department superintendent and Brewer was the shift foreman. The guy walked out of there with tears in his eyes. He was hurtin'. Needed his job. Bad, you know. Charley Brewer turned around to Sowers and said, "He kind of had the 'hot ass,' didn't he?" I thought, "Why—" Of course, I couldn't afford to say what I felt. I wanted to say, "Why you son-of-a-bitches, if you was in his shoes, you'd have the same 'hot ass,' too."

Brewer got hurt durin' the big strike. He climbed the fence. He was comin' in there to work and he climbed the fence and fell and injured himself quite a little bit.[15] He wasn't a kid. He was a man fifty years old or older. He was scabbin' in there while we was on strike. He climbed the fence instead of goin' in the front gate because the front gate, they wouldn't let him in. The strikers was out there in front. He was afraid to go in. He climbed one of them big wire fences and fell off and hurt himself pretty bad.

So we had a company union at that time. Sponsored by the company. The men elected representatives. They elected a senator and congressman or whatever. A representative and a senator, I guess. And they had an office in the building of some type. A fellow by the name of Graham was our representative—our bailiwick there. So I went to him and I said, "I want to go home and they won't give me time off. They're layin' off people. Can you do anything about it?" He said, "I'll try." So, in about a week, they give me a notice that I can go for three weeks, see. But this son-of-a-bitch, he'd laugh at this poor guy for getting' layed-off.

We needed a union. We needed it bad because conditions were terrible, terrible, terrible. There's always, in any labor job (and most any other job), there's people who excel in that. Now, in the tire building, you've got two hundred men in a room who are building tires. Well, they're not all as physically as good or mentally as good or whatever the word is. So one guy is always ahead. He'd get more tires than anybody around him because he's big, strong and able and smart and knows how to do it. When they got ready to set a rate, they set it by his work—not by mine or yours. We couldn't cut it like that. Not by an average, but by Jim Hoover.

We had this Jim Hoover in there. He could get more money, so who blamed him? Nobody particular blamed him. We had no limit. We finally put a limit on it after we got a union to fifty-six tires for an eight-hour shift. Well, six hour shift. Six hour shift.

We still worked six hours for a year or so after the strike. Fifty-six for six hours. When I started buildin' tires (of course, they built a different method), we built sixteen tires in eight hours. Well, then, they changed the style and the method of speedin' the machines and this, that, and the other. Various other things that speeded it up.

Well, Jim Hoover'd get seventy tires a day with no problem. He could build that many. And he built a good tire. He wasn't cheatin' on 'em. But most guys couldn't do that. He was about twenty-seven, eight years old. I was— Well, we went on strike in '36. I was thirty-eight years old, see. I wasn't a kid anymore.

I worked 'til '37 and things went down hill and I got laid off.[16] I think I got laid off on the 12th of November and I had started to work on the 17th or somethin' like that. I lacked that much of havin' ten years' service when I got laid off.

CHAPTER FORTY-THREE

RELIEF AND PUBLIC WORKS

Initially, as the reality of the Depression began to set in, Washington attempted to help the needy and unemployed through the Federal Emergency Relief Administration (FERA). Given a start-up budget of $500 million, FERA gave aid directly to the states, which then channeled the funds through local relief bureaus and welfare departments to fund work projects, as well as distribute cash, clothing and food. Within five months, six states counted half of their urban population on unemployment relief. With its formerly heavy industrial base, Ohio was ranked as #4 with 12.5% of the U.S. population on relief in its urban areas.[1] Of those, 34,437 individuals were in Summit County with 29,414 residing in Akron.[2] As author Karl Grismer noted:

> Relief money from the federal government began flowing into Summit County on November 20, 1933. During the following winter and spring more than 4,000 unemployed were furnished three days' work a week, six hours a day, at 50 cents an hour, thereby enabling them to receive $9 a week. There were few planned projects. Many of the men were assigned to cleaning out ditches, mowing weeds or raking leaves, or some other equally useless task. This was when the word "boondoggling" first came into use.[3]

By April 1938, 12,504 families were getting direct relief from either Summit County or its cities. Provided through the county or individual cities, "families on direct relief were given 12 cents a day for each person in the family, 4 cents a meal. They also got some free surplus food."[4] Money from the city came through a special excise tax and the sale of delinquent tax bonds. Money from the county came from the sale of poor relief bonds, paid out of tax revenues.

Apple sellers first appeared on downtown streets on December 3rd [1930] the apples being provided by the Citizens Unemployment Committee. To get the jobs of selling apples, 700 applicants appeared—200 were chosen. Within a month, 350 families were dependent upon sales.

Karl Grismer
Akron and Summit County

From the start of The Depression on October 29th to the end of the year, it was estimated that 1,400,000 people lost their jobs.[5] And unemployment exploded from an estimated 3 percent of the population to a high of 24.9 percent in 1933.[6] Just as in the depression of the early 1920s, however, the U.S. government actually had no idea of how many workers were unemployed.[7] As late as 1937, Harry Hopkins, the Administrator of the largest public works program in the country would note:

> At the present time all we have are estimates of unemployment in addition to our relief figures, which show how many unemployed are receiving public assistance. But we know that many, certainly millions of other workers have no jobs and receive no public aid. How large this group is we don't know. We should find out.[8]

To help battle the massive unemployment, Washington instituted a variety of just-as-massive make-work programs. The passage of the National Industrial Relief Act of 1933 did more than just grant workers the rights to organize.[9] It also created the Public Works Administration (PWA). Funded by some $3.3 billion dollars, it ultimately completed over 34,000 major, make-work projects across the country, including schools, water treatment plants, dams, post offices and bridges. As successful as it was over the long-term, its slow but deliberate pace under administrator Harold Ickes frustrated President Roosevelt

Transferring nearly a third of its funds to the Civil Works Administration (CWA), Administrator Harry Hopkins was tasked with the goal of putting 4 million people back to work. He accomplished the task in an astonishing two months.[10] Before the program ended just five months later due to charges of socialism and outrage that blacks would be paid the same as whites, "The CWA laid 12 million feet of sewer pipe and built or made substantial improvements to 255,000 miles of roads, 40,000 schools, 3,700 playgrounds, and nearly

1,000 airports (not to mention 250,000 outhouses still badly needed in rural America)." Incredibly, of the nearly $1 billion invested, nearly 80 percent went directly into worker's pockets. The majority of the remainder went to purchase equipment. And less than 2 percent paid for administrative costs.

The ongoing Depression led to the creation of the most successful and most recognized of the make-work programs just a year later in the spring of 1935—the Works Progress Administration (WPA).[11] Modeled on the success of the CWA and led, once again, by Harry Hopkins, it offered employment on an unprecedented scale including building and highway construction, reforestation, slum clearance, and rural rehabilitation. During its 8-year history, it created more than 8 million jobs—today's equivalent of more than 20 million jobs.[12] And it "built 651,087 miles of highways, roads, and streets; and constructed, repaired, or improved bridges, 125,110 public buildings, 8,192 parks and 853 airport landing fields."[13]

The first WPA project in Summit County began on August 12th, 1935.[14] By the end of the first week, 2,000 were employed.[15] Providing public work opportunities for the unemployed, it paid $55 a month for unskilled workers, $85 for skilled workers and $94 for professional and technical workers.[16] October of 1938 saw peak employment in the county through the WPA with jobs being provided for 21,829. In addition to relatively mundane tasks such as clearing snow for city streets, literally hundreds of major projects were also completed by WPA workers including the construction of the Rubber Bowl, the renovation of school buildings, the installation of 40 miles of sewer pipe and waters lines, the construction of 55 bridges and improvements to over 600 miles of city streets and country roads. With the country's entrance in World War Two and the end of the need for WPA, more than 30,000 individuals were assisted in Summit County— which did not include the thousands of other families who received direct relief.[17] With each worker representing a family of four, it's believed that WPA helped some 120,000 people in the area. By the time it went out of existence in Summit County in January 1943, it had spent some $51,000,000. Of that amount, $35,000,000 went to Akron.[18]

Florence: That was a time was worse than it's been in any time in these last years. I'm tellin' you, people had a hard time gettin' along.

Haskell: They didn't have all these relief agencies in those days. They're "Johnny-come-lately's." They're all new. They had soup kettles downtown. If you couldn't get to the soup kitchen you was out of luck 'cause they didn't bring it to ya'. They had a lot of fella's peddlin' apples down on the street on— Oodles and oodles of 'em sellin' apples for a dime apiece. They'd have some big Washington apples. They'd buy 'em for about a nickel and sell 'em for a dime on the street. They'd have a little box somewhere and be sellin' apples. And everybody worked that could find anything to do for a few cents. But there wasn't much to do. The factories weren't busy, so all the related industries weren't busy. Akron was a rubber town in those days. Everything depended on the rubber.

Tallmadge, O.
June 4th, 1930
Dear Mary:

I'm tired as a dog tonight, but it looks like if I wait till I have time and feel like writing I'll never write.

I have to water our flowers every night now it is so dry and tonight I only pumped and carried 22—12 qt. sprinkler's full or 66 gallons. You can imagine what a job it was. I have also made two pairs of curtains, fixed a dress over for Jean and stuck my sweet peas since four o'clock this afternoon . . .

Tom has never got work and Mattie and Grace have to keep things going.

The shops are not hiring at all. They said 1600 passed through the Goodyear employment office Mon. morning and not a one was hired . . .

Will close for this time.

Love to all,
Florence.

Tallmadge, O.
Aug 6th, 1930.
Dear Mary:

I'll try to write a few lines tonight, but havn't been in a writing way. . . .

It has been awful hot here, most of the time, since we got back. Have had a few cool days, but most every day the temperature has been around a hundred. It was a hundred two days, and Monday it was 101° and a hard hot wind with it. It almost ruined things. Another day like it would have dried up everything. It has been a little cooler since and no wind to amount to anything. If it don't rain pretty soon we won't have vegetables much longer, my early cabbage is most gone and beans about dried up. The corn field beans are just beginning to bloom and would make plenty beans with a good rain. We have had tomatoes for two weeks, on our early vines, but just enough for table use.

I havnt seen Barton and Margaret for two weeks. The baby sure looked good when I saw him last. He is still real good. Barton is back on second shift on piece work.

Work at the Goodyear is fair now, but they will have a ten day lay off the first of Sept. They are working 8 weeks and taking a week off along till work picks up.

Firestone is more slack than usual. Mrs. Jones has had to quit housekeeping for they couldnt keep her going. We have had to take Tom and Henry . . .

. . . I must close for I want H. to mail this as he goes to work.

Love to all,
Florence.

Florence: Jean went to school a few days before she thought about whether the people was poor or whether they wasn't, I guess. She came home one day, tears in her eyes. She says, "Mama, are we poor white trash?" I said, "Honey, what makes you ask me a question like that?" She said, "Well, I know we're poor." And says, "Some of those kids at school call some of the others 'poor white trash.' I know we're poor, but," says, "are we 'poor white trash'?" I said, "Don't ever get that into your head." I said, "We're poor, but we're not trash." She said, "Well, I knew we was poor." I said, "I want you to look at it this way. Everybody that's poor not trash by any means 'cause there's more poor people than any other kind." I said, "Don't you ever be guilty of calling any of 'em 'white trash'—no matter what you think of 'em. They're just people. Like we are." And that settled everything for her. She never worried anymore about it.

The kids worked for first one and then another little job they could pick up here. And they had good clothes all the time. I made part of Jean's. I'd buy this material in the store for a little bit and I could make her pretty little dresses. And Donald would help the farmer that lived by us. They'd do a little farm or help somebody mow a little and he'd buy clothes. And those kids, they went to school lookin' nice all through. There's a lot of kids that didn't have clothes that were very good. No way of gettin' 'em.

(L-R) Donald and Barbara Jean Jones.

I'd just made Jean some new dresses and she'd wore one of 'em to school. And we had a P.T.A., I guess. I was talking to a teacher and she asked me, said, "Mrs. Jones, where do you get Jean's clothes?" I said, "I make 'em." She said, "You make 'em?" I said, "Yes." She said, "Well, she has the prettiest dresses of any kids in my room." It's a good thing I could sew or she wouldn't have had many dresses of any sort, I'll tell ya'. But as it was, she didn't have a lot of 'em, but she had plenty and they always looked nice. I could buy a yard of good material to make dresses for her for a few cents a yard and it didn't take very much to make her dresses. I even made some of Donald's shirts at that time.

Haskell: You could make a pretty good dress for a dollar. Gingham and stuff like that. Twenty-five, twenty, twenty-five cents a yard. Buy a package of buttons for a nickel. Spool of thread for a nickel.

I had rough days and rough times, but I don't think I ever got— In The Depression when I was completely out of money and had a family and had no job, you had to be a little down-hearted. You couldn't be too cheerful when you was like that. But I worked at every little odd job I could get and made a dime here and a dollar there. Always made a garden and we always had somethin' to eat. We didn't have any money. Never went to bed hungry or cold. They always had somethin' to eat. Wasn't always what you wanted, but it was always filling. Kids were dressed well. Florence made their clothes and they were as neat lookin' as anybody in the county. Had good credit. And that was one thing. And I don't know how I got it. But the coal man and the grocery man was always sympathetic. When I finally went back to work, I owed both of 'em about four hundred dollars. In those days that was a lot of money.

Florence: We always had a whole bunch, seemed like, that we knew come in for dinner. On Sunday—

Haskell: We lived in the country.[19] They thought our food was free. We owned a garden and the rest of 'em lived in town. And this is Depression days, see. They come out to get a good meal that they couldn't afford at home.

I think durin' The Depression, people had no money for bought entertainment so they went to each other's house and played bridge or cards of some kind and enjoyed the association. Florence and I used to go here and there and play bridge Saturday night. After you get money, people don't associate. They go buy entertainment here and there. A show or some place of that kind, you know. But when they had no money, they had to depend on their friends for entertainment. It was a pretty good life—even though it was hard. But people survived. They came through and they enjoyed each other.

One time Mom [Florence] made a couple pies during hard times. She'd make it out of anything she had you could make it. Somebody gave her a recipe for green tomato mincemeat. And the pie wouldn't have been too bad, but she didn't do a very good job on the crust. Something unusual for her because she always made good crust. But that day they didn't turn out good. They was hard. So, we didn't eat 'em. She cut one and we nibbled on it a little bit and the other one set there for a day or two. A tramp came to the door one day and wanted something to eat so Mom gave him that pie.

I kidded her 'til yet about it [at the time of the recording]. I told her the poor guy went out to the road somewhere and ate it and died. But he was probably tickled to death to get it. It wasn't bad. If the crust had been good, we probably would've eaten it. But she failed for once at makin' a piecrust.

The woman across the road— A guy had come there one day and wanted something to eat and all she had was homemade bread and butter. So, she told him that's all she had. "Well, that'd be fine." So, she sliced a big slice of that homemade bread and smeared it with butter. And he walked out by the side of the road and opened the bread and took the butter out and greased his shoes with it. His feet were hurtin' him.

Jean: Instead of sitting around now and feeling sorry because nobody cares, back in those days, people helped each other. I remember we didn't have people standing on the corners begging, but we had— We called them "tramps" that came and knocked on the door and asked for something to eat. Mother fed a lot of tramps. Nobody ever did us any harm. They didn't break in and steal— There wasn't much to steal, anyway.

Florence: Talkin' about when we were livin' up there— The people that lived across the street from us, the Sacketts, they were awful nice.[20] And our two kids loved to go over there and visit with 'em. They got along real good. And Mrs. Sackett was borrowin' something always and never brought it back. So, one day I went to bake something. I think it was a pie pan.

Haskell: Bread pan! You'd loaned her your bread pans.

Florence: Yeah. Donald was out playin' with the kids that lived next door. He was just a little boy. Looked down the field and saw her comin' across. And he'd gone over in the yard and was meetin' her and she said, "I come to bring your mother's bread pans back." Says, "I never bring anything back, do I?" Donald says, "That's what Mother says."

Haskell: Believe it or not, she borrowed Mom's clothesline. Cotton clothesline. Her old clothesline. In the fall Florence hung her clothes in the basement. Well, Mrs. Sackett borrowed those clotheslines in the fall and she strung 'em up out there in the yard and they hung there all winter long. The coal soot down on 'em all winter. You couldn't have used 'em. They was just as black as a harness. So, in the spring, why, Mom needed her clothesline. She sent Donald (he was a "carrier") over to get her clothesline. She knew where they were. And Mrs. Sackett said, "Well, they're not fit to use. I'll go get you some more."

So she went to Kramer's.[21] Big store there. She run up there and got her some clothesline but she didn't get herself any. Pretty soon she was borrowin' Mom's again. They lived pretty hard. They didn't have much money. Piddled around out there farmin'—milked a bunch of cows, raised a few chickens and pigs. They wasn't rich by any means.

Jean: Kramer's had a big variety of things. Kramer's store was very important in our life. They kept us in food during the bad days and let us put everything on credit. I'm happy to say that we paid back every penny of it. But there were times when there wouldn't have been food on our table if it hadn't been for Kramer's.

I think about that today. There aren't any stores like that anymore. And if people are in a situation like we were back then (and some of them are now), they didn't have that possibility. At Kramer's we got groceries and Henry Bierce we got coal. Same deal. We weren't the only ones, not by a long way. I was talking to somebody about those days and I said, "We still had a very good life. We weren't poor. We just didn't have any money." But things were done that we could go ahead and live and not suffer too much.

Haskell: Terrible, Terrible thing! The people that lost their homes then— That was a bad thing. I always felt that would be the most worst blow in the world, outside of a death in the family, was to have a home partially paid for and they kick you out in the street 'cause you couldn't pay for it, see—through no fault of your own. They just— Job folded up and you didn't have any.

Florence: Donald just about burnt that house down. This was in the fall of the year. I was cannin' and doin' stuff and I'd gone back in the garden to pick some extra beans I needed and left Jean and him at the house. They was just little kids and I'd always put 'em to bed in the afternoon. And they were real good. They'd go in their beds and go to sleep. And I thought no longer than I'm gonna' be gone, they can't get into anything today. So I run back and grabbed off what beans I needed and started to the house and I see Jean comin' to meet me—cryin'.

Oh, well, I guess they've had a fight. But I hurried to her and she says, "Mother, brother has set the house afire and he won't come out!" So there I was with some beans hurryin' to get to the house. And I meet her and I really hurried then. I got to the house and run upstairs. Now, this is a crazy way that they built the house. There's two closets but you had to go through the one closet to get in the other closet. Well, when I got there, I guess Jean had shut the door that came into the hall. And I guess a good thing it was.

I opened the door and called to Donald. It was so full of smoke I couldn't see where he was. And I called to him so I could find him. I got an answer from him and I said, "Where are you!?" Said, "In my bed." I knew where the bed set (and from his voice, too) and I felt my way through the smoke over to his bed and found him and took him out.

They didn't go to sleep like they was supposed to. They went in the closet and was playin'. And there's always some matches around where Haskell was, where he smoked all the time. They had got some matches and was playin' with the matches. I don't know if you've see this kind of fireworks that you could strike a match and stick to 'em and look like a snake crawlin' out. They saw the kids across the road have some and they didn't know what was made 'em crawl like they did. They just thought it was a rolled-up piece of paper. So, he strikes this match and sticks it to a piece of paper that was in the closet. I used to sew a lot and I had these patterns in a basket or a box settin' against the outside wall. Well, he stuck this match to some of that paper. "Thought it would make a snake," he said.

So, this blaze started. And I had clothes hangin' all along the wall in there—my winter coat and different things. So, these blazes come up and burnt some of those clothes to make this awful smoke. I got them out and I didn't know anything I could do. I told Jean (she was just a little thing), I said, "You run up to Mrs. Vannoy's and tell her what's happened and to send her husband down here right quick!" And so, there was Charley Knapp. He was an old man, lived with the Keller's. He was related to 'em. He was workin' in the field out there and he saw the smoke and he came running.

We didn't have any water only where you had to pump it. And one of 'em pumped water in a tub while the other one was bringin' the ladder and Charley was gonna' pump water. So, Kenner brought the ladder and set it up. Charley was pumpin' all the time and I'd take it over to the ladder. We was lucky enough that the three of us, together, put the fire out by openin' up the outside window right in the right spot.

I think it was Labor Day and everybody was gone from home or asleep—one or the other. Usually, Haskell would have been home, but he had some kind of electrical work he had to do that day and all the neighbors were gone but Vannoys. Ooh, I never was as scared in my life I don't think. I thought that he would be burnt to death before I get up them steps. But when he answered me, and I could find him, I could grab him and run out with— But I thought, "Well, if everything else burns up, I've got my child." And, so, we sure had a time around there.

And there's a man comin' along in a truck. We had gotten the fire out but he knew somethin' had happened because we had the ladder up against the house and the buckets out there. And he said to me, "Are you sure you have the fire out?" And I said, "Yes, it's out O.K." And he said, "Well, it's too often you think the fire's out and it'll break out somewhere close by later." Said, "Do you care if I climb up this ladder and look in there where the fire was?" And I said, "No, I don't care. I'd be glad for you to." I said, "I know that it's out. I just feel sure that it's out but I'd hate for somethin' to happen and it'd break out again after I said that I knew it was out." But I said that, "I'll be glad for you to look."

So, he come down and he said, "Well," said, "I want to tell ya' somethin'." Said, "there's a good job been made." Said, "There's no sign of fire in anyway—only just the black." So, Haskell was doin' some work over in Akron. 'Course when he got home, things was kind of a mess. He was really shocked.

Well, I'll tell ya', we've gone through some pretty hard times during The Depression. Some pretty hard times. We was lucky to come through it as good as we did.

Haskell: I made a garden and we canned everything we could can. Florence would have five or six hundred cans of fruit every year in the fall. Fruit cellar full. And we had somethin' to eat. I ate so many green beans I don't relish 'em too much anymore. If Florence cooked 'em, I like 'em. She was the best. Never seen anybody that cooks beans like Florence did. I guess her mother did, but I don't remember. She took a lot of pride in her cookin'. That was her "bag" —was make a good meal.

After Roosevelt got in there and they got organized after a year or so, why, they begin to take hold and they had a lot of programs that was— They had some surplus clothes. They had surplus groceries and things of that kind that they had various— Every little place like Tallmadge had a distribution point, see, and you go there and you get surplus groceries. You get a bag of flour and some potatoes and some butter and whatever they had.

Donald: They gave out surplus food at the Circle. When they gave that out and we were getting that, dad wouldn't go down and get it. I had to go down and get it. He didn't want anybody to see him getting it.

Haskell: I worked 'til '37 and things went downhill and I got layed off. Then, I didn't have any work and I got on W.P.A. and any old job I could pick up here and there. Digging ditches alongside the road. We worked up at Tallmadge school. Whatever I could do. For about three years.

W.P.A. was a national make-work program. We got fifty-two dollars and twenty cents a month. We worked five days a week for twenty days for $52.20. If you worked every day. $52.20. And you had to be there every day. Wade mud hip-deep. Ditches. Terrible! Terrible! Terrible! After so long a time I got on a county workforce. I was workin' on county roads for the county road department under the county engineer.

We worked up at the Tallmadge school when they graded that schoolyard down from that north building, up there. Worked there some through the winter, one winter. But we worked on the roads around town here—digging and graveling roads and stuff of that kind.

Shoveling snow on Tallmadge Circle for the WPA in 1936. Tallmadge Town Hall is to the left. The Circle Restaurant and hotel, with U.S. Stoneware behind it, is in the background (Lawrence Collection, Akron-Summit County Public Library).

There, we got $75.00 a month. That's all we could collect. We could work more and pile it up and take it off, but we couldn't get a check for more than $75.00. If we had like fightin' snow or something like that, you might work long hours and earn more than the $75.00 a month, but you couldn't collect it. You had to take time off and you could get it that way—make up a garden.

One time they wanted to form a union and I said the hell with it. I ain't gonna' bother with a union. What are you guys gonna' do? You're on your knees. Got a little job here for $75.00 a month. You want to go and join a union? They didn't bother me, but we had an Italian foreman. A nice guy. A heck of a nice guy. Named Dominick Alteri. I remember his name. Dead now. He was our foreman and all he did was tell us what to do, not how much of it. He didn't push any-body. We was all workin' for the same deal. So, one mornin' over there on North River Road, they're gonna' run him off the job because he won't join the union. I said, "Why don't you try runnin' me off? I don't want to join, either. Nah," I said, "That guy's a good—" Supervisor, I guess. He wasn't a foreman. "He don't bother anybody. What the hell do you want to bother him for?" I said, "If you gonna' give him trouble, you're gonna' give it to me. I'm puttin' in with him." And they didn't bother him. Ah, I'm a screwball. I don't like to see somebody ganged up on.

None of us wanted to stay on that job any—not one day longer than we have to. I don't know what kind of work they did before they was on this county job, but they was just like me. They was tickled to death to get out of W.P.A. and get about twenty dollars a month more. Twenty-two-*fifty*. Nah, I stuck my neck out a lot of times. But that's the way I believe.

Finally, the guy that married one of those women that owned our house got out of work. She got out of work. They was livin' in the Falls and rented a house. They couldn't pay the rent so they wanted that house so they could live in it. So, we had to get out.

I had a nice garden started. We were gettin' a little stuff out of there. I said, "O.K." I owed 'em a little rent because times had been tough and I hadn't kept my rent up all the time. I owed 'em maybe sixty, seventy dollars. I didn't pay much rent, but whatever it was. I said, "I owe ya' some rent and I'll give ya' the garden and we'll be even." So I never did pay 'em any more rent. I never did get a dun for it. Nobody ever asked me for it. So they got the garden and we moved to Akron and stayed a few months.

We didn't want to live in Akron. So I found that little old house over by the schoolhouse (where the town hall is now). I don't know

(L-R) Barbara Jean Jones, Marjorie Jones and Donald Jones with Queenie in the yard of their home next to the Tallmadge High School (seen in background).

what the hell I was workin' at—if any. There wasn't much work.

Florence: We were lucky. We didn't have to pay much rent. The old house was in bad shape. Dirty. It hadn't been lived in for four or five years, I think. And we all got busy (Haskell and me and the brothers and all) and got that cleaned up so we could move into it.

Haskell: We stayed there from thirty-eight to forty-three, I think. Forty-three, we went down to Thomas Road and rented that old house.[22]

Florence: We rented it and we lived in it for 25 years. We did quite a bit of work on it. The whole place looked pretty. Haskell worked the outside of it. The grass was kept mowed, cut out all the old bushes and briars and everything and it was pretty.

* * *

Haskell: I was off 'til to about November 1940 when they called me back. I'd been laid-off for three years and I went back and work was good. I knew how to build a tire but I'd been out of it so long and I wasn't gettin' any younger. I was havin' some hemorrhoid trouble. We had great big rolls of stock to pick up and put on a machine. And it's hurtin' me. I'm bleedin' like a sick walrus. I was havin' a hard time makin' out. Specification was very rigid. They had a spec man runnin' up and down the line checkin' your work all times. And you never knew when he was comin'. He'd check for any little fault in it. If it wasn't good, then he made you repair it. It had to be good. And we had minute inspections after the tire was built and put on the conveyor to be cured. Very close.

Well, I said to my supervisor, Mike Mitchell (a good man.)— I said, "I'm havin' a hard time makin' out, Mike, gettin' my—" what I was supposed to make. He said, "I've been watchin' and I know what the trouble is." I said, "What is it?" He said, "You're tryin' to build 'em too good." Said, "They don't build 'em that a way here anymore." Said, "Let it go. Let it go. Let it go. Anything that'll pass, let it pass." Well, I wasn't used to buildin' 'em like that.

I'd worked nine weeks and I'd made an application for this police job in Tallmadge. That come up and I was appointed policeman. So I quit and went to that job. And that was a dumb thing. I should've jumped off a bridge somewhere instead of takin' that job.

PART SEVEN

**TALLMADGE, OHIO
1941**

CHAPTER FORTY-FOUR

THE CIRCLE

Haskell: The old hotel building we had in Tallmadge where Standard Oil is set out there on the corner.[1] They had a feed store in it. They had a barber shop in it. They had a bootleg joint in it. They had a restaurant in it. They had a cat house in it. They had a gamblin' joint in it. It had quite an unsavory reputation. They stayed open all night. They didn't sell anything but booze much. A little sandwiches or somethin'. It was called the Kentucky Tavern, by the way. I can't think of who run it. I s'pose they had that there until Prohibition come back and then they closed it up.

Jack Sperry's family owned that corner. About the time we came here, gasoline become a worthwhile commodity. So, they had the old hotel building moved back. Old man Bunting built a great, long building there and put a fruit stand into it to start with and Aber worked for him.[2] Well, that was a mistake. They didn't have that much business for a fruit stand. They cut it in two then and rented the back end of it to a grocery. They had an I.G.A. Grocery in there. And the front end, they rented for a restaurant and a three-two beer joint. They put a little gas station—just a little bit of an eight by ten job there. They're all drunks. Everyone of 'em.

Durin' the Depression, that little old gas station wasn't big enough hardly to work out of—let alone have people come in it. But everybody was out of work and they had to go somewhere to relieve the pressure. Guys would come in there.

Girl Hiker's Nerves Break Under Strain
Red Eyes, Drawn Face Tell Story of Murder Charge's Effect
Asserts Act Justified
"No Jury Will Ever Convict My daughter," Says Mrs. Boyle.
By Clyde E. Schetter, Beacon Journal Staff Writer

FRANKLIN, PA., Sept. 17.—"I had to shoot to save myself."

Thus, simply, does pretty Miss Loveda Boyle, 18-year-old Oil City high school graduate and divorcee, explain why she fired the shot that resulted in the death of Robert McCormick, 21, Akron automobile salesman, Saturday morning.

"I shot in defense of my honor," she says. "Even then I didn't shoot to kill."

Is Showing Signs

Auburn haired, blue eyed and neat in appearance despite her confinement in Venango county's none-too-inviting jail, Miss Boyle is beginning to show signs of the strain she is under. . . .

. . . . Mrs. Boyle also related that her daughter called her by long distance telephone from a farmhouse near the scene of the shooting Friday morning. "Loveda called me but we had such a poor line I could not make out what she was trying to tell me. . . .

Akron Beacon Journal
Sept. 17, 1928

Haskell: Some girl come in there one night. She was hitchhikin' from Oklahoma and somebody dropped her off there at the Circle. She saw the lights on at this place. She went over there and got a cup of coffee and told the night man who was workin' there that she was tryin' to get to Oil City, Pennsylvania. So, two rounders come in just as she left. Him and his buddy— They'd been out prowlin' around.[3] She's goin' down by the railroad there to try to thumb a ride to Oil City, Pennsylvania, see. So, these guys saw her and they went in and asked the bartender who she was. This guy said, "Well, she came in here and got a bite to eat. She's tryin' to thumb a ride to Oil City, Pennsylvania." Well, they got the big deal. So, they go drivin' down there and stop and she asks 'em where they're goin' and they said, "Oil City, Pennsylvania." "Hop in." She got right in and they hadn't got to the top of the hill when one of these guys started tryin' to pull her clothes off and she shot and killed him. We was livin' on the hill. So, this girl— The guys stopped and let her out.

She went in the Rutherford's poundin' on the door and they got up and let her in.[4] She called the Sheriff's office and told 'em she'd just shot a guy. Well, the guy took him to the hospital. He didn't know whether he was dead or not. She didn't kill him outright. It was a small gun. Shot him in the belly. She stayed there for several hours and the sheriff's deputy never came out. So, she said the hell with him. I'm goin' home. So, she left her name and address and everything and went out and thumbed a ride to Oil City.

Well, the guy died and then finally the sheriff gets all the stuff together. They went over to Oil City and brought her over here and had a little preliminary hearing— Turned her loose and told her to go home. Twenty-eight, twenty-nine—somewhere along there.

Old man Aber was an alcoholic. He'd drink all the time. He'd drink anything, everything, anytime he'd get it. It didn't make no difference. Worked in a gas station in his later years. Worked nights. When the morning come, he'd stand around the gas station (We didn't have any booze joints in Tallmadge) 'til he had a customer— or somebody he knew, was going to Leon's or to the Roosevelt (which was down the south road).[5] One or the other. It didn't make any difference to him. "Are you goin' up—?" "Yeah." "Well, I'll ride up with ya'." So he'd go up there and he'd stay two or three hours (heisted quite a few) and catch a ride back. He lived right by the Circle. You could throw a rock to his house. So he'd go to bed. About one or two o'clock in the afternoon he'd wake up, take a bath, clean up, shave. Neat, clean guy. Always clean. Eat a little—very little. Go back down to the station, wait for another ride—somebody goin' this way or that way. He'd catch a ride and go back.

But he went to work at eleven o'clock at night. Got off at seven in the morning. So, he'd stay up there and play euchre or play cards or something and drink a lot. Then about six o'clock, he'd catch a ride home. Come home pretty well loaded, go to bed. Ten o'clock, he'd wake up again, go take a bath again and clean up, get awake, go over to the gas station and go to work.

He had a habit of always carryin' a half-pint bottle in his coat-pocket. Before he left up at Leon's, he'd walk down to the end of the bar and hand this half-pint bottle around the corner and they'd fill it up, and he'd pay for it and go on home. Well, after he went to work, and got squared away there in a little while, he'd take a sip—about a tablespoon full, see. That first one wouldn't stay down. As soon as he did it, he'd go around back of the station and leave a ka-hoop! The next one would stay a little longer. 'Bout two he'd heave up. Stomach was on fire. He never'd drink much on the job. He'd nip along—just a little sip, now and then. Well, it was morning and by that time he'd cleaned up his bottle.

He was quite an independent cuss. A lot older than I was when I was policeman. I'd go in the station eleven or twelve o'clock and old Aber's in there and I can tell right away— He forgot to get his bottle filled. He got too much while he was there and somebody come along to take him home and he'd forget it. And he can't hardly make change. He's in bad shape. I said, "Aber, you look like you need a little of the hair of the dog that bit you." He said— (And tears would come in his eyes.) He said, "I do, Jonesie. Would you go get me a bottle?" I'd say, "Yeah. I'll go get you a bottle. Give me your bottle." I'd go up to Leon's and stick the bottle behind the bar and say, "Aber's dry. Fill his bottle up." I said, "He'll be here to pay for it tomorrow." They'd fill it up and I'd stick it in my coat pocket and go back and give it to him.

One Saturday night he come in there and go to work and he come in on the early shift. His boy worked on the first shift. Somebody else was workin' nights, workin' late. So Newland and I and his boy were gonna' go down to the Roosevelt. That was before I was the policeman. We was gonna' go down to the Roosevelt and get a beer. And Aber run out to wait on a customer out at the gas pumps. Newland knew where his bottle was. Picked it up and hid it behind something else—right there in the station. So we went down to the Roosevelt and had a couple of beers and we bought a couple bottles of beer and brought them out to him.

We come back there and he is madder than a Georgia hen! He was boilin'. He knew what happened. He thought we drank his whiskey. We didn't touch it. Somebody said, "We brought you a couple of beers." And he told us what we could do with the beers. He said, "I got to work here tonight and you guys can go and get a drink anytime you want it. But I got to stay here." And he was— He was boilin'. So he got out and waited on another car and they took his whiskey and put it back where it belonged, where it was originally. He finally come back in and he looked up and sees it. But that man was mad, I'll tell you! Poor, old Aber. He was a character.

Witty. He looked just like Will Rogers exactly. People— Customers would— Strangers— I was standing there and a crew of colored people got out and got some gas. And one of these boys was about fourteen or fifteen years old. Just went into shock. Said "He looks just like Will Rogers!" And he did. And he was just as witty as Will Rogers, I'll telll ya'. As a comedian, he would've been a champion, see. Looked like him and talked like him.

When they moved this buildin' off, there was a basement under it and it set there for some time before they did anything. Somebody was in there and Aber was always about half tight. Somebody said, "Aber, what are you goin' to do with that old basement?" "Well," he said, "They're goin' to cut it up into post holes and sell it to farmers."

They had a Lebanese [Abraham Massad] that ran that old Roosevelt down there.[6] Aber would go down there one or two mornings a week and drink a dollar or two's worth of booze. He went down there one morning and this guy said, "Mister Aber, I've got a new drink." He said, "Yeah, what's that?" He said, "Well, it's an ale. They call it a nut-brown ale." Said, "It's a new drink and I like for you to try it." And Aber says, "O.K." He thinks he's gonna' get a free drink. This Arab pours him out a double tablespoon full in a glass and hands it to him to taste. To hear Aber tell this story—what he thought about this guy. He's been spendin' money with this guy for years and he gives him a "taste" of beer. Not a draft. Give him a little thing. Couple of tablespoons full to taste. He was quite a character.

I went in there one night and a fellow named Bill Shakespeare— Played football around there in his youth, but Bill was an alcoholic. Good mechanic. Worked for a big machine company and did a lot of trouble-shooting. They'd sell a machine and if there was anything that went wrong they'd send Bill to get it fixed. He was a good mechanic. But he'd been in the workhouse for drivin' drunk. They give 'em thirty days back in those days. I come in the gas station. It was cold, winter time. And he's layin' behind that stove, wrapped around it just like a dog. Drunk. On his way home. He hadn't got home from the workhouse, yet, see. I said, "Abe-e, it looks like you got a customer." He said, "Get him out of here if you can. Get him out of here." So I dragged Bill out. I said, "C'mon, Bill. I'll take you home." He lived over in Munroe Falls on River Road that goes back down in there by the County House. I knew where he lived. So I took him home.

I had a Frick guy. He lived down there in front of the Stoneware. One of the old Frick family, there. But he was an alcoholic. He didn't have much control of himself. Worked at Stoneware. He went down to the Roosevelt and got drunk and eat a bowl of chili. Comes back up to the gas station and loses it right— right in the middle of the entrance. As you go open the door— Ka-loop! I come in and Aber's cleanin' it up with a broom, tryin' to clean up the place a little. "Jonesie, why can't they eat somethin' besides chili?" That was a mess, I'll tell you.

Art Pfeifle run that restaurant. I don't know whether it had a name. Just a restaurant. A three-two beer joint.[7] Charlie Mills run the gas station.[8] But he used to hang around there a lot. He lived in the old building that was an old feed store in back of it. He had a pretty good building there. You could go in there and go into the beer joint.

I had a buddy. Bill Perry was his name. Bill and I had been friends for a long time. Heck, I hauled him up that hill when he was goin' with that Crites girl. He went with Wanda for nineteen years. Never could get enough money to get married. She finally give up on him and married somebody else. He always went up there in the evening, stay there a little while and get a little lunch, lay down on the davinette and sleep 'til ten o'clock. She'd finally wake him up and say, "Bill, you'd better go home. I got to go to bed." The whole family loved him. Every one of 'em. There was a house full of girls. And they all loved Bill. He was a nice guy in a lot of respects. But he was a character.[9] He was a lady's man.

He'd walk back down the hill there to the restaurant and pick up one of the girls that worked in the restaurant and shack up with her durin' the night. Every night, nearly. Every night. I remember one time these people had a gas station on the corner of Newton and Ninety-one. Pretty good-sized gas station. They did some repair work. Both drunks. Both of 'em. Anyway, they'd close up about twelve o'clock at night and they'd go over to the Roosevelt and get higher than a Georgia pine. Roosevelt closed at one. One o'clock, they'd come up to the three-two beer joint and shoot the ox around there. Have a few beers.

Charlie Mills used to hang around there a lot. He lived in the old building that was an old feed store in back of it. Gone now. So Charlie was drunk and old man Beddington (I'm gonna' say. I don't think that's his name), was drunker than a hoot owl and she was drunk. This guy and Charles are out there havin' a conversation and cryin' on each other's shoulder. And Bill's got this guy's wife in the back room on a pile of Sunday papers givin' her the "hot oil treatment," you know. But he was a character, I'll tell ya'. One of 'em is out there in the yard settin' on a pile of gravel cryin'. And the other one is in there gettin' the treatment. But that Bill was a character.

CHAPTER FORTY-FIVE

THE TALLMADGE POLICE DEPARTMENT: ONE MAN

Following the impact of The Depression, the 1940 Census of Akron revealed "a sorry picture indeed, [with] declining production figures, slumping employ-ment totals and dimin-ishing industrial income."[1] Out of a population of 244,791, there were only 29,000 factory employees. And some 1,397 vacant houses.[2] By comparison, Tallmadge was not much better off. Its population had fallen by nearly half to 3,452, even less than that of Mayfield, Kentucky's population of 4,081 of 1900.[3] Everything, how-ever, was about to change. Again.

With war already raging in Europe and England, Akron was about to experience its biggest boom (and face its greatest challenges) ever. Many of its workers would find a home in Tallmadge. And many more would travel through Tallmadge on their way to that work. That's because as small as Tallmadge was, its historic, nearly century and a half old traffic circle was also a critical transportation hub for the area. There, spoke-like from the center of the township, 8 major roads radiated in different directions to the rubber, armament and aircraft factories of Akron, the steel mills and shipping industries of Cleveland on the Great Lakes and northeast to the Army's massive 24,000-acre Ravenna Ordnance Center, as well as the steel plants of Youngstown.

Located in the center of this traffic circle, was the Tallmadge Town Hall, a historic structure dating back the middle of an overgrown swamp and was of such ill repair that it had actually been officially condemned in 1936.[4] In addition to Council Chambers, it also served

Haskell A Jones in backyard of the family's home off Tallmadge Circle, adjacent to the high school. Their home was located on the site of the present-day Tallmadge Police Department building.

as the offices of the Tallmadge Police Department. There, beginning in 1941, that entire depart-ment would consist of just one man, Haskell Jones.[5] On call 24 hours a day, seven days a week, he would be required to supply his own uniform and gun, as well as his own police car. If a prisoner required transport to the jail, he would be responsible for taking them into Akron, as well, as Tallmadge didn't offer a holding cell, let alone a jailhouse.

Despite the initial challenges of the position (and many more which were to materialize as the country entered into World War II), one thing was to become abundantly clear to the citizens of Tallmadge. As a current history of the Tallmadge Police Department notes, "Police work in Tallmadge began in 1941 when Haskell Jones served as the lone officer and Town Marshal in the village of Tallmadge."[6]

Haskell: When the city was incorporated, they never had had a policeman. They had a constable. He was an elected man. And they never had a town marshal—never had a town. So, when the city was incorporated in 1936, they appointed Harley Crislip town marshal. He

403

"Tallmadge Circle, 1933." Tallmadge High School is seen in the top left of the photo. The home which Haskell and Florence rented sits directly adjacent to it, between the school and the Congregational Church on The Circle (Lawrence Collection, Akron-Summit County Public Library.

wore a policeman's uniform and a police badge and did police work, see. But he was a rat.

He was taggin' motorists and givin' 'em a ticket and takin' the money and never turnin' it in. He caught some man from over east—Youngstown, Pittsburgh. Somewhere over there. Some travelin' man. Caught him speedin' one night and took a ten dollar bond—which *I* did. I took bonds from 'em because it was a convenience to the man. You either had to hold him or take a bond. And in the middle of the night, you can't get a hearing. You have to put him in jail for a lousy ten-dollar bond, see. So, it was a common practice. Everybody did it. They still do it. Some places.

So, this man (when he got back to his office), he had this ticket for ten dollars that he paid the policeman over here for a speedin' ticket. And he gave it to his boss to be reimbursed. So, the boss said O.K. He evidently was a right kind of a guy, so he put the ticket in an envelope and wrote to the mayor and wanted to know if this ten dollars that the guy had posted was sufficient to take care of the deal. So, they wrote him a letter and said yes. It wasn't more than a month 'til he caught the

Tallmadge Town Hall, c. 1920 (Summit County Historical Society).

same guy—done the same thing. He didn't recognize the fellow, see.

So, when he gets back over there, his boss does the same thing. He puts the ticket in an envelope and mails it to the mayor. Here's the mayor got two tickets over about a month's time for ten dollars apiece that hadn't been turned in. So, he talked to the council about it and they decided to give him another month just to see, maybe, that he'd overlooked it for some reason—that he didn't turn it in.

He didn't turn it in so after a council meeting one night, why, they called him into a special session and wanted to know if he ever gave Joe Blow a ticket from Youngstown, Pittsburgh, wherever it was and Harley didn't remember anything about it.

"You don't remember givin' this man a ticket—takin' a ten dollar bond?" "No." He'd give the ticket and wrote on it and give it to them, but he tore up the duplicate. They laid these tickets out on the table and said," Is this your handwritin'?" He couldn't deny it, see. They said, "Well, the end of the month, turn in your tools and you're done."

Mr. Mills moved to adopt the following resolution. That in view of the resignation of Marshal Crislip, effective January 1, 1937 that the Mayor shall appoint one police office [sic] for the Village of Tallmadge and that the Mayor shall notify council of said appointment for further action or conformation [sic] by council. Seconded by Mr. Barnes; carried unanimously.

Mr. E. O. Windsor was designated by council as their choice for appointment.

S.A. Schlup, Clerk
Village of Tallmadge, Ohio
Council Minutes

December 15, 1936

Haskell: So, they appointed a man by the name of Oscar Windsor. He come out of the sheriff's department.[7] He was from my home county down in Kentucky. Nice guy. A helluva' nice guy. He was a nice policeman. Did a good job.

I was willing to do anything that was better than what I had. And I had a hunch that I'd like to be a police officer. So the job came up for election. I run against him for policeman and he beat me—which was all right. I told him, I said, "Hell, you're a good man and I don't mind you winnin'." But I was workin' on W.P.A. at the time. What the heck? I'm tryin to do a little better.[8] Well, Oscar had a heart attack or somethin' and died.

Then they appointed this fellow by the name of Carter, Lloyd Carter. His brother was a deputy sheriff.[9] But anyways, he had a little pull downtown and he got the job. He had a small insurance agency, too, and it grew a little bit. He tried to be a policeman and have an insurance business over on Exchange and Summit. Somewhere over there. He worked about three or four months (six, at the most) and he quit both jobs and went to Texas.

I applied for this job again. I had a petition with three hundred names on it from people in town and petitioned Mayor Ritchie to appoint me to the job—which he did.[10] I started on the last day of 1940. New Year's Eve. And I was a policeman 'til the last day of June 1944. About nine months after he appointed me to the job, the state legislature outlawed the job of town marshal statewide. They made it a chief of police job rather than a town marshal job. In most cases, they only had the one man, but some places they had more than one. They had two men, but the marshal was the headman. So I was then the chief of police. Now they've got an army doin' the same job I did and not much more than I did. That's the truth. Not much more.

Mr. Mills moved to adopt ordinance #106, which provides for the hiring of a police officer for the Village of Tallmadge. Seconded by Mr. Sperry. Carried unanimously.
. .
Mr. Mills moved the passage of the following resolution. Be it resolved by Council of the Village of Tallmadge that the Village Police Officer secure insurance on his car in the amount of ten and twenty thousand dollars, the policy to be filed with the Village Clerk. Further that the officer, provide and pay for and maintain a car, telephone, uniform, and all other necessary equipment. Motion seconded by Mr. Sackett. Carried unanimously.
Mayor Ritchie appointed Haskel [sic] Jones as Police Officer of the Village of

Tallmadge in accordance with Ordinance No. 106 and the above resolution. Mr. Sperry moved to approve the appointment. Seconded by Mr. Sackett. Carried unanimously.

S.A. Schlup Clerk
Village of Tallmadge, Ohio
Council Minutes
December 23, 1940

In each village there shall be a marshal, who shall be designated chief of police, who shall be an elector thereof, appointed by the mayor with the advice and consent of council . . ."

Revision to the Ohio General Code, Section 4384
Ohio Senate Bill No. 3
Enacted on September 5th, 1941

Mr. Belden reported that he had conferred with Mr. Zook State Examiner, located in Akron, with regard to the position of Marshal and compensation therefore. According to the opinion given Mr. Belden by Mr. Zook, the Marshall's salary can lawfully be set from month to month. It may be reduced or raised at any time during the Marshal's continuance in office.

Mr. Cunningham moved that the salary of the Marshal be fixed at $225.00 per month. That at that amount the Marshal be required to furnish everything pertaining to the job. Seconded by Mr. Mills. Messrs. Carter, Cunningham and Mills voted aye. Messrs. Ripley and Sackett voted no.

Mr. Ripley moved to fix the pay of the Marshal at $200.00 per month, and that the officer furnish everything pertaining to his job except the bond which should be furnished by the Village. Seconded by Mr. Carter. Carried unanimously.

Ordinance No. 124 providing for hiring of a Marshal, was introduced. Mr. Mills moved that the ordinance be adopted but that the same should be rewritten and section six providing for upkeep of Marshal's car be eliminated. Messrs. Carter, Cunningham, Mills, Ripley and Sackett voting aye.

Mayor Sperry appointed Haskell A. Jones in accordance with the terms of Ordinance No. 124.

Mr. Mills voted to approve the appointment of Mr. Jones as Marshal. Seconded by Mr. Ripley. Carried unanimously.

S.A. Schlup Clerk
Village of Tallmadge, Ohio
Council Minutes
January 26, 1942

Haskell: I should've jumped off a bridge somewhere instead of takin' that job. I never made enough money on it to pay my bills. I got $225 a month and I furnished my own car. They furnished the repairs, gas and oil and washin' and whatever I needed. But it was my car. And I had to make payments on my car. They paid for the insurance on it. Worked seven days a week about sixteen hours a day. On call all hours of the day and night.[11]

Florence: He was apt to get called out any time of day or night.

Haskell: And all alone, too. No radio to let you know what's goin' on in the country.[12] You didn't have any radio to know if they had a big holdup in Akron, a killing, or nuthin'! You was "cold turkey" everywhere you went. You just on your own. Had to use your head or run—one or the other. That's about all.

You go to bed at night and two o'clock in the morning, some bastard's run into a pole down here and they call me to come out. They got an accident out there. Some man is fightin' with his wife at four o'clock in the mornin' and he calls me and he wants me to come out there and keep her from killin' him. You didn't get any rest. You had a hard time with it. You patrolled the place from nine-thirty, ten o'clock in the mornin' 'til about two, three o'clock in the mornin'. Supervised the road department. Was a fireman. I was in charge of organizin' the fire department, organizin' the auxiliary police department (We didn't use 'em much. Didn't need 'em. There was nothin' happenin'. But the firemen, we did.).[13] Everything that went along with Civilian Defense. I was in charge of it, see. Worked my ass off eighteen, twenty hours a day.

Buttons from Haskell's police uniform.

But you don't know. You think you'll try and you do the best you can. I learned a lot and got to be acquainted and knew a lot of people and liked a lot of people and so forth. But in the meantime, I didn't make any money.

When I was policeman, I damn near run the town. Me and the Clerk, Sam Schlup. There wasn't anybody else to run it. They had a Council, but everybody was workin'. It was durin' the war when I was a policeman. Everybody was workin'. Nobody had time. Shit, they was all runnin' their ass off doin' somethin' else. Sam and I was the only ones that had any time. He was the Clerk and I was the policeman. He was a full-time man in the Hall and I was a full-time policeman.

Old Ma Baker give me the low-down.[14] She was the town scandalmonger. Knew everything about everybody in town. Knew when they went to the toilet and how long they set on the throne. She didn't have a telephone. Didn't go out. Didn't have a car. Never left the house more than three times a year and knew everything that went

on in town. I was the policeman. I didn't know half as much as she did, though. She was a character of first-water.

She was the neatest lookin' old lady you ever saw. Clean as a pin. Always dressed like a nice, old lady should be dressed. The foulest mouth you ever heard of. I think he [her husband had] got her out of a cat-house in Canton. He must have. I don't know where else. But she was ornery. Oh, my goodness! Drink everything and anything.

They had a government project on that gravel back in Roosevelt's days. The F.E.R.A. Federal something. I don't know what. But they hired a bunch of these young guys. And the guys had old trucks that was haulin' gravel gravelin' that road. First guy that was headin' back toward the gravel bank, Mrs. Baker come out and flag him down. She'd have a dollar bill. She'd say, "Stop at the schoolhouse and bring us a bottle." Then the guy would stop and get it and when he'd come back with a load, he'd stop and they'd each cut down on that bottle. "Now, you so-and-so, next trip you bring one!" She'd cuss 'em out. But she was always lookin' for a bottle.

I went up to the Hall and stayed awhile and wait for a call and do my bookwork or whatever. We had an extension in the restaurant at night. I don't know whether the restaurant had a name. Art Pfeifle ran it, but I can't tell you if it had a name. Just a restaurant. A three-two beer joint. [15] They had a little gas station there. Charlie Mills run the gas station. Eight square feet. The girls at the restaurant didn't answer the phone durin' the daytime. The Clerk went home at 4:30 in the afternoon. Why, from then on, they would answer the phone 'til about one in the morning and then they went home. Then, the bastards would get me out of bed every time somebody bent a fender or something. Family fight or somethin' of that kind. But that was kind of my headquarters when the Hall was closed.

Sec. 1706. [Officers of villages.] The officers of a village shall consist of a mayor, clerk, sealer of weights and measures, treasurer and marshal, and the council may, when in its opinion expedient, create by ordinance the offices of solicitor and street commissioner, or when no territory is attached to a village for road purposes, may provide by ordinance that the marshal shall in addition to his duties prescribed by law perform the duties of street commissioner. . .
The Annotated Revised Statutes of The State of Ohio.
Including All Laws of a General Nature In Force
January 1, 1900.

Mayor Sperry appointed Haskell Jones as Road Superintendent. Mr. Cunningham moved that the appointment be approved and that Mr. Jones be allowed 100 gallons of gasoline monthly for his car. Seconded by Mr. Ripley. Mr. Youngen did not vote. Mr. Carter voted no. Messrs. Sackett, Mills, Youngen and Cunningham voting aye.

Mr. Mills moved that road committee be authorized to expend not more than $475.00 for a truck. Seconded by Mr. Carter. Carried unanimously.[16]

S.A. Schlup Clerk
The Village of Tallmadge
Council Minutes
March 9, 1942

Haskell: As a policeman, I had charge of the streets, too. That was a job. I had to look after that and recommend repairs and buy gravel and supervise the maintenance of the streets. That was a gratis job. I didn't get paid for it and not much thanks. You can't believe how we tried to take care of the roads around here. In my department, we had two old men with shovels and a grader. We didn't even have a truck then.

In the wintertime the road crew couldn't work outside—too much bad weather. No nothin' but a pick and a shovel. We had a road grader. And one of us suggested we excavate under that Town Hall and put a basement under there. Needed a new furnace.

So, we took the road crew and we started excavatin' that.[17] The wall underneath the Town Hall originally didn't go down the full depth—like the basement. It only went down, say, three feet underground. So, we had to dig back away from that and leave that dirt underneath that foundation. Then we stepped back in about two and a half feet, thirty inches, somethin' like that, and built a cement block wall up all the way and put a new furnace in it.

That was a coal furnace they was usin'. They eventually put two gas furnaces in there, but at the time, we didn't use the upstairs for anything only meetings. And usually, the council meeting was held down in the council chambers they called it, where the clerk and I had our offices—just one side of the bottom. They didn't have toilets in the Hall. They had two inside/outside toilets. They were in the corners in the front and the back—man and woman. And they were just a scuttle-hole or toilet built in there with a one-eye job. You went in from the inside.

But they had to have somebody clean it periodically. It was not used very much. So, we put a toilet and a sink back in the back corner back there. I don't know what they got in there now. They probably got up-to-date showers and everything for the police.[18] But at that time, we didn't have but one policeman. And he never took a bath. But we did at least have a toilet, see.

Then we did some remodelin' in the Hall. We put our offices on the opposite side of the hall and dropped the ceiling so we could heat it. The ceiling was about fourteen feet high in that main room, I suppose. Maybe sixteen. It's high. And we put a false ceiling in there. Dropped ceiling.

The Councilmen were not full-time. They're not yet. In those days, hell, they met twice a month. Spent two, three hours in the meeting and that was about all they ever did. Passed a few ordinances. We proposed or dug up the facts for 'em, so they could tell what they wanted to do.

We had a Court regular Friday night. Seven o'clock, 7:30. But if we had an emergency come up, why, I'd call the mayor over and we'd take care of it then. He lived right across the street from the Hall at that time.

My first mayor— A fellow by the name of Ritchie was mayor. He was the first mayor they had. He didn't last too long. He died, I think, in April after I took the job in the first of the year. Went to Columbus for some business meeting and died down there with a stroke or heart attack or something.[19]

Mayor Charles Ritchie

Haskell: His folks had made the money. He'd never made any money in his life. He was fifty-five, sixty years old. His dad, old man Ritchie (Sam Ritchie), had been a salesman for the U.S. Stoneware and he'd gone to Louisville, Kentucky and sold a bunch of sewer pipe. And the man didn't have enough money to pay for it. So old man Ritchie took a thoroughbred stallion of some kind in on trade and he was going to ship it back to Tallmadge to the company. It was the company's horse.

So, on his sales trip, he gets into Canada. Sold a big jag of stoneware to somebody. And this man told him that he was lookin' for that same kind of horse that he'd picked up in Louisville. So, he traded him the horse for a big tract of land in Canada. Wilderness. Then, he paid the company for the horse. Whatever the man owed on the order of sewer pipe. This is before the turn of the century, way back.

They later discovered iron and nickel on this land and he became rich. And Ned [Mayor Ritchie] told me his dad had sold some of the land for something. Maybe to pay for the horse. I don't know. Said if he'd of kept it all, they would've been the richest family in the United States. Maybe the world. But they didn't.

That Hale farm down there in the Valley belonged to his mother's family. They weren't particularly rich, but they had the big farm down there in the Valley. And there was some iron down in the Valley. I'm sure it was on the Hale farm. It was not good iron ore, but it was workable. They used it for pots and stuff of that kind. Had a small smelter out there and smelted that iron. Cheap ore. A lot of rock in it. So, he'd never had to work.

But Ned was this man that was Mayor. They always called him "Ned." I never heard of anything else. Ned Ritchie. He had good judgment on a lot of things when you pinned him down to make a decision, but general behavior was rather erratic. He did a lot of stuff for Tallmadge and would've done some more if hadn't some of the guys hadn't wanted to tell him how to do it. But they kind of pissed him off because he wanted to furnish the money to do it the way he wanted to do it and they wanted to tell him how they wanted it, see, instead of lettin' him go ahead.

That Circle was a swamp when we moved out there. There was cattails growin' in the Circle. What wasn't a swamp was just a field and had so many dandelions in it, in the spring you could almost walk over the top of the dandelion blossoms. It was just solid yellow. It looked just like a big chunk of butter. And they'd mow it with a field mower and a team of horses just before Decoration Day and just before Labor Day. Twice a year. And they'd just let the stuff lay. Let the grass grow back up through it again. It was a hell of a hazard. A fire hazard and everything else.

Well, when he got to be Mayor, why, he bought dirt— And, well, first they started a federal relief program called F.E.R.A. Now I don't know what it stood for. Federal something. Relief Agency. I don't know. I guess Federal Emergency Relief Agency. Sound like about right. Anyway, they hired a lot of younger guys to work. A few old ones. And did some road work and cut some brush and stuff of that kind. So, they was doin' a project back in there along the railroad. There was a bluff in there and they cut that down. They hauled the rough dirt into the park and scattered it out. And he bought "Certified Soil." It'd been treated for weeds. And covered that whole park. Had it seeded. Put a curb around it, sidewalks through it. Did a lot of stuff around

Haskell Jones and his '41 Plymouth P11-D DeLuxe police cruiser with side bumpers used for running traffic violators off the road. $764 new, he paid for it (and the side bumpers) out of his own pocket.

there.

I had borrowed a gun from Neil Jones and I carried it for about a year and finally Mrs. Ritchie (that was the mayor's wife), she gave me this gun I've got now—one of his guns.[20] He had a whole mess of 'em. She said, "Take your choice." The President of Council became mayor then. A fellow by the name of Sperry. Jack Sperry.[21] Jack was a pretty good Joe.

I furnished my own car. It wasn't really a police car. Real red. Maroon red only it was redder than maroon. Forty-one Plymouth. Seven hundred and sixty-four dollars. [22] Everybody knew that red Plymouth. It had side bumpers on it. The only ones I ever saw. Never saw another car with side bumpers. A young fellow I knew that lived up on the hill this side of Leon's was workin' for some supply house and they had some. He said to me one day, "Hey, I've got something you'd like. I've got some side bumpers." He kind of explained it to me and I got a low price on 'em. I think I paid seven dollars for 'em. Of course, that was in the early forties when the price of seven dollars was pretty big. Wasn't much trouble to put 'em on and I kept 'em on there until I quit usin' the car for a police car. Was real neat.

They were on the side of the runnin' board. They was nice and

413

May- 17- 42 — 4:29 A.M. Witness (ST4060 Kisane) 4:00

accident on Triplett Blvd. car turned over 2 or 3 times
Driver Jack Kay Howell, Stow Rd Tallmadge O
Sweeneys ambulance to City Hosp.

Police Officers made Report - (Tinnell & Patrick)
Approximately $3,200 missing from Purse when admitted to Hosp 176 - 182
Bob Smith of Tallmadge was with Howell when
Purse not missing
Howell got into his car and who followed him
another car to State Rd 241- Says that Howell had this
money when he got into his car at the corral Hamburger
Place on N. Arlington St.

C Margaret Kisane - lives first house W. of scene,
Telephone - ST 4060 Says that
she did not see anyone touch Howell But ambulance
attendants, she was there when Police arrived
(she is not Positive that Police did not Remove
Purse) Night nurse at Emergency Room at
City Hosp. Says that Howell had no money
when he arrived at Hosp.

The sole surviving police report from the earliest years of the Tallmadge Police Department (on the back of Village of Tallmadge letterhead). It only survived because driver Jack Howell was boarding with Haskell and Florence at the time.

smooth and there was no place to hang on 'em. If you needed to crowd a drunk off the road, you just simply cut in front of him and that bumper cut against his tire and it headed him toward the ditch. You picked a place where you could crowd him off without runnin' him out in the ditch and wreckin' him. But it was a pretty good arrangement for a police car.[23]

I used 'em more than once. You'd pull up alongside of the guy and blow the horn and motion for him to stop and he'd just keep on goin', see, 'cause he thought it— Lot of people think traffic laws that if a police officer is following 'em, when they get over the line into the next subdivision, the police officer can't arrest them. Well, that's a fallacy because a police officer can follow you as long as he can keep you in sight. For a misdemeanor. Of course, for a felony, he can follow you whether you're in sight or not—long as he can imagine where you are. But for a misdemeanor, like a traffic violation, why, as long as he keeps you in sight, he can follow you as long as you stay in this state.

So, I run a lot of 'em out of this county. Kent, East out— Almost to Palmyra out here. I caught 'em out there. Some of 'em would give you a pretty good chase. Traffic interfered with a police officer more than it did with a wild driver because he'd cut in and out where a police officer wouldn't take a chance to kill somebody just to catch a nut, see.

This one guy passed a school bus there at the corner of Munroe and Eighteen. I was followin' the bus and I took after him. There was a little snow on the ground—just a little "skiff" here and there. He went through the light at Brimfield like there wasn't any light and I slowed down for it to catch it green because he went through on the tail end. I had the siren, had a little advantage. Through Rootstown, Edinburgh, and I caught him out there beyond Wicke's Lumber. There was a big truck goin' up a hill and traffic was heavy comin' down and he couldn't get by. He knew I was after him. He was from Detroit. I had some wild rides. Some of 'em I didn't catch.

Had one smart cookie get away from me one night and I didn't know where he went. He disappeared with me chasing him, right behind him. He was goin' out Eighteen, just crossed Munroe, got down in that little flat. There was a big truck. They used to have a lot of "doubles" in those days. They don't pull many of 'em anymore, but they— Big, high sides. They pull one and tow another one, pull doubles.

Well, he got around this outfit and somebody was coming and I had to slow up. When I got around it, he's not there! And it's flat from there to the Portage County line. You could see a car anywhere! There

Mr. Jones—

One of our good milk customers was given a ticket for not stopping for school bus... He is a reliable honest man + we would appreciate... treating him with courtesy. He has never received a ticket before. As long as no damage was done it seems as if it might be overlooked.

The reason... Tallmadge didn't see fit to even play square when our little girl was almost killed + nothing was done, the man was left off without even a fine.

Mrs. Earnest Atwood

A letter from Mrs. Earnest Atwood asking Chief of Police Haskell Jones for a little "courtesy" for one of their customers. As Haskell would later note, "We gave him courtesy. But we didn't fix his ticket."

ain't any car there! It's a nice moonlight night— Disappeared! He's going too fast to turn in a driveway. He's almost going fast enough to take off, but he didn't.

So I went out to the Portage County line lookin' for him and, naturally, I didn't find him. And, after a lot of good, hard studying, I found out what he did.

He pulled past that big tractor and trailer, pulled over on the berm, and stayed alongside that tractor and trailer while I went around the tractor and trailer. But I just laughed about it. What the heck? It didn't bother me anyway. But I rode around for a few hours 'til I figured out what he did. Said, "Which way did he go, George?" It was comical. So what? He got a big laugh out of it and I do, too.

Marge: When I was little and he was the policeman, I used to love to ride in the car with him. I liked to go with him anyway. I liked going with him to the hardware store, Tallmadge Lumber, on Saturday morning. He was fun to go around with. I was in the police car with him one time and he was taking me to a birthday party for Margie Pfeifle. Going up Northeast Avenue, somebody flagged him and pulled him over and said that some wild driver had forced an ambulance off the road that had come to take one of the local girls, "Happy" Huffman. I don't know what Happy's first name really was.[24] She had been stricken with polio and they were taking her in and this guy had forced it off the road. Described the car and we took off in pursuit with me in the car. I can't remember if he found him or not. I don't know. I don't know. But I remember the chase up the road.

Haskell: I had a lot of experiences. I learned a lot. I enjoyed helpin' people if I could help 'em. I didn't enjoy givin' a man a ticket for a violation. I didn't enjoy that. I had to do it, but I didn't particularly get any kick out of it. But if I could pick up a man that was out of gas on the road in the middle of the night and I could take him down to a gas station and get him some gas, I enjoyed doin' that. I could help somebody. But to give tickets, I never— I give many of 'em. Many, many, many of 'em. I never did get any thrill out of it. A few people that was sassy and ugly, why, I didn't mind it. But ordinarily, a citizen, I didn't particularly like it.

Marge: If there was a situation he'd do what he needed to do to help people. Very much wanted to do that. There were occasions where we had a homeless man sleeping out in the shed there on Thomas Road. He'd been sleeping in some cardboard box, I think. Covered with cardboard anyway up in the field behind our property and it was getting cold. Dad knew him and knew what his circumstances were and he had straw in the shed. Let him come and sleep in the shed some. I think we got a real appreciation of people of all kinds because of dad. He had friends from high to low. And definitely he was not one to say well, he's beneath me. Can't be friends there or whatever. He was pretty good. He had his prejudices, certainly, but– Just really learned to appreciate people and to know that we didn't all have to be just alike.

Haskell: I took quite a few drunks home. People'd dump 'em off at that restaurant on the Circle. Somebody they'd been out with. And they lived in the area somewhere. Some of 'em, they didn't even know where they lived. But if they could get to Tallmadge, they could get home. Some of these guys were completely paralyzed. "Well, c'mon. I'll take you home." What the heck? I had to do something.

Boy, 16, Held as Car Rams Into House

A 16-year-old Kent youth, arrested on a delinquency charge, will go before Judge Oscar Hunsicker Monday to tell his part in a twist of "the man who came to breakfast."

According to Marshal Haskel [sic] Jones, of Tallmadge, the youth will also be held to account how he happened to ram himself and his car into the living room of the home of Mr. and Mrs. Eugene Fritch [sic], on the Tallmadge-Cuyahoga Falls rd., early Saturday while the couple was eating breakfast in their kitchen.

The early morning visitor rudely jolted the attention of the couple away from coffee and cakes when his car zoomed off the road, skidding about 275 feet and landed in the front room of the house, Jones said.

The Fritch [sic] couple jumped up from the breakfast table to see who their caller was and found that his car had struck the house broadside and had catapulted through the wall into the front room, demolishing furniture and leaving the home precariously on its foundation.

Marshal Jones said the youth driving the car—a borrowed one—was intoxicated, had been absent from work at Goodyear Aircraft Corp. and was going about 80 miles an hour when the machine went out of control. He is being held in county jail.[25]

Haskell: I arrested Gene Fritsch's stepson for drivin' drunk one time. Kenney Rollins. He was old Fritsch's wife's son. I had to hit him. He tried to hit me when I was tryin' to open the door and I kept twistin' his arm to turn him away him and he kept tryin'— I said, "I'm gonna' slap the piss out of you if you don't open up that door and behave yourself."

So, he took another swing at me and I slapped him open-handed right on the side of his face. Pow! Just about as hard as I could hit him. I slapped his glasses from one end of that town hall to the other. They just went like a paper airplane. Zooomph! I thought, "Ooooh, they're broken!" But they didn't break. I took him inside and while he was gettin' his breath, I got the door unlocked and took him in and he still wants to fight. I got him in front of a hard bottom chair and hooked my heel behind his heels. Pushed him backward enough to get him over-balance and— I doubled him up in that chair and I took— I could've broke his back. I said, "Now next time you get out of that chair, I'm gonna' hit you with a club. I'm tired of hittin' you with my fist."[26]

They didn't have a jail cell then at the Town Hall. I used to have to take 'em to Akron Summit County Jail. They got that jail cell after Mike come there.[27] Some time. They haven't had that too many years.

The next night I went down to jail to get him and bring him out for a hearin'. We're comin' along up there about the Akron city limits on 261. I catch up with another drunk—windin' all over the road. So, I run him down and stop him and got out and checked him out and he's blind. I told this guy, I said, "You bring my car on to the Hall. I'm gonna' take this guy in." So, he brought my cruiser on up to the Hall.

Willie Jackson. Yeah, old Willie didn't have money to pay his fine, so he said he had a new suit and if I'd take him downtown and get the suit and go to Sam's (a pawn shop) he'd hock the suit and pay the fine. So, I took him down to his room and got the suit and went down to the pawnshop and hocked it and got the fine money. Not long after that, he got sent to the penitentiary for robbin' an old couple out in the country toward Medina somewhere. He went out there and broke in the house (him and another guy), beat this old couple up and they sent him to the pen.

Never shot anybody. Had a mean one one time I had to cool down a little. He killed somebody right after that in downtown Akron. He'd hit a car and I arrested him. Hit somebody on the railroad over by Stoneware and hurt somebody. Hit the Crites girls, I believe. I think it was Wanda and Wilma.[28] I took 'em to the hospital. I took him along on the way to jail. The mayor wasn't available for a hearing or anything. Had to put him in jail, see.

So I got him over to Saint Thomas Hospital and he got tough. I took my gun out and I says, " I'll shoot you right through the belly! Now, shut-up! I don't want to hear any more out of you!" He shut up and I took him down to the jail. The mayor fined him and he paid the fine. It wasn't very long after that he killed somebody in an alley down here back of the Mayflower Hotel. Somewhere in there.[29] Sent him to the pen.

* * *

Haskell: Tallmadge had a small airfield in those days. It was just very small private field.[30] Belonged to a fellow by the name of Jim Snodgrass. And he did some flyin'. I don't know whether he ever owned a plane or not. He had a fight down there with some fella' about a plane that I had to be the "moderator."

They had bought a plane that had been damaged. I don't know whether it had been wrecked or wind-damaged or what, but it'd been damaged. Jim had done a lot of the work and furnished the place to do the work and the other guy had paid for the plane. But they had fallen out about who the thing belonged to. So, the man wanted to fly it away from there and Jim wouldn't let him fly away.

So, the man went to the Justice of the Peace and got an order from the court. He showed him the papers that the plane belonged to him. The order's from the court to permit him to fly that plane away from there— Take it away. I don't think he specified that he could fly it away, but he could take it away. It belonged to him. So, Jim said he could take it away if he had to haul it. He couldn't fly it away. So, I was the policeman and they got the papers and brought 'em to me to serve on Jim—that he should let the man take the plane away from there because that's what the court said.

So, I go down there Sunday afternoon and this fella's there with the plane and he's got it warmed up. Got two or three buddies with him. They're hagglin' about it and the man wants to know what I can do about it. I said, "I can't do anything. The court says that you can take the plane away from here and that I'll let you do. But it don't say how you can take it away from here." I said, "You didn't get that specified. If you can fly it out of here, it's all right with me. I won't let anybody bother you." "Well," he said, "O.K."

So, he prepared to fly the plane up. They had it backed up in the field as far as they could. It was a short runway (not very long). When Jim saw that the guy was gonna' fly it away from there, him and some of his buddies started diggin' a ditch in front of it. It was sandy soil, see, and they started diggin' this ditch. The two or three— They dug there like mad.

The fellow got in there and got the thing warmed up and his buddies pulled it across the ditch. It wasn't very heavy. It was just a light plane, anyway. And they pulled it across the ditch. They lifted it up as it went across and got on the other side of the ditch and then they held it 'til he revved it up in high speed and he took off with it. He cleared a fence about that much down at the lower end of that thing.

Jim was mad at me a long time about that. But what could I do? All I was down there was to stop a riot. I wasn't down there to take any sides or anything.

Huband Seized in Wife Shooting
Deputies Surround Theater to Make Arrest After Phone Tip

Steve Nuss, 30, of Tallmadge, sought for the shooting of his estranged wife, was captured by sheriff's deputies last night as he emerged from an East Akron theater.

Nuss was armed with a fully loaded .38 caliber revolver, but offered no resistance. Sheriff Walter P. O'Neil said Nuss readily confessed the shooting.

An anonymous telephone call to police headquarters informed police that if they wanted Nuss they would find him in the theater.

Deputies Bob Smith, Fred O'Toole and Jonathan Jarvis surrounded the theater. When the show ended, Nuss was one of the last to leave the theater. He was arrested in the lobby and immediately admitted his identity.

Wife in Hospital

Nuss' pretty 26-year-old wife, Yolanda, who is a serious but not critical condition at St. Thomas hospital, was shot shortly after midnight Friday as she drove her car into the driveway of the home of her parents at Atwood Corners, Tallmadge.

Her husband emerged from the shadows and fired a .32 caliber revolver, the bullet penetrating her chest.

After the shooting, Nuss told deputies, he ran to the home of a former employer, Charles Miller, on route 18 two miles east of Tallmadge.

Not finding the Millers at home, Nuss said he entered the house, hid the gun in the attic and stole the .38 caliber revolver which was found on him when he was arrested.

He told deputies he was hiding inside the house when they went there early Saturday morning looking for his footprints in the snow.

After staying at the Miller home for a few hours, Nuss said he walked downtown "to see a movie."

Akron Beacon Journal
Sunday, January 5, 1941

Haskell: I was cruisin' at night one time when I was a policeman. Snow on the ground. And I met this man, walkin', comin' up the road facin' me—which was rather unusual at that time of night. One o'clock in the morning, probably. And I wondered about him. And I cut the car away from him and cut it back so my headlights would shine on him, but I didn't know who he was. So I went on about my business.

Later I got a call that a woman had been shot up the street a little ways. Maybe a block or two. I went there with a deputy sheriff name of Nolan. Nolan. Big Irishman. We searched around. We couldn't find the man. He had shot his former— I guess she was still his wife. She was an Italian girl. But I can't remember her name. They had separated. He was livin' in town and she was livin' with her mother. So he hid and waited for her to come home and run up and shot her through the door of the car—which didn't do too much damage to her.

He disappeared and we looked for him and couldn't find him. We knew his name by that time. Nuss. N-U-double-S. Nuss. A Hungarian or hunky name of some kind. We went to his home over in East Akron and searched the house. We found his brother, but we didn't find him. The next morning, the deputy (Bob Smith) called me and said, "I found out where that man might be, that Kuss. A place where he had worked as a chicken-picker." He might be at Jim Hazen's. That was the Miller's but the house belonged to Jim. So we went there to search the property.

They told us we could get in the house if we wanted to. It wasn't much trouble to force the kitchen door. We went there, went in the basement, went through the outbuildings and found no trace of him. We decided not to go in the house. We found out later, when he was arrested, that he was in the house with a gun in his hand waitin' for us. And we went away and they picked him up that evening and sent him to the pen for three years. But he was asked if he would've shot us and he said he didn't know.

He had thrown his gun away and stole one out of that house— which he had when they arrested him, to the best of my knowledge. That's the same man I met and I knew he was suspicious. I knew he didn't belong in that neighborhood. They sent him to the pen. But we didn't get shot, anyway. We might well have been.

"Queenie"

Haskell: That little Queen dog— Kermit and Bill [Jones] had an apartment out around a lake somewhere.[31] They saw this woman throw a milk bottle at her and hit her. And it fractured her leg. She was a pretty little pup. So they brought her out to me and said, "You want a pup?" Says, "She's got a broken leg." I said, "Yeah, I'll take her." And I wrapped something around her leg.

A dog's smart. You can break that dog's leg and he'll lay still for a week until it heals up. Two weeks. He won't move. They know that.

They know that if they don't move, it'll heal. So I took her and fed her and she was doin' all right.

She gets hit with a car one day. So she runs in the sewer under the driveway. We had a ten or twelve inch sewer under the driveway. And she runs in there and I couldn't get her out. Hell, the thing's fourteen feet long and she's in the middle of it. So we had one of them old open cellar doors on the side of the house. It was a gutter run up into the back door, cellar door, a low spot. A bank on each side. So I left the door open. And she'd been sleepin' in the basement.

The next morning I went and looked in the sewer, she isn't there. So I go down in the basement and look. And there she is, behind the chimney, back of the furnace—between the furnace and the chimney. I had thrown some old burlap bags in there for her to sleep on. She's layin' on that. So I talk to her and she won't get up. She just lays and looks at that leg. Go back and look at that leg, look at that leg. "Look what happened to me." So I took some food down and put it in front of her. And water. I bet she laid there for two weeks and never moved. One day she

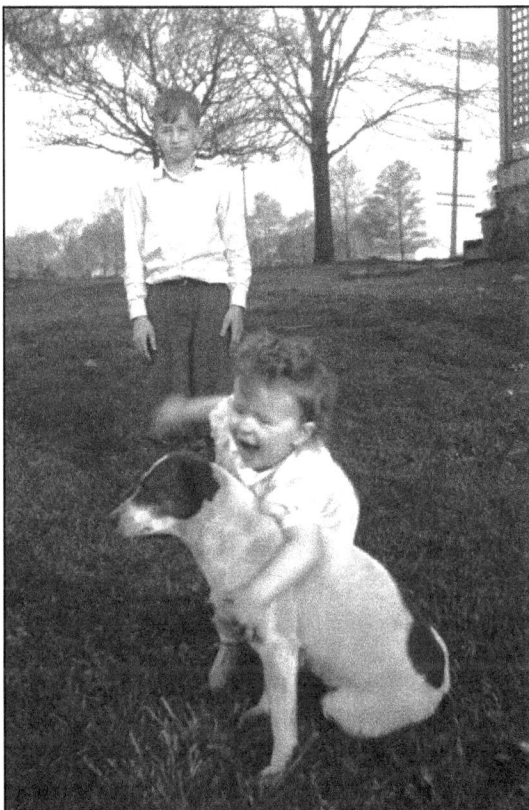

Donald Jones, Marjorie Jones and "Queenie."

come out. She limped. She had a short leg. It wasn't as well as the other ones. But she never had any more problems as long as she lived.

She was a good huntin' dog. She had some bird dog blood in her 'cause she'd point at stuff. She wasn't big enough to be a bird dog. Couldn't track too good. Didn't have enough nose. But you could shoot a pheasant and it'd fly from here to downtown and she'd go straight to it. She could watch 'em and she had an uncanny sense of tellin' where they fell. In a thicket, in a woods or wherever the hell they fell, she'd go straight to 'em. If it was alive yet, she'd catch it. If it was dead, she'd stand beside it. She wouldn't touch it. She was white and you could find her because you could see her up there.

Ralph and Jack took her huntin' and lost her. She got gun-crazy. Every time a gun'd shoot around her, she'd want to run over there to see what happened. They was huntin' in a swamp out there on the west side and she run away from 'em. Run over to somebody else and they kept her. So they come home and told me they'd lost my dog. Well, what the hell, you can't do anything about it. They didn't intentionally do it.

Next day was Sunday. They hunted Saturday. We went out there and looked all over and couldn't find her. Called, whistled and looked all over where they'd hunted. So we give up. She's gone. I give up.

In exactly thirty days— One morning Florence heard something scratching at the door. Said, "That sounds like Queen." So, open the door and there's Queen. She comes walkin' in. Thirty days later. She'd been lost all that time. Her feet— The pads was worn out 'til she was actually bleedin'. Ain't no tellin' how far she went, lookin' and tryin', huntin' that place. But she found it. Florence was so proud of her. Margie was as crazy about any kind of a dog. So she thought Queenie was the best dog in the world. And Don and Jean did, too.

Florence: Ruth and Ralph lived up the road from us.[32] And Marge went up there one Sunday afternoon for a little while. They was havin' a mad-dog scare at the time. You had to keep your dogs in or tied up— one or the other. And we had put Queenie on a line that was in front of the house so she couldn't get away. We could tell she wasn't too peppy anyway. And when time come and she came home, she saw Queenie laying on the ground. She wasn't up and moving around like she always was. And Marge came into the house crying and said, "Mama! Something's the matter with Queenie! She's laying down and she won't get up!" And says, "There's flies on her." And I thought, "Oh, she's dead." I went out and looked and sure enough, she was.

I didn't hardly know how to tell her. She didn't know about dead things—especially things that she liked. And I said, "Well, honey, I hate to tell you, but Queenie's gone." I says, "She's dead, but it's just like you when you're asleep—only you wake up. But Queenie won't ever wake up."

Haskell: Marge was about five, probably. Born in thirty-six. She was about four or five years old.

Florence: She says, "Everything happens when there's nobody here but me and you." Says, "Daddy's never home when we want him and he's a policeman." I said, "Well, brother's here. He's up in his bedroom asleep." He was workin' nights then and he wanted to sleep a little. And I said, "So you can go up there and wake him. It's about time for him to go wake up."

Marge went upstairs and she's cryin'. She told him that Queenie was dead and he says, "Well, don't cry. I'll go with you and we'll put her away." Said, "We'll have to dig a hole and put her in it and cover her up." So, he went out with her and dug a hole to bury her. When they got her buried, they picked some flowers and put flowers on the grave. Marge felt better 'cause she was covered up and had flowers over her. Yes, sir, "Everything happens when there's nobody here."

Marjorie Kathleen Jones.

Haskell: When I come home they said, "Queenie's dead." "What happened?" "Well, she was out on the front porch." Marge brought her there and tied her around the porch post and left her on the front porch in the shade. I said, "Marge, was she all right when you put her on there?" She said, "Dad, she fell down two or three times while I was leadin' her from back there to the porch." Well, the poor old dog was dyin' and she was honest enough to keep tryin'. She'd fall down and get up and Marge put her on that porch and she'd conked out, see. But she was a true, little dog.

She must've been the most variety of any dog in the United States, I'll tell you. She looked like everything. She was a 97 varieties or a 110. Short hair. She had two or three messes of pups. Cur-dogs would get to her. Had some pretty weird lookin' pups, I'll tell ya'.

She was a good dog.

CHAPTER FORTY-SIX

"WAR FARERS"

Even before the United States entered World War Two, Akron was gearing up for war production. And with America's entry into the war after Pearl Harbor, it was reckoned by the head of Civil Defense in Ohio that, "Akron, Cleveland, Lorain and Toledo are just as much war fronts as Bataan, Port Moresby and Port Darwin."[1] Then, even as the city was being warned of potential air raids, undergoing a simulated "bombing attack," testing blackouts, practicing driving under blackout conditions and establishing the standards by which civil defense efforts would be coordinated across the country, its factories were put under military protection.[2] In fact, the fear of an air attack on the U.S. mainland was so great, that it was forbidden to publish any weather news in the

"The Second Front is Right Here!" Office for Emergency Management. War Production Board (U.S. National Archives).

427

newspaper other than that which had occurred locally until October 1943.[3]

On the ground, the F.B.I. was also paying special attention to Akron and the surrounding area, doubling its presence and providing special training to local police departments in preventing espionage and sabotage, as well as monitoring the foreign-born population and the impact of soldiers and sailors returning home on leave or traveling through the area.[4] And there was a particularly good reason that the Axis powers would want to target Akron.

In addition to a production goal of more than 1,000,000,000 tires a month just for essential civilian use, Akron's factories were furiously churning out products of war 24-hours a day.[5] "Here in a community that once spoke of tires by the millions," one article noted, "hundreds of different types of implements for a modern fighting machine are rolling out at a rate that overshadows anything ever anticipated."[6]

Goodyear Tire & Rubber was making the largest non-rigid patrol blimps ever used to combat enemy submarines off the coasts.[7] General Tire was building barrage balloons to protect against enemy air attack.[8] Goodyear Aircraft was building Corsair fighter planes with a goal of completing one every eight minutes—putting it "on a footing that almost overshadows the giant rubber business." [9] And Firestone was manufacturing nearly as many Bofors 40 mm anti-aircraft guns in 24 hours as a comparable English plant could do in a month.[10] That was just one "of more than 200 other war products which Firestone is making . . . keyed to the same tempo."[11] In fact, one federal director reckoned Akron as "one of the most important war production centers in the world."[12] And by early 1944, the dollar amount of defense contracts in the area surpassed one billion dollars—or over 24 billion dollars in today's dollars. [13] Even Summit Beach Park got into the business of war production as it rebuilt one of its airplane rides, painting the planes in camouflage colors.[14]

With local economy once again booming, cars with license plates of the new "War Farers" from New York, Tennessee, California, Texas and a dozen other states began to fill the parking lots of the rubber factories. [15] With an additional 25,000 workers required at the start of the second half of 1942, it was projected that "125 to 175 workers must be assigned every working day for the remainder of the year."[16] By September 10th, it was reckoned that Akron factories were hiring 1,000 a week.[17] Just three days later, on September 13th, it was reported that

Goodyear Aircraft alone was hiring an additional 1,000 a week— making it "Akron's No. 1 war industry."[18] By the end of October 1942, less than a year after Pearl Harbor, there were 70,600 clock card workers at the five major rubber companies— breaking Akron's employment record of 1920.[19]

Just as had occurred during the First World War, however, a twofold crisis existed. The first was in both finding and keeping enough employees to fill the available jobs—making it "undisputably the tightest labor market area in Ohio."[20] The second, even larger problem was ensuring that any of those employees migrating to Akron could find adequate housing.

Akron's Wartime Workforce

At its heart, it wasn't that there weren't enough workers in the Akron area to meet the massive human resource requirements of the factories—despite the record number of employees. It's just that Akron was once again experiencing the same issues it had during the First World War; job shopping; absenteeism; and replacing workers who just walked off the job, often without giving any notice whatsoever. In fact, during the last two months of 1942, "there were 17,764 new hires and 12,534 losses—leaving industry a net gain of 433 workers."[21] It was more than just a human resource nightmare. To the despair of management and labor, Akron was suddenly "blacklisted" by the federal government. No more contracts would be awarded, the city was told, until the employment crisis was solved.[22] This was no minor issue when millions of dollars in government contracts were up for grabs.

In a desperate attempt to halt the exodus, some 135,000 essential area workers had their jobs "stabilized." Under the plan set forth by labor and management under the War Manpower Commission (the "most drastic measure of its type in this war production center's history"), all workers were frozen in their jobs, unable to transfer jobs without first obtaining a "certificate of availability." To further stabilize the employment market, it was decided to close the doors to employment from anyone except skilled labor from outside the Akron area.[23] These orders were then followed within days by yet another. Under federal directive, "all employment" in Akron and 31 other cities was ordered to go on a minimum 48-hour workweek. This even included domestic servants.[24] Under this "Vast New Experiment,"[25]

"Deputy War Manpower Chairman Fowler W. Harper said war industries now were working an average 45.7 hour work week and that if all persons working over 30 and under 48 hours were moved up to the higher figure, there would be an additional 1,500,000 workers released for the war effort."[26]

As a result of these actions, the ban was lifted in March of 1943. By the time they were successful in meeting their goal, however, an estimated $20,000,000 in contracts had been lost. [27] Even then, the respite was short lived. Ironically, the city was facing still yet another challenge—an "out-migration" of workers who had been recruited away and were packing up and leaving for the cities that had gotten the contracts that would have gone to Akron.[28] Two months later, the ban was back in place.[29]

Desperate to tap every locally available labor source, Akron's war industry began hiring between 2,500 and 3,000 area boys over age 16 and girls over age 18 ("Since 14 and 15-year-old children are permitted to work no later than 6 p.m. employers prefer not to hire them," one article in the *Beacon* later helpfully noted). [30] But even that number wouldn't be enough.[31]

In a last ditch effort to balance the profitable war contracts against available workers and suitable housing, War Manpower director Harry C. Markle presented a carefully laid plan of stabilizing the area workforce at 116,000 before tire company and government officials in June of 1943. Before the meeting was over, however, the government dropped the biggest bombshell of all, "blasting to bits carefully laid plans for pulling the city out of the WMC 'critical labor area' classification."[32]

With the production of synthetic rubber now a reality, Rubber Administrator William Jeffers ordered Akron rubber companies to produce 3,000,000 synthetic passenger tires by the end of the year. And some 18,000,000 in 1944. To do so, it was estimated that the factories would need 5,000 to 10,000 more tire builders.

By January 1944, it was obvious that Akron would be in a critical labor classification for the duration. The rubber companies were begrudgingly given permission to start recruiting as far south as Florida—even as rubber company management were embroiled in heated discussions with unions over decentralizing their plants and moving them south. [33]

Housing

The critical shortage of workers was exacerbated by one problem—and it was a big one. Akron was experiencing "the worst housing shortage since the war days of 1917-18".[34] Once again, it was "S.R.O."—Standing Room Only in Akron. "'It's a mystery to me where those out-of-town people will be housed,' said one employment manager. 'We're losing skilled workers every day because they cannot find houses in which to live. If we can't take care of the people here now, how in heaven's name are we going to take care of additional thousands?'" As columnist Helen Waterhouse noted, "there are limits to the stretching potentialities of even a 'rubber city'—and from all indications, those limits already have been reached, if not exceeded."[35] Between alleged miscommunication on the part of the federal government as to the size of the workforce that would eventually be required when the defense program started up in 1940, rubber factories too immersed in war production to get into the housing business again and federal restrictions on new home building due to rationing, there would be no immediate easy answer forthcoming.[36]

The crowded conditions in Akron were as bad, if not worse than they were during World War I. Twenty-three people were found crowded into one nine-room home under "horrible conditions." At another location, four adults and twelve children were crowded into one room and 37 people shared the same bathroom.[37] Unable to find even those miserable conditions, workers began moving into storerooms, former sandwich shops and abandoned gas stations.[38] Those that couldn't find either began returning home. Charities Director J.M. Zang reported that many families "are living in quarters unfit for animals" and pronounced that the ability to find any suitable housing "requires something akin to clairvoyance."[39]

With spare rooms in otherwise occupied homes eventually being branded as "Slacker" rooms by the *Beacon Journal*, local residents were asked to voluntarily divide up homes into multiple family dwelling units.[40] They were also pressed to simply accept "war guests" into their own homes.[41] Among the thousands of people who became temporary landlords were Haskell and Florence Jones who took in Jack Howell and Joe Barry Young from Graceville, Florida (who both worked at Goodyear Aircraft), as well as a woman named Madge whose last name has been long forgotten. "The only thing I remember about her specifically," daughter Marjorie later recalled," was that she spilled fingernail polish on the bedspread. That's my memory of her."

Unlike the boom years of the First World War, however, the landlords weren't getting rich this time around. Beginning April 1, 1941, the federal government established rental-ceiling rates for landlords. However, in Akron, those rates didn't even allow for necessary repairs, let alone a profit. In fact, a comprehensive survey showed that after allowing for the effects of the Depression, the new "fair rent" level was equal to that charged in 1931—and not even equal to the rates allowed at a federal defense housing project in nearby Massillon.[42] "H.T. Waller, OPA rent director, refused to accept responsibility. 'Our job is to protect renters—not manage properties,' he asserted."

Despite protests to the contrary, the government was already planning to get into managing properties in a big way. The following January, the government announced plans to lease and remodel 4,000 properties.[43] By early February 1943 (in a presage to FEMA), "the first consignment of house trailers for the Akron Metropolitan Housing Authority's new trailer camp on Arlington st., south of Wilbeth rd., was hailed by housing officials as more tangible evidence of government aid toward solving the acute housing shortage in Akron."[44] The very next day, a contract for the construction of 500 temporary homes was announced which would cover 40 acres. By April, there were an additional five projects in the works providing accommodations for 1,240 families in the works.[45] By the spring of 1944, the U.S. government would become Akron's largest landlord, "providing roofs over heads of more than 13,000 members of war-working families, and collected rental on a basis of more than $1,000,000 a year."[46]

Women in the Workforce

Despite the severe housing shortage during the initial years of the war (or perhaps because of it), there was another major positive impact on the area, as well as the nation as a whole. As there was insufficient housing for the "war-farers", factories were forced to turn to a previously purposely untapped local labor pool of existing residents already established in housing.[47] As one article noted, "Handicapped men and women and Negroes also are finding work opportunities opening to them as never before, and persons who want to learn trades are welcomed into scores of special schools set up throughout the state to supply industry with workers."[48] While African-Americans still found themselves primarily relegated to janitorial positions in the rubber factories (despite an Executive Order 8802 prohibiting discrimination in the defense industry) and the "handicapped found jobs made for them," it was the role of women in America's workforce that was about to change forever—and Akron had a leading role in causing it to occur. [49]

Dating back to the early 1920s, Ohio's labor laws forbade women from being employed in dozens of specific jobs, limited their hours of work and precluded them from lifting anything that weighed over twenty-five pounds. Along with being prohibited from positions at blast furnaces or quarries, they were also forbidden from driving taxicabs, school buses, bakery or floral delivery trucks. They couldn't work in saloons, bowling alleys or poolrooms and they were only allowed to work as ticket sellers or bellhops if it was between the hours of 6:00 a.m. and 10:00 p.m. "Some of these prohibitions, for which the reasons are obvious, are good and should not be discarded, everyone agrees. The reasons for others are obscure," columnist Marion Hopwood noted.[50]

Wartime realities, however, were beginning to set in. With Goodyear Aircraft estimating that it was losing "1 1-2 to 2 per cent of its men employes each month to the armed services," they projected that more than 50 percent of their payroll would be comprised of women when their production peak was reached. "In the barrage balloon division at the Firestone Tire & Rubber Co., 85 per cent of the workers [were] women while in the pontoon boat department, the number is 80 per cent."[51] Throughout the factories, "Inspection—except the final one on direct ordnance items—[was] 100 per cent by feminine hands and eyes."[52] "The junior leaguer, the lady who used to grace the society pages, holds the bucking plate for the riveting of the young migrant girl from the Tennessee hills who's having her first taste of city life," columnist Ben Williamson noted.[53] By October of 1942, women were being hired in Akron factories at the rate of 1,500 a month.[54] That didn't even include all the other area businesses.

Haskell: I saw one of those women drove durin' the war after men was pretty scarce— Everybody was in the Army. They put women on these trucks, sellin' bread. I was settin' in the H & H Restaurant havin' a cup of coffee. They had a big window in the front. You could look right out in the street. Settin' there and I hear a bang. Look up and the dust hadn't cleared away and a woman barreled out from behind that wheel on one of the Nichols' bread trucks and run around and looked and she had a flat tire. The tire blew out on her. I bet she was rollin' in ten minutes. She run out and put a jack under there and jacked that up and grabbed a spare tire and stuck it on and bolted it in and throwed the other in there. I never— I never saw a man do a quicker job in my life. She sure changed that tire in a hurry.

* * *

By April of 1943, even as Summit Beach Park was highlighting women's work clothes in its Easter Parade, women were taking on new roles in Akron that would literally shift the balance of power in the Pacific during the war.[55] This, as Goodyear Aircraft announced a new contract that would require the hiring of an additional 3,500 workers for the production of the new FG-1 fighter plane, the Corsair. And the majority of employees to be hired were women.[56] Then, by mid-July, what had previously been unthinkable in Akron was revealed. Under the pressures of the acute manpower shortage and the demand for civilian tires, the B.F. Goodrich Co. was forced to turn to womanpower. It hired its first female tire builders.

Lest the reportage of this momentous event sound too overconfident (or bruise too many feelings among what had once been "rubber shop royalty"), the news was buried in the *Beacon* on page 22.[57] The paper was apparently happier to report that the "Silk Shirt Era" may have once again returned as women war workers, flush with money, "are paying as much as $150 for a custom-made suit. They're buying their soldier boy friends all-silk ties at $15 apiece. They're spending $100 for dresses." *That* made page one.

CHAPTER FORTY-SEVEN

THE HOME FRONT

Rationing

Ironically, that same wartime economy also meant that those who had driven so far, surmounted so many barriers in search of employment and earned enough money to buy a new silk tie or dress couldn't buy a new set of tires for the car that had taken them to work. With the rubber plantations of the Dutch East Indies now in the hands of the Japanese, rubber tires were one of the first items to be rationed. As of January 5, 1941, you first had to appear before the ration board at your local school to prove that your existing tires were completely worn out to receive retread tires (which were also rationed) or purchase used tires (which had their prices frozen).[1] And then, you could only purchase "mounted tires." The purchase of spare tires was not allowed.

The "C" Gas Ration Sticker. Displayed in the front window of a car, it was issued primarily to professional people in 17 different job categories.

As The United States moved onto a war footing in 1942, it was soon determined that the most immediate way to curtail the general public's rubber consumption would be by mandatory gasoline rationing, which began in seventeen eastern states on May 15th, 1942. With the Baruch Rubber Report of September 1,

435

1942, however, it was concluded that meeting the enormous needs of the military would be impossible unless nonessential driving was *completely* eliminated. To ensure that goal was met, President Franklin Roosevelt bypassed Congress on November 26th to order that mandatory gasoline rationing began nationwide on December 1, 1942.[2] Once gasoline rationing took effect, those with a ration book and a windshield sticker bearing an "A" classification were entitled to three to four gallons of gas per week (or about sixty miles of driving at the time). A "B" classification entitled the owner to eight gallons a week. A "C" classification went to individuals essential to the war effort such as doctors and war workers, while class "T" included all truck drivers and "X' was reserved for police, firemen, civil defense and other "important people." (The last three categories, however, were not subject to gasoline restrictions.) By July, B and C book holders were being warned that they wouldn't even get gas unless they were sharing the ride.[3]

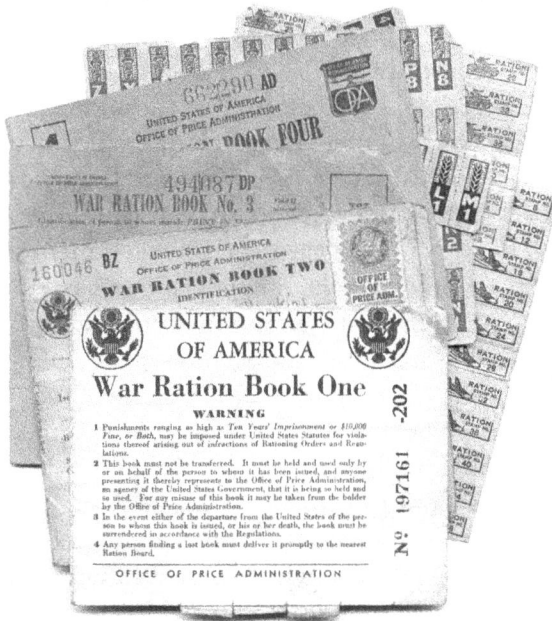

War Ration Books and stamps. During World War II, there wasn't much you could buy without them.

To further reduce the possible consumption of gas, any tires owned in excess of five had to be sold back to the government, a national speed limit of thirty-five mph was established for the duration of the war and, for a brief period in 1943, all pleasure driving was made illegal.[4] Anyone that violated the speed regulations was subject to losing their ration cards. The worst offenders could lose them for "the duration."[5] To help ensure an uninterrupted flow of workers to the factory gates, a bus line began operation from General Tire, Goodyear and Goodrich to Tallmadge

Circle.[6]

As one news article entitled "Less Comfort Will Be The Rule," reported, "Tire rationing is only the beginning."[7] It went on to note that, "The war demands of the nation are about to take from the civilian market most of the supply of metal, rubber and other materials that go into washing machines, sweepers, electrical appliances and home heating units, refrigerators, sewing machines and many other household articles now standard equipment in the majority of American homes. Taking new products off of the market is only half the story, for the dwindling supply of parts on hand to repair these machines will not be replaced.

"That means when the electric washer goes on the blink in the near future it will remain out of use possibly for the duration, unless you can obtain a part from a friend or dealer who happens to have a used part."

Food would be another item to be rationed—with each member of a family being issued their own ration book—and forced to become familiar with an entirely new

OFFICIAL TABLE — No. 12—EFFECTIVE March 5, 1944
CONSUMER POINT VALUES FOR MEAT, FATS, FISH AND DAIRY PRODUCTS

The Consumer Point Value chart as printed in the Akron Beacon Journal. Just the listing for meats, fats, fish and dairy, it took up most of a full page.

437

concept, a point system. The *Akron Beacon Journal* attempted to explain this new concept, noting that, "Akron housewives, along with others throughout the country, are on the verge of having their old established marketing routine almost completely revolutionized." The article went on to explain that:

The related chart for Processed Foods was as equally detailed and difficult to use.

At the grocery store she will match the point value of a commodity as closely as the price—even more so because in most cases she'll have more dollars than ration coupons.

She will be forced to budget her ration coupons as carefully as her marketing money—or more so. She will have to do all her buying for a month within the points allowed for each month by each ration book issued for each member of her family.

In reading market and grocery advertising, she will observe the listed point value of each commodity as carefully as the price or more so. Because if cheese, for instance, is rationed, a pound of American cheese may be worth so many points one week and a different number the following week. Its point value will be established from time to time by the government according to the amount of American cheese on hand and the demand for it . . ."[8]

By February of 1944, rationing was so much a part of daily life that ration tokens were issued for use as change in purchases—all but replacing the use of currency. This alone was expected "to save retailers at least $35,000,000 annually in terms of time now spent in counting and sorting stamps."[9]

For a short time, even sliced bread was unavailable. It was explained that "Heretofore, all bread which had been sliced had to be wrapped in a double layer of waxed paper. With slicing eliminated, about half of the total paper used will also be cut out. Elimination of the extra moment used to slice each loaf of bread, including slicer operators and electricity to run the machines is expected to pile up a goodly savings by the end of the year, too."[10] For the consumer, having already survived the Depression and just able to once again purchase the things they desperately needed, it would be a very long war indeed. This would even be true for the children on whom the war also had a lasting impact.

Office of Price Administration (OPA) ration tokens. Commonly called OPA's, they were used as change for food purchases. If you look closely, you'll see each has different coding in the center for different purchases. There were 34 different red tokens and 24 blue ones.

Marge: Homer Emmit had a variety store there on the Circle.

Jean: Kramer's had a big variety of things, but Homer's was just a little small convenience store.

Donald: He had a kind of a variety store, nick-knack thing, but he didn't have any groceries. He wasn't much of an operator. He was kind of a piddler but he got by. That was where the first fire station used to be.

Marge: During the war, things were very restricted as to what was available. Chewing gum or candy. Those were— Sugar was rationed. You just didn't get that kind of stuff. Homer would get candy bars in (A few, you know) and he kept a little notebook. If you bought a candy bar, he wrote your name down in the notebook. If you tried to buy another one that week, he'd check his notebook and say, "No, you already bought one this week. You can't." So he had his own rationing system.

Chewing gum just wasn't available. They sold long sticks of pink wax, flavored, and it was kind of like chewing a candle. It hurt your jaw. I never became really a gum chewer and I think that's why. It would just wear your jaw out to chew that stuff.

We'd go down to Kramer's grocery and Mom would go to the meat counter and they would give her something wrapped and she wouldn't know what she had until she got home. They would kind of tuck a few things away for favored customers, I think. So she might have a little beef roast or a little pork roast, but she just didn't know. Open it up and see what she had. We had butter and not margarine through them, too. I can remember only a time or two of her mixing that margarine.

A Gas Mask requires 1.11 pounds of rubber

A Life Raft requires 17 to 100 pounds of rubber

A Scout Car requires 306 pounds of rubber

A Heavy Bomber requires 1,825 pounds of rubber

America needs your
SCRAP RUBBER

War Production Board. Bureau of Industrial Conservation (U.S. National Archives).

Since it was white, they gave you a color capsule that mixed in with it that made the color in it. You'd knead it together. I think there was a government law or something that they couldn't sell it colored at that time. The dairy farmers would want to do that.

I think it was the Jewel Tea Company that would come around to the house. They sold some kind of pudding mix in a canister. Kind of a cocoanut flavored stuff. Sugar, you had a hard time buying, but this was sweet. Mother had a recipe from probably the same company that sold the stuff that you could use it to make cookies. And she would buy that so she could bake cookies for us. Meat and butter were very much scarce.

You wouldn't think of it, but even the color of cloth was affected by the war. Anything that went into making a khaki color, I guess. The fabric that you'd find in the stores just didn't have those colors. Things were mostly a yucky dark red and maybe a dark navy blue. They weren't very pretty. The particular dies that were used in army uniforms during the war—the greens and yellows and all, we just really didn't have that available. It was always going to do army khaki colored stuff. Things were really restricted. Mom made most of my clothing. It was a treat when colorful fabrics became available again.

Scrap Drives

To complement rationing, massive scrap drives began across the country—aluminum, scrap metal and tin were all collected—leading to the irony of a "Tin Can Campaign" to collect what had once been carelessly discarded and poetically referred to as "Akron Wildflowers" during the boom years of World War I.[11] With some 90 percent of the country's tin coming from Pacific Islands now in the hands of the Japanese,

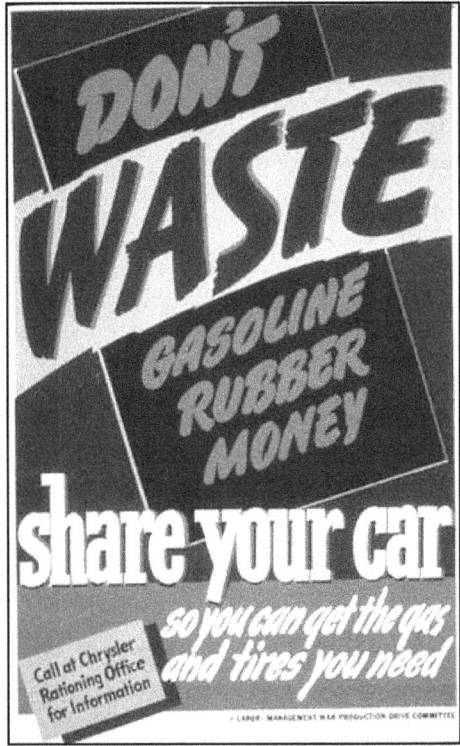

"Don't Waste Gasoline, Rubber Money." The Chrysler Rationing Office Labor-Management War Production Drive Committee (U.S. National Archives).

however, no one was laughing.[12] Even unused keys were collected for their precious nickel alloy—with six tons of over 360,000 keys turned in during one drive.[13] But in the Rubber Capital of the World, the most sought after (and easily obtainable) scrap commod-ity was rubber. "So impor-tant to the national economy has scrap rubber become," one article noted, "the tire beads, which were formerly burned on the outskirts of the city, now are being conserved. Not only is the rubber reclaimed, but the wire in the beads is being salvaged."[14]

In fact, the search for scrap rubber in the city led to the startling discovery of "6,000 to 10,000 pounds of industrial scrap rubber flowing through Akron sewers every day" and the equally startling discovery of rubber "mines" on the sites of abandoned factory sites, dumps and river beds.[15] The Palace Theater offered free admission for an old tire or tube and Summit Beach Park offered free rides to children who brought a pound of rubber to the admission gate.[16] The offer was so popular that it netted two tons of scrap rubber in one day.[17]

Marge: My high school class did scrap metal drives and fundraisers to earn money for putting on the prom.[18] Juniors, I think, were responsible for the expenses. Had quite a few scrap metal drives as fundraiser stuff. They were still doing quite a bit of that. They did newspapers. They did cooking grease. They took in tin cans.

We also collected milkweed pods because they used the fluff in the pod in life vests. Ordinarily, it would have been kapok filled, but they needed a lot of them during the war and that was also a commodity that was hard to get because of the shipping dangers. So we took whatever we could find of collections of milkweed pods to school.[19]

Haskell: They had a rationing board. Then they had deputies. Florence was on that. She used to go to school every week. One day a week to issue food stamps or— Gee, I can't remember. I hadn't thought about it in years. But if you wanted tires on your car, you had to go to the ration board and they would look at 'em. And if they thought they could go another hundred miles, they wouldn't give you tires. You had a helluva' time. Being the policeman, I never had much problem. One guy at the ration board wanted me to take recap tires. And I said, "No way. I'm chasin' speeders. I'm the guy that's tryin' to keep the gas consumption down and stuff like that. [20] And you want me to drive recap tires? I won't take 'em!" "Oh, well—" And they give me new tires, see. But they give me all the gas stamps I

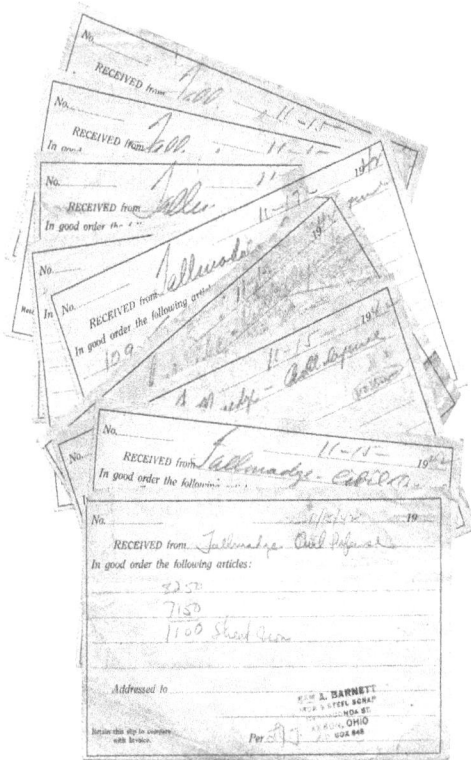

Receipts from Tallmadge Scrap Metal Drives.

442

wanted.

I always had surplus stamps. Always had 'em. Everybody in town knew I had 'em. And I would only give 'em to guys in the army. Young guys would come home from the army for a five or six-day furlough. They would give them <u>five</u> gallons of gas for the whole week or ten days or whatever they had. Five gallons. Well, that would take 'em about three days runnin' around with their girlfriend and they were out of gas.[21]

So, the word got around— "See Jonesie." I knew all these young guys that was in the service in our town. So they'd come to see me and they'd say, "Jonesie, somebody told me I could see you and you might be able to fix me up with a little gas." I said, "Well, when are you going back to camp?" "Well, I got (four days, three days, nine days or whatever it was)." Nobody went anywhere much. There wasn't much to do. I mean the country was dead. There was nothin' to do much. Drive out in the brushes somewhere and park with your girlfriend. "Well, how much you need?" "Well, if I had five gallons, I could make it," see. "O.K. Here's five gallons. Forget where you got it." But they didn't always forget.

They passed the word on to their friends. I don't know how much I gave away, but <u>a lot</u> of it. One afternoon, Sunday afternoon, I'm home eatin' dinner (summertime), knocks on the door. I go to the door and here's an army— I think he was a lieutenant. And I come out and I said, "What's the problem?" He says, "Well, I'm in trouble." I said, "What do you mean?" He said, "I'm supposed to be back in camp in New Jersey tomorrow afternoon. I'm sittin' here at your place out of gas."

They wouldn't give you gas in a gas station unless you had stamps because they had to account for their gas allotment. "The man down at the gas station told me to come and see you." I said, "O.K. Where ya' goin'? You got to go to Hoboken (Or wherever the heck it was. I don't remember.). How much gas you think you need?" He said, "Oh, maybe fifteen gallons would get me there." I said, "Well, here's twenty-five. And I hope you make it and live the rest of your life." That guy could have kissed me. He had his family in the car. He'd been up in Detroit somewhere to see his parents and so forth and he was headin' back East. He never did forget me, I know, because if he's livin' today, he still remembers that that old man gave him some gas, see, and got him straightened out.

But I wouldn't sell it. A guy would offer to give me every kind of deal to "Sell me—" "Hey, sell me some of this stuff. I'll give you ten dollars apiece for 'em." "Up your ass. You ain't gonna' get 'em. No way." A guy's in the service, then I would give it to him. And word got around and I gave away many gallons. But I wouldn't give it to strangers or somebody like that. I give it to this guy because he was a man in uniform and he showed me his credentials and everything else. He said, "I'm in trouble. I went up there and I overextended myself. And I've got to be back there tomorrow afternoon." So, what the heck am I doin'? Sittin' in there and say, "So what? You can starve for all I care." No way. No, I didn't do that. Maybe I was cheatin'. But if I was cheatin' for a good cause, I didn't care.

I registered in World War Two. I was forty-five, six years old. Forty-five. You had to be up to forty-five. I was almost forty-six,

Private Barbara Jean Jones upon induction into the U.S. Marines.

probably, when we registered. I don't remember what it was. Never classified, see. Never was called. I just registered and that's the last I heard of it.[22]

Our daughter Jean was in the Marines.[23] She was in the service the same time Donald was in the Army.[24] I don't know whether she went in first or he went in first. I can't tell ya' that. I don't know.[25] But I know they both were in there at the same time. After she went to basic training and got out of the East Coast, she went to Norman, Oklahoma and was there for a while. She was in a repair gang repairin' airplanes. Then she went to California and she was over there for some time.

444

Donald went somewhere in Alabama.[26] He got basic training for maybe six weeks or somethin' like that. I think he went from there right on to Jersey or somewhere and caught a boat overseas.[27] He went to England and was there for a while. He wasn't in the invasion. He was in there durin' the second wave. They had it pretty rough. Things was pretty hot over there about that time.

Florence: We got a call when Donald had been wounded and we didn't know how bad or anything for a little bit. I believe a man came by the next day and talked to us about it. Said so far it wasn't too bad.

Private First Class Donald A. Jones, 309th Infantry, 78th Division.

Haskell: Wasn't wounded bad to start with. We'd get a letter from him every few days, week, ten days, two weeks. He'd tell us what was goin' on. I guess he had a little rough time. He was pretty fortunate. His outfit just about got wiped out and he was in the hospital with minor problems. Pneumonia. A couple times, wounded. Small. Not bad. While he was in there, hell was poppin', I'll tell you.

We had quite a few guys killed there. It's been so long I'd forgotten. There was a kid on Thomas Road. Jimmy Shears got killed. Lived on Ferguson Drive. Ahh, Imhoff. Two of the Rutherford boys got killed. Art Rutherford. His cousin. They were glider operators and they— When they went in that time under the Germans, why, they killed 'em like flies. They didn't have a chance.

I can't remember all of 'em. It's been so long. Been a long, long time. Geez, that's many, many years ago. The Army sent somebody to the house and notified the parents or wife or whoever it might be. They didn't notify me.[28]

F.B.I. Training

Members of the American law-enforcement profession ranging from village constables to metropolitan police chiefs are being thoroughly prepared to meet and master any emergency which international developments may bring. Last fall, two-day administrative training schools for police executives were held at 54 field division headquarters of the FBI, and were attended by over 5,000 police chiefs and other executive heads of police agencies. These schools were followed by more detailed six-day courses for selected subordinate officers of local and state police forces which were conducted by the FBI in 260 key cities throughout the nation and were attended by about 30,000 law-enforcement officers.

"Policing a Nation at War"
Popular Science
February 1942

Haskell: I went to school to an F.B.I. school for some time. We had school for a week up in Cleveland and then went back every three months for a refresher course. It was good trainin' but, ah, mostly recital. They couldn't give you much in a week's time. They give you a lot of pointers. It had to do with the war effort to some extent. The sheriff would take over if I was gone.

Civil Defense in Tallmadge. With the threat of war a very real possibility, Haskell Jones completed F.B.I. Civil Defense training three weeks before the United States entered World War II. By May of the following year, operations in Tallmadge were in full swing, with every home having been contacted for assistance.

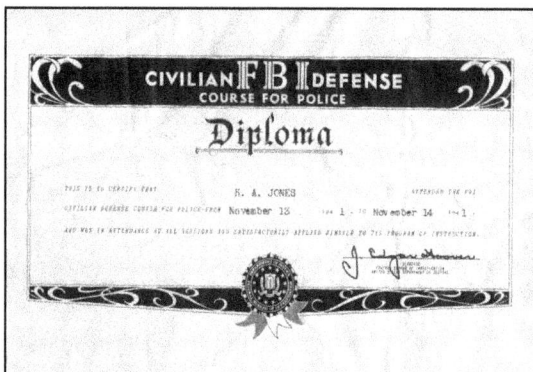

Mayor John Sperry was in charge of the Tallmadge Civilian Defense Council, town clerk Sam Schlup coordinated civilian defense, Wiley Smith directed transportation of scrap material to area salvage yards, Dale Powers was in charge of volunteer participation and Earl J. Raess, chairman of public relations, headed up a committee of 35 members tasked with contacting every home in Tallmadge to obtain war bond pledges.

In addition to these positions, V.N. Ziegler headed up an auxiliary police division of 42 local men (who were the first in Summit County to complete training), Mrs. Wesley Page was in charge of the local branch of the American Red Cross (with Mrs. Edith Spring in charge of knitting and Mrs. J.C. Baldwin over sewing), Dr. R.L. Ross supervised the Tallmadge medical division and Mrs. H. O. King managed the civilian defense welfare program.

Their efforts were all part of an overall plan for Summit County created more than a year before—which was recognized as so successful in coordinating resources and eliminating duplication of efforts that it became the pattern for the nation.[29]

War Traffic Control. While this might at first seem to be of little more than standing at intersections waving traffic through, it was actually of critical importance to the

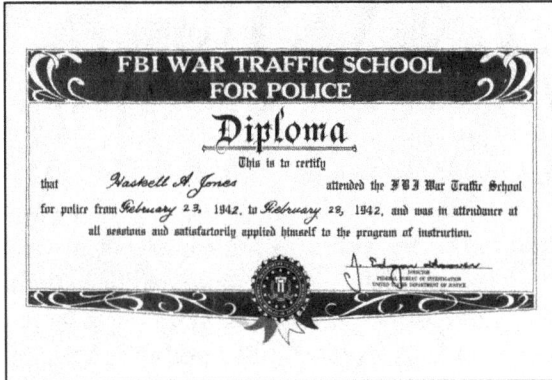

war effort. So much so, in fact, that training lasted six full days vs. the civilian defense training of only two days in duration.

Lieutenant E. L. Engelhart (One of the Akron police officers tasked with training the Tallmadge auxiliary police force in May of 1942) noted, "There is no more important lesson in the entire auxiliary police course than that dealing with 'War Traffic Control and Duty." In an article in the *Akron Beacon Journal*, he went on to point out that, "failure to handle traffic on the streets and highways of France and Belgium contributed largely to the downfall of those two countries.

"Following the first bombardments," he continued, "inhabitants put all their possessions into carts, motor vehicles, hay wagons and other conveyances and flocked out onto the streets and highways blocking them so effectively that troops, convoys and military supplies could not reach the fighting men at the front.

"This was done so effectively that ammunition and supplies were kept from the points where they were so badly needed.

"When the Germans occupied the same territory they knew what to do. They used tanks and heavy trucks to sweep fleeing civilians off the roads so their troops could get through without interference."[30]

Haskell: We had a guy up there who was the F.B.I. man. Name was Bergman. Smarter than a whip. Smarter than hell. A memory that didn't forget. When you went in there and registered, he was right there by the side of the register where you signed your name when you come in—your department, where you come from and so forth. Chief, lieutenant or whatever you were. And that guy never forgot that. The next day you come in and you walked in, he said, "Hello, Jones. How's things down in Tallmadge?" "How's things in Canton?" "How's things in Pittsburgh?" How's things here? How's things there? He knew everybody, where he come from and what the hell he was doing. He was really a brain. Bergman was his name. We'd go back every— It seems to me like three months. We went back for a refresher course. They give you a little later information on what was goin' on. Didn't make any difference. He knew you the minute you come in. He knew exactly. He really was a brain.

Bergman was tellin' us a story about chasin' a supposedly German collaborator. They'd chased him around over the United States here, there and everywhere. And, finally, they hurried him up in some town. He told us where it was. I don't remember. So he knew where he went in the hotel and checked in and went out to eat. They went into his room and went through his suitcases and so forth and checked him. And he had a bottle in there with somethin' in it. No label on it or anything. He thought it was invisible ink. He said, "So we sent it to the F.B.I. laboratory in Washington to be tested to find out what it was. Come back and said it was 'clap' medicine." We laughed. They spent days trailin' this guy all around and they— They thought he was a secret agent or somethin'. He was a travelin' man, doin' somethin'. Havin' a good time. Yeah, he had clap medicine.[31]

"For Their Sake . . . Avoid Venereal Disease." Along with preparations for civil defense against an attack by Axis forces, Summit County (along with every other major industrial city in the country) suddenly found itself fighting another battle—that against gonorrhea and syphilis.

"Why?" an article in the *Akron Beacon Journal* questioned.[32] "The war is the answer. The same thing that happened in 1917-18 is happening all over again—only public health officials hope that this time it won't be as bad.

"'Venereal disease always shoots upward in time of war and preparation for war,'" Dr. [L.I.] Thomas [head of the city health department's venereal disease clinic] observed. "Industrial expansion in Akron and vicinity has brought thousands of young men into the city. For many of them this is the first time in years that they have had money in their pockets."

For their sake...
AVOID VENEREAL DISEASE

With gonorrhea recognized as a "crippler" that could only be cured with a 10-day regimen of the "modern" sulfa drugs, syphilis was a well-known "killer"—requiring the patient to be under a doctor's care for at least 18 months. As a result, the loss of valuable industrial manpower could be tremendous.

"To what extent prostitution figures in the increased venereal disease rate in Akron is not known," the article continued. "Thomas says that the number of syphilis cases contracted from prostitutes is negligible when compared with other sources of infection. "From what I learn from male patients, most of them get the disease from 'pickups' who," he said, "are not necessarily professionals."

That was seconded by, "Sherman Gandee, head of the police vice squad, [who] said he has seen no noticeable increase in prostitution in Akron since industrial expansion began to reach its peak. However, he said, there was little doubt that a number of "floaters"—prostitutes who travel from city to city—have moved into Akron.

That being said, the article also helpfully noted that "While the more established houses of prostitution in Akron operate unmolested except for an occasional raid, those prostitutes who are arrested and found infected are held for approximately seven weeks. During this time they are examined and given tests for gonorrhea and syphilis. If either of the diseases is detected, and attempt is made to render it non-infectious. However, this procedure is only partially successful."[33]

"What can be done about it?" the article once again questioned. "Education, says Dr. Thomas, helps, but the fundamental in the campaign against syphilis still is, 'Find 'em and treat 'em.'"

To that end, the Office of War Information kicked off a nationwide educational campaign and (among other grants) the federal government offered an additional $10,000 in funds to the Akron clinic, provided that it be greatly expanded. The local school system even got involved with "The most extensive program of social hygiene education . . . at Central high school."

In a foreshadowing of Haskell's F.B.I. training on the subject, "We decided from the start not to mince words," said [school principal R.J.] Stine, "and the course has been well received by everybody concerned, including the parents."

Haskell: Generally speakin', the venereal disease was so bad with the guys that was in service from— They come home. And here and there and the girls in the cathouses and this, that and the other. They all had gonorrhea or worse.[34] The idea was to kind of keep these guys out of there if you could. Keep these places out of business, if you could, in your area. It didn't affect my area too much as it did the bigger town. But I went through the same training, see, and stuff of that kind. It was mostly that.

I remember we had an old army colonel. Merrifield, I think his name was. Old Southern guy. And he makes us a speech to us about this situation—what's goin' on and how it affected people and so forth. I don't know where these women come from, but they're policewomen. They'd been invited like the men were invited. It was a little early for women to get involved in things like this, but it was the beginning of it.[35] So, there's forty, fifty of us policemen from all over

Portage, Summit and half a dozen, fourteen counties around Cleveland area who were invited to this thing. And these women are right on the front seat. Nice-dressed, good-lookin' women in uniform and so forth—deputy sheriffs or whatever they were.

So, old Merrifield, he didn't like 'em bein' there. He was an old rough talkin', old medical man. Old Southern doctor. An old Army man. So he rolls a big chart out here and he unrolls the chart and turns it down and— I can remember his words and he (I don't know if you should copy it or not)— He said, "Now, most of you people have had the 'clap'." That was his openin' statement. "But the few of you who haven't, I can tell you somewhat as to what it's like." And he run over to another page and here's a big colored guy with a "john" about that long. Half of it's eaten up with syphilis.

Well, these women were sittin' here and he's tellin'— He don't pull any punches. He don't call "piss" anything else but "piss." He don't mess around. So, finally, we have a little recess. They left and never did come back. He really sanded 'em down. You could tell when he got up there that he didn't want anything to do with this bunch of women. It wasn't routine. It wasn't what he was used to.

I had to check the aliens. If they had an alien in town, I had to check 'em every so often.[36] It didn't mean nothin', but it was part of my duty. I had to do it. Every month or so, I had to go make a round around like a census. I got to your house and I say, "I understand you're not an American citizen. You're an alien?" "Yeah, that's right." Well, your name is Joe Blow— "What's your family status?" And "When'd you come here?" Fifteen, twenty. Somethin' like that. Not too many. I had to get all that on a sheet and send it to the F.B.I. see.

Cigarettes

Following the rationing of first rubber and then gasoline, the concept was extended in early May of 1942 to butter, beef, coffee and sugar— among other items.[37] Each required a visit to your local school for ration stamps and books. Even if you found you had sufficient cash and the appropriate ration stamps when you visited your neighborhood store, however, that didn't mean you could find the desired item. As agricultural and factory output was being redirected to meet the needs of the troops overseas, many items were in short supply.[38]

Although tobacco wasn't among the rationed items, 18 percent of the production of premium brand cigarettes was going overseas to GIs as part of their daily C-rations by mid-1943—while those on the home front had to make do with off brands such as Rameses, Pacayunes or Marvels.[39] The result was a shortage of tobacco on the home front that made any cigarettes highly coveted among smokers—and a great opportunity for anyone that found themselves in possession of any excess quantity.

Haskell: Old man Beers that lived on Thomas Road— He had a daughter that worked up there where Samir's is now.[40] That was the H & H, then. And he had driven her up there to leave her off in the morning. He was an old man. It was terribly foggy. Ooooh, it was terrible!

So, on the way back, he was followin' along the curb tryin' to find out where his road was. There wasn't any flashin' lights or anything to go by. When he saw where there was a gas station on the right-hand side and he saw where he was, he cut across the road.

This guy with a load of cigarettes was goin' west. He couldn't see him in the fog. The old man pulled right in front of him and that truck driver knocked him up in the yard there. Drove him way up in that yard and killed the old man. But, set the load of cigarettes afire.[41]

They was as cheap cigarettes as was on the market. It was during the war when cigarettes was a premium. Not because they were good, but because nobody had any. They were Marvels. They've been off the market ever since that day, I think. But they were a cheap cigarette with a real thin tissue paper wrapper around— It wasn't tissue. It was a vinyl of some kind around 'em that wasn't very good.

So, the front end of that van caught afire and I got called out. And a fellow named McNellis (He was a deputy sheriff from Akron)— He came out and we was there all day long keepin' the people off those cigarettes. The firemen had pulled a bunch of 'em out and threw 'em—[42] Just cases of 'em, see. They was in big cases. There was two hundred cartons in a case and they'd pulled 'em out so they could get to the fire. The fire was in the front end of the trailer, inside. But the whole thing was smoked up, stunk.

We worked there all day and in the evening, the insurance adjuster come out and got everything cleared up. They was transferring it into another truck and I told him, I said, "'Mac' and I would like to have some of those cigarettes. We've been here all day long." And he said, "Take all of 'em you want." Said, "They're junk. The insurance company's gonna' have to pay for 'em, anyway. So go ahead and take 'em."

I hollered to Mac, "Back your cruiser up here." So each one of us took a case of those cigarettes and I sold mine for two hundred dollars. Mac sold his for probably fifty cents a pack in the jail down there because he had an "out," see. They could peddle 'em to prisoners in the jail. But I bought Mom [Florence] a set of teeth with the money.

Florence Grace Jones

Money was a little hard to come by. That's how she got her teeth. Didn't have very many left and she had them pulled and some new ones put in.

Florence: We didn't have much. He wasn't makin' enough to make a livin' and, as far as teeth went, I just had to do without. People that didn't just know about me, how awful my teeth were (that I'd got new teeth) wouldn't believe that they were false teeth. When I went to get 'em, your grandfather told me, "Now, when you go to get these teeth made, you tell 'em to put 'em (these two in front) just a little crack between 'em." That's the way my real teeth were. So, this dentist kinda' thought I was nutty, I guess, when I told him. He said, "Well, what do you want that for?" I said, "Well, that's the way my real teeth were!"

So, he made 'em that way and there's a lot of people would say, "Well, you're— You've got the nicest teeth. Your teeth look so nice." Maybe I'd say, "Well, they ought to. I paid for 'em" or something like that. "You don't have false teeth!" And they said, "But you don't look like you got false teeth." Said, "Whoever saw teeth made like that!"

Mayor Vincent Ziegler

Haskell: The man that was the mayor then (a fellow by the name of Ziegler), him and I didn't get along worth a crap.[43] He was a Republican and I'm a Democrat. He didn't like me for that. He wanted me to arrest everybody that come through town that made a technical break. I wouldn't do it. So he give me a bad time. When I wanted a raise, he fought the raise. He did me a favor. But I didn't know it then.

I started out with less than $200 a month. I forgot what it was. I didn't make a livin' on that job. I lost money every day I was on that job. I think when I quit, I asked for $275.[44] I was gettin' two and a quarter a month. And I'm workin' ungodly hours—day and night. I did it all myself. By myself. With no help and no training. Didn't get hurt. Didn't get killed. Never shot anybody. Never hit anybody. Only slapped a couple people, see. People liked me. I liked them. I did the best I could for 'em. I worked about sixteen, eighteen hours a day—which was not right. But I did it.

Bunch of old buzzards on the city council thought fifty cents an hour was enough for a man workin' on the street. I had old men workin' on the street with a shovel— They didn't have much equipment. They had to clean out the gutters and the sewers and the streets and patch the holes and so forth. And they was gettin' fifty cents an hour. I was tryin' to get 'em ninety cents an hour. I go to council and I say, "My crew of men here—" I had old men. Every young guy was in the army. They were workin' in a shop somewhere. There was no free labor around. You'd get whatever you could get.

I said, "I can't get any more help. I got these two old men. And they're only gettin' fifty cents an hour. I got to get 'em more money." In fact, that was more than I was gettin' (to tell the truth about it). And old Phil Youngen (He was a councilman. Dirty, cheap Dutch son-of-a-bitch.), "Why, fifty cents an hour is enough for any man workin' with a shovel." He worked for Bierce. He was haulin' coal for Bierce and that's probably about all he got.[45] Well, I was— I was disgusted. I asked for a raise and they wouldn't give it to me. So I said, "Quit." I give 'em thirty days and at the end of thirty days, they could get somebody else to do the job.

Council adjourned to meet in executive session. The matter of acting upon Mr. Jones request for a raise in salary and reconsideration of his resignation was discussed. Council reconvened. All members present. Mr. Watts moved that Officer Jones request for a raise in salary be considered. Sec by Mr. Smith. Mr. Wolcott no, Mr. Youngen no, Mr. Watts no, Mr. Smith no. Mr. Burns no. Mr. Page no.

Mr. Watts moved that the resignation of Mr. Haskell Jones be accepted as of June 15th. That Mr. Jones be paid for the first half of June. Sec by Mr. Smith, Mr. Wolcott, aye, Mr. Youngen aye, Mr. Watts aye, Mr. Smith aye, Mr. Burns aye, Mr. Page Aye.

S.A. Schlup Clerk
Village of Tallmadge, Ohio
Council Minutes
June 12, 1944

I was a policeman 'til the first day of July 1944—and the night before. Did I work that day? I don't know. No, I don't think I worked that day. I think I— The last day of June 1944. Maybe I worked 'til midnight. That, I can't remember. But that's when I quit.

One time (a year or so later) we were huntin' with a group down the western part of the state and just by chance, [Ziegler] and I had to come back together. I rode with him or he rode with me. I don't remember which. He was tryin' to apologize to me. He said, "You know, I made a mistake when—" Said, "My mother-in-law and my wife really give me hell about my treatment of you." I said, "You did me a favor. I'm a helluva' lot better off than I was on that job. Nah, you did me a favor. But," I said, "you didn't intend to. It wasn't because you wanted to."

He died not long after that. He went out and shoveled snow in his driveway and (SLAPS HANDS TOGETHER) boom, he died. If I'd've been there, I'd've hit him in the ass with the shovel.

CHAPTER FORTY-EIGHT

THE TALLMADGE FIRE DEPARTMENT

Without even the basics of a volunteer fire department, Tallmadge might have been expected to turn to its largest, closest and most experienced neighbor, Akron, for assistance. Unfortunately, Akron's fire department was not much better off. Having suffered financial neglect due to voter apathy at the polls, its condition may have actually been worse.[1] In Akron, people could only rely upon the fire department's antiquated, underpowered equipment to respond in an emergency. In Tallmadge, residents relied upon Akron, but they could also rely upon the nearby township of Stow, as well as the cities of Kent or Cuyahoga Falls—each of which, ironically, boasted better fire protection equipment than Akron.[2] As the United States entered World War II, however, the deficiencies of Akron's fire department were suddenly forced to the forefront of the city's agenda in a major fashion. And while the development of the Akron Fire Department would be critical to that of Tallmadge's, ensuing events in Tallmadge would prove critically important to Akron.

With the protection of plants critical to war production suddenly at risk (as well as a booming billion dollar economy wholly dependent upon workers who were living in cramped, overcrowded quarters), Akron was suddenly shocked into reality by an insurance underwriters' report.[3] In stark terms, it "condemn[ed] the 22-year old pumpers, a fire signal system that is unintelligible if two alarms are sounded at once, personnel 70 men below standard, and an almost complete absence of satisfactory aerial ladders. The city would be helpless if two major fires occurred at the same time, it was pointed out . . ."[4] "Modern pumpers have 240 horsepower engines," a writer for the *Beacon Journal* continued, "and that's 200 more horsepower than some of our engines have."[5] A city councilman added to the condemnation with his declaration that "'Akron has no fire department at all,' so antiquated are some of the trucks."[6] Despite being known throughout the nation as the "Rubber Capital of the World," the underwriters' report flatly downgraded Akron to a "fifth class city."[7]

If that report were not enough, Akronites only had to read the *Beacon Journal* on a daily basis to see the effects of years of neglect. One article noted that a pumper broke down on the way to an emergency call and had to coast downhill to the scene of the fire.[8] Just a week later, a second pumper broke down on the way to another fire call—closing the fire station and leaving the entire West Hill section without fire protection.[9] Yet a third article noted, "the company operating the city's obsolete aerial ladder frequently has to call on bystanders to help raise it once they get to a fire."

The situation was so embarrassingly bad that Fire Chief R.M. Clark of Kent called Akron's fire protection equipment "an outstanding disgrace" and "declared he would not accept for service in his community of 8,500 a single piece of the equipment Akron sends to its fires."[10] Fire Chief Louis P. Seiler of Cuyahoga Falls noted that his fire department had "14 of the new 'fog' hose nozzles for its lines, while all of Akron's fire hoses combined can boast of but one."[11]

Responding to the crisis, a citizens' committee only underscored what was already becoming widely known following their own investigation. In "six closely typewritten pages" the report was "unique for its outspoken frankness [and] detailed weaknesses in every engine house the city has."[12] Among other items, Lon G. Tighe, head of the advisory citizens' committee "discussed Kenmore district's 'pumper' which is so underpowered it detours [around] the hills north of Kenmore blvd., and once at a fire is of little value because it won't pump," as well as the weakened floor of engine house No. 2 at E. Market and S. Arlington.[13] "It's no exaggeration to say that we'll find the engine down in the basement one of these days," Tighe commented.[14]

With the city fathers and the citizen's action committee mobilized to solve the crisis, a tax increase was placed on the November ballot to help rebuild the fire department and a delegation was sent to

Washington in May to petition the War Production Board for permission to purchase four new pumpers.[15] The subsequent contribution of four "grim looking" olive drab "lease lend" pumpers from federal funds in October (perhaps "the first city in the country to get such equipment"), gave Akron hope that a crisis had been averted.[16] As a result, its antiquated pumpers were sent to the scrap heap[17] to support the war effort.[18] When the votes were tallied after the November election, however, the shock, despair and disbelief at City Hall was palpable:

> Jacob C. Mong, city finance director, observed sadly that the federal government defeated the fire levy when it sent in four emergency fire-pumpers on loan for the war's duration.
>
> "Some people seem to think we have enough fire protection now," Mong said, "although the great majority of our equipment still is more than 20 years old and likely to fail us at any moment.
>
> Mayor George J. Harter accepted the outcome as final and announced flatly that he is done with attempts to get a fire levy passed.
>
> "Apparently we'll have to have a major catastrophe before anything is done," the mayor said.[19]

Akron, in short, was a "major catastrophe" waiting to happen. The housing shortage in Akron had already led to instances such as four adults and 12 children living in one room and 23 crowded in a nine-room home.[20] What's more, with a wartime draft in place, the city was losing experienced firefighters quicker than they could be replaced.[21] Now, without funding, Fire Chief Frank Vernotzy began closing fire stations and relocating personnel.[22] Even the new pumpers, while a much-appreciated addition, weren't ready for immediate use. Manufactured to current standards, their hose connections were threaded differently than that on Akron's antiquated water supply system—as would also be the case when the local Office of Civil Defense (OCD) received the first of 53 skid-mounted pumpers in early December.[23] In every instance, adapters first had to be fashioned out of scarce rationed materials before the equipment could ever be put into service.[24] Mayor Harter's fears were very real. In fact, during the last half of 1942, major catastrophic fires were suddenly occurring across the northeastern United States and Canada with frightening regularity.

Since early August, the country had seen disastrous fire after disastrous fire make front-page news. The first occurred in nearby

Cleveland as a fire at "The Greatest Show on Earth" killed 100 animals in their cages as 5,000 onlookers stood by utterly helpless.[25] In late November, some 478 Thanksgiving partygoers burned alive when The Cocoanut Grove nightclub caught fire in Boston.[26] A little more than one week later, on December 8th, over 100 died in Newfoundland as "Flames And Stampede Turn Servicemen's Hostel Into Hall Of Death."[27] Just three days after that, a 6-story department store burned in Boston, injuring 65 and causing $1,000,000 in damage.[28] Each event made Akron's shortcomings all the more pressing. And ominous.

In mid-November, "An investigation of fire hazards in crowded Akron rooming houses" began.[29] Two weeks later, in response to the Cocoanut Grove disaster, Mayor Harter ordered "Akron's undermanned fire and building inspection staffs, already weighted down with a checkup of overcrowded apartments and lodging house . . . [to make] a survey of night clubs, restaurants and lodge halls in the wake of the Boston fire disaster."[30] With only four fire inspectors at his disposal,[31] Fire Chief "Vernotzy renewed his plea for passage of a fire prevention ordinance . . . which would give his department six more inspectors "so that we could adequately take care of inspections of apartments, night clubs and the like."[32] With the issue locked in petty City Council bickering since August, however, there were no signs of any immediate passage. As a result, "Fire Warden Harold Brannon asserted that he [would] be unable to obtain a complete report of fire hazard conditions in Akron night clubs for at least two months."[33] An initial preliminary review with city building inspector James A. Easton was far from encouraging. They found that, "Most of Akron's night clubs violate safety provisions" as "Doors on nearly all clubs swing in, and some clubs are decorated with easily inflammable materials."[34]

Everything augured for a fire of catastrophic proportions in Akron before additional housing could be built to relieve the overcrowded conditions, countless fire safety violations could be uncovered and remedied and the fire department could be properly equipped and staffed—except that the next major fire to make front-page news didn't take place in Akron. It took place in Tallmadge. And it nearly had the same fatal consequences as the other fires.

Haskell: The Whispering Pines Dance Hall was a shell of a building—just a shell. There was no ceiling in it. They only used it one or two night a week. Saturday— I can't remember whether they had dances on— Sometimes on Friday nights, I believe. But the building stood there empty all week. It was cold weather and they had it festooned with paper (crepe paper) hung all over the joists up here to dress the place up a little. To keep it from lookin' so bare. Loaded with paper festoons hangin' down. A few rows of bells and so forth like that—a regular firetrap.

So, a man named Bauman was the fire marshal in this district (state fire marshal) and I called him up and I told him, I said, "You ought to check out that old dance hall up here (It was a public building). It's gonna' burn down and kill a lot of people." All they had was a small door at each end. And he said, "Well, what's it like?" And I explained it to him. He said, "O.K. When can I come out there and meet you?" I said, "Well, the place is locked up except for Saturday night." At that time, I think it was Saturday. Yeah, I know it was. And he said, "Well, What time do they open?" I said, "Well, they go in there early in the afternoon to build a fire and warm the place up." They had a great big pot-bellied stove in there, see, and they fired it up pretty hard and got it warmed up to some extent. He said, "O.K., I'll be out there about six o'clock." Said, "Fine."

So, about four-thirty, I called him up and I said, "You can scrub that call out here to Tallmadge." He said, "Why?" I said, "She burnt down this afternoon." He said, "Good."

$6,000 Fire Levels Frame Dance Hall

A tragedy that might have been similar to those that recently struck places of amusement in Boston and St. Johns Newfoundland, was averted Saturday night when the Whispering Pines dance hall on route 91, a mile southwest of Tallmadge, burned to the ground before an expected crowd of 250 to 500 frolickers got there. Pvt. Clyde Morris, son of O.M. Morris, 938 Concord av., Akron, owner of the building, said the frame building was valued at $6,000.

The flames, which had completely enveloped the building by the time firemen arrived, was fought by two fire companies, one from Akron, the other from Stow.

Firemen could not determine the cause of the fire, since nothing but two chimneys remained standing. An adjacent dwelling, home of Mrs. Lewis Mayer, who summoned the fire departments, was saved by an east wind that blew the flames away from it.

Akron Beacon Journal
Sunday, December 20, 1942

On January 19th, 1943, one exactly one month to the day after the fire, Akron City Council suspended a rule of Council and passed ordinance No. 25-1943 by 12-0 "creating a Bureau of Fire Prevention in the Fire Department providing for the assignment of the City Fire

Warden to such bureau as Chief Inspector; prescribing the powers and duties of the Bureau; making it unlawful to create or maintain fire hazards; providing rules and regulations for the recharging of fire extinguishers; providing for fire drills in schools; making it unlawful to block stairways, elevators, fire escapes, passageways, doors or windows, exits; authorizing the investigation of fires; providing penalty for the violation thereof; and repealing all ordinances and parts of ordinances inconsistent therewith."[35] The era of modern fire prevention in Akron, as well as Tallmadge, had begun.

Haskell: They started this Civilian Defense thing during the war and after so long a time, we became interested in a Fire Department. I was a policeman and our mayor, Jack Sperry, was a businessman. Pretty good-sized businessman. And he depended on me a lot. I pat myself a little on the back. "Now," he said, "Haskell, I can not and I don't want to be bothered with this thing. I can't handle it. I've got work to do day and night in my business. Now you are able to take over and now you will be the administrator (I guess you'd call it)." Anyway, I was the one guy without a steady job. I was not tied down all the time like everybody else, so he give me the job.

I went out and hustled men who could be volunteer fire department firemen and I got together some fifteen, twenty— Some were day and some were nights. I mean they were available durin' those hours. At first, all the young guys was in the army. So I had to go out and get old guys. We had guys forty, fifty years old who agreed to be volunteer firemen. When the siren sounded, they'd come and help put the fire out.

Dick Sokol was one of the firemen. I appointed 'em. But I don't know what their names were, all of 'em. Some of 'em. Gone. Many of 'em's gone. Over the hill, see. Some left town. Some died. Some moved away. A few of 'em I could name, but I couldn't name 'em all. Hated lead pencils, so I didn't write things down very good.[36]

They lasted for ten, fifteen years 'til we finally got the young boys back and they begin to get interested and come in. We got younger guys in there. But I didn't want to wave a flag sayin' I did this or I did that. I tried. I did a good job. And I was proud of what I did. But I didn't— Nobody knows what I did.

The mayor, Jack Sperry, and I had a conference and he said, "How are you gettin' along with the Fire Department." I said, "Well, I have got these men who have agreed to answer the call." And he said, "Who you got for Chief?" I told him Dave Bierce and he said, "No, you can't have him." I said, "Why?" He said, "He's my nephew." I said, "So what?" "Well," he said, "everybody's gonna' say I've appointed my nephew as Chief." (It was his job to appoint somebody. It was my job to select him.)

I said, "You don't have anything to do with this, do you? You told me it was my job. If you don't want me to do it, now's a good time to say so. I'll quit right now. I don't get anything out of this, only headache." "Oh, no," he said, "I didn't mean that." But said, "I'm gonna' get a lot of criticism." I said, "Well, lay it back on me if you do." So he walks across the street and saw Dave and told him he wanted him to be Chief of the Fire Department. He was a good man. Did a good job. But Jack wouldn't let me tell him. He had to tell him himself.

Through the good graces of Gerald Vernotzy, who was the head of the Akron Fire Department,[37] he guided us. He was the dispenser of Civilian Defense materials—pumps and hoses and ladders and stuff like that. They all had to be cleared through him. He was the big chief of this area. So, we got a CD pumper and we bought an old truck and built the thing up and put the pumper on it.[38]

Bought it from Pierson Ford Agency down in Mogadore.[39] They had an old gasoline truck and we cut the tank in two. It was too big for the truck to haul water in and put the other equipment, put a pumper on it. So, we cut the old chassis down, rebuilt it completely. Had some pretty good "jack-leg" mechanics.

Barney Goff and Danny Sekulich worked through a machinist and some of the guys worked day and night tryin' to get the thing built. They rebuilt that old truck and we put the pumper on it. It had about a thousand gallon, I s'pose, pump tank on it and we cut it down to five-hundred and put the pumper on the back end, did the plumbing, everything, and the wiring—got it to work. We saved some houses with that old thing. We called it the "Milk Wagon."

We had wooden sides, about so high—big enough to put our hose inside and shovels and what-have-you, axes and whatnot. We used it a couple of years. Put out a lot of grass-fires, of course. We had some of these Indian pumper cans. What'd they call 'em? I don't know. But we had pretty good luck with that old clunker.

Ray Paulus was a garage mechanic. Him and some of the other

guys, they rebuilt this motor. I didn't get much credit. I didn't want credit. I wanted cash, but I didn't get cash, either. One of the guys died just not long ago in the last three months [at the time of the recording in the early 1990s]. Vern Morris. He was a machinist and the top machinist in the country. Top. But I knew Vern. I got him and another guy who owned a machine shop to build the deck around this old Chevy we finally got.

Lee Herman that owned the Herman Machine give us a lot of help.[40] He was a good man. A lot of help. He turned that shop over to us. We had one of his employees who worked in there in the fire department. Good mechanic. Would make anything we needed. He said, "I've got iron of any kind you need. I've got channel iron. I've got this. I've got that. Whatever you want, take it. Put it on there. You don't have to worry about where it come from or anything." He was a prince of a man. Many a night, two or three o'clock in the morning, me and Danny (was the guy that worked for him), went in there to make a hose connection or whatever we need. I went to Barberton, here, there and everywhere else huntin' screws, bolts or nuts—whatever we needed all day long.

I worked hard. And I hustled things and material and everything else to get this thing goin'. During the war, you couldn't find any metal parts, wood, or nothing else. Did my best and I guess I did a pretty good job. I still got some of the papers where we had a scrap metal drive to get money to help booster the fire department.

I hustled material— Material was scarce. You couldn't buy a bolt in a store. You needed a quarter-inch bolt that long and you couldn't find it. I went all over the county (hardware stores here and there) just to get some three-quarter inch bolt or half-inch bolt or one-eighth inch bolt or whatever we needed.

Me and Sam Schlup stole the siren off of Coventry High School for a fire siren. They wouldn't give you a nickel to help do anything civically. "We haven't got any law that says we should do this." "We can't do anything." "We can't bend over." "We can't take a chance or nothing."" We bought an old garage down there where the library is now.[41] It had been a gas station. It was a pretty good-sized buildin'. Big enough. We added an addition to it to put two trucks in it. I wired it. But we had to have a siren.

So the city don't have any money. They can't borrow any to give us. We got no siren. A siren cost a hundred and fifty bucks, maybe.

The light company said they'll give us a pole. They come out and set us a pole. A big one. I'll bring the wirin' out of the station, underground, over to that. Boys dig the trench and we carried it over there and put pipe in there and pulled wire through it and left it there.

So I talked to Gerald Vernotzy. I said, "Gerald, we need a siren. How can we get one? He said, "I'll tell you where there is one. Belongs to Civilian Defense.[42] They put it on top of that Coventry High School. There's an air raid siren. Says, "They'll never need it. If you can get it off there, you can have it." I said, "We'll get it." So Sam Schlup was the clerk of the town. I said, "Sam, we've got a little job." He said, "What?" I said, "We've got to go out there and get that siren off of that school-house at Coventry Township at the high school." Well, "Can we do it? Can we—" Ahhhhh, everybody was afraid they can't do it, can't do it, can't do it. I said, "C'mon, we'll do it." I'm in uniform with a badge on and a gun on my side.

We drive out there and pull up in front of the schoolhouse on a Saturday afternoon about four o'clock. Go up and the front door is open. We go in and the janitor's in there cleanin' up the place. 'Cause I come in there with a police uniform on he's a little bit in awe.

I said, "We come to get that siren off the schoolhouse up there." "O.K.," he said, "I'll show you how to get up there. I got a ladder." We had to go up in the hall upstairs and through a scuttle-hole up in the roof. It was sittin' on a platform up there where it was wired. So, we go up and I disconnect it and take a rope and put on it and let it down through the hole and Sam takes it. I come down and I put it in my car and bring it over— They don't know, yet, what the hell happened, see. But we got the siren. And they're still usin' it.

Gee, how many years? That's in the forties. That's fifty years ago, plus. So anyway, we did things like that. But you couldn't be a pantywaist and be afraid to do somethin'. You had to do the best you could do. So anyway, I worked my butt off and when I was gone, nobody cared. We got it done and we got a fire department. And we got a nice fire department now, but I was the seed. I was the seed. I didn't ask for credit. All I wanted to do was get the thing goin'.

When the Village Fire Siren Blows
By Keith Spriggel

"Whoo-ee-ee-ee!"

The siren atop the fire station split the air with a shrill blast.

It rising shrieks vibrated through the general store on the corner. It echoed among the walls of the kilns down by the brick yard. Further down the street, two mechanics in the repair garage heard the signal. A few rods away, a farmer reined in his team and stopped cultivating.

It was the signal to get going—and quick. The butcher behind the counter at the store ripped off his apron and raced toward the door, ignoring customers. Brick workers poured from the yard. The auto mechanics jumped in their tow car and shot it into gear. The farmer tied up his team and started his truck.

All of them converged on the fire station across from the general store. One of the mechanics leaped into the driver's seat of the pumper truck. The others grabbed slickers and helmets and hung on the rear of the truck as it shot from the station.

"Where is it?" roared a brick worker, red faced from the heat . . . . [43]

"When the Fire Siren Blows.
County's Minute Men on Alert to Answer Call
for Protection of Lives and Property."
The Akron Beacon Journal
Sunday, July 4, 1948

Haskell: I can't remember the first fire.[44] A lot of grass fires in those days. I remember the first house we saved. A fellow by the name of [George] Mast—who was later the town clerk. Was an old school teacher and a very educated old man. He was an accountant, a bookkeeper, whatever you call 'em. I guess accountant. Knew facts and figures, anyway. If he had a account that come up one penny short, he spent three weeks huntin' that penny—instead of takin' it out of his pocket and puttin' it in there. I'd've found some way to do it, but he did not. His house caught afire and we put it out.

City bought the old gas station from Henry Bierce where the number one station was. That belonged to Henry Bierce. Neil Jones gave us the lumber for that thing. He run the Tallmadge Lumber at that time and—

Florence: He was a Kentuckian and came from the same place we did.

Haskell: He was just about as close to a brother to me as he could be without being any kin at all. So, we got that fire station built. There was a high bank behind it. We couldn't drive around behind the fire station because there wasn't any room back there. So, I engineered another gratis job. We'd dig that out and level it back of the fire station, see, so we could park back there and have a place to get around. And Bierce furnished the trucks one Sunday morning. About twenty-five, thirty of us went down there and I guess we used the city backhoe, I guess, or grader or somethin' and cut it down and loaded it in those trucks and hauled it away.

"Here they go! On the running board of the big truck as it leaves the Tallmadge station are Wilburn Crites and Raymond Paulus. Behind the wheel is Chief Dave Bierce and at his side is Jack Platz." (*Akron Beacon Journal*)

It was just half of that building there originally. Just the side next to the circle. Then they built this other side and we wanted heat in there.[45] They built the new building and we was heating it with a "Warm Morning" coal stove, and I gave 'em that. One we'd taken out of the house we lived in on Eighteen. We used that a couple winters. By that time, I wasn't a policeman anymore. I was workin' for the furnace company. I helped buy the furnace and put it in. Got it for as cheap as I could. I was still in the fire department. I was in it for twenty-five years.

Then, we needed a fish fryer. I was a chiseler. I was always chiselin' stuff. Well, I got two big long furnace burners from the furnace company and we got a piece of decking plate, thick, to make the table out of. Somebody brought a torch in and cut it to fit the pans. We had pans made that was about eight inches wide and eight inches deep to cook fish in.

A friend of mine was the foreman down at Bellows Sign and I said, "Mike, we need a hood for our fish fryer." And he said, "Well, what've you got to make it out of?" Buford Finney was a foreman down at the Goodrich over the salvage department and he got the— I don't think he stole it. They probably give it to him because he was a yard foreman down there. But anyway, he said they had some of this aluminum. We got enough of that aluminum to make that hood out of. So, we took it down to Mike and they made this big hood to fit over that thing. It's about eight feet long and it fitted in the end so we could put an exhaust fan to take the fumes out, the grease. Cook fish down there.

We made some fish fries and stuff and made a lot of money.[46] We made a lot of money. We served seven hundred, eight hundred pounds of fish down there one day. We had that place so full of people you can't believe!

We didn't have anything only the old pumper. So we told the city if they'd buy us a Chevy chassis, we'd build it up and we'd put the furnace in. So the city paid for the furnace and I don't know whether we paid for that ductwork or if they paid for it. Anyway, we did the work. We put the furnace in. I engineered the job. I was workin' for a furnace company and I knew somethin' about it, see. So, we put the furnace in there, the ductwork in.[47]

Built another addition to it and finally, the city bought us a Chevrolet truck—just a bare truck. We put one of these tanks in there and put one of these CD pumpers on it. I think they're still usin' it. It was the best piece of equipment we ever had in Tallmadge. Even though they paid twenty-five, thirty, forty thousand dollars for a piece of equipment, this Chevy would do anything it would do. And quicker.

We had various fires. We never had any serious fire. I didn't. I was workin' one day and they had a fire out here at—toward where Barton lives.[48] Somewhere out there. And it burnt up a guy in a trailer house out there. I wasn't on the call. I was workin' at the shop then. Furnace work or electric work. I'm glad I wasn't. They say it smells bad. Oh, we saved a few buildings. A lot of grass fires in those days. We don't have so many anymore. Don't have so many grass fires.

We finally got a dollar for a fire for the first hour. And after that, you got paid so much for the second hour. But the first hour was a dollar. Even if it was only thirty minutes, you got the dollar or whatever it was. I don't remember. It wasn't too much. It was whatever it was.

So, I was a fireman for about three to five years. I wanted to quit and they said, "You haven't got twenty-five years in yet." I said, "Well, I'll stay another year or two." But I didn't do much. I got too old to take one of them five-gallon buckets of water and put it on your back and run from here down to that cross-road down there and put out a grass fire or somethin' of that kind. It was too much for me. I couldn't do it anymore and I just kinda' was one of the firemen in name only—but I was still a member.[49]

CHAPTER FORTY-NINE

THE FURNACE COMPANY

Haskell: They had government-paid watchmen in every machine shop and the Stoneware and everywhere.[1] They needed 'em like I need a hole in my head, but they thought they— They didn't want somebody to blow the shop up that was makin' critical war material. I used to stop every night and check these guys. They were in my circuit. I'd stop and spend a few minutes with 'em and see if everything was goin' all right. Go on to somewhere else and about my business. So, I knew this guy quite well and I told him I was quittin'. He had worked for this outfit and he said, "You go over there and you can get a job."

So I went over to Curt Collins the next day. Within twenty-four hours, I had another job for a furnace company, which was makin' me twice as much money as I was makin' as a policeman, see.[2] Didn't get rich at it, but it was a lot better. And I could pay some of my bills— which I had accumulated while I was tryin' to be a policeman.

I went to work wiring furnaces and burners. Stuff of that kind. Doin' service work—which I knew nothin' about. On top of that, <u>they</u> didn't know anything about it. The foreman or the man that owned the building—didn't neither one know anything about how to wire a furnace. Only a little common sense was all I had—and very common. They had nobody to teach me. But they'd give you a print.

With every piece of equipment come a print. I'd never read a blueprint in my life. I didn't know a blueprint from a blue sky. So I had to set down and try to iron out these blueprints. How this thing was wired and how everything else— So I could wire it all right. But when it come to wirin' or makin' it work properly, sometimes I was lost.

I couldn't tell 'em, "I don't know what the hell this thing is. I don't know how to do this." I didn't tell 'em that. I took it out and I did the job. And I learned how to do it. On my own. Strictly with no help, see. I mean definitely with no help. And nobody on the job but me.

They send me out to wire a big boiler in a factory or in a schoolhouse or wherever it might be with a lot of controls on it and so forth. I had done electric work back in the twenties. But I hadn't done it for years. And I'd never read a blueprint. I didn't know what a blueprint was. I'd heard of 'em, but that's about all.

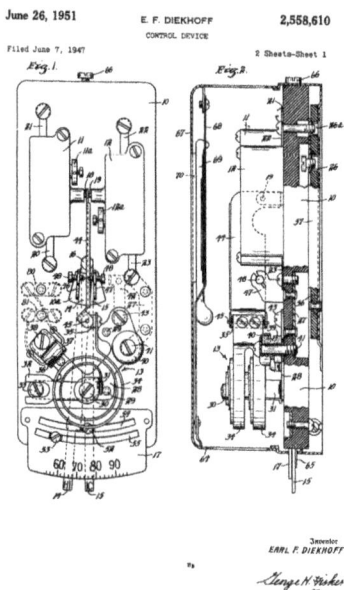

U.S. Patent No. 2,558,610. Control Device, Earl F. Diekhoff, assignor to the Minneapolis-Honeywell Regulator Company (USPTO).

Sometimes, I'd get stuck. I'd get stuck. I'd go in the shop and I'd say, "How 'bout—" What's this—" "I don't understand this." "I got a problem out here." "I can't do this." The boss used to say, "Call Buffalo." "Call Chicago." The factory. I said, "The hell with Chicago and Buffalo. I'll figure it out. If you can' tell me, I'll go figure it out myself. I might be out there for a week, but I'll finally figure it out. But I ain't callin' the factory to find out which screw to turn and which wire to add here." I never did. I never called once. Not once.

But I beat my brains out and I was considered one of the top trouble-shooters and wiring operators. I had men from various companies want to hire me that come in there for various things. So, I wasn't a dummy. But I was not educated in that line, see.

Finally, they got an engineer in there. A fellow by the name of Paul Frampton. Nice guy. He was generally a salesman. But he was an engineer. He had a little more finesse than I had. Not always was he right, because he had never had training in this line, see. But he could theorize and get things— Sometimes when we didn't know, we'd mess up. But, he'd come out and help me. And between the two of us, we could iron the bug out of it, see. But he wasn't available part of the time. I finally developed into a pretty good serviceman. I was able to work out most bugs and surprised 'em quite a lot. Some of my discoveries I wouldn't even tell 'em.

We had a gas valve that was a self-generating job. The pilot generated the electricity to operate the valve—the gas valve that open and shut to control the furnace flame, on a gas burner. And we had a tremendous job of puttin' burners in old coal furnaces 'cause gas was fairly new and they finally loosened it up durin' the middle of the war. There was more gas than there was coal. This thing had a stem on the valve that went up and down. When the thermostat was satisfied and it was hot enough the thermostat shut off and it dropped down and shut the gas off. That stem was stickin' in the housing. And we almost burnt houses up.

People'd wake up in the middle of the night and it was a hundred and twenty degrees in the house. This thing wouldn't shut off. The thermostat would say quit and it don't quit. The thing is stuck open. It was a delicate thing. You couldn't adjust it in the field. There was no way. It was too delicate an arrangement.

So I brought one of 'em home with me. Tore it apart and found out what was happenin'. The stem come up instead of goin' down. It was wedgin' in the housing. So I find me a very, very, very thin washer off somethin' that would go over that stem. And the next one that fouled, I took it apart on the job and I put that washer on it and put it back together.

So, problem. I couldn't find these washers. It had to be real thin. So I started makin' 'em out of sheet metal. I take a drill and drill a hole in a piece of sheet metal, then take snips and trim it to the right size. It didn't have to fit anything. It just had to be a shim.

They had about four or five other servicemen. I was top serviceman, but they had others. So, one day the boss called me in and said, "What are you doing to these general valves?" I says, "What do you mean?" He said, "We haven't had a call back on one you've been on for months. The other guys can't seem to do anything with 'em." I said, "I don't know. I just adjust 'em." "Well," he said, "I think you're doin' somethin' else and you owe me and you should tell me what you're doin'." I said, "No. I just sell you my labor. I ain't gonna' sell you my brains—if I've got any." And I never did tell him.

I imagine eventually they might've took one apart to see what the heck was goin' on—if they knew enough to do that. But generally, all they'd do was put a new one on and in two months, it'd do the same thing, see. It'd stick again. I never told 'em. And I worked there for about four years.

They send a couple engineers and they go out with me to help me wire this equipment. They was out of Minneapolis from— What's the big people in Minneapolis? Not Minnesota Mining, is it? Nah, these people make control equipment. Thermostats and whatnot. Ahh, I can't think what the hell the name is. I ought to. They're the kind of things I can't remember. Anyway, it don't make any difference.

They were engineers. They knew what the hell they was doin'. But they knew only how to take this piece of paper and read that print and do that. But it didn't tell you how to get through this buildin'. Where the wires are or whatever. Where the service came from or anything else. They didn't know that. They knew this. This is just the furnace proper. They knew that. So I knew how to get through a house like a rat. And I would figure out these jobs and go and do 'em.

Well, these guys couldn't understand that. They were amazed at some of the things I did. I'll never forget it. Here's a great big basement. The furnace sits in the back end and there's no ceiling. This is all sealed over here and plastered and finished. Way over here, up above this three or four feet, is the thermostat. This thermostat has to be taken off and you have to change it. Well, this is plastered underneath.

So we go to drill a new hole up there. Got to run a new wire, see. So I measure. I measure from here to yonder, to here to yonder and back again. Fourteen times. Fifteen, twenty, thirty times, I measured. Well, I come up to the figure myself. Right here, you drill through the ceiling. Right above that is a wall. There's plate under the wall. You drill up through that and you can get up here. And I go upstairs and I drive a nail right under where I want this thing to be. Used a long finishin' nail and drive it through the floor. And I go down underneath and I take my drill (I got an auger about that long) and I drill up through there and I shine a flashlight and I missed that nail about an inch.

These boys was dumbfounded. "How—? How—? How—? How—?" I says, "This, I've been doin' for years. That I can do. This thing you got here is a little foggy for me. But this— This part I can handle. This end of it." Said, "Why don't you work for us? We'll give

you a good job. You can travel with us and you can help install these."
I said, "I can't do it. I've got a wife and kids and a home. I've got to
live here. I can't run around with you guys." "But we'll make it worth
your while." I said, "I'd love the money, but I can't take it."

Some of our crew had put a day and night thermostat on the wall
to operate a furnace and shut it off at night and open it up in the
morning and stuff of that kind. Great, big thing. As big as a shoebox.
They call me and I go out there.

So, this old lady (And she was much older than I was at that time),
she said, "This thing isn't workin'. They put it on here a few days ago.
I'll show you what's the matter with it." This is a woman sixty-five years
old. "Show me, granny." So she says, "You take the cover off and I'll
show ya'. Up in there, you see that cam and that shaft and so forth?
That cam is slippin' on the shaft." "O.K." So I check it and she's right.
It's slippin' on the shaft. It isn't doin' its stuff.

I told her, "I'll take it off, put a regular thermostat on and we'll
send this back to the factory." I said, "I can't fix it. I don't know
anything about it." So I took it off and took it back to the shop. So,
not long after that, I get another call back there and this same
thermostat that I put on there is in there and she said, "We got
trouble." I said, "What's the trouble?' Said, "Somewhere in that wall,
between the thermostat and the basement, is a loose connection." Said,
"It chatters." When the furnace comes on, it goes off, comes on, goes
off, this vibration— If somebody went down the street with a truck or
somethin', it chattered. Said, "There's somethin' wrong between that
thermostat and down there at the furnace because I've checked it." I
said, "Well, we'll find out."

I tie a new piece of thermostat wire on it here, I pull it down in the
basement and there's a thumbnail splice. The guy didn't even tape his
joints. He staggered 'em, but he didn't tape 'em. I repaired it and said
"How do you figure out these things? Where do you get the mechanical
knowledge?"

She said, "My father was old man— (Told his name. I can't
remember.) Had fifteen hundred patents, probably. He was a
mechanical engineer. Worked for Goodrich. But on the side, he made
patents of his own model in his own head." She said, "I worked with
my dad when I was a kid from day to dawn or whenever I had spare
time. I worked with him in his lab and in his machine shop and
whatever. And when a service man comes out here and says, 'I did so-

and-so,' he better do it. 'Cause <u>I know</u> whether he did it or not because I know what I'm talkin' about."

She could've been a million— I said, "I'll tell you, we could use you down at the shop." I said, "We haven't got too many mechanics down there. We've got a lot of screwdriver mechanics, but they're not really industrial mechanics. We could take you down there." But she knew exactly what she was talkin' about—better than I did.

The woman who managed the company was a Kentucky highbred and had a very, very high opinion of herself. She thought she was a big operator. And they had about thirty people workin' for 'em in the field and office.

She gets a brilliant idea. They paid us in check and everybody had to come in on a Friday evening and stand in line while she handed out the checks. Get in there by alphabetical order. And here's twenty-five, thirty people come in there to get a check. Why don't one of 'em get in a car and go around to their jobs and pass out their checks and the guys could go home? I got tired of it. I said one evening, "This is ridiculous. Come in here and stand in line for fifteen minutes to get a check." And it irked her to no end, I'll tell ya'. A couple weeks later I got laid off.

CHAPTER FIFTY

TALLMADGE CITY COUNCIL

Even before World War II was two months old, economists were forecasting massive unemployment and a return to The Depression when the war was over. Echoing the impact on the economy at the end of World War I, it was reckoned that "After the close of the war, there will be a rush of civilian goods output to fill the unsatisfied demand of war-rich consumers. That will employ workers discharged from armament factories. But there will soon be an overproduction of civilian goods. Result: In about nine months after the close of war, the unemployment crisis will be as severe as in 1932 when the New Deal was swept into power."[1] Fortunately, it didn't occur. Instead, the United States was swept into one of the greatest periods of economic growth in its history.

As the factories switched over from wartime production to consumer goods, the returning soldiers, as well as the general public, wanted both cars and tires. Akron continued its boom. And Tallmadge continued to grow. By the Census of 1950, the population of Tallmadge had shown a dramatic reversal compared to that of 1940. With an influx of factory workers and returning veterans looking to live in Tallmadge, the village would soon celebrate the status of city—and with that would be massive visible change in everything from paved roads (much of it on an emergency basis), to new housing developments (such as Atwood, Knollwood, Maca and Stillmeadow) and the delivery of mail (but only after the houses were numbered) to its first shopping mall, drive-in theater and city bus service.[2] More importantly, as the only city in Ohio without a municipal water system, the Council forced a water system through against voter's wishes, oversaw the installation of gas mains, sewage disposal and a contract for garbage collection.[3] For the new city employees, it also established paid holiday and sick leave, as well as a police pension fund.[4]

As an elected member of Tallmadge City Council, Haskell Jones would be in the middle of all of it. First elected in 1949, then re-elected in 1953 and 1955 (each time with the greatest number of votes cast for a Council candidate), Haskell helped define the infrastructure on which today's modern city is built.[5] In effect, the "hillbilly" who grew up without an outhouse, drank water out of a filthy cistern and traveled on nearly impassable roads helped ensure that a modern city had pure water, a modern sewer system and paved streets.

Son Donald later remembered, "It was busy. There was an awful lot of land that had never been developed that was farmland or near farmland in the town. And the way the roads were laid out it left a lot of land in between those roads to be worked up. It was quite a change."

Haskell: I guess somebody asked me to run or somethin'. I don't know why. I served eight years. It must've been about '47 I ran for council. Got more votes than anybody that run. I know I was Councilman when it became a city. It became a city when the '50 Census gave us 10,000 people, see.[6] That's what makes you a city. And I'd been on Council for some time.

RE-ELECT

| X | Haskell A. Jones |

Member Democratic County Central Committee
Tallmadge Vil., Precinct D
My name will appear in the lower right hand corner of the DEMOCRATIC Ballot.
PRIMARY ELECTION — TUESDAY, MAY 2, 1950
Endorsed by Regular Democratic Organization
[7]

I run the next time and got more votes than anybody that run. Anywhere. In any district. The first two or three years, I went as a council at large. Everybody in town could vote for council at large. And I beat everybody that run in Tallmadge. We had a Presidential election. I got more votes in the town than the President counted that was elected President. I got more votes than him. I run four years and I got more votes every time than anybody that run in the town or for any county office in the town.

Was nothin' but a hole down there where that "Y" [YMCA] is. That belonged to the Ritchie family and there wasn't anything down there but two big holes. And I mean they were big holes! And water in it. One kid drowned down there that I knew. I was on Council at the time. We filled those holes. We built two ballparks in there. That one hole next to 261. Built a little clubhouse down in there. Just a basement clubhouse on the hill. And Emmett Orr finagled a guy who was a business agent of the operating engineers to get a bunch of equipment.[7]

So, they come out there on Saturdays and Sundays. Various contractors donated the equipment and the operators come and ran the equipment. They pushed the banks down in there and cut a lot of trees and got 'em out of the way. Made some ballparks there. Softball parks. That's where the kids play ball. Then, later, in the last few years, they've gone with a little more of a clubhouse. Put a top on it. It was just a basement for a long time. Then they built the Y later. I guess it's a continuing fund from the Ritchie Association to maintain the Y activities.

16A AKRON BEACON JOURNAL   Sunday, March 6, 1955

GOOD MORNING

YOU CAN'T BEAT Tallmadge Councilman Haskell Jones for getting to the bottom of things. During a discussion of an ordinance to restrict dogs from running at large, Jones pointed out that most of the complaints were about injuries to evergreens.

Referring to the law requiring muzzling of dogs on public roads or unenclosed lots he said, "So we muzzle the dogs. That won't stop the damage to the evergreens. The dogs will still run over the gardens. Maybe we're muzzling the wrong end."

FOLKS around Killbuck are beginning to look on the strange white robin that returns each year to nest in the Methodist Church yard tree as sort of a good luck omen. Last week the creamy robin soared into the village right on schedule as it has for the last three years. Mrs. Owen Smith reported that she saw the robin near her home in the company of an ordinary robin believed to be its mate. The bird usually spends the Summer within a two-block radius of the church. The robin's body is white but the ends of its wings are dark and there is a small patch of red on the lower part of its breast...

HASKELL JONES

Tallmadge Erases City Hazard
Volunteers Fill in Water Hole, Make Park
By John Fowler

TALLMADGE—A dozen bulldozer operators and $100,000 worth of equipment have eliminated this city's most feared hazard in three Sundays of free work.

Volunteers of Local 18, International Union of Operating Engineers (AFL), put and end to a water hole 14 feet deep in Tallmadge Veterans' Memorial Park. They manned contractor-donated equipment in shoving a hill into the pond . . . .

Now that the pit is filled the board is anticipating laying out a baseball diamond on the west side and a softball field on the east side . . . .

Since citizens decided to turn the park into a living memorial to the dead of all wars the ground floor of a shelter house has been built by donated funds. The

476

board expects to build a second story to the building when funds become available
. . .

Akron Beacon Journal
Monday, December 10, 1951

Haskell: Then I didn't run anymore. I was disgusted and I quit. I ran for mayor after council, but I didn't get elected. And I was glad. I'm glad now I didn't. A bus driver beat me.[8] He knew all the kids. And all the people in town knew all the kids. And they all voted for the bus driver, see. So, I was lucky I didn't get it. I was lucky I didn't get it. I'm glad. I'm glad. Very glad. Very glad. Paul Hill. Lived next door to Barton.

Dumber than an ox. But he belonged to the Boy Scouts and this, that and the other. They elected him and he couldn't've done any worse if they went all over town huntin' for a bad guy. They couldn't've done any worse. He was dumb as an ox.[9] Never did anything worthwhile. He was the mayor for two terms, I think. And they just went down the hill as far as the

HASKELL JONES
FOR MAYOR
Well Qualified
By Experience

Chief of Police . .	3½ Years
Road Supervisor . .	3½ Years
Fireman	15 Years
Councilman-at-Large .	8 Years

Tallmadge Resident Since 1926
DEMOCRAT

town was concerned. We lost it.[10] But, in the meantime, I'm workin' the electric trade and I don't want to be bothered with these guys and I don't worry about 'em or nothin' else.

Marjorie: I think he thought that people still all knew him and that he didn't have to campaign. So he wouldn't go out and do any campaigning whatsoever and he got defeated and it hurt his feelings. At one time everybody in town did know him. But by that time, he'd been out of the police department. Of course, he'd been on city council for quite a while, but the town had grown a lot. So then not as many people knew him as he thought.

CHAPTER FIFTY-ONE

RETROSPECTIVE

"When you get to be 91, ain't no use to bullshit yourself, you're getting old."
Haskell Jones
March 29, 1990

Haskell and Florence Jones in their garden, Tallmadge, Ohio.

Haskell: I went back to construction work doin' electric work from then on for first one thing and another. I worked for many different companies. Short time. Long time. Worked for one outfit nine years and lost two days on account of no work. I'd go home early if the work was scarce. After I'd finish a job I'd go home early. But I had good work. So I made out all right.

Stayed with the electrical work for twenty years and retired an old man. Seventy-three years old when I retired. Well, I wouldn't say it thataway. I was not seventy-three when I retired, I was seventy-three when I officially retired. The last year I didn't work. I only paid my dues and when my name'd come up for a job, I'd turn it down. You get to do that and go back to the bottom of the list, see, 'til I got my twenty years service in. Then I quit and got my pension. Man, that was one of my lucky days. Gettin' a hundred and seventy dollars a month pension. It helps out a whole lot. Puts a little butter on your bread. Started keepin' house and workin' the garden. That's about it.

Florence Jones

"When I visit her at the nursing home, she's either tied into a chair or on a bed. If she's gonna' die, she's gonna die in my arms."

Haskell A Jones
February 11, 1983

Following a fall at home and a broken hip, Florence's health rapidly declined, leaving Haskell to take care of her. Over numerous stays at area nursing facilities, first her memories were stolen from her, then her dignity. Finally, even her false teeth, which she had been so proud of, were stolen. She passed away on July 17, 1984. She was 88 years, 3 months, 9 days old.

Haskell: She had a kidney problem. She had leukemia. She fell and got hurt a couple times. So she had a combination of things. She couldn't take anesthetic. She had some anesthetic and it knocked her out every time. Every time. Well, she had two of these hip operations and had to be under anesthetic for a long time. They just absolutely ruined her. They— She couldn't take it.

They never said Alzheimer's. Never. Nobody mentioned that. But she got to where she was unreasonable to live with. You couldn't imagine how bad. I tried, but I couldn't make it. I got help. I got girls come in here two or three times a week to clean her up and clean the bed and everything. She was so damned contrary, she wouldn't cooperate in any manner with me. I couldn't do anything with her.

She was out here at Edwin Shaw for two months. I went every day. Most days, twice went out there. Every day. Every day and never missed one. But most time, I'd go in the morning and again toward the evening. Did all I could do. Took her out for walks and rides— She had to go in a wheelchair. She couldn't walk. Pushed her all over that area. I don't think she was mentally alert enough to appreciate it at all, see. Which made it bad. But she was a good woman. She'd done a good job. She should've killed me long ago, but she didn't do it.

We made out. We enjoyed each other many, many years. We worked our butts off to try to feed the kids and ourselves. And we managed to do it. Raised three nice kids. Grandchildren. Great-grandchildren. That's a little spot in the history of the world, right there. Just a little bit, you know. It wasn't much. But we wasn't ashamed of it. We lived together some million years and didn't have any problems we couldn't surmount. Sixty-four years and six months exactly.

* * *

In April of 1990, Tallmadge Grange No. 2589 recognized Haskell Jones with its Community Citizen Award for his service as the last marshal, first chief of police, village road superintendent, head of civil defense, volunteer fireman, city councilman, member of the city charter commission (which determined the form of government Tallmadge now has) and, even after his "retirement," city electrical inspector and member of the city planning and zoning commission.[1]

"It's in a nice folder," Haskell would later comment. "Plastic and so forth. Nice. Then some of the people got up and told what they thought of me. Which I paid 'em to before the thing started. It cost me a lot of money." For that occasion, his daughter Marjorie penned the following tribute:

> I see in Sunday's paper that a book titled "Everything I Ever Need to Know I Learned in Kindergarten" is still on the best-seller list. If that were true for everyone, being a product of the Tallmadge school system in the days before kindergarten was provided, I'd be up the proverbial creek. Fortunately, I didn't miss much, though, for I learned everything I need to know from my father, Haskell Jones.
>
> I learned to treasure books and music, to try new things, to enjoy people who were unique, and to keep my lawn mowed. I learned to weather adversity, to hold my head high, to use my brain, and to love trees.
>
> He also taught me to give a full day's work for my pay. If he hadn't done such a good job of that, I might be with you tonight. Instead, I was at work today in Clearwater, Florida preparing twenty-three first graders for their first formal achievement testing, and trying to pass on some of the lessons my father taught me.
>
> I'm very proud that you have chosen my father as Citizen of the Year. To me, though, he's Citizen of the Century!
>
> Very truly yours,
> Marjorie (Jones) Knapp

Haskell: Settin' here, I don't feel any different than I did when I was fifty. But when I get up and try to walk, I know I'm older. Balance is bad. I stagger and fall around. I've got to watch myself <u>awful</u> close that I don't fall. Awful close! Umh! I

head down into the basement, I got to watch I don't fall off of the damn steps. And right here, I might start over there and I lose my balance and have a little time of gettin' my balance back. But part of life, I guess. I don't cry about it. I laugh about it. Walk out to the mailbox in the wintertime to get the mail and there's snow on the ground. Turn around to walk back and I said, "Look where you walked." All over the driveway, you know.

I use a cane most of the time. I'm a little unsteady when I first get up in the morning than I am later in the day. I get a little more acclimated, I guess. Fell twice. I fell down in Kentucky and I fell down in Florida. Lucky I didn't get killed both times. Umh! But settin' here, I feel perfectly normal. At ease. Nothin' botherin' me. So I guess you'd call me a "sittin' duck." Sittin' here. Sittin' here. Sittin' here. Sittin' here all the time. I still like to work. I go out and run my mower. I can run it for hours. I come in, I'm tired. But it don't particularly bother me or anything like that.

I run that tiller in that garden this year and come out of there and my arms tired. And butt tired. And legs tired and everything else. Physically, I'm kinda' busted up. But I keep goin'. What the hell? Umh! So— Can't go on forever. Some morning, I'll wake up dead and I'll say, "What the hell happened?" The doctor, last time I was there said, "Your heart is beatin' perfect and your blood pressure's perfect." But I wake up in the morning a lot of times (and sometimes when I go to bed) and that heart's goin' "Boom-boom-boom-boom. Boom-boom-boom-boom-boom." Just racin', you know. Don't hurt. Don't hurt me a bit. Kinda' alarms me a little bit sometimes. They put me in the hospital one time on account of that about ten years ago. Fifteen. So what? Time keeps rollin' by. They say you can't stay here forever.

My dad told me about a man that worked for them when he was a kid. He was a horse trainer. I think he worked for them. Or, if not, for a neighbor. Man who broke wild horses for people and stuff like that. But he went to work for some farmer around there. And he had an old mule. Old mule. He'd been out and worked and at noon or in the evenin' he's comin' in from the field or somethin'. He's settin' sideways on this old mule. And the old mule stumbled over somethin', threw him off against a tree and killed him.

This man is an— This man is an expert horseman, but he's careless. He's settin' up there, ridin' along, relaxed, and the old mule dumps him off and he happened to hit a tree. It's part of fate. You don't know when you're gonna' go. Might be this quick. You don't know. I don't want to live in a rest home. The hell with that. The day they want to take me to a rest home, I want 'em to take me to a bridge somewhere so I can jump off.

Oh, well, so what? We went around. It's a great life. But we've lived

it a long time. We've had good times and bad. Never bothered me. I don't have any regrets. I don't worry about it. I think about, "Boy, you was lucky. You was lucky. You was lucky. You were a little bit smart a few times, but lucky all the time." In other words, I say, "I have covered the waterfront." Some of it was full of sticks.

But I had a lot of fun in my life, I'll tell ya'. I liked a lot of people and I knew a lot of people. A million of 'em. A million of 'em. And people liked me—'cause I didn't bother 'em. I helped 'em if I could. I did what I could. Was kinda' congenial in help. Information-wise or labor-wise or anything else. If I could help 'em, I helped 'em. Some of 'em, I didn't agree with everything they did, but I didn't hate 'em because of that. I figured that's their business. Not mine. If they bothered me, I fought 'em. If I could whip 'em, I did. And sometimes I didn't win. But that's the way life goes.

Oh, a lot of water's gone under the dam. Oooh, oooh, ooooh, ooooh, ooooh, ooooh, oooh! And I lived in the best years this country will ever see. They'll have more sophisticated machinery and equipment and every-thing else in the world from now on than I'll ever know of or heard of or thought of. But they'll never have the freedom we had. The ambition we had. Now, I got along with no education because I came at a time when all they wanted was muscle. But that time is gone, see. They don't need that muscle. They got a machine doin' that muscle now. They need somebody that can think. In today's market, I couldn't've made it.

Ahh, I've walked the waterfront and I don't— I don't have any regrets. Some things I've had to do, I wouldn't do or I'd do 'em better —or more of it. But life goes on. When I'm gone, I'll be forgotten in ten years. Nobody'll say, "Wonder whatever become of that old guy? He's been dead, ain't he?" "He's dead." "Yeah, I think he's dead." "I ain't too sure, but I— I never heard about him dyin'. But he died, I think." And they're gone. They're forgotten. Generations are forgotten. Generations. You know, when your old grandfather dies, a lot of history is gonna' go down the drain. I don't know whether you can use it or not, but I hope you can. Someday.

I kinda' believe in Abou Ben Adhem. Did you ever read Abou Ben Adhem? I can't repeat it. I can give a little bit of history of this. He woke up one night and the angel was in his bedroom. The angel was writing. And he asked what the angel was writing. And the angel said, "I'm writing the ones who love the Lord." And the angel writes. Abou said, "Write me up as a man who loves his fellow man. "So the next night the angel comes back to read the list of people who love the Lord. And he said, "Does my name appear in this list?" The angel said, "No, but you're the top of the list. Because you are the man who loves his fellow man." So it goes like that. I can't get it verbatim. It's in one of these readers.

Yeah. Abou Ben Adhem. May his tribe increase. It was a good poem. I don't know who wrote it. I can't remember. But I subscribe to that theory—that I love my fellow man. I loved everybody. I never hated anybody. I didn't mistreat anybody too bad—I don't think. Some people who mistreated me, I tried to hate 'em, but I couldn't. They were only human. And humans are subject to all kinds of problems of every kind. I think the man that loves his fellow man and does what he can for his fellow man has got some place to go. May not get on the front seat, but I think he'll get in there anyway. So if I don't get there, why, they can tell me I tried. It's a great life. But it's about over. And I know that, too.

Naah, life's been good to me. I've laughed. I've laughed. Enjoyed every inch of it. Ain't nothin' we can do about it anymore. Part of life. Part of life. I've told you everything I know. Twice. Shut that recorder off. You're drivin' me to drink.

ABOU BEN ADHEM (may his tribe increase!)
Awoke one night from a deep dream of peace,
And saw within the moonlight in his room,
Making it rich and like a lily in bloom,
An angel writing in a book of gold.

Exceeding peace had made Ben Adhem bold;
And to the presence in the room he said,
"What writest thou?" The vision raised its head,
And, with a look made of all sweet accord,
Answered, "The names of those who love the Lord."

"And is mine one?" said Abou. "Nay, not so,"
Replied the angel. Abou spoke more low,
But cheerily still; and said, "I pray thee, then,
Write me as one that loves his fellow-men."

The angel wrote, and vanished. The next night
It came again, with a great wakening light,
And showed the names whom love of God had blessed;
And, lo! Ben Adhem's name led all the rest.[2]

—James Henry Leigh Hunt

EPILOGUE

Haskell: I dreamed I was workin' on a construction job of some kind and it was terribly muddy. Me and some other fellow that I have known in the background some time. And the boss, the big-shot, came and he wanted us to come to his house. So, we went and I got through the front door and my shoes were so muddy I couldn't come in the house. I scraped and scraped and I finally got inside and I— There was a couch or daybed or somethin' just inside of an entry and I sat on that and with a spoon I would scrape for an hour gettin' the mud off my shoes. They were terrible! And finally, they said come out to dinner. I don't remember the other guy. He disappeared in the meantime. I don't remember him bein' in after that.

But I went in and I told the lady I had to wash my hands. And I felt this was the most elegant house I've ever been in my life. Everything in it was out of this world. I'd never seen anything like it in my life. So, they had two little boys— And the little boy was gonna' show me where to wash and he went around and through the dining room to a stairway that went upstairs and he told me there was a bath up there. And by the stairway was a little half-bath.

Oooooh, was it— It was outfitted with the most elegant stuff you ever saw. My hands were muddy. I just went in there and washed my hands and I hated to dry on the towel. Everything was so exquisite, you know.

So, I went back to the table. Everybody else was seated, but I went back to the table. When I sat down, they had a steak this long and about this thick and that was the whole meal for everybody. Beautiful!

Beautiful! Best lookin' steak I ever looked at. And all at once I remembered I didn't have my teeth.

Man! I felt bad that I sat there and I— I didn't want to say I didn't have 'em. I didn't know how I was gonna' make out with that meat. It was a killer! But they gave me a piece of meat and I can remember that I could eat it because it was so tender. It was so nice. I told Mom [Florence] from now on, "I'm gonna' put my teeth in and sleep with 'em in. I might get invited out to eat." Oh, man, that was a dandy!

* * *

Haskell: I can't put it together very good. I dreamed I was in the Goodyear workin'. And I had dreamed about that several times. I always get lost in that factory in my dreams—mammoth big factory. I couldn't get out of there.

I dreamed a half dozen times that I worked at Goodyear. Never rang a clock card. Everybody else rang the clock card. I just walked through the card rack, went on down. Every week I got paid. Never turned in any time, just continually got paid. I've dreamed that half a dozen times.

Last night I was millin' around. I didn't seem to have anything to do. I was kind of a "squad man" or handyman. Everybody else seemed to be busy, but I wasn't doin' anything. Just millin' around 'til finally, the foreman said, "Every time I come down here, I'd see you standin' around and wonder why." I said, "Well, nobody tells me what to do. So without some instructions, I can't just start to work." "O.K.," he said. And away he went. He didn't say any more.

So, finally, somebody brought me a bag of papers—leather bag with the newspapers that was supposed to go to each office in the shop. But I didn't know where the offices were. I didn't know where to look for 'em. I didn't know how to begin. So, I didn't do anything. I just walked around with that bag on my shoulder. Finally, I tried to get out of there at four o'clock. Couldn't find my way out. And I asked some old "gooney" at the top of the steps about gettin' out of there and he started tellin' me a big story about a twenty-three-foot fish his wife saw. I was a little perturbed with him so I walked away. I don't know whether I ever got out or not. That was about the end of it. I just woke up. I'm still there, as far as I know.

I was born to work, I guess, because that's— That's what I dream about more than anything else—workin'.

* * *

Summit Beach Park, where Haskell, Hoolie, Hound Leg and the other rubber workers spent their free time has been closed and demolished for decades. Four concession stands and a warehouse in the shuttered park were burned by vandals in the winter of 1959-60. To prevent the same fate to the wooden roller coaster, the owners had it torn down the following July. Wreckers were not as quick with the roller rink. It burned later the same month. Fearing the same end for the remainder of the park, it was completely leveled, the property eventually sold for low-income housing.[1] Some say the old grounds are haunted.[2]

Most of the rubber industry for which Haskell and the others worked is long gone, as well. Due to outdated facilities, union demands, corporate raiders, restructuring and recalls, tire manufacturing in the one time "Rubber Capital of the World" slowly ceased and moved elsewhere.[3] Massive, painful layoffs occurred, plants were shuttered and then demolished. Even the corporate headquarters were relocated.

General Tire, where son Donald Jones had found employment after returning from World War II, was the first to move in 1978. B.F. Goodrich followed suit in 1986. Firestone Tire & Rubber, where Donald found employment after General, left in 1987, only to be bought out by the Bridgestone Corporation, a Japanese company.[4] That left the corporate offices of Goodyear Tire & Rubber Company as the only standing evidence that tires had ever been built in Akron.[5]

Finally on October 2, 1991, following a series of medical errors related to surgery for an aneurysm, Haskell Jones left Akron and Tallmadge behind. When he went into the hospital, doctors said he had the health of a 65-year old. He was 93, 2 months and 7 days old. As had been his birthday tradition, he had stood on his head one last time just two months before. He rests at the Tallmadge cemetery next to Florence, his days of work over.

Today, the Old Town Hall and Police Department in Tallmadge is a museum with limited hours. The new Town Hall and City Police Department both sit, literally, on the footprint of the home in which Haskell and Florence raised their children while he served as the entire police force. Like other parts of the country, the economy has not been kind to the area.

As the area weathered the last of yet another recession, Akron, unfortunately, led the nation in the number of foreclosures in 2013.[6] As a result, many of the homes that were just being built in Goodyear Heights when Haskell, Florence, Barton and the others arrived some 100 years ago are being torn down. Among those homes were 36 West Miller, where Haskell first roomed when he moved to Akron and 678 Blaine Avenue, the home the entire extended family shared (and in which son Donald was born) before Haskell and Florence moved to Tallmadge.

"They definitely took their time with craftsmanship and workmanship," City Development Manager Abraham Westcott, Jr. noted recently of one home that had been leveled. Nonetheless, it only took the Bob Bennett Construction Company thirty-one minutes to render one into rubble. Ironically, the offspring of those who came to build the city are now employed to level it. Bennett's children (who are now running the company) are the great-grandchildren of Haskell's father, E. A Jones. Their mother, Sarah, is the daughter of Haskell's brother, Ralph.

"You are right-sizing your city because of population," City Development Manager Abraham Westcott, Jr. explained. In 2010, that population was 199,110—which hadn't been that low since 1910.[7] Before the first rubber boom began. Before the farm boys, the "singing soldiers," began to arrive by the thousands from the hills and the hollows of the South. Before Haskell Jones boarded a train with six dollars in his pocket and hope in his heart. But then, all it would take to recover is another boom. And, as history proves, it's happened before.

"ça va"

ABOUT THE AUTHOR

Tom Jones was born in Akron, Ohio when it was still "The Rubber Capital of the World" and the acrid smell of sulphur in the air was a matter of civic pride. Like his grandfather and his father before him, he, too, was employed at Firestone Tire & Rubber as a young man, where he helped key in thousands of dealer adjustment forms for the disastrous Firestone 500 Steel Belted Radial.

Following his graduation from Kent State University, he packed his Chevette, fled what was then rapidly becoming known as "the rustbelt" and (like his grandfather before him) headed to a boomtown—Houston. Following the collapse of the oil industry, he found employment within the advertising industry in San Antonio as a nationally award-winning copywriter.

Tom is also the author of *Waldo Maccabees, In the Footsteps of Christ*—a fictional tale of Jesus' ministry as seen through the eyes of His dog.

Tom lives in New Braunfels, Texas, with his wife, Steffanie. For questions or comments, Tom can be contacted at Tom@OnABurningDeck.com

SELECTED BIBLIOGRAPHY

Archives, Museums and Organizations
Akron Summit County Public Library, Special Collections, Akron, Ohio
Arkansas Historical Association
Graves County Schools, Mayfield, Kentucky
Kentucky Historical Society, Frankfort, Kentucky
Kentucky State Archives, Frankfort, Kentucky
Library of Congress, Washington, D.C.
National Archives and Records Administration, Washington, D.C.
Summit County Historical Society, Akron, Ohio
The University of Akron Archives
The University of Kentucky Libraries
The University of Kentucky Libraries Digital Library Services
United States Census Bureau
Washington University in St. Louis, St. Louis, Missouri

Books and Reports
A Centennial History of Akron, 1825-1925. Summit County, Ohio: Summit County Historical Society/Akron Beacon Journal Company, 1925.
A History of Tallmadge, Ohio. Tallmadge, Ohio: The Tallmadge Historical Society, 1957.
An Atlas of Graves County, Kentucky From Actual Surveys Under the Direction of B.N. Griffing. Philadelphia, PA: D.J. Lake & Co., 1880.
Biennial Report of the State Board of Health of Kentucky, 1908-1909. Louisville, Kentucky: The Continental Printing Company, 1909.
Bogart, Charles H. *Yellow Sparks Over the Bluegrass, Streetcars and Interurbans of Kentucky, Volume Two.* Frankfort, KY: Yellow Sparks Press, 2011.
Brainerd, Elizabeth and Mark V. Siegler, "The Economic Effects of the 1918 Influenza Epidemic," June 2002.
Caron's Directory of the City of Paducah. Louisville, Kentucky, Caron Directory Company, Vols. 1920-1923.
Child Welfare in Kentucky: An Inquiry by the National Child Labor Committee for the Kentucky Child Labor Association and the State Board of Health. New York: National Child Labor Committee, 1919.
City of Tallmadge, Ohio, Council Meeting Minutes. Tallmadge, Ohio: 1948-1960.
Connelly, Mark Thomas. *The Response to Prostitution in the Progressive Era.* Chapel Hill, NC: University of North Carolina Press, 1980.
Cunningham, Bill. *On Bended Knees, The True Story of the Night Rider Tobacco War in Kentucky and Tennessee.* Nashville: McClanahan Publishing House, 1983.
Davis, Judy Anne. *A History of Tallmadge Coal: A Tale of Woodchucks, Welshmen and a Canal.* Stow, Ohio, 2006. http://sc.akronlibrary.org/files/2011/09/TallmadgeCoal_.pdf
Davis, D. Trabue. *The Story of Mayfield Through a Century, 1823-1923.* Melber, Kentucky: Reprinted Simmons Historical Publications, 1990.
Endres, Kathleen L. *Rosie the Rubber Worker.* Kent, Ohio: The Kent State University Press, 2000.
Firestone, The Colossus of Roads. A Visit With the Firestone Organization, Its Men, Its Factory, Its Branches. (Approximately 1916, No Copyright Date or Location of Publication)
Francis, Diane DeMali and David W. Francis, *Summit Beach Park: Akron's Coney Island.* Akron: Summit County Historical Society, 1993.
Glazier, Jack. Been Coming Through Some Hard Times. Race, History, and Memory in Western Kentucky. Knoxville: The University of Tennessee Press, 2012.

Grismer, Karl H. *Akron and Summit County*. Akron: Summit County Historical Society, c. 1950.

Hunt, James Henry Leigh, "Abou Ben Adhem." As quoted in "Lesson XXVI. Abou Ben Adhem," Wm. H. McGuffey, LL.D., *McGuffey's Fifth Eclectic Reader, Revised Edition* (New York, Cincinnati, Chicago: American Book Company, H.H. Vail, 1920).

Johnson, Susan Allyn. "Industrial Voyagers: A Case Study of Appalachian Migration to Akron, Ohio. 1900-1940. Dissertation. Ohio State University, 2006.

Klotter, James C. *Kentucky, Portrait In Paradox, 1900-1950*, Kentucky Historical Society, Frankfort, Kentucky, 1996.

Lewis, Clarice Finley. *A History of Firestone Park*. Akron: Firestone Park Citizens Council 20th Anniversary 1966-1986.

Lightning, The History of the 78th Infantry Division. Nashville: The Battery Press, 2000.

Love, Steve and David Giffels, *Wheels of Fortune, The Story of Rubber in Akron*. Akron, Ohio: The University of Akron Press, 1999.

Lucas, Marion Brunson and George C. Wright, *A History of Blacks in Kentucky: Pursuit of Equality, 1890-1980, Volume 2*. Kentucky Historical Society, The University Press of Kentucky, 1992.

Lucas, Marion B. "Kentucky Blacks: The Transition from Slavery to Freedom," *The Register of the Kentucky Historical Society, Vol. 91, No. 4* (Autumn 1993), pp. 403-419. Accessed September 17, 2014. Article Stable URL: http://www.jstor.org/stable/23383193

Marshall, Suzanne. *Violence in the Black Patch of Kentucky and Tennessee*. Columbia, Missouri: University of Missouri Press, 1994.

Meyer, Bruce M. *The Once and Future Union, The Rise and Fall of the United Rubber Workers*, 1935-1995. Akron, Ohio: The University of Akron Press, 2002.

Mills, Hubert Howard. "The History of Education Of Graves County," Thesis, University of Kentucky, Graduate School, College of Education (Lexington, KY: 1928).

Moore, Lucas. *Twelfth Biennial Report of the Bureau of Agriculture, Labor, and Statistics of The State of Kentucky*. Louisville, Kentucky: The Geo. G. Fetter Printing Company, 1897.

Newhall, Elizabeth Bliss. "Schools," *Child Welfare in Kentucky: An Inquiry by the National Child Labor Committee for the Kentucky Child Labor Association and the State Board of Health*. New York: National Child Labor Committee, 1919.

Official Akron City Directory Supplemented by Directories of Barberton, Kenmore and Cuyahoga Falls. Akron: Burch Directory Company, Vols. 1917-1946.

O'Reilly, Maurice. *The Goodyear Story*. Elmsford, New York: The Benjamin Company, Inc., 1983.

Public Education in Kentucky, A Report by the Kentucky Educational Commission, Prepared Under the Direction of the General Education Board. New York: General Education Board, 1921.

"Report and Recommendations of the Paducah Vice Commission." Paducah, Kentucky, 1916, 44.

Rubber, Its History and Development. Akron, Ohio: The Firestone Tire and Rubber Company, 1922.

Simmons, Don. *Graves County Newspaper Genealogical Abstracts,* Melber, Kentucky: Simmons Historical Publications, 1988-1993.

"Tom Tinker," *Graves County, Kentucky*. Paducah, Kentucky: Turner Publishing Company, 2001.

Tully, John. *The Devil's Milk*. New York: Monthly Review Press, 2011.

Village of Tallmadge, Ohio, Council Meeting Minutes. Tallmadge, Ohio: 1936-1944.

Waldrep, Christopher. *Night Riders. Defending Community in The Black Patch, 1890-1915*. Durham and London: Duke University Press, 1993.

Walsh, Rita. *The World War II Ordnance Department's Government-Owned Contractor-Operated (GOCO) Industrial Facilities: Ravenna Ordnance Plant Historic Investigation*. U.S. Army Materiel Command Historic Context Series Report of Investigations, Number 7A. Gray & Pape, Inc., Under subcontract to Geo-Marine, Inc. Plano, Texas, 1995.

Which Shall it be Home or Hovel? Akron: Goodyear Heights Realty Company, 1918.

Wolf, Howard and Ralph Wolf. *Rubber, A Story of Glory and Greed.* New York: Covici Friede Publishers, 1936.

Wright, George C. *Racial Violence in Kentucky, 1865-1940, Lynchings, Mob Rule, and "Legal Lynchings."* Baton Rouge: Louisiana State University Press, 1990.

Newspapers

The *Akron Beacon Journal,* Akron, Ohio

The Mayfield *Daily Messenger,* Mayfield, Kentucky

The Mayfield *Saturday Messenger,* Mayfield, Kentucky

The Mayfield *Weekly Messenger,* Mayfield, Kentucky

The *Paducah Sun,* Paducah, Kentucky

Websites

Ancestry.com

Books.Google.com

ChroniclingAmerica.com

Ebay.com

FindAGrave.com

Newspapers.com

NOTES

ABBREVIATIONS USED

ABJ	*Akron Beacon Journal*, Akron, Ohio
ACD	*Official Akron City Directory Supplemented by Directories of Barberton, Kenmore and Cuyahoga Falls*
BLEW	"The City That Blew Itself Up," *The American Mercury*, February 11ᵗʰ, 1926.
BRAIN	Brainerd, Elizabeth and Mark V. Siegler, "The Economic Effects of the 1918 Influenza Epidemic," June 2002.
CAR	*Caron's Directory for the City of Paducah*
CEN	*A Centennial History of Akron, 1825-1925*
CITY	"Minutes," Tallmadge City Council
CON	Mark Thomas Connelly, *The Response to Prostitution in the Progressive Era*
CWK	*Child Welfare in Kentucky: An Inquiry by the National Child Labor Committee for the Kentucky Child Labor Association and the State Board of Health*
DAV	Judy Anne Davis, *A History of Tallmadge Coal: A Tale of Woodchucks, Welshmen and a Canal*
EQUA	Marion Brunson Lucas, George C. Wright, *A History of Blacks in Kentucky: Pursuit of Equality, 1890-1980, Volume 2*
FRAN	Diane DeMali Francis and David W. Francis, *Summit Beach Park: Akron's Coney Island*
GRIS	Karl H. Grismer, *Akron and Summit County*
HOME	*Which Shall it be Home or Hovel?* Akron: Goodyear Heights Realty Company, 1918.
JOH	Susan Allyn Johnson. "Industrial Voyagers: A Case Study of Appalachian Migration to Akron, Ohio, 1900-1940." Dissertation. Ohio State University, 2006.
KLO	James C. Klotter, *Kentucky, Portrait in Paradox*
LAW	Frank E. Lawrence, *About Old Tallmadge*
LIEF	Alfred Lief, *The Firestone Story, A History of the Firestone Tire & Rubber Company*
LUCAS	Lucas, Marion B. "Kentucky Blacks: The Transition from Slavery to Freedom," The Register of the Kentucky Historical Society, Vol. 91, No. 4.
LUCAS/WRIGHT	Lucas, Marion Brunson and George C. Wright, *A History of Blacks in Kentucky: Pursuit of Equality, 1890-1980, Volume 2.*
MAR	Suzanne Marshall, *Violence in the Black Patch of Kentucky and Tennessee.*
MDM	*The Daily Messenger*, Mayfield, Kentucky
MEM	*Memories of Tallmadge. Recalling Our Past; Celebrating Our Bicentennial (1807-2007)*
MILLS	Hubert Howard Mills, *"The History of Education Of Graves County"*
MIT	H.H. Mitchell, M.D. "Health, School Hygiene," *Child Welfare in Kentucky: An Inquiry by the National Child Labor Committee for the Kentucky Child Labor Association and the State Board of Health*
MDM	*The Daily Messenger*, Mayfield, Kentucky
MM	*Mayfield Messenger*, Mayfield, Kentucky
MSM	*The Saturday Messenger*, Mayfield, Kentucky
MWM	*The Weekly Messenger*, Mayfield, Kentucky

NEW   Elizabeth Bliss Newhall, "Schools," *Child Welfare in Kentucky: An Inquiry by the National Child Labor Committee for the Kentucky Child Labor Association and the State board of Health*

NYT   *The New York Times*, New York

NS   *The News Scimitar*, Memphis

ORE   Maurice O'Reilly, *The Goodyear Story*

PDS   *The Paducah Daily Sun*

PEK   *Public Education in Kentucky. A Report by the Kentucky Educational Commission. Prepared Under the Direction of the Commission by the General Education Board.*

PES   *The Paducah Evening Sun*

PS   *The Paducah Sun*

REP   *Report and Recommendations of the Paducah Vice Commission*, Paducah, Kentucky, 1916.

ROB   John E.L. Robertson and Ann E. Robertson, *Paducah, Kentucky, A History*, The History Press, Charleston, SC (2014).

RRPVC   "Report and Recommendations of the Paducah Vice Commission"

SIHH   *A Survey of Industrial Health Hazards, Ohio State Board of Health, February 1915*

SIM   Don Simmons, *Graves County Newspaper Genealogical Abstracts*

SKR   Quentin R. Skrabec, Jr. *Rubber. An American Industrial History*. Jefferson, North Carolina: McFarland & Company, 2014

TALL   *A History of Tallmadge Ohio*

TULL   John Tully, *The Devil's Milk*

VILL   Village of Tallmadge, Ohio, Council Meeting Minutes

WAL   Walsh, Rita. *The World War II Ordnance Department's Government-Owned Contractor-Operated (GOCO) Industrial Facilities: Ravenna Ordnance Plant Historic Investigation*. U.S. Army Materiel Command Historic Context Series Report of Investigations, Number 7A. Gray & Pape, Inc., Under subcontract to Geo-Marine, Inc. Plano, Texas, 1995.

WHE   Steve Love and David Giffels, *Wheels of Fortune, The Story of Rubber in Akron*

WOLF   Howard and Ralph Wolf, *Rubber, A Story of Glory and Greed*

WOOL   Edward Mott Wooley, "Akron: Standing Room Only!"

WRIGHT   Wright, George C. *Racial Violence in Kentucky, 1865-1940, Lynchings, Mob Rule, and "Legal Lynchings."*

FRONTPIECE
[1] Lesson LV. "Casabianca," Wm. H. McGuffey, LL.D., *McGuffey's New Fourth Eclectic Reader* (Cincinnati: Winthrop B. Smith & Co., New York: Clark, Austin, Maynard & Co., 1857), 173-174.

PREFACE
[1] James N. Gregory, *The Southern Diaspora, How the Great Migrations of Black and White Southerners Transformed America* (Chapel Hill: The University of North Carolina Press, 2005), 4.

[2] Gregory, ibid, 78. "In fact, white out-migrants outnumbered blacks during every decade and usually by a very large margin. In the Great Migration era of the early twentieth century, when African Americans moved north for the first time in large numbers and established much-noticed communities in the major cities, less-noticed white southerners actually outnumbered them roughly two to one." James N. Gregory, *The Southern Diaspora, How the Great Migrations of Black and White Southerners Transformed America* (Chapel Hill: The University of North Carolina Press, 2005), 15.

[3] JOH, pg. 18.
[4] JOH, pg. 8.
[5] TULL, 52.

INTRODUCTION

[1]   http://aconerlycoleman.wordpress.com/2010/02/21/james-baldwins-reaction-to-malcolm-xs-assassination-feb-21-1965/ Accessed March 7, 2012.
[2] TULL, 144.

CHAPTER ONE: "HILLBULLIES

[1] WRIGHT, 190.
[2] Tandy Ellis, *Report of the Adjutant General of the State of Kentucky, Confederate Volunteers, War 1861- 1865* (Frankfort, 1915); M. Juliette Magee, *Ballard's Brave Boys* (Wickliffe, Ky., 1974), 25; Lowell H. Harrison and James C. Klotter. *A New History of Kentucky* [Lexington, 1997), 195. As cited by Berry F. Craig. "The Jackson Purchase Considers Secession: The 1861 Mayfield Convention." *The Register of the Kentucky Historical Society, Vol. 99, No. 4* (Autumn 2001), 360-361. Accessed September 15, 2014, http://www.jacksonpurchase history.org/wp-content/uploads/2011/02/Craig3.pdf
[3] LUCAS, 411-412.
[4] Robert M. Ireland. "The Debate over Whipping Criminals in Kentucky." *The Register of the Kentucky Historical Society. Vol. 100, No. 1* (Winter 2002), pp. 25. Accessed September 18, 2014. Article Stable URL: http://www.jstor.org/stable/23384457; Generally supported by Democrats and opposed by Republicans, legalized whipping ceased with the adoption of a new general criminal statute enacted after the adoption of a new constitution in 1891. Ireland, 21; Although whipping ceased to be a legal alternative after 1891, this did not mean that it ceased to be a practice. Just as the illegal lynching became legal lynching, the judiciary in Mayfield found creative ways around the law. Instead of having the justice system administer the whipping, they prevailed upon the parent to do so. "Roosevelt Purdue, a 13 year old negro boy who stole a bicycle from the drug store of Evans and Covington recently, was allowed to go free from jail Wednesday afternoon but not until he had felt the effect of fifty licks from a buggy whip laid on with a lavish hand by his mother, who lives in Fulton, and who came to do a good job and get her son out of prison. The lash was so effectively applied that the young negro could not occupy a chair with much ease and pleasure following the last application of the raw hide instrument. It was the order of the court that the boy be released from further prosecution provided the mother would apply the lash. The 'impressive' ceremony was performed in the county court room, the only eye witness who acted as referee being Deputy Jailer Jim Byrne and he says the woman certainly did a good job of it. The act occurred at 2:15." "Negro Boy Released When His Mother Applies a Buggy Whip." *MDM*, March 24, 1915, Vol. XIV, No. 163, 1.
[5] Relations between the races would not see immediate improvement within the Bluegrass State. Kentucky was the next to last state to ratify the 13th amendment abolishing slavery—in 1976, some 111 years after its passage. Only Mississippi surpassed this record, officially voicing its approval in 1995. Greg Kocher, "Kentucky Supported Lincoln's Efforts to Abolish Slavery—111 Years Late." *The Lexington Herald Leader*, February 23, 2013. Accessed September 3, 2014. http://www.kentucky.com/2013/02/23/2528807/kentucky-supported-lincolns-efforts.html
[6] LUCAS/WRIGHT, 79-80; Author Lucas posits a substantially higher number of lynchings in another work, noting, "One black-owned newspaper placed the number of blacks murdered in Kentucky between 1869 and 1885 at 1,405" Louisville *Commercial*, July 21, 1870; E.H. Fairchild, *Baccalaureate Sermon by E.H. Fairchild, of Berea College, Preached, June 30, 1878* (Boston 1878), 7; Louisville *Bulletin*, September 24, 1881; New York *Freeman*, July 3, November 27, 1886. As cited in LUCAS, 403-419.

[7] WRIGHT, 251.

[8] "Wore Masks. Henry Finney, Colored, Riddled With Buckshot." *PDS*, Vol. 1, No. 85, Saturday, December 19, 1896, 1; "Third Outbreak. Mayfield Mob Follows Murder With Arson." *PDS*, Vol. 1, No. 87, Tuesday, December 22, 1896, 1; "A Mob's Awful Work. A Mob's Lawless Deeds Bring on a Race War. Over at Mayfield. Armed Men Patrol the Streets and a Fight is Momentarily Expected. Both Races Are Now Fully Organized." *Weekly Kentucky New Era, Volume XXVII, No. 26, Friday, December 25, 1896, 2.* Accessed October 23, 2014.

[9] "All Mayfield Under Arms. Excitement Over the Kentucky Race War." *NYT*, December 24, 1896.

[10] "Peace Reigns at Mayfield," *NYT*, December 25, 1896.

[11] LUCAS/WRIGHT, 84.

[12] Cooler heads would prevail once again in June 1905, to prevent the lynching in Mayfield of Charley Parker, believed to be guilty of killing engineer John Bobbitt. In the face of a mob, Judge Webb ordered Sheriff J.N. Harris to transfer Parker to an unknown location until he could be tried in a calmer atmosphere. "Parker Taken Away on Indication of Mob." *MDM*, Vol. V, No. 269, Wednesday, June 14, 1905, 1.

[13] WRIGHT, 1. This armed stand in defense of their homes and families by the black population may well have prevented the expulsion of blacks from the county that occurred in adjacent Marshall County in 1908. In 2007, the black population in Marshall County stood at 37, while that of Graves County was 1,600. Elliot Jaspin, *Buried in the Bitter Waters: The Hidden History of Racial Cleansing in America.* (New York: Basic Books, 2007), 7.

[14] "The Complete 1898 Lynching Report," Historical Crime Detective, http://www.historicalcrimedetective.com/the-complete-1898-lynching-report/ Accessed August 7, 2016.

[15] The historical record spells his last name both as "Mathias" and "Mathis." "Arraigned, Tried, Convicted and Executed in Fifty-Five Minutes." "Speedy Justice for Allen Mathis," *PES*, Vol. XVIII, No. 186, Wednesday, August 1, 1906, 1, 4.

[16] "Coming After a Hangman's Rope." *MDM*, Vol. IX, No. 134, Thursday, June 10, 1909, 1; "Scaffold Ready for Next Victim of the Civil Law. Constable A.C. Shelton Will Construct Instrument of Death. Will Be Left Standing for Next Term. Rope Purchased by Sheriff." *PES*, Saturday, June 12, 1909, 1.

[17] In addition to *The Daily Messenger* (which began operations in 1900), there were three other papers published in Mayfield at the time, "the *Mirror*, a semi-weekly, the *Index Democrat*, a weekly, and the *Monitor*, a weekly." Being the only daily published in Mayfield, the *Messenger* was not a paying concern and was about to be shuttered until it was sold to J.R. Lemon and W.K. Wall on April 16, 1901. Under their direction, the paper steadily grew from some 200 subscribers in 1900 to nearly 1,000 by 1909. *The Weekly Messenger*, first published on May 9, 1901, required a press run of over 3,500 copies over the same time. "Eighth Anniversary Under Present Management," *MDM*, Vol. IX, No. 86, Friday, April 16, 1909, 1; On Tuesday, July 6th, 1909 the *Daily* and *Weekly Monitor* ceased publication in Mayfield, leaving *The Messenger* (which eventually published *The Daily Messenger*, *The Saturday Messenger* and *The Weekly Messenger*) the only newspaper in Mayfield. "Editor W.K. Wall Makes An Assignment." *MDM*, Vol. IX, No. 156, Tuesday, July 6, 1909, 1; "Secured Hangman's Rope." *MDM*, Vol. IX, No. 135, Friday, June 11, 1909, 1.

[18] MILLS, 6.

[19] MAR, 113.

[20] MAR, 114. Steven Laurence Danver, *Revolts, Protests, Demonstrations, and Rebellions in American History, Volume 1*, "Black Patch War (1909)". (Santa Barbara, California: ABC-CLIO, LLC, 2011), 698.

[21] R.R. Hubbard, "Night Riders and Hillbillies: The Kentucky Tobacco War," Saturday, March 20, 2010. SnusCentral.org. http://www.snuscentral.org/feck-rr-hubbard/kentucky-

tobacco-war-american-tobacco-trust-imperial-tobacco-war-on-tobacco.html/ Accessed July 9, 2011; "Black Patch War." Tennessee4me. http://www.tn4me.org/article.cfm/era _id/6/major_id/20/minor_id/56/a_id/139 Accessed July 9, 2011; "Night Riders & The Equity" http://www.nkyviews.com/Other/text_night_rider%20movement.htm/ Accessed July 9, 2011.

[22] "A Common Scene." *MSM*, Vol. V, No. 245, Saturday, May 27, 1905, 1.

[23] "Four Big Barns Now in Ashes." *MDM*, Vol. IX, No. 82, Monday, April 12, 1909, 1. This is not to say that Mayfield was totally immune. As late as 1920, when most of the nightrider activities throughout the state had passed into history, "the lawless element among the farmers burned a loose leaf chute in Mayfield, Ky., on April 7, 1920." Report of the Federal Trade Commission on the Tobacco Industry: December 11, 1920. Government Printing Office. Washington: 1921, 127-28. The destruction of the barns and their contents was indeed the direct result of arson. However, a subsequent trial found that the motive was to collect the insurance money, which would have been more profitable than selling the contents at the prevailing market rate. "Allen v. Commonwealth," *The Southwestern Reporter*, Vol. 196, West Publishing Company, 1917, 161-69; One winking mention in the *Messenger* regarding Haskell's grandfather, Robert James, does bear mention here. "Henry Theobald left Mon. for Trigg Co. to visit for ten days. He says he wants to take one more degree in night riding and then he will return to ornagize [sic] here. Bob James, he says, will be one of the charter members." [23] *MM*, June 6, 1910. SIM *Vol. 9*, 65.

[24] MAR, 154; "Farmers Must Organize." *MWM*, Vol. No. 49, Thursday, April 4, 1907, 4; Farmers, Stand by Your Organization." *MWM*, Vol. No. 7, Thursday, May 16, 1901, 1; "Urges the Farmers to Join the Association and Aid in Advancing the Prices of Tobacco." *MWM*, Vol. No. 7, Thursday, May 16, 1901, 1; "A Few Pointers for the Farmers to Read. A Short Talk on What Tobacco Association Has Done in Way of Securing Good Prices." *MWM*, Vol. VIII, Thursday, Feb. 11, 1909, 1; "Tobacco." *MDM*, Vol. XIV, No. 69, Friday, December 4, 1914, 1.

[25] "How is This for Pistol Toting?" *MDM*, Vol. IX, No. 87, Saturday, April 17, 1909, 1.

[26] "Bootlegging Whiskey Dwindling Here," *MDM*, Vol. XIII, No. 48, Saturday, November 8, 1913, 1.

[27] "Pistols and Whisky on Easter Day," *MDM*, Vol. IX, No. 82, Monday, April 12, 1909, 1. This was hardly unique to Graves County. Addressing the Black Patch as a whole, author Suzanne Graham writes, "Malevolent behavior, vandalism, and boyish pranks were also very common in the region as they were in the South as a whole. Often bearing the brunt of such attacks were institutions of authority in the society, such as the church and the school. Adolescent and young adult white men committed these acts at community gatherings. Nearly any political meeting, religious revival, neighborhood party, or school social could be the setting for random shooting sprees outside the gatherings, loud talk, crude jokes, and bouts over honor among the young men." MAR, 98.

[28] MAR, 104.

[29] "Three Escaped. Prisoners Made a Break for Liberty at Mayfield." *PS*, Friday, July 11, 1902, 6; "A Big Jail Delivery. Several Prisoners Escaped From the Jail at Mayfield. They Filed the Steel Bars and Five Were This Morning Missing. None Are Recaptured Yet." *PS*, Saturday, July 19, 1902, 1; "Night Guard at the Jail." *PS*, Thursday, July 31, 1902, 5; "Soon Overhauled. Mayfield Prisoner Attempted to Outrun the Officer." *PS*, Monday, December 1, 1902, 1; "Jail Delivery. Frustrated at Mayfield by Prompt Act of Deputy Jailer." *PS*, Monday, October 16, 1905, 1.

[30] "The Jail is Unsafe. Guard May Be Necessary to Keep Mayfield Prisoners In. Dave Johnson of McCracken, Declined to Escape with the Others Saturday. Tom Tinker Playing Bad." *PS*, Monday, July 21, 1902, 3; "Three Prisoners Escape From the Benton Jail. Lindo Murphy Refuses to Go." *MDM*. Vol. VI, No. 96, Wednesday, November 15, 1905, 1.

[31] "Tom Tinker Lynched Here Last Night," Editorial, *MDM*, Wednesday, February 10th, 1915, 1.

[32] Ancestry.com. *1860 U.S. Federal Census - Slave Schedules* [database on-line]. Provo, UT, USA: Ancestry.com Operations Inc., 2010. Original data: United States of America, Bureau of the Census. *Eighth Census of the United States, 1860*. Washington, D.C.: National Archives and Records Administration, 1860. M653, 1,438 rolls. http://search.ancestry.com/cgi-bin/sse.dll?db=1860slaveschedules&h=1710969&ti=0&indiv=try&gss=pt Accessed July 24, 2016.

The nickname "Devil" comes courtesy of Bepgjones of Salem, Indiana who noted in personal correspondence of February 26, 2012 that, "My husband is Robert Jr., his dad was called Rob, his dad was James Glover, who was a brother to your Joseph H. who everyone called "Little Joe" As far as the "Devil Joe" nickname; I don't know if it is documented or not but that's what my husband's dad (Rob) called him. Devil Joe would have been his grandfather. Also every one of their cousins first, second and third that still live in the area all called him by that name so it has been handed down."

[33] **Haskell:** [Uncle] Tom [Jones] got killed in it. Uncle David got killed in it. Uncle James got killed in it. Uncle Len got shot up and lived about five or six years after the war was over before he died.

[Uncle] Miles [James]. He was younger than my grandfather. My grandfather was born in forty-eight and Miles, I think, was born in fifty. [ED. Census records show he would have actually been born c. 1844-5] But he died in a soldier's home.

[34] Labon Galbreath, was the brother of Florence's grandmother, Effiah (Galbreath) Jones who lived with both her and her husband, Joseph Jones, at the time of the 1860 Census (at which time Joseph is recorded as owing 31 slaves). Labon (1834-78) and "mulatto" Amanda Rives (1848-1898) would have six children together, William Rivas (aka Rives, Reeves), 1866-? Leslie T. Galbraith (1868-?), Clarence Galbreath (aka Rives, Rivas, Reeves), 1871-1914, Mamie (aka Rivas, Rives, Reeves) Galbreath-Price, 1872-1922, Sallie (aka Rivas, Rives, Rivas) Galbreath-Taylor, 1874-1928 and Thomas Rivas (aka Rives, Reeves) 1875-?

[35] *The Daily Messenger* went so far as to refer to "Col. Bob" as "one of the pioneer carpenters of the county, having come to this section away back in the 30's." "Warm Times." *MDM*, Vol. V, No. 304, Wednesday, July 26, 1905, 1; "Enlarging." *MDM*, Vol. VI, No. 40, Tuesday, September 12, 1905, 1; "Bob James Injured." *MSM*, Vol. VI, No. 133, Saturday, December 30, 1905, 1; "Guard at the Jail," *MDM*, Vol. 3, No. 282, Wednesday, July 30, 1903, 1; Or, as *The Daily Messenger* noted, "R.C. James in the past day or so, has been acting in various official capacities. He is special policeman, deputy chief of police, deputy jailer and many other deputies and specials too numerous to mention, but notwithstanding the variousness of his work he performed it all to the 'dot.'" "Acting in Many Capacities," *MDM*, Vol. 3, No. 280, Monday, July 28, 1902, 1.

[36] "Guard at the Jail," *MDM*, Vol. 3, No. 282, Wednesday, July 30, 1903, 1.

[37] **Haskell:** I used to ask mom if she was kin to Jesse James and she got real embarrassed and she was insulted. She was immediately mad. She shut up. She didn't say anything. She wasn't that type. But that embarrassed my mother. So, I kinda' believe she knew. But she didn't want to admit it.

[38] "Jail Delivery. Averted by Acting Jailer Robert (Jesse) James Friday." *MSM*, Vol. VI. No. 69. Saturday, October 14, 1905, 1; "A Frog Story." *MDM*, Vol. 3, No. 227, Saturday, May 24, 1902, 1; "Last of the Coon." *MDM*, Vol. 4, No. 15, Monday, September 22, 1902, 4.

[39] Robert James' brother, John shot two men, killing one, at a "blind tiger" he operated in 1903. "Killing," *MDM*, Tuesday, March 3rd, 1903. John's son, William James, was subsequently killed in an exchange of gunfire with sheriff's deputies in 1954. "Oak Ridger Victims of Blazing Gunfight," *Clinton Courier News*, Clinton, Tennessee, Thursday, October 28, 1954, 1.

[40] As a member of the financial court, the magistrate was considered one of the two most important positions in the county by *The Daily Messenger* (a member of the county school board being the other). "Yes, Without Exception," *MDM*, Vol. XVI, No. 239, Thursday, February 22, 1917, 1.

[41] MAR 38-39.

[42] "Sheriff's Sale for Taxes," *MDM*, Vol. XIV, No. 91, Wednesday, December 30, 1914, 3; "Notice. Graves Circuit Court. E. A. Jones' Admr. & c., Plaintiffs, vs. His Heirs and Creditors, Defendants." *MDM*, Vol. XIV, No. 49, Tuesday, November 10, 1914, 7; Sixty-four Acres were put up for auction at the court house door on December 21st, 1914. Of this thirty-five acres were deducted, having been sold to Annie Lassiter on April 27, 1912. "Also deducted from the above described real estate the new barn built on same and the . . . land upon which E.A. Jones built a new barn." "Commissioner's Sale." *MDM*, Vol. XIV, No. 73, Wednesday, December 9th, 1914, 3; At the public auction, the remaining thirty acres were sold to U.E. Kennedy for $650. "Sales Made Monday by Master Commissioner," *MDM*, Vol. XIV, No. 85, Wednesday, December 23, 1914, 3.

CHAPTER TWO: ORIGINS

[1] A horizontal wooden or metal bar between the wagon and the horse used to balance the pull of the horse's alternate shoulders as it walks.

[2] "An attempt was made in 1870 by the legislature to provide professional training for teachers by the adoption of the County Institute system. Institutes were held annually for a period of five days. All teachers and those who wished to be examined for a certificate to teach were require to attend and pay a fee to be used meeting the expense of the institute." MILLS 24.

[3] Now lost to history in all but the most obscure reference works, Swan was the site of a U.S. Post Office as early as 1851. *Table of Post Offices in The United States on the First Day of January, 1851, Arranged in Alphabetical Order, and Exhibiting the States, Territories, and Counties in Which They are Situated, with the Names of the Post Masters; also an Appendix Containing a List of the Post Offices, Arranged by States and Counties, to which is Added a List of the Offices Established, Changed, or Discontinued to May 31.* (Washington: W. & J.C. Greer, Printers, 1851), 366, 600; Although the Mayfield *Daily Messenger* would occasionally reference the community well into the early 1900's, it was apparently of such little importance that its existence was not even recognized on *An Atlas of Graves County, Kentucky From Actual Surveys Under the Direction of B.N. Griffing.* (Philadelphia, PA: D.J. Lake & Co., 1880); *The Daily Messenger* offers conflicting spellings of the little town's name, alternately spelling it "Swan" or "Swann"—often in the same article. "Young Lady Dies Near Swan." *MDM*, Vol. IX, No. 102, Tuesday, May 4, 1909, 1.

[4] From 1893 until 1904, the term for a common school was five months. It changed to 6 months in 1904. MILLS 70, 74.

[5] The county was actually named for Charles R. Haskell, a casualty of the Goliad Massacre in 1836 in the fight for Texas Independence. "Haskell County," Texas State Historical Association, https://tshaonline.org/handbook/online/articles/hch10. Accessed April 17, 2017.

[6] Founded as the United States Indian Industrial Training School in 1884, the name was changed in 1887 to honor U.S. Representative Dudley Chase Haskell. "School of Business, History of Haskell's Business Department." http://www.haskell.edu/academics/business /history/ history-hinu-business/ Accessed April 17, 2017.

[7] *The Daily Messenger* went so far as to refer to "Col. Bob" as "one of the pioneer carpenters of the county, having come to this section away back in the 30's." "Warm Times." *MDM*, Vol. V, No. 304, Wednesday, July 26, 1905, 1; "Enlarging." *MDM*, Vol. VI, No. 40, Tuesday, September 12, 1905, 1; "Bob James Injured." *MSM*, Vol. VI, No. 133, Saturday, December 30, 1905, 1.

[8] Known as "commutation," it allowed for an individual to pay $300 for a substitute to go in their place and avoid service for three years in each of four drafts. This was roughly equal to the annual wages of an individual employed in manufacturing. Timothy J. Perri, "The Economics of US Civil War Conscription." Appalachian State University, www.appstate.edu/~perritj/CWC.pdf. Accessed March 11, 2012.

[9] Reparations for horses stolen by Union troops were still being addressed some 35 years later as one local resident finally received notice that he would be paid $175 for his horse, bridle and saddle in late 1902. "James Barber To Be Paid for His Horse After 35 Long Years," *MDM*, Vol. 3, No. 292, Monday, August 11, 1902, 1.

[10] "Although Graves County was not a large slaveholding county, the county's sympathies seem to have been most firmly rooted in Southern family ties." "Graves County's Confederate Monument." *Graves County Kentucky, History & Families.* Graves County Genealogical Society (Paducah: Turner Publishing Company, 2001), 57

[11] The mother-in-law, Mary Kesee, is recorded as living with Haskell's grandparent's, Robert C. and Martha James, in the 1880 Census. 1880; Census Place: Wingo, Graves, Kentucky; Roll: 416; Family History Film: 1254416; Page 360A; Enumeration District: 095; Image: 0122. http://search.ancestry.com/cgi-bin/sse.dll?db=1880usfedcen&h=11697438 &ti=0&indiv=try&gss=pt

[12] Although his grandmother may have admitted to one slave, there is evidence in the 1860 Slave Schedules that her husband, William Buntin Jones, owned eleven slaves in Montgomery County, Tennessee, about the time they married. Ancestry.com. *1860 U.S. Federal Census - Slave Schedules* [database on-line]. Provo, UT, USA: Ancestry.com Operations Inc., 2010. Original data: United States of America, Bureau of the Census. *Eighth Census of the United States, 1860.* Washington, D.C.: National Archives and Records Administration, 1860. M653, 1,438 rolls.

[13] "In Middle Tennessee, the 'Little red cob,' or Willis corn, is a favorite with almost everyone. As a rule this is a gourd seed and the ear is nearly all grain, as the cob is very small, while the grains are very long and have very fine tips, barely touching the cob and crowding outward. The white cob is generally a flint, and makes excellent bread, giving less bran than the gourd seed, but from the hardness of its grains is not so well suited for horses." Joseph Buckner Killebrew, *The Grasses of Tennessee; Including Cereals and Forage Plants,* The American Co., 1878, 352; A 1905 bulletin from the Kentucky Agricultural Experiment Station entitled "14697 Red Cob Willis," notes, "The sample consists of two ears of corn obtained from Isaiah Bowden, Sedalia, Graves County, Kentucky. Yield, 60 to 65 bushels per acre; Grown on bottom land, soil about twelve inches deep, heavy, no sand; dark red sub-soil." *Bulletin - Kentucky Agricultural Experiment Station, Issues 118-132,* University of Kentucky, 1905, 167; The seed for Red Cob Willis was frequently found for sale in the pages of the *Messenger* in the mid-teens. "Red Cob Seed Corn." *MDM*, Monday, March 13, 1916, Vol. XIV, No. 281, 1.

CHAPTER THREE: PUBLIC EDUCATION IN KENTUCKY

[1] Haskell, being two years younger, would not enter school for another two years. "School Teachers and Money." *MDM*, Vol. 3, No. 287, Tuesday, August 5, 1902, 4. Until 1909, each District consisted of a population of 100 school-aged children—whether they attended school or not. KLO 146; A complete listing of all school names and numbers appears in The Weekly Messenger in 1918 in regards to the results of a bond drive during World War 1. "Standing Of School Districts To Date On Liberty Loans." *MWM*, Vol. XVIII, No. 13, Thursday, May 2, 1918, 1. With the enactment of the Day Law in 1904, schools would be officially segregated, prohibiting blacks and whites from attending either the same schools or schools that were located less than 25 miles apart. "Berea College V. Kentucky," Law and Higher Education, http://lawhigheredu.com/17-berea-college-v.-kentucky.html Accessed July 31, 2016.

"Beginning shortly after the Civil War, the Kentucky General Assembly mandated that the support of black schools derive exclusively from black tax revenues. The racialization of tax collection and tax allocation for education resulted in a gaping discrepancy between funds available for the support of black and white schools." Although a federal court ruling in 1882 was to declare this illegal, it would continue throughout the history of segregated education in Kentucky. What more, prior to 1916, there was no secondary education for black students. GLAZ, 116-117, 133.

2 This would remain the case throughout Kentucky until 1950. *Child Welfare in Kentucky*, 52; Postwar Planning Commission *Report*, 70; Ligon, *PEK* 138. As cited by KLO 146.

3 "Kindergarten School." *MDM*, Vol. XII, No. 785, Thursday, April 10, 1913, 1.

4 "Graded School 18 Months Old." *MDM*, Vol. IX, No. 302, Tuesday, December 28, 1909, 1.

5 The passage of the School District Law in 1907 (more popularly known as the Sullivan Bill, after Richmond legislator and lawyer J.A. Sullivan) mandated that each county establish a high school within two years. KLO 148-49; "Mayfield High School." *MWM*, Vol. VIII, Thursday, September 16, 1909, 2.

6 "County School Board and the County School Business." *MWM*, Vol. XI, Thursday, May 16, 1912, 4; "Parent-Teacher Body Offers Three Petitions." *MDM*, Vol. XII, No. 223, Tuesday, May 27, 1913, 4.

7 NEW 50.

8 "Measuring Worth" http://www.measuringworth.com/uscompare/relativevalue.php Accessed March 5, 2013.

9 "School Teachers and Money." *MDM*, Vol. 3, No. 287, Tuesday, August 5, 1902, 4; "The Monthly Average Price Of School Teachers." *MDM*, Vol. 4, No. 58, Tuesday, November 11, 1902, 4.

10 "Unlettered Laborers Paid More than Schoolteachers. Kentucky School Superintendent Plans Methods Whereby Educated Rural Teachers May Not Have To Bear the "premium of ignorance" Any Longer." *MWM*, Vol. XVII, No. 51, Thursday, January 23, 1919, 6.

11 "Teachers' Salary to Be Held Back. Supt. Gilbert Claims Only Part of Money Available Before June 30." *MDM*, Friday, March 10, 1916, Vol. XIV, No. 279, 3; A report later in the year would record revenue into the school fund from the dog tax in Graves County to be $1,527.53 ("after deducting payments for sheep killed"). "Dog Licenses Net $45,949. State School Fund Enriched by Tax." *MDM*, Friday, August 11, 1916, Vol. XV, No. 80, 3.

12 "Pay for County Teachers Is Delayed." *MWM*, Vol. XVII, No. 37, Thursday, October 11, 1917, 4.

13 NEW 58.

14 MILLS 39.

15 Local practicality led to the discovery in 1914, however, that there were over 5,000 school trustees in Kentucky who could neither read nor write. Ligon, *PEK* 118, Hamlett, *History of Education*, 198; James Sill, *The Wolfpen Notebooks* (1991), 98. As cited by KLO 147.

16 KLO 146-47. The passage of the Sullivan Bill also reduced the number of trustees from three to one and required that they had to be literate. Obviously, as noted in the text, this was not always the case. KLO 149. "State funds might be used to pay teachers, but, from the organization of the system, local school units have been responsible for school grounds, buildings, equipment and incidental expenses . . . In fact, up to 1908, rural districts rarely levied a school tax." "Local School Support," *PEK* 141.

17 "County Organization and Administration," *PEK* 28.

18 "Local Organization," *PEK* 36; "Present Condition of Schools," *PEK* 9.

19 KLO 160-61.

20 KLO 146.

21 KLO 147; "The Elementary School," *PEK* 92.

22 "The Elementary School," *PEK* 91-92.

23 NEW 65.

24 "Local Organization," *PEK* 36-37.

25 "The City Schools." *MDM*, Vol. V, No. 222, Monday, May 1, 1905, 1.

26 "Buildings, Grounds, and Equipment," *PEK* 72-73.

27 "Buildings, Grounds, and Equipment," *PEK* 72.

28 "Buildings, Grounds, and Equipment," *PEK* 73-74.

29 NEW 52.

30 KLO 159.

31 *CWK* (New York: National Child Labor Committee, 1919).

32 MIT 39.

33 "In the Schools. High School News." *MDM*, Vol. XIII, No. 166, Friday, March 27, 1914, 3; Having been born on January 24, 1894, she was four years older than Florence and would have just turned 20 years old; She is noted as having enrolled at the Graves County Teachers' Institute that July. "List Of Teachers Who Are Attending Graves Co. Institute," *MDM*, Vol. XIII, No. 272, Wednesday, July 29, 1914, 1.

34 "In the Schools. Mayfield High School News." *MDM*, Vol. XIII, No. 118, January 30, 1914, 2.

35 "New State Laws Now Effective." *MDM*, Vol. XI, No. 140, Friday, June 14, 1912, 1.

36 "Does Not Apply to Public School. Attorney General Gives Opinion Regarding Drinking Cup Law." *MDM*, Vol. XI, No. 169, Friday, July 19, 1912, 1.

37 "The Drinking Cup." *MWM*, Vol. XI, Thursday, June 6, 1912, 2.

38 "Boil the Ice." *MDM*, Vol. XV, No. 90, Wednesday, August 4, 1915, 4.

39 "Will Banish Cup of Death." *MDM*, Vol. XI, No. 173, Wednesday, July 24, 1912, 3.

40 "Graves Has Lead in High Schools. According to Prof. Coates it Has Eleven— Teachers' Pay." *MDM*, Vol. XV, No. 85, Thursday, August 17, 1916, 2.

41 "Present Condition Of Schools," *PEK* 3.

CHAPTER FOUR: EDUCATION

1 Graded schools were introduced in Mayfield in September 1909. "Graded Schools 18 Months Old. *MDM*, Vol. IX, No. 302, Tuesday, December 28, 1909, 1.

2 Written by Augusta Jane Evans in 1866, this melodramatic Victorian novel follows the romantic travails of Edna Earl as she struggles to become a world famous novelist. Along the way, she witnesses a duel, survives a train wreck and is taken in by a stern wealthy dowager whose troubled son, St Elmo, catches her attentions. Believed to have been inspired by Jane Eyre, the work is an early example of feminist writing (although Edna raises her voice against suffrage). "St Elmo, by Augusta Jane Evans," Vintage Novels, Travel Through Time and Space." http://www.vintagenovels.com/2013/08/st-elmo-by-augusta-jane-evans.html/ Accessed November 30, 2015.

3 Attendance for most of the time Florence and Haskell attended school was purely voluntary. Compulsory education for the county schools wasn't the law until June of 1912. "New State Laws Now Effective," *MDM*, Vol. XI, No. 140, Friday, June 14, 1912, 1.

4 The Vital Statistics Law of Kentucky, which legalized the registration of births and deaths, was enacted in 1910 and went into effect January 1, 1911. "Kentucky Vital Records." Accessed October 22, 2014. http://www.kentuckygenealogy.org/vitalrecords.htm/ It's enactment, however, was not a matter of civic duty in any normal sense. W.L. Helser, the State Registrar of Vital Statistics saw its importance in classifying the race of any child born to protect against any possible mixture of the races. He considered it a "real peril" that our "grandchildren and great grandchildren will be marrying persons having negro blood in their

veins." "Sees Race Mixture Through Lax Laws. Kentucky Official Points Out Danger in Failure to Register Negro Births." *MDM*, Vol. XVI, No. 185, Saturday, December 16, 1916, 1.

[5] Had Claude indeed attacked the teacher, it wouldn't have been without precedent in the area. *The Daily Messenger* noted a local incident in 1902 in which a 15 year old boy "whipped out a knife and stabbed the teacher in the side" after having been corrected. The teacher would survive his wounds, but "School was adjourned . . . on account of the teacher's condition." "Teacher Stabbed," *MDM*, Vol. 4, No. 45, October 27th, 1902, 4; Another incident, reported in 1917 by *The Daily Messenger*, also played to the adage of "turnabout is fair play"—even though the sides were decidedly unfair at the start. "From reports," the article noted, "it seems that several of the larger school boys decided to give the teacher a whipping, and when they began to gather around Prof. [Roscoe] Reed, the latter backed away and in doing so picked up a piece of a bench and in the encounter a young man named Davidson got his arm broken. A warrant was issued for Prof. Reed, who came to the city Monday and employed Attorney Pete Seay to defend him at the trial. The school came to a close last Friday." "Teacher and Pupils Have Trouble at Dogwood," *MDM*, Vol. SVI, No. 243, Tuesday, February 27, 1917, 1; On a related note, a teacher could be criminally charged with punishing a pupil "too much." An example was recorded of one such instance when one local teacher "was tried on a charge of having punished a girl pupil unmercifully through the application of the switch." "Charged with Punishing a Girl Pupil Too Much." *MDM*, Vol. IX, No. 98, Saturday, December 21, 1912, 1.

[6] Kentucky Death Records note Josh Boyd died August 29, 1946, age 69, of congestive heart failure in Graves County. Haskell would have been 48 years old and would have completed his term as Chief of Police of the Tallmadge Police Department when his mother slapped him. *Vital Statistics Original Death Certificates – Microfilm (1911-1955).* Microfilm rolls #7016130-7041803. Kentucky Department for Libraries and Archives, Frankfort, Kentucky.

CHAPTER FIVE: TOBACCO

[1] Patton, Janet. "Documentary Film Focuses on Western Ky.'s Black Patch Tobacco Farmers," *Lexington Herald Leader.* http://www.kentucky.com/news/business/article 44402640.html, Accessed February 4, 2017.

[2] Reid, Yolanda C. and Rick S. Gregory. *Robertson County Tennessee.* Tennessee: Robertson County Historical Society, 1996, 90.

[3] MAR 110, 108.

[4] "Industrial Kentucky (1870-1970) – Tobacco Traditions." http://athena.uky.edu/kyleidoscope/industrialky/tobacco/tobacco.htm Accessed July 4, 2014.

[5] "A Common Scene in the Tobacco District in West Mayfield, the Largest Loose Tobacco Market in the World." *MSM*, Vol. V, No. 245, Saturday, May 27, 1905, 1.

[6] "Tobacco Hornworm Damage." http://www.uky.edu/Classes/ENT/574/insects/tobacco_insects/tobacco_hornworm/thw_damage.htm Accessed July 8, 2014; "A Talk on Worms." *MWM*, Vol. VIII, Thursday, March 11, 1909, 2.

[7] "A Talk on Worms." *MWM*, Vol. VIII, Thursday, March 11, 1909, 2.

[8] Reid, Yolanda C. and Rick S. Gregory. *Robertson County Tennessee.* Tennessee: Robertson County Historical Society, 1996, 92-93

[9] "Dog That Beats Paris Green for Tobacco Worms." *MDM*, Vol. XV, No. 94, Monday, August 28, 1916, 1.

[10] "Tobacco Hornworm Moth (Manduca Sexta)." http://www.insectidentification.org/insect-description.asp?identification=Tobacco-Hornworm-Moth Accessed July 8, 2014.

[11] "House burn" can occur if the leaves are not shaken before being hung which allows them to stick together, ruining the texture and elasticity of the leaves. W.H. Scherffius, H.

Woolsey and C.A. Mahan, "The Cultivation of Tobacco in Kentucky and Tennessee," Farmer's Bulletin 343, Issued January 20, 1909, 23. Washington: United States Department of Agriculture, 1909.

[12] W.H. Scherffius, H. Woosley and C.A. Mahan, "The Cultivation of Tobacco in Kentucky and Tennessee," Farmer's Bulletin 343, Issued January 20, 1909, 27. Washington: United States Department of Agriculture. 1909; Bill Maksymowicz. "Harvesting, Curing and Preparing Dark-Fired Tobacco for Market." Cooperative Extension Service, University of Kentucky, College of Agriculture, 1997. http://www.leffingwell.com/agr152.pdf Accessed July 8, 2014.

[13] *Reid, Yolanda C. and Rick S. Gregory.* Robertson County Tennessee. *Tennessee: Robertson County Historical Society, 1996, 95-96.*

[14] A 19th century term for the lowest grade of tobacco. "The lowest qualities of shipping tobacco are called *lugs*, and these are distinguished into 'factory lugs' and 'plantation lugs,' both being the stems, strippings, and broken leaves attached to them. The best full leaves are usually packed separately as 'wrappers,' and the value of these last is six to ten times as great as the lowest 'lugs.'" Johnson's New Universal Cyclopaedia: S-Z (New York: Alvin J. Johnson & Son, 1877), 877.

CHAPTER SIX: WORK

[1] "Each bur contains two brown to black achenes (seeds), one above the other. The lower seed can germinate immediately; the upper seed is dormant and does not germinate until months or often years later." "Common Cocklebur," PennState Extension, http://extension.psu.edu/pests/weeds/weed-id/common-cocklebur/ Accessed December 7, 2015.

CHAPTER SEVEN: HEALTH

[1] After a visiting nurse made her report public on the front pages of *The Daily Messenger* in 1916, it was appallingly obvious as to why. "In Interest of Public Health Our Visiting Nurse is Requested to Give an Outsider's Point of View." MDM, Vol. XIV, No. 327, Friday, May 5, 1916, 1.

[2] "Perry Taylor Meets Tragic [sic] Death Wednesday." MDM, Vol. XV, No. 169, Thursday, November 4, 1915, 1; "Toy Pistols Cause Death of Two Colored Boys of Farmington," MWM, Vol. 5, No. 38, Thursday, January 17, 1907, 5; "Deadly Toy Pistol. Fatal Tetanus Claims Victim as Result of Demonstration to Prove it Harmless." MDM, Vol. IX, No. 302, Tuesday, December 28, 1909, 1; "Door Slam Causes Death." MDM, Vol. XII, No. 176, Monday, March 31, 1913, 2; "Explosion Of Gasoline Iron," MDM, Vol. IX, No. 171, Friday, July 23, 1909, 1.

[3] Intermittent Fever is "an attack of malaria or other fever, with recurring fever episodes separated by times of normal temperature" whereas Remittent Fever is "one that shows significant variations in 24 hours but without return to normal temperature," http://medical-dictonary.thefreedictonary.com/ Accessed December 2, 2011.

[4] 5th Sergeant Simeon Carman "was wounded and captured at the Battle of Fishing Creek, Kentucky, on January 19, 1862. He was sent [to] a prison hospital at Somerset Kentucky. He escaped when able to travel and he re- joined the regiment. He was wounded at Murfreesboro, Tennessee, on December 2, 1863 during Breckinridge's Charge and received a belly wound. He was wounded in the right leg at Chickamauga, Georgia. He received wounds and was captured at Missionary Ridge, Tennessee, on November 25, 1863. The mini ball in his right leg was never removed." E.J. Keen, 20th Tennessee Infantry Regiment, http://freepages.genealogy.rootsweb.ancestry.com/~providence/cw_20k.htm, Accessed March 12, 2012; Sergeant Simeon A. Carman served with the 20th Tennessee Infantry

Regiment, Company K and was captured at Harrison's Landing on November 27, 1863. He was transferred to the Rock Island Prison on December 12th and released on oath March 11, 1865. *Civil War Prisoner of War Records, 1861-1865* [database on-line]. Provo, UT, USA: Ancestry.com Operations Inc., 2007; Although he was a "major hater of the Yankees," he apparently did not take part in any of the annual reunions of his Company or Regiment in Nashville. Printed in 1904, the *History of the Twentieth Tennessee Regiment Volunteer Infantry, C.S.A.,* notes it was compiled with the assistance of all in attendance over the past two reunions. However, on page 180, it incorrectly records his middle initial and notes he had died since the end of the war—when he was still alive until October 4, 1921. He died at age 93.

   [5] A severe bacterial skin infection treated by antibiotics today, its impact would have been extremely frightening at the time—particularly in a child. "The temperatures observed in erysipelas are often extreme: 106° is not at all rare. The highest we ever saw was 107.2°. While the erysipelas continues or is spreading, the fever is seldom continuous, nor are the remissions insignificant . . . The headache is often intense . . . The patient may be very restless, excited, and wakeful. At night there may be mild or even violent delirium; or there may be decided stupor. . . . There is constipation; or there may be quite severe diarrhea . . . The entire duration of the disease varies greatly in different cases. A very light case may get well in a few days. Most cases of average severity last a week or ten days. Erysipelas migraine may continue for many weeks." Adolph von Strumpell, "Acute General Infectious Diseases," *A Text-Book of Medicine for Students and Practitioners,* Third American Edition (New York: D. Appleton, 1901), 65-66.

   [6] For the responsible males in such a situation, the "Ugly Charge" of bastardy still existed in Kentucky as late as 1905, as one man who fled to Graves County to avoid the charge was aware. "Arrested on Ugly Charge." *MDM*, Vol. V, No. 134, Tuesday, January 17, 1905, 1.

CHAPTER EIGHT: THE POLITICIAN

   [1] Known as "The Great Commoner," Democrat William Jennings Bryan was elected to Congress in 1890 and 1892 before running for President as a Populist in 1896 and again in both 1900 and 1908 as a Democrat. The first candidate to travel extensively in search of voter support, he delivered hundreds of speeches across the country. A staunch advocate of free silver and anti-imperialism, he founded the *Commoner* in 1901, which he continued to publish for 12 years. "William Jennings Bryan," United States History, http://www.u-s-history.com/pages/h805.html/ Accessed November 29, 2015.

   [2] *The Yellow Jacket* was published from 1895-1953 in Moravian Falls, North Carolina, by R. Don Laws and James Larkin Pearson. Distributed on a national basis, it was known for its radical political agenda that included socialism. http://chroniclingamerica.loc.gov/lccn/sn85038642/ Accessed July 21, 2012.

   [3] In fact, Graves County was so staunchly Democratic that it received national recognition in nothing less venerable than *The Saturday Evening Post.* In the issue of September 7, 1912, an unknown contemporary author noted, "Graves County, Kentucky, is, or was, the banner Democratic county of the state." "The Wild Ass of the Bleachers," *The Saturday Evening Post*, Volume 185, No. 10, September 7, 1912 (Philadelphia, Pennsylvania: The Curtis Publishing Company, 1912), 31. Another modern-day historian went so far as to call it "The Democratic Gibraltar of the West." Cunningham, Bill. *On Bended Knees, The True Story of the Night Rider Tobacco War in Kentucky and Tennessee.* (Nashville, McClanahan Publishing House: 1983), 113.

   [4] In a very lengthy piece in 1909, *The Daily Messenger* editorialized against this noting, "For a man, or any number of men, in order to get votes, to go about over the country trying to prejudice the minds of the country people against the town people, without cause, is certainly very reprehensible. There are just as good people live in the country as live in the towns, they

are all neighbors and relatives and simply because a man is in business in town that he is a worse man than the man who lives in the country is simply a ridiculous idea." "Editorial. Very Bad Politics." *MDM*, Vol. IX, No. 242, Saturday, October 16, 1909, 1.

⁵ Sam Galloway shot and killed Sheriff John T. Roach on March 6, 1922. Upon his death, his widow, Lois Roach, was appointed sheriff in his stead making her the first and only female sheriff in the country at the time. D. Trabue Davis, *The Story of Mayfield Through a Century, 1823-1923*. Reprinted Simmons Historical Publications (Melber, Kentucky: 1990), 10. After unsuccessfully pleading "self-defense" under the guidance of ever-present attorney for the defense, Pete Seay, Galloway was convicted and sentenced to 7 years in prison. "Galloway Given 7 Years in Pen For Roach Death. Slayer of Graves Sheriff Found Guilty Today by Carlisle Jury. Second Trial Success. Jurors Deliberated 22 Hours, May Not Take Appeal." *PES*, Volume XLV; No. 186, Friday, August 4, 1922, 1.

⁶ "Campaign Committee Has Money Left." *MDM*, Vol. XIII, No. 47, Friday, November 7, 1913, 1; "Fast Old Boy. Printers Too Fast for the Business Manager," *MDM*, Vol. 3, No. 267, Saturday, July 12, 1902, 1; "The Mayfield Papers And The Sheriff's Race." *MDM*, Vol. VI, No. 55, Thursday, September 28, 1905, 1; "Newspaper Deal On. The Mirror and Monitor Likely to Consolidate and L.A. Chandler Retire." *MDM*, Vol. VI, No. 83, Tuesday, October 31, 1905, 1.

⁷ Not that any of this was unusual in the day. An article in The Messenger less than 10 years later noted there was "only one republican paper in the state." "Republican Papers." *MDM*, Vol. XIV, No. 67, Wednesday, December 2, 1914, 1.

⁸ "Shall Negroes or White People Name Governor of Kentucky?" *MDM*, Vol. XV, No. 166, Monday, November 1, 1915, 1.

⁹ "Buried at Former Home, Benton." *MWM*, Vol. XVII, No. 32, Thursday, January 30. 1919, 1.

¹⁰ "The People. On South Tenth Street Greatly Excited by a Lively Run Away All Caused by a Republican Horse." *MDM*, Vol. V, No. 274, Tuesday, June 20, 1905, 1.

¹¹ "Digging Their Own Grave." *MDM*, Vol. IX, No. 24, Friday, January 29, 1909, 1.

¹² "Democrats, Don't Be Deceived." *MDM*, Vol. IX, No. 228, Thursday, September 30, 1909, 4.

¹³ "Editorial. Races for Sheriff." *MDM*, Vol. XVII, No. 128, Wednesday, October 10, 1917, 1.

¹⁴ "County Officers and Their Pay," *MWM*, Vol. IX, Thursday, November 25, 1909, 6.

¹⁵ "'The General Green' Makes Successful Voyage up the Perilous Salt River." *MDM*, Vol. IX No. 263, Wednesday, November 10, 1909; Even that slim a margin was too much for Haskell's grandfather, Robert James. In an article on the front page of *The Daily Messenger*, it was noted that "Bob James was in the city Tuesday and in speaking of the recent election said that he learned that Mayfield was Democratic by only sixteen majority since he moved away. And he stated that if he had known that such a thing would have happened that he would have moved considerably further away from the city when he did." "Too Much for Him." *MDM*, Vol. IX, No. 262, Tuesday, November 9ᵗʰ, 1909, 1.

¹⁶ "Commissioners Make the Official Count." *MDM*, Vol. XIII, No. 47, Friday, November 7, 1913, 1. "Graves County Democracy Still Solid as Steel." *MDM*, Vol. XIII, No. 45, Wednesday, November 5. 1913, 1.

¹⁷ "Editorial." *MWM*, Vol. XVII, No. 41, Thursday, November 8, 1917, 1.

¹⁸ The magistrate or justice of the peace was "paid by fees and commissions that result from their courts, except that they receive $3 per day for the time spent in holding the fiscal courts." Each magistrate received $3 per day when the fiscal court was in session. In 1909, they were in session 19 days. "County Officers and Their Pay." *MDM*, Vol. IX, No. 270, Friday, November 19, 1909, 1. "Fiscal Court Meetings." *MDM*, Vol. IX, No. 285, Friday, December 3, 1909, 1.

[19] The situation became so bad that the Commonwealth eventually made it law for property owners to clear the brush back on any land bordering public roadways. "Fair Warning." *MWM*, Vol. XVI, No. 52, Thursday, July 3, 1919, 7.

[20] Isaac B. Potter, *The Gospel of Good Roads, A Letter to the American Farmer* (New York: The Evening Post Job Printing House), 1891.

[21] "Gravel the Roads." *MDM*, Vol. 4, No. 12, Thursday, September 18, 1902, 4.

[22] "Coldest in History. Was Weather for Five Months Just Past." *MWM*, Vol. XI, Thursday, April 11, 1912, 6; "April Rainfall Was Heaviest for Years." *MWM*, Vol. XI, Thursday, May 9, 1912, 2.

[23] "Lynnville, Route 3." *MWM*, Vol. XI, Thursday, April 11, 1912, 6.

[24] "Horse Falls in Mud Hole; Dies." *MWM*, Vol. XI, Thursday, March 28, 1912, 3.

[25] "Livery Horse Almost Drowns in Mud Hole." *MWM*, Vol. XI, Thursday, March 28, 1912, 4.

[26] "Thrilling Experience in Treacherous Mud Hole." *MDM*, Vol. XI, No. 101, Monday, April 29, 1912, 1.

[27] "Emergency Action Taken on Roads. Each Magistrate Calls for Bids for the Letting of Contracts at Once—Total Damage Over Five Thousand Dollars. Travel Over County Badly Crippled." *MWM*, Vol. XI, Thursday, April 11, 1912, 2.

[28] "Fish Found in Public Road; Men Go Fishing." *MDM*, Vol. XI, No. 103, Wednesday, May 1, 1912, 1.

[29] "The Value of Deep Mud Holes Demonstrated." *MDM*, Vol. XI, No. 167, Wednesday, July 17, 1912, 1.

[30] "Crops in The County Are Not Looking Well." *MWM*, Vol. XI, Thursday, Aug. 8, 1912, 3; "Large Sum for Roads. Fiscal Court Appropriates $3,500 to Each District at Meeting." *MWM*, Vol. XI, Thursday, Aug. 8, 1912, 2.

[31] "Roads so Rough Eggs Cannot Be Brought Here." *MDM*, Vol. XII, No. 199, Monday, April 28, 1913, 1.

[32] "Why Not Try Oil on Mayfield's Streets?" *MDM*, Saturday, May 3, 1913, 1.

[33] "Good Roads Celebration. Citizens of Graves County Take Notice—Important!" *MDM*, Vol. XII, No. 305, Tuesday, September 2, 1913, 1.

[34] "Graves County Has Good Roads Fever All Over." *MDM*, Vol. XIII, No. 1, Saturday, September 13, 1913, 2.

[35] "Speaking Places and Speakers for Saturday." *MDM*, Vol. XIII, No. 6, September 19, 1913, 1; "Town and County Get Together." *MDM*, Vol. XIII, No. 2; He also spoke at one of mass meetings at the Court House, reporting, "We met at our school house Saturday night, and while we took no definite steps, everybody is going to joining in the work with the exception of a few who are never in favor of doing anything that they think will benefit their neighbors. Now, one thing that may set back the road work, is the probability of frost on the 15th and 16th. If the weather turns off cool just the day before, the farmers are going to be too busy cutting their tobacco to work on the roads. The moon will be full about that time. But if a frost scare comes before that time nine-tenths of the men of the county, I believe, will work the roads." "Multitudes of Men Will Work." *MDM*, Vol. XIII, No. 16, Wednesday, October 1, 1913, 1.

[36] "Attend Mass Meeting Court House Tonight." *MDM*, Vol. XIII, No. 11, Thursday, September 26, 1913, 1; Splitting the difference, County School Superintendent W.D. Dodds, took out a notice in the paper a few days later. "While it is not thought best to dismiss the schools," he wrote, "it is recommended that all boys attending all city and graded and rural school be allowed and encouraged to work on these days and be given credit in their classes for the time." "Notice to Teachers." *MDM*, Vol. XIII, No. 15, Tuesday, September 30, 2.

[37] "Colored Men Willing to Assist in Work." *MDM*, Vol. XIII, No. 12, Friday, September 26, 1913, 1.

[38] "Thousands of Men Are at Work on the County Roads. Never Before Was There Such Unity for Good Cause—Every Man in Earnest. First Day Grand Success." *MDM*, Vol. XIII, No. 27, Wednesday, October 15, 1913, 1.

[39] "Roads Are in a Good Condition." *MDM*, Vol. XIII, No. 29, Friday, October 17, 1913, 1.

[40] "Former Sheriff, W.L. Brand, is Being Tried for Embezzlement." *MM*, Wednesday, March 12, 1913. SIM *Vol. 36*, 51.

[41] An extremely oddly titled article in *The Daily Messenger* records in the first paragraph, "On motion of Justice Jones, it was ordered that R.G. Robbins be allowed $1,250 on his account for taking depositions in the cases of Graves County against W.L. Brand, the same to be issued in two warrants; $500 was ordered paid now, and the $750 warrant to be held by him for 30 days before presented for payment." "No Road Machinery Will Be Bought." *MDM*, Vol. XII, No. 307, Friday, September 5, 1913, 1.

[42] "Brand Suits Have Been Finally Settled." *MDM*, Vol. XIII, No. 148, Thursday, March 5, 1914, 1.

[43] "Seven Ex-Sheriffs Are Now Residents of the City of Mayfield and Are Very Handsome." *MWM*, Vol. No. 15, Thursday, July 18, 1907, 1.

[44] "Sheriff Potter Must Pay Back." *MDM*, Vol. V, No. 194, Wednesday, March 29,1905, 1; "Special Venire to Try Brand Case." *MDM*, Vol. XII, No. 158, Friday, March 7, 1913, 1; "Former Sheriff is Being Tried." *MDM*, Wednesday, March 12, 1913, 1.

[45] "Foreman of Grand Jury Refused to Issue Subpoenas for Witness to Investigate the Official Conduct of County Officials." *MDM*, Vol. V., No. 211. Tuesday, April 18, 1905, 1.

[46] "Local Organization," *PEK* 42.

[47] "Auditor After Sheriffs." *MWM*, Vol. VIII, Thursday, May 13, 1909, 1.

[48] Sam Douthitt is recorded as being a former sheriff in 1902. "City Democratic Primary Election Called." *MDM*, Vol. 3, No. 299, Thursday, August 19, 1902, 4; J.N. Harris is recorded as being the current sheriff in *MDM* in 1902; J.N. Harris is also recorded as being the current sheriff in *The Daily Messenger* in 1905. "City and County Directory." *MDM*, Vol. V., No. 164, Tuesday, February 21, 1905, 1; W.L. Brand served as sheriff of Graves County during 1906, 1907, 1908 and 1909. "Instructions Given in W.L. Brand Case." *MDM*, Friday, March 14, 1913, 1. "Officers." *MDM*, Vol. 3, No. 108, Monday, January 6, 1902, 1; Sheriff Rafe B. Wallace was elected to office November 4th, 1909 to replace outgoing Sheriff W. L. Brand. "Democratic Victory! The Farmers Stood Loyal to Their Ideals and Carried Rafe B. Wallace Safely to Office of Sheriff." *MWM*, Vol. IX, Thursday, November 4, 1909, 1.

[49] "Sheriff Reports Condition of Books." *MWM*, Vol. XI, February 29, 1912, 4.

[50] Sheriff William Franklin Housman was elected in 1891, "Houseman/Brooksire/Jones/Sneed," *Graves County Kentucky, History & Families*. Graves County Genealogical Society (Paducah: Turner Publishing Company, 2001), 296.

[51] "County Attorney Writes Regarding Frost Tax Bill." *MWM*, Vol. XI, Thursday, April 4, 1912, 5. It would also eventually recognized that the sheriff had never been required to actually provide receipts for any of his travel expenses, giving ample opportunity to pad his expense account. "Editorial." *MDM*, Vol. XIV, No. 259, Wednesday, February 16, 1916, 1.

[52] "Ex-Sheriff Harris Pays $7,000 Cash to County." *MWM*, Vol. XI, Thursday, March 14, 1912, 1.

[53] "Former Sheriff Acquitted." *MDM*, Vol. XI, No. 276, Friday, November 22, 1912, 1; Richard Jackson Bugg, Circuit Judge of the First Judicial District of Kentucky. "Judge R. J. Bugg Died at Home in Bardwell." *MDM*, Vol. XIII, No. 185, Saturday, April 18, 1914, 1.

[54] "Sheriff Wallace Fined $400." *MDM*, Vol. XI, No. 275, Thursday, November 21, 1912, 1.

[55] "Special Venire to Try Brand Case." *MDM*, Vol. XII, No. 158, Friday, March 7, 1913, 1.

56 "Former Sheriff is Being Tried." *MDM*, Wednesday, March 12, 1913, 1.

57 "Instructions Given in W.L. Brand Case." *MDM*, Friday, March 14, 1913, 1.

58 "Candidate Fires the Opening Gun." *MDM*, Vol. XII, No. 175, Saturday, March 29, 1913, 1.

59 "Sheriff Replies to Judge Monroe." *MDM*, Vol. XII, No. 193, Saturday, April 19, 1913, 1.

60 "No Road Machinery Will Be Bought." *MDM*, Vol. XII, No. 307, Friday, September 5, 1913, 1; Shortly after this appropriation, Editor Lemon would note that the cost of the ongoing investigations would be total at least $30,000. "Editorial. Counting The Cost." *MDM*. Vol. XIII, No. 2. Monday, September 15, 1913, 1.

61 *Kentucky Birth, Marriage and Death Records – Microfilm (1852-1910).* Microfilm rolls #994027-994058. Kentucky Department for Libraries and Archives, Frankfort, Kentucky.

62 "Settlement of the W.L. Brand Case." *MDM*, Vol. XIII, No. 142, Friday, February 27, 1914, 1. While this may seem a piddling sum by today's standards, the economic value of $14,000 in today's dollars is a staggering $6,390,000. http://www.measuringworth.com/uscompare/relativevalue.php Accessed July 19, 2014.

63 "Editorial. The Suits Against W.L. Brand and Others." *MDM*, Vol. XIII, No. 117, Thursday, January 29, 1914, 1.

64 "Brand Suits Have Been Finally Settled." Vol. XIII, No. 148, March 5, 1914, 1.

65 "Commissioner's Sale. J.L. Stunston Against W.L. Brand, G.B. Allen and Others." *MDM*, Vol. XIV, No. 73, Wednesday, December 9, 1914, 3; Somewhat ironically, he had placed the property in the name of Maggie B. Brand (which may have been either his sister, Maggie, wife, Margaret B., or daughter, Margaret) to protect it, a common technique at the time. Just two years before, he had filed suit against E.E. Wilson, Julia E. Wilson, Lester E. Wilson and H.E. Wilson for $540. The court records noted that "The plaintiffs seek to have deeds recently transferred to Julia E. Wilson be declared null and void . . ." "Clay Company Sued For Large Amount." *MWM*, Vol. XI, Thursday, June 6, 1912, 1.

66 "Commissioner's Sale. E.A. Jones' Admr. & c. Against His Heirs and Creditors." *MDM*, Vol. XIV, No. 73, Wednesday, December 9, 1914, 3.

67 Though the Commonwealth and the City may have been done with him, the former Sheriff was not through with trials. He would undergo two more embezzlement trials. The first would end in a hung jury. The second would see charges dismissed after the defense (mysteriously and quite belatedly) produced county warrants which showed there had been no embezzlement in the first place. "No Jury Secured in Brand Case. 125 Men Tested and All But Six Excused Wednesday. 113 More Summoned." *MDM*, Vol. XIV, No. 401, Wednesday, June 23, 1915, 1. "Speaking Began in the Brand Case." *MDM*, Vol. XIV, No. 403, Friday, June 25, 1915, 1. "Brand Case is Given to Jury." *MDM*, Vol. XIV, No. 404, Saturday, June 26, 1915, 1. "Jury Failed to Reach a Verdict." *MDM*, Vol. XIV, No. 60, Monday, June 28, 1915, 1. "Cases Set For Trial." *MDM*, Vol. XIV, No. 178, Saturday, November 13, 1915, 1. "Moorman Moves Brand Case Be Dismissed." *The Paducah Evening Sun*, Vol. XXXV, No. 125, Saturday November 27, 1915,

68 "Eleven Sales Were Made Monday by Master Commissioner." *MDM*, Vol. XIV, No. 186, Tuesday, April 20, 1915, 1; "Deed, Fannie Lowe to Mrs. E.A. Jones," August 6, 1914.

69 *MDM*, Friday, May 2, 1913.

70 E.A. Jones announced in candidacy for County Judge on January 9, 1913 and passed away on January 27, 1914 at 51 years of age. "Prominent Citizen of County Died Tues. Night." *MDM*, Vo. XIII, No. 116, Wednesday, January 28, 1914, 1.

71 *The Daily Messenger* kicked off its subscription contest on Saturday, May 17th, 1913. Two pianos and four diamond rings were awarded to the women who brought in the most subscriptions over a six-week period. "Great Opportunity Offered to the Ladies By The Messenger." *MDM*, Vol. XII, No. 215, Saturday, May 17th, 1913, 1.

[72] Following his death on January 27th, 1914 the official cause given by Dr. Fuller was "Pulmonary Tuberculosis." *Kentucky Death Records, 1852-1953* [database on-line]. Provo, UT, USA: Ancestry.com Operations Inc., 2007.

[73] As shocking as this might be to modern sensibilities, it was all too common—even within the public schools of the time. "Dr. McCormack, Secretary of the State board of Health, estimates that at least one-third of the schools have no toilet or privy at all." MIT 39; "As late as 1940, some 97 percent of Kentucky farms had not indoor plumbing." KLO 125.

CHAPTER NINE: RECREATION

[1] Ben Morris was apparently more than just a "devil in the seine." *The Daily Messenger* reprinted an article from the *Paducah News-Democrat* about his actions outside the seine.

"Ben Morris, of Hickory Grove, while attending a moonlight picnic at St. John last night, engaged in an altercation with John Wilkins, from Graves County, near Hard Money, which resulted in a fight. The two combatants were going for each other before bystanders comprehended that there was even an argument between the two. Wilkins was getting decidedly the best of the fight when Morris drew his knife and stabbed his opponent in eight different places in the back, the neck, the chest and the abdomen. The last mentioned cut was very deep and may prove fatal, as the way the wound bled indicated that the knife had reached a vital place. Wilkins fell to the ground, blood bushing from nearly every wound, and Morris hurried to his buggy and left the scene before he could be apprehended by an officer.

"Dr. R.D. Harper, of St. Johns, who luckily was at the picnic, was immediately called and attended Wilkins, stopping the flow of blood as much as possibly, and he gave it as his opinion that the chances for the recovery of the young man were very slim, and that it would be at least three days before he would know whether Wilkins would live or not.

"No one could tell the cause of the trouble, though there were a number present who saw the two at the beginning of the fight. Wilkins was unable to talk and so nothing could be learned from him. It has been established that the trouble was from no bad blood previously existing between the two, as they saw each other last night for the first time, and the supposition is that some word or act of one of the young men, whether intentionally or accidentally, aroused the ire of the other and the fight ensued.

"The Graves County authorities were notified last night and were looking for the cutist at an early hour this morning.

"Morris, it is understood, is a young lawyer, and had been admitted to the bar recently."

"Graves County Boys Fight at Picnic." *MDM*, Vol. XII, No. 292, Monday, August 18, 1913, 1; "Graves County Youth Held for Cutting." *MDM*, Vol. XII, No. 308, Saturday, September 6, 1913, 2; Wilkins apparently survived as Morris, initially charged with "malicious cutting" saw the charge reduced to "the one of cutting in sudden heat and passion, for which he was fined $100." "Ben Morris Fined in Paducah Court," *MDM*, Vol. XIII, No. 189, Thursday, April 23, 1914, 2.

[2] "Matty Matsuda. Lightweight champion wrestler of the world, with the Metropolitan Shows here next week. Matty will meet all comers up to 150 pounds. His weight is 130. If you are a lover of the boxing and wrestling sports you will be sure to see some of the best at the fair next week." "Matty Matsuda," *MDM*, Saturday, September 23, 1916, Vol. XV, No. 116, 4.

CHAPTER TEN: JUSTICE

[1] The attack was extensively covered in the pages of the *Messenger* and *The Paducah Evening Sun*. "Henry Campbell Victim of Operation By B.E. Choate. Unprecedented Operation is Crudely Performed in Big Road. Victim Quietly Submits When Choate Presents a Pistol and Knife and Asks Which is Preferred." *MDM*, Wednesday, July 19, 1916, Vol. XV, No. 60, 1. "Choate Trial Goes Over Day. Fifty More Men Summoned For Jury Service." *MDM*, Vol. XVI, No. 250, Wednesday, March 7, 1917. "Choate Seizes Upon Insanity Plea for His Justifi-

cation. Springs Surprise in Trial for Mutilation by Saying He Was Insane. Claims Intimacy Between Campbell and His Wife and Admits Action on Day of Cutting." *The Paducah Evening Sun*, Vol. XXXVIII, No. 59, Friday, March 9, 1917, 1. "Choate's Insanity Plea is Hotly Attacked by Lawyers. Claim Mutilation of His Victim Proved He Was Calm." *The Paducah Evening Sun*, Vol. XXXVIII, No. 60, Saturday, March 10, 1917, 1. "Choate Gets 3 Years and 4 Months for Mutilation. Jury in the Mayfield Mayhem Case Brings in Its Verdict Today. An Appeal is Next Step." *The Paducah Evening Sun*, Vol. XXXVIII, No. 61, Monday, March 12, 1917, 1. "Campbell Suit for Mutilation Ends in Compromise. $750 and Costs Accepted by Victim from Choate Who Was Convicted." *The Paducah Evening Sun*, Vol. XXXVIII, No. 97, Monday, April 23, 1917, 1; After much legal maneuvering, he was eventually sentenced to three years. "Choate's Three-Year Sentence Affirmed," *MDM*, Vol. XVII, No. 33, Wednesday, June 20, 1917, 1.

2 "B.E. Choate is Given Pardon." *MWM*, Vol. XIX, No. 25, Thursday, November 28, 1919, 3.

3 "Seeking to Secure Pardon for Choate; Now in Mayfield Jail." *MWM*, Vol. XVII, No. 31, Thursday, September 6, 1917, 1.

4 "The maiden name of Tinker's mother was Marge Fisher. She was married first to Watson and later to Joe Drew. Tinker first took up the name of Fisher and later Watson but came to be called 'Tinker' as a nickname on account of his work as a tinker on various kinds of instruments." "Tom Tinker Lynched Here Tuesday Night," *MDM*, Wednesday, February 10, 1915, 4; The 1910 Census shows a Tom Watson, 33, as a prisoner at Eddyville, Lyon, Kentucky.*1910*; Census, Place: *Eddyville, Lyon, Kentucky*; Roll: *T624_492*; Page: *6B*; Enumeration District: *0110*; Image: *614*; FHL microfilm: *1374505*.

5 Eddie B. Rogers, 18, is recorded in the 1910 Graves County Census. *1910*; Census Place: *Magisterial District 7, Graves, Kentucky*; Roll: *T624_475*; Page: *2B*; Enumeration District: *0084*; FHL microfilm: *1374488*.

6 The Certificate of Death for Tom Tinker Fisher, approximate age 41, dated February 9, 1915, gave the cause of death as "Homicide. Hung by a mob." Place of death was noted as the "Courtyard" in Mayfield. *Kentucky Death Records, 1852-1953* [database on-line]. Provo, UT, USA: Ancestry.com Operations Inc., 2007; There is no evidence that the jailer suffered any repercussions from allowing the mob to take the prisoner and no reason at that time to believe he would have. The State of Kentucky had passed a series of anti-lynching laws over the years and, depending upon which party was in office, had subsequently repealed them. The first anti-lynching laws were passed in May of 1897 under W.O. Bradley, Kentucky's first Republican Governor. Under these laws, officials could be fined $500 and removed from office if they did not resist the action of a mob. As a result, there were only 25 lynchings in Kentucky during Bradley's 4-year term as compared to 56 under the previous Democratic administration of J.Y. Brown. On March 17, 1902, under Democratic Governor J. C. Beckham, those provisions were eliminated. Although a bill to remove any jailer who allowed a lynching to occur was discussed in 1916 and there were instances in the Commonwealth where the Governor, judges and prosecutors stood up to the mob to prevent or investigate a lynching, it wouldn't be until March 22, 1920 under the next Republican administration of Governor Edwin Morrow that anti-lynching laws were reinstated. Personal communication with Anthony Curtis, M.A., Kentucky Historical Society, Thomas D. Clark Center for Kentucky History, (undated). Also: KLO 68; "History of Kentucky Governors, William O. Bradley," http://www.historykygovenors.com (Accessed December 22, 2012); "Threats Made to Go After Judge Reed. Receives Letter Telling Him He Will Be Killed Unless Mob Inquiry Dropped." *MDM*, Vol. XV, No. 147, Monday, October 30, 1916, 1; "Judge Gardner Suggests Bill to Avoid Lynching. Wants Statute Making Removal Automatic for Surrendering Prisoners." *MDM*, Vol. XVI, No. 197, Friday, December 29, 1916, 2; "Dramatic Appeal of Governor Stanley Had Desired Effect. Offered to Sacrifice Own Life to Save Name of

Calloway County." *MWM*, Vol. XVII, No. 3. Thursday, January 18, 1917, 5; "Did Not Yield to the Will of the Mob at Murray." *MWM*, Vol. XVII, No. 3, Thursday, January 18, 1917, 8.

[7] The double hanging of Tom Tinker on February 9, 1915 and the resulting photograph remain perhaps the most infamous event in local history. Arriving late for the first hanging, photographer E.G. Burton allegedly ordered one of the local boys on the scene to rehang Tinker. The photograph was taken and Burton began selling copies of the photos for fifty cents each. When Sheriff W.B. Sullivan found out what had occurred, he ordered Burton to stop, buy back any outstanding photos and then destroyed them. "Tom Tinker," Graves County, Kentucky (Paducah, Kentucky: Turner Publishing Company, 2001), 53-54.

[8] Such establishments were also known as "blind tigers."

[9] "Mayfield was the first town in the state to effect local option. In the Spring of 1874 the first vote on the prohibition question was taken . . . A law was passed, which restricted the selling of liquor only to a certain extent. The law was not enforced, and whiskey could be easily bought. It was not until 1884, ten years later, after 7 or 8 votes on the question, that liquor and open saloons were successfully barred." D. Trabue Davis, *The Story of Mayfield Through a Century, 1823-1923*. Reprinted Simmons Historical Publications (Melber, Kentucky: 1990), 26.

[10] "The train's very apt nickname was "Whiskey Dick," after one of Bret Harte's most comically solemn tosspots [drunkards]. That name nowadays has been transferred to an Illinois Central freight train running out of Louisville in delicate allusion to the quantities of bourbon produced in that city." Albert Botkin, A Treasury of Railroad Folklore: the stories, tall tales, traditions, ballads, and songs of the American railroad man (New York, Crown Publishers, 1953), 490; With the men away in the service during World War I, Prohibition in effect and little drunkenness on board, *The Messenger* coyly suggested it be renamed "Water Dick." "Let Name Be Changed." *MWM*, XVIII, No. 38, Thursday, November 14, 1918, 5.

[11] Though the reference would have also been somewhat "before his time," there were apparently a number of brothels operating in Mayfield in 1907. "'Niggers Read and Run'" or How Sam Schofield Wrecked Mayfield Dive—R.E. Tribution Overtook Him." *The Paducah Evening Sun*, November 23, 1907, 1.

[12] The 1922 Paducah City Directory shows Bird Lytton and wife Jennie operating a "boarding house" at 204 Monroe. U.S. City Directories, 1821-1989 [database on-line]. Provo, UT, USA: Ancestry.com Operations, Inc., 2011.

[13] Emma, "a keeper of a house in the new "Red Light" district at 1020 N. 10th street" in Paducah attempted to commit suicide by taking a dose of morphine in May 1907. "Attempted Suicide." *MWM*, Volume Number 9, Thursday, May 30, 1907, 4; In the 1916 Paducah City Directory, Bessie and Ruth are residing at 1018 Murrell Blvd. Emma is listed at 1016 Boyd's Alley. *CAR 1916*, 321-22. Neither is listed in the 1918 directory.

[14] As colorful as this story of retrieving the pocketbook of money may be, it appears to be somewhat of a conflated "rural legend." There *was* a train accident involving the famed "Whisky Dick" with fatalities in which Ms. Martin (alternately referred to as "Ruby" or "Ruth") who worked in a house of "ill fame" suffered an injury to her leg. Although Ms. Martin did attend to Queenie McClure as *she* lay dying that was about where the truth of Haskell's version ended. The *Messenger* recorded that "The party were doubtless out for a joy ride, for beer and whisky bottles, cigars and cigarettes were scattered in all directions from the automobile by the collision . . . The McClure and Martin women were inmates of houses of ill fame in the section of Paducah known as the 'gash.'" Ruth Martin later filed suit against the railroad claiming permanent injury, a laceration to her leg. "Two Killed When Train Hits Automobile From Paducah. Z.C. Graham, Jr., and Queenie McClure Victims of Accident. At Gravel Pit Crossing. Lance Fox of Obion and Ruby Martin, Also in Car, Escape Practically Uninjured." *MDM*, Thursday, August 10, 1916, Vol. XV, No. 79, 1. Kentucky, Death Records, 1852-1953 [database on-line]. Provo, UT, USA: Ancestry.com Operations Inc., 2007. "Third Damage Suit Comes of Illinois Central's Accident. Ruth Martin Sues for $5,000—Makes

Aggregate of $90,000 Asked." *MDM*, Wednesday, September 20, 1916, Vol. XV, No. 113, 1.

[15] "Paducah, Ky., Feb. 2—Richard Iseman, 37 years old, one-armed, was shot down when in Theodore Peters saloon to-night by an unidentified bandit, who entered the saloon and ordered everyone to 'throw up your hands.' Iseman refused to hold up his single arm and the bandit shot him through the left temple, killing him.

"'See what a fool gets,' he remarked as he turned to the bartender. 'Give me that gun in that drawer and hand over the money,' he commanded. The bartender, Al Redmon, complied and the highway-man backed out the door.'"

"'Throw Up Your Hands!' One-Armed Man Slain." *The Hartford Herald*, 42nd Year, No. 6, Wednesday, February 09, 1916, 1; The saloon was located at 1049 Kentucky Avenue and a man positively identified by witnesses as Iseman's killer, Harvey Kissner, met the same fate when attempting to rob Schmidt's saloon at 1100 South Eleventh the following month. "Played it Once Too Often. Paducah Bandit Tackled the Wrong Man in a Saloon Hold-Up." *Hopkinsville Kentuckian*, Vol. XXXVII, No. 35, Tuesday, March 21, 1916, 8. "Paducah's Lone Bandit Meets Violent Death." *The Hartford Herald*, 42nd Year, No. 12, Wednesday, March 22, 1916, 1. *CAR* 1916-17, Vol. VII" (Louisville: 1916), 673. Despite the positive identification, however, another man ("a well known police character") was charged and convicted of the crime based on circumstantial evidence. "The Iseman Murder Case. Will Malone Makes Clean Breast and Tells About Preparations. Elmendorf is Held. Startling Admissions Made in the Sensational Trial in Paducah Tuesday." *MDM*, Vo. XIV, No. 259, Wednesday, February 16, 1916, 1. "Elmendorf is Charged With Murder." *MDM*, Vol. XIV, No. 318, April 25, 1916, 3. "Convicted of Murder. Ernest Elmendorf Sentenced at Paducah to Prison for Life." *MDM*, Vol. XIV, No. 322, Saturday, April 29, 1916, 1. Protesting his innocence to the end, Ernest Elmendorf died in prison at Eddyville, age 47. "Ernest Elmendorf Dies at Eddyville. Death Comes In Few Hours After Stricken With Fatal Illness." *MWM*, Vol. XVII, No. 47, Thursday, December 20, 1917, 6.

CHAPTER ELEVEN: THE SOCIAL EVIL

[1] *REP*, 4, 7.

[2] "Blind Tiger Put Out of Business, 100 or More Citizens Organize Themselves and Raid Made Monday Afternoon. House Near Fair Grounds Visited and 'Red Eye' Confiscated. Ministers and Citizens Announce They Inted [sic] To Stop Illicit Sale of Whisky." *MDM*, Vol. IX, No. 76, Tuesday, April 6, 1909, 1. "Another Effort to Reduce License on Pool Rooms. Negro Pool Room and Restaurant Promises to Leave Broadway for Other Location." *MDM*, Vol. XIV, No. 270, Tuesday, February 29, 1916, 1. "Editorial. The Pool Room Agitation." *MDM*, Vol. XIV, No. 273, Friday, March 3, 1916, 1. "Settled as to Pool Rooms. City Council Deals Death Blow to Lowering License to $100." *MDM*, Vol. XIV, No. 276, Tuesday, March 7, 1916, 1. "Editorial. After the Skating Rinks." *MDM*, Vol. XV, No. 65, Tuesday, July 25, 1916, 1. "Council Gives Permit for Skating Rink on West Water Street," *MDM*, Vol. XVI, No. 239, Thursday, February 22, 1917, 1. "Fancy Farm Druggist Claims He Has Right to Sell Soft Drinks on Sunday," *MDM*, Vol. XV, No. 65, Tuesday, July 25, 1916, 1.

[3] *REP*, 40

[4] "Voice of the People. The Fight Against the Bawdy Houses—A Statement." *PES*, Monday, December 3, 1906, 4. "Best Town in Kentucky," *PES*, Thursday, November 29, 1906, 4.

[5] "Voice of the People. The Fight Against the Bawdy Houses—A Statement." *PES*, Monday, December 3, 1906, 4.

[6] "Red Light's Doom Will Be Sounded. People Are in Earnest About Cleaning Up District." *PES*, Wednesday, August 1, 1906, 1. "Red Lights Go Out on December First. Judge Reed Orders Disorderly Houses on Kentucky Avenue to Abate Nuisance." *PES*, Wednesday, September 19, 1906, 1.

[7] *REP*, 17. "The Exodus," *PES*, Friday, November 16, 1906, 4. "Cairo Protests Against Invasion. Sends Paducah Women Out of That City." *PES*, Monday, December 3, 1905, 1. "Some Policemen and Cab Drivers said to Know About Location of Bawdy Houses." *PES*, Friday, December 14, 1906, 1.

[8] "Fiat and Sentiment," *PES*, Tuesday January 15, 1907, 4.

[9] *REP*, 23

[10] ""City Ordinance," *PES*, Friday, August 20, 1909, 8.

[11] CON, 26. Although prostitution is, perhaps, more easily defined today, that was not the case in progressive America during the early 1900's. In fact, even within the pages of the vice report on the metropolitan city of Chicago, it's author's struggled to come to terms with a definition. In *The Response to Prostitution in the Progressive Era* by Mark Thomas Connelly, the author notes that ". . . in the moral world of The Social Evil in Chicago, potentially all sexual activity unsanctioned by marriage could be characterized as prostitution." The reports of other cities were no more precise. Author Connelly comments that, "Each could have applied, with rough accuracy, to a professional streetwalker, a sexually active or promiscuous young woman, a married man or woman in an extramarital affair, or even a married couple practicing birth control." As hard as it is to grasp now, the moral culture of the period would not allow a more precise definition. The vocabulary just didn't exist. There was simply either a "good girl" or a "bad girl." A more precise definition would only occur after the social scientists and sex researchers of the middle 20th century had more thoroughly delved into the topic. CON, 28.

[12] *REP*, 41

[13] Not that pastor Quin came to Paducah with any illusions in the first place. "Frankly, it's one of the roughest spots in the diocese—the community, I mean," he was warned by Bishop Woodcock, before continuing, "There are a lot of undisciplined, self-indulgent people in Paducah." Alan L. Chidsey, *The Bishop: A Portrait of the Right Reverend Clinton S. Quin*, Houston, TX: Gulf Publishing Co., 1966, p. 71 as cited in "Fifth Sunday After Epiphany," Grace Episcopal Church, Accessed November 18, 2014, http://www.gracepaducah.net/resources-2/sermons/fifth-sunday-after-the-epiphany/ "Mayor Paducah to Appoint Vice Commission That Will Investigate the Social Evil." *MDM*, Vol. XIV, No. 261, Friday, February 18, 1916, 1. "Vice Commission. Named By Paducah Mayor. Prominent Men and Social Workers Appointed." *MDM,* Vol. XIV, Saturday, March 4, 1916, No. 274, 3.

[14] *Report and Recommendations of the Paducah Vice Commission.* Paducah, Kentucky, 1916, 5

[15] CON, 37. *REP*, 46, 29, 7.

[16] *REP*, 4, 11

[17] "Red Light Resorts Must Be Closed if Cantonment is Established in Louisville," *MDM*, Vol. XVII, No. 39, Wednesday, June 27, 1917, 3. *REP*, 39.

[18] *REP*, 11-12, 42

[19] *REP*, 33-35

[20] CON, 89. *REP*, 21.

[21] *REP*, 8. *REP*, 32. *REP*, 16. *REP*, 7.

[22] ROB.

[23] ROB.

[24] "Bawdy Houses To Be Closed In Paducah." *MDM*, Vol. XV, No. 68, Friday, July 28, 1916, 2.

[25] "Charges Against Five Women Are Erased By Judge. Crossland Says There Is No Law Against Playing Pianos In Bawdy Houses And He Will Not Fine." *MDM*, Vol. XV, No. 71, Tuesday, August 1, 1916, 2.

[26] "Southern Hotel Is Too Hot For Rev. Mr. Myrick. Calvert City Minister Declares Porter Offered To Provide Him With A Woman As He Goes To Room." *MDM*, Vol. XV, No. 103, Friday, September 8, 1916, 2.

27 "Business So Good Madam Wanted To Add Ten Rooms." *PES*, Vol. XXXVIII, No. 2, Tuesday, January 2, 1917, 2.

28 "Rebuke Paducah Fathers. Rev. Clinton S. Quin Uses Strong Language in Resigning." *MDM*, Tuesday, December 26, 1916, 3.

29 "Last Sermon by Rev. C.S. Quin. Beloved Rector of Grace Church and Vigorous Apostle." *PES*, Vol. XXXVIII, No. 6, Saturday, January 6, 1917, 5. Fred Gus Neuman, *The Story of Paducah*, Young Printing Company, 1927, 176. Accessed November 18, 2014, http://books.google.com/books?ei=V6VrVKSqKYO3yAT0gIKgCA&id=KPETAAAAYA AJ&dq=Clinton+S.+Quin+paducah&focus=searchwithinvolume&q=Clinton+S.+Quin+ Among a lifetime of other achievements, Bishop Quin would be instrumental in the founding of St. Luke's Episcopal Hospital in Houston. "St. Luke's Episcopal Hospital," *Texas Monthly*, July 1990, 106.

CHAPTER TWELVE: MIGRATION

1 "The block-long Merit Manufacturing Company Building at Fifth and South Street was the site for over seventy years of one of Mayfield's most important industries. The original Merit Pant Company was organized on October 1, 1899 and began business in an upper story room. In 1900 the company was incorporated and the two-story brick factory on Fifth Street built. A stone plaque above the entranceway to the factory recognizes D.R. Merritt as president and Z.T. Long as vice-president of the company. The company manufactured such products as 'American Gentlemen Trousers', 'Pony Boy Suits', and 'Merit Hi-School Suits'. Merit pants were known all over the nation. In 1923 it was estimated that 7,500 merchants sold Merit pants and one million men wore them. The Merit Company continued to operate until the late 1970s." National Register of Historic Places Inventory—Nomination Form, completed July 31, 1984. http://pdfhost.focus.nps.gov/ docs/NRHP/Text/84001477.pdf Accessed May 12, 2012.

2 Samuel Benson "Uncle Ben" Wright (10/4/1828-6/24/1913), one of the original settlers of Graves County. "S.B. Wright Died Today," *MDM*, Tuesday, June 24th, 1913, 1.

3 Florence graduated May 18, 1917. She then took and successfully passed the examination for county Teachers' certificate over June 15 and 16th, 1917. "Successful Persons In Teachers' Examination," *MDM*, Vol. XVII, No. 37, Monday, June 25, 1917, 1; "Miss Florence Jones was one of the successful teachers who made a first-class teachers' certificate in the examination last Friday and Saturday. Her average was 95 2-10. She will teach at Boswell's school this time." "Mayfield Route Four." *MDM*, Vol. XVII, No. 39, Wednesday, June 27, 1917, 3.

4 In rural school districts, the one-room school was the norm throughout Kentucky. "The usual type is a one-room frame house lighted from both sides. According to the report of the state superintendent of education in 1917, out of 8,115 houses, 7,025 were one-room buildings of which 123 were located in ordinary log cabins. Many are situated far from the road and in most inaccessible spots. The grounds are barren of trees and grass. The houses themselves are in poor repair with broken windows, torn shades, and often broken benches, and there is a general sordidness about them." NEW 52; "In the school laws can be found this provision:

'The County Board of Education shall furnish each schoolhouse with at least the following articles of furniture and apparatus: teacher's desk and chair, a seat, patent or otherwise, with back, for each child, the height of the seat and its back to suit the age of the child; no desk or bench to be made to accommodate more than two children; writing desk for all pupils; blackboard space of at least fifty square feet; water stand.

'Even these few articles are missing in many of the schools. In only two schools visited were adjustable seats found. In five others there were seats of varying size, but in all the rest benches were of one size and unfitted for many of the children. In place of ordinary blackboards, one side of a room in painted black and used for writing purposes. Often there is no desk for the teacher, who is compelled to use one of the desks provided for the children. In many schools three children are accommodated on the same seat.'" NEW 54; Graves County had over 150 one-room schoolhouses. Personal email communication with Debbie Smith, Graves County School District, January 15, 2011.

CHAPTER THIRTEEN: "SINGING SOLDIERS"

[1] SKR 27.

[2] SKR 113, 116.

[3] Ralph C. Busbey. "Rubber," A Centennial History of Akron 1825-1925, Summit County Historical Society, 1925, 313-345. Accessed December 12, 2014. http://www.akronhistory.org/busbey_rubber.htm

[4] *CEN* 113 & 119; Clarice Finley Lewis, *A History of Firestone Park* (Firestone Park Citizens Council 20th Anniversary 1966-1986. n.p., n.d.), 16.

[5] CEN, 344; WOOL, 13.

[6] GRIS, 349.

[7] Edwin Balmer. "Akron—Suzerain of Rubber." *Collier's Weekly*, December 29, 1917, Volume 60, No. 16, 13-14.

[8] Balmer, Ibid.

[9] "The City That Blew Itself Up," *The American Mercury*, February 11th, 1926, 176-177.

[10] "The City That Blew Itself Up," *The American Mercury*, February 1926, 176; TULL, 133.

[11] GRIS, 377.

[12] TULL, 133.

[13] WOLF, 337.

[14] Jon C. Teaford, *Cities of the Heartland: The Rise and Fall of the Industrial Midwest* (Indiana University Press: Bloomington, Indiana, 1993), 108

[15] WOLF, 499-500.

[16] WOLF, 362.

[17] Although abortive attempts had been made to organize the rubber workers by the AFL and the IWW (or "Wobblies"), their efforts would not bear fruit for another 20 years. Bruce M. Meyer, *The Once and Future Union, The Rise and Fall of the United Rubber Workers*, 1935-1995 (The University of Akron Press, 2002).

[18] Malcolm Gladwell "Harlan, Kentucky," *Outliers, The Story of Success*. (New York: Little, Brown and Company, 2008), 170.

[19] "Disabling Sickness Among Employees of a Rubber Manufacturing Establishment in 1918, 1919, and 1920." *Public Health Reports*, Vol. 37, No. 50, December 15, 1922, 3085; One historian calculated that Akron's murder rate increased by 457 percent between 1914 and 1920. Even if you took the city's growth rate of 202 percent between 1910 and 1920 into consideration, the toll was still staggering. John Hevener, "Appalachians in Akron, 1914-1945: The Transfer of Southern Folk Culture," TMs [photocopy], p. 6, Box 17, John Hevener Papers, Southern Appalachian Archives, Special Collections, Berea College. As cited in JOH, 106.

[20] *Akron Evening Times*, April 13, 1920. As cited in JOH, 107.

[21] *Akron Evening Times*, April 11, 1920. As cited in JOH, 110.

[22] *ABJ*, March 23, 1916. As cited in JOH 98.

[23] *ABJ*, April 27th, 1920. As cited in JOH, 103.

[24] "Home."

[25] WOOL

[26] WOOL

[27] WOOL

[28] Steve Love and David Giffels, "Building Communities Goodyear, Firestone Offer Homes, Strong Bonds," *ABJ*, March 30, 1997.

[29] BLEW, 176.

[30] WOLF, 438.

[31] WOOL

[32] Greg Grandin. *Fordlandia, The Rise and Fall of Henry Ford's Forgotten Jungle City.* Metropolitan Books, Henry Holt and Company LLC: New York, 2009, 272.

[33] SKR, 121.

[34] *The Work of the Labor Division.* Goodyear Tire & Rubber, Co. (Akron: 1920) 63-64.

[35] HOME, 3; This despite the fact the architect of the plan was simultaneously telling the business world that it was "practical welfare work . . . primarily designed to create a proper organization, loyal to his company's interests . . . ." "Houses in Akron, Ohio." *The Intelligencer,* June 9, 1917, Volume XI, Number 8. Metropolitan Life Insurance Company, New York, 12.

[36] HOME, 4.

[37] HOME, 4.

[38] *A Wonder Book of Rubber* (Akron: Superior [B.F. Goodrich Company]. 1917), 33 as cited in SKR 70

[39] SKR 101.

[40] Jim Carney, "Homes Demolished in Minutes as Akron Wipes Out Pieces of History, Moves Forward," *ABJ,* December 19, 2011; TULL, 143.

[41] JOH, 99

[42] JOH, 103

[43] Alfred Winslow Jones, Life, Liberty, and Property: A Story of Conflict and a Measurement of Conflicting Rights (New York: J.B. Lippincott Co., 1941), 62-63. Cited in JOH 66.

[44] Allen Sinsheimer. "Giving Permanency to Keeping Men at Their Jobs," *Automobile,* March 8, 1917, 524-8. As reported in Business Digest, Vol. 3, pg. 394; In today's dollars, calculated by Production Worker Compensation that would be valued at $295,000,000. http://www.measuringworth.com/uscompare/ Accessed September 3, 2011.

[45] SKR, 120.

[46] WOLF, 437.

[47] WOOL

[48] JOH, 99.

[49] Charles T. Hutchison, "The Business Outlook," *Mining and Scientific Press,* November 27th, 1920, Vol. 121, 755; Herman Fetzer, "An Outline of The City's History," *Centennial* (Summit County, Ohio: Summit County Historical Society/Akron Beacon Journal Company, 1925), 118; WOLF, 437.

[50] Allen Sinsheimer. "Emulation. The Mainspring of Efficiency," *Automotive Industries,* May 3, 1917. Volume 36, Issues 3-18, 880.

[51] JOH, 43.

[52] "Immigration dropped from 1.2 million in 1914 to only 110,000 in 1918." James N. Gregory, T*he Southern Diaspora, How the Great Migrations of Black and White Southerners Transformed America* (Chapel Hill: The University of North Carolina Press, 2005), 24. JOH, 38; At Goodyear, alone, some 6,200 employees were either drafted or volunteered. O'Reilly, *Goodyear,* 44.

[53] Paul W. Litchfield, *Industrial Voyage: My Life as an Industrial Lieutenant* (New York: Doubleday, 1954), 175. As cited in JOH 86.

[54] WHE, 125; ORE, 44; TULL, 145; Even at the height of World War II War Production, the majority of blacks hired in the rubber shops were for janitorial positions. H.B. "Doc" Kerr, "On The Home Front. Rural Route Mail Service Adds One Rubber Ball To Scrap Pile; Negroes Aid Industry." *ABJ,* 103rd Year, No. 220, Monday, July 13, 1942, 3; The first African American tire worker was actually hired in 1955. TULL, 146.

[55] Personal communication with Steve Love, May 30, 2017.

[56] TULL, 144.

[57] TULL, 146.

[58] Arthur Kornhauser, *Detroit as People See It: A Survey of Attitudes in an Industrial City* (Detroit: Wayne University Press, 1952), 46-47. As cited in JOH, 15-16.

[59] Clyde B. McCoy and Virginia McCoy Watkins. "Stereotypes of Appalachian Migrants." *The Invisible Minority: Urban Appalachians*, eds. William W. Philliber and Clyde B. McCoy, 20-31. Lexington, Ky.: University Press of Kentucky, 1981. As cited in JOH, 15-16.

[60] Dan M. McKee and Phillip J. Obermiller, *From Mountain to Metropolis: Urban Appalachians in Ohio* (Cincinnati: Ohio Urban Appalachian Awareness Project, 1978), 1. As cited in JOH, 17.

CHAPTER FOURTEEN: ARRIVAL

[1] This would appear to be Francis G. Hannah (wife Bessie) who lived at 136 Crescent Drive in Akron. He is first listed in the Akron City Directories as in 1920 as working at Firestone and again in 1922. In 1926 he is recorded as a department manager.

[2] The *Akron City Directory* notes this as being the "Richmond Stag Hotel" and was located at 591 S. Main. *ACD*, 1372.

CHAPTER FIFTEEN: THE MILLER RUBBER COMPANY I

[1] Saturday, March 17th, 1917. St. Patrick's Day.

[2] "Carbon black, obtained by the incomplete combustion of natural gas . . . has increased, immensely, the life expectancy of tires . . . . To color these gray or white casings black, the manufacturers took to adding small quantities of carbon black. At about the same time in 1912, however, several observers . . . discovered that this coloring stuff was not only a reinforcing medium, but the best one that ever had come the tire maker's way. Gradually amounts used were increased, and today [1936] twenty per cent by volume of carbon black goes into the long-wearing treads to aid in resisting the abrasion of road upon tire." WOLF, 355.

[3] "In addition to the rubber there are . . . other materials common to every rubber article . . . . If tires, for instance, were to be made of pure rubber with only enough sulphur for vulcanization and nothing else, they would run no more than a few hundred miles . . . . Carbon black . . . is doubly valuable, for it is cheaper than the rubber it replaces and at the same time it increases tremendously the strength of the compound in which it is used." WOLF, 359.

[4] From the description of the use of lampblack, the steel rolls and the resulting fatality, this would appear to be a roller mill, the second stage in the processing of rubber after it has been received and washed. Here, the crude rubber was mixed on a series of steel rollers along with shovelfuls of sulphur, lampblack and other dry powders to produce seven-foot rolls of usable stock. WOLF, 361-362.

CHAPTER SIXTEEN: FIRESTONE TIRE & RUBBER

[1] "The creel room is the only quiet spot in the factory. In it demurely sit thousands of cones of stout cotton cord, each silently delivering it eight-mile long content at the behest of a nearby giant—the calender. Through a central gathering comb, a wide flat band of many cords is pulled over a heated roll and in between the bottom rolls of the calender. This consists of three heavy vertical rolls operating at different speeds. Rubber compound is fed between the two top rolls, is carried around the middle cylinder and is wiped off by the cord passing through at the bottom. The sheet of rubbered cord is rolled up in cloth treated to prevent its sticking, and taken to the bias cutter, where, as it is unwound, a cutting knife lops off strips at an angle. These strips, of the proper width to form a ply in the carcass of the tire, are joined together, then cut to proper length and carried off to the tire builder." WOLF, 363; "Articles of a more complicated cross section are shaped by forcing them out of a 'tubing' machine.

This might be likened to a giant sausage grinder—a revolving screw squeezing rubber out through a die of any desired design. In this way are all kinds of tubing and hose, strips for auto windows and insulated electric wire produced. Too long to be cured in molds, the articles, after being shaped by the tuber, are vulcanized in hot air or steam. Rubber bands and jar rings are first made as long tubes and, after vulcanization, are placed on lathes and cut by sharp knives." WOLF, 362.

CHAPTER EIGHTEEN: FIRESTONE TIRE & RUBBER II

[1] Per Haskell, this was his last name; The *Akron City Directory* for 1917 records a James G. Bartholmew working at Firestone. *ACD*, 1917, 342.

[2] The B.F. Goodrich Co. alone reported 9 homicides in the workplace in the four and a half years from November 1, 1915 through May 1, 1920. That was two more than the number they reported killed in industrial accidents. "Disabling Sickness Among Employees of a Rubber Manufacturing Establishment in 1918, 1919, and 1920." *Public Health Reports*, Vol. 37, No. 50, December 15, 1922, 3085.

[3] Per the 1930 Census, Albert A. Spitznas, 39, was classified as an "Employment Agent" at a "Rubber Shop." *1930*; Census, Place: *Akron, Summit, Ohio*; Roll: *1880*; Page: *7B*; Enumeration District: *154*; Image: *821.0*; FHL microfilm: *2341614*

[4] The only person by the name of Buckmaster working at Firestone recorded in the Akron City Directories from 1918-20 is Lelland S. Buckmaster, who resided at 150 W. Miller, just a few doors down from Haskell. During this time period, he is only recorded in the 1920 directory. *ACD*, 1920, 479.

CHAPTER NINETEEN: ROOMMATES

[1] E.R. Hayhurst, A.M., M.D., "The General Principles of Industrial Hygiene," *SIHH*, 10-11.

[2] The *Akron City Directory* for 1917 shows the address listed to H. H. Jackson. *ACD*, 1917, 175.

[3] The 1917 Akron City Directory lists Mrs. Martha "(wid George W)" Pennington at 56 W. Miller Ave. *ACD*, 1917, 1416.

[4] For a scientific explanation of why this occurs, see Esther Ingles-Arkell. "Why Grease Kills the Head on a Beer." http://io9.com/why-grease-kills-the-head-on-a-beer-1680239372 Accessed February 10, 2015.

[5] His estimate was "spot on." Just between Goodrich (located at 444-586 S. Main) and Firestone (at 1286 S. Main), The *Akron City Directory* of 1918 records 30 saloons—and 20 "Billiard Rooms"—over the 1 ¾ mile distance. This does not include establishments that may have had their physical address on a corner side street. By 1919, after Prohibition, there was not a single saloon listed. *ACD*, 1918, 1528, 1575-76.

[6] Per the *Akron City Directory*, this would be the Canellos & Chakiris Billiard Room. *ACD*, 1918, 1528.

[7] Per a reverse search of a billiard room at 1105 S. Main, in the 1918 *Akron City Directory* the proprietors are Steve Canellos and James Chakiris, both also residing at 1105 S. Main. "Jimmy the Greek" would therefore have to have been James Chakiris. *ACD*, 1918, 508, 530; Although the restaurant section of the 1917 *Akron City Directory* ties 1101 S. Main to Steven Canellos (without a specific restaurant name) and pages are missing in the restaurant section of the online 1918 Akron Directory, 1101 S. Main is tied to S. Canellos and 1105 S. Main as Canellos & Chakiris in that edition. It would appear that the Billiard Room was at 1105 and the Manhattan Restaurant at 1101. *ACD*, 1918, 158; World War I Draft Records show a Demetrio James Chakiris as a resident of Akron, Ohio, residing at 1101 S. Main on June 5, 1917. His birthplace is listed as Greece and he is employed as a waiter at the Manhattan Café. World War I Draft Registration Cards, 1917-1918. FHL Roll Number 1819511, Draft Board

4.

[8] **HASKELL:** Me and another guy went to Barberton and got drunk once. Got off the streetcar and walked about halfway home. I was sick. He said, "I'll get that out of you." We stopped at a little, old restaurant over there in Kenmore and he went in. Take me in with him. A little bit of a restaurant about half— About this wide. Said, to the guy, "You got any cream?" And the guy said, "Yeah." And he said, "Give 'em here." A glass of cream. "Well," he said to me, "you drink this and get the hell out of here." So I turned it up and I drank it all. I wanted to get better. I was not feelin' real— I headed for that door and I just pushed the screen door open and I heaved as far as from here to that door—clear out to the car-track. Whooooom! Man, I really unloaded. It took that whiskey out of me, I'll tell you. Oooh! I can remember that. I could go back to that neighborhood within fifty feet of where that little, old restaurant was now.

[9] FRAN; Indeed, opportunities for recreation were so poor that Summit County wouldn't even have a public park until a small tract of land was donated in 1925. Cheri Goldner, Librarian Akron-Summit County Public Library, "The History of Metro Parks." http://www.summitmetroparks.org/insidemetroparks/History.aspx Accessed July 2, 2014.

[10] Summit Beach Park opened for the first time on the last Saturday in June, 1917. "Park Celebrates Sliver Anniversary." *ABJ*, 103rd Year, No. 205, Sunday, June 28, 1942, 12A.

[11] At the time, the "Over The Top Coaster" was billed as the fastest and steepest roller coaster in the country. Four passengers eventually died and eleven were injured. FRAN 42-43.

[12] Originally built for the adjacent Lakeside Park, which was subsequently absorbed by Summit Beach Park, the Casino had seating for 1,900 and 12 private boxes. Admission to see concerts, summer stock theater, animal acts, circus performers and vaudeville's best acts was twenty cents for reserved seats and ten cents for general admission. FRAN 23-24.

[13] Actually, there were just two brothers, Willie (born Wilhelm Levkowitz) and Eugene. Comedian Fred Allen recalled that "Willie Howard was a great artist. He was a fine comedian, an accomplished dramatic actor, an excellent singer, and a versatile mimic," before adding that he, "wasted most of his professional life impersonating actors who didn't have a fraction" of his talent. Willie and his brother may well have been the inspiration for Neil Simon's "The Sunshine Boys." Benjamin Ivy, The Schmooze: Your Jewish Pop Culture Fix. "Willie Howard, More than Just a Sunshine Boy. July 30, 2012. http://forward.com/schmooze/160194/willie-howard-more-than-just-a-sunshine-boy/ Accessed April 18, 2017.

[14] Authors Francis and Francis note, "The roller skating rink was among the largest in the Midwest." FRAN, 38.

[15] One website references the skater in black tights during the 1920's, quoting an undated photograph and article from the *Akron Beacon Journal*, referencing a now broken link: "The acrobat's steel skates glinted in the spotlight as he steadied himself on a 3/8-inch wire about 50 feet above the crowd. The taut cable made a steep descent from theater balcony to orchestra pit . . . . Near the halfway point, the audience exhaled. Cheers rippled below. The crowd burst into applause. By the time Lowther hit bottom and skated onstage, the roar was deafening. The Akron man's famous "Slide for Life" routine dazzled audiences around the globe. As world roller-skating champion, Lowther never failed to impress." http://www.rubberbuzz.com/2005/04/roller-skating.html Accessed November 4, 2011.

CHAPTER TWENTY: WORLD WAR ONE

[1] "Lucille, the five-year-old daughter of Arthur Scott, living six miles northwest of Mayfield, was burned to death Sunday by her dress catching fire from an open grate. The child was burned at 10 o'clock and lingered in terrible agony until 7:30 p.m. She was horribly burned from her knees up and part of the hair of her head was also burned off. Drs. Neal and Shelton of Mayfield were summoned immediately following the accident, but the burns were so serious that the child's life could not be saved. Burial occurred at 2 o'clock Monday afternoon at the

Dowdy graveyard." "Five-Year-Old Girl Burned to Death," *MWM*, Vol. XVII—No. 47. Mayfield, Kentucky, Thursday, December 20, 1917, 2.

² Now Western Kentucky University; Tuition for teachers was free and many Graves County teachers enrolled between sessions of their rural schools. MILLS 77.

CHAPTER TWENTY-ONE: THE SPANISH FLU

¹ "The Influenza Pandemic of 1918." http://virus.stanford.edu/uda/ Accessed August 28, 2011.

² Rodolfo Acuna-Soto, C. Viboud, G. Chowell (2011) "Influenza and Pneumonia Mortality in 66 Large Cities in the United States in Years Surrounding the 1918 Pandemic." PLoS ONE 6(8): e23467. doi:10.1371/journal.pone.0023467Accessed October 30, 2014. http://chowell.lab.asu.edu/publication_pdfs/Influenza%20and%20pneumonia%20mortality%20in%2066%20large%20cities%20in%20the%20United%20States%20in%20years%20surrounding%20the%201918%20pandemic..pdf

³ "Top 10 Facts About the 1918 Flu Pandemic." http://www.toptenz.net/top-10-facts-about-the-1918-flu-pandemic.php Accessed August 28, 2011.

⁴ BRAIN; John M. Barry, "The Story of Influenza," The Threat of Pandemic Influenza. Are We Ready? U.S. National Library of Medicine, National Institutes of Health (Washington, DC: National Academies Press, 2005) http://www.ncbi.nlm.nih.gov/ books/NBK22148/ Accessed September 3, 2011.

⁵ John M. Barry, "The Story of Influenza," The Threat of Pandemic Influenza. Are We Ready? U.S. National Library of Medicine, National Institutes of Health (Washington, DC: National Academies Press, 2005) http://www.ncbi.nlm.nih.gov/books/NBK22148/ Accessed September 3, 2011.

⁶ In fact, it became known as the "Spanish Flu" because Spain was a neutral country in World War I. As such, it had no censorship of the news, giving the disease it widest and most reliable coverage. John M. Barry, "The Story of Influenza," The Threat of Pandemic Influenza. Are We Ready? The Story of Influenza. U.S. National Library of Medicine. National Institutes of Health (Washington, DC: National Academies Press, 2005) http://www.ncbi.nlm.nih.gov/books/NBK22148/ Accessed September 3, 2011.http://www.ncbi.nlm.nih.gov/books/NBK22148/ September 3, 2011.

⁷ "The Public Health Service," *Scientific American* 86:343, 30 Nov 1918. As cited by Carla R. Morrisey, RN, BSN. "The Influenza Epidemic of 1918," The Navy Department Library, Department of the Navy, Naval Historical Center. http://www.history.navy.mil/library/online/influenza%20epid%201918.htm August 28, 2011.

⁸ Previous dates on June 5ᵗʰ, 1917 and June 5ᵗʰ, 1918 (including a supplemental registration on August 24, 1918) were only for men aged 21 and over. Kimberly Powell, "WWI Draft Registration Records," http://genealogy.about.com/od/records/p/ wwi_draft.htm Accessed September 4, 2011.

⁹ The Public Health Service. *Scientific American* 86:343, 30 Nov 1918. As cited by Carla R. Morrisey, RN, BSN, "The Influenza Epidemic of 1918." The Navy Department Library, Department of the Navy, Naval Historical Center. http://www.history.navy.mil /library/online/influenza%20epid%201918.htm August 28, 2011.

¹⁰ Some 3,631 men registered in Graves County on that date. "Registration of September 12ᵗʰ." *MWM*, Vol. XVIII, No. 33, Thursday, September 19, 1918, 6.

¹¹ "Fort Knox May Never Have Been Built if it Were Not for Camp Zachary Taylor," Camp Zachary Taylor Historical Society, January 21, 2010. http://camptaylorhistorical.org/page/2/ Accessed August 28, 2011.

¹² "The Great Pandemic. The United States in 1918-1919. Kentucky." http://1918.pandemicflu.gov/your_state/kentucky.htm Accessed August 28, 2011.

¹³ "Doctors Called to Camp Taylor." *MWM*, Vol. XVIII, No. 36, Thursday, October 10,

1918, 3.

[14] Keith L. Runyon, Opinion: "1918: When Influenza Paralyzed Louisville," *Louisville Courier Journal*, April 28, 2009. http://legacy.kctcs.edu/todaysnews/index.cfm?tn_date= 2009-04-28#20951 Accessed September 3, 2011.

[15] "Death List at Camp Taylor is Near 800." *MWM*, Vol. XVII, No. 38, Thursday, November 21, 1918, 8.

CHAPTER TWENTY-TWO: CAMP KNOX

[1] In fact, if he were to have enlisted at the time, he would have had the opportunity to join his neighbors as a company of soldiers was being organized for "Graves county boys to go in a body." "Graves County to Organize Company for New 4th Kentucky Regiment." *MWM*, Vol. XVII, No. 22, Thursday, July 5, 2017, 6.

[2] In efforts to protect the soldiers and the war effort from the effects of venereal disease, the Commission on Training Camp Activities was created in 1917 to protect all military encantonments. With the authority of the Chamberlain-Kahn Act and the Selective Service Act that banned any form of prostitution within five and sometimes ten miles around a camp, military police had carte blanche to enact whatever measures they wished against the civilian population without due process, legal representation or trial. Based on the merest suspicion of their activities, women could be rounded up off the streets and tested for venereal disease. A positive test was considered positive evidence of prostitution and they were put into custody for "rehabilitation." Lacking appropriate medical facilities, the county jail in Louisville was one such place of rehabilitation (though there was a move to transfer "white women" to the City Hospital). The legalities of the enforced quarantine were upheld by the courts and the city fathers, not wishing to lose the financial benefits of the nearby encantonment, were happy to go along. CON 136-150. Fricks, L.D. & Stuart Graves. "The Fight Against Venereal Disease in the Encantonment Zone About Camp Taylor," *The American Journal of Syphilis*. St. Louis: C.V. Mosby Co., Vol. III, January, April, July, October 1919, 280-290.

[3] Ironically, Mary's father appears to have died less than a year after Haskell had broken off the relationship of "Acute Bright's Disease" with a secondary cause of "Malarial Fever." *Kentucky Death Records, 1852-1953* [database on-line]. Provo, UT, USA: Ancestry.com Operations Inc., 2007.

[4] Haskell Jones' draft registration shows the date to actually be one month later on September 12th, 1918.

[5] "Three Thousand Blacks to Be Trained, New Order Says." *MWM*, Vol. XVII, No. 38, Thursday, October 18, 1917, 3.

[6] The war ended on Monday, November 11, 1918. Haskell would have left Camp Knox after being paid on Saturday, November 16th. All physical examinations for the service ceased the following Thursday. "No More Examinations by Local Draft Board." *MWM*, Vol. XVIII, No. 38, Thursday, November 21st, 1918, 1.

[7] While the toll in Mayfield and Graves County from the Spanish Flu has not been found (with even a contemporary history of Mayfield, written in 1923, failing to record it), the number of those who died in military service is recorded—9 from Mayfield and 20 from Graves County. Of those 6 in Mayfield died of disease, with only one stateside. Within Graves County, 18 died of disease, 12 of which died stateside at a military encampment. D. Trabue Davis, *The Story of Mayfield Through a Century, 1823-1923*. Reprinted Simmons Historical Publications (Melber, Kentucky: 1990), 8.

[8] "Influenza. An Advisory Proclamation by the State Board of Health." *MWM*, Vol. XVIII, No. 35, Thursday, October 3, 1918, 1.

[9] "County Schools Ordered Closed for One Week." *MWM*, Vol. XVIII, No. 36, Thursday, October 10, 1918, 3; "Flu Causes Jury Dismissal. Judge Gregory Acts on Advice of the Health Board. Cannot Afford to Take Chances and Jeopardize Health of Community."

MWM, Vol. XVIII, No. 40, Thursday, December 5, 1918, 1.

[10] "The Messenger's Troubles." *MWM*, Vol. XVIII, No. 36, Thursday, October 17, 1918, 1.

[11] "Ban Outside of Mayfield. Widespread Epidemic of Influenza Causes This Action." *MWM*, Vol. XVIII, No. 40, Thursday, December 5, 1918, 7.

[12] Preliminary Vital Statistics Report for 1918 and Tables for 7 Years, 1911-1917 Inclusive. Bulletin of the State Board of the Health of Kentucky. Vol. IX, No. 4, April 1919, Louisville, Kentucky, 1919, 3; Due to the impact of the flu, accurate public health reports were obviously among the casualties. In Graves County, no cases of either flu or pneumonia were reported in the latter months of 1919, while total documented in the weekly reports during early 1920 were only listed sporadically. *Public Health Reports*, United States Public Health Service, Vol. 34, Part 2, Numbers 27-52, July—December, 1919. *Public Health Reports*. United States Public Health Service, Vol. 35, Part 1, Numbers 1-26, January—June, 1920, Washington, Government Printing Office, 1920, 140, 234, 407, 468, 719.

[13] "Much School Time Lost This Term." *MWM*, Vol. XVII, No. 50, January 6, 1919, 5; While the influenza epidemic was more likely to strike those in the prime of life, this closure may well have had a major impact on the reduction of deaths from flu among school-age children, as well. The mortality rate in Kentucky for under age 6 was 971 per 100,000 and 563 per 100,000, it was only 219 per 100,000 in the group aged 6 to 16 years. Preliminary Vital Statistics Report for 1918 and Tables for 7 Years, 1911-1917 Inclusive. Bulletin of the State Board of the Health of Kentucky. Vol. IX, No. 4, April 1919, Louisville, Kentucky, 1919, 2; Throughout the Commonwealth, some 7,917 will be reported dead from the beginning of the epidemic just through December 1st. "Mortality Report for Kentucky From Beginning of Flu Epidemic to December 1." *MWM*, Vol. XVII, No. 48, Thursday, January 2, 1919, 5.

[14] "Buried at Former Home, Benton." *MWM*, Vol. XVII, No. 32, Thursday, January 30, 1919, 1.

CHAPTER TWENTY-THREE: RETURN

[1] ORE, 46.

[2] WOOL 13.

[3] BLEW, 176.

[4] H. Earl. Wilson, "Good Old Days' Embraced Rugged War Time Doings—Flu Horror," *ABJ*, February 8, 1934. As cited in TULL, 143.

[5] GRIS 384; Astonishingly, as late as 1945, with the end of World War II, no organization or newspaper in Summit County kept a tally of those local men and women who died in military service, either. GRIS 506n.

[6] The Metropolitan Life Insurance Company noted in 1919 the death rate among the company's insured in Ohio was 6.7 per thousand in Cleveland and 6.5 in Akron. Akron's population of 210,000 in 1920 would have resulted in 1,365 deaths. One should also consider that many of the "hillbillies" may not have carried life insurance and, if they did, it probably would have been payable to survivors in their home state. In Kentucky, the incidence was 7.4 in Louisville and 8.0 in Paducah. Lee K. Frankel and Louis I. Dublin, "Influenza Mortality Among Wage Earners and Their Families," (New York: Metropolitan Life Insurance Company, 1919), http://pds.lib.harvard.edu/pds/view/7302859?n=3 Accessed October 2, 2011.

[7] GRIS 384.

[8] The 1918 *Akron City Directory* shows the home listed to W. E Heminger. *ACD*, 1919, 13.

[9] "When a teacher does not live at home, she pays from $16 to $20 a month for board, and spends the six months when she is not teaching either with her family or at some other occupation." NEW 57.

CHAPTER TWENTY-FOUR: PROHIBITION

[1] This would reference the temporary Wartime Prohibition Act, which banned the sale of beverages having an alcoholic content greater than 2.75%. Intended to save grain for the war effort, it was actually passed after the Armistice was signed and before the 18th Amendment to the Constitution was ratified. It actually took effect on June 30, 1919, with July 1, 1919 becoming widely known as the "Thirsty-First." The state of Ohio had actually instituted its own version of Prohibition earlier, on May 26th, 1919. At the time, there were 178 saloons in Akron.

"The Thirsty First," https://calibredkuku.wordpress.com/2014/04/11/the-thirsty-first/ Accessed December 17, 2015; "The Mixer and Server, Official Journal of the Hotel and Restaurant Employes' International and Bartenders' International League of American," Vol. XXVII (Cincinnati: Roessler Bros); GRIS. 26.

[2] There were actually two Jake Schaefers who were considered brilliant billiard players. Jake, Sr. and Jake, Jr. Jake Schaefer, Sr. was considered "A player whose super-brilliance with a billiard cue won for him the sobriquet of 'Wizard,'" while Jake, Jr. is ranked as "the greatest of the American Balkline players." "Hall of Fame Inductees: 1966-1968," Billiard Congress of America, http://home.bca-pool.com/displaycommon.cfm?an=1&subarticlenbr=31, Accessed February 19, 2012.

[3] The 1919 City Directory lists John Bryer's billiard hall at 20 E. Miller Ave. *ACD*, 1919, 1721.

[4] Although a later newspaper does record that John killed himself, his end was not quite that simple. In an article in the Massillon (Ohio) Evening Independent of July 13, 1922 headlined, "2 Dead, One Wounded in Akron Battle," the full story came out:

AKRON, JULY 13. –Detectives Wednesday night were still unable to explain a three-cornered gun battle at 632 Euclid court which resulted in the death of two men and the wounding of a third late Wednesday afternoon.

Sigmund Kuhn of 632 Euclid court and John Bryer, former proprietor of the Ohio hotel, same address, are dead.

Anton Pearlman, who is said by police to have had no fixed Akron address, is at People's hospital, where it is expected he will recover from a bullet wound in his neck.

According to a story related tonight to detectives and representatives of the county prosecutor's office at police headquarter by Mrs. Sarah Kuhn, wife of Sigmund, Bryer appeared suddenly at the Euclid court home Wednesday afternoon and started an argument which led to the shooting. She says the dispute started when Pearlman accused her husband and Bryer of tipping police off to a Barberton affair which led to Pearlman's recent arrest on a swindle charge and his later release under bond of $3,000 pending a grand jury investigation.

She says there was a struggle and that John Bryer drew a revolver and started shooting.

After her husband had been killed and Pearlman wounded she says Bryer retreated into a hallway at the head of the stairs and turned the weapon on himself.

Detective William McDonnell says that wrecked furniture and broken windows in the second floor apartment occupied by the Kuhn family and Bryer bear witness to a protracted fight previous to the shooting.

In the hall, near Bryer's body, he says he found six empty shells. In a 32 caliber revolver clutched tightly in Bryer's hand, he found two more empty shells and four loaded ones, he states.

Detectives who interviewed Pearlman at the hospital say his stories of the struggle are so conflicting that they can credit none of them. "2 Dead, 1 Wounded in Akron Battle," *Massillon Evening Independent*, July 13, 1922, 7.

[5] The 1919 *Akron City Directory* records Harry B. Haberman associated with Justrite Tailoring Co., 1160 S. Main. *ACD*, 1919, 849, 1782.

CHAPTER TWENTY-FIVE: MARRIAGE

[1] Haskell and Florence married Saturday, January 17th, 1920.

[2] This would have been the death of Claude M. Parkhill, 49, on January 14, 1920. Kentucky, Death Records, 1852-1953 [database on-line]. Provo, UT, USA: Ancestry.com Operations Inc., 2007. He was the Mayor of Mayfield from 1910-1918. D. Trabue Davis, *The Story of Mayfield Through a Century, 1823-1923*, 61.

[3] The son's draft registration card, dated Sept. 12, 1918, is made out in the name of Estil Haskell McNutt, but signed Estle Haskell McNutt. *World War I Draft Registration Cards, 1917-1918* [database on-line]. Provo, UT, USA: Ancestry.com Operations Inc., 2005.

[4] Florence was born on April 8, 1896, while Haskell was born on July 25, 1898, making their difference in age just 2 ½ years; Although Florence would have been nearly 24 years old and Haskell nearly 21 ½ (a reasonable age at which to marry today), girls as young as 12 and boys as young as 14 were permitted to marry in Kentucky at the time with the consent of their parents. By those standards, as well, Florence was indeed old. *CWK*, 9.

CHAPTER TWENTY-SIX: LUCK

[1] Florence may well have benefited from an open position due to teacher losses as a result of enlistment into World War I and deaths from the Spanish Flu. After the war ended, there was a statewide shortage of over 2,000 teachers. Although many may have temporarily entered government work, the number lost to the Spanish Flu would be uncountable. KLO, 160; She may have also benefited from the fact that in 1919 there was a teachers' strike in Mayfield. With a minimum salary of $45 and a maximum of $55, "all high school teachers, except two, left." NEW, 78; "A study of salaries reveals one of the chief reasons for the general inefficiency of the rural school teacher. They are so inadequate, in almost no instance a living wage, that one wonders how even poor teachers are procurable. Although the state law sets as a minimum salary $45 a month, salaries range from $35 to $70 a month, the greatest number of teachers receiving from $46 to $57. As the school term lasts only six months, the annual salary is quite insufficient. No wonder the county superintendent and the trustees complain that they cannot secure enough teachers and that in many places schools have been closed because of this lack. The superintendent in one county told the investigator that 60 per cent. of his schools for the coming year were still without teachers and even without candidates . . . . one asks, "But how do they live?" Obviously, they do not depend upon their salaries for full support. Many live at home and do not pay for their board. In fact, many teachers are selected for this very reason. As one trustee said, "She doesn't need any more money. Her father keeps her." NEW, 56-57; "In Hopkinsville the average annual salary is $540. The superintendent made an investigation in that city and found that negro women who were stripping tobacco in a factory were earning more money per day than the grade teachers. This, of course, is based on working days in the year, not school days." NEW, 78.

CHAPTER TWENTY-SEVEN: "THE LITTLE DEPRESSION"

[1] Ralph C. Busby, "Rubber," *CEN*, 343.

[2] FRAN, 45.

[3] Nolen, John. *City Plan for Akron, Prepared for Chamber of Commerce*. Akron: Akron Chamber of Commerce, 1919.

[4] *ABJ*, August 5, 1919, 13, August 11, 1919, 9, August 22, 1919, 15.

[5] *ABJ*, August 5, 1919, 13, August 14, 1919, 19, August 20th, 1919, 9.

[6] GRIS, 409.

[7] GRIS, 392.

[8] *The Work of the Labor Division* (Akron: The Goodyear Tire & Rubber Co., 1920), 17.

[9] SKR, 130.

[10] ORE, 48.

[11] SKR, 128.

[12] GRIS, 410.

[13] "Air Seiberling Fight in Court," *ABJ*, June 1, 1940, 1.

[14] Victor Zarnowitz, *Business Cycles*, University of Chicago Press, 1996. As cited on Wikipedia, Depression of 1920-1921, http://en.wikipedia.org/wiki/Depression_of_1920 %E2%80%9321#cite_note-Vernon-1. Accessed on February 1, 2012; The Annual Consumer Price Index for the United States, 1774-2010, http://measuringworth.com /uscpi/ As cited on Wikipedia, Depression of 1920-1921, http://en.wikipedia.org/wiki/ Depression_of_1920%E2%80%9321#cite_note-Vernon-1. Accessed on February 1, 2012; J.R. Vernon, "The 1920-21 Deflation: The Role of Aggregate Supply. Economic Inquiry, Vol. 29, 1991. As cited on Wikipedia, Depression of 1920-1921, http://en.wikipedia.org/ wiki/ Depression_of_1920%E2%80%9321#cite_note-Vernon-1. Accessed on February 1, 2012; BRAIN.

[15] Anthony Patrick O'Brien (1997). "Depression of 1920–1921". In David Glasner, Thomas F. Cooley. *Business cycles and depressions: an encyclopedia*. New York: Garland Publishing. pp. 151–153. As cited on Wikipedia, Depression of 1920-1921, http://en.wikipedia.org /wiki/Depression _of_1920%E2%80%9321#cite_note-Vernon-1. Accessed on February 1, 2012.

[16] JOH, 119; U.S. Census Bureau. U.S. Census of Population and Housing. Volume 3. Population, 1920. Composition and characteristics of the population by states. Ohio, Table 8. Age for cities of 10,000 or more, 772.

[17] JOH, 118.

[18] 117,262 individual names were listed in the directory. "Akron and Summit County During the Last Decade," *Akron Official City Directory Supplemented by Directories of Kenmore, Barberton and Cuyahoga Falls, 1920.*

[19] A total of 85, 705 were enumerated in the 1922 Directory. *ACD*, 1922.

[20] WOLF, 445.

[21] GRIS, 410.

[22] ORE, 48.

[23] The story was later told that Goodyear President Frank Seiberling ran into Harvey Firestone when he was visiting the financial district in New York in a futile effort to secure financial support. "Harvey," Seiberling was reported to have said, "you take that side of the street. I'm taking this side." ORE, 49.

[24] LIEF, 130.

[25] LIEF, 130.

[26] "Tire Prices Drop to Lowest Levels. Goodyear, Miller and General Reductions Range from 10 to 30 Per Cent." Automotive Industries, Vol. XLV, No. 20, The Class Journal Company, Detroit, November 17, 1921, 992.

[27] Harvey S. Firestone, *Men and Rubber: The Story of Business*. New York: Doubleday, Page, 1926, 9. As cited in SKR, 133.

[28] Greg Grandin, *Fordlandia, The Rise and Fall of Henry Ford's Forgotten Jungle City*. Metropolitan Books, Henry Holt and Company LLC: New York, 2009, 57-58; Anthony Patrick O'Brien (1997). "Depression of 1920–1921". In David Glasner, Thomas F. Cooley. *Business cycles and depressions: an encyclopedia*. New York: Garland Publishing. pp. 151–153. As cited on Wikipedia, Depression of 1920-1921, http://en.wikipedia.org/wiki/Depression_of of_1920%E2%80%9321#cite_note-Vernon-1. Accessed on February 1, 2012.

[29] ORE, 47.

[30] *Our Glorious Century* (Pleasantville, New York: Reader's Digest Association, 1994), 140.

[31] With a Census estimate of 41,614,248 "Persons 10 Years of Age and Over Engaged in Gainful Occupations" during the first two weeks of January, this would translate into an unemployment rate of 13.78%. *1920 Census of Occupations*, pg. 33 as recorded by Leo Wolman

in "Chapter II. The Working Population in the United States," *The Growth of American Trade Unions, 1880-1923* (National Bureau of Economic Research, 1924), 69-71.

[32] Economist and author John Steele Gordon notes that while the Great Depression was technically over by 1933, the ongoing economic malaise was problematic. "Indeed," he writes, "in 1937, when the economy suddenly turned south again, there was a problem: what to call the new downturn. Most people thought the country was still in a depression, so that word wouldn't do. But economists, delighted to have a problem that they could actually solve, came up with the word 'recession,' and that's what we have been using ever since." "Economic Lessons from American History," *Imprimis*, July/August 2012, Volume 41, Number 7/8, 7. (Hillsdale College: Hillsdale, Michigan, 2012) Adapted from a lecture delivered on February 27, 2012, aboard the Crystal Symphony during a Hillsdale College cruise from Rio de Janeiro to Buenos Aires.

CHAPTER TWENTY-EIGHT: THE CLAY PITS

[1] An in-depth discussion of the constituency of this clay can be found in "Hickory Grove, Graves County," High-Grade Clays of the Eastern United States With Some Notes on Western Clays. H. Ries, W.S. Bayley, and Others. Department of the Interior, United States Geological Survey, Bulletin 708 (Washington: Government Printing Office), 1922, pg. 280; "The United States government department of the interior in its report from the bureau of mines and technology has the following to say under the head of ball clays:

Ball clays are being mined in the United States that are equal or superior to any European clay as regards color. Inplasticity and bonding strength they are slightly inferior to a few but equal to most of the imported ball clays.

The ball-clay mines in the United States that are now being worked are located in Calloway and Graves counties, Ky., and Henry county, Tenn.

The centers of the ball-clay industry in Kentucky are Calloway and Graves counties. This clay occurs in much larger masses than do the ball clays of England and is mined by open pits, whereas in England the clay is taken out through small shafts.

The deposits are more or less stratified, yielding several grades of clay suited to various industries.

These ball clays can be substituted for English ball clays with success in most industries, as their colors when burned, bonding strength, and shrinkages are very similar to those of the imported clays. They are slightly more refractory than the English ball clay, and this must be taken into consideration when a substitution is made.

The companies that the bureau of mines knows to be in active operation in the field at the time this paper is printed are:

Kentucky Construction and improvement Co., Mayfield, Graves county, Ky. Cooley, Ball and Sagger Clay Co., Hazel, Calloway county, Ky.

The ball clay mines in operation in Tennessee are in Henry county in the neighborhood of Paris. The deposits, which are similar to those of Kentucky, consist of several strata of clays that differ slightly in physical and pyrometric properties." "Ball Clay Mines in Graves, County." *MDM*, Friday, April 30, 1915, Vol. XIV, No. 195, 2; "Work on New Pit Progressing Rapidly. Sixteen Feet of Fine Quality Clay Near Pryorsburg." *MWM*, Vol. XVII, No. 19, Thursday, June 14, 1917, 7.

[2] Looking back in 1922, the effect on the agricultural economy had been devastating. In an article entitled "Crop Decline is Unparalleled in History of U.S.," the authors noted:

There is no parallel in the records of the bureau or markets and crop estimates to the fall of $21.22 or 59 per cent, in the average value per acre of the ten crops constituting nine tenths of all crop production which occurred in the two years from 1919 to 1921, it was announced today by the department of agriculture. The decline was found by the department to have been from $35.74 in 1919 to $14.52 in 1921.

The general trend of the average was downward, the department's figures show, from about $14 per acre in the years immediately following the civil war, to $8 in 1896, the lowest point in the industrial depression of that time, it was said. The average per acre advanced to $16.49 in 1913 and reached the "peak," $35.74, in 1919.

The fall in average the department said, after 1919 was more rapid than the ascent at the beginning of the war, even more rapid than the ascent when this country became a belligerent—if the average value per acre went "up like a rocket" it came "down like a stick."

"Crop Decline is Unparalleled in History of U.S.," *The Paducah Evening Sun*, Volume XLIV; No. 176, Saturday, January 21, 1922, 9.

CHAPTER TWENTY-NINE: THE ROAD WEST

[1] This would have been the construction of the Albert Pike Free Bridge or as it was known at the time it was being constructed, "The Million Dollar Bridge." This, when a million dollars was still a sizable amount of money. 3,173 Feet long, it would be the first highway crossing of the Arkansas River into Oklahoma at Fort Smith, Arkansas, opening up trade west. Before its construction the Helen Gould Railroad Bridge served double duty as it was planked to allow wagons to cross. There was, however, a toll. The Albert Pike bridge was replaced in the 1960s (as were all other navigable channels of the Arkansas) to better allow for barge traffic. Gene McCluney, "Arkansas River Bridge," http://bridgehunter.com /ar/sebastian/arkansas-river/, Accessed January 9, 2012; Prokes, C.A. "Building a Rib-Arch Concrete Bridge in Arkansas," Engineering News-Record, Feb. 23, 1922, Vol. 88, No. 8, pg. 306.

[2] Looking back in 1922, the effect on the agricultural economy had been devastating. In an article entitled "Crop Decline is Unparalleled in History of U.S.," the authors noted:

There is no parallel in the records of the bureau or markets and crop estimates to the fall of $21.22 or 59 per cent, in the average value per acre of the ten crops constituting nine tenths of all crop production which occurred in the two years from 1919 to 1921, it was announced today by the department of agriculture. The decline was found by the department to have been from $35.74 in 1919 to $14.52 in 1921.

The general trend of the average was downward, the department's figures show, from about $14 per acre in the years immediately following the civil war, to $8 in 1896, the lowest point in the industrial depression of that time, it was said. The average per acre advanced to $16.49 in 1913 and reached the "peak," $35.74, in 1919.

The fall in average the department said, after 1919 was more rapid than the ascent at the beginning of the war, even more rapid than the ascent when this country became a belligerent—if the average value per acre went "up like a rocket" it came "down like a stick."

"Crop Decline is Unparalleled in History of U.S.," *PES*, Volume XLIV; No. 176, Saturday, January 21, 1922, 9.

[3] The 1910 Census for Davidson County, Tennessee, records the population of the Tennessee Industrial School on Murfreesboro Pike, 2 ½ miles outside of Nashville. Both Rollie Frey, 15, and Roy Frey, 15, are listed among its hundreds of pupils. *1910*; Census Place: *Civil District 6, Davidson, Tennessee*; Roll: *T624_1496*; Page: *3B*; Enumeration District: *0094*; Image: *1191*.

[4] Per the 1910 Census of Graves County, his father was Samuel R. Douthitt, 48. His son, Reed, 12, is also listed. 1910, Census Place: Mayfield Ward 1, Graves, Kentucky; Roll: T624_ 475; Page 20B, Enumeration District: 0083; Image 1000; FHL microfilm: 1374488.

[5] This would reference the shooting of Jake L. Hamon, "oil and railroad millionaire and Republican National committeeman," on November 21st, 1920, by Clara Smith Hamon, who was married to his nephew. Her subsequent capture, trial and acquittal on March 18th of the following year, made national news. "Clara Hamon Will Leave Ardmore to Begin Life Again," *PES*, Vol. XLV, No. 61, Friday, March 18, 1921, 1; Before his death, Jake Hamon was in line

for the position of Secretary of the Interior with the incoming Harding administration, a position eventually taken by Albert Fall of Teapot Dome notoriety. Laura Wilkerson, "Republican Follies of 1920" http://open.salon.com/blog/laura_wilkerson /2011/04/05/republican_follies_of_1920, April 5, 2011.

[6] Despite all efforts, I was unable to find any record of this man or company in Oklahoma City at that time.

CHAPTER THIRTY: MEMPHIS

[1] The streetcar tracks head north to eventually meet up with the Hollywood Line (No. 18) following first Chelsea Avenue to the northeast and then to the New Raleigh Road (present day Peres Avenue) before ending in a loop just west of the tracks of the northbound Illinois Central Railroad, just behind the present-day Archer Daniels Midland Company).

CHAPTER THIRTY-ONE: THE "MELTIN' POT"

[1] "Census of Unemployed Shows Paducah Has Few Idle Men." *PES*, Vol. XLVI, No. 93, Monday, October 17, 1921, 10.

[2] "Liquor Traffic is Growing, Police to Redouble Efforts." *PES*, Vol. XLVI, No. 45, Monday, August 22, 1921, 1.

[3] "First Panel of Women on Jury says Man 'Not Guilty.' Mesdames Lally, Post; Miss Husbands Win Honor of Serving on McCracken's Initial Mixed Panel." *PES*, Vol. XLV, No. 87, Monday, April 18, 1921, 5.

[4] "Negroes To Hold Fair, Races On August 10 To 12. City Sanctions Effort, 10th to Be Official Negro Holiday." *PES*, Volume XLVI, No. 29, Wednesday, August 3, 12.

[5] "Exposition Reveals Wonders to Big Crowd. Brilliant Spectacle is Thrown Open for Public's Inspection. Exhibits All in Place. Thousands of Twinkling Lights Cast Their Radiance Over Indoor Fairyland.' *PES*. Volume XLIV. No. 106. Tuesday, November 1, 1921, 1; "Exposition Will Be Open Monday to Colored Folk. Continuation of Exhibit at Their Request Is Decided Upon." *PES*. Vol. XLIV, No. 109, Friday, November 4, 1921, 1.

[6] "Notice to White People." *PES*, Volume XLVI, No. 34. Tuesday, August 9, 1921, 2.

[7] "Take 'Leggers' to Be Judged." *PES*, Vol. XXXV, No. 138, Monday, December 13, 1915, 1.

[8] Public transportation by streetcar in Paducah underwent a number of name changes from its inception. From 1887 until 1898, it was known as the Paducah Street Railway Co. From 1898 until 1902, it was referred to as the Paducah Railway & Light Co. From 1902 until 1905, it was called the Paducah City Railway. From 1905 until 1919 (under the ownership of Stone & Webster) it was known as Paducah Traction & Light Co. From October 1919 through 1925, Stone & Webster continued to offer transit services through the Paducah Electric Company and its subsidiary, the Paducah Railway Company. From 1925 through 1944, public transportation went by the name of Kentucky Utilities Co. (under Middle West Utilities Co.) Finally, in 1932, streetcar service was discontinued as buses took their place. "Transit Systems in Kentucky," http://web.me.com/willvdv/chirailfan/ aatky8.html, Accessed January 1, 2012. *Stone & Webster Electric Railway, Electric Lighting, Gas and Water Power Properties*, 1920. Boston, 1920, 55-56, "New Franchise in Paducah," *Electric Railway Journal*, Vol. 54, July to December, 1919. (New York: McGraw-Hill), pg. 477. "Public Utilities," *Poor and Moody's Manual Consolidated*, Vol. 21, Part 2, (New York: Poor's Publishing Company, 1920), 361.

[9] Lovett Bryant, 51, in 1920. He is recorded as a widower at this time. *1920*; Census Place: *Paducah, McCracken, Kentucky*; Roll: *T625_588*; Page: *3B*; Enumeration District: *152*; Image: *1008*.

[10] Rothrock's Cafe ("Delightful meals served in pleasant surroundings.") was located at 516 Broadway. *PES*, Vol. XLV; No. 136, Thursday, June 8, 1922, pg. 10.

[11] The car barn was listed as being located at 1400 Broadway at 14th Street (the site of

the present-day Paducah Police Department) as the Paducah City Railway Shops and Car Barn on the 1906 Sanborn map. In the 1918-1919 *Caron's Directory for the City of Paducah* it is shown at 1342 Broadway as the Paducah Traction Co. Car Barn and Shops. By 1926-27, the same address is listed as the Kentucky Utilities Car Barn and Shops. Vonnie Shelton of the McCracken County Public Library believes the mailing address changed from the original location, but not the physical location. Personal communication with Vonnie Shelton, Local and Family History Librarian, McCracken County Public Library, March 1, 2011. *Caron's Directory for the City of Paducah for 1922-1923* verifies 1342 Broadway as the location of the "Paducah Ry Co car barn and shops" at the time, pg. 602. It also lists 406 Broadway as the location of the Paducah Electric Company and the Paducah Railway Company, pg. 600. U.S. City Directories, 1821-1989 (Beta) [database on-line]. Provo, UT, USA: Ancestry.com Operations, Inc., 2011. The original car barn still exists and is used by the Paducah Police Department for storage. Personal communication with Pam Spencer, Public Information Officer, City of Paducah, June 21, 2012.

[12] An advertisement on behalf of the utility profiled Bethel in 1922:

Electrac "Bill"

Mr. W.H. Bethel, or "Bill", as he is best known to the patrons of the Third street line, has been in the service of the Paducah Railways since 1883. During the thirty-nine years that he has been in the service, Bill has never been suspended from work and has held a remarkably low record for accidents.

When Bethel entered the service there were two street car systems in Paducah. One operated between Rowlandtown and Ninth and Trimble streets, and was known as the Rowlandtown Line. The other system was controlled by the People's Railway Company, which operated a line between Fountain Avenue and the river, on Broadway, a line on South Sixth street to the junction of Sixth and Willie streets and another line on North Sixth street to Trimble street, thence West on Trimble street to the Cemetery. The cars were drawn by mules and moved on regular schedule and in accordance with a published time table . . . .

Bill, who by reason of his length of service, is an authority on the history of the local street railway system, says that first electric car was operated in Paducah in 1885. The electric street car system of the city was one of the first constructed in the United States and Mr. Bethel has operated an electric car for thirty-six years.

"The Electrac News," *PES*, Volume XLV; No. 153., Wednesday, June 28, 1922, 8.

[13] A receipt to Haskell from the Paducah Electric Company for payment on a stove records their address on May 4, 1922 as 421 Kincaid [sic] Ave. A search of Google Earth shows this single-story house to be still standing. This should make it the address of the third and final home as the first house was "ready to fall down," the second house was two stories and 1922 was the final year they lived there. Haskell is listed as working for "Pad Ry Co". Brother Ralph is listed as residing at 1637 Washington, pg. 304. U.S. City Directories, 1821-1989 (Beta) [database on-line]. Provo, UT, USA: Ancestry.com Operations, Inc., 2011.

[14] "Electric Journal Praises Paducah Railway Co., for Safety Campaign," *PES*, Friday, July 7, 1922, 8. The copy of *AERA* (Volume 10, July 1922, 1074-75) in which this article appeared, along with photographs of the signage, can be found through Google Books.

[15] Single truck cars were normally less than 30 feet long and seated 25 to 30 people. The undercarriage consisted of a single bogie or "truck" of two axles that did not swivel in respect to the body of the car. Double truck cars were 35 to 50 feet long, seated 45 to 70 people and offered a more comfortable pair of two-axle trucks that swiveled as the car made its way along the tracks. "APTA Streetcar and Heritage Trolley Site." http://www.heritagetrolley.org/defHeritage.htm Accessed August 7, 2014.

[16] Barron Gift Collier. An early advertising entrepreneur, he became the largest property owner and developer in Florida, acquiring some 1.3 million acres of land. "The Barron Collier Story." Barron Collier Companies. http://www.barroncollier.com /Default.aspx?id=11.

Accessed December 17, 2015.

[17] "As all trolley companies needed a destination for its riders to visit on Sundays and holidays, a trolley park was developed on the outskirts of Paducah near 32nd and Broadway. First opened in 1890 as LaBelle Park this 75-acre park was renamed Wallace Park in 1900. Besides having well-kept lawns and shade trees to encourage picnicking, the park had a 200-by-500 foot artificial lake for rowing and swimming, a dance hall and a baseball field." The park was sold in 1925 for residential development. Charles H. Bogart, "Paducah Was First in its Region to Lay Rails for Streetcar System." The Kentucky Explorer, March 2004, 23-26; "In a neighborhood currently across from Clark Elementary School (roughly bounded by Buckner Lane, Lone Oak Road, Maple Avenue, and Forest Circle), there once stood a park, a quite large park called Wallace Park. In the early decades of the 20th century, Wallace Park marked the outskirts of the Paducah city limits. It was quite literally the end of the line. For a nickel, you could ride the rail car from the foot of Broadway to its culmination at the park and then turn around and come back again." Matt Jaeger, "4000 Easter Eggs!?!" Local and Family History, April 16, 2014, Accessed August 15, 2014, http://mclib.net/blogs /history/?tag=wallace-park

[18] This fare was actually a point of great contention between the company and the City of Paducah. A lawsuit determining the fare made it to the U.S. Supreme Court in 1923. CITY OF PADUCAH v. PADUCAH R CO, 261 U.S. 267 (1923) 261 U.S. 267. CITY OF PADUCAH et al. v. PADUCAHRY. CO. No. 243. Argued Jan. 18, 1923. Decided Feb. 19, 1923. http://caselaw.lp.findlaw.com/scripts/getcase.pl?court=us&vol=261&invol=267 Accessed June 20, 2012.

[19] Motorman Walters would not be the only member of the group to accidentally kill a pedestrian with his streetcar. Motorman Lonnie B. Ragland hit and killed Josephine Williamson, 73, dragging her body some 30 feet before stopping. PES, Vol. XLV, No. 94, Tuesday, April 26, 1921, pg. 1 and Monday, May 6, 1921, pg. 9.

[20] More than 90 railroad cars of strawberries were shipped out of Paducah in 1922. Neuman, Fred Gus, Paducahans in History, (Paducah: Young Printing Company, 1922), 132.

[21] These cars were phased out for the "modern 'pay-as-you-enter' cars" in 1912. "Modern Cars on Paducah Traction Lines." MDM, Vol. XI, No. 116, Thursday, May 16, 1912, 1."

[22] From the route map of the Paducah Railway Company, this would appear to be Oak Grove Cemetery.

[23] The murder of Calvert City farmer Joe Daniels, 63 was first reported in PES on March 28, 1921. The actual trial was held over to the September term of the Grand Jury; In October, Van Daniels was sentenced to life. "Life Term Given Van Daniels For Death Of Parent. Jury Holds Defendant Is Guilty Of Murder And Apply Life Term." PES, Vol. CLVI, No. 83, Wednesday, October 5, 1921, 1.

[24] In fact, during the earliest days of the line, instances had occurred where bricks had been placed on the tracks, as well as a "railroad signal torpedo." When the former event occurred, the driver was pitched through the front window at the mule drawing the trolley along the tracks. When the latter event occurred as the car ran over the signal torpedo, it was with such force that both driver and passengers tumbled out of the car and the employees of a nearby bank believed they were the target of an attempted bank robbery. ROB, 104

[25] Haskell: His name was Tandy Neil. Old man Stubblefield was his uncle. Old Tandy Stubblefield was his uncle so they named him "Tandy Neil." He never used it. He didn't like it. He never used it. But he went under the name of "T. Neil." The "T." was an initial. Then Neil.

[26] The 1920 Census shows two owners of King Lumber, Charles H. King, 60, and Fain W. King, 32. As this particular story referenced "Old Man King," it would most probably refer to Charles H. King. 1920; Census Place: Paducah, McCracken, Kentucky; Roll: T625_588; Enumeration District: 147; Image: 881.

27 Per the 1920 Census, Rinaldo and Elizabeth had 2 daughters, Olevia, 17, and Myola, 23. Ollie Barnett, 32, is recorded living with them.1920; Census Place: Paducah, McCracken, Kentucky; Roll: T625_588; Page: 2A; Enumeration District: 132; Image: 525.

28 Deputy Marshal Ollie Barnett officed out of the Custom House and resided at 166 Farley Place. Also residing at 166 Farley Place was Rinaldo S. and Elizabeth E. Barnett. Rinaldo is noted as operating a general store at 240 Farley Place. *CAR 1923.*

29 When Rubel's arrest was first reported, he faced more than a hundred federal fraud charges. "M'Neill's Arrest Exposes General Scheme of Fraud. Federal Officers Detain W.R. McNeill of Boaz, Graves County. To Face Indictments. Claim He Fleeced Victims Through Mails, Obtained Large Sums." *PES*, Vol. XLVI, No. 88, Tuesday, October 11, 1921, 1.

30 Young Rubel was indeed a prolific letter-writer, with his missives having frequently previously appeared in The Messenger. After he enlisted in the Army during World War I, he dutifully documented his service—as well as his subsequent desertion and descent into crime, as well. "Rubel McNeil Joins Army." *MWM*, Vol. XVII, No. 38, Thursday, October 18, 1917, 1. "Rubel McNeil Writes of War and Slackers." *MWM*, Vol. XVII, No. 38, Thursday, October 18, 1917, 2. "Rubel McNeil Writes From Great Lakes, Ill." *MWM*, Vol. XVIII, No. 27, Thursday, August 8, 1918, 5. "Soldier's Letters. Rubel McNeill." *MWM*, Vol. XVIII, No. 40, Thursday, November 28, 1918, 3; The arrest, imprisonment and subsequent trial of young Rubel McNeill, 22, is one of the more interesting and engaging reads in *The Paducah Evening Sun*—even at a time when the paper was filled with tales of moonshine and bootlegging. After being arrested on October 11, he cheerfully admitted everything (in great detail) to reporter Sidney Snook who filed a profile on October 15, 1921. At the conclusion of his trial on Tuesday, November 22, 1921, he smiled as he was being sentenced to five years in prison. "When he left the court room," the coverage notes, "McNeill was heard to say pleasantly, 'Yes, I got off light, all right.'" "Sentence Rubel McNeill To Five Years In Prison. Grand Jury Indicts Another Youth On Same Count." *PES*, Vol. XLIV, No. 124, Tuesday, November 22, 1921, 1.

31 Apparently the heavy controller handle found common usage as a makeshift weapon among the motorman. *The Paducah Evening Sun* reported an argument over transfers in which Robert E. Nelson asked motorman D.H. Rowlett "for a transfer to Tyler, the police said, and Rowlett replied that he didn't have any transfers. The men are said to have argued about the transfer and Nelson, it is alleged, thought Rowlett was about to strike him with a car controller. The switchman struck Rowlett on the head with an unopened knife, the police allege." *PES*, Vol. XLV, No. 65, Wednesday March 23, 1921, 12.

32 This would appear to be Henley M. Franklin, listed as a detective in the 1920 Census. *1920*; Census Place: *Paducah, McCracken, Kentucky*; Roll: *T625_588*; Page: *3B*; Enumeration District: *132*; Image: *528*. By the time of the 1922 City Directory, he is recorded as chief of police. *Caron's Directory for the City of Paducah for 1920*. U.S. City Directories, 1821-1989 (Beta) [database on-line]. Provo, UT, USA: Ancestry.com Operations, Inc., 2011

33 Counterfeiting pocket change would appear to have been common in Paducah at the time. *The Paducah Evening Sun* reports a counterfeit dime being passed on a streetcar in 1916. "Police Court in Eight Rounds. Biff! Bing!---Minute Rounds and No Rest. All the Ingredients of a Free-For-All. Every Lick Worth Dollar." *The Paducah Evening Sun*, Vol. XXXVI, No. 117, Tuesday, May 16, 1916, 8.

34 T.A. Jones & Sons was located at 2103 Bridge. *CAR 1923*, 703.

35 The Southern Hotel was located at 101-107 Broadway and apparently had a bit of a reputation before this encounter. During an ill-fated campaign against "the social evil" of Paducah in 1916 a visiting member of the clergy chanced to stay at the hotel. Briefly. He quickly fled after the porter kindly offered to arrange female companionship for him. *CAR 1923*, 500. "Southern Hotel Is Too Hot for Rev. Mr. Myrick. Calvert City Minister Declares Porter Offered to Provide Him with a Woman as He Goes to Room." *MDM*, Vol. XV, No. 103, Friday, September 8, 1916, 2.

[36] Dickerson had apparently been at it for some time, with evidence of his gaming "said to have been operated over a pool room near Fourth and Kentucky Avenue" being reported in the Mayfield *Daily Messenger* as early as 1912. "Paducah Police Department Has Severe Shake-Up." *MDM*, Vol. XI, No. 275, Thursday, November 21, 1912, 1; Dickerson died on Sept. 30, 1922 of a pistol wound. *Kentucky Death Records, 1852-1953* [database on-line]. Provo, UT, USA: Ancestry.com Operations Inc., 2007.

[37] "On July 3, 1902, the City of Paducah awarded a streetcar franchise for a route known as the Broadway-Third Street Line. This route ran down Broadway from First Street to Fountain Avenue, down Fountain Avenue to Park Avenue, then up Park Avenue to Sixth Street. The conditions for this streetcar line were that it was to run at least once every hour from 6:00 a.m. to 10:00 p.m.; it was not to run at a speed exceeding 8 miles per hour; and the fare was not to exceed five cents per person. Later, after the turn of the century and the advent of the automobile, the streetcar lines were taken up. On Fountain Avenue and on Jefferson Street from 18th Street to Central Avenue, the medians holding the streetcar lines were converted into green areas. Here trees, grass and bushes have been planted to create a picturesque park area. This boulevard effect is one of the distinctive and beautiful features of the Jefferson Street-Fountain Avenue area." "History of the Fountain Avenue Area (Taken in part from the Application to the National Register of Historic Places—Richard Holland, 1978)." The City of Paducah, 2007. http://www.fountainave.com/history.php

[38] "Mule" was slang for illicitly distilled bootleg whiskey.

[39] Frederick William "F.W." Katterjohn served as mayor of Paducah from 1920-1924. He was followed by Jacob N. Bailey who was elected on November 6, 1923. http://politicalgraveyard.com/geo/KY/ofc/paducah.html

[40] This would appear to be Benjamin H. Moredock, listed in the 1930 Census as a traveling salesman for a hardware company. *1930*; *Paducah, McCracken, Kentucky*; Roll: *768*; Page: *4B*; Enumeration District: *0009*; Image: *559.0*; FHL microfilm: *2340503*.

CHAPTER THIRTY-TWO: RETURN

[1] The 1924 Akron City Directory shows Haskell and Florence living at 193 E. Archwood. He was noted as working at the Miller Rubber Company. *ACD*, 1924, 745. The property is listed to J.T. Wynn. ACD, 1924, 77.

[2] Vodre Sylvester "Jack" Jones. Not a relation, but a close family friend. **Haskell:** Jack was like a brother to us. His folks married in a double ceremony [with my parents] and Jack and I was always good friends. His real name was Vodre. His dad had a brother named that. I guess he didn't like Vodre so they called him "Jack." Most people didn't know he had any other name. He lived with us. He had a room at the same place. Ate with us, you know. Two, three or four times. He'd leave and go somewhere and come back. He always come back to our house. It was home to him. My mom was like his mom.

CHAPTER THIRTY-THREE: THE MILLER RUBBER COMPANY II

[1] "Labor Supply Scarce," The Magazine of Wall Street, Vol. 30. No. 1, May 13, 1922 (New York: Colonial Communications Corp., 1922), 259.

[2] Discrimination against Catholics within the rubber industry was, in fact, so pervasive that employment opportunities were about as limited as those of blacks until General Tire was established in Akron on St. Michael's Day in 1915 by Irish Catholic William O'Neil. SKR 101, 123-25.

[3] The 1925 Akron City Directory shows Haskell and Florence residing at 678 Blaine Ave. He is noted as working at Miller Rubber at the time. *Official Akron City Directory Supplemented by Directories of Barberton, Kenmore and Cuyahoga Falls*, 1925, (Akron: Burch Directory Company, 1925), 840. The 1926-27 Akron City Directory Still shows Haskell and Florence residing at 678 Blaine. However, now Haskell is listed as an electrician. *Official Akron City Directory*

Supplemented by Directories of Barberton, Kenmore, Cuyahoga Falls, Etc., 1926-27, (Akron: Burch Directory Company, 1926), 628. This residence no longer exists (December, 2011). The address is now an empty lot. Per the Summit County Fiscal Office 678 Blaine is last listed as a residential property in 2006. By 2007, it was a vacant lot. http://fiscalweb.summitoh.net/clt/refintg3.main Accessed January 21, 2012.

[4] Louia W. Jones, son of Garland and Lillie M. Jones, was Barton's aunt and uncle through his father Joseph Jones.

CHAPTER THIRTY-FOUR: DUTY AND JONES

[1] World War I draft records show Homer Elijah Duty as a lineman with the N.A.T. & L. Co., a precursor to the modern Ohio Edison. World War I Draft Registration Cards, 1917-1918 [database on-line]. Provo, UT, USA: Ancestry.com Operations Inc., 2005.

[2] Sam survived the airplane ride to be assigned to the detective bureau of the Akron Police Force on Jan. 1, 1939. He was killed November 16, 1941 in a car accident on the way to a hunting trip in New London, Ohio. He had just finished building a new home for his wife and two daughters and they were planning on moving into it the following Friday. "Akron Detective, Truck Driver Killed In Traffic," *ABJ*, Monday, November 17, 1941, Vol. 102, No. 347, 1.

CHAPTER THIRTY-FIVE: TALLMADGE

[1] GRIS 37, 56.

[2] Ohio Dept. of Natural Resources, GeoFacts No. 14., as referenced in DAV, 6; In fact, it had only been incorporated from a township to an Ohio village by special election on January 1, 1936. *TALL*, 74.

[3] Constructed in 1841 and pulled by teams of horses or oxen, it transported coal to the nearby canal for shipment to Akron. DAV, 21. It failed by only five years to be the first railway in Ohio. The honors for this went to the horse drawn Erie and Kalamazoo Railroad that began operation on November 2, 1836. "Lake Shore and Michigan Southern Railway," http://en.pedia.org/wiki/Erie_and_Kalamazoo_Railroad, Accessed January 15,2012 and "Mad River and Lake Erie Railroad," http://en.wikipedia.org/wiki/Mad_River_and_Lake_Erie_Railroad, Accessed January 15, 2012.

[4] In 1806 David Bacon purchased a twenty square mile tract of land that would define the boundaries Tallmadge. William B. Shreve & Howard C. Barnes, "Political History of Tallmadge," *TALL* 74; "Akron and Summit County During the Last Decade," *ACD*, 1920.

[5] "Tallmadge Seeks Wider Annexation by Akron Council. Will Ask Village Be Taken In or Township Left Entact [sic]." *ABJ*, Thursday, March 27, 1930, 31.

[6] GRIS 43. Those commuters from Akron often took the train. In fact, as late as 1900, the tracks from New York City ended in Akron, with 5 trains arriving each day. Sometime around 1912, as Akron began to boom again, an additional car was added at the Akron station to handle the number rubber workers returning home. James P. Emmitt, "Horsepower Replaces Horses," *TALL* 50.

[7] The 1924 Akron City Directory records Jacob and Pauline Krauss as proprietors of the Jacob Krauss Electric Co. at 341 W. Bowery. *ACD*, 1924, 785.

[8] Per the 1930 census, this would appear to have been the home of Lewis and Eva H. Keller. His occupation was noted as "Farmer." "Population Schedule," Fifteenth Census of the United States: 1930. Department of Commerce—Bureau of the Census. Tallmadge Township, Summit County, Ohio, Enumeration District 77-207, April 1930, Sheet 15B.

[9] With the end of Prohibition on December 5th, 1933, alcohol could once again be legally purchased and consumed in Akron. In Tallmadge, however, the Village instead chose to remain dry. And in that Polish immigrant Leon Kubalak saw an opportunity. He purchased

property at the intersection of 1349 East Tallmadge Avenue and Brittain Road (when the location was so far out in the country it didn't even have a street number) at the very edge of the Akron-Tallmadge city limits. There, he first established his home and then, with the help of his son, Leonard, a business that would grow into an area institution. For decades, Leon's offered a good place to eat—and the closest place to buy a drink if you lived in Tallmadge.

The Akron city directories chart his offerings from a simple lunch counter at the very depths of The Depression in 1934-35 to a lunch counter and auto service station by 1937, Leon's Tavern by 1939-40, Leon's starting in 1952-53 and finally Leon's Restaurant beginning with the directory of 1960-61. By that time, Leon's was firmly established at what had become a major intersection. It was also adjacent to two of the area's first shopping malls, Midway Plaza and Chapel Hill Mall.

Leon eventually retired to Florida where he died in 1969, leaving his son Leonard to operate the restaurant until his death in 1994. It continued in operation for the remainder of the decade until the property was sold to McDonald's. After tearing down the old building, they opened their own restaurant (#26655) on the site in 2001—ironically the same year that Tallmadge voted to allow liquor sales. Leon's had had a good run.

CHAPTER THIRTY-SIX: THE MILLER RUBBER CO. III
[1] Verified by his granddaughter through personal email communication. Also, in 1925, per the Akron City Directory, the only Dickson (Dixon) listed as working as a foreman at the Miller Rubber Co. was Elisha H. Dickson who resided at 354 E. Crosier. *Akron Official City Directory Supplemented by Directories of Kenmore, Barberton and Cuyahoga Falls.* 1924. (Akron: The Burch Directory Company, 1923.), 6777.

CHAPTER THIRTY-SEVEN: PROHIBITION II
[1] The 1926-27 Akron City Directory shows this to be Grover C. and James H. Andrus who operated the Andrus Brothers billiard room at 1227 S. Main. *ACD*, 1926-7, 296, 1340.

[2] The Hotel Frederick was located at 1229 ½ South Main Street, *ACD*, 1920,1372.

[3] George Thomas, husband of Haskell's sister, Mattie.

[4] Per the 1930 census, this would appear to have been James T. McAleese, 56. His occupation was noted as "Patrol Man" with the "City Police." His father, John H. McAleese, 64, was noted as having been born in Northern Ireland. "Population Schedule," Fifteenth Census of the United States: 1930. Department of Commerce—Bureau of the Census. Akron, Summit County, Ohio, Enumeration District 77-2, April 1930, Sheet 21A; Per the 1930 census, his brother's name would appear to have been Patrick McAleese, 33. He is noted as being a "Policeman" on the "City Police Force." Fifteenth Census of the United States: 1930. Department of Commerce—Bureau of the Census. Akron, Summit County, Ohio, Enumeration District 77-120, April 1930, Sheet 44A.

[5] Haskell: Bill Jones. Florence's uncle. His name wasn't Bill. His name was Bryan. B-R-Y-A-N. But they called him Bill. Everybody knew him as Bill. Garland Jones [was his father].

[6] 878 Northeast Avenue.

[7] The 1940 Census shows Eugene Fritsch, 44, and his wife, Tamar, 51, at 20 Cuyahoga Falls-Mogadore Road. At that time, his occupation was listed as "Laborer" on the "School Project." National Archives, Seventh Census of the United States, 1940, Ohio, Summit County, Tallmadge, S.D. 23, E.D. No. 77-80, Sheet 1B, April 16, 1940.

[8] The very last story Haskell told during the period the tapes were being made was that of an incident in this department. Although the tape recorder had already been shut off and packed away, I pulled it out again as I was leaving the house to record it in my own words so that we might revisit the story the next time I spoke with him on tape. That next time never happened. In lieu of his words, I'll simply quote what I recorded at the time:

When he worked at Miller around '26 or '27 in the bathing shoe and cap division, it was a department filled mostly with women. Fairly rough. He said they would tell stories he wouldn't even repeat to his dog. When he first got there, he was assigned a woman partner to work with from Kansas City who warned him if the power ever went off (which it did frequently), to dive under the table and hide. Because the department would be in pretty much total darkness and the women who were there would strip him naked. They would do that to the rookie men who were assigned to the department. The first time the lights went out, he did dive under the table and heard all the women scuffling, asking, "Where is he?" "Where is he?" "Where is he?" When the lights came back on, they found him under the table. One of the women told his partner, "You told him! Didn't you, you bitch!"

CHAPTER THIRTY-NINE: THE DEPRESSION

[1] Charles B. Coates, "Labor Boomerang in Akron," Factory: Management and Maintenance 96 (July 1938): 38-39. Quoted in JOH, 140.

[2] Barry Machado, "Farquhar and Ford in Brazil: studies in Business Expansion and Foreign Policy," PhD dissertation, Northwestern University, 1975, p. 201; Nevins and Hill, *Ford*, pp. 396-97; Royal Davis, "Cycles in the Automobile Pneumatic Tire Renewal Market in the United States," *Journal of the American Statistical Association*, vol. 26, no. 173, Supplement: Proceedings of the American Statistical Association (March 1931), pp. 10-19. As cited by Greg Grandin, *Fordlandia, The Rise and Fall of Henry Ford's Forgotten Jungle City*. Metropolitan Books, Henry Holt and Company LLC: New York, 2009, 23.

[3] ORE, 69.

[4] SKR, 129.

[5] SKR, 133.

[6] JOH, 142.

[7] Mary J. Drucker, *The Rubber Industry in Ohio* (Columbus, Ohio: National Youth Administration in Ohio, 1937), 38. Quoted in JOH, 141-142, footnotes.

[8] Mansel G. and K. Austin Kerr, B.F. Goodrich: Tradition and Transformation, 1870-1995 (Columbus, Ohio: Ohio State University Press, 1996), 117-118. Quoted in Susan Allyn Johnson. "Industrial Voyagers: A Case Study of Appalachian Migration to Akron, Ohio, 1900-1940." (PhD diss., Ohio State University, 2006), 141 (osu1140124259). http://rave.ohiolink.edu/etdc/view?acc_num=osu1140124259. Accessed September 28, 2011.

[9] "70,600 Workers Set Akron Mark." *ABJ*, 103rd Year, No. 362, Wednesday, December 2, 1942, 1. This *does not reflect the numbers who remained on at part-time hours*. GRIS 458.

[10] William E. Leuchtenburg, "The Wrong Man at the Wrong Time," *American Heritage*, Summer 2009, Vol. 59, Issue 2, http://www.americanheritage.com/content/wrong-man-wrong-time, Accessed January 9, 2012. SKR, 161.

[11] WHE, 89; Leuchtenburg, ibid.

[12] GRIS, 459.

[13] Karl Grismer. "Ghost City? Not Akron! Population: 278,903? Barometers Used In Estimates Vary; 34,112 Increase Seen Here Since 1940." *ABJ*, 103rd Year, No. 317, Sunday, October 18, 1942, 1; "Comprehensive Rental Survey Shows Akron Back to '31 Level." *ABJ*, 103rd Year, No. 240, Sunday, August 2, 1942, 10C.

[14] Grandin, ibid, 23; This was largely due to the fact that federal highway funds became available to the states with the passage of the Federal-Aid Road Act of 1917 and the Federal Highway Act of 1921. "Brief History of the Direct Federal Highway Construction Program." U.S. Department of Transportation, Federal Highway System. Accessed September 17, 2014. http://www.fhwa.dot.gov/infrastructure/blazer01.cfm/

[15] WOLF, 465-466.

[16] WOLF, 509.

17 WOLF, 499-500.

18 WOLF, 509

19 An early proponent of scientific management, Bedaux started his company in nearby Cleveland, quickly becoming a millionaire after introducing his techniques to B.F. Goodrich in 1917. "How Bedaux Got Rich," *Mansfield News-Journal*, November 8, 1937, 1 & 5. http://www.newspaperarchive.com/SiteMap/FreePdfPreview.aspx?img=10317264 Accessed Saturday, October 1, 2011. WOLF, 509-510.

20 United States Senate, Seventy-First Congress, Third Session, *Unemployment and Relief. Hearings Before a Special Committee to Investigate Unemployment and Relief, Volume 2, February 8 to April 8, 1938*. Washington, DC: GPO, 1938) 1344. http://fraser.stlouisfed.org /publications/sen_unemprel/ Accessed September 5, 2011.

21 Both Goodyear and B.F. Goodrich opened new plants in Los Angeles before 1929. This was followed by another Goodyear plant in Gadsen, Alabama in 1929, a Goodrich plant in Massachusetts in 1930, a Firestone plant in Memphis in 1937 and another Goodrich plant in Clarksville, Tennessee in 1939. Ralph William Frank, "The Rubber Industry of the Akron-Barberton Area: A Study of the Factors Related to Its Development, Distribution, and Localization" (Ph.D. diss., Northwestern University, 1952), 25 as cited in JOH, 127 and 140 (footnotes). SKR, 108. "History by Year," "Goodyear Corporate." Accessed December 15, 2015. http://www.goodyear.com/corporate/history/history_byyear.html. Interestingly enough, General Tire of Akron would eventually open a tire manufacturing plant in Graves County, Kentucky in 1960, the very county in which Haskell and his family had once lived before moving to Akron. It, too, was eventually closed in 2006.

CHAPTER FORTY: THE HARDEST OF TIMES

1 Per the 1930 census, this would appear to be Harry J. Hazen, age 35, with wife Kathleen, age 36. "Population Schedule," Fifteenth Census of the United States: 1930. Department of Commerce—Bureau of the Census. Tallmadge Township, Summit County, Ohio, Enumeration District 77-207, April 1930, Sheet 18B.

CHAPTER FORTY-ONE: LABOR

1 *National Industrial Recovery Act,* Ch. 90, 48 Stat. 195, Title I, Sec. 7(a); Unfortunately, The Wagner Act did little to advance the cause of black Americans (or other minorities) as it did not prohibit racial discrimination in union membership—this courtesy of pressure from the American Federation of Labor. As existing racism effectively blocked membership in unions, it prohibited employment. It also banned "company unions, unions that were more racially egalitarian than affiliated unions, and made the hire of strikebreaking workers, usually African American more difficult. The NLRA, in essence gave unions governmental validation to exclude black workers from labor agreements." These shortcomings would only be addressed by the Taft-Hartley Act of 1947. Charles Gallagher and Cameron D. Lippard, "New Deal," *Race and Racism in the United States, An Encyclopedia of the American Mosaic* (Greenwood, an imprint of ABC-CLIO, LLC, Santa Barbara, CA, 2014), 883. "Closed Shop," "The Free Dictionary by Farlex." Accessed December 5, 2014. http://legal-dictionary.thefreedictionary.com/Closed+Shop/

2 TULL, 167.

3 SKR, 176.

4 WHE, 89.

5 SKR, 161.

6 Ruth McKenny, "Uneasy City," *The New Yorker*, December 19, 1936, 56. Quoted in JOH, 162.

7 WOLF, 522.

[8] The first possible "sit-down" strike took place at Mansfield Tire & Rubber in Mansfield, Ohio, on May 15th, 1933. Factory management was "perplexed" at the technique, not knowing how to react. They made no effort to expel the workers settled with them shortly after pickets began to appear outside. Daniel Nelson, *American Rubber Workers & Organized Labor, 1900-1941* (Princeton University Press, Princeton, 1988), 133. The first important "sit-down" occurred on June 19, 1934 against General Tire and Rubber Company. Bruce M. Meyer, *The Once and Future Union, The Rise and Fall of the United Rubber Workers*, 1935-1995 (The University of Akron Press, Akron 2002), 56.

[9] TULL, 177; GRIS, 482; Akron Rubber Strike of 1936. Ohio History Central, An Online Encyclopedia of Ohio History, The Ohio Historical Society. http://www.ohiohistorycentral.org/entry.php?rec=461 Accessed September 11, 2011.

[10] Aaron Brenner, Benjamin Day, Immanuel Ness, *The Encyclopedia of Strikes in American History* (New York, M.E. Sharpe, Inc., 2009), 404.

[11] GRIS, 482.

[12] ORE, 73.

[13] SKR, 170.

[14] "Marker #32-77, 1936 Akron Rubber Strike," Remarkable Ohio, The Ohio Historical Society, http://www.remarkableohio.org/HistoricalMarker.aspx?HistoricalMarker Id=991. Accessed January 5, 2013.

CHAPTER FORTY-TWO: STRIKE

[1] The United Rubber Workers organized on September 12, 1935 in Akron, Ohio.

[2] James S. Jackson, "Plant 2 Tire Workers Idle," *ABJ*, Friday Evening, February 14, 1936, 1, 14.

[3] Kenneth Nichols, "Biography in Brief. Fred Climer." *ABJ*, No. 198, 103rd Year, Sunday, June 21, 1942, 5D.

[4] James S. Jackson, "Ousters Seen After Sitdown," *ABJ*, Saturday Evening, February 15, 1936, 1-2.

[5] Per the 1940 Census, Adrian E. Bethel was a "foreman tire room" in the rubber industry. 1940; Census Place: Akron, Summit, Ohio; Roll: T627_3178; Page: 3B; Enumeration District: 89-149.

[6] An 1896 graduate of the Massachusetts Institute of Technology, Paul W. Litchfield joined Goodyear in 1900. Over the course of his 59-year career with the company, he became president in 1926 and its first Chief Executive Officer and Chairman of the Board in 1930. "Goodyear Corporate." http://www.goodyear.com/corporate/bios/litchfield.html Accessed July 11, 2012.

[7] The 1937 Akron City Directory shows Ormond R. Bethel of 80 Briner Avenue as a clerk at the *ABJ*. *ACD* 1936, 154; The 1920 Census of Belmont, Ohio, shows Ormond R., 11, and Adrian, 15, as brothers. Year: 1920; Census Place: Flushing, Belmont, Ohio; Roll: T625_1349; Page: 8B; Enumeration District: 3; Image: 150.

[8] James S. Jackson, "Blockade Goodyear; 8,000 Idle," *ABJ*, Tuesday Evening, February 18, 1936, 1.

[9] WHE, 94.

[10] Bruce M. Meyer, *The Once and Future Union, The Rise and Fall of the United Rubber Workers*, 1935-1995 (The University of Akron Press, Akron 2002), 49.

[11] Ruth McKenney, *Industrial Valley* (Greenwood Press, New York: 1939), 373.

[12] TULL, 337.

[13] *ABJ*, February 16, 1938. Quoted in JOH 169.

[14] Per the 1930 census, this would appear to be Charles R. Brewer, 36, who is listed as a "Supervisor" in the "Tire Dept Rubber Factory." Fifteenth Census of the United States: 1930. Department of Commerce—Bureau of the Census. Akron, Summit County, Ohio,

Enumeration District 77-181, April 1930, Sheet 11B; Per the 1930 census, this would appear to be Walter C. Sowers, 29, who is listed as a "Supervisor" in the "Rubber Mill." Fifteenth Census of the United States: 1930. Department of Commerce—Bureau of the Census. Akron, Summit County, Ohio, Enumeration District 77-26, April 1930, Sheet 13B.

[15] Brewer would appear to have been a member of Goodyear's "Flying Squadron," a cadre of workers cross-trained in all aspects of tire manufacturing as a pathway to managerial positions. During the strike Squadron members climbed the fences to operate machinery and smuggle supplies past union members who patrolled the perimeter with baseball bats and pool cues. SKR, 170, 174.

[16] Just as the economy was gaining ground, another recession hit in early fall of 1937. This time, it was so severe that the demand for tires was halved by the end of the year. Once again, thousands more were laid off. GRIS, 486.

CHAPTER FORTY-THREE: RELIEF AND PUBLIC WORKS

[1] Harry L. Hopkins, *Unemployment Relief Census: October 1933* (US, Federal Emergency Relief Administration, 1933), 4. Federal Reserve Archival System for Economic Research, http://fraser.stlouisfed.org/publications/urcen/ Accessed October 2, 2011. Hopkins, *Unemployment Relief Census*, 13. Among the rural population, more than half the population was concentrated in nine states. Kentucky was #2.

[2] Hopkins, *Unemployment Relief Census*, 177, 216

[3] Grismer, *Akron and Summit County*, 460.

[4] Grismer, *Akron and Summit County*, 461.

[5] United States Senate, Seventy-First Congress, Third Session, *Unemployment and Relief. Hearings Before a Special Committee to Investigate Unemployment and Relief, Volume 2, February 8 to April 8, 1938*. Washington, DC: GPO,1938), 7. http://fraser.stlouisfed.org/publications /sen_unemprel/ Accessed September 5, 2011.

[6] This statistic includes those on work relief programs. If they are not included, the unemployment rate was still 20.6%. Robert A. Margo, "Employment and Unemployment in the 1930s," *Journal of Economic Perspectives*, Volume 7, Number 2. Spring, 1993, 41-59. http://fraser.stlouisfed.org/cbt/browse.php?collection_id=5&browse=title September 5, 2011.

[7] Harry L. Hopkins, Administrator, Works Progress Administration, "The Realities of Unemployment." (Washington, DC: Works Progress Administration, 1937), http://fraser.stlouisfed.org/publications/roune/ Accessed September 5, 2011.

[8] Hopkins, ibid.

[9] Later shortened to the more familiar NRA. National Industrial Recovery Act of 1933. The Social Welfare History Project. http://www.socialwelfarehistory.com/events/national-industrial-recovery-act-of-1933/ Accessed September 10, 2011.

[10] As a percentage of the population, that would be equivalent of putting some 10 million people to work today. Charles Peters and Timothy Noah, "Four million jobs in two years? FDR did it in two months," *Slate*, January 26, 2009. http://www.slate.com/ id/2209781/ Accessed September 11, 2011.

[11] Economist and author John Steele Gordon notes that by June of 1932, the stock market had bottomed out, down 90% from its high in September of 1929. And by March of 1933, The Great Depression was technically, at least, over. In fact, 1933 would be the second best year for the Dow Jones average in the 20th century. However, recovery was still very slow. "Unemployment," he records, "over 25 percent in 1933, was still at 17 percent as late as 1939. Indeed, in 1937, when the economy suddenly turned south again, there was a problem: what to call the new downturn. Most people thought the country was still in a depression, so that word wouldn't do. But economists, delighted to have a problem that they could actually solve, came up with the word 'recession,' and that's what we have been using ever since." "Economic

Lessons from American History," *Imprimis*, July/August 2012, Volume 41, Number 7/8, 7. (Hillsdale College: Hillsdale, Michigan, 2012) Adapted from a lecture delivered on February 27, 2012, aboard the Crystal Symphony during a Hillsdale College cruise from Rio de Janeiro to Buenos Aires.

[12] Peters and Noah, ibid.

[13] The Works Projects Administration in Indiana. http://www.indiana.edu/~liblilly /wpa/wpa_info.html Accessed September 11, 2011.

[14] GRIS, 460.

[15] GRIS, 460.

[16] GRIS, 460.

[17] GRIS, 462.

[18] Karl Grismer. "WPA Dies Today After Spending $51,000,000 in County." *ABJ*, 104th Year, No. 55, Saturday, January 30, 1943, 2; The WPA went out existence nationwide in May. John Grover, Associated Press Feature Service Writer. "WPA DIES; Not Even Funeral; Biggest Employer Unmourned." *ABJ*, 104th Year, No. 147, Sunday, May 2, 1943, 6D.

[19] Per the 1930 census, they paid monthly rent of $25. "Population Schedule," Fifteenth Census of the United States: 1930. Department of Commerce—Bureau of the Census. Tallmadge Township, Summit County, Ohio, Enumeration District 77-207, April 1930, Sheet 18A.

[20] This would have been the family of Francis and Katherine Sackett. Children in 1930 were noted as Howard T., Elmore E., Elizabeth B. and Bruce C. Sackett. "Population Schedule," Fifteenth Census of the United States: 1930. Department of Commerce—Bureau of the Census. Tallmadge Township, Summit County, Ohio, Enumeration District 77-207, April 1930, Sheet 18A.

[21] The 1940 Census records Bruce Kramer, 42, as "Owner" of a "grocery." National Archives, Seventh Census of the United States, 1940, Ohio, Summit County, Tallmadge, S.D. 23, E.D. No. 77-82, Sheet 1A, April 2-3, 1940. It was located on East Avenue, just off Tallmadge Circle. Today, the site is occupied by the parking lot of the Rite-Aid Pharmacy at 45 East Avenue.

[22] The physical address was 74 S. Thomas Rd., the very base of "Coal Hill." 100 years earlier, what would eventually become Thomas Road was the bed of Summit County's first railroad servicing the coal mines on the hill behind the house. Frank E. Lawrence, About Old Tallmadge, The Tallmadge Historical Society, 1984, 4. Judy Anne Davis, "A History of Tallmadge Coal: A Tale of Woodchucks, Welshmen, and a Canal" (Stow, Ohio: 2006), 9. The windows on the ground floor to the left of the front door were in the living room; to the right was the dining room. Upstairs were three bedrooms. The addition to the rear of the home was the site of the kitchen and, many years later, its first indoor bathroom. The house was torn down after the property was sold for apartment development in the late 1960s.

CHAPTER FORTY-FOUR: THE CIRCLE

[1] At the time of the recording in the mid-1980s. Located on Tallmadge Circle between Southeast and East Avenues, it is now a parking lot.

[2] The 1930 U.S. Census shows Mahlon Bunting, 48, as a "Gas man" at a "Gas Station." Year: *1930*; Census Place: *Tallmadge, Summit, Ohio*; Roll: *1882*; Page: *18B*; Enumeration District: *207*; Image: *662.0*; FHL microfilm: *2341616*.

[3] McCormick's companion in the attempted assault was A.J. Ritchie, which took place after they left a "roadhouse" named as the White Pond Inn. The events were described in *ABJ* throughout the second half of September 1928.

[4] Per the 1930 Census, the household of Clyde, 42, and Ruth M. Rutherford, 38. They had three Children, Arthur, 18, Glenn, 14, and Dorothy, 12. They were next-door neighbors to Haskell and Florence when they lived on 18. *1930*; Census Place: *Tallmadge,*

Summit, Ohio; Roll: *1882*; Page: *18A*; Enumeration   District: *207*; Image: *661.0*; FHL microfilm: *2341616*.

⁵ The 1939-40 Akron City Directory shows the Roosevelt Restaurant at 313 Darrow Road. *Akron, Barberton and Cuyahoga Falls Official City Directory 1939-40* (Akron, Ohio, Burch Directory Co., 1939), 1018.

⁶ The 1939-40 Akron City Directory shows Abraham Massad as proprietor of the Roosevelt Restaurant at 313 Darrow Road in Akron. *Akron, Barberton and Cuyahoga Falls Official City Directory 1939-40* (Akron, Ohio, Burch Directory Co., 1939), 1018.

⁷ Son Donald later remembered, "That restaurant was the Eagle Café. It was on the corner of East Avenue and the Circle. It was back just a little bit. It was between there and the Stoneware. The food wasn't anything. In fact, a guy come in there and asked Art one time where was a good place to eat and he told him to go across the street."

⁸ 1930 U.S. Census records show Charles E. Mills, 46. At the time, he was employed as a carpenter. Year: *1930*; Census Place: *Tallmadge, Summit, Ohio*; Roll: *1882*; Page: *30B*; Enumeration District: *232*; Image: *740.0*; FHL microfilm: *2341616*.

⁹ Son Donald seconded that opinion, later remembering, "That Bill Perry— He was up there at his girlfriend's one night. It was cold, cold wintertime. He went out— He had an old Plymouth and his car wouldn't start. He tried to start it and he tried to crank it and he couldn't get it started. He took the crank and knocked out both the headlights and threw it through the windshield. He was [quite the character]."

CHAPTER FORTY-FIVE:
THE TALLMADGE POLICE DEPARTMENT: ONE MAN

¹ "'39 Slump Pictured in Census Figures," ABJ (June 28, 1942), quoted in TULL 333; "Rubber Plants To Hire 37,000. Record Number Of Jobs Expected To Open Before July. 60,000 Now On Payrolls." *ABJ*, 103rd Year, No. 279, Thursday, September 10, 1942, 1.

² "Flash!! 1,397 Vacant Houses in Akron—In April, 1940." *ABJ*, 103rd Year, No. 345, Sunday, November 15, 1942, 18A.

³ Akron, too, had seen a dramatic population decrease of 10,249 or 4% from 1930 to 1940. "1940 U.S. Census of Population. Ohio. Table 2. Population of cities of 10,000 or more from earliest census to 1940," 814. http://www.census.gov/prod/www/abs/decennial/1940.html Accessed September 17, 2011.

⁴ "The Committee was informed that in 1936 the Hall had been condemned by the State Department of Industrial relations but that various organizations had been permitted to use the Building regardless of the order issued by the state." CITY, 1.

⁵ Other than Council documentation, no official written records of the Tallmadge Police Department exist for the period when Haskell Jones was first marshal and then chief of police. All records have been destroyed per a record retention schedule. Telephone conversation with current Chief of Police, Donald J. Zesiger, 7th chief of police, City of Tallmadge, Tuesday, December 6th, 2011.

⁶ "The History of the Tallmadge Police Department, The City of Tallmadge, History Moving Forward." http://tallmadge-ohio.org/Government/Police-Department/Police-Department-History.aspx Accessed April 7, 2012.

⁷ "Ex-Officials Hunting Jobs. Deputy Windsor First of Ousted County Employees to Find New Employment." *ABJ*, Saturday, January 2, 1937, 11.

⁸ The 1940 Census records Haskell Jones, 41, working as "Labor" on "County Road Work" earning some $800 a year while Marshall Oscar Windsor, 43, is recorded having an annual income of $1,560. National Archives, Seventh Census of the United States, 1940, Ohio, Summit County, Tallmadge.

⁹ Oren D. Carter is recorded as a deputy sheriff in the 1939-40 Akron City Directory (No publisher or copyright date recorded on a scanned copy in possession of Akron Summit County Public Library), 481.

[10] Haskell was not the only person interested in the position. The former Sheriff of Summit County also had his eyes on the position but was ultimately turned down. H.H. Harriman, "Jim Flower's Eyes on Job of Marshal." *ABJ*, Sunday, December 8, 1940, 51. "Miscellany," *ABJ*, Sunday, January 5, 1941, 46. Party affiliation may well have had a deciding role in that selection process. While Flower would appear to have been a Republican, Haskell was a solid Democrat, having been elected to the county central committee in May of 1940. "Win Committee Posts in Hotly Contested Races," *ABJ*, Wednesday, May 15, 1940, 26.

Charles Edward Ritchie "was elected the first mayor of Tallmadge when the village was incorporated in 1935 and served in this position until his death in 1941. He spent more than $100,000 of his own money in the restoration of historic buildings on the Circle and in other public improvements. His widow, Mabel Marsh Ritchie, left a fortune to Summit County, with Tallmadge to share in benefits from the income." Dee Buente, "Tallmadge Personalities of Particular Note," *TALL*, 21.

[11] As tight-fisted as the Village appeared (and was), their method of remuneration (or lack thereof) was not without precedent. An article in the *ABJ* in April of 1940 noted, "Akron has 210 policemen who are paid, most of them, less than rubber workers when the latter draw full pay.

"The highest paid patrolmen are men with four years or more service. They get $1,923 a year. That's $37 a week.

"For that $37, the veteran officers, nearly all with families, must buy their own uniforms, guns and ammunition . . .

"Men with three years' service draw $1,860 a year; two years, $1806, and one year, $1660. A first-year man gets less than $32 a week."

The same article went on to note that "The minimum requirement recommended by all types of safety associations is one policeman for every 1,000 persons . . .

"Dollar for dollar the police department probably gives more visible service than any other city department.

"Yet, discounting entirely the risk of life and limb present in all police work, the cop is paid less than most city employes [sic] except firemen."

At $225 a month or $2700 a year by the time he resigned after 4 ½ years' service, Haskell *was* at face value paid considerably more than the "highest paid patrolmen" of Akron. However, he also had to pay for the additional cost and upkeep of his car for which Akron cruisermen were not responsible. As the same article went on to note that the cost of operating each of the Akron Police Department's motor vehicles to be roughly $790 a year, his net pay actually would have dropped to some $1910 a year.

In April of 1944 during the salary negotiations that would lead to his resignation, city councilman Watts could truthfully claim, "that Marshal Jones is paid somewhat higher wages than Akron cruiserman." However, Councilman Watts also managed to ignore the obvious that Haskell was far from just a "cruiserman" by that point in time. He had become the Village's last marshal, its first chief of police and undergone F.B.I. training, while also being tasked with managing the road crew and organizing civil defense operations (which included establishing the volunteer fire department and running scrap drives for the war effort). All on 24-hour a day basis.

Then there's that other minor point that the "minimum requirement recommended by all types of safety association is one policeman for every 1,000 persons." In effect, the Village, with its population of 3,452, had been getting quite the deal—however they defined his position. Kenneth Nichols, "Akron's Police Below Minimum," *ABJ*, 101st year, No. 135, April 14, 1940, 1-2.

[12] Two-way radios were such a novelty at the time that the installation of one in an Akron police cruiser merited a large photo in August 1940. "New 'Black Maria' Boasts Two-Way Radio," *ABJ* August 26, 1940, 25; Even as late as June 1942, The Summit County Sheriff's

Department was forced to rely on the sales of advertisements in a self-published yearbook to finance the purchase of their own first two-way radio system. This after Summit County Commissioner's found it was impossible to find the funds in their budget for such an idea. "It's Not on the County. Sheriff Buys Equipment." *ABJ*, 103rd Year, No. 193, Thursday, June 16, 1942, 26.

[13] The auxiliary police in Tallmadge were actually the first to be trained in the county and the first to "go on duty" as traffic officers. Although Haskell's full role in its organization is unknown, a contemporary news article recognized Mayor John Sperry as head of the Tallmadge civilian defense council, Sam Schlup as coordinator of civilian defense, V.N. Ziegler (who would later become mayor and opponent of Haskell) as head of the auxiliary police, Dale Powers, chairman of the committee on volunteer participation, Wiley Smith, director of transportation and Earl J. Raess, public relations director. It also recorded that "Mrs. Wesley Page is chief of the Tallmadge Red Cross branch and has two able aides in Mrs. Edith Spring and Mrs. J.C. Baldwin. Mrs. Spring has charge of Red Cross knitting. Work in the sewing division, headed by Mrs. Baldwin, has temporarily suspended until autumn." H.B. "Doc" Kerr. "On The Home Front. Tallmadge Auxiliary Police First in County to Display Their Skill." *ABJ*, 103rd Year, No. 160, Thursday, May 14, 1942, 8.

[14] There are only two adult women with the last name of Baker in the 1940 Census of Tallmadge: Susan, 49, at 286 Mogadore-Cuyahoga Falls Road and Ona, 72, at 381 Monroe Falls Road. Ona would be the most likely reference. National Archives, Seventh Census of the United States, 1940, Ohio, Summit County, Tallmadge, S.D. [Unrecorded], E.D. No. 77-83, Sheet 7A, April 29, 1940.

[15] Son Donald later remembered, "That restaurant was the Eagle Café. It was on the corner of East Avenue and the Circle. It was back just a little bit. It was between there and the Stoneware. The food wasn't anything. In fact, a guy come in there and asked Art one time where was a good place to eat and he told him to go across the street."

[16] Village of Tallmadge, Ohio, Council Meeting, March 9, 1942 (Tallmadge, Ohio: 1942)

[17] The basement was excavated and "restrooms" were installed in 1943. Frank E. Lawrence, *About Old Tallmadge*, Tallmadge, Ohio, 1984, pg. 26.

[18] The Police Department moved out of the building to their new offices (on the site of the Jones residence next to the schoolhouse) on April 3rd, 1980, after this recording was made. Frank E. Lawrence, *About Old Tallmadge*, Tallmadge, Ohio, 1984, pg. 26.

[19] Charles Ritchie died March 13, 1941. "Ritchie Dies at 63; Rites in Tallmadge," *ABJ*, Friday, March 14, 1941, 1-2.

[20] Per the 1930 census, her name would have been Mabel E. Ritchie. "Population Schedule," Fifteenth Census of the United States: 1930. Department of Commerce—Bureau of the Census. Tallmadge Township, Summit County, Ohio, Enumeration District 77-207, April 1930, Sheet 23B.

[21] John A. "Jack" Sperry. Mayor of Tallmadge from 1942-1943.

[22] Model verified through personal communication by Jim Benjaminson, Mem. Sec., Plymouth Owners Club, Inc. Haskell's memory of it being $764 would tend to verify the model as being the P11 DeLuxe Club Coupe. "1941 Plymouth Series P11 Deluxe and P12 Special DeLuxe," http://www.autogallery.org.ru/ply1941.htm Accessed March 6, 2017.

[23] In contrast to today's litigious society, Ohio law leaned decidedly in favor of such an arrangement at the time as "Ohio law says that [the private citizen] has no legal claim against the city if he suffers personal injury or damage to his car as the result of collision with a police or fire department car used in line of duty . . ." "Police Cruisers Crash Too Often. Slusser Asked to Discipline Driver after Mishaps." *ABJ*, Thursday, April 6, 1944, No. 122, 105th Year, 3.

[24] As there was only one Huffman family listed in Tallmadge in 1940 and they only had one child, a girl, this would have to be Elizabeth A. Huffman, 10. Parents Francis and Clara

resided with Elizabeth on Kent Road, today's Northeast Avenue. 1940; Census Place: Tallmadge, Summit, Ohio; Roll: T627_3154; Page: 61A; Enumeration District: 77-78.

[25] "Boy, 16, Held as Car Rams Into House." *ABJ*, Sunday, August 15, 1943, 2.

[26] Although harsh by today's standards, it could be considered comparatively mild by the standards of the day. The trial of Akron policeman Jacob Yingling for a fatal blow with a blackjack to prisoner Walter Lamb resulted in his acquittal. Although the blow "fractured the skull and tore the brain" the court ruled the officer "was permitted to use whatever force was necessary to subdue Lamb when he resisted officers who were attempting to lock him in a cell at city jail." "Lamb's Widow Files Suit Against Officer." *ABJ*, July 22, 1942, 7. Yingling Freed in Lamb Death." *ABJ*, 103rd Year, No. 236, Wednesday, July 29, 1942, 1; As regards prisoner's civil rights, it was also an era when a prisoner in Akron could be bound over to a grand jury for a murder trial "after almost a week of incessant questioning" by a team of detectives. "Woman, 48 Faces Murder Charge. Mrs. Lexie Isley Bound Over in Melton Stabbing." *ABJ*, 103rd Year, No. 210, Friday, July 3, 1942, 12.

[27] This would have referred to Mike Dremak, who became chief of police in 1961. "Police Department Helps Preserve Small Town Flavor of Growing City." *MEM*, 37.

[28] The 1940 Census of Tallmadge lists Wanda, 27, and Wilma, 24, daughters of James and Iva Crites. 1940; Census Place: Tallmadge, Summit, Ohio; Roll: T627_3154; Page: 19A; Enumeration District: 77-83.

[29] This could well be the stabbing murder of George Reynolds by Whitney Jones in the Maiden Lane alley near E. Exchange Street. "Canton Father of Six Killed in Akron Fight," *ABJ*, 103rd Year, No. 113, Saturday, March 28th, 1942, 9. "Stabbing Suspect Held for Grand Jury," *ABJ*, Tuesday, March 31, 1942, 19.

[30] According to the recollection of Donald Jones, it was located between Southwest Avenue and the B&O Railroad tracks near the Tallmadge City Limits and could have been accessed via Osceola Avenue. Personal communication with Donald Jones, January 12, 2013.

[31] "Bill Jones. Florence's uncle. His name wasn't Bill. His name was Bryan. B-R-Y-A-N. But they called him Bill. Everybody knew him as Bill. Garland Jones [was his father]," Haskell Jones.

[32] Haskell's brother Ralph Jones and his wife Ruth (Thomas) Jones.

CHAPTER FORTY-SIX: "WAR FARERS"

[1] "Area to Get OCD Equipment Within 30 Days. Aid Promised by J.M. Landis. Initial Shipments to Include Helmets, First Aid Materials. Delay Fire Apparatus." ABJ, 103rd Year, No. 117, Wednesday, April 1, 1942, 17.

[2] "Bombing of Akron Held Possible." *ABJ*, 103rd Year, No. 139, Thursday, April 23, 1942, 18; Ray C. Sutliff, "Akron Shows Ohio How to Combat Air Raid," *ABJ*, 103rd Year, No. 155, Saturday, May 9, 1942, 1; Ray C. Sutliff, "Electric Signs Mar Black-Out. Rest of Akron Turns Off Lights in First Test." *ABJ*, 103rd Year, No. 218, Saturday, July 11, 1942, 1; "Second Black-Out Set for Tuesday." *ABJ*, 103rd Year, No. 296, Sunday, September 27, 1942, 1; "Surprise Black-Out is Next for Akron. Public Failures to Cooperate Assailed as OCD Checks Tuesday Night Test." *ABJ*, 103rd Year, No. 299, Wednesday, September 30, 1942, 1; "Summit Awaits Signal for First General Blackout. Alert Sounds in 29 Counties. Raid Siren Here Scheduled to Shriek Warning at 9:25 P.M. 'All Clear' Set for 9:55." *ABJ*, 104th Year, No. 87, Wednesday, March 3, 1943, 15; "Black-Out Tonight—Lights Out 9:25-9:55; Other Rules." ABJ, 104th Year, No. 87, Thursday, March 4, 1943, 1; "OCD Sees Need of 500 Drivers. Prepares to Extend Corps to All Areas of County. First Night Test Held. Extra 'Gas' Rations Reported for Volunteers Who Qualify." *ABJ*, 104th Year, No. 5, Friday, December 11, 1942, 25; "Summit Defense Plans Made National Pattern." *ABJ*, 103rd Year, No. 180, Wednesday, June 3, 1942, 23; "Army Directs Plant Guards. Protection of Akron Defense Factories Will Be Under Military Control. 10 Companies Affected." *ABJ*, 103rd Year, No. 231, Friday, July

24, 1942, 21.

[3] "U.S. Lifts Ban on Publishing Weather News." By United Press. *ABJ*, 104th Year, No. 311, Tuesday, October 12, 1943, 1-2; It wasn't until April 1944 that the diminished threat of air raids allowed "Summit county civilian defense official to place thousands of trained volunteers on a reserve, or 'inactive' basis.'" "Thousands in OCD to Go on Reserve List. Need for Raid Wardens Eases. Diminished Peril of Bombing Causes Changes; Many Units Retained." *ABJ*, Thursday, April 6, 1944, No. 122, 105th Year, 21.

[4] Helen Waterhouse. "Guard on Spies Doubled Here," *ABJ*, March 10, 1940. All F.B.I. records relating to this training were destroyed in 1996 per record retention and disposal schedule. Letter from David Hardy, Section Chief, Record/Information Dissemination Section, Records Management Division, F.B.I. March 11, 2011, While today it might seem far-fetched, there *was* evidence of a Japanese spy network in Akron for a period of ten years preceding the war. "Jap Spies Worked in Akron, Says FBI." *ABJ*, June 4, 1942, 32.

[5] Ray C. Sutliff. "Goal for October is Set At 250,000. Million a Month is Ultimate Output Level." *ABJ*, 103rd Year, No. 313, Wednesday, October 14, 21.

[6] Joseph E. Kuebler. "War Tools Rolling Off Akron Lines. Tire Capital Wining Fame With Diversity of Its Industries." *ABJ*, 103rd Year, No. 184, Sunday, June 7, 1942, 1-2; During a rubber workers strike in 1943, the *Beacon* listed some of the products that were no longer being produced in Akron due to the stoppage. It included, "Half-tracs and padding for tanks, gas masks, barrage balloons, self-sealing fuel tanks, bridge pontoons, blimp bags, de-icers for aircraft, machine gun clips, Bofors guns, airplane wings, life boats, life rafts, life belts, aircraft tires and tires for military trucks, artillery, jeeps, peeps and other rolling equipment, molded and extruded plastics for planes and land vehicle, shatter proof oxygen cylinders, parachute seats and backs, crash pads, pilot seats, tank turrets, Bogie roller, life suits, hose of all types, synthetic rubber and products made of it, and some articles of clothing." "Here is List of War Products on Which Strike Halts Work." *ABJ*, 104th Year, No. 170, Tuesday, May 25, 1943, 2.

[7] "Officials Discuss New Blimp Plans. Navy Party Visits Goodyear Officials in Akron." ABJ, 103rd Year, No. 162, Saturday, May 16, 1942, 18.

[8] H.B. "Doc" Kerr. "On The Home Front. That 'Necessity is Mother of Invention' Proved in Making U.S. Barrage Balloons." *ABJ*, 103rd Year, No. 206, June 21, 1942, 3.

[9] While the manufacture of aircraft would appear to be an odd combination for a rubber company, Goodyear actually had deep roots in aviation having manufactured tires for aviation pioneers the Wright brothers, Glenn Curtiss & Glenn Martin. This was followed with the construction of both rigid and non-rigid airships. SKR 150; Joseph E. Kuebler. "Mystery Cloak Hiding 8-Ball Is Ripped Off." ABJ, 103rd Year, No. 131, Wednesday, April 15, 1942, 1-2; By October 1943, overall U.S. airplane production was turning out close to one completed aircraft every five minutes. "Plane Every Five Minutes Near Realization in U.S. Wilson Outlines Huge War Output. WPB Man Gives FBI Credit for Production Aid. By United Press." *ABJ*, 104th Year, No. 322, Saturday, October 23, 1943, 3; While turning out a new Corsair ever 8 minutes was an admirable goal, actual production would fall short. Nonetheless, it did reach a very respectable height in 1944 as one new Corsair was completed every 168 minutes of every working day. Joseph E. Kuebler. "A New Corsair is Born Every 168 Minutes Now!" *ABJ*, Thursday, April 20, 1944, No. 136, 105th Year, 1-2.

[10] In fact, by 1944 Firestone's "achievement was hailed by the army ordnance department as one of the outstanding production records of the war" after having built more anti-aircraft guns than all of the Allied nation combined." Matt Hall. "Akron Makes 25,000 Bofors. Firestone Celebrates as Factory Tops Entire World in Production." *ABJ*, Sunday, April 2, 1944, No. 118, 105th Year, 1A, 6A.

[11] Joseph E. Kuebler. "War Tools Rolling Off Akron Lines. Tire Capital Wining Fame With Diversity of Its Industries." *ABJ*, 103rd Year, No. 184, Sunday, June 7, 1942, 1-2; One of the many diverse tasks Firestone was assigned was to manufacture wings for the "world's

largest transport plane," the C-46 Commando. And one of their inspectors would be a young Virginia Lois Dille, who would go on to marry Donald Jones after the end of the war. "New War Job for Firestone. Firm to Build Major Parts for World's Largest Transport Plane." *ABJ*, No. 240, 103rd Year, Sunday, August 2, 1942, 1.

12 "Portable Home Locations Set. Speedy Installation of 500 War Workers' Houses Promised Akron. Hint More Dwellings." *ABJ*, 104th Year, No. 334, Thursday, November 4, 1943, 1.

13 "Summit War Contracts Pass Billion Mark." *ABJ*, Friday, January 14, 1944, No. 39, 105th Year, 1-2; Measuringworth.com Accessed February 2, 2014.

14 Kenneth Nichols. The Town Crier. What Happens to an Amusement Park in Wartime—Should Happen To It." *ABJ*, 103rd Year, No. 160, Thursday, May 14, 1942, 21.

15 "Meet the War Farer: A New Kind of Migrant, Hunting a War Job in Scores of Boom Towns." *ABJ*, Sunday, May 3, 1942, 6D; "License Plates Reveal Newcomers. Akron Draws Workers From Everywhere." *ABJ*, Tuesday, March 31, 1942, 19.

16 "Akron to Need 25,000 More Workers in 1942." *ABJ*, 103rd Year, No. 163, Sunday, May 17, 1942, 8C.

17 "Rubber Plants to Hire 37,000. Record Number of Jobs Expected to Open Before July. 60,000 Now on Payrolls." *ABJ*, 103rd Year, No. 279, Thursday, September 10, 1942, 1.

18 Joseph E. Kuebler. "Aircraft Hires 1,000 Weekly. Pay Roll at Akron's No. 1 War Industry is Nearing 20,000 Total. Production Mounting. Peak In Operations Expected Next Spring, Says Litchfield." *ABJ*, 103rd Year, No. 282, Sunday, September 13, 1942, 1; "Akron Hiring 2,000 a Week. War Industries Continue to Drain City's Worker Reservoir. 8-Hour Day Ordered. Agents From Other Industrial Centers Seek to Hire Men Here." *ABJ*, 103rd Year, No. 303, Sunday, October 4, 1942, 1.

19 "70,600 Workers Set Akron Mark." *ABJ*, 103rd Year, No. 362, Wednesday, December 2, 1942, 1.

20 "Akron Boom Leads State." *ABJ*, Wednesday, April 26, 1944, No. 142, 105th Year, 1-2.

21 Rayy Mitten. "Labor Leaving Akron District. WMC Sees New Peril in Call From Other Towns." *ABJ*, 104th Year, No. 130, Saturday, April 15, 1943, 1-2. Ed. Note: Mitten's math is wrong. It would be a net gain of over 5200.

22 Lisle Croy. "Blythe Analyzes House Shortage. Unpredictable Expansion of Aircraft Contributes." *ABJ*, 103rd Year, No. 291, Tuesday, September 22, 1942, 24; "Akron Cited in Shortages. Labor, Housing Problems Here Termed Serious by WMC Chief. May Affect War Work." *ABJ*, 103rd Year, No. 314, Thursday, October 15, 1942, 1; "Akron 'Blacklisted' on War Contracts." ABJ, 103rd Year, No. 314, Thursday, October 15, 1942,1; "Akron Facing War Work Cut." *ABJ*, 104th Year, No. 27, Saturday, January 2, 1943, 1, 4; Rayy Mitten. "Labor Classification Robs Akron of Plant." *ABJ*, 104th Year, No. 87, Wednesday, March 3, 1943, 1-2.

23 Rayy Mitten. "WMC Outlines Job Benefits. Stabilization Plan Offers Seniority Advantages, Says Committee. Rehiring is Provided." *ABJ*, 104th Year, No. 38, Wednesday, January 13, 1943, 1; "Must First Use Available Labor." *ABJ*, 104th Year, No. 130, Saturday, April 17, 1943, 13.

24 "This Will Answer Your Questions on New Manpower Order." *ABJ*, 104th Year, No. 66, Wednesday, February 10, 1943, 2.

25 Thomas L. Stokes. "U.S. Embarks on Vast New Experiment With Workers." *ABJ*, 104th Year, No. 66, Wednesday, February 10, 1943, 3.

26 Lyle C. Wilson, United Press Staff Writer. "Akron to Go On 48-Hour Week. McNutt's Order Affects Employment in 32 Cities. Time and One-Half Pay Retained; Return to Farm Sought." *ABJ*, 104th Year, No. 66, Wednesday, February 10, 1943, 1-2; The 48-hour work week would have little impact in Akron, however. Most of the area war plants were already on

a 49-hour workweek, with some departments at B.F. Goodrich working as many as 57 to 70 hours. "Akron Shift to 48-Hour Week Will Be Gradual, Markle Says. Most War Plants on New Schedule. WMC Official Sees 2,000 Here Affected by Order." *ABJ*, 104th Year, No. 85, Monday, March 1, 1943, 2; Ben Williamson. "48-Hour Ruling Confuses Akron?" *ABJ*, 104th Year, No. 80, Wednesday, February 24, 1943, 4; "Little Aid Seen in Hours Edict. Manpower Gains Soon to Be Wiped Out by Draft." *ABJ*, 104th Year, No. 68, Friday, February 12, 1943, 1.

[27] That would be the equivalent of $1.6 billion dollars of purchasing power in 2013. "Measuring Worth." http://www.measuringworth.com/uscompare/relativevalue.php Accessed September 29, 2013; Rayy Mitten. "Labor Classification Robs Akron Of Plant." *ABJ*, 104th Year, No. 87, Wednesday, March 3, 1943, 1-2; Rayy Mitten. "Akron Critical Labor Area Ban Lifted. Order Checks Contract Loss. WMC Opens Way for Industries to Bid on New Government Needs. Worker Surplus Seen. City To Remain On 48-Hour Week, Washington Official Say." *ABJ*, 104th Year, No. 100, Tuesday, March 16, 1943, 1.

[28] Rayy Mitten. "Labor Leaving Akron District. WMC Sees New Peril in Call From Other Towns." *ABJ*, 104th Year, No. 130, Saturday, April 15, 1943, 1-2.

[29] "Akron Moved Back to 'Critical Labor Area' Class. Cuts All Bids on War Orders. Action Follows Plant Reports Showing Need of 7,500 More Workers. Layoff Fears Are Aired." *ABJ*, 104th Year, No. 166, Friday, May 21, 1943, 21; Rayy Mitten. "Plants Facing Contract Loss. War Order Cut-Back, 48 Hours Are Urged." *ABJ*, 104th Year, No. 168, Sunday, May 23, 1943, 1; "Akron Officially Put in 'Critical Labor Area.'" *ABJ*, 104th Year, No. 169, Monday, May 24, 1943, 1.

[30] Mize, Lea. "Production Lines, Stores, Offices Provide Employment. Schoolgirls Take War Jobs, Continue With Studies." *ABJ*, 104th Year, No. 351, Sunday, November 21, 1943, 19A; Rayy Mitten. "2,500 Boys And Girls Get Jobs At Aircraft." *ABJ*, 104th Year, No. 189, Sunday, June 13, 1943, 1A.

[31] The need to tap what previously had been considered child labor reached far beyond the Akron city limits. 'More than 500 have been brought in from neighboring southern states, chiefly West Virginia, and still more are to come." columnist Rayy Mitten noted in the *Akron Beacon Journal* before continuing, 'On Monday mornings at the bus and train stations, one gets the impression that a youth convention is about to be held here." Rayy Mitten. "2,500 Boys and Girls Get Jobs at Aircraft." *ABJ*, 104th Year, No. 189, Sunday, June 13, 1943, 1A; Four-hour factory shifts were slated for high school students when school resumed in September. Rayy Mitten. "Part-Time Workers Pool is Proposed for Akron." *ABJ*, 104th Year, No. 259, Sunday, August 22, 1943, 1; Still more workers were heavily recruited from out of state, boarding buses and trains for Akron by the hundreds—many who could not even read or write. Helen Waterhouse. "Akron—'Induction Center' for War Workers." *ABJ*, 104th Year, No. 337, Sunday, November 7, 1943, 1, 14; By November, the factories began to hire local girls as young as 14, as well. "Aircraft Will Hire Teen-Age Girls." *ABJ*, Wednesday, November 17, 1943, 5. Lea Mize. "Production Lines, Stores, Offices Provide Employment. Schoolgirls Take War Jobs, Continue With Studies." *ABJ*, 104th Year, No. 351, Sunday, November 21, 1943, 19A; Desperate to replace workers lost to the military draft, local companies also started visiting prisons to interview inmates about to be paroled. Waterhouse, Helen. "Akron—'Induction Center' for War Workers." *ABJ*, 104th Year, No. 337, Sunday, November 7, 1943, 1, 14.

[32] Rayy Mitten. "Tire Order Rips Akron Manpower Plan. Factories in Need of 5,000 to 10,000 More Workers to Fill U.S. Program." *ABJ*, 104th Year, No. 198, Saturday, June 22, 1943, 1, 5.

[33] Rayy Mitten. "Labor Recruiters Push Farther Into South as City's Worker Shortage Continues Acute." *ABJ*, Sunday, January 9, 1944, No. 34, 105th Year, 2A; "Heated Session

Expected Over Tire Plant Locations." *ABJ*, 104th Year, No. 267, Monday, August 30, 1943, 1.

34 "City Must Solve Its Own Housing? Report U.S. Unlikely to Intervene Unless Asked." *ABJ*, 103rd Year, No. 156, Sunday, May 10, 1942, 1.

35 Helen Waterhouse. "S.R.O. Sign Up On City Homes. House Shortage in Akron Irks Newcomers." *ABJ*, 103rd Year, No. 247, Sunday, August 9, 1942, 6A.

36 Karl Grismer. "House Shortage Drives Workers to Other Cities. No. 1 of a Series." *ABJ*, 103rd Year, No. 252, Friday, August 14, 1942, 1; Karl Grismer. When Information, Vision Are Lacking, So Are Homes. No. 2 of a Series." *ABJ*, 103rd Year, No. 253, Saturday, August 15, 1942, 1; Lisle Croy. "Blythe Analyzes House Shortage. Unpredictable Expansion of Aircraft Contributes." *ABJ*, 103rd Year, No. 291, Tuesday, September 22, 1942, 24.

37 "Housing Probe Pushes Ahead. Woman Arrested When 23 Are Found in Nine-Room Home. Other Areas Checked. Basements, Attics Being Used as Living Quarters, Says Report." *ABJ*, 103rd Year, No. 351, Saturday, November 21, 1942, 9.

38 Helen Waterhouse. "Vacated Store Rooms Prove Haven for Few." *ABJ*, 103rd Year, No. 271, Wednesday, September 1, 1942, 1; Helen Waterhouse. "'They Don't Sell Gas Here Anymore.' Filling Station Becomes a Cozy Home. Housing Problem Solved for Four. War Worker, Two Children, Sister Occupy Building." *ABJ*, 103rd Year, No. 352, Sunday, November 22, 1942, 13C.

39 L.C. Croy. "House Shortage Creates New Welfare Problems. Some Families Live in Places Unfit for Animals, Charities Director Zang Reports." *ABJ*, 104th Year, No. 133, Sunday, April 18, 1943, 5C.

40 L.C. Croy. "Conversion of Dwellings Urged in Housing Crisis. Akron Real Estate board Proposes Method To Alleviate Home Famine." *ABJ*, 103rd Year, No. 268, Sunday, August 30, 1942, 12C; L.C. Croy. "Akron Approves Conversion Plan. Similar Program Sponsored Locally Two Years Ago." *ABJ*, 103rd Year, No. 268, Sunday, August 30, 1942, 12C, "Home Conversion Here Leads State. Akron Campaign Shows Best Results in Ohio." *ABJ*, 104th Year, No. 56, Sunday, January 31, 1943, 7C.

41 L.C. Croy. "Housing Problem Gets More Acute. Owners, Realtors Asked to Furnish Rooms." *ABJ*, 103rd Year, No. 294, Friday, September 25, 1942, 34; Lisle Croy. Realtors Study Housing Problem. Gallagher Tells Group More Homes Must Open. *ABJ*, 103rd Year, No. 333, Tuesday, November 3, 1942, 28.

42 "Comprehensive Rental Survey Shows Akron Back to '31 Level." *ABJ*, 103rd Year, No. 240, Sunday, August 2, 1942, 10C; "Landlords Map New Rate Fight. Admit Federal Figures 'Fair,' Call Local Scale Unjust." *ABJ*, 103rd Year, No. 274, Saturday, September 5, 1942, 2.

43 "Government to Lease and Remodel 4,000 Properties." *ABJ*, 104th Year, No. 37, Tuesday, January 12, 1943, 32.

44 "Government House Trailers Delivered." *ABJ*, 104th Year, No. 63, Sunday, February 7, 1943, 7C.

45 "240-Unit Trailer Camp Ordered for Barberton. Work to Start in Two Weeks. Akron Metropolitan Housing Authority In Charge Of Development. Will Construct Houses." *ABJ*, 104th Year, No. 125, Saturday, April 10, 1943, 7.

46 William V. Wallace. "Projects Give Home (Illegible) 13,000. U.S. Preparing to Collect Million In Rent From Akron." *ABJ*, Sunday, January 9, 1944, No. 34, 105th Year, 1A, 8.

47 Ben Williamson. "Akron Sets Pace, Provides Pattern in Design for Women in War." *ABJ*, 103rd Year, No. 319, Tuesday, October 20, 1942, 2.

48 Gordon C. Nixon. "Jobs Opening Up for Unskilled. Demand For Negroes, Handicapped Also Grows." *ABJ*, 103rd Year, No. 296, Sunday, September 27, 1942, 11A.

49 "Executive Order 8802," "U.S. History in Context." Accessed December 1, 2014. http://ic.galegroup.com/ic/uhic/PrimarySourcesDetailsPage/DocumentToolsPortletWindo w?displayGroupName=PrimarySources&u=silv39674&u=silv39674&jsid=38f0d798b286b7 471c6b1d2efed2b251&p=UHIC&action=2&catId=&documentId=GALE%7CCX2687400

084&zid=f406e2b9f842dcb3d75acfb705e47b66; H.B. "Doc" Kerr, "On the Home Front. Rural Route Mail Service Adds One Rubber Ball To Scrap Pile; Negroes Aid Industry." *ABJ*, 103rd Year, No. 220, Monday, July 13, 1942, 3; "Negro Manpower Board Selected. Rev. R.L. Robinson Named Chairman of Group." *ABJ*, 104th Year, No. 59, Wednesday, February 3, 1943, 18; "Hiring of More Negroes Urged. Ohio WMC Director Calls for More Jobs for Minority." *ABJ*, 104th Year, No. 175, Sunday, June 6, 1943, 16A; Ben Williamson. "Akron Sets Pace, Provides Pattern in Design For Women in War." *ABJ*, 103rd Year, No. 319, Tuesday, October 20, 1942, 2.

50 "Aged Laws Bar Women in Ohio Jobs." *ABJ*, 103rd Year, No. 276, Monday, September 7, 1942, 13.

51 Joseph E. Kuebler. "Is Akron on the Job? Women Play Varied, Vital Role in Production Battle." *ABJ*, 103rd Year, No. 241, Monday, August 3, 1942, 2.

52 Ben Williamson. "Women Better Than Men in Many Akron War Jobs. Writer's Survey Finds They Can Do Any Task Not Requiring Heavy Lifting." *ABJ*, 103rd Year, No. 320, Wednesday, October 21, 1942, 11; One of these inspectors was Virginia Lois Dille, who inspected aircraft wings for the C-46 Commando at Firestone Tire & Rubber. She would later marry Haskell and Florence's son, Donald.

53 Ben Williamson. "Akron Sets Pace, Provides Pattern in Design For Women in War." *ABJ*, 103rd Year, No. 319, Tuesday, October 20, 1942, 2.

54 Ben Williamson. "Akron Sets Pace, Provides Pattern in Design For Women in War." *ABJ*, 103rd Year, No. 319, Tuesday, October 20, 1942, 2.

55 "Work Clothes to Have Place in Summit Beach Easter Parade." *ABJ*, 104th Year, No. 134, Monday, April 19, 1943, 20.

56 "Goodyear Aircraft to Hire 3,500 More, As Demand for New War Goods Grows. Women Mostly Will Get Jobs. Added Force Scheduled to Build FG-1 Planes." *ABJ*, 104th Year, No. 138, Friday, April 23, 1943, 2.

57 "100 Women at Goodrich Work as Tire Builders." *ABJ*, 104th Year, No. 221, Thursday, July 15, 1943, 22.

CHAPTER FORTY-SEVEN: THE HOME FRONT

1 "Tire Retreads to Be Rationed." *ABJ*, 103rd Year, No. 68, Wednesday, February 11, 1942, 1-2; "Prices Frozen On Used Tires. Henderson Orders Ceiling As Of Last October; Effective Monday. Hits at Profiteering. Cost of second-Hand Rubber to Be Scaled on Size and Condition." *ABJ*, 103rd Year, No. 96, Wednesday, March 11, 1942, 1A.

2 Rayy Mitten. "Here's Data on Probable Gasoline Rationing Setup. Answers to Questions Based on Plan Now Being Used in Eastern States." *ABJ*, 103rd Year, No. 324, Sunday, October 25, 1942, 12A; Rayy Mitten. "Akron Drivers Growl Over Weary Hours In Line To Get 29,000 Gas Ration Books." *ABJ*, 103rd Year, No. 349, Thursday, November 19, 1942, 1; "Begin Rationing Gas Dec. 1'—F.D.R. Presidential Edict Rules Out Possibility of Delay." *ABJ*, 103rd Year, No. 357, Friday, November 27, 1942, 1; "Full 'Gas' Rationing Dec. 1 Ordered By The President," *NYT*, Friday, November 27, 1942, 1; Clifford A. Prevost. "You Got Headaches Now? Wait Till 'Gas' is Rationed. Giant Army Of Mechanics Will Be Needed to Service Cars; Just Try to Find One." *ABJ*, 103rd Year, No. 338, Sunday, November 8, 1942, 1, 14.

3 "No Riders, No 'Gas', B and C Book Holders Warned." *ABJ*, 104th Year, No. 231, Friday, July 30, 1943, 1.

4 Tony Long, "This Day in Tech. Dec. 1, 1942: Mandatory Gas Rationing, Lots of Whining," Updated November 30, 2009, http://www.wired.com/thisdayintech/2009/11/1201world-war-2-gasoline-rationing/; Carl Zebrowski, "Enough to Go Around," America in WWII, June 2006, As referenced on http://www.americainwwii.com/stories

/enoughtogoaround.html, Accessed December 29, 2011; "This Day in History, May 15, 1942, Seventeen States Put Gasoline Rationing into Effect," http://www.history.com/this-day-in-history/seventeen-states-put-gasoline-rationing-into-effect, Accessed December 29, 2011; Adams, Cecil, "How Was Gas Rationing Handled During World War II?" http://www.straightdope.com/columns/read/353/how-was-gas-rationing-handled-during-world-war-ii, Accessed December 29, 2011; With the onset of World War II, gas and tire rationing, ticketing speeders became a national defense priority. Individuals caught violating the national maximum speed limit of 35 miles per hour could also be found guilty of "tire abuse" and be denied both tires and gas ration books in the future. "Law Violators Face Tire Bans. Ration Boards Will Maintain Accurate Checkups." *ABJ*, 103rd Year, No. 265, Thursday, August 27, 1942, 1; "No Speeder to Get Tire or Recaps. Akron Ration Boards Ready to Crack Down." *ABJ*, 103rd Year, No. 287, Friday, September 18, 1942, 5; "4-Gallon 'Gas' Ration Set for Nov. 22. 35 MPH Speed Limit Ordered. Fuel Plan To Be Merged With Rubber Program, Says Henderson. Tires to Be Checked. Bans Expected To Reduce Travel Of Passenger Cars 60 Per Cent." *ABJ*, 103rd Year, No. 296, Sunday, September 27, 1942, 1; Ray C. Sutliff. "War Pinch Felt as U.S. Restricts Speed, Gas, Oil." 103rd Year, *ABJ*, No. 300, Thursday, October 1, 1942, 1; "Gasoline. OPA Sets Up 5-Tire Limit. Nation-Wide Rationing is Due to Go Into Effect on Nov. 22. Penalties Established. Violators of Rubber-Saving Dictum May Lose Fuel Books." *ABJ*, 103rd Year, No. 312, Tuesday, October 13, 1942, 1; "'Greatest Tire Sale Begins' in Akron With Uncle Sam Only Buyer. Autoists Must Turn in Extras. Only Five Per Car is New Federal Regulation. *ABJ*, 103rd Year, No. 314, Thursday, October 15, 1942, 2; "Drivers Rush to Sell Tires. Akron Machinery Function In U.S. Plan to Buy Extra Casings. Five Only for Each Car. Rubber Company Official is First to Volunteer His Equipment." *ABJ*, 103rd Year, No. 315, Friday, October 16, 1942, 25; "35 M.P.H. Limit is Answer to Traffic Cops' Prayers." *ABJ*, 103rd Year, No. 317, Sunday, October 18, 1942, 12A; Traffic Fines Based on Rates of Speeding." *ABJ*, 103rd Year, No. 316, Saturday, October 17, 1942, 13; "10,000 Tires Already Sold to Uncle Sam." *ABJ*, 103rd Year, No. 332, Monday, November 2, 1942, 1-2; Rayy Mitten. "'Fill 'Er Up' Cries Stilled. Gasoline Rush Sets Record as Motorists Beat Ration Deadline. Busses Are Crowded. Demands for Ousting of Henderson Sounded in Congress." *ABJ*, 103rd Year, No. 361, Tuesday, December 1, 1942, 1-2.

[5] "Formulate Plan to Check Speed. OPA, Police Agree on System Of Restraint." *ABJ*, 104th Year, No. 139, Saturday, April 24, 1943, 16; "'Gas' Violators Feel Crackdown." *ABJ*, 104th Year, No. 142, Tuesday, April 27, 1943, 1.

[6] "Workers' Bus Line Serves Tallmadge." *ABJ*, 103rd Year, No. 260, Saturday, August 22, 1942, 8.

[7] Clifford A. Prevost, "Less Comfort Will Be Rule. Housewives Facing Loss of Washers, Sweepers, Refrigerators. Parts to Be Cut Off. Tire Rationing Only Beginning; Return to Old-Fashioned Methods Looms." *ABJ*, Monday, December 29, 1941, No. 24, 103rd year, 15.

[8] Rayy Mitten. "Food Ration Book No. 2 to Change Buying Habits." *ABJ*, 104th Year, No. 7, Sunday, December 13, 1942, 5C.

[9] "OPA Puts Chips in Home Front War Game. Rationing Goes into Token Stage with Fiber Disks Used as Change." *ABJ*, Sunday, February 27, 1944, No. 83, 105th Year, 4C.

[10] Jane Reiker. "Steady Hand, Sharp Knife Kitchen Need." *ABJ*, 104th Year, No. 28, Sunday, January 3, 1943, 1-2; This experiment in savings last just over two months. "Bread Slicing Devices Ready to Cut Again." *ABJ*, 104th Year, No. 93, Tuesday, March 9, 1943, 2.

[11] "Aluminum Dive Far From Goal," *ABJ*, 103rd Year, No. 196, Friday, June 19, 1942, 21; L.C. Croy, "Akron Auto Graveyards Yield 400 Tons Monthly. Steady Flow of Much Needed Scarp Metal Moves to Mills; Cannons Now May Be Sold." *ABJ*, 103rd Year, No. 226, Sunday, July 19, 1942, 11C; Harold Lengs. "50,000 Children to Help Bury Axis in Scrap." *ABJ*, 103rd Year, No. 293, Thursday, September 24, 1942, 1; Harold Lengs. "Every Home in Area

Asked for 50 Pounds Of Metal." *ABJ*, No. 294, 103rd Year, Friday, September 25, 1942, 1; Harold Lengs. "50,000 Pupils Heap Scrap in County Schoolyards. Homes Are Scoured in Hunt for Metal. Tons of Junk Are Started on Way to Become Tanks, Guns for America." *ABJ*, 103rd Year, No. 305, Tuesday, October 6, 1942, 1; "Pupils Hand Axis 250-Ton Blow In Scrap Drive." *ABJ*, 103rd Year, No. 306, Wednesday, October 7, 1942, 1; "Akron Won't Hold Tin Can Campaign." *ABJ*, 103rd Year, No. 188, Thursday, June 11, 1942, 21; "Tin Can Campaign Begun At Goodrich." *ABJ*, 103rd Year, No. 185, Monday, June 8, 1942, 19; "Tin Savers Are Miners in This War." *ABJ*, 104th Year, No. 9, Tuesday, December 15, 1942, 30; "Tin Can Party Saturday; Are You Boys, Girls Set?" *ABJ*, 104th Year, No. 11, Thursday, December 17, 1942, 1; "Children Pile Tin Cans High at Theater Parties." *ABJ*, 104th Year, No. 13, Saturday, December 19, 1942, 12.

[12] Harold Lengs. "First Tin From Akron's Food Can Mines Will Be Collected on Jan. 18." *ABJ*, 104th Year, No. 33, Friday, January 8, 1943, 15.

[13] "Kids! See Free Show, Help Beat Hitler! Three Old Keys Admit You to Movies Saturday Morning." *ABJ*, 103rd Year, No. 315, Friday, October 16, 1942, 1; Harold Lengs. "We're Getting in The Scrap! Thousands At Key Shows; Drives to Continue." *ABJ*, 103rd Year, No. 316, Saturday, October 17, 1942, 1; "Six Tons of Keys Join War Metal. Judges Begin Selection of Campaign Winners." *ABJ*, 103rd Year, No. 336, Friday, November 6, 1942, 30; "See Yours In This Pile? Keys—360,000—On Way To Refinery." *ABJ*, 103rd Year, No. 341, Wednesday, November 11, 1942, 13.

[14] L.C. Croy, National Scrap Rubber Drive May Be Needed. Akron Dealers Report Collection Decline About 50 Pct.; Vast Quantity Available." *ABJ*, 103rd Year, No. 135, Sunday, April 19, 1942, 8C.

[15] Kenneth Nichols, "Akron Rubber Prospectors Hit 'Pay Dirt.' 40,000 Pounds of Scrap Taken From 'Mines'" *ABJ*, 103rd Year, No. 195, Thursday, June 18th, 1942, 1-2.

[16] "Scrap Tire or Tube Accepted For Movie," *ABJ*, 103rd Year, No. 140, Friday, April 24, 1942, 12; "Scrap Rubber Wins Rides At Summit Beach," *ABJ*, 103rd Year, No. 216, July 9, 1942, 9.

[17] "Summit Beach Offer Nets 2 Tons Of Scrap," *ABJ*, 103rd Year, No. 218, Saturday, July 11, 1942, 5; While the drives for scrap rubber may have been successful in cleaning up the environment, their actual effectiveness in reclaiming usable rubber was debated even at the time of the drives. Later, this was proven true as it was disclosed in 1944 that some 19,000 tons of salvaged rubber "consisting of old garden hose, rubber toys, hot water bottles and similar items" still sat in great piles in Cleveland alone, completely unusable. "'We Told You So!' Much Scrap Rubber Is Found Unusable." *ABJ*, Saturday, February 5, 1944, No. 61, 105th Year, 1-2; While the government paid and "over-generous price of $25 a ton for it, it was figured that it wouldn't be worth more than $1 a ton on resale after discovering it was mostly unusable. "Washington Calling. Japs Depending on 'Inner Ring'? U.S. to Sell Scrap Rubber Discard." *ABJ*, Sunday, March 5, 1944, No. 90, 105th Year, D5.

[18] Having been born in 1936, Marjorie wouldn't have been attending high school during the war, but would have been aware of the activities with through her older brother and sister, as well as the fact that the school was located next door to their home.

[19] The benefits of milkweed in replacing kapok were first recognized in early 1943. "Milkweed Plant New Farm Crop." *ABJ*, 104th Year, No. 109, Thursday, March 25, 1943, 4.

[20] With the onset of World War II, gas and tire rationing, ticketing speeders became a national defense priority. Individuals caught violating the national maximum speed limit of 35 miles per hour could also be found guilty of "tire abuse" and be denied both tires and gas ration books in the future. "Law Violators Face Tire Bans. Ration Boards Will Maintain Accurate Checkups." *ABJ*, 103rd Year, No. 265, Thursday, August 27, 1942, 1; "No Speeder to Get Tire Or Recaps. Akron Ration Boards Ready to Crack Down." *ABJ*, 103rd Year, No.

287, Friday, September 18, 1942, 5; "4-Gallon 'Gas' Ration Set For Nov. 22. 35 MPH Speed Limit Ordered. Fuel Plan to Be Merged With Rubber Program, Says Henderson. Tires to Be Checked. Bans Expected to Reduce Travel of Passenger Cars 60 Per Cent." *ABJ*, 103rd Year, No. 296, Sunday, September 27, 1942, 1; Ray C. Sutliff. "War Pinch Felt as U.S. Restricts Speed, Gas, Oil." 103rd Year, *ABJ*, No. 300, Thursday, October 1, 1942, 1; "Gasoline. OPA Sets Up 5-Tire Limit. Nation-Wide Rationing is Due to Go into Effect On Nov. 22. Penalties Established. Violators of Rubber-Saving Dictum May Lose Fuel Books." *ABJ*, 103rd Year, No. 312, Tuesday, October 13, 1942, 1; "Traffic Fines Based on Rates of Speeding." *ABJ*, 103rd Year, No. 316, Saturday, October 17, 1942, 13; In one article, the forced reduction in speed was reckoned as the "Answer to Traffic Cops' Prayers," and referred to speeders as "Hitler's little helpers." "35 M.P.H. Limit is Answer to Traffic Cops' Prayers." *ABJ*, 103rd Year, No. 317, Sunday, October 18, 1942, 12A.

21 It wasn't until March of 1943 that consideration was given to providing *any* gasoline to servicemen on furlough. "Men on Furlough May Get Gasoline." *ABJ*, 104th Year, No. 98, Sunday, March 14, 1943, 2A; "Here Are 'Gas' Regulations Which Tie Hands of Panels." *ABJ*, 104th Year, No. 130, Saturday, April 15, 1943, 34; "Extra 'Gas' Is Assured Furloughed Servicemen." *ABJ*, 104th Year, No. 136, Wednesday, April 21, 1943, 1; "'Gas' for Men on Furlough Delayed a Bit." *ABJ*, 104th Year, No. 138, Friday, April 23, 1943, 21; An allotment of five gallons was finally allowed in May of 1943. "Servicemen on Furlough to Receive 'Gas' Ration." *ABJ*, 104th Year, No. 156, Tuesday, May 11, 1943, 23.

22 Haskell would have registered on Feb. 16, 1942, during the 3rd draft registration for men ages 35-44. Having been born July 25, 1898, he was one year shy of the limit for the "old man's draft" for men ages 45-64 on April 27, 1942. Kimberly Powell, "World War II Draft Registration Records," http://genealogy.about.com/od/records/p/wwii_draft.htm, Accessed January 9, 2012; While one might assume police officers would be automatically deferred from the draft, that wasn't the case at all. In fact, the local civil service commission pressed Akron Mayor George J. Harter to fight for a deferment for members of both the police and fire departments. He declined the invitation. "No serious emergency is yet in sight," the mayor declared. "We are still able to replace all the men who are leaving for military service. It seems as though half the young fellows in town would like to get jobs in the departments. Last Saturday, 30 took examinations for five vacancies in the fire department." "Harter Refuses Deferment Plea. Mayor Says City Still Able to Replace Policemen." *ABJ*, 103rd Year, No. 332, Monday, November 2, 1942, 20; While the Akron mayor may have been confident in the number of officers on duty, the police chief wasn't. Less than one month later, "Chief Rae M. Williams Saturday raised the distress signal for more policemen as five men prepared to leave Monday for naval service, cutting the force to 15 below its full strength off 210." "Williams Cites Police Shortage." *ABJ*, 103rd Year, No. 352, Sunday, November 22, 14A.

23 Available U.S. Marine Corps Muster Rolls first show Barbara J. Jones having mustered in during October 1944. At that time, she is a private in Squadron 23, MAD, Naval Air Technical Training Center, Norman, Oklahoma. Ancestry.com. *U.S. Marine Corps Muster Rolls, 1798-1958* [database on-line]. Provo, UT, USA: Ancestry.com Operations Inc., 2007; Available muster rolls last record her as a private in October 1945 at Aviation Women's Reserve Squadron Ten, Air Base Group Two USMCAS, El Toro, California. Ancestry.com. *U.S. Marine Corps Muster Rolls, 1798-1958* [database on-line]. Provo, UT, USA: Ancestry.com Operations Inc., 2007.

24 Donald received his draft notice on April 1, 1944, and served as a private in the Army's 78th Infantry Division, First Battalion, 309th Infantry Regiment, A Company, First Platoon, First Squad. He served until April of 1946.

25 Donald later remembered, "She went in after I did and was home before I was."

26 Donald first went to Camp Benjamin Harrison (from which he mailed birthday and

Easter wishes home to Florence, her birthday being on the 8th and Easter falling on the 9th) and then Camp Atterbury in Indiana. From there he was subsequently transferred to Fort McClellan, Alabama, for basic training, then Camp Pickett in Virginia. After that, he was transferred to Kilmer, New Jersey before embarkation out of New York. "A lot of people went out through Dix in New Jersey. But we didn't go out as replacements. We went out as a Division."

[27] Donald left the states on the John Ericsson, a former ocean liner on October 14th, 1944. "I think it was eight days or something like that. They stripped all the good stuff out of them and had bunks about four high, close together as they could get 'em," he later remembered. "I think it was eight days or something like that. We went into Southampton. Then we went from there up to Bournemouth. We were in Bournemouth for about a month, I guess, somewhere along there. But going across the Channel was really rough. The weather was bad. We were on there like three days or something like that just going across the Channel. Then we went out of there into LeHavre and went into France there and stayed not too long in France and went on into Belgium—the border there. Stayed another week or so there and went on up into the Front."

Departure date confirmed in the Divisional history. *Lightning, The History of The 78th Infantry Division.* (Nashville: The Battery Press, 2000), 17.

[28] As late as 1945, with the end of World War II, no organization or newspaper in Summit County had kept a tally of those local men and women who died in military service. GRIS, 506n; The Veteran's War Memorial on Tallmadge Circle lists eleven who lost their lives in World War II from Tallmadge: Claude W. Hoffman, David Jost, Mike Milnar, Arthur E. Rutherford, John W. Rutherford, Robert P. Pitkin, Herbert Von Gunteen, William Fox, James R. Shears, Doyle Simpson, Robert M. Imhoff. One name possibly missing is that of P.F.C. Franklin R. Crislip, noted in a casualty list in *The Akron Beacon Journal* as from Tallmadge and killed at Tarawa in 1944. However, Haskell's son Donald recalls that Crislip had moved from Tallmadge to Akron during the thirties. "Taps," *ABJ*, Sunday, February 6, 1944, 40.

[29] H.B. "Doc" Kerr. "On The Home Front. Tallmadge Auxiliary Police First In County To Display Their Skill." *ABJ*, 103rd Year, No. 160, Thursday, May 14, 1942, 8. H.B. "Doc" Kerr. "On The Home Front. Tallmadge Civilian Defense Workers Make Enviable Record; Sell War Bonds." *ABJ*, 103rd Year, No. 165, Monday, May 18, 1942, 13.

[30] H.B. "Doc" Kerr. "On The Home Front. Tallmadge Auxiliary Police First In County To Display Their Skill." *ABJ*, 103rd Year, No. 160, Thursday, May 14, 1942, 8.

[31] A similar story of an espionage investigation gone awry is reported in a 1942 newspaper article entitled "Spy Suspect Had Needles For Proof." The article notes, "It looked like the beginning of a fine espionage case, with a Mata Hari angle, when Seattle police arrested an attractive brunette for a minor law infraction: She carried a little black book with such mysterious inscriptions as 'K1, P2, CO 8, K 5, YO, K 3, P 2, DECR. 6, K 5, INC. 4.' Neither police nor federal agents were able to "decode" the inscriptions. Finally they called in the suspect and began to question her. She giggled. 'Oh, that,' she replied. 'Those are my knitting instructions. They mean knit one stitch, purl two, cast on eight, knit five, yarn over, knit three, purl two, decrease six, knit five, increase four.' "Spy Suspect Had Needles for Proof." *ABJ*, No. 121, 103rd Year, Sunday, April 5, 1942, 5.

[32] "Venereal Peril Gains. Rate Of Infection Reverses Trend, Shoots Upward." *ABJ*, 103rd Year, No. 58, Sunday, February 1, 1942, D5.

[33] While Akron's brothels may have been operated "unmolested," that didn't mean they were a house of pleasure for all employed there. In a 5-state white slavery trial, one worker testified that she found one Akron house of prostitution "Too tough to stand more than five days" This, "because there were several fights each night." "U.S. To Subpoena Vice Operators. Akron In Spotlight During White Slave Trial." *ABJ*, 103rd Year, No. 286, Thursday, September

17, 1942, 39.

34 Before the era of modern antibiotics, venereal disease was particularly difficult to treat and cure. An effective treatment for syphilis took 18 months under a physician's care while gonorrhea (8 to 10 times more prevalent in Akron at the time) could be effectively cured in 85% of recognized cases in 10 days with sulfa drugs. Prostitutes who were arrested and found to be visibly infected were placed in quarantine for seven weeks. The impact on both the newly wealthy workforce and healthcare professionals was tremendous. "Venereal Peril Gains. Rate of Infection Reverses Trend, Shoots Upward." *ABJ*, 103rd Year, No. 58, Sunday, February 1, 1942, D5.

35 As a result of the manpower shortage, Akron began actively recruiting women to the police force in April 1944. The starting salary was $135 a month. "The policewomen are expected to assist in the drive to curb juvenile delinquency, and to patrol areas like bus terminals and stores in which the work is not hazardous," an article in the Beacon noted. "Not Many Women Seeking Police Jobs." *ABJ*, Sunday, April 16, 1944, No. 132, 105th Year, 6C; "Policewomen Tests Set For Wednesday." *ABJ*, Sunday, May 14, 1944, No. 160, 105th Year, 8C.

36 Of Tallmadge's population of 3,452 in 1940, 240 or nearly 7% were classified as foreign-born. "1940 U.S. Census of Population. Volume 2. Characteristics of the Population. Ohio. Table 30. Composition of the population, for incorporated places of 2,500 to 10,000: 1940," 661. http://www.census.gov/prod/www/abs/decennial/1940.html Accessed September 17, 2011.

37 With sugar shipments from the Philippines cut off, the mandate to ration sugar was far more important than just the culinary needs of the troops. As one newspaper article of the time noted, sugar is used as "Motive power for torpedoes, solvents in gelatine dynamite and smokeless powder, detonators that ignite shells, "dope" used in the fabric coverings of airplane wings—all come from alcohol made from sugar. One firing of a 16-inch gun eats up the distilled product of a fifth of an acre of sugar cane. If you hoard nine-tenths of a pound of sugar you hold back enough alcohol to manufacture a pound of smokeless powder." Morry Rabin. "What About This Sugar Shortage? Four Reasons Why You Go on a Ration Card System Next Month." *ABJ*, 103rd Year, No. 121, Sunday, April 5, 1942, 5D.

38 Carl Zebrowski, "Enough to Go Around," America in WWII, June 2006, As referenced on http://www.americainwwii.com/stories/enoughtogoaround.html, Accessed December 29, 2011; "Rationing, World War II, United States," http://conservapedia.com/Rationing, Accessed December 29, 2011.

39 Heimann, Robert Karl, Tobacco and Americans, 1960, New York, McGraw Hill, p. 231-32, as cited in Betsy Gohdes-Baten, Greenville, NC Tobacco Warehouse Historic District: National Register of Historic Places Registration Form, 1997, Joyner Digital Library, http://digital.lib.ecu.edu/exhibits/tobacco/htmlFiles/NREG2.html#tag39, Accessed December 29, 2011; The Cigarette Camps. The U.S. Army in the Le Havre Area. http://www.skylighters.org/special/cigcamps/ Wednesday, November 10, 2010; Mark R. Henry, The US Army In World War II, Osprey Publishing, 2001, p 23, As cited on http://www.ww2incolor.com/forum/showthread.php?3551-US-Army-Rations-World-War-II, Accessed December 29, 2011.

40 At the time of the recording in the 1980s. Located at 67 West Avenue in Tallmadge, it is currently the site of Delanie's Neighborhood Grill.

41 "Crash Injuries Kill H.B. Beers. Goodyear Aircraft Worker Is County's 58th Traffic Victim. Car Struck During Fog. Seven Persons Are Injured In two Accidents On Akron Streets." *ABJ*, No. 253, 103rd Year, Saturday, August 15, 1942, 9. "Vital Statistics. 1—Death Notices. Beers." *ABJ*, No. 253, 103rd Year, Saturday, August 15, 1942, 12.

42 Until The Tallmadge Volunteer Fire Department was organized in 1943, the adjacent

city of Stow provided fire protection from 1934 to 1943. Wilburn Crites, "Fire Protection," *TALL* 77.

43 Vincent W. Ziegler. Mayor of Tallmadge from 1944-1947.

44 The issue of raises for both the road crew and the Police Chief came up again and again during Haskell's tenure on the Village and then City Council. One of the first times it occurred was in September of 1950 following discussion on an increase in wages for the Road Supervisor from $260 to $275 per month with "Mr. Jones stating $275.00 per month is not a living wage today." Curiously, he did not hold that same view when it came to the Police Department.

Immediately following the approval of that increase the discussion turned to an increase in wages for the Police Chief and Patrolman. Ordinance #360 provided "for a $15.00 per month raise for Chief of Police and $13.50 per month for Patrolman was read. Discussion followed on unequal basis for raises, as the ranged from $13.50 to $30.00 per mo. for approximately equal work. Mr. Jones states the Chief of Police is overpaid as his position could be filled on a moment's notice, a road grader operator could not be replaced so easily. However, no consideration was given to increasing a patrolman's rate—a rate of $265.00 per month having been recommended. Moved by Mr. Lang, sec. by Mr. Jones to accept the rates of $310.00 per month for Police Chief and $265.00 per month for Patrolman." After his initial "Aye" vote in favor resulted in a tie vote, he changed his mind and voted "No" to any increase. VILL, September 28, 1950.

45 The 1940 Census records Phillip Youngen, 52, as a "Driver" for a "Coal Co." He was reported to be earning $1,640 a year. National Archives, Seventh Census of the United States, 1940, Ohio, Summit County, Tallmadge, S.D. 23, E.D. No. 77-82, Sheet 1A, April 2-3, 1940; Ironically, the tables would also eventually be turned on Councilman Youngen when it was his turn to ask for a raise for the road crew. Still a Councilman in March of 1950, he was also now Road Committee Chairman. "Mr. Youngen reported road men request raise and recommends the following raises; Mr. Pletcher - $5.00 month – no overtime; 10¢ hour for Mr. Reynolds." His motion was tabled for further study. VILL March 9, 1950.

CHAPTER FORTY-EIGHT: THE TALLMADGE FIRE DEPARTMENT

1 " . . . voters turned down a bond issue a year ago to remedy the situation. They turned thumbs down on the charter amendment to refurbish the fire department and an out-of-date sewage treatment plant as well." William V. Wallace. "What Price Economy If Our War Industry Is Destroyed By Fire?" *ABJ*, 103rd Year, No. 157, Monday, May 11, 1942, 1-2.

2 William V. Wallace. "Falls, Kent Have New Type Trucks. Citizen Committee Promises Modern Pumpers." The *ABJ*, 103rd Year, No. 163, Sunday, May 17, 1942, 2A, 9.

3 William V. Wallace. "What Price Economy If Our War Industry Is Destroyed By Fire?" *ABJ*, 103rd Year, No. 157, Monday, May 11, 1942, 1-2.

4 William V. Wallace. "Pumper Truck Order Pushed. Council Wants New Fire Equipment Bought Without Legal Ruling. Rowe is Urging Speed. Special Bond Issue May Be Asked at August Primary Elections." *ABJ*, 103rd Year, No. 160, Thursday, May 14, 1942, 21.

5 William V. Wallace. "What Price Economy If Our War Industry Is Destroyed By Fire?" *ABJ*, 103rd Year, No. 157, Monday, May 11, 1942, 1-2.

6 William V. Wallace. "Fire Purchase Speed Urged. Tighe Calls Committee to Recommend Equipment for Akron. Reports on Inspection. Mong Asserts Legality of $100,000 Expenditure is Still Open." *ABJ*, 103rd Year, No. 162, Saturday, May 16, 1942, 9.

7 William V. Wallace. "Pumper Truck Order Pushed. Council Wants New Fire Equipment Bought Without Legal Ruling. Rowe is Urging Speed. Special Bond Issue May Be Asked at August Primary Elections." *ABJ*, 103rd Year, No. 160, Thursday, May 14, 1942, 21.

8 "Pumper Engine Breaks Down—Coasts to Fire." *ABJ*, 103rd Year, No. 117, Wednesday, April 1, 1942, 1. "Dodge Av. Pumper In Repair Shop." *ABJ*, 103rd Year, No. 126,

Friday, April 10, 1942, 23.

[9] "Dodge Av. Pumper in Repair Shop." *ABJ*, 103rd Year, No. 126, Friday, April 10, 1942, 23.

[10] William V. Wallace. "Falls, Kent Have New Type Trucks. Citizen Committee Promises Modern Pumpers." *ABJ*, 103rd Year, No. 163, Sunday, May 17, 1942, 2A.

[11] William V. Wallace. "Falls, Kent Have New Type Trucks. Citizen Committee Promises Modern Pumpers." *ABJ*, Sunday, May 17, 1941, 103rd Year, No. 163, Pg. 9, 2A.

[12] William V. Wallace, "Fire Pumpers Assured Akron. Tighe's Report Brings Fast Action; Harter Praises Committee's Work. Bond Issue is Favored. Group Sent to Washington to Obtain A-1A Priority Rating for City." *ABJ*, 103rd Year, No. 166, Wednesday, May 20, 1942, 1-2.

[13] In fact, the pumper was of so little use that after it was replaced by a loaner from the federal government, it was donated in its entirety to a scrap drive. "Fire Engine No. 10 to Go on Scrap Pile." *ABJ*, 103rd Year, No. 320, Wednesday, October 21, 1942, 5.

[14] Following the failure of a levy to secure additional funds for the fire department in early November, Fire Chief Frank Vernotzy permanently closed the fire station on November 23rd, much to the ire of "J.C. Fry, president of the Rental and Home Owners' league, who inquired, 'Are you not, by this method, gambling with the lives and property of the people served by this station?'" "The floor has settled an inch since we attempted to shore it up," the chief commented in response. "The roof is bad, and there's a second floor concrete slab that's likely to fall at any moment." "Fry Hits Closing of Fire Station. Chief Vernotzy Holds Action Was Safety Move." *ABJ*, 103rd Year, No. 353, Monday, November 23, 1942, 16.

[15] Akron to Vote on Fire Needs. Council to Place $400,000 Bond Issue on Ballot at Fall Elections. To Meet with Experts. Issue, if Passed by Voters, Would Provide Funds for New Equipment. *ABJ*, 103rd Year, No. 178, Monday, June 1, 1942, 13; William V. Wallace. "Only Four Pumpers Permitted Now. 1943 Budget Will Call for 35 to 40 More Firemen." *ABJ*, 103rd Year, No. 191, Sunday, June 14, 1942, 10A.

[16] U.S. Promises Akron Fire Aid. "Heavy Piece of Equipment," Now in Detroit, To Be Brought Here. FWA Orders Transfer. Harter, Tighe in Cleveland Seeking Share Of Small Pumpers From OCD." *ABJ*, 103rd Year, No. 167, Thursday, May 21, 1942, 21; "Delivery of New Pumpers Speeded." *ABJ*, 103rd Year, No. 216, July 9, 1942, 5; "Four New Pumpers Due in 'A Few Days'" *ABJ*, 103rd Year, No. 286, Thursday, September 17, 1942, 8; "City Gets New Fire Pumpers. Engines Are Delivered Here Through Lease-Lend Agreement. Two More Promised. Trucks Will Augment Akron's Protection to Vital War Industries." *ABJ*, 103rd Year, No. 308, Friday, October 9, 1942, 25; "Two More Pumpers Received By City." *ABJ*, 103rd Year, No. 315, Friday, October 16, 1942, 25.

[17] "Fire Engine No. 10 to Go on Scrap Pile." *ABJ*, 103rd Year, No. 320, Saturday, October 17, 1942, 13.

[18] The city would be given the authorization for a new aerial ladder truck the following March, as well as a second allotment of fire-fighting equipment. "Within 30 days the city will receive two of the 750-gallon-per-minute pumpers and two of the 500-gallon pumpers, and 4,000 feet of hose." "Delivery Seen Within Month. Mayor Harter Told Priority Granted City in Appeal For New Equipment. Ladder Truck O.K.'d. Better Protection is Seen for Vital War Industries of District." *ABJ*, 104th Year, No. 92, Monday, March 8, 1943, 13; William V. Wallace, "Fire Pumpers Assured Akron. Tighe's Report Brings Fast Action; Harter Praises Committee's Work. Bond Issue is Favored. Group Sent to Washington to Obtain A-1A Priority Rating for City." *ABJ*, 103rd Year, No. 166, Wednesday, May 20, 1942, 1-2; The city was finally able to order its first new piece of fire-fighting equipment in five years in April 1943. It would be an aerial ladder truck that carried a 65-foot automatic ladder "which can be raised in one-tenth the time required for the one piece of similar equipment which now serves

the city." "City Places $19,979 Order for 12-Cylinder Fire Truck." *ABJ*, 104th Year, No. 122, Wednesday, April 7, 1943, 17; The truck was delivered the following November. "Firemen Just Push Button, Up Goes 65-Foot Ladder." *ABJ*, Wednesday, November 17, 1943, 17.

[19] William V. Wallace. "Fire Levy Loses; Jobs Are Opened." *ABJ*, 103rd Year, No. 334, Wednesday, November 4, 1942, 1.

[20] "Housing Probe Pushes Ahead. Woman Arrested When 23 Are Found in Nine-Room Home. Other Areas Checked. Basements, Attics Being Used as Living Quarters, Says Report." *ABJ*, 103rd Year, No. 351, Saturday, November 21, 1942, 9.

[21] "Harter Refuses Deferment Plea." *ABJ*, 103rd Year, No. 332, Monday, November 2, 1942, 20.

[22] "Fry Hits Closing of Fire Station. Chief Vernotzy Holds Action Was Safety Move. *ABJ*, 103rd Year, No. 353, Monday, November 23, 1942, 16.

[23] OCD Gets Pumps—New Problems. Transportation is Needed for Equipment. *ABJ*, 104th Year, No. 2, Monday, December 8, 1942, 10.

[24] "Fire Engine No. 10 to Go on Scrap Pile." *ABJ*, 103rd Year, No. 320, Saturday, October 17, 1942, 13; OCD Gets Pumps—New Problems. Transportation Is Needed For Equipment. *ABJ*, 104th Year, No. 2, Monday, December 8, 1942, 10.

[25] Fire Kills 100 Ringling Animals. Loss $125,000 at Cleveland. Terrified Beasts Burn in Cages As 5,000 People Stand Helpless. Gargantuas Are Safe. Victims Shot by Police; 'Greatest Show' to Go on in Akron." *ABJ*. 103rd Year, No. 242, Tuesday, August 4, 1942, 1.

[26] "150 Believed Dead in Night Club Fire. Blaze Sweeps Boston Resort. More Than 200 Reported Injured as Flames Strike Spot. Celebrate Grid Victory. Navy Officers Believed Among Victims; Five Alarms Sounded." *ABJ*, 103rd Year, No. 359, Sunday, November 29, 1942, 1; James L. Kilgallen, Akron Sailor Among 478 Fire Dead. Prank is blamed in Boston Night Club Tragedy." *ABJ*, 103rd Year, No. 360, Monday, November 30, 1942, 1-2, 13; Herbert Richardson, "Bodies Block Doorways, Trap Screaming Victims." *ABJ*, 103rd Year, No. 360, Monday, November 30, 1942, 1-2, 13.

[27] John Meany, "Flames and Stampede Turn Servicemen's Hostel into Hall of Death. Fire Ruins Give Up Bodies of 100 Merrymakers." *ABJ*, 104th Year, No. 8, Monday, December 8, 1942, 1.

[28] "65 Injured in $1,000,000 Boston Fire. Blaze is City's Third In Month. Coast Guardsmen Summoned to Fight Flames In Department Store. 6-Story Building Burns. Conflagration Follows Night Club Disaster That Killed 488." *ABJ*, 104th Year, No. 10, Wednesday, December 16, 1942, 1.

[29] "Fire Trap Checkup to Begin Monday." *ABJ*, 103rd Year, No. 345, Sunday, November 15, 1942, 2A.

[30] "Fire Hazard Check Opens. Mayor Orders Survey To Determine Akron's 'Danger' Spots. Aims At Public Places. Entire Fire And Building Inspection Staffs Put On Job." *ABJ*, 103rd Year, No.. 360, Monday, November 30, 1942, 1-2, 13.

[31] "Night Clubs Held Safety Violators. Inspectors Find Few Spots Adhering To Laws." *ABJ*, 104th Year, No. 7, Sunday, December 13, 1942, 11C.

[32] "Fire Hazard Check Opens. Mayor Orders Survey To Determine Akron's 'Danger' Spots. Aims At Public Places. Entire Fire And Building Inspection Staffs Put On Job." *ABJ*, 103rd Year, No. 360, Monday, November 30, 1942, 1-2, 13.

[33] "Fire Hazard Remedy Lags. City Officials Stage Dispute Over Provisions Of New Ordinance. Check Of Clubs Is Slow. No Hope Of Speed Unless More Help Is Hired, Brannon Says." *ABJ*, 103rd Year, No. 36, Thursday, December 3, 1942, 25.

[34] "Night Clubs Held Safety Violators. Inspectors Find Few Spots Adhering To Laws." *ABJ*, 104th Year, No. 7, Sunday, December 13, 1942, 11C.

[35] "Minutes." Akron City Council January 19, 1943, 307; Chief Vernotzy's fire ordinance would finally get a nod from Akron City Council on January 6, 1943, two weeks after the dance

hall fire, the first meeting of the new year after the holidays had ended. William V. Wallace. "Council Pledges Passage of New Fire Prevention Measure. Vernotzy Asks Bill Adoption. 56-Page Ordinance Covers Possible Hazards In Homes, Businesses. Last Reading Is Due." *ABJ*, 104th Year, No. 30, Wednesday, January 6, 1943, 15; It would be passed on January 19, 1943, exactly one month to the day from the Whispering Pines fire. "Council Puts O.K. on Fire Ordinance." *ABJ*, 104th Year, No. 44, Tuesday, January 19, 1943, 23.

36 "In addition to Fire Chief Bierce, the original Tallmadge Volunteer Fire Department of 1943 had 15 firemen: Si Young, Dan Sekulich, Haskell Jones, H.O. King, J.C. Thomas, E.J. Ilg, Robert Young, A.L. Smith, S.A. Schlup, Bernard Goff, Thomas Diesz, Roy Diesz, Howell Acken, Norman Sylvester, and Joseph Hickey." *TALL*, 77.

37 Both the 1943 and 1946 Akron City Directories list G.F. Vernotzy as captain of the Training School (There are no directories for the years in between. Publisher and copyright data not included in scanned copy available through Akron Summit County Public Library.), F.C. Vernotzy is listed as Chief, 8; Fire Captain Gerald F. Vernotzy was the head of the Akron Fire Department Training School. In addition to these responsibilities, he taught tens of thousands of citizens, auxiliary firemen, civil defense and other OCD members the basics of fighting fires in wartime. "Their Help Worthwhile." *ABJ*, 103rd Year, No. 323, Saturday, October 24, 1942, 14; Gerald was also the son of Akron Fire Chief Frank Vernotzy. "Vernotzy Heads Fire Department." *ABJ*, 103rd Year, No. 270, Tuesday, September 1, 1942, 7.

38 Fire Captain Gerald Vernotzy received his first shipment of 17 skid-mounted pumpers for the area's civil defense firefighters in late 1942. The first of 53 such units on order, they were capable of pumping 500 gallons of water a minute. "OCD Gets Pumps—New Problems. Transportation is Needed For Equipment." *ABJ*, 104th Year, No. 2, Monday, December 8, 1942, 10; By March of 1943, the *Beacon* could now boast that "Summit county has fifty 500 gallon pumpers, 8,284 pump tanks that throw a stream of water 40 feet, thousands of feet of hose, and quantities of medical supplies and cots as a result of the civilian defense preparation for emergency . . . To operate the OCD equipment in Summit county is a force of 17,000 men and women, the Akron OCD office reports. It released figures showing the organization has 4,500 firemen, 3,200 policemen, 5,000 air raid wardens, with the balance of the total being in communications, medical assistance, and other specialized units." "Fire Protection Surveyed by OCD." *ABJ*, 104th Year, No. 102, Thursday, March 18, 1943, 23.

39 "The first fire truck was a '34 Ford chassis equipped with a 500 gallon water tank and pumper, built by the firemen." Wilburn Crites, "Fire Protection," *TALL*, 77.

40 Manufacturing tank and aircraft parts under defense contracts, Herman Tool & Machine Co. of Tallmadge played a substantial role in the war effort. In addition to helping the local volunteer fire department, the company was awarded the army-navy "E" in April 1943 in recognition of their efficiency, was the first to go "over the top" in Summit County's Bond Drive (purchasing some $28,050 worth of bonds over an initial goal of $15,000) and later purchased $33,000 worth of bonds in memory of a former employee during the Sixth War Loan—some 183% over quota. "Herman Plant Flies 'E' Flag." *ABJ*, 104th Year, No. 138, Friday, April 23, 1943, 21. *ABJ*, Monday, January 24, 1944, 2. "Herman Machine Goes Over Bond Goal Again." *ABJ*, Wednesday, November 22, 1944, 9.

41 At the time of the recording in the early 80s. Approximately 32 South Avenue. The Village of Tallmadge advertised for bids for the construction of a building on Thursday, July 15, 1943. "Notice for Bids," *ABJ*, Thursday, July 15, 1943, 27.

42 Akron received its first Civil Defense fire siren almost a year to the day from Pearl Harbor, on Sunday, December 6, 1942. Costing about $4,200 installed and having a range of approximately one and one-half miles, the siren was purchased by the Summit county civilian defense executive council. In tests prove satisfactory, others for locations in the four outlying sections of Akron, and for Barberton and Cuyahoga Falls may be bought, OCD officials said.

The siren is mounted on a turntable and has two gasoline motors, and eight-cylinder engine to power the siren itself and a smaller motor to run the air 'Chopper' that revolves in front of the siren's mouth, causing the sound breaks that bolster the range." Lots Of Noise Due In City! Siren Arrives." *ABJ*, 103rd Year, No. 365, Sunday, December 6, 1942, 11A; Happy with its new purchase, Akron City Council "appropriated $1,250 for purchase of two steam-powered air raid sirens for test purposes. They will supplement the $4,200 gasoline-driven Victory siren being mounted atop the city building . . ." "Akron OCD Tops State for Speed. Has Fastest Mobilization in Test Monday." *ABJ*, 104th Year, No. 3, Wednesday, December 9, 1942, 1-2.

[43] Supplementing the article that profiled the area volunteer fire departments were 4 photos of the Tallmadge Volunteer Fire Department in action. Members of the fire department that were pictured included: John Crossen, D.E. Fenn, Clayton Young; Wilburn Crites, Raymond Paulus, Chief David Bierce and Jack Platz. Keith Spriggel, "When the Village Fire Sire Blows," ABJ, Sunday, July 4, 1948, 11.

[44] The first fire has been recorded as being on May 28th, 1944 to the Stella Sparhawk residence on East Avenue. Wilburn Crites, "Fire Protection," *TALL*, 77. Ironically (for a couple of reasons) son Donald later recalled that that particular fire call "was to the house where we'd lived up on East Avenue."

[45] "A Gas Station, the building now part of No. 1 Fire Station, was purchased and remodeled." Wilburn Crites. "Fire Protection." *TALL*, 77.

[46] "Purchase of part of the equipment was made possible through an organized Civil Defense Unit of which the Government paid a part — other purchases and improvements made by the firemen have been made possible by the department holding public fish suppers. These have been widely supported by the citizens of Tallmadge by their attendance and generous donations of food and personal help." *TALL*, 77.

[47] "An extention [sic] was added to Fire Station 1 in 1945 to house the additional trucks. The present heating system, a gas furnace, was purchased and installed by the firemen." Wilburn Crites, "Fire Protection." *TALL*, 77.

[48] Florence's brother Barton and his wife Margaret lived on Southeast Avenue at the railroad tracks just before entering Mogadore.

[49] Supplementing the article that profiled the area volunteer fire departments are four photos of the members of the Tallmadge Volunteer Fire Department at work. Keith Spriggel, "When the Village Fire Siren Blows," *ABJ*, Sunday, July 4, 1948, 11.

CHAPTER FORTY-NINE: THE FURNACE COMPANY

[1] Located just off Tallmadge Circle, U.S. Stoneware Co. manufactured acid-proof chemical stoneware under defense contracts during the war, some of which were used in the development of the atom bomb. "Defense Work Finds an Echo in Tallmadge," ABJ, Wednesday, February 12, 1941, 13. "Akron Helped in Preparing of Atom Bomb," *ABJ*, Sunday, August 12, 1945, 41.

[2] The Curt Collins Heating Company, 391 S. Maple at Five Points and 521-525 W. Exchange. *ACD, 1946*, 624.

CHAPTER FIFTY: TALLMADGE CITY COUNCIL

[1] Schneider, Lou. "Big Unemployment Crisis Seen Shortly After War." *ABJ*, 103rd Year, No. 47, Wednesday, January 21, 1942, 18.

[2] CITY, October 8, 1953, 1-2; May 9, 1950; October 11, 1951, 2; April 12, 1956; November 9, 1950, 2; April 8, 1954, 4; September 29, 1953, 2; May 25, 1950, 2; July 10, 1952, 3; May 27, 1954, 1; February 28, 1952, 2.

[3] CITY, December 30, 1953, 3; November 13, 1952, 3; December 4, 1952, 2; January 25, 1951; May 24, 1956, 2; February 11, 1954, 2.

[4] CITY, November 8, 1956, 1; July 29, 1954.

5 "Orr Wins Race for Mayor in Tallmadge," *ABJ*, 110th Year, No. 338, 4; "Tallmadge Keeps Orr as Mayor," *ABJ*, 114th Year, No. 333, Wednesday, November 4, 1953, 14; "Orr is Upset in Tallmadge," *ABJ*, 116th Year, No. 338, Wednesday, November 9, 1955, Night Final, 20.

6 "In Ohio, a village reaching a population of 5,000 automatically becomes a city, and a city falling below 5,000 becomes a village. There is no act of incorporation, simply a change acknowledged by the Secretary of State after census figures have been published." "1940 U.S. Census of Population. Ohio. Table 8. Area and population of counties, urban and rural: 1920 to 1940. Minor Civil Divisions," 817. http://www.census.gov/prod/www/abs/decennial/1940.html Accessed September 17, 2011; 793.01 "Ohio Revised Code, Title [7] VII Municipal Corporations, Chapter 703:01 Classification-federal census," Lawriter, Ohio Laws and Rules, http://codes.ohio.gov /orc/703.01, Accessed October 30, 2011.

7 Jane Rieker, "Tallmadge Boy Drowns; Fifth Victim of Year," *ABJ*, Thursday, June 13, 1940, 1. "Friends Morn Boy's Death. Bicycle Remind of Drowned Playmate," ABJ, Thursday, June 13, 1940, 40.

8 School bus driver and Goodyear Tire & Rubber employee Paul C. Hill was elected mayor of Tallmadge in an upset election over three-term Mayor Emmitt Orr in 1955. "Orr is Upset in Tallmadge," *ABJ*, 116th Year, No. 338, 20.

9 Although Haskell's comments might be ascribed to having been the loser in the recent election, City Council minutes may indicate something else. By the time Mayor Hill took office, council minutes had changed from the somewhat chatty tone of previous years to a stark point-by-point recitation of ordinances and committee reports. As a result, the contrast was all the more astonishing to read one particular exchange between Mayor Hill and his new Council shortly after he began his first term in the approved city minutes:

"14. Mr. Porter reported sewers. City to be set up as one sewer district, then divided into sub-districts, this needed in order in include everyone. #1 area to be Tallmadge Center including West Avenue. #2 Area to be six Corner area. #1 area is a little advanced from other sub-district as engineers have been figuring and working on plans. A scale agreement should be made with Barstow and Associates.

15. Mayor Hill brought to councilmen's attention that they have a new council table. As to the health and sanitation condition existing on South Munroe Road, the County Health Department gave these people thirty days to correct the situation. Reports from neighbors show these people have started to comply with Health Department's ruling." CITY, January 26, 1956; Likewise, it is equally striking to read to Mayor's Report a month later. Normally a place for the mayor to either announce his agenda for the City for the year or note pressing important concerns on which he has been working during the course of the year, the "Mayor concluded his report with a request that a place or way be considered for councilman [sic] have a place to hang their coats." CITY, February 23 and March 1, 1956.

10 It was under the administration of Mayor Hill that Tallmadge lost much of the historic character and charm of Tallmadge Circle as the rush to allow commercial investment in any form overrode structures there since the early to mid-1800s. As a recent history of Tallmadge delicately phrased it, "During that time, many changes were made to the city with the construction of new buildings and businesses and the razing of the old. The Circle was changed forever by the razing of the Methodist Church and the Hine property. A bank, Amy Joy Donuts, the Atlantic gas station, and a Burger Chef Restaurant provided a new look for the historic circle." *MEM* 11.

CHAPTER FIFTY-ONE: RETROSPECTIVE

1 "Struggles on Charter Commence," *ABJ*, Friday, November 30, 1962, 67.

2 "Lesson XXVI. Abou Ben Adhem," Wm. H. McGuffey, LL.D., *McGuffey's Fifth Eclectic*

Reader, Revised Edition (New York, Cincinnati, Chicago: American Book Company, H.H. Vail, 1920), 95-96.

[1] Diane DeMali Francis and David W. Francis, Summit Beach Park, America's Coney Island, The Summit County Historical Society (Akron, Ohio: 1993), 146.

[2] John Albrecht, Jr. "Hunting The Haunted: Akron's Summit Beach Park." http://www.examiner.com/article/hunting-the-haunted-the-history-of-akron-s-summit-lake Accessed June 29, 2014.

[3] The author of this book actually honed his skills at keyboarding while processing dealer adjustment forms for the Firestone 500 Steel Belted Radial in the late 1970s. During that time, the product caused thousands of accidents, hundreds of injuries and over 40 known fatalities. This, even as the company was offloading the remaining defective inventory in half price sales. Facing charges of using the public as "guinea pigs" to test tires, this forced recall of 14.5 million tires stands as the largest tire recall in history. In an effort to shield the company from lawsuits, its historical archives at Akron University were permanently closed to researchers. "Firestone 500 Steel Belted Radials," The Center for Auto Safety, https://www.autosafety.org/firestone-500-steel-belted-radials/ Accessed March 9, 2017. Personal communication with John Ball, Library Associate Senior, Archival Services—University Libraries, The University of Akron, March 14, 2016.

[4] Steve Love and David Giffels, *Wheels of Fortune, The Story of Rubber in Akron*, Beacon Journal Publishing Company (Akron, Ohio: 1999), 230-231.

[5] The corporate offices of Goodyear are there to remain, with a new 639,000 square-foot North American and global headquarters currently under construction. Jim Mackinnon, "Progress Continues at New Goodyear Headquarters," *ABJ Online*, Thursday, July 5, 2012. http://www.ohio.com/news/top-stories/progress-continues-at-new-goodyear-headquarters-1.318236. "Goodyear Holds Grand Opening of New Global Headquarters." Babcox AMN Aftermarket News. May 10, 2013. http://www.aftermarketnews.com/Item/113417/goodyear_holds_grand_opening_of_new_global_ headquarters.aspx Accessed May 10, 2013. Today, overall union membership in the United States has fallen to a 97-year low of just 11.3%—the same as it was in 1916, the year before Haskell arrived in Akron.[5] By 2016, the total number of manufacturing jobs in the tire industry stood at 43,197 throughout the entire United States. Don Lee, "Limited Success of Chinese Tire Tariffs Shows Why Donald Trump's Trade Prescription May Not Work," Los Angeles Times, July 24, 2016, Accessed January 2, 2017, http://www.latimes.com/business/la-fi-tariffs-trade-analysis-20160724-snap-story.html

[6] "Foreclosure Rates Stay High in Nevada and Florida: RealtyTrac." 24/7 Wall Street. May 9, 2013. http://247wallst.com/2013/05/09/foreclosure-rates-stay-high-in-nevada-and-florida-realtytrac/ Accessed May 10, 2013.

[7] Jim Carney, "Homes Demolished in Minutes as Akron Wipes Out Pieces of History, Moves Forward," *ABJ*, December 19th, 2011.

INDEX

A

A History of Blacks in Kentucky, 3

A History of Tallmadge Coal: A tales of Woodchucks, Welshmen and a Canal, 336

A.I. Smith, 247

Aber, Marian D., 396, 398, 399, 400

Abou Ben Adhem, 484

Agee, James, 30

Aikins, Andrew "Duke", 284, 288

Akron Beacon Journal, iii, iv, 142, 167, 184, 369, 370, 372, 373, 376, 430, 431, 434, 438, 447, 448, 456, 459, 464

Akron Lamp, 162

Akron Municipal Airport, Akron, Ohio, 334

Akron, Ohio, iii, vi, viii 12, 92, 129, 138, 139, 140, 141, 142, 143, 145, 146, 147, 148, 149, 150, 151, 167, 169, 173, 180, 182, 185, 187, 194, 196, 200, 207, 208, 210, 220, 221, 225, 227, 228, 231, 234, 235, 236, 237, 239, 245, 246, 269, 310, 312, 313, 324, 325, 326, 331, 334, 336, 337, 338, 347, 356, 357, 361, 362, 363, 364, 365, 366, 367, 369, 373, 375, 376, 377, 380, 382, 383, 389, 392, 402, 403, 407, 408, 419, 421, 422, 427, 428, 429, 430, 431, 432, 433, 434, 438, 441, 447, 448, 449, 451, 455, 456, 457, 458, 459, 460, 461, 474, 488, 489, 538, 539, 547, 548, 559, 560, 564

Alabama, iii, 149, 179, 344, 445

Allen, Jack, 181

Allen, Richard, 5

Alliston, Sheriff George, 306

Alteri, Dominick, 391

American Red Cross, The, 446

American Revolution, The, 236

American Tobacco Company, The, 6, 7

Andrews, Saul W., 283, 288

Andrus, Grover C., 346

Andrus, James H., 346

Appalachia, iii

Arant, Thomas E. "Tom", 283, 288

Arizona, 99

Arkansas, 67, 196, 244, 245, 249, 250, 253, 254, 257, 531

Ashbrook, Riggs,

288

Atchison, Hugh,
111

Austin, John, 202,
203

Averitt, Anna
(Jones), 117

B

B.F. Goodrich
Company, The,
138, 139, 142,
146, 150, 177,
178, 234, 316,
327, 328, 356,
434, 436, 466,
472, 488

B & O Railroad,
196

Baker, Ona "Ma",
408, 409

Bald Knob,
Arkansas, 250,
253

Balderson, Frank
L. "Red", 319

Baldwin, James, viii

Baldwin, Mrs. J.C.,
446

Ball, George, 174

Ballard County,
Kentucky, 111

Ballew, Handsel,
172

Bannerson, Deputy
Sheriff Bob, 309

Barberton, Ohio,

237, 462

Barnes,
Councilman, 405

Barnett, Ollie, 296

Barnett, Rinaldo,
294, 296

Bartholomew,
James G., 167,
168

Bauman, State Fire
Marshal, 459

Beasley, Lillian, 284

Beasley, Lube L.,
284

Bedaux, Charles E.,
358

Beddington
(surname), 401

Beers, Harry
Blachard, 451

Belden,
Councilman, 407

Belgium, 447

Bellows Sign,
Akron, Ohio,
465

Bennet, Bob, 489

Benton, Kentucky,
306

Bergman
(surname), 447,
448

Berkley, Kentucky,
103

Bethel, Adrian E.
"Whitey", 372,
373

Bethel, Ormond
R., 372

Bethel, William H.
"Uncle Billy",
272, 283, 288

Bierce, Fire Chief
Dave, 453, 461

Bierce, Henry, 387,
464

Bittner, Harry, 353

Black Patch, The,
6, 7, 8

Blackburn, United
States
Commissioner
Walter A., 306

Blancett, Emmet,
181

Blanks, Robert, 5

Blue, Surgeon
General Rupert,
194

Boaz, Kentucky,
113

Bob Bennett
Construction
Company, 489

Bondurant,
George, 309

Boston,
Massachusetts,
193, 285, 458,
459

Bowling Green,
Kentucky, 191,
192

Boyd, Josh, 45, 46

Boyle, Loveda, 397, 398

Brand (surname), 85

Brand, A.L. "Art", 87

Brand, W.L. "Will", 92, 93, 94, 95, 96, 97

Brannon, Fire Warden Harold, 458

Brewer, Charles R. "Charley", 378

Brian, Goebel A., 293, 294, 295

Bright, Ambrose, 46

Bright, Claude, 45, 46

Bright, Mary Ann, 46

Brimfield, Ohio, 415

Brown, Earnest, 70

Brown, Silas, 70

Bryan, Bill, 284

Bryan, William C., 283

Bryan, William Jennings, 83

Bryant, Lovett "Uncle Love", 268, 269

Bryer, John, 218, 219, 220

Buchanan, Vera, 199

Buckmaster, Lelland S., 170

Bugg, Judge, 95

Bull Durham tobacco, 57

Bunting, Mahlon, 396

Burger Iron, Akron, Ohio, 353

Burns, Councilman, 454

Burns, Mayor Frank N., 128

Burton, Susan E., i

C

California, 58, 146, 196, 428, 444

Calloway County, Kentucky, 3, 111

Camp Funston, Kansas, 193

Camp Knox, Kentucky, 194, 197, 201, 204, 209

Camp Taylor, Kentucky, 194, 195, 204

Campbell, Henry, 112

Canton, Ohio, 187, 324, 409, 447

Carey, Ohio, 220

Carlisle County, Kentucky, 103

Carlton Clothes, Akron, Ohio, 162

Carman, Charles, 74

Carman, J.E., 91

Carman, Simeon Augustus, 74, 75, 76, 77, 115

Carmen, Simeon Augustus, 9

Carter, Councilman, 407, 410

Carter, Deputy Sheriff Oren D., 406

Carter, Ed, 113

Carter, Lloyd, 406

Casabianca, vii

Central High School, Akron, Ohio, 449

Chakiris, James "Jimmy the Greek", 180, 222

Chambers, Tom, 4

Chester, Harvey, 211, 228

Chicago, Illinois, 112, 185, 222, 266

Chickasaw Indians, 2

Child Welfare in Kentucky, 31, 32,

34, 43, 71
Choate, Bird, 112
Cincinnati, Ohio,
196
City Bakery,
Akron, Ohio,
340
City Hospital,
Akron, Ohio,
181
Civil War, The, 2,
4, 9, 15, 17, 76,
84, 118, 123
Civil Works
Administration
(CWA), 381, 382
Clark, Deputy
Sheriff Charles,
309
Clark, Fire Chief
R.M., 456
Clark, J.W., 307
Clark, James
"Mike", i
Clay,
Commissioner
of Public Safety
Sanders E., 16,
127
Clearwater, Florida,
481
Cleveland Rubber
Corporation
Company, The,
235
Cleveland, Ohio,
187, 402, 427,

446, 450, 458
Climer, Fred, 369,
370
Clinton, Ohio, 345
Coal, 221, 261
Cobb, Irvin S., 2
Cocoanut Grove,
Boston,
Massachusetts,
458
Cole, Julian, 283,
284, 288
Coleman, Hobart,
204
Collier County,
Florida, 278
Collier, Barron
Gift, 278
Congress of
Industrial
Organizations
(CIO), 377
Copeland, May,
111, 112
Coventry High
School,
Coventry, Ohio,
462
Crislip, Marshal
Harley F., 403,
404, 405
Crites, Wanda, 401,
419
Crites, Wilma, 419
Crittenden County,
Kentucky, 3
Cross, Lexie W.,

288
Cross, Night Police
Captain Lige,
309
Crossland, Judge
Caswell B., 127
Cuba, Kentucky,
75, 89, 192
Cumberland River,
The, 2, 266, 310
Cunningham,
Councilman Rob
Ray, 407, 409,
410
Curd, Johnny, 110
Curt Collins
Heating
Company, The,
468
Cuyahoga Falls,
Ohio, 237, 328,
392, 418, 455,
456

D

Daniels, Joe, 291
Daniels, Van, 291
Davis, "Biddy",
313
Davis, Bill, 313
Davis, Judy Anne,
336
Davis, Marie, 313
Democratic Party,
The, 2, 11, 83,
84, 86, 87, 88, 96
Denny, William E.

"Bill", 372

Detroit, Michigan, 129, 143, 220, 221, 234, 415, 443

Devine, Jessie "Jess", 322

Diamond Match, 138

Diamond Rubber Company, The, 138, 139

Dick (mule), 67, 68, 69

Dick (surname), 113

Dickerson, Clarence L. "Poker Dick", 306, 307, 308, 309

Dickson, Elisha H. "Dice", 343

Dill, Boge, 70

Dill, Fred, 70

Dill, Sterlin, 70

Dill, Troy, 70

Dodd, H.R., 261

Dodd, Mary, 261

Dorpinghaus, Sarah M., i

Douthitt, Reed, 246, 248, 249, 255

Douthitt, Samuel R., 92, 94

Dowdy, Dell, 308

Doyle (surname), 69

Dublin, Kentucky, 38, 134

Dunaway, Detective John, 306

Dunn, Deborah M. "Shell", i

Dutch East Indies, 435

Duty, Homer Elijah, 329, 330, 331, 332, 333

Dyersburg, Tennessee, 121

E

Eaker, Police Chief James W., 127

Easton, James A., 458

Eddyville State Prison, Kentucky, 116

Edinburgh, Ohio, 415

Edwin Shaw Rehabilitation Hospital, Akron, Ohio, 480

Emmit, Homer, 439

Engelhart, Lieutenant E.L., 447

England, 402, 445

Europe, 89, 185, 402

Everything I Ever Need to Know I Learned in Kindergarten, 481

F

Falls Rubber Company, The, 328

Fancy Farm, Kentucky, 89, 91, 198

Faulkner, William, 58

Federal Bureau of Investigation (FBI), 428, 446, 447, 448, 449, 450

Federal Emergency Management Agency (FEMA), 432

Federal Emergency Relief Administration (FERA), 380, 409, 412

Ferguson, Edwin, 74, 75

Ferguson, Mary Enola "Nola" (Carman), 74, 75

Ferrell, Edward R., 283

Ferris, H.P., Jr.,
187
Finley, Henry, 4
Finney, Buford,
466
Firestone Bank,
Akron, Ohio,
178, 221, 222
Firestone Park,
Akron, Ohio,
143, 313, 314,
338
Firestone Tire &
Rubber
Company, The,
139, 143, 149,
153, 158, 160,
162, 166, 167,
169, 170, 177,
178, 229, 236,
238, 314, 316,
317, 323, 324,
325, 327, 328,
330, 356, 357,
369, 384, 428,
433, 488
Firestone, Harvey,
238
Fletcher, J.W., 283
Florida, 278, 363,
430, 431, 481,
482
Folsomdale,
Kentucky, 95,
112, 113, 114
Forest Hill, Akron,
Ohio, 235

Fort Smith,
Arkansas, 244,
245, 531
Frampton, Paul,
469
France, 447
Franklin, Detective
Henley M., 300
Franklin, Detective
Kelly, 306
Franklin, Police
Chief Henley,
127
Frederick Hotel,
Akron, Ohio,
346
Frey, Rollie, 245,
246
Frey, Roy, 245
Frick, Ralph W.,
400
Fritsch, Eugene
"Gene", 349,
418
Fuller, Dr. George,
72
Fulton County,
Kentucky, 3
Fulton, Bain
Ecarius
"Shorty", 334
Fulton, Kentucky,
4
Fuqua, Willie, 47
Futrell, Etheledied
"Lenny", 288

G

Gable, Clark, 146
Galbreath
(surname), 9
Galloway, Sam, 85
Gammon, Johnny,
258
Gandee, Sherman,
449
Garnett, State
Attorney
General, 35
Gates and Kittle,
Akron, Ohio,
146
General Tire and
Rubber
Company, 428,
488
Georgia, 149, 150,
178
Giffels, David, iii
Gilbert, Elvis
"Doot", 70
Gilbert, Jeff, 65
Gill, Purley, 344,
345
Glenn, Marshal
Joe, 261, 262
Glick, (surname),
362
Glisson, Hardy, 70
Goff, Bernard
"Barney", 461
Goins, Lee, 113
Goodyear Aircraft
Corporation,

418, 431, 433, 434

Goodyear Heights Realty Company, The, 138, 143

Goodyear Heights, Akron, Ohio, 143, 489

Goodyear Tire & Rubber Company, The, 139, 143, 145, 146, 163, 166, 182, 188, 235, 236, 237, 327, 328, 334, 350, 351, 354, 356, 357, 365, 366, 367, 368, 369, 370, 371, 372, 373, 374, 376, 377, 383, 384, 428, 429, 436, 487, 488, 489

Gorman (surname), 197

Gossett, Cordie, 216

Gossett, George, 48

Grace, Jim, 47

Graceville, Florida, 431

Graham (surname), 379

Graves County, Kentucky, 2, 3,

4, 6, 8, 11, 12, 15, 30, 31, 34, 36, 55, 83, 86, 90, 92, 93, 94, 95, 96, 111, 113, 114, 118, 119, 123, 128, 129, 131, 204, 239, 240, 326

Great Depression, The, ii, iv, 236, 337, 350, 356, 357, 362, 368, 380, 381, 382, 385, 390, 396, 402, 432, 439, 474

Great Lakes, The, 138, 402

Great Migration, The, iii

Green, J.W., 87

Green, Joe, 295

Green, Robert, 191

Greene, Marcus, 262

Gregory, County Judge Voris, 96, 98

Gregory, James N., iii

Gregory, Rick S., 50, 52, 55

Grismer, Karl, 380

Gulf of Mexico, The, 58, 266

H

H & H Restaurant, Tallmadge, Ohio, 373, 433, 451

Haberman, Harry, 222

Haines, Ralph "Gob", 211, 212, 213

Hale Farm and Homestead, Summit County, Ohio, 412

Hamilton, Clyde, 260, 261, 262

Hamlett, State Superintendent of Public Instruction Barksdale, 35

Hannah, Francis G., 149, 169, 327, 328

Harper, Fowler W., 430

Harper, Harry, 283

Harris, J. Newt, 94, 95

Harter, Mayor George J., 457, 458

Haskell College, 15

Hazen, Harry J. "Jim", 360, 361, 362, 422

Hazen, Kathleen,

361

Herman Tool & Machine Co., Tallmadge, Ohio, 462

Herman, Lee, 462

Hickman County, Kentucky, 3, 113

Hickory, Kentucky, 113

Hill, Paul, 477

Hites, Oliver, 162

Holifield, County Attorney M.B., 94

Holland, Kelley, 105

Holmes, Thomas, 5

Holyer, Bull, 113

Homer, Winslow, 30

Hoover, Jim, 379

Hopkins, Harry, 381, 382

Hopwood, Marion, 433

Houseman, Bill, 94, 118

Houston, Texas, 128

Howard, Willie, 184

Howell, Jack, 431

Huddleston, Gardner, 40

Huff, William, 283, 284, 288

Huffman, Elizabeth A. "Happy", 417

Hunsicker, Judge Oscar A., 418

Hunt, James Henry Leigh, 485

I

Ickes, Harold, 381

Illinois, 118

Illinois Central Railroad, 196, 244, 255, 256

Imhoff, Robert M., 445

Index Democrat, The, 86

Industrial Valley, 377

Industrial Voyagers: A Case Study of Appalachian Migration to Akron, Ohio, 1900-1940, iv

Ireland, Robert M., 3

Iseman (surname), 121, 122

J

Jackson Purchase, The, 2, 3

Jackson, H.H., 171, 172

Jackson, James S., 369, 371, 376

Jackson, Mississippi, 92

Jackson, President Andrew, 2

Jackson, Willie, 419

James Hotel, The, Akron, Ohio, 150

James, "Colonel" Robert "Bob", Cook 10, 11, 16, 114, 115

James, Frank, 283, 284, 288

James, Jesse, 11

James, John, 118

Jamestown, Virginia, 50

Japan, 185

Jarvis, Deputy Jonathan, 421

Jeffers, William, 430

Jewel Tea Company, Akron, Ohio, 340, 440

Johnson, "Drap", 105, 106

Johnson, Dave, 113

Johnson, Emmet, 283, 284, 288

Johnson, Susan Allyn, iv, 377

Jones School,
Graves County,
Kentucky, 15,
99, 213, 214, 229
Jones, "Alan", 343
Jones, Barbara
Jean, 324, 339,
374, 383, 384,
385, 388, 389,
424, 444
Jones, Barton
Augustus, 275,
276, 277, 326,
328, 337, 347,
348, 362, 363,
364, 375, 383,
466, 489
Jones, Bryan "Bill",
348, 422
Jones, Charlie, 66
Jones, Clarence,
215
Jones, Clyde, 66
Jones, Donald
Alan, 326, 337,
338, 339, 374,
375, 384, 385,
387, 388, 390,
423, 424, 425,
444, 445, 475,
488, 489
Jones, E. (Edwin)
A, 5, 11, 12, 13,
15, 16, 17, 19,
21, 23, 24, 26,
28, 31, 47, 56,
57, 60, 61, 64,

65, 66, 67, 68,
73, 83, 84, 85,
86, 88, 92, 93,
97, 98, 99, 100,
101, 110, 201,
226, 262, 426,
489
Jones, Ethel
Carman, 275
Jones, Frances
Carolyn
"Fanny", 35, 62,
74, 98, 117, 192,
225, 226, 227
Jones, Grace Inez,
16, 99, 214, 303,
324, 325, 337,
383
Jones, Grover, 16
Jones, Henry
Bascom, 99, 182,
214, 262, 325,
384
Jones, Herbert
"Hub", 66
Jones, Hollie, 66,
151, 174, 209
Jones, Howard,
328
Jones, James, 216
Jones, Joseph, 25,
26, 37, 62, 63,
64, 79, 226, 227,
275, 326
Jones, Joseph
"Devil", 9
Jones, Joseph Huel,

227
Jones, Josephine
(Stubblefield), 82
Jones, Kermit
Eldridge, 26,
226, 326, 355,
422
Jones, Laban, 172
Jones, Lawrence,
16
Jones, Lillian
Roberta, 99, 214,
215, 325
Jones, Louia
Walton, 326, 328
Jones, Luther, 80,
81
Jones, Margaret
June (Wright),
375
Jones, Marian
Gertrude
(Carman)
"Mammy", 26,
78, 226, 227, 364
Jones, Marjorie
Kathleen
"Marge", i, 374,
375, 376, 424,
425, 426, 431,
481
Jones, Mary Effie,
74, 117, 275,
362, 363, 383
Jones, Mary
Genevieve, 15,
194, 198

Jones, Mattie
  Keesee, 99, 198,
  199, 214, 324,
  325, 337, 383
Jones, Neil, 216,
  295, 464
Jones, Ola, 216
Jones, Oscar, 216
Jones, Ralph
  Edwin, 13, 17,
  67, 68, 69, 70,
  99, 100, 117,
  135, 182, 205,
  209, 225, 229,
  230, 231, 240,
  242, 243, 267,
  268, 269, 283,
  284, 288, 303,
  304, 313, 315,
  316, 324, 325,
  334, 337, 347,
  375, 424, 489
Jones, Ruth
  (Thomas), 375,
  424
Jones, Sarah
  (Bennett), 489
Jones, Sarah Ellen
  (Wright), 17, 20,
  21, 29, 101
Jones, Steffanie, B.,
  i
Jones, Thomas
  "Tom", 16, 19
Jones, Thomas
  A.R., 99, 182,
  214, 215, 325,

384
Jones, Vodre
  Sylvester "Jack",
  315, 326, 424
Jones, Will, 16
Jones, William B.,
  9, 18, 215
Jones, William
  Pinkney, 70
Jones, Willie
  (James)
  "Granny", 11,
  12, 13, 14, 24,
  28, 41, 44, 46,
  47, 56, 57, 60,
  62, 72, 83, 100,
  117, 182, 198,
  226, 230, 268,
  303, 325, 326,
  337, 347, 384
Jones, Zack, 66, 67

K

Kansas, 83, 193
Keller, Eva H., 339
Keller, Lewis &
  Eva H., 389
Kelly, E.B., 261
Kenmore, Ohio,
  237, 324, 456
Kennedy, "Uncle"
  Clay, 16
Kennedy, "Aunt"
  Kate, 16
Kent, Ohio, 415,
  455, 456
Kentucky, iii, v, 2,

3, 5, 7, 8, 9, 12,
  21, 30, 31, 32,
  33, 34, 36, 42,
  50, 71, 86, 94,
  111, 118, 123,
  124, 129, 131,
  148, 149, 194,
  204, 209, 210,
  229, 277, 378,
  411, 473, 482
Kentucky Tavern,
  Tallmadge,
  Ohio, 396
Key, Evalina, 45
Kimbell, Deputy
  U.S. Marshal
  R.W., 307
King, Charles H.,
  295
King, Clide, 106
King, Mrs. H.O.,
  446
Kirk (surname),
  352
Knapp, Charley,
  389
Koch (surname),
  298
Kohout, F., 290
Kolb Park,
  Paducah, 285
Kramer's (store),
  Tallmadge,
  Ohio, 387, 439,
  440
Krauss, Jacob
  "Jake", 338, 343

574

Krauss, Pauline "Polly", 338, 343

L

Lackey, Mayor Ernest, 127
Lakeside Casino, Akron, Ohio, 183
Lakeside Park, Akron, Ohio, 183
Landrom, Dick, 172
Lassiter, Annie, 72, 215, 216
Lawrence, Alice, 331
Lawrence, George R., 139
Lebre (surname), 53
LeMay, Janie, 210
Lemon, Clifton "Hennyburger", 488
Lemon, James Robert, 7, 9, 35, 86, 87, 89, 90, 91, 92, 93, 97, 204
Leon's/Tavern/Restaurant, Akron, Ohio, 342, 398, 399
Leonard, George, 19

Lewis, John L., 367
Lindsay, Pres, 274
Litchfield, Paul W., 372
Little Cuyahoga River, The, 140
Little House on the Prairie, 30
Lorain, Ohio, 427
Louisville, Kentucky, 83, 119, 149, 194, 196, 197, 266, 267, 411
Love, Steve, iii
Lowes, Kentucky, 85, 91, 111
Lowther, Lloyd, 185, 186
Lucas, Marion, 3
Lucas, Marion Brunson, 3, 4
Lucy, Tennessee, 259
Lyman, Joseph B., 13
Lyman, Laura E., 13
Lytton, Jenny, 121

M

MacAleese (surname), 347
MacAleese, Jim, 347
MacMillan (surname), 320

MacMullin (surname), 322, 323
Maderite Tire and Rubber, 235
Madge (first name), 431
Magaren, Frances Catherine "Aunt Fanny" (Jones), 78, 79
Magaren, Hugh Dudley "Uncle Dud", 79, 80
MaGennis Heights, Akron, Ohio, 235
Malone, Effie, 211, 212
Manhattan Restaurant, The, Akron, Ohio, 178, 179
Maplehurst Allotment, Akron, Ohio, 235
Markle, Harry C., 430
Marshall, Suzanne, 8, 11
Martin Heights No. 2, Akron, Ohio, 235
Martin, Bess, 121
Martin, Emma, 121, 127

Martin, Ruth, 121

Mason, Jack, 179

Mason, Lee, 179

Mason, Maude, 44

Mason, Richard "Slim", 178, 179, 180, 183

Massad, Abraham, 400

Massillon, Ohio, 432

Mast, George, 464

Mathias, Allen, 5, 6

Matlock, E.C., 285, 286, 288

Mayer, Mrs. Lewis, 459

Mayfield Monitor, The, 109

Mayfield Woolen Mills, The, 131

Mayfield, Kentucky, i, 4, 5, 7, 8, 14, 33, 35, 38, 62, 63, 75, 83, 86, 89, 90, 92, 93, 95, 98, 109, 112, 113, 114, 115, 116, 118, 119, 120, 121, 125, 129, 131, 149, 174, 178, 187, 190, 194, 196, 199, 204, 214, 225, 240, 244, 255, 262, 275, 284,

308, 346, 402

Mayflower Hotel, Akron, Ohio, 419

McAllen. A.B., 3

McCain, F. Marion, 87

McCarter, John, 162

McClure, Clarence, 173

McClure, Queenie, 127

McCormick, Robert, 397, 398

McCracken County, Kentucky, 5, 8, 93, 113, 123, 267, 306, 309

McGrath, Joseph "Joe", 351, 352, 354, 355, 371

McGuffey's Readers, vii, 42

McKenny, Ruth, 366, 377

McNeely, Superintendent of Transportation Jasper W. "Mister Mac", 277, 286, 287

McNeill, Rubel, 296

McNellis, Deputy

Sheriff Frank H. "Mac", 451, 452

McNutt, Haskell, 226

McNutt, Marshal/Chief of Police Charles H., 5, 112, 113

McNutt, Thomas, 226

Medina, Ohio, 419

Memphis, Tennessee, 244, 249, 251, 255, 258, 266

Merit Pant Company, Mayfield, Kentucky, 131

Merrifield (surname), 449, 450

Merritt, Dr. B.R., 19

Middlebury (Akron), Ohio, 336

Middleton, Ben, 48

Mill and Mine Supply, Paducah, Kentucky, 305

Miller (surname), 245

Miller Rubber Manufacturing Company, The, 138, 145, 146,

151, 152, 153, 160, 167, 178, 297, 316, 317, 319, 323, 327, 329, 343, 346, 349, 356

Miller, Charles, 421, 422

Millington, Tennessee, 259, 260

Mills, Councilman Charles E. "Charlie", 401, 405, 406, 407, 409, 410

Minneapolis, Minnesota, 471

Mississippi River, The, 253, 266, 310

Mitchell, H. H., 34

Mitchell, Mike, 393

Mogadore, Ohio, 461

Mong, Jacob C., 457

Monroe, County Judge J.W., 95, 96

Montenegro, 167

Montgomery County, Tennessee, 180

Moore, Addie, 187

Moore, Lelland, 187, 188

Moredock, Benjamin H., 309, 310

Morris, Ben, 105, 106

Morris, L.F., 309

Morris, O.M., 459

Morris, Pvt. Clyde, 459

Morris, Vern O., 462

Murray, Kentucky, 116

Myrick, Reverend A.A., 127

N

Naples, Florida, 278

Nashville, Tennessee, 266

National Child Labor Committee, The, 34

National Industrial Recovery Act (NIRA), 365

Nell (horse), 62, 63, 64

Nelson, Detective Jack, 306

Nero (dog), 24

New Braunfels, Texas, v

New Jersey, 163, 196, 443, 445

New York, 428

New York, New York, 285

Newfoundland, 458, 459

Newhall, Elizabeth Bliss, 32, 189

News Scimitar, The, 262

Nichols Bakery, Akron, Ohio, 341, 434

Nichols, Manager Alfred S., 277, 278

Nolan, Deputy Sheriff, 422

Nolan, John A., 297

Norman, Oklahoma, 444

Norman, Robert "Bobby", 106, 108

North Hill, Akron, Ohio, 325

Nuss, Steve, 421, 422

Nuss, Yolanda, 421, 422

O

O'Neil, Sheriff Walter P., 421

O'Toole, Deputy Fred, 421

Office of Civil

Defense (OCD), 457

Office of Price Administration (OPA), 432

Office of War Information (OWI), 449

Ogilvie, Sheriff, 5

Ogles, Neal, 306

Ohio, 12, 253, 266, 312, 316, 324, 336, 362, 363, 364, 380, 407, 409, 427, 429, 433, 475, 529

Ohio Edison, 330

Ohio River, The, 266, 291

Oil City, Pennsylvania, 397, 398

Oklahoma, 244, 245, 246, 247, 248, 249, 257, 397, 444, 531

Oklahoma City, Oklahoma, 245, 247, 249

Old Black John, 29

Orr, Emmett, 476

Owensboro, Kentucky, 199

Owsley, Dennis "Hound Leg", 213, 220, 221, 222, 488

P

Paducah News-Democrat, The, 90

Paducah Railway Company, The, 268, 277, 283, 288

Paducah, Kentucky, 5, 8, 17, 18, 90, 100, 111, 112, 113, 114, 115, 118, 119, 120, 121, 123, 124, 125, 126, 128, 129, 266, 267, 268, 269, 274, 275, 277, 278, 293, 298, 303, 304, 306, 309, 310, 325, 374

Page, Councilman, 454

Page, Mrs. Wesley, 446

Palace Theater, Akron, Ohio, 441

Palmyra, Ohio, 415

Paris Green, 52-53

Parks, William, 283

Patterson (surname), 338

Paulus, Raymond F. "Ray", 461

Payne, Joe Lee, 173

Payne, Tom, 172, 173

Pearl Harbor, Hawaii, 249

Peary, Constable, 113

Pennington, Martha, 173

Pennsylvania, 83, 149

Pennsylvania Railroad, 196

Perry, Bill, 401

Pfeifle, Arthur F. "Art", 401, 409

Pfeifle, Marjorie "Margie", 417

Phillips, Lexie, 283, 284

Pierson Ford Agency, Mogadore, Ohio, 461

Pittsburgh, Pennsylvania, 404, 405, 447

Planter's Protective Association, The, 6, 7

Port Darwin, Australia, 427

Port Moresby, Papua New Guinea, 427

Portage County, Ohio, 188, 415, 416, 450

Portsmouth, Ohio,

253, 257, 259
Potter, Sheriff, 113
Potter, William B.,
300
Pottsville,
Kentucky, 83
Powers, Dale, 446
Price, Joe, 108
Prohibition, 217,
218
Pryorsburg,
Kentucky, 89,
113
*Public Education In
Kentucky*, 32, 33,
93
Public Works
Administration
(PWA), 381

Q

Quaker Oats,
Akron, Ohio,
138
Queenie, 422, 423,
424, 425
Quin, Reverend
Clinton S., 125,
126, 127, 128

R

R.J. Reynolds
(tobacco), 57
Radcliff (surname),
283
Raess, Earl J., 446

Ragland, Lonnie
B., 283, 288
Rat (dog), 24
Ravenna Ordnance
Center, 402
Ray, Flora, 45
Rectenwald,
Miranda, i
Red Cob Willis, 28
Reed, Circuit Judge
William, 124
Reelfoot Lake,
Tennessee, 112
Reeves, George,
256, 261, 262
Reid, Yolanda G.,
50, 52, 55
*Report of the
Commissioner of
Education Made to
the Secretary*, 43
Republican Party,
The, 5, 84, 85,
86, 87
Richmond Hotel,
The, Akron,
Ohio, 151
Rickman, James,
305, 306, 309
Riffner, Boldizres,
167
Rinehart, George
R., 322
Ripley, Councilman
Elton C., 407,
410
Ritchie (surname),

476
Ritchie, A.J., 397
Ritchie, Mabel E.,
413
Ritchie, Mayor
Charles Edward
"Ned", 406, 411,
412
Ritchie, Sam, 411
Roach, Sheriff
John T., 85, 86
Robbins, R.G., 96
Roberts, Will, 113
Rock Island
Railroad, 244,
250
Rock Island Slim,
250
Rock Island,
Illinois, 9, 76, 77
Rogers, Ed, 116
Rogers, Will, 399
Rolfe, John, 50
Rollins, Kenney,
418, 419
Roosevelt
Restaurant,
Akron, Ohio,
398, 399, 400,
401
Roosevelt,
President
Franklin D., 381,
390, 409, 436
Rootstown, Ohio,
415
Rose, Clarence C.,

288
Ross, Dr. R.L., 446
Rothrocks Cafe, Paducah, Kentucky, 270
Rubber Bowl, Akron, Ohio, 382
Rubber: A Story of Glory and Greed, 141, 357
Rush (dog), 24
Rutherford, Arthur E. "Art", 445
Rutherford, Clyde, 397
Rutherford, John W., 445

S

Sackett, Councilman Claude, 339, 407, 410
Sackett, Katherine, 339, 386, 387
Saint Elmo, 41
Saint Louis Post Dispatch, The, 83
Saint Louis, Missouri, 253, 278, 309
Saint Thomas Hospital, Akron, Ohio, 419
Samir's Restaurant, Tallmadge,

Ohio, 451
San Antonio, Texas, Public Library, i
Sawyer, 113
Schaefer, Jake, 218
Schlup, Council Clerk S.A. "Sam", 405, 408, 409, 410, 446, 454, 462, 463
Schneider, George W., 161, 162
Scotland, 351
Scott, Lena, 215
Seay, "Pete", 111, 112
Sedalia, Kentucky, 62, 75, 90, 92
Seiberling, Frank, 236, 237
Seiler, Fire Chief Louis P., 456
Sekulich, Dan "Danny", 461, 462
Sellers, Albert, 38
Sellers, Alta, 38
Sellers, Essie, 38
Sellers, Roy, 38
Sellers, Will, 38
Sellors, George, 45
Shaffer, John, 65
Shakespeare, Bill, 400
Shaver, John, 187
Shaw, Alden, 261

Shaw, John, 309
Shears, James R. "Jimmy", 445
Shelton (surname), 222, 223
Sherbondy Rubber Co., The, 139
Sherman, E.N., 162
Shreveport, Louisiana, 197, 211
Silver Lake Estates, Akron, Ohio, 235
Sims, George, 226
Skinner, Carl, 194
Sladon, Dan, 274
Sledd, Newman, 306
Slim (nickname), 300, 301
Smith, Councilman, 454
Smith, Deputy Robert L. "Bob", 421, 422
Smith, Dewey, 178
Smith, Sheriff R.F., 261, 262
Snodgrass, James "Jim", 420, 421
Sokol, Dick, 460
South Carolina, 2
Southern Hotel, Paducah, Kentucky, 303
Spalding, John

Bernard, 199, 288

Spalding, Mary Vincent, 198, 199, 200, 205, 207

Spanish Flu, The, 193, 194, 204, 236, 275

Sparhawk (surname), 361

Speers, James W. "Jim", 323

Sperry, Mayor John A. "Jack", 396, 406, 407, 409, 413, 446, 460, 461

Spicer, H.C., 142

Spitznas, Albert A., 169, 170

Spriggel, Keith, 463

Spring, Mrs. Edith, 446

St. Louis Republic, The, 109

St. Louis. Missouri, 266

Stelzle, Charles, 217

Stephens, Ann, 45

Stewart, Sheriff Roy, 306, 309

Stillenbauer, Gus, 349

Stine, R.J., 449

Stone, Jim, 4

Stout, "Slim", 323

Stow, Ohio, 455, 459

Streit, Rudolph "Rudy", 297

Suet, Will, 4

Sullivan, W.B., 87

Summit Beach Park, Akron, Ohio, 173, 182, 183, 184, 428, 434, 441, 488

Summit County, Ohio, 182, 336, 380, 382, 419, 446, 447, 448, 450

Summit Lake, Akron, Ohio, 182

Swan, Kentucky, 14

Swinehart Rubber Company, The, 327

T

T.A. Jones & Sons, Paducah, Kentucky, 301

Tallmadge, Ohio, vi, iv, 295, 331, 336, 337, 338, 349, 372, 383, 390, 391, 393, 396, 398, 402, 403, 405, 406, 407, 410, 411, 412, 417, 418, 420, 421, 436, 446, 447, 454, 455, 458, 459, 460, 464, 466, 474, 475, 476, 480, 481, 488, 489

Tally (surname), 113

Tennessee, 2, 77, 112, 118, 121, 149, 178, 180, 225, 428, 433

Tennessee River, The, 2, 266

Texas, 99, 428

The American Mercury, 234, 235

The Commoner, 83

The Daily Messenger, i, 5, 7, 8, 10, 11, 31, 33, 35, 53, 83, 86, 89, 90, 93, 95, 96, 97, 111, 114, 115, 116, 118, 119, 129, 507

The Debate Over Whipping Criminals in Kentucky, 3

The Devil's Milk, iv

The Gospel of Good Roads, A Letter to the American

Farmer, 89

The New York Times, 2, 4

The Paducah Evening Sun, 109, 124, 266, 267, 278

The Philosophy of Housekeeping, 13

The Reivers, 58

The Saturday Messenger, 11, 51

The Southern Diaspora, How the Great Migrations of Black and White Southerners Transformed America, iii

The Weekly Messenger, 31, 35, 52, 93, 94, 95, 199

The Yellow Jacket, 83

Thomas, Dr. I.L., 448, 449

Thomas, George Christopher, 334, 347

Thomas, Sam, 329, 334

Thurmond, Allen, 118

Thurmond, B.S., 118

Tighe, Lon G., 456

Timbuktu, 285

Tinker, Tom, 8, 9,

112, 113, 114, 115, 116, 117

Tobe (mule), 67

Toledo, Ohio, 427

Tolleson, Mike, i

Travis, Lee, 283, 288

Tubb, Hal, 89

Tuberculosis ("T.B.", "consumption"), 324

Tucker, Ed, 225

Tucker, Nigel (Sullivan), 225

Tully, John, iv

Turk, Lucian, 111

Turner, William T., 50

U

U.S. Stoneware, Tallmadge, Ohio, 337, 400, 419, 468

Ufford, C.P., 142

Union County, Kentucky, 3

United Mine Workers (UMW), 367

United Rubber Workers (URW), 366, 377

United States Steel Corporation, The, 236

University of Kentucky Libraries, i

V

Van Noy Railway News and Hotel Company, 251

Vannoy, Kenner C., 389

Vannoy, Thelma L., 389

Vernotzy, Fire Chief Frank, 457, 458

Vernotzy, Gerald, 461, 463

Victory Park, Akron, Ohio, 235

Violence in the Black Patch of Kentucky and Tennessee, 8

W

Wallace Park, Paducah, Kentucky, 282

Wallace, Dell, 283, 288

Wallace, Rafe B., 94, 95, 96

Waller, H.T., 432

Walpole, Norman, 113

Walters, Felix, 283,

284, 285, 288

War Between the States, The, 6

War Manpower Commission, The, 429

Ward, Sylvester Denny "Vester", 283, 288

Washington University Libraries, i

Water Valley, Kentucky, 4, 118

Waterhouse, Helen, 431

Watson (surname), 170

Watts, Councilman, 454

West Memphis, Arkansas, 253

West Virginia, iii, 179, 343

West, Carl H., 343, 344

Westcott, City Development Manager Abraham, Jr., 489

Western Kentucky State Normal School, 191

Wheels of Fortune, The Story of Rubber in Akron,

iii

Whiskey Dick, 119

Whispering Pines Dance Hall, Tallmadge, Ohio, 458, 459

Whitaker, T.L., 307

White Cob Willis, 28

Whittemore, Chief of Police Charles, 309

Wilkerson, Rudolph John "Stud", 268, 269, 271, 284, 288

Williams Rubber Company, 327

Williams, Duke, 283, 286, 287, 289

Williams, John B. "Happy", 283, 284

Williamson, Ben, 433

Wilson (surname), 199

Wilson, Annice, 45

Wilson, Aubrey, 45, 47

Wilson, Matt, 47, 48

Wimberly, Harry, 90

Windsor, Marshal E.O. "Oscar"

Windsor, 405, 406

Wingo, Kentucky, 4, 14, 89, 219

Winona, Mississippi, 261

Wolcott, Councilman, 454

Wolf, Howard, 141, 143, 357, 358, 366

Wolf, Ralph, 141, 143, 357, 358, 366

Wolfe, Raymond "Ray", 178, 179

Woods, Dick, 345

Wooldridge, Gladys, 180, 222

Wooldridge, Jim, 180, 209, 210, 211, 222

Woolley, Edward Mott, 143

Wooster Avenue Allotment, Akron, Ohio, 235

Works Progress Administration (WPA), 382, 390, 392, 406

World War I, 146, 148, 152, 168, 169, 187, 188, 205, 229, 243, 320, 429, 432

World War II, 376,
382, 444, 455,
474

Wotts, Moses, 167

Wright, Bob, 174

Wright, Clarence
"Hoolie", 174,
175, 176, 178,
180, 181, 213,
488

Wright, Earl, 45

Wright, George C.,
3, 4

Wright, Rev. D.C.,
124

Wright, Samuel
Benson "Uncle
Ben", 131

Wright, Wilson, 47,
174, 175, 276

Wynn, Mr. & Mrs.
J.T., 314, 315

Y

Yates, Samuel L.,
344

Young, Bill, 270,
286

Young, Joe Barry,
431

Youngen,
Councilman
Phillip "Phil",
410, 453, 454

Youngstown,
Ohio, 324, 402,
404, 405

Z

Zang, Charities
Director J.M.,
431

Ziegler, Mayor
Vincent W.
"Zig", 453, 454

Ziegler, V.N., 446

Zook, Abner D.,
407

www.ingramcontent.com/pod-product-compliance
Lightning Source LLC
Chambersburg PA
CBHW071845090426

42811CB00035B/2333/J